D1125963

PERSONNEL
AND
INDUSTRIAL
RELATIONS:
A Managerial Approach

PERSONNEL
AND
INDUSTRIAL
RELATIONS:
A Managerial Approach

John B. Miner

Professor, University of Maryland
Consultant to the Firm, McKinsey & Company, Inc.

The Macmillan Company, New York
Collier-Macmillan Limited, London

WILMINGTON COLLEGE Library WILMINGTON N C

© Copyright, The Macmillan Company, 1969

All rights reserved. No part of this book may be reproduced or transmitted in any form or by any means, electronic or mechanical, including photocopying, recording or by any information storage and retrieval system, without permission in writing from the Publisher.

First Printing

Library of Congress catalog card number: 69–10416

THE MACMILLAN COMPANY, NEW YORK
COLLIER-MACMILLAN CANADA, LTD., TORONTO, ONTARIO

Printed in the United States of America

HF5549
· M522

51480

To Mary

PREFACE

It has become common practice to utilize the preface of a book for at least two purposes. One is to acknowledge assistance in the preparation of the volume, and thus to give due credit to individuals who have made significant contributions. The second is to provide some indication of the type of book that follows.

Both the beginning and the final chapters of this book were written with considerable assistance from others. The early drafts of Chapters 1 through 6 were prepared by Abraham K. Korman, who is currently on the faculty of New York University. With training in economics, industrial relations, and industrial psychology, Professor Korman is ideally suited to write on topics in the personnel area, and it is unfortunate that he was not able to continue working on this volume to its completion. However, other commitments and interests made that impossible. Certainly the two introductory chapters, as well as those on individual differences, the external milieu of personnel management, and legal considerations, are far more informative as a result of his efforts than would otherwise have been the case.

The second coauthor, Mary Green Miner, made essentially the same contribution to the chapters of Part VI. Drawing on her experience as an editor and writer in the labor relations field at The Bureau of National

Affairs, Inc., and as an editor of company publications, she prepared the original drafts of the chapters dealing with labor relations, fringe benefits, and internal communications; she also contributed to the revisions of other chapters. This assistance proved invaluable. Without it the final chapters might never have been completed; surely they would not have achieved their current level.

What follows is intended as a comprehensive introduction to the field of personnel management. However, in view of the variety of books bearing a personnel title that have appeared in the last few years, it is important to indicate where within this dissimilar array the present volume falls. It does not include an extended consideration of existing knowledge in the broad area variously described as organization theory, management, administrative science, organizational behavior, or human relations. It assumes that personnel management represents a relatively circumscribed field within the broader organizational framework and that the student will take other courses dealing with the more general managerial processes and organizational functions.

Organization theory has had a major impact on the presentation, but primarily as it provides a framework for analysis and a method of defining the limits of the personnel management field. Although this has not been attempted as yet, organization theory could perform the same function for books on other aspects of business administration—marketing, production management, and accounting, to name some examples that come readily to mind.

This stress on the organization as the unit of analysis yields some rather distinctive advantages. Among these, the most significant appears to be the provision of a value system in terms of which the techniques and procedures of personnel management may be appraised. Thus, in the following pages, reference to the fact that a personnel manager *should* do this or that means that by doing so he will in all probability contribute most effectively to the goals of the organization and thus to the fulfillment of his managerial responsibilities. The frame of reference is the organization, the company, and not the individual employee or the total society. The values of the social system as a whole are reflected in what is described as the constraint structure, but they do not provide a primary focus. It is this stress on the organization as the unit of analysis that leads to the subtitle—"A Managerial Approach." The *manager's* job is to make his *organization* as effective as he possibly can.

An additional feature is a major concern with managerial problem solving, rather than descriptions of existing practice. The goal is to provide the reader with sufficient knowledge of approaches and relevant considerations so that he may develop appropriate strategies for solving a company's personnel problems.

Because much of our current knowledge in the personnel area derives from behavioral science research, this research has been incorporated extensively in many parts of the book. Yet the intent is to deal with problems of human resources utilization in all of their manifestations. The behavioral sciences of psychology, sociology, political science, and cultural anthropology have contributed solutions to these problems in an extremely uneven manner. In some areas behavioral science research provides practically all that is known; in other areas behavioral scientists have done almost no research at all. Knowledge in the field of personnel management derives from a host of disciplines. In what follows, every effort has been made to present the best information available irrespective of its disciplinary origins.

A further point involves the order of presentation. The various topics are grouped in accordance with the dictates of the systems-orientated conceptual model that provides the framework for the book. The result is a sequence of chapters that departs in certain respects from traditional ordering. In addition, the model itself is developed on a piecemeal basis as appropriate to the topic under discussion. Chapter 22 does, however, contain a complete statement of the model, and there is no reason it cannot be read in conjunction with the two chapters of Part I. Furthermore, it may be desirable to group Chapter 5, dealing with labor relations law, with Chapter 19, which covers other aspects of labor relations. For some purposes Chapter 3, on individual differences, might well be read along with Chapter 13, on psychological testing; and portions of Chapter 6, on legal constraints in the employment area, along with Chapters 16, 17, and 18, on wages, safety, and performance control. Yet for most purposes the existing chapter sequence does appear to be the most meaningful.

This book and *Personnel Psychology* are published as parallel volumes to satisfy particular course needs and disciplinary interests. Their content is frequently overlapping. *Personnel and Industrial Relations* is the more general, dealing with the personnel process broadly defined. *Personnel Psychology* is more specific, covering those topics within the larger volume that are primarily of psychological concern.

J. B. M.

CONTENTS

I

The Emerging Profession of Personnel Management

1

The Role of
Personnel Management

On what basis should individuals be hired? What is the best way of training employees? How can a company's work force be motivated to higher levels of performance? How can acceptance of company goals be increased?

These questions and others like them are heard almost every day within the confines of all business organizations. They have stimulated, concerned, and at times plagued managers from time immemorial, and they will no doubt continue to do so. Such questions persist because almost everyone recognizes that company success depends in large part on the manner in which they are answered.

People are the essential ingredient in all organizations, be they business, educational, governmental, or religious, and the way in which people are recruited and utilized by the leadership largely determines whether the organization will survive to achieve its objectives. It is not too surprising, therefore, that business management is constantly concerned with the company's human resources—with the way in which these resources are developed and utilized, with the assumptions made about them, with the formulation of personnel policy, with the methods and procedures used in dealing with the work force. It is important that the company utilize the best available manpower in as effective a manner as possible. The purpose of this book is to assist in the accomplishment of this goal.

The Personnel Management Profession

The profession of personnel management may be defined as involving the development, application, and evaluation of policies, procedures, methods, and programs relating to the individual in the organization. This definition applies whether the specific individual involved is a blue-collar factory worker, a female clerical employee, a member of top management, or a research chemist.

In the relatively large organization personnel management activities are characteristically carried out by a separate component having a title such as Personnel Department, Industrial Relations Department, or Employment Relations Department; the specific designations vary from company to company. On occasion, however, personnel functions may be performed under a different organizational structure. Some firms have established two separate departments to deal with the utilization of human resources: one concerned entirely with the relationships between the company and the various labor unions which represent its employees, and the other with all remaining functions. The former may be called the Labor Relations Department and the latter the Personnel Department. In other instances there has been a movement toward consolidation rather than fragmentation of components. Thus employee relations, public relations, and government relations all may be combined in a single Relations Department.

Another approach is often used in large decentralized organizations, where separate personnel groups tend to appear as an integral part of each of the major departmental segments. In most such instances there is, in addition, another similar group at the very top corporate level, although the individual working in this corporate unit may carry out slightly different functions than those in the various departments.

More recently with the advent of the systems concept as a major approach to the organization of work (1,2), this decentralized pattern for allocating personnel management activities has taken on a somewhat different look. When a firm is organized on this basis, personnel groups are formed within each of the major project systems. These groups carry out all the functions required to provide for effective utilization of human resources within the system. Individuals are actually assigned to work within a specific project system, however, by a manpower allocation group which performs its function quite independent of the various systems making up the firm's operational component. This continuing allocation or placement activity is, of course, an aspect of personnel management also.

In smaller organizations the personnel management function may not be clearly differentiated from other organizational functions. Individuals with additional responsibilities in areas such as purchasing, sales, or accounting may also take on many duties in the personnel area, or personnel management functions may be distributed rather widely throughout the company. Often a number of activities of this kind, especially those related to organization planning and labor relations, are carried out by those holding positions at the very top of the firm's structure.

Whether the formulation of policies and methods related to human resources utilization is assigned to a personnel specialist who devotes all his time to this kind of work or to a man with many hats, the nature of the field remains essentially the same. Thus, the profession of personnel management must be defined in terms of a specific set of activities and functions, and not with reference to the organizational locus where the work is performed.

A further point regarding the profession concerns the nature of its influence on the attainment of company goals. Personnel management has generally been considered, in traditional terms, a *staff* function within the organization. In the newer systems terminology it is said to have a *support* role. This means that the job of personnel management is not to produce the goods and/or services which are the company's products. Activities of this kind are reserved to the *line* or primarily *operational* components. Rather the aim of personnel management is to develop conditions within the firm which will facilitate the production of the goods and services in a manner which will be of optimal benefit to the organization. Thus, in an automobile manufacturing company the personnel component might well recommend policies and procedures related to the training of production employees; it might even conduct such training, but it would not become directly involved in the process of actually manufacturing the automobiles.

Within the company large enough to have a separate personnel department, the way in which the field has been defined has important implications for the relationships existing between personnel managers and other managers in the organization. The fact that personnel management is generally considered a staff activity means that the individual working in this area is expected to serve as an advisor, consultant, and expert to other managers, but has no direct formal authority to obtain compliance with his recommendations. If others wish to reject his advice, they are free to do so, and the assumption is that no sanctions will be invoked against them for their recalcitrance.

In actual practice, however, this limitation upon the authority vested in the personnel function is often not nearly as pronounced as the staff designation would seem to imply. For one thing, although personnel managers may not have formal authority to enforce their recommendations, they do have, or should have, an equally important type of authority. This derives from their specialized knowledge in the field of personnel management. Managerial jobs have become increasingly complex over the years with the advent of more sophisticated mathematical techniques, electronic computers, and a generally more advanced technology. For this reason many managers have been only too happy to delegate certain aspects of their work to qualified specialists. To the extent a personnel manager actually possesses superior competence in his field of specialization, and can convince others of the value of his contribution, his "advice" may well acquire the ring of authority. Line managers are often, although perhaps not universally, glad to defer to the judgment of a man with expert knowledge when decisions with regard to human resources must be made.

In addition to this authority by virtue of greater information, personnel managers may also possess another type of authority, which is often designated in a very specific and formal manner. Such activities as benefit planning, accident prevention, wage and salary administration, and establishing staffing ratios are entirely the responsibility of the personnel department in many firms. Top management expects representatives of this department to make the crucial decisions in these areas and will support the right of personnel managers to exercise unilateral control over such matters. A similar type of authority resides in the manpower allocation group when the firm is organized on a systems basis. The extent of this more formal type of authority appears to vary tremendously from company to company. In some instances, especially among the highly decentralized firms, personnel management remains a basically consultative process. In other cases almost all decisions relating to human resources are made by specialists in the field. The determining factor is the extent to which top management wishes to employ its personnel department for the purpose of exercising manpower control.

One further point regarding the relationship between the personnel function and other functions within the company deserves mention. While the other departments, i.e., the line organization and the various staff groups, are, in this view, the consumers of the specialized competencies of the personnel manager, it should be emphasized that they are also his critics. It is their responsibility to provide the necessary feedback regarding the effectiveness of personnel programs and policies. Personnel managers are, all too often, in no position to determine for themselves what the actual consequences of their recommendations and directives are. Consequently, they badly need someone to relay information back to them. Only on the basis of such feedback can the required modifications in procedures be introduced and adjustments to changing circumstances carried out.

For this feedback and correction process to operate with maximum efficiency, a degree of mutual cooperation and understanding must exist. Personnel specialists need to be informed regarding the work performed by the various groups within their area of jurisdiction. And the managers of these groups need to know, at least in a general way, what the personnel manager is attempting to accomplish, as well as what techniques he has available to him. The former requirement means that specialization in the field of personnel management should not be so narrow as to preclude a broad education covering the major functional areas of business—manufacturing, marketing, accounting, and so on. The latter requirement means that those who specialize in one or the other of these various functional areas should also have a knowledge of personnel management, at least to the extent provided in this volume.

The Goals of Personnel Management

Although the methods used to achieve them are different, the goals which personnel management seeks to achieve within the organization are the same as the goals of management in general. Personnel managers carry out a unique set of activities having to do with the utilization of human resources, activities which are not duplicated in other components of the organization. But this work is done with a view to accomplishing exactly the same objectives as is the work of all other managers.

There appear to be two interrelated but distinct categories or types of organizational goals involved here. The first of these is to maximize the productivity of the organization. This is, of course, no new concept. It has been generally recognized as a major goal of business and most other organizations for a long time. Some, in fact, have considered it the only goal worth mentioning. In the business world, of course, productivity must be considered in relation to earnings and long-term net profit.

In its most general sense this objective refers to the whole gamut of procedures and activities which management carries out to maximize the attainment of the stated functional purpose of the organization. This purpose may be to manufacture and sell automobiles, or to provide a valuable stock market investment counseling service, or to produce missiles for the national defense effort. Some of the larger corporations have become so complex and their product lines so diversified that a full statement of this productivity objective can become quite lengthy. Yet in all instances the company is devoted to producing something that presumably has value for other people, and that therefore has some prospect of yielding a profit. In this sense there is always a task objective.

The procedures used to compute or identify the extent to which this type of goal attainment has actually occurred vary considerably from firm to firm. Thus, in manufacturing it is not uncommon for management to determine productivity by computing the number of units produced per man-hour worked. This figure may be modified to take the quality factor into account by putting the percentage of all units produced which meet previously established standards of excellence in the numerator, and then dividing by the number of man-hours. A department store on the other hand may establish productivity in terms of the dollar volume of sales divided by the man-hours worked, or perhaps the dollar value of goods returned per man-hour, or over a given time period. Sometimes much more complex procedures are introduced which take into account investments, depreciation allowances, share-of-the-market factors, and company growth curves of one sort or another. Whichever method is used, the guiding assumption behind them all is similar: A major goal of management is to maximize the attainment of the stated functional purposes of the organization.

Since, as previously stated, the goals of personnel management are identical with those of the rest of the management team, productivity at a profit also becomes a major concern of those engaged in carrying out the personnel function. It is their responsibility to develop and recommend policies and procedures which will contribute to this goal. In addition, they have the task of evaluating and applying certain programs and methods which were devised with this objective in mind. Personnel managers are frequently called upon to develop techniques for measuring the degree of impact their activities have on attainment of the productivity goal. To accomplish this, methods of evaluating *individual* job performance must often be developed. In this way indexes of the contributions made by specific members to the productivity of the total organization can be obtained. Later chapters will deal with this matter of measuring individual productivity, or performance, at considerable length.

The second major goal of management is one which is related to the first, but can be distinguished quite clearly from it. It has been recognized much more recently, and is probably still not nearly as likely to be given explicit statement as that of organizational productivity. It is, nevertheless, of equal, and perhaps even greater importance. Stated most simply, this objective is to maintain the organization as an ongoing unit in the face of internal and external pressures and stress. The term *organizational maintenance* is often used to refer to this particular type of goal.

The importance of this goal began to be appreciated in the period following World War II when shortages of talent developed and there was strong competition for the talent that was available. During this period management started to realize that if it was to maintain a loyal work force which would remain with the company, an active effort would have to be made to establish working conditions within the organization which would contribute to job satisfaction and thus facilitate talent retention.

Recently management has become much more aware that increased effort must be devoted to problems of organizational maintenance if the company is to remain intact under the stresses of a changing labor force, automation, and technological innovation. These factors have brought about sizable alterations in many firms, and in the process their organizational structures have often been strained to the breaking point. New occupational groups have appeared from nowhere to demand a position, often of considerable importance, within the existing hierarchy. At the same time other groups, many with a declining role to play insofar as the company is concerned, have been striving to maintain their traditional status.

Management has also come to realize that practices developed during a period when large numbers of relatively poorly educated employees made up the work force are no longer suitable when a sizable percentage of the employees are as well educated as the top management group itself. But this realization has on occasion lagged well behind the actual changes in the composition of the labor force, and major problems of organizational maintenance have developed as a result. Stress situations such as these place an enormous strain on any social group and may even absorb so much attention that the productivity goal is almost entirely forgotten for long periods of time.

As might be anticipated, personnel management has an extremely important role to play in creating conditions which will contribute to the stability of the organization. It is the responsibility of personnel managers more than any other group to recommend policies, procedures, and programs which will make the company an attractive place to work, and at the same time serve to minimize internal dissension and conflict which might threaten the firm's very existence. When these efforts are successful, and internal stability has been achieved, the organization will be in a better position to maintain itself against external stress also.

As we shall see in subsequent chapters, major contributions in the area of organizational maintenance have been made by the basic behavioral sciences of psychology and sociology. Research and theory derived from these fields have been extremely helpful to personnel management in that they have provided a variety of procedures for measuring and quantifying such concepts as job satisfaction, organizational commitment, and morale. In addition, work in these disciplines has contributed to a much greater understanding of how group and organizational dynamics may be modified so as to foster stability and continued existence. Just as economics has made its greatest contribution in providing a knowledge of the ways in which *external* stresses have an influence on a company's capacity for survival, psychology and sociology have been particularly valuable as sources of information regarding the nature of *internal* pressures and stresses.

The Work of Personnel Management

Having reviewed, at least briefly, the position of personnel management in the modern business organization and the goals which personnel managers attempt to achieve, let us now turn to the actual content of the work. At this point only a brief preview is possible, because much of the remainder of this volume will, in fact, be devoted to a detailed description of the activities which make up the profession of personnel management. Yet it is important at the outset to get a general feeling for the type of work involved and to gain some appreciation of the more important functions performed.

ORGANIZATION PLANNING AND JOB ANALYSIS. One of the major activities is the study and analysis of jobs throughout the company in terms of the various tasks and duties required, as well as the personal characteristics needed for effective performance. This involves an initial analysis of each individual position. Then these separate studies are combined and compared to provide information regarding the interrelationships between jobs. Groupings are developed on various bases—in terms of the difficulty of the work, in terms of the specific tasks performed, in terms of the characteristics required for successful performance. In this way it is possible to use job analysis data in establishing wage and salary scales, as a guide when transferring employees, in promoting employee health and safety, and for many other purposes.

Organization planning and job analysis have much in common, since both are concerned with establishing what a person is expected to do. Organization planning, however, focuses specifically on managerial activities. It provides a structure for the company by identifying the various subgroupings headed by individuals in managerial jobs. Thus, while organization planning serves to define what is expected at the upper levels of the hierarchy, job analysis carries the process down through the organization.

APPRAISAL AND EVALUATION. Once a job has been established and some definition of what the incumbent is expected to do developed, it is then possible to evaluate the performance of an individual against these expectations. A great variety of measurement techniques have been invented for this purpose, and not all of these are normally administered by personnel managers. Industrial engineers, for instance, are likely to be responsible for developing measures of output, waste, and so on, for production employees; accountants set up systems for determining profitability which are used to evaluate department managers. Yet many techniques, especially those involving some type of rating, are clearly within the province of personnel management.

It is characteristic for management appraisal programs to be administered separately from procedures applied to those at lower levels in the company. This is in part because of the differing requirements of the two. A major approach in management appraisal is to evaluate the manager in terms of the productivity and the attitudes of his group. To what extent is the particular function supervised contributing to the goals of the organization? Nonmanagerial employees, on the other hand, must be evaluated directly, rather than through knowledge of the performance of others.

Yet, whatever the level and technique, the purposes of appraisal and evaluation procedures remain much the same. The resulting information is used to establish pay, to make personnel placement decisions, to determine the degree to which training is needed, and for a number of other purposes. In recent years there has been considerable interest in the values and problems associated with feeding back appraisal information to the employee himself with a view to stimulating greater effort and helping him to perform more effectively.

SELECTION. Among the most important responsibilities of personnel management are those relating to the selection of those specific individuals who will actually work for the company from among the usually much larger number applying for positions. There is reason to believe that more problems of human resource utilization have their origins here than in any other area (3). Thus, the selection policies and procedures utilized by an organization are of major importance, and it is within a personnel department that the technical skills needed to deal with this problem are located. It is there that the responsibility for developing recruiting procedures which will ensure an adequate supply of applicants is usually assigned. And it is there that the analyses required to develop satisfactory techniques for choosing among applicants are normally carried out. Advances in methods of selecting employees are being made at a rapid rate, and for this reason the demands currently being made on personnel managers, so that they may keep abreast of new developments in this particular aspect of the work, are especially pronounced.

In developing a selection system, personnel managers must keep both of the major types of company goals discussed in the preceding section in mind. It is not enough merely to determine whether an individual has the characteristics needed to perform the work effectively, and thus to contribute to the overall productivity of the organization. There is also the question of his contribution to the goal of organizational maintenance. Will the person remain sufficiently satisfied in his new position so that he will stay with the company? Will he work effectively with others or will his presence be a source of dissension? Is he likely to do anything of a dishonest or disloyal nature that might serve to undermine the firm's very existence? These are important questions for any organization, and it is impossible to dismiss them as merely reflecting an excessive concern with matters of conformity.

There are some types of selection procedures which are used almost exclusively to identify those individuals who will contribute the most in terms of productivity. Other techniques are characteristically used to select those who will not threaten the organization in any way or leave it before a reasonable period of time has elapsed. Although some of these latter procedures, such as the employment interview, are not widely recognized as performing the function that they do, they remain important to the total selection process. Subsequent discussions will cover the whole range of techniques and procedures in this area, while at the same time attempting to specify exactly what objectives are achieved by each approach.

TRAINING AND DEVELOPMENT. Another task of personnel management is to serve as a source of specialized information in the area of employee and management training and development. On occasion this involves actually teaching various courses for company personnel. To carry out their responsibilities in this area, irrespective of the specific nature, personnel managers must be thoroughly informed regarding relevant research findings in the fields of education and psychology, as well as those developed in the industrial training field itself. Often considerable knowledge of the various fields of business study such as accounting, management, and marketing may be required as well.

The specific nature of the training programs developed will, of course, depend on the organizational objective to be served. Training may be used to directly increase the job skills of a group of individuals by teaching them how to perform their tasks more effectively. Thus, production workers may learn how to operate a new type of equipment or new supervisors how to handle certain bookkeeping details associated with their work. Here it is clear that the training primarily contributes to the productivity goal. In other instances, however, the educational process is used in connection with the organization maintenance function, as when production foremen are taught how to handle various types of labor relations problems or when a number of managers participate in a sensitivity training laboratory in order to increase their ability to work cooperatively with one another.

WAGE AND SALARY ADMINISTRATION. Central to the operation of any organized group activity is the existence of some type of reward structure which will be viewed by the members as fair and equitable, and which is sufficient to induce individuals to contribute their efforts toward the common goals. Although in recent years there has been some tendency to place increasing stress on nonmonetary considerations, the major formalized reward system used by business organizations remains the wage and salary structure. Therefore, it is not too surprising that personnel management is heavily involved in this area. Monetary payments must be adequate to serve as a reward for productive effort, but they must also be scaled among individuals and jobs in a manner which will minimize jealousy and dissension. The development of such a system is a complex undertaking involving considerable research and analysis.

As part of the whole process of wage and salary administration, those engaged in carrying out the personnel function must conduct a continuing audit of wage structures in the community, and often in the specific industry as well. In addition, employee responses to the company's wage structure must be investigated through a study of formal grievances under the union contract, turnover and absenteeism rates, and various other indexes of dissatisfaction. It is important that wage and salary administration be viewed not only as a system of incentives contributing to productivity, but also as an essential means of achieving the organizational maintenance goal. This can be accomplished only if a continuing effort is made to establish payments at a level which will be generally perceived as equitable.

HEALTH AND SAFETY. Although the primary specialists are medical doctors and safety engineers, health and safety matters are a major concern of personnel managers. The objective here is to keep employees in physical shape to continue working. American industry has been very successful in this regard, to the point where many factories are in fact safer than the homes to which employees return at the end of the work day.

The approaches used to achieve this result are varied. They include safety training, posters, contests, and equipment design. In addition, physical examinations are used to place employees in jobs where their disabilities will not produce a safety hazard. And industrial medicine has done a great deal as well to create safe working conditions and to introduce measures which protect against disease. Although the physician and others involved in this overall health and safety effort are often specialists in every sense of the word, their primary concern is still with an aspect of the utilization and development of the company's human resources. Thus, the safety and medical groups within a company usually report to the man in charge of personnel and industrial relations.

COUNSELING, DISCIPLINE, AND TRANSFER. When a man is not doing well on his job, something must be done to change the situation. Of course, he may be fired and that, like hiring, is basically a personnel function, but there are a number of other alternatives.

Some kind of counseling may be introduced in the hope that the man can come to understand the source of his difficulties and correct them. This is a costly approach from a company viewpoint and as a result it is now usually restricted to highly trained employees, such as research and development groups, legal departments, and the like. In these cases the demand for manpower of a kind which is in short supply makes replacement difficult, and thus investment in retention procedures such as counseling is deemed worthwhile.

Discipline and job change are additional procedures for improving unsatisfactory employees. Discipline may take the form of a warning or of suspension without pay, or, in extreme cases, of discharge. The specific approaches are usually spelled out in considerable detail in the union contract and the procedures involved tend to be rather legalistic. Transfer, on the other hand, at least as it relates to ineffective performance, is primarily an attempt to overcome the errors of initial placement. Thus, an effort is made to shift the man to a type of job in which the expectations are more consistent with his capabilities and desires.

LABOR RELATIONS. Another area of major concern involves dealing with the labor union or unions which represent the company's employees. Yet this concern is not entirely restricted to those firms which have been unionized. Even in those instances where a union is not present, there is always the prospect that the situation may change at some later date. As a result, the personnel department may devote considerable effort to the development of strategies designed to forestall such an event and in conducting attitude surveys to determine whether it might be imminent. When a union does represent a sizable segment of the company's labor force, collective bargaining, grievance procedures, arbitration, court cases, and other related activities may absorb much of the personnel manager's time.

To carry out the necessary planning and minimize errors in decision making, it is essential that a sizable proportion of the company's total management group be involved in the various aspects of labor relations. Yet it is also true that those with specialized knowledge in the area of human resource utilization will almost invariably have a central position. In most companies the primary responsibility for advising on labor-management problems is allocated either to an industrial relations specialist or to a person who has been trained in the intricacies of labor law. In many instances these two are actually one and the same person. In any case the function performed is basically a component of the personnel management profession.

Because the ultimate goal of management's efforts with respect to labor relations is the minimization of internal conflict without sacrificing profitability and productivity in the process, labor relations activities can be viewed as serving a primarily organizational maintenance function. There are a number of firms which have completely disappeared under the pressure of extreme labor-management stress. In these instances the organizational maintenance goal of the personnel component has clearly not been achieved.

BENEFIT PLANNING. The total compensation package typically consists not only of wages and salary, but also of a variety of benefits and services. These include payments for time not worked such as holidays and leaves, group insurance, retirement plans, and a great variety of special services from recreation programs to employee discounts. In some instances such as group insurance and pension planning, the work is highly specialized, requiring the services of lawyers, actuaries, and accountants; in other cases it is not. In any event the problems of working out agreements with unions in these areas and integrating benefits and services into the total personnel program are very much those of the personnel manager.

Although included in total compensation, benefits are not normally intended as a means of encouraging work effort and productivity. In this sense they differ from wages, salaries, and incentive payments. Rather, the primary objective is to further organizational maintenance by fostering high morale and a sense of economic security. There is some reason to believe that they may contribute to longer employment tenure and that they may provide an added inducement in recruiting new employees.

COMMUNICATIONS. Like employee benefits, communications procedures are used primarily for purposes of organizational maintenance. In many instances they play a major role in labor-management relationships, communicating the company viewpoint on issues which are in dispute. Even where this is not the case, the goal is to create a sense of belonging in relation to the firm—to pull the total organization together as a cohesive unit. Downward communication programs of this kind can include the use of company magazines and newspapers, bulletin boards, meetings, handbooks, and certain other approaches.

But organizational maintenance is not most effectively fostered by a total emphasis on downward communication. In addition, procedures are needed which will permit dissatisfactions, questions, and ideas to flow upward. This is one objective of attitude surveys, counseling, grievance procedures, and suggestion systems. Unfortunately techniques of this latter kind which will provide valid feedback to management on the consequences of its policies and decisions have not been developed to the same degree as have downward communication mechanisms.

These, then, are the major activities which comprise the profession of personnel management, and which will be discussed in greater detail in the chapters to follow. It should be emphasized, however, that not all aspects of the work to be considered are performed by all personnel managers. There is, in fact, a tendency toward considerable specialization within the field as a whole, with specific individuals concentrating on training, labor relations, and so on. In addition, the way in which the various activities are combined into specific jobs varies from company to company. And some firms may not make any formal provision for the performance of a given personnel task at all. As previously indicated, the profession is defined by a set of activities and not by how it is performed in a specific situation or organization.

Before taking up the activities that go to make up the profession, however, several chapters will be devoted to the context within which the practice of personnel management occurs. First, the historical background of the field will be reviewed to provide a better appreciation of the traditions, precedents, and loyalties which influence the profession today. Second, a chapter will be devoted to those particular constraints or restrictions which a personnel manager faces in his work merely because of the wide variations in ability and personality characterizing the human resources that may be available to him. These are the variations which psychologists study under the heading of *individual differences*. It is evident that no personnel manager can do any better in contributing to his company's productivity and survival than is permitted by the raw material available to him in the form of human capabilities. Third, there will be some discussion of the constraints outside the organization that may operate to restrict and channel a personnel manager in his work. These include the customs, mores, norms, and laws of the larger society, as well as the restrictions imposed by virtue of economic conditions and the actions of other, often competing, companies. With this backlog of information regarding the context in which the profession is practiced, we will be in a better position to take up specific activities as they contribute to productivity and organizational maintenance.

References

1. Johnson, R. A., F. E. Kast, and J. E. Rosenzweig, *The Theory and Management of Systems*, 2nd ed. New York: McGraw-Hill, 1967.
2. McDonough, A. M., *Information Economics and Management Systems*. New York: McGraw-Hill, 1963.
3. Miner, J. B., *The Management of Ineffective Performance*. New York: McGraw-Hill, 1963.

Questions

1. Imagine that you were asked to develop specific measures that could be used to determine whether the productivity goal was being attained in a department store. What are some of the measures you might suggest? What are some of the measures you might suggest to ascertain whether the organizational maintenance goal was being attained? List as many measures as you can.
2. What are some of the stresses in our society today that might have an influence on the work of the personnel manager? Discuss each of these and how they might operate.

3. There is considerable diversity among companies in the way in which the personnel function is organized and the various activities are allocated. What are some of these organizational patterns and what are some of the advantages and disadvantages of each, from the viewpoint of effective implementation of the personnel management function?

2

The Historical Development of Personnel Management

There are probably few fields of organized human endeavor which have developed in a really pure state, uninfluenced by other areas of knowledge. Sociology was affected by history and social work, psychology developed from a merging of philosophy and physiology, engineering is primarily an amalgam formed out of the traditional physical sciences such as physics and chemistry combined with the demands of the business enterprise. Many other examples could be cited.

Personnel management is no exception. The field as it currently exists represents a crystallization of a variety of historical and contemporary influences, among them economics, psychology, social work, engineering, and accounting. Together these influences have combined in a complex fashion to bring the profession to its current position in the management framework. The purpose of this chapter is to trace these historical roots and show how they have contributed to the growth and current status of personnel management.

In general it appears that there have been two major traditions or trends within personnel management over the years. One of these, stemming largely from economics and accounting, emphasized a hardheaded, profit-minded approach to the utilization of human resources; the other, with its origins in social work and certain subfields within psychology, took more of a social welfare viewpoint. This duality of approach appears to have hampered the development of the profession within certain segments of American industry, and the signs of the split have still not entirely disappeared. The social welfare tradition has been viewed as antithetical to the "real" organizational goal of productivity by many managers both within and outside the personnel field. On the other hand, the feeling among those with a social welfare orientation has been that management generally emphasized productivity and profit too much and employee satisfaction too little.

Only in relatively recent years has there been some lessening of this conflict as an increasing number of firms have come to accept the view that there are really two primary types of organizational goals—productivity *and* maintenance. Both appear to be essential, yet some policies and procedures which maximize one may well do so at the expense of the other. Out of this increased understanding regarding the nature of company objectives has come an opportunity for personnel management to make peace with itself. As a result the future of the profession looks considerably brighter than its past.

The Beginnings

Interest and concern with the utilization and organization of human resources has been in evidence since antiquity. The topic appears in the philosophic, religious, and military writings of both ancient and medieval times, and certain aspects of current practice can be traced directly to origins in Europe during the 1400's (14). Yet the history of personnel management as a distinct managerial specialty does not extend back nearly that far. In fact, the field as a separate entity is actually of relatively recent origin. Its development had to await the growth of the business unit and the consequent emergence of at least some degree of managerial specialization. This type of growth did not begin to occur until the years between the close of the Civil War and the early part of the twentieth century (8).

It was during this period that a significant increase in the size of the organizational unit began to take place, and it was then that departments devoted to such specialties as finance and accounting, production, and marketing came on the scene. These three were the most common subdivisions at that time. There is no evidence that separate departments devoted to the personnel function were in existence during this post-Civil War period (8).

Industrial Engineering

A small group of managers who were very much concerned with developing techniques for the maximization of the productivity goal through the effective utilization of human resources did begin to emerge, however. These were the industrial engineers, among whom Frederick W. Taylor (19) is perhaps best known. According to these people, the contribution of the human factor to the attainment of high productivity levels could be increased sizably through the appropriate use of selection, training, and monetary incentives.

Although Taylor and the other industrial engineers of the time, such as Frank and Lillian Gilbreth and Henry Gantt, had little interest in the formation of personnel departments as such, they did make a major contribution to that end through their insistence that management must pay attention to such matters as the selection of employees, proper training methods, and the development of appropriate compensation programs. This was in relation to a predominant concern with how machinery might be used most effectively.

The key components of this early industrial engineering approach were the emphasis on identifying the ideal physical conditions and methods of work and the concern with developing monetary incentives for the worker that would be both satisfying and effective. In this way it was felt that there would be benefits to both the company and the individual. This movement, which was named Scientific Management by Taylor (2), became an extremely important force in American industry during the latter part of the nineteenth century and the early twentieth century. It constituted the first real attempt, originating from within management itself, to achieve a means of utilizing human resources that would be optimal from both the company and the individual viewpoints. It is interesting to note that Scientific Management was, nevertheless, a continuing object of severe attack by workers and worker groups for many years, in spite of the fact that it gave important consideration to the welfare of the individual employee.

The Labor Movement

A second major influence during this period was the growth of the organized labor movement in the United States. Because the new unions were continually making demands for economic concessions from management, the history of the labor movement becomes almost inevitably intertwined with the history of personnel management. To understand the nature of these employee demands, why they became largely economic rather than social in nature, it is necessary to review, at least briefly, the background of unionism in the United States.

A trade union movement can be found in this country as far back as the late eighteenth century, when organizations were formed in a number of cities to represent the printers, carpenters, and shoemakers. These unions were local in nature, with few financial resources to call on, although they did resort to strikes on a number of occasions even in those early years (1786, 1799, and 1809). They operated under one major handicap, however, during this period. All unions were considered under the English common law to be conspiracies against the public, because it was presumed that their purpose was to benefit the membership at the expense of society. Not until 1842 in the famous case of *Commonwealth v. Hunt* did this interpretation of the legal status of trade unionism begin to change. At that time a precedent was established that a union was no longer illegal in and of itself, but the means that it used to gain its ends (strikes, boycotts, and so on) might well provide a basis for legal action.

As a result of this decision and the rapid industrial expansion of the mid-nineteenth century, the number of trade unions increased significantly, both along the eastern seaboard and in the developing areas around the Great Lakes. By the end of the Civil War there were approximately 300 local unions, and national organizations had been formed by such groups as the printers, stonecutters, hat finishers, machinists, locomotive engineers, plasterers, cigar makers, and bricklayers.

The next step was the development of some type of national labor federation and the fifteen years following the war saw several attempts of this nature, all of which eventually foundered. Although the reasons for failure varied from case to case, there was a common thread through all these efforts. All represented an intermingling of political goals, aimed at achieving a major change in the social order, and economic objectives such as higher wages and better working conditions. The most famous of these attempts involved the Noble Order of the Knights of Labor, founded in 1869 by Uriah S. Stephens in Philadelphia, which claimed 700,000 members by 1886. This early success was shortly dissipated, however, as a result of internal conflict between leaders who were interested in economic issues and others who were concerned primarily with political questions and with producing basic changes within the social system itself.

It was in 1886 that a number of leaders left the Knights of Labor and joined with a relatively small group of unions that had been formed five years before under the title Federation of Organized Trades and Labor Unions. The result was the American Federation of Labor (AFL), devoted to the purely economic objectives of increased wages and better working conditions and composed largely of unions organized along craft lines (cigar makers, printers, carpenters, and so on). The spokesman for the organization was Samuel Gompers, and under his presidency it grew rapidly in size and solidified its position despite considerable employer opposition. By 1917 total union membership in the United States, most of it within the AFL, was over three million. The growth of the union movement during this period produced an increasing concern throughout American industry with questions relating to manpower utilization and with what we would now call personnel policy.

The Welfare Secretaries

One response to this growth of trade unionism was the emergence of the so-called social or welfare secretaries, starting just prior to 1900. Although the major stimulus for the creation of these positions was without doubt management's need to find some means of stemming the union tide, it is also true that employers were increasingly concerned over the growing size of their organizations and the fact that it was becoming more and more difficult to maintain close personal contact with employees.

The welfare secretaries were expected to assist the workers by suggesting improvements in working conditions and in any other way that they could. It is largely from these individuals and to some extent from Taylor, although he is much more widely known for his emphasis on improved work methods, that the social welfare tradition in personnel management first developed. The welfare secretaries concerned themselves with helping workers with such matters as housing, medical care, educational facilities, recreational activities, and in the various other areas that have become the province of the social workers of today. They were, in actual fact, engaged almost entirely in promoting the organizational maintenance objective, although this was not widely recognized.

The Early Personnel Departments

It was from a merging of these various developments that the first recognizable personnel departments began to appear in the period between the turn of the century and World War I. In 1902 the National Cash Register Company established a Labor Department that was responsible for such matters as wage administration, grievances, employment, sanitary and working conditions, record keeping, and worker improvement (8). Other companies gradually followed suit, and by 1912 the first employment managers association was founded (4). By 1917 this increased to ten associations, with over one thousand member companies (21).

Although the work performed in these early departments varied somewhat from company to company, there was a common core of activities that were almost invariably present. These were selection, recruiting, record keeping, training, time and motion studies, welfare, and, generally, union relations. The primary stated goal of the personnel function in this pre-World War I period, as with most other aspects of the business enterprise, appears to have been productivity or profit. Welfare activities as well as methods improvements were evaluated either explicitly or implicitly in terms of their contribution to this objective. The organizational maintenance goal as such was not widely recognized or accepted, except among a rather limited group of individuals within the personnel area itself.

Early Industrial Psychology

During this same period some developments were occurring within certain American universities that were to have a profound impact on the future course of personnel management. The science of psychology had had its beginning on the European continent as a combination of physiology and philosophy. By 1900 it had penetrated the United States and had become well established in a number of major universities. Although originally defined as the study of consciousness or conscious experience, this emphasis soon began to fade in the utility-minded American environment (6). Men like James Angell and John Dewey at the University of Chicago started to talk about the *uses* of consciousness and its functions. And psychology began to move to a much greater concern with practical problems.

Cattell and Muensterberg

This utilitarian approach was taken up shortly on the East Coast, particularly by James McKeen Cattell at Columbia University and by Hugo Muensterberg at Harvard. Both of these men made significant contributions to early industrial psychology in the period when the possibility of applying the still adolescent science to industrial problems was just beginning to be recognized. Subsequently their ideas became part of the developing body of knowledge in the field of personnel management as well.

Cattell was a psychologist who had had his early training in the German laboratories where a purely descriptive, nonutilitarian approach to the study of conscious experience prevailed. However, this contact with German psychology apparently did not elicit a very favorable reaction from the young man; he clearly viewed the experimentation as sterile and of little practical value. Spurred on by contacts with Sir Francis Galton, the brilliant British nobleman who had been active in the eugenics movement and who had made many contributions to statistical methodology, Cattell soon turned his attention almost entirely to ways in which psychology could be of use to society. By 1890 he had coined the term *mental test* and had assumed the chairmanship of the psychology department at Columbia University.

During the ensuing years, while in this position, Cattell continued to actively encourage research and interest in the applications of psychology to practical problems. Although some of the early research attempts by students under his direction were notably unsuccessful (22), Cattell remains of great importance historically because of his role as a stimulus in the development of applied psychology. He is also important as the founder, in his later years, of the Psychological Corporation, one of the first consulting firms providing psychological services to the business world and a major publisher of psychological tests for industrial use.

In an even more direct line with the development of personnel management are the activities of Hugo Muensterberg at Harvard University. Unlike Cattell, Muensterberg was German born and raised, but both men received their training in the German laboratories and both were dissatisfied with the nonutilitarian approach that they found there. During the first fifteen years of the twentieth century, Muensterberg developed an extremely active interest in seeking out ways in which psychology could be applied to the problems of business and industry and wrote extensively, expounding his views (16). He was also able to put a number of his ideas to good use within several firms in the Boston area. Perhaps his most famous study involved the development of a selection test for electric-streetcar operators. Throughout Muensterberg's research and writings a strong emphasis on empirical analysis and statistical validation appears continually. This emphasis has now rather thoroughly permeated the methodology of personnel management.

Psychology in World War I

The most historically significant contributions that psychology has made to the origins of the personnel field occurred during World War I. Cattell and Muensterberg were important, but it was not until the war period that objective psychological tests were used on a major scale to facilitate the effective utilization of human resources within a large organization.

The Army was faced with a very difficult problem. It had to train and place the millions of men who were coming to it as a result of the draft. But which recruits should be sent to Officer Candidate School, which to technical specialty schools, which to training of a less complex nature? The Army turned to the American Psychological Association with a request for assistance with this problem. Subsequently a special committee of psychologists was appointed to determine what could be done.

Starting with the assumption that the more intelligent and able individuals should be the ones to attend the Officer Candidate Schools and the higher-level technical training programs, the committee set out to develop a short psychological test that would measure a person's general intelligence. This test was to be given to all recruits at the time of induction into the Army and was to be used as a basis for assigning individuals to the various types of training programs.

THE ARMY ALPHA. This definition of the problem and an approach to its solution were only the beginning. The only intelligence measures in existence at the time were the Binet tests, which were in French, and their translations. But these had to be administered to one person at a time and therefore were completely impractical for military purposes. Thus, a completely new test had to be devised.

Using as their base an experimental instrument that was being developed by Arthur Otis, a Cleveland psychologist, the American Psychological Association committee constructed the Army Alpha, the first group intelligence test and a milestone in the methodology of psychological test construction. Immediately pressed into service, Army Alpha proved extremely valuable as a means of placing draftees and is estimated to have saved the United States government many millions of dollars in training and replacement costs. It also provided a spur for additional developments that subsequently came to have considerable significance for personnel management.

THE ARMY BETA. During the course of a large number of Army Alpha administrations, it became apparent that a surprisingly large number of recruits were scoring at the zero point or very close to it. Investigation revealed that many of these individuals were illiterate and that Army Alpha presumed a certain amount of literacy. This led before long to the construction of a second test, Army Beta, that was specifically designed to provide information regarding the intelligence of those who were not able to read and write well enough to complete Army Alpha. The new instrument proved invaluable as an aid in the placement of less well-educated recruits. It subsequently found wide usage in the postwar years in the testing of immigrants who came to the United States with little knowledge of the English language.

Results obtained with Army Alpha and Army Beta made it clear that although illiteracy was rather widespread at that time, this did not necessarily mean that the intelligence of these people was extremely low. Many had the ability to learn rapidly. It seemed worthwhile therefore to attempt the construction of quick and economical training programs that could bring draftees to at least a certain minimal level of literacy. The courses that resulted were to have considerable impact in years to come on the development of training techniques for use in industry.

Personnel Management in the Interval Between the Wars

The 1920's

As a result of steadily increasing growth prior to the war, the success of the Army personnel program, and the general business boom, personnel management grew rapidly during the 1920's. Many companies added personnel departments for the first time, and a number of colleges and universities began to offer training in the area. Personnel consulting firms began to appear, one of the first being the Scott Company, which was formed by a group of people who had worked on the Army Alpha and Beta during the war years. Personnel research studies were initiated in a variety of settings. The work done at Carnegie Institute of Technology dealing with manpower utilization in the sales management field is particularly noteworthy (10).

The personnel departments of this period looked very much like many that exist today. The major areas of specialization were selection, recruiting, training, methods improvement, and employee welfare. The last activity was strongly supported during the 1920's.

Probably the most important factor contributing to this welfare emphasis was the very intensive campaign that management mounted aimed at discouraging the growth of the labor unions. This became possible after the government-sponsored and -enforced agreements that had been in effect during the war period were permitted to expire. Many companies used both positive incentives, such as benefit and recreation programs, and negative sanctions in their efforts to keep the unions out. This was the period of the· so-called *yellow-dog* contracts, under which the worker agreed, as a condition of employment, not to join a union. At this time also *company unionism* reached its peak. Management-sponsored employee groups of this kind were particularly prevalent in the petroleum industry.

Thus, the welfare programs of the 1920's represented in large part an attempt to eliminate employee dissatisfaction thereby minimizing the conflict-producing impact of the union movement. But this conflict-reduction objective was not the only one involved here. There was a general feeling, which is still popular in some quarters today, that "a happy employee is a productive employee." Thus, the welfare programs were considered to be good for productivity and were justified as such by the personnel departments of the period.

Toward the end of the 1920's a series of experiments began at the Hawthorne plant of the Western Electric Company near Chicago that were to extend over several years and to have a substantial impact on the field of personnel management. Briefly, these experiments, which have been described and discussed at length in other publications (5,12,17), were initiated in order to study the effects of physical factors such as lighting and ventilation on worker productivity. As time went on, it became increasingly apparent that productivity was primarily affected by the emotional state of the employee; by his relationships with other people, particularly those with whom he worked; and by the amount and kind of attention he received from his superiors.

These findings served as the basis for what has since come to be called the *human relations* movement in American industry. For our purposes, however, it is most important that they provided personnel managers with a major justification for their welfare programs. Here was some real evidence that factors in the realm of employee attitudes and motivation did make a difference insofar as performance and productivity and profits were concerned.

The Depression Years

Whereas the 1920's were a time of growth, the 1930's were just the reverse. With the great reduction in business activity throughout the world came a sharp emphasis on cutbacks and savings. Managements were almost universally interested in doing all they could to reduce costs and to eliminate activities that were not absolutely necessary. The welfare programs of personnel management had had some difficulty justifying their existence in times of prosperity; in a time of depression they were clearly in serious trouble. In many companies it soon became apparent that they were definitely expendable.

Gradually, therefore, the welfare tradition began to lose out within personnel management, and in many cases whole personnel departments went with it. Those that remained were in most instances rather drastically reoriented and reorganized. The stimulus for this change came in part from government, both Federal and state, and in part from the labor unions.

Under the pressures of the depression a number of laws were passed that placed the unions in a much more advantageous position than they had held previously. Among the most important of these were the Norris-LaGuardia Act of 1932 and the Wagner Act of 1935. The former drastically limited the use of court injunctions as a method of preventing work stoppages. The Wagner Act went much further and guaranteed the right of workers to organize into labor unions and to bargain collectively with their employers. (These laws will be discussed further in Chapter 5.)

The stimulus provided by this new legal environment produced mass unionization drives in a number of industries that had never previously been organized—automobiles, aluminum, and rubber, among others. These new unions were in many instances of a very different nature than those that had existed since the nineteenth century. Increasingly, management found itself faced with demands from *industrial unions* that included all types of workers from a given industry, regardless of specific occupation. Almost all unions, previously, had been of the *craft* variety and had contained workers in a single occupation irrespective of the industry in which they worked.

By 1941 the total number of union members had increased from the 1933 low of 2,973,000 to a very respectable 8,614,000 (3), and there were now two major national labor federations, the American Federation of Labor and the Congress of Industrial Organizations (CIO). The former still stressed the old concept of craft unionism, whereas the CIO was made up in large part of a group of industrial unions that had seceded from the AFL in 1935.

As a consequence of this tremendous growth in the size and power of the union movement, major changes had to be made in whatever remnants of the earlier personnel departments remained by the mid-1930's. Increasingly, personnel managers found that they had to concern themselves with developing recommendations and evaluating policies designed to deal with the resurgent labor unions. Individuals with legal training began to find positions in personnel departments, and the attention of the personnel field as a whole became riveted on the labor relations problem. Other duties assumed a distinctly secondary role under these new legal constraints (see Chapters 5 and 6).

World War II

Although World War I had a sizable impact on the development of personnel management, the significance of World War II was infinitely greater. One reason was that World War II was conducted on a considerably larger scale and as a result the need for effective manpower utilization was much more pronounced. Second, the demand was not only greater in a quantitative sense, but more complex in a qualitative sense. Weapons and machinery were of a much more advanced design and the airplane in particular had introduced a new set of manpower problems.

Thus, the early 1940's saw a sudden shift away from the labor relations emphasis that had permeated personnel management during the preceding decade. Now problems of selection, training, and leadership became paramount.

Military Research on Selection and Placement Procedures

The assignment given the military personnel researchers of World War II was much more complex than that during World War I, although the basic requirements were much the same. Now, however, the number of technical specialties had increased sizably, so that the placement problem had assumed much greater proportions. As a result, a great variety of psychological tests had to be developed to aid in the process of allocating individuals to training programs and to specific duty assignments.

An example of what was achieved is provided by published reports concerning research undertaken with the Army General Classification Test (AGCT), the World War II successor to Army Alpha (1). Studies carried out in the Engineer, Ordnance, Signal Corps, and Coast Artillery Officer Candidate Schools indicated that scores on this test were related to successful completion of the training, and thus the receipt of a commission, in the following manner:

1. If an individual scored above 125 on the AGCT, the probability that he would eventually graduate and receive his commission was .90, or 90 out of 100.
2. If he scored between 110 and 124, the probability of graduation was .69.
3. If the score was between 100 and 109, the probability was .46.
4. If the score was between 90 and 99, the probability was only .26.

Thus, it is clear that by adopting this test as a screening instrument and accepting only those above a certain score level, it was possible to eliminate many individuals who would have failed. Considerable savings in training time and expense were achieved as a result; the only major cost was that some men who would have succeeded and achieved a commission were not permitted to enter the schools at all and thus were lost to the officer ranks.

Developments in the Training Field

In addition to the very great strides in the theory and technique of psychological measurement that occurred during the war years, there were also some significant developments in the training area. The complex technological innovations of the period fostered considerable emphasis on an applied science of learning. Simplified models representing aspects of the actual combat work situation became quite popular as training devices. So, too, did films, discussion groups, role playing, and other variants of the traditional educational procedures. Many of the training techniques introduced by the armed services at various points throughout the war subsequently found their way into the business world and had a profound influence on industrial training and management development.

THE TRAINING WITHIN INDUSTRY PROGRAM. There was, however, one major development that occurred within the civilian sector itself. Various training programs were systematized and clarified so that they could be used by people who were not particularly experienced or knowledgeable as trainers. Thus, it was possible to convert the large numbers of individuals, many of them women and older people, who flocked into the defense industries into satisfactory workers within a relatively short period of time. And this was accomplished by trainers who in many instances had had no prior experience in the instructor role (14).

Among the most famous of these programs were the Job Instruction Training (JIT) sessions conducted by the Training Within Industry

Division of the War Manpower Commission. Guidelines to be used during the training process were developed in considerable detail. These subsequently provided a basis for many skill training programs in industry; in fact, much the same approach is still employed by many companies today.

Concern with Leadership and Supervisory Techniques

A third development of the World War II years with implications for the future of personnel management was the greatly increased interest in problems of work group effectiveness and the techniques of leadership. The forces behind this trend were several in number. One was the widespread dissemination among personnel managers of the Hawthorne findings, which were taken to indicate that more permissive supervision was far superior to an authoritarian approach. These results did not achieve a major impact throughout industry generally until the early 1940's.

Second, the very facts of the war itself instigated a revulsion against the traditional strong-man theory of leadership that had been accepted in many segments of the business world. There was as a result a widespread search for a theory of leadership more in keeping with American democratic values.

Finally, many of the individuals in charge of the manpower utilization programs of the armed services were psychologists who were thoroughly familiar with the controlled experimental studies conducted by Kurt Lewin and others at the University of Iowa. These studies seemed at the time to indicate clearly the superiority of democratic as opposed to authoritarian leadership techniques.

All these factors combined, plus others, gave a strong impetus to the concern with effective supervisory behaviors. How should a manager treat his men to induce them to contribute maximally to the company's goals? There was a strong suspicion that he should be as permissive and democratic as possible. Perhaps this particular viewpoint was overemphasized, but in any event a strong interest in problems of leadership was initiated that has continued to the present.

The Postwar Decade

The first ten years after the end of World War II represented a period of growth for the profession of personnel management. There was almost constant expansion in nearly every segment of the economy and in the educational system as well. The personnel field shared in this expansion and perhaps even gained proportionately over other areas. But by the mid-1950's it had become increasingly apparent that the superstructure had not been built on a really solid foundation. Some reordering of the general bases of the personnel profession was definitely needed. Let us take up these developments in greater detail, and in the order of their occurrence.

Developments Within Industry

By the end of the war the newly developed personnel selection and assignment procedures had clearly proved themselves. Furthermore, training methods had become generally available which were adequate to the task of converting inexperienced workers into competent employees capable of operating very complex equipment. Finally, attention had been focused on the problem of effective industrial leadership within a democratic society, and preliminary results from experimentation involving democratic and autocratic techniques seemed to indicate that progress was being made in this area.

Many firms installed comprehensive selection systems, utilizing the new theoretical and methodological developments that were emerging from universities and research centers. Training and management-development programs became a standard and integral part of the personnel program. There was a particularly marked increase in the number of human relations courses for supervisors. The latter had their origins in the Hawthorne findings and more recently in the democratic type of leadership theory that had become popular during the war. These training programs were very much in the welfare tradition of personnel management, emphasizing as they did the importance of consideration and kindness in dealing with subordinates. Treating employees in this manner, it was argued, would increase their satisfaction with the work situation and thereby contribute to more effective performance and higher profits. Thus, the productivity objective was still generally considered to be the only really important goal of the business enterprise, or at least it was the only goal that had the stamp of legitimacy and that, therefore, could be openly discussed. A number of personnel managers were, however, beginning to shape their actual behavior in terms of organizational maintenance considerations as well.

Other developments within the business world included a major expansion of health and welfare programs, retirement plans, and various other so-called *fringe benefits*. These were extremely costly to management, but the pressures from the unions, the employees generally, and the society as a whole were so strong that they could not be denied. The labor unions became particularly militant during the late 1940's, after the hiatus of the war period, and made increasing demands on industry. Many of these demands were granted, but only after lengthy strikes and extended negotiation. Thus, labor relations once again became a major area of concern within personnel management, but now in conjunction with other areas as well.

This growth within the personnel field took place against a background of continued business expansion and an ever-increasing demand for skilled manpower. By the early 1950's shortages of human resources had become acute, especially in the technical and engineering occupations. Management was increasingly faced with the problem of attracting and holding highly skilled employees at a time when the supply was limited by the low depression birth rate and the third of a million deaths that had occurred among members of the armed services during World War II. Organizational maintenance problems came to the fore during this period and combined with the already existing union and other pressures to foster a continued expansion of fringe benefit programs. Management hoped that these benefits would help in recruiting and also induce present employees to remain with the company. Yet the organizational maintenance goal was still not generally recognized as a major company objective, separate and distinct from productivity.

Developments Within the Universities

There was also considerable growth within the colleges and universities, where personnel management became clearly established as a distinct management specialty. Two aspects of this growth can be distinguished. One was a sharp increase in the number of courses dealing with manpower utilization and the various aspects of the personnel function. Practically every major school of business administration had a curriculum in personnel management by the end of the postwar decade. Graduate programs, in particular, were attracting sizable numbers of students.

A second major development was the establishment, at a number of universities, of various research centers and institutes specifically devoted to the study of manpower problems within business and industry. Among the first of these were the School of Industrial and Labor Relations at Cornell University (1944), the Institute of Labor and Industrial Relations at the University of Illinois (1946), and the Industrial Relations Center at the University of Minnesota (1945).

Although these centers have been most important in their role as agents in the search for basic knowledge, they have also made a significant contribution in attracting a number of capable individuals to the personnel field. Scholars from a variety of disciplines have been brought together in the industrial relations centers with the result that a multidimensional approach to the problems of the field has been encouraged. Most prominent among the participants have been economists, psychologists, sociologists, industrial engineers, political scientists, and lawyers. The research emerging from this amalgamation of basic disciplines has proved to be of inestimable value to the practicing professionals of personnel management.

The Period of Reevaluation

By the mid-1950's, in spite of the tremendous growth that had occurred since the end of the war, personnel management was once again in trouble. This time, however, the problem was not organizational in nature: It was not a matter, as during the depression, of whether the personnel function would continue to be represented in the business world. Rather the difficulties were largely conceptual.

One major problem involved the human relations approaches that had been adopted on the advice of their personnel managers by many companies as a means of increasing productivity. It now became evident that whereas human relations techniques might well raise the general level of job satisfaction, and even foster better emotional adjustment among employees, they did not necessarily contribute anything to productivity. Research increasingly indicated that the long-accepted assumption of a constant, positive relationship between job satisfaction and work output was basically incorrect (7). In some instances worker satisfaction did seem to contribute to increased productivity, but almost as often it produced the reverse. Generally the studies yielded no evidence for a relationship of any kind.

A second type of difficulty appeared as research evidence began to pile up regarding the relative effectiveness of the various procedures and techniques employed by the personnel profession. A number of practices that had become widely accepted seemed to be accomplishing their stated objectives in a much less satisfactory manner than had been assumed. The selection interview, which had been in use for many years (20), came under particularly severe attack. The basic complaint was that, at least as an information-gathering device, the interview was sorely deficient in a number of respects (15). Considerable research appeared to be needed before definitive conclusions could be reached regarding the relative advantages of the interview as compared with other methods of achieving the same objectives.

An additional source of concern was the area of labor-management relations. The unions had continued to grow in the postwar period, from 12,724,700 members in 1945 to over 17 million by 1954 (11), and this growth was paralleled by a similar increase in union power. Furthermore, the two major federations had merged into one in 1955, thus reducing the internal dissension that had often plagued the labor movement and presenting management with a more unified type of opposition. Yet no major advances in knowledge had occurred that might provide a greater understanding of labor-management conflict and thus offer the prospect that more peaceable answers would eventually be available in this area.

Finally, the stresses and strains associated with manpower shortages and technological change were increasing, and few companies had been able to find adequate solutions to the problems thus created. By the mid-1950's experienced men with the skills appropriate to a semiautomated or totally automated production process were in extremely short supply. Also, an almost infinite variety of human problems had emerged with the new technology, including a need for a redistribution of manpower resources within many firms, for extensive retraining, and in a number of instances for major changes in organization structure.

These difficulties were further compounded as a consequence of some major shifts in the composition of the postwar labor force. As compared with the prewar period, the workers now available were much better educated and had had a considerably broader spectrum of experiences. Then there were the increasing numbers of women who were seeking and finding employment in the business world. Clearly many of the personnel policies developed in an earlier period were not adequate to the new task.

The Recent Past: Clarification of Goals

Although many of these problems remain today and the reevaluation process is not yet at an end, there has been some conceptual clarification. As a result, personnel management now appears to be in a better position to meet the challenges of the future than at any time in the past.

What has happened is that the idea of multiple organizational goals has finally achieved a degree of acceptance (9). At least within personnel management, and increasingly throughout the rest of management as well, there has come a general recognition that productivity and profit, although extremely important, are not the only factors that must be considered when developing company procedures and policies. The task of keeping the organization together as an ongoing entity in the face of external and internal stresses is also of considerable import.

It has become evident that the kinds of managerial policies and programs that will maximize one type of goal attainment may have little or no relevance for the other. Thus, a policy designed to soften the impact of a major change in production methods might be extremely successful in keeping anxiety and dissension to a minimum and yet have no direct effect on performance levels and productivity. Turnover and union difficulty could be reduced by such a policy without there being any change in worker energy expenditure and effort.

This clarification of the nature of organizational goals, along with the realization that procedures intended to contribute to one type of goal might not be of much value in achieving another and might even on occasion be detrimental, appears to have derived from two major sources. For one thing a number of practicing personnel managers have gradually moved to this position as a result of their experiences in dealing with specific manpower problems. The most explicit statement of this viewpoint, however, seems to have come from the universities, where a good deal of relevant research has been in progress for some time.

The most significant studies were those conducted at the University of Michigan (13) and at Ohio State University (18). Both of these research programs produced considerable evidence, largely as a result of field studies carried out in ongoing business organizations, indicating that organizational maintenance was, in fact, an important and independent factor in business success. The results demonstrated that where employees were satisfied with the company, their jobs, and their relationships with each other, and where the individual was made to feel that he was a valuable and trusted member of the organization, the company was most likely to withstand external and internal stresses effectively. Turnover and absenteeism could be expected to be low and the organization would be in a position to maintain itself as a stable entity. However, policies which lead to this condition need not have a positive effect on productivity. In fact, the reverse *can* be true.

Thus, the frequently conflicting traditions within personnel management, productivity (or profit) maximization and welfarism, seem to have achieved some reconciliation, at least for the moment. Both are seen as important factors, which need not be either positively or negatively related. A happy employee is not necessarily a productive one, but this does not mean that programs that attempt to increase employee satisfactions are inevitably wasteful.

References

1. Bellows, R., *Psychology of Personnel in Business and Industry.* Englewood Cliffs, N.J.: Prentice-Hall, 1961.
2. Bendix, R., *Work and Authority in Industry.* New York: Wiley, 1956.
3. Bernstein, I., "The Growth of American Unions," *American Economic Review,* Vol. 44 (1954), 303–304.
4. Bloomfield, M., "The Aim and Work of the Employment Managers' Associations," *Annals, American Academy of Political and Social Science,* Vol. 65 (1916), 77.
5. Blum, M. L., *Industrial Psychology and Its Social Foundations,* Rev. ed. New York: Harper & Row, 1956.
6. Boring, E. G., *A History of Experimental Psychology.* New York: Appleton-Century-Crofts, 1950.
7. Brayfield, A. H., and W. H. Crockett, "Employee Attitudes and Employee Performance," *Psychological Bulletin,* Vol. 52 (1955), 396–424.

8. Eilbert, H., "The Development of Personnel Management in the United States," *Business History Review*, Vol. 33 (1959), 345–364.
9. England, G. W., "Organizational Goals and Expected Behavior of American Managers," *Academy of Management Journal*, Vol. 10 (1967), 107–117.
10. Ferguson, L. W., "The Development of Industrial Psychology," in H. Gilmer (ed.), *Industrial Psychology*. New York: McGraw-Hill, 1961.
11. Gitlow, A. L., *Labor and Industrial Society*. Homewood, Ill.: Irwin, 1963.
12. Landsberger, H., *Hawthorne Revisited*. Ithaca, N.Y.: Cornell Univ. Press, 1958.
13. Likert, R., *New Patterns of Management*. New York: McGraw-Hill, 1961.
14. Ling, C. C., *The Management of Personnel Relations—History and Origins*. Homewood, Ill.: Irwin, 1965.
15. Mandell, M., "The Group Oral Performance Test," *Personnel Administration*, Vol. 15 (1952), 1–5.
16. Muensterberg, H., *Psychology and Industrial Efficiency*. Boston: Houghton Mifflin, 1913.
17. Roethlisberger, F. J., and W. J. Dickson, *Management and the Worker*. Cambridge, Mass.: Harvard Univ. Press, 1939.
18. Stogdill, R., *Individual Behavior and Group Achievement*. New York: Oxford, 1959.
19. Taylor, F. W., *The Principles of Scientific Management*. New York: Harper & Row, 1911.
20. Wagner, R., "The Employment Interview: A Critical Summary," *Personnel Psychology*, Vol. 2 (1949), 17–46.
21. Willits, J. H., "Development of Employment Managers' Associations," *Monthly Labor Review*, Vol. 5 (1917), 497–499.
22. Wissler, C., "The Correlation of Mental and Physical Traits," *Psychological Monographs*, Vol. 3 (1901).

Questions

1. Discuss the contributions of J. McKeen Cattell and Hugo Muensterberg to the growth of personnel management.
2. Trace the "welfarism" tradition in personnel management from its beginnings to its current status. Emphasize the rational justifications for this tradition in business and how they have changed over the years.
3. Discuss the similarities and differences between the effects of World War I and World War II on the growth of personnel management.
4. Of what importance was the depression during the 1930's to the growth of personnel management? Do you think that a depression today would have the same effect on the field?
5. Who was F. W. Taylor and of what importance is he to personnel management?

II

**Constraints on
Personnel Decisions**

3

Internal Constraints:
Individual Differences

People differ from one another. They differ in an almost infinite number of respects, including aspects of their intelligence, personality, and physical makeup. This fact of difference is something of which we are all aware to the point that we generally tend to take it for granted, yet the practice of personnel management is influenced as much by this diversity of human characteristics as by any other factor.

At any given point in space and time the decisions that a personnel manager makes and can implement, in his efforts to maximize the attainment of productivity and organizational maintenance goals, are severely restricted by the specific nature of the human resources available to him. He has at his disposal a limited set of abilities, specialized knowledges, motives, and muscular skills that characterize the individuals working for the company. His freedom to make and carry out decisions, to initiate programs, and to implement policies is confined within an area determined by existing potentialities for certain types of behavior. Thus, a major scientific research effort cannot be mounted immediately by a firm devoid of employees with advanced training in the sciences, and an effective office-machine unit cannot be achieved within an organization that lacks people with very high levels of work motivation, or industriousness, to operate the machines (27,28). It is in this sense that individual differences act as constraints on personnel decisions.

Yet constraints of this kind are not so rigid that there is no possibility of modification. At a given point in time, with one's perspective limited to a specific organization and the individuals constituting it, these constraints do tend to appear insurmountable. But given a longer time span and the possibility of utilizing human resources outside the existing firm, many can be made to disappear. Thus, it is important to know not only how people differ in those characteristics that are related to the attainment of organizational goals, but also how various types of individuals may be changed—at what cost, under what circumstances, and in how short a period of time. Which of the constraints within the company are for all practical purposes absolute, because no matter where one searches in the national labor force or what type of change procedure is introduced, the restrictions imposed are not likely to be overcome? Which internal constraints are relatively resilient, given the opportunity to go outside the confines of the existing organization and to extend the change process into the future?

This chapter represents an attempt to answer these questions. An effort will be made to review some of what is currently known about the differences that exist between various major groups in our society. In the process the reader should gain an understanding of many of the human factors that play an important role in determining whether an organization will survive and attain high levels of productivity. In addition, an attempt will be made to indicate which factors are susceptible to change and to at least note in passing how these modifications may be brought about. Subsequent chapters, however, will take up the personnel manager's role as a change agent in much greater detail. The primary emphasis here must be on the *degree* to which internal constraints of the kind represented by individual differences are, in view of the present state of our knowledge, subject to alteration and circumvention.

In this review no effort will be made to cover the entire field of differential psychology, the scientific specialty that deals with individual and group variability, because the area is far too large and complex (2,38). An attempt will be made, however, to take up those factors that are of primary significance for the practice of personnel management.

Individual and Group Differences

Because the major problem insofar as a personnel manager is concerned is to determine where within the labor force as a whole a given level of ability or a given characteristic is most likely to be found, the discussions that follow will deal primarily with group differences. If a department within the company contains individuals of a particular age, sex, occupational group, or social class, it is important to know what human characteristics might be expected to predominate in such a group. Similarly, if one wants to overcome a constraint imposed as a result of these characteristics being available, rather than others, by recruiting individuals from the outside, it is desirable to know where to look for the kinds of skills that are lacking (in which groups these skills are most likely to be found).

An important limitation of this type of analysis, however, stems from the fact that groups are generally described in terms of some average value, usually the *mean*. Thus, we shall be concerned primarily with differences among group means and with contrasting trends among groups. This is not the same as talking about individuals. Not all members of a group are likely to be at the average; rather they will be distributed above and below the mean, often in a pattern similar to the bell-shaped *normal distribution*. Thus, generalizing from knowledge about a group to specific individuals within the group can become a rather hazardous affair. And it is not necessarily true that, because two groups have distinctly different means, two individual members of the respective groups will invariably differ in the same manner.

Anastasi (2) makes this point clear in discussing a research study that required that a test of arithmetic reasoning ability be administered to 189 boys and 206 girls in the third and fourth elementary grades. It was found that the boys had a mean score on this particular test of 40.39, whereas the girls had a mean score of 35.81. The difference between the two groups appeared to be substantial. (It was significant at the .01 level, and thus would be expected to occur less than once in a hundred times if a mere chance fluctuation rather than a real and basic difference between boys and girls were responsible for the result.)

However, the author goes on to emphasize that even in this instance of a highly reliable group difference, 28 per cent of the girls reached or exceeded the median score for the boys, a figure that was, of course, exceeded by 50 per cent of the boys. The significance of this for a personnel manager is that, if these differences are retained into adulthood (and other evidence would indicate that they are), he will find a greater concentration of high levels of arithmetic ability among males. But many females may also possess comparable ability. Thus, in times of talent shortage this source might be well worth investigating; previously male jobs might be staffed with individuals of both sexes. Furthermore, it is clear that one cannot classify an individual in terms of arithmetic reasoning competence merely on the basis of knowledge regarding his or her sex. Many of the girls scored higher than a number of the boys. Apparently, therefore, in this area at least, group differences cannot be translated directly into individual differences.

This point emerges even more clearly from a study made by the U.S. Army Personnel Research Office (9). The researchers knew that on a number of the aptitude tests used for assigning Army recruits to occupational specialties males performed significantly better than females in terms of average scores. The problem posed was, given this fact of a clear-cut sex difference, how many females would be able to meet various required minimum acceptable levels of test performance (cutoff scores) in times of talent shortages. The results of the study are presented in Table 3-1.

Table 3-1.   Sex Differences in Qualifications for Three Aptitude Areas

Aptitude area	Per cent qualifying for aptitude area with cut-off score of 90		Per cent qualifying for aptitude area with cut-off score of 100	
	Females	Males	Females	Males
Electronics	55	93	19	76
General maintenance	27	88	5	70
Motor maintenance	14	85	2	52

Source: E. F. Fuchs and C. H. Hammer, "A Survey of Women's Aptitudes for Army Jobs," *Personnel Psychology,* Vol. 16 (1963), p. 153.

It is apparent that there are a number of female recruits who could qualify for work in the areas represented, especially electronics, without time-consuming and costly training. Yet it is also clear that under normal conditions of manpower availability males are most likely to be equipped to perform effectively in the type of position under study. One would have to search much less widely among recruits of the masculine sex to find a specified number of acceptable workers.

Differences Between the Sexes

In view of the major differences in the upbringing of members of the two sexes and in the roles they play in adult life, it seems important to extend our discussion of the relative positions of males and females, especially in those areas that are closely related to the goals of business organizations. This is a field that has received considerable attention from researchers, and consequently a good deal of information is available.

Differences in Abilities

The sexes do not appear to differ very much, if at all, in terms of the most important type of mental ability in our society, verbal ability. In a nationwide survey of intelligence, using a short vocabulary test that is apparently very similar to most measures of general intelligence, the mean score for the 721 males was 10.75 and for the 779 females 10.78

(26). This difference is of no significance and is typical of most that have been obtained, although another national survey did produce a somewhat larger discrepancy in favor of the female sex (39). In any event such differences as may exist in the ability most closely associated with general intelligence do not appear to be sufficient to influence personnel decisions.

There are other abilities, however, where important differences do exist (2). In the area of manipulative abilities, for example, there is evidence that women are clearly superior, both in the speed of their movements and in their accuracy. Female groups consistently score higher on the standard measures in this area such as the O'Connor Finger Dexterity Test, the O'Connor Tweezer Dexterity Test, and the Purdue Pegboard. In addition, women generally excel on tasks relating to the rapid perception of details. On the Minnesota Clerical Aptitude Test, which requires the checking of similarities and differences between lists of names and numbers, only 16 per cent of the male working population scored above the level attained by the average female.

However, the ability to pay attention visually to some specific object without being disturbed by the surrounding context, an occupational skill of some importance in these days of dial-watching and automated equipment, is much more pronounced among males. In fact men generally do somewhat better than women on tasks related to the spatial and mechanical abilities, apparently because of the differences in what society expects of members of the two sexes. As indicated previously, men tend to be rather markedly superior in activities involving the use of numbers and arithmetic or mathematical reasoning.

Finally, the average female is superior insofar as abilities related to artistic and musical performance are concerned, although the predominance of males at the very top levels in these fields suggests that the amount of time and effort devoted to learning is an important consideration. When an individual man or woman is willing to break through the sex role constraints, he or she may well achieve a great deal. Yet in an overall sense it seems to be generally true that men are more skillful in those areas that have traditionally been defined as masculine in nature, and women exhibit greater competence when the abilities relate directly to tasks that society considers essentially feminine. It appears likely, therefore, that the differences noted will remain, as long as there is no major change in the way children are raised in this country and in the things they are taught.

Differences in Personality

Among the many differences that have been found between men and women, a pattern that is manifested again and again is the generally much stronger social orientation of members of the female sex. This greater concern with and for other people begins early and continues throughout life. It is evident both within and outside the work situation.

Two examples may serve to illustrate the relevance of this difference for personnel management. The first derives from a research study dealing with the introduction of automated office equipment in an insurance company (16). Here it was quite apparent that the female employees developed highly negative attitudes toward the change because they were afraid that social relationships in the office would be upset. In another study (24) females were found to be much more oriented toward attempting to gain high scores on a specially constructed test when their superior performance might lead to social, rather than intellectual, acceptability. Men, on the other hand, were much more strongly oriented toward achievement and advancement in an intellectual sense.

This pattern, with social orientation paramount among women and achievement orientation more pronounced among men, receives further substantiation from research that has been done with a variety of psychological measures. On the Kuder Preference Record men tend to obtain higher scores on the mechanical, persuasive, computational, and scientific scales, whereas women exhibit greater interest in the literary, musical, clerical, social service, and artistic areas (2). Similarly, with the Study of Values men score higher on the Theoretical, Economic, and Political indexes and women on the Aesthetic, Social, and Religious ones (1). In general the evidence from a number of studies indicates that women are more concerned with such matters as spiritual values, the enjoyment of artistic experience, and the welfare of others. In contrast men tend to have a greater desire for prestige and power, as well as more appreciation of abstract knowledge and understanding. There is, however, considerable overlapping on all these characteristics. Thus, it should not be surprising to find a number of success-oriented women in any group of reasonable size. In fields such as retail sales, where women have considerable opportunity to advance, the incidence would appear to be quite high (30).

Another important difference that probably has both biological and cultural origins is the greater aggressiveness of the masculine sex (2). This consistent trend manifests itself in a variety of ways, suggesting that internal stresses tending to divert a company from its maintenance goal will be at a maximum in the primarily male organization or department. On personality inventories this factor apparently accounts for the fact that males usually score higher on scales measuring ascendance and dominance, traits that appear to have much in common with aggression (11,12).

Finally, a very important difference between the sexes occurs in the area of emotional adjustment. There is good reason to believe that many more women than men experience considerable emotional distress and that symptoms of an emotional nature are also more prevalent among women (13). Although a greater sensitivity to internal feelings generally and a greater willingness to report such feelings to others may account in part for these findings, the evidence suggests that women are actually less well adjusted as a group in our society than men. The implications of this difference for employment are discussed at some length toward the end of this chapter.

The Prospects for Removing Constraints

It appears, then, that there are certain types of work for which women are much less likely to be qualified than men, and other types where the reverse is true. This fact may well serve to limit the alternatives open to a personnel manager as he attempts to solve the problems facing him. Thus, if a company employing primarily semiskilled female workers engaged in individual manual assembly tasks wishes to move to an automated production process requiring primarily spatial and mechanical skills of the operators, the existing work force could constitute a major problem. There is every reason to believe that the abilities required for the change would not be available in sufficient quantity among the present employee group. To circumvent this constraint, it would be necessary to either go outside the company, presumably so as to keep recruiting costs at a minimum among the male population, to find the skills now required or perhaps something could be done to overcome the barrier imposed by the existing characteristics of the present employee group. Perhaps the abilities of the women could be changed.

What are the chances that constraints of this kind can be removed by changing people? In general the prospects, insofar as various intellectual abilities are concerned, do not appear to be very good. Although learning is clearly involved here, this learning tends to occur at the most rapid rate during the formative years while the individual is devoting his energies almost entirely to his education. Probably if a similar amount of time were allocated to the learning process in adult life, changes could be produced then, and many women could develop their mechanical, spatial, and numerical abilities to a much higher level. This assumes, however, that they would also *want* to learn in these areas. In actual fact the time involved and the problem of motivation present almost insurmountable barriers in adult life as our society is now structured.

Unfortunately for any attempt at change, most differences between the sexes are firmly embedded in the culture. In spite of some recent changes, we still have rather deeply rooted concepts of the male and female role, of the things men and women should be good at. Because the members of the two sexes want to meet these role prescriptions, it is very difficult to induce a sizable number of males to develop skills and personality characteristics they consider basically feminine, and it is equally difficult to get women to acquire behavior patterns that are generally designated as masculine.

It is also true, of course, that certain of the abilities we have discussed may well be determined in large part by biological factors which are sex linked. This would seem to be particularly true in the physical area, insofar as such things as physical strength and manipulative skills are concerned. Here the chances for major change would seem to be small, although training can make some difference.

Yet the prospects for removing internal constraints by changing members of the existing work force are not quite all bleak. There is reason to believe, for instance, that the relative lack of success and achievement motivation among women can be overcome to some degree. One way in which this may be accomplished is to open up to women some of the more challenging higher-level positions that have been denied to them in many companies. The increase in level of expectations resulting should contribute to an overall rise in achievement motivation throughout the female work force. In addition, the greater opportunity will attract to the firm women who want to attain occupational success.

If this greater opportunity within the company can be coupled with attendance at adult education or university courses, the prospects for change would seem to be even better. A number of university programs designed to facilitate the return of married women to the labor force have been developed in recent years. Personnel managers can help to bring these programs to the attention of their employees and in the process contribute to a much more pronounced success orientation.

The degree to which women can be changed in this respect is best illustrated by reference to a specific study (30). Forty-one college women moved from an initial mean score of 1.59 to a score of 4.24 on a measure of motivation to assume management responsibilities and exercise power after completing a course specifically designed to produce this type of change. The increase is highly reliable and thus cannot be attributed to chance. The women clearly did change, even though, as might be expected, they held rather unfavorable attitudes toward managerial work at the outset and were still somewhat negative after the training. Other evidence indicates that these changes can be retained over a considerable period of time.

Age Differences

Among the group differences that are of significance for personnel management, those related to age rank toward the very top. Pension plans and retirement policies must be formulated with specific reference to variations in the degree to which older and younger workers can contribute to company objectives. In addition, replacement planning should be carried out with a view to constraints imposed by differences between age groups. If, for instance, younger workers can generally contribute most effectively in certain areas, it is important that whenever possible they be brought into the company to fill vacancies that occur because of retirement or for other reasons. Without this the average age of the work force may creep up to the point where only the skills of older employees are available. Eventually a time will come when practically all employees are eligible for retirement and the company will lack adequately trained replacements.

Differences in Abilities

For many years the belief among psychologists and educators in this country was that general intelligence (primarily verbal ability) showed a steady rise until the late teens and then began a decline that extended throughout the rest of life. Recent advances in research methodology and a greater sophistication in the use of research tools, however, have led to a drastic revision of this belief. It is now recognized that those studies which seemed to demonstrate a decrease in intelligence with increasing age may have turned out as they did largely because older people in our society usually have less education. When the older and younger groups are equated in terms of education, no evidence of decline can be found (26). In fact it appears that, at least among those with high school or college training, there is actually a slight tendency for intelligence to rise throughout adult life. Many such people apparently have greater ability toward the end of their occupational careers than at the beginning. These findings have received support from other studies in which the same individuals were tested at various times over the life span (3,32).

Thus, at present there seems little reason to expect any decline in general intelligence or verbal ability with age, and in fact at the higher occupational, educational, and intellectual levels there should be an increase. On the other hand it is true that, because of their somewhat lower average educational level, older people generally do score below the peak age group (individuals in their late thirties and early forties).

Other abilities do not follow quite the same pattern; there does seem to be a decline in many cases. In most areas other than the verbal, people tend to become somewhat less competent after their mid-twenties, although in individual cases where the skills are continually practiced, this drop-off may well not occur. A rather pronounced decrement with age is particularly likely to appear on tasks that emphasize speed. Here there seems little doubt that significant decreases do occur—partly as a consequence of reduced efficiency in visual perception and partly as a result of a falloff in the rapidity with which muscular responses can be carried out.

None of this should be taken to imply that older workers cannot be taught new skills. Such problems as do arise in this regard appear to be primarily attributable to inappropriate motivation rather than to a lack of the ability required for learning. Older people have had an opportunity to develop rather definite attitudes as a result of their extensive work experience. Over the years beliefs regarding the correct way to do things have been reinforced again and again, to the point where they become firmly entrenched in the personality. For this reason individuals who have been in the labor force for a considerable period often fail to appreciate the value of new techniques and procedures. They fail to learn new skills largely because they do not believe such learning is desirable, rather than because of a lack of ability. This is an important point to keep in mind during this particular period in our history when, because of technological change and the introduction of automated equipment, retraining is a constant fact of life in most companies.

Insofar as work performance is concerned, it seems clear that problems are most likely to arise when an older worker is employed in a factory job, or something similar, which requires extensive physical activity. After the age of about forty-five it becomes very difficult to carry out repetitive physical activities at a rapid pace (40). Thus, the quality of work done may be maintained at a high level, but the quantity of output is likely to fall off. In office jobs, however, and in managerial or professional positions, where intellectual and, particularly, verbal abilities take on more significance, performance should not decline with age. In fact in many managerial positions there may be a steady improvement as a result of increased verbal competence and experience.

Differences in Personality

We have already noted that there is a tendency for older people to hold onto previously established attitudes and to oppose the introduction of new work procedures. This pattern of resistance against the unfamiliar, the unforeseen, and the novel is not, however, restricted to the occupational sphere. It appears to be true generally (36), and may take on a uniquely personal tone, so that an experienced employee can stand out alone as being somewhat obstructionist even when almost everyone else favors a new approach.

Research has revealed a number of additional changes that tend to occur with age (37). The work motivation of the average person in the United States, for instance, rises during the teens and reaches a high point in the early twenties. After that there is a decline, at first precipitous and then more gradual, that continues throughout the years of employment. Thus, people tend to be most devoted to their work and presumably most interested in accomplishment shortly after entering the labor force. The average person, however, becomes less and less industrious as he continues in his occupation.

Interest in people and thus the desire to be with other human beings follows just the opposite course. It rises from a low point in the early twenties to a maximum just prior to the time of retirement. As people decline in work orientation, they seem, in a great many instances, to shift toward a much more pronounced social orientation. This is not to say that they conform more to social pressures, however. In general the tendency to follow the lead of the group—to go along with what is socially accepted and think like other people—is most characteristic in the early years. Sometime around thirty, or shortly thereafter, a decline in conformity sets in that continues uninterrupted throughout the remaining years of employment. Individualism is most likely to emerge later in life when a man's station has become reasonably well established and when he has less to lose by repudiating some of the widely established social norms.

Taken as a whole these data seem to imply that the commitment to the company's productivity goal will be greatest among younger employees and considerably less in the older age groups. Perhaps this accounts in part for the resistance to innovation we have noted in this latter group. Work, productivity, and profit are not considered important enough to warrant all the effort involved in learning and becoming accustomed to the new procedures.

The commitment to organizational maintenance, on the other hand, would seem to be less directly related to age, although a change in the basis for this commitment may well occur over time. In the early years an individual avoids behavior that would produce conflict and dissension within the organization, not because he likes the people around him but because he feels a need to conform to socially accepted behavior patterns. Later on intracompany stress may be minimized by the positive feelings toward each other that people develop with increasing age. Many older employees may care very little about conforming but still not want to do anything that might disrupt their extensive network of friendships in the work situation.

Removing Constraints

In general the constraints imposed on personnel management as a result of age differences can be overcome—either by going outside the firm to hire new employees, thus maintaining a balanced work force appropriate to the tasks to be performed, or by carrying out various changes within the company.

The decline in visual perception that usually comes with age need not result in a major decrement in performance on the part of the worker.

To a considerable extent job restructuring and redesign can mitigate the effects of these losses in perceptual abilities. Such restructuring now appears to be possible in many cases where it was not considered feasible previously. To take an example, an individual may be required to react to various dials on a dashboard and have difficulty doing so accurately and quickly. A simple repainting of the dashboard may serve to make the dials stand out more vividly and thus reduce the effects of poor visual perception.

Similarly the decline in muscular speed among older employees may be compensated for by emphasizing the penchant for accuracy that also appears to develop with age. In many instances a reduced quantity of output per individual becomes acceptable if waste and breakage are almost completely avoided and errors are rare. Often a separate inspection job can be eliminated entirely when older workers are engaged in the production process; the duties of the inspector are taken over by the production workers themselves, thus reducing the need for extremely high output rates.

Even the resistance to change and novelty that seems to characterize many older employees at all levels within a company can be overcome under appropriate circumstances. There is a growing body of research dealing with procedures for inducing attitude change, and if the personnel manager keeps himself informed regarding this work, there is every reason to believe he will find considerable opportunity to put his knowledge to good use. Although later chapters of this book take up this area much more thoroughly, it is important to note here that some general principles are beginning to emerge from the research that can be put to use by practitioners, not only in the field of personnel management but in areas such as advertising, sales promotion, public relations, and so on.

Geographical and Racial Differences

Another set of constraints on personnel decisions arises because of the specific location of the company installation. If a plant is located in a rural area, the employees are likely to possess any characteristics associated with the rural population; if it is located on the West Coast, then anything that is distinctive among residents of this region can be expected to emerge in the employee group as well. The resulting homogeneity may act to make certain alternative courses of action impossible, at least without some change in the composition of the work force.

Because in the United States the major racial differences that are of significance for personnel management involve Negroes and whites and because the Negro population still tends to be clustered on a largely geographical basis (in the South and in the large cities), it seems appropriate to take up racial variations in conjunction with those related to location.

Differences in Abilities

There can be little disagreement, among those conversant with the research literature, regarding the fact that major differences along geographical and racial lines do exist in the United States. The differences in mental abilities seem to be narrowing in practically all areas, but true equalization has not yet occurred. Changes over the last thirty years or so have been sufficient to produce a sizable overlap, however. Even the most deprived geographical area can now be presumed to possess many individuals who are intellectually superior to the national average. The same pattern emerges from the numerous studies in which Negro and white groups have been compared.

GEOGRAPHICAL AREA. One significant finding involves differences in general ability among the various major regions of the United States. Although there are sizable variations among areas within each region, it is still true that when these internal fluctuations are averaged out regional differences do remain (26). The highest level of ability has consistently been found in the three West Coast states. The other areas of the country do not appear to differ a great deal, except for the Deep South, where studies have repeatedly indicated that the general level of intelligence is well below the national average. Interestingly this tendency to low scores does not seem to extend to the Border South: Virginia, North Carolina, Kentucky, Tennessee, Oklahoma, Texas, and Florida.

When the country is cut up in another manner on the basis of the population of the area, i.e., when rural-urban differences are studied, significant findings again emerge. In general, lower average scores are found in the rural areas—in farming country and in the small towns under 2,500 population (25,26). The highest levels of ability are found in the suburban areas around the largest cities. With the demise of the one-room school house and the general improvement of education throughout the less populous parts of the country, this difference seems to be decreasing, however.

In the past there has been a tendency for individuals of higher intelligence to migrate from rural areas where opportunity was at a minimum to the cities, and this trend is probably still continuing to some degree. Yet it is also true that with the advent of large-scale farming in the West and Middle West, there has been a major increase in opportunity within the rural areas. The rewards for those intellectually and educationally qualified to engage in large-scale farming have become sizable. Thus, in many areas the drain-off of the upper levels of talent is probably minimal now, if it exists at all.

On the whole it is probably true that differences associated with specific localities are larger and more important insofar as personnel management is concerned than those found when the major regions of the country or various groupings based on population density are compared. Local circumstances affecting the caliber of education and the patterns of migration, either in or out of an area, seem to be the really crucial factors insofar as geographical differences are concerned.

NEGRO-WHITE DIFFERENCES. There can be little doubt that there does exist a significant difference on general ability tests between Negroes and whites in the United States today. Typical of the many studies reporting such a result is one based on the short vocabulary test mentioned previously. Samples of 1,347 whites and 153 Negroes, both of which were selected to be typical of the two racial groups throughout the United States, yielded mean scores of 11.06 and 8.08, respectively (26). The difference is large enough so there is little possibility that a chance fluctuation associated with these specific samples could account for the result.

In part, however, findings of this kind reflect the influence of regional factors. Negroes on the West Coast score well above those in the Deep South. Because many more Negroes reside in the South, where the whites also appear to be somewhat less intelligent on the average, comparisons based on samples drawn to represent the country as a whole tend to overemphasize Negro deficiencies. A much greater proportion of low-ability southern Negroes is included than would be appropriate if an estimate of racial differences within a local labor market were desired. In a given area the Negro population can be expected to score somewhat below the white, but the difference may not be very large. Usually it is this local situation that matters most to personnel managers.

Also, these racial differences have apparently been decreasing in recent years as more and more Negroes emigrate to the cities of the South and North from the rural South (19). In the cities their children have characteristically received somewhat better schooling, and intelligence levels have improved as a result (22). Thus, there is reason to believe that in spite of the existing Negro-white differential, the future may see a narrowing, perhaps even an elimination, of the gap. Even at the present time there is reason to believe that a large percentage of the Negroes employed in any given company are, at least intellectually, capable of higher-level positions, just as are many whites (26).

Differences in Personality

GEOGRAPHICAL AREA. Relatively little is known about regional and rural-urban differences in personality characteristics. There is some basis for concluding that such differences do exist, but their nature has not been established with any certainty. One of the few studies bearing on this problem was carried out in the warehouse installations of the McKesson and Robbins Company throughout the United States (18). The findings indicate that both the overall level of employee satisfaction and the quantity of work produced were higher in small-town locations, rather than in the larger cities. Thus, it would appear that the commitment to the goals of organizational maintenance and productivity may well be greater in rural locations.

This conclusion receives some support from the history of unionization in the United States. It seems clear that the union movement has had its greatest successes in the large metropolitan areas. In the rural parts of the country, especially in the South, the unions have had much more difficulty, and many workers in these areas are still not represented by any organized labor group. It would appear, therefore, that there must be geographical differences in those personality characteristics that contribute to labor-management conflict within an organization and thus to deviation from the maintenance goal.

NEGRO-WHITE DIFFERENCES. Racial differences in personality characteristics, on the other hand, have been studied rather extensively, and in at least one instance have been tied in with the geographical factor as well. It seems clear that there are few real differences between Negroes and whites insofar as attitudes and values are concerned. The major factor that differentiates the groups is that being a Negro is of much greater relevance and importance to the Negro than being a white is to the white person. The Negro tends to be more conscious of his specific group membership and to view events within this particular focus (7,33).

Probably the most comprehensive piece of research in this area was carried out with a view to identifying personality differences between whites and Negroes, and within the Negro population between northern and southern Negroes (17). One of the most striking results was the finding that the differences that emerged when northern whites and southern Negroes were compared also appeared when the southern Negroes were compared with northern Negroes. Thus, in the North the evidence seemed to indicate that racial differences were minimal. On the other hand the traits identified as typical of southern Negroes seemed to suggest considerable personality disorganization. Most pronounced was a tendency to pretend that feelings of aggression and the aggressive acts of others did not really exist at all—to blot out and deny anger and hatred as if it did not occur in the world. This characteristic appears to be so pervasive among Negroes in the rural South that almost all emotion is restricted and inhibited. The fear of the consequences of aggression is so pronounced that it has spread into other areas as well, and all emotional expression tends to be held in check. In the urban areas of the South this suppression of emotion seems to be less drastic: Although anger is held back, it does tend to emerge eventually, sometimes long after the event that provoked it and often toward someone who was not originally involved. Only the northern Negro appears to feel sufficiently free to express his emotions in a manner comparable to whites.

As might be expected from these findings, the incidence of emotional disorder among Negroes does appear to be considerably higher than for whites, and even more important from the point of view of personnel management, a great many more cases go untreated and remain in the labor force. Yet even here the influence of regional differentials is evident. It appears that although northern Negroes are more likely to require hospitalization for emotional illness than northern whites, this difference is entirely attributable to the Negroes who have migrated to the North from the South. Negroes born in the North are not particularly prone to disorders of this kind (17).

Removing Constraints

Little need be said here about removing constraints imposed by geographical differentials. The personnel manager who finds his freedom of action restricted because of characteristics of his work force that are indigenous to the area is not likely to be able to circumvent these constraints by recruiting new employees from the local labor market. The same limitations will be found outside the company as within. Geographical differences of the kind discussed are in fact as much external constraints as internal. For this reason any treatment of methods for dealing with them will be delayed until the next chapter.

Racial differences, too, may not be subject to elimination by the simple expedient of going outside the company. Increasingly, external constraints are being imposed by society that for all practical purposes require companies to include Negroes as part of their potential labor force. Thus, a firm that seeks to overcome any limitations imposed as a result of the presence of a primarily Negro work force by hiring whites only is likely to run into considerable difficulty on legal grounds and in other respects as well. These external pressures will be discussed in the chapters that follow, but their consequence is that personnel managers would do well, if they do go outside the company, to seek out those Negroes who have the abilities and personality characteristics that are in short supply.

The alternative is to attempt some change in the existing employee group. In a sense the differences between the southern and northern Negro that have been noted can serve as a model here. Outside the South, in those areas where the fear of emotional expression has been removed, the level of emotional adjustment is considerably higher. Outside the South, in those areas where educational opportunities are better, the level of intelligence is higher also. This would suggest that a company can improve the caliber of its Negro work force, if this appears necessary, by reducing those conditions that act to arouse anger, while at the same time serving to suppress emotional expression, and providing extensive training in areas where knowledge is lacking.

Occupational Differences

A final area of major concern for personnel management involves the differences in abilities and personality that exist among the various occupational groups within a company. This, of course, is relevant in reaching decisions with regard to the selection and placement of employees at all levels of the organization. It is crucial to have people working in jobs where their abilities and personality characteristics will contribute to success.

However, our primary concern here is with the way in which an existing employee group may serve to limit the freedom of personnel action because only a specific set of occupations is represented and these occupations characteristically attract individuals with particular skills and talents. Thus, the emphasis here is on the factors that discriminate *between* occupational groups, rather than between successful and unsuccessful employees *within* occupational groups. If, for instance, a company wishes to expand rapidly, it will need large numbers of managers that it does not currently possess. Is it likely, in view of what is known regarding the characteristics of employees working below the managerial level, that the needed talent can be found within the present nonmanagerial work force? Will the abilities and personality traits prevailing in existing occupational groups act as a constraint on the expansion decision?

Differences in Abilities

Perhaps the most striking ability difference between occupations involves the association between the level of the job and general intelligence. There is no question but that intelligence test scores are much higher among those in the more skilled occupations, in the professions, and in management. Table 3-2 serves to illustrate this point. The test scores are those obtained when these individuals were inducted into the armed forces.

A similar pattern is found when occupations are grouped according to the classification system used by the Bureau of the Census. Table 3-3 contains the results obtained when the short vocabulary test was administered to a nationwide sample of 745 individuals. This sample may be considered typical of the national labor force.

In general, a similar pattern has been found for the other intellectual abilities—numerical, spatial, mechanical, and so on. This does not mean,

Table 3-2. Army General Classification Test Scores Classified by Civilian Occupation

Civilian occupation	Number of cases	Mean score
Accountant	172	128.1
Lawyer	94	127.6
Public relations	42	126.0
Auditor	62	125.9
Draftsman	153	122.0
Pharmacist	58	120.5
Sales manager	42	119.0
Manager	234	116.0
Radio repairman	267	115.3
Teacher	256	112.8
Toolmaker	60	112.5
Foreman	298	109.8
Electrician	289	109.0
Mechanic	421	106.3
Carpenter	451	102.1
Bartender	98	102.2
Welder	493	101.8
Chauffeur	194	100.8
Cook and baker	436	97.2
Truck driver	817	96.2
Barber	103	95.3

Source: T. W. Harrell and M. Harrell, "Army General Classification Test Scores for Civilian Occupations," *Educational & Psychological Measurement,* Vol. 5 (1945), pp. 231–232.

Table 3-3. Intelligence of Occupational Groups, Census Classification

Census classification number	Classification title	Number of cases	Mean score
0	Professional	68	14.56
1	Farmers	45	10.22
2	Managers	78	12.60
3	Clerical	102	12.40
4	Sales	48	11.52
5	Craftsmen	102	10.62
6	Operatives	154	10.02
7	Service	81	9.19
8 and 9	Laborers	67	9.63

Source: J. B. Miner, *Intelligence in the United States.* New York: Springer, 1957, p. 73.

however, that there is not a very sizable overlap. There are many individuals in lower-level jobs who possess the abilities required for performance much farther up in the hierarchy. Whether or not these people can be expected to possess the other characteristics required for effective performance at higher levels in the organization is another question, however. Let us turn now to the data on occupational differences in personality.

Differences in Personality

The idea that there are basic differences in the personalities of members of different occupations has its roots in the writings of the Greek philosophers and continues to be of interest today. Thus, a considerable amount of research into the interests, attitudes, motives, and emotional adjustment of various occupational groups has been carried out by a number of investigators, and as a result a number of generalizations that are important for personnel management can be made in this area.

INTERESTS. Turning first to the research dealing with interests, it has been firmly established that the higher-level occupational groups in our society can be clearly distinguished from one another on this basis. For example, the Strong Vocational Interest Blank can now be scored for 47 male occupations such as architect, musician, certified public accountant, and so on (6). This means that members of at least 47 different occupations responded in a consistently different manner to the 400 questions on the test, thus establishing a pattern of responses that was typical and unique for their type of work. The test asks for a like-indifferent-dislike categorization of a variety of activities.

Some of these occupations, however, are more different from each other than others, at least insofar as the Strong Vocational Interest Blank responses are concerned. Thus, the higher-level occupations tend to cluster into a smaller number of groupings. Table 3-4 lists the groups that had been clearly identified by the late 1950's and some of the occupations in each category.

It has also been shown that occupational groups at lower levels seem to have some significantly different interest patterns (5). Thus, there are indications that people such as plasterers, bakers, and truck drivers do differ substantially from one another in the pattern of their interests. Also, it appears that there are significant differences in interests between the higher level occupations generally and those at lower levels. Thus, business and professional men tend as a group to have very different types of preferences than unskilled workers.

The implication of these findings for personnel management is that it may be very difficult to get an individual to perform in a job that deviates in many ways from his personal pattern of interests. People are not in any sense perfectly interchangeable across jobs. A man may be shifted to a job in the same interest grouping without much difficulty insofar as his levels of satisfaction and performance are concerned. But transferring him directly into work that normally satisfies a very different set of interests may well be accomplished at considerable cost to organizational goal achievement.

Table 3-4. Vocational Interest Groups as Measured by the Strong Vocational Interest Blank

Group	Group title	Occupations
1	Creative-scientific	Architect, dentist, psychologist
2	Technical	Mathematician, engineer, chemist
3	Production manager	Production manager
4	Subprofessional technical	Farmer, carpenter, aviator
5	Uplift	Personnel manager, social science teacher
6	Musician	Musician
7	Certified public accountant	Certified public accountant
8	Business detail	Accountant, banker
9	Business contract	Sales manager, life insurance salesman
10	Verbal	Lawyer, journalist
11	President of manufacturing firm	President of manufacturing firm

Source: L. J. Cronbach, *Essentials of Psychological Testing*, 2nd ed. New York: Harper & Row, 1960, p. 410.

ATTITUDES. There seems little doubt on the basis of the research evidence that there is a strong relationship between occupational groupings and general socioeconomic attitudes. In a typical study a nationwide sample of the adult white male population was subdivided into the following occupational groups: large business, professional, small business, white collar, skilled manual, semiskilled manual, and unskilled manual (4). This breakdown was then related to socioeconomic attitudes.

The greatest conservatism was found in the two business groups and among the professionals, the greatest radicalism among the manual workers, and the greatest variation among the white-collar workers. Apparently many white-collar employees identify with the business management and professional groups, whereas others react in a manner commensurate with their income levels. Taken as a whole, these results provide some indication of the amount of unconflicted support for organizational goals, especially the productivity or profit goal, that may be expected in different occupational groups.

MANAGERIAL CHARACTERISTICS. Research indicates that managers as a group have a homogeneous set of values that are highly pragmatic in nature (8). Furthermore, top-level managers differ significantly from middle managers in that they view themselves as being more dynamic, daring, and less cautious (34). And this trend extends on down in the organization. A direct positive relationship exists between both self-assurance and initiative and the level of job held in the hierarchy (10). The evidence on this last point is contained in Table 3-5.

Table 3-5. Mean Scores on Self-Assurance and Initiative for Various Occupational Levels

Occupational level	Number of cases	Self-assurance score	Initiative score
Higher management	110	28.56	32.46
Middle management	67	24.27	29.51
Lower management	87	24.14	29.07
Line workers	152	23.22	26.75

Source: E. E. Ghiselli, "The Validity of Management Traits in Relation to Occupational Level," *Personnel Psychology*, Vol. 16 (1963), p. 110.

Other studies have indicated that there is a similar positive association between the motivation to assume managerial responsibilities and to exercise power over others and actual managerial level. The extent of the relationship is indicated by the fact that the correlations obtained have consistently been in the low .40's (30). Furthermore, graduate business students who aspire to managerial positions have more such motivation than those who do not (31).

There is also some research evidence available regarding this factor of power motivation as it appears in different types of managerial groups. The results of one such study are contained in Table 3-6. It is clear that whereas the sales managers are strongly motivated to exercise power, the research managers are much less so.

Table 3-6. Miner Sentence Completion Scale Scores in Various Corporate Manager Groups

Group	Mean score	Number of cases
Sales management	8.94	35
Engineering management	6.35	43
Research management	4.45	40

Source: J. B. Miner, *Studies in Management Education*. New York: Springer, 1965, p. 200.

Results of the same kind have been obtained with business school students majoring in different areas (20,30). Thus, it seems likely that differences between managers working in the various areas of specialization are not entirely a consequence of experiences occurring *after* managerial responsibilities have been assumed. Men who choose sales work, for instance, are not the same as those who prefer other fields.

A particularly extensive study of occupational personalities at the higher levels of management involved the administration of a number of personality tests to a large group of executives, followed by a comparison of the results obtained by those working in different specialties (15,35). Among the tests used were the Minnesota Multiphasic Personality Inventory, Bernreuter Personality Inventory, and Thematic Apperception Test. The results are summarized, in a general way, as follows:

1. Sales managers tend to be highly dominant, sociable, thick-skinned, people-oriented, and to some extent self-centered.
2. Production managers are somewhat defensive in nature and are marked by strong self-control; they shy away from self-analysis and tend to prefer the practical.
3. Administrative and accounting managers are not very creative or original and are given to moods of depression.

It is clear from the studies described that managerial positions do contain individuals with certain specific personality characteristics, and there is reason to believe that major differences exist among managers working in different areas. For this reason a company that had always operated within the marketing segment of its industry might have considerable difficulty expanding into the production and research areas. Similarly, individual and group differences can serve as a constraint against too rapid growth of any kind, because many of the characteristics noted appear to be required for all managerial work, and a small company is simply not likely to have these resources available in sufficient quantity to staff a greatly expanded management group.

An additional constraint on rapid expansion derives from what is known about emotional illness and the symptoms of emotional disorder. It is clear that emotional problems are most prevalent among people in lower-level occupations—among those in unskilled and routine semi-skilled jobs in particular (21). They develop much less frequently in the more highly skilled and in management (29).

Other evidence indicates that symptoms of emotional illness do not tend to have negative consequences for performance when the work is of a routine, repetitive nature. But they do interfere drastically when frequent decision making is required and a variety of problems must be thought through. Thus, a company staffed with a high proportion of minimally skilled employees will not need, and probably will not have, a work force that is extremely stable and well-adjusted emotionally. If, however, a sizable upgrading of skills should appear desirable, as with the introduction of automated equipment, this reduced level of emotional stability could serve as a major limitation on management's freedom of action.

Removing Constraints

In one sense the constraints that have been described are of a kind that personnel management may well prefer not to remove. Many of the abilities and personality characteristics noted are not only prevalent in the occupational groups where they occur, but are also essential for effective performance there. Thus, it would in many instances be disastrous for a company to attempt to eliminate them. Too much homogeneity within a total work force can be a source of difficulty in and of itself.

Yet it is also true that if an organization is to promote from within it must have in lower-level positions individuals who possess the abilities and other characteristics required for performance at higher levels. This means in the case of the factors associated with managerial work that some overstaffing or stockpiling is usually necessary. A company needs more people with high intelligence, managerial interests, and a desire to exercise power than it can use at a given point in time, because a continuous flow of replacements must be maintained.

Of course, where provision is not made for an adequate internal supply of the resources needed to permit a smooth managerial replacement process, the resulting constraints can be overcome by hiring managers from outside the company. A number of firms do in fact follow this procedure as a matter of policy. There are some disadvantages, primarily the lack of incentive for those at lower levels, when promotion from within is not the policy, but this is certainly one possible way of overcoming the restrictions imposed by an inadequate supply of managerial talent.

An obvious alternative is to attempt to change existing employees who do not possess the managerial characteristics, so that after the change process they are more fully qualified for this type of work. In the case of intellectual abilities this appears impractical, if not impossible, so that stockpiling on intelligence would appear to be essential. But the personality factors discussed are in many cases subject to modification.

Interests are known to shift rather frequently early in life, although they do become stable in adult life. Thus, there is some reason to believe that changes can be produced purposefully if the right conditions are established. However, little actual research has been done on this specific problem. Socioeconomic attitudes clearly may be altered, although the ease with which this may be accomplished varies from individual to individual. There is some reason to believe that considerable change occurs normally as a function of the first promotion into the ranks of management (23). Certain of the other personality characteristics discussed can apparently be changed as a result of management-development programs (30). Specific details on this will be covered in Chapter 14. In the case of some traits the evidence that change can be produced is extremely strong; in other instances we do not really know yet whether management development can be effective or not. Finally, emotional stability can be improved and symptoms reduced through individual and group psychotherapy. The process may not be a short one and it may never succeed with certain people, but it is possible to bring about a considerable change in emotional adjustment given the appropriate circumstances.

This concludes our necessarily brief survey of the nature of individual and group differences in American society. The intention has not been to provide a separate course in differential psychology, but rather to make the individual with an interest in personnel management aware of the large number of consistent and significant differences that do exist and of the way in which these differences may act as constraints to limit the freedom of personnel decision making.

As indicated, many of these constraints can be circumvented. As this is written, it is quite likely that some of the differences described are no longer as significant as they were and that some are even more so. Much of this change occurs as a result of forces that are beyond the personnel manager's control—but by no means all. A personnel manager can, by assuming the role of a change agent within his organization, do a great deal to remove internal restrictions on his freedom of decision.

References

1. Allport, G. W., P. E. Vernon, and G. Lindzey, *Study of Values: Manual of Directions*, rev. ed. Boston: Houghton Mifflin, 1951.
2. Anastasi, A., *Differential Psychology*, 3rd ed. New York: Macmillan, 1958.
3. Bentz, V. J., "A Test-Retest Experiment on the Relationship Between Age and Mental Ability," *American Psychologist*, Vol. 8 (1953), 319–320.
4. Centers, R., *The Psychology of Social Classes*. Princeton, N.J.: Princeton Univ. Press, 1949.
5. Clark, K. C., *Vocational Interests of Non-professional Men*. Minneapolis: Univ. Minnesota Press, 1961.
6. Cronbach, L. J., *Essentials of Psychological Testing*, 2nd ed. New York: Harper & Row, 1960.

7. Dreger, R. M., and K. S. Miller, "Comparative Psychological Studies of Negroes and Whites in the United States," *Psychological Bulletin*, Vol. 57 (1960), 361–402.
8. England G. W., "Personal Value Systems of American Managers," *Academy of Management Journal*, Vol. 10 (1967), 53–68.
9. Fuchs, E. F., and C. H. Hammer, "A Survey of Women's Aptitudes for Army Jobs," *Personnel Psychology*, Vol. 16 (1963), 151–156.
10. Ghiselli, E. E., "The Validity of Management Traits in Relation to Occupational Level," *Personnel Psychology*, Vol. 16 (1963), 109–114.
11. Gordon, L. V., *Gordon Personal Profile: Manual*. New York: Harcourt, Brace & World, 1953.
12. Guilford, J. P., and W. S. Zimmerman, *The Guilford-Zimmerman Temperament Survey: Manual*. Beverly Hills, Calif.: Sheridan Supply Company, 1949.
13. Gurin, G., J. Veroff, and S. Field, *Americans View Their Mental Health*. New York: Basic Books, 1960.
14. Harrell, T. W., and M. S. Harrell, "Army General Classification Test Scores for Civilian Occupations," *Educational and Psychological Measurement*, Vol. 5 (1945), 229–239.
15. Huttner, L., S. Levy, E. Rosen, and M. Stopol, "Further Light on the Executive Personality," *Personnel*, Vol. 36 (1959), 42–50.
16. Jacobsen, E., D. Trumbo, G. Cheek, and J. Nangle, "Employee Attitudes Toward Technological Change in a Medium Sized Insurance Company," *Journal of Applied Psychology*, Vol. 43 (1959), 349–354.
17. Karon, B. P., *The Negro Personality*. New York: Springer, 1958.
18. Katzell, R. A., R. S. Barrett, and T. C. Parker, "Job Satisfaction, Job Performance, and Situational Characteristics," *Journal of Applied Psychology*, Vol. 45 (1961), 65–72.
19. Klineberg, O., "Negro-White Differences in Intelligence Test Performance: A New Look at an Old Problem," *American Psychologist*, Vol. 18 (1963), 198–203.
20. Korman, A. K., "Self-esteem Variable in Vocational Choice," *Journal of Applied Psychology*, Vol. 50 (1966), 479–486.
21. Kornhauser, A., *Mental Health of the Industrial Worker*. New York: Wiley, 1965.
22. Lee, E. S., "Negro Intelligence and Selective Migration: A Philadelphia Test of the Klineberg Hypothesis," *American Sociological Review*, Vol. 16 (1951), 227–333.
23. Lieberman, S., "The Effects of Changes in Roles on the Attitudes of Role Occupants," *Human Relations*, Vol. 9 (1956), 385–402.
24. McClelland, D. C., J. W. Atkinson, R. A. Clark, and E. L. Lowell, *The Achievement Motive*. New York: Appleton-Century-Crofts, 1953.
25. McNemar, Q., *The Revision of the Stanford-Binet Scale*. Boston: Houghton Mifflin, 1942.
26. Miner, J. B., *Intelligence in the United States*. New York: Springer, 1957.
27. Miner, J. B., "The Concurrent Validity of the PAT in the Selection of Tabulating Machine Operators," *Journal of Projective Techniques*, Vol. 24 (1960), 409–418.

28. Miner, J. B., "The Validity of the PAT in the Selection of Tabulating Machine Operators: An Analysis of Predictive Power," *Journal of Projective Techniques*, Vol. 25 (1961), 330–333.
29. Miner, J. B., *The Management of Ineffective Performance*. New York: McGraw-Hill, 1963.
30. Miner, J. B., *Studies in Management Education*. New York: Springer, 1965.
31. Miner, J. B., "The Early Identification of Managerial Talent," *Personnel and Guidance Journal*, Vol. 46 (1968), 586–591.
32. Owens, W. A., Jr., "Age and Mental Abilities: A Longitudinal Study," *Genetic Psychology Monographs*, Vol. 48 (1953), 3–54.
33. Pettigrew, T. F., *A Profile of the Negro American*. Princeton, N.J.: Van Nostrand, 1964.
34. Porter, L. W., and E. E. Ghiselli, "The Self-Perceptions of Top and Middle Management Personnel," *Personnel Psychology*, Vol. 10 (1957), 397–406.
35. Rosen, E. H., "The Executive Personality," *Personnel*, Vol. 36 (1959), 8–20.
36. Toch, H., "Attitudes of the Fifty Plus Age Group: Preliminary Considerations Toward a Longitudinal Survey," *Public Opinion Quarterly*, Vol. 17 (1953), 391–394.
37. Tomkins, S. S., *Affect Imagery Consciousness, Vol. II: The Negative Affects*. New York: Springer, 1963.
38. Tyler, L., *The Psychology of Human Differences*, rev. ed. New York: Appleton-Century-Crofts, 1956.
39. Wechsler, D., *The Measurement and Appraisal of Adult Intelligence*, 4th ed. Baltimore: Williams & Wilkins, 1958.
40. Welford, A. T., *Aging and Human Skill*. New York: Oxford, 1958.

Questions

1. Discuss the relationship between age and the various abilities. What influence does the degree of education appear to have on this relationship?
2. What are some of the important sex differences? Which of these differences appear to be susceptible to change by the personnel manager?
3. Discuss the general notion of geographical constraints on the practice of personnel management. What are the major dimensions of this factor in the United States and what can the personnel manager do to overcome them?
4. What are the general characteristics of different types of managers? What are the implications of these differences for personnel policy and practice?
5. What do we know about the prevalence and consequences of emotional disorder in the world of work? What is the significance of this problem for personnel utilization and planning?

4

External Constraints:
Cultural, Geographical,
and Industry Characteristics

In Chapter 3 we discussed the various internal constraints, in the form of individual differences, that may operate to limit personnel decisions. In this chapter and the two that follow, attention will focus on the various factors in the external environment that may serve to restrict a personnel manager's freedom of action. The latter constraints exist because all organizations must carry on their activities within a much larger context—a cultural milieu, a geographical environment, an industry structure, and numerous governmental jurisdictions. No company is an island unto itself. The programs and policies of the firm must reflect these various environmental pressures as they exist at a given point in time and in a specific location (4).

To be more specific, let us cite as a hypothetical example the XYZ Company that employs approximately 2,000 people, manufactures aluminum widgets, and has its principal facilities located in the heart of New York City. With this information alone, it is possible to identify a number of external constraints that may be presumed to operate in a restrictive manner on decision making within the company's personnel department:

1. Personnel policies must reflect the laws and customs of the United States, rather than those of Canada, the Soviet Union, Great Britain, or some other country.

2. Personnel policies must reflect the laws and customs of New York State and New York City, rather than those of New Jersey, Massachusetts, Texas, or California.
3. Personnel policies must reflect the local and Federal laws that relate directly to the aluminum industry. The extent to which these policies will be affected by laws relating to other industries is determined by the extent to which the products of these other industries are relevant in the production of aluminum widgets.
4. Personnel policies must reflect the level and type of technological development that has been attained in the aluminum industry.
5. Personnel policies must reflect the nature of the labor market in the New York City area in terms of its social, economic, and psychological characteristics, rather than the labor market as it exists in Los Angeles, Seattle, Houston, or Atlanta.

As with internal constraints, those in the environment outside the company are far from absolute. They can be overcome if there is time to devote to the task before a decision must be reached. Either the business activity may be relocated in a new environment where the identical restrictions do not appear, or an attempt may be made to alter those forces that served to produce the particular external constraint in the first place. Laws can be changed, labor market characteristics can be modified, and so on. But these things take time; meanwhile the personnel manager's freedom of decision and action may be very severely limited.

In this chapter the discussion will concentrate initially on the roles various cultural factors may have in personnel decisions, with special attention given to those factors that characterize whole nations. Next, the perspective will be narrowed, and a somewhat smaller unit of analysis will be employed, as the focus shifts to the various geographical regions and locations within the United States. Finally, the restrictions that may operate within specific industries such as petroleum and automobiles will be taken up. Constraints of a specifically legal nature will, however, be reserved for discussion in the two chapters that follow.

Cultural Characteristics as They Affect International Business

Knowledge regarding the influence that differences in national culture may have upon personnel management is of considerable importance to American companies today. International trade has reached a record peak with the countries of Europe, Latin America, and the Far East and promises to attain even higher levels as the underdeveloped nations rush toward economic self-sufficiency and higher standards of living. Thus, large numbers of American firms are faced with the problem of staffing overseas offices and in many cases manning major production and distribution facilities in foreign countries (13). If these international operations are to be managed in a way that will maximize organizational productivity and maintenance, a very high priority must be given to the development and utilization of knowledge that might indicate how the management process should be varied in the light of cultural considerations.

That cultural variations do exist, even at the managerial level, can no longer be doubted. In one study of managerial attitudes sharp differences were found between Nordic-European countries (Norway, Denmark, Germany, and Sweden), Latin-European countries (France, Spain, Italy, and Belgium), the United States and Great Britain, a group of developing countries (Argentina, Chile, and India), and Japan, which stood alone. Managers in these countries did hold many attitudes in common, but there were also a number of specific findings characteristic within each cultural grouping. Thus, whereas attitudes in the three developing countries tended to be on the autocratic side, Japanese managers gave evidence of a considerably greater democratic trend (6).

How, then, do these cultural factors impinge upon personnel practices? What are the specific characteristics of a culture that can be expected to influence the way in which human resources are utilized? A descriptive framework for answering these questions is provided in Table 4-1.

Table 4-1 was originally devised with reference to the production process (16). However, it is clear from the last column that many of the activities and areas described as being subject to influence by cultural factors fall within the domain of personnel management. Among these are management development, safety programs, supervisory selection, layoff policies, incentive systems, labor relations, merit evaluations, policies on absenteeism, promotion procedures, job description, and fringe benefits. It seems evident that people in other parts of the world can view things very differently than we do in the United States, and they may have very different conceptions of what is right and what is wrong.

Japanese Culture

A good example of the way in which cultural considerations may serve to condition personnel decisions comes from Japan. In connection with a research study, some 2,000 production workers, divided equally between the United States and Japan, were surveyed (20). The firms studied in the two countries were essentially comparable. Some of the questions dealing with personnel practices and policies that were asked of the workers in both countries are noted in Table 4-2.

Table 4-1. The Cultural System As It Affects Production Management

Differences in these cultural factors—	. . . affect a people's values and habits relating to—	For example, the local employee might feel that—	. . . and this would tend to affect approaches in these (and other) areas of manufacturing management—
I. Assumptions and attitudes	Time	Time is not measured in minutes, but in days and years.	Production control, scheduling, purchasing
	One's proper purpose in life	The only purpose which makes sense is to enjoy each day.	Management development
	The future	The future is not in man's hands.	Short- and long-range planning
	This life vs. the hereafter	Life and death are completely ordained and predetermined.	Safety programs
	Duty, responsibility	Your job is completed when you give an order to a subordinate.	Executive techniques of delegation and follow-up
II. Personal beliefs and aspirations	Right and wrong	I give the boss inventory counts that please him.	Inventory control system
	Sources of pride	A college degree places one higher in society for life.	Selection of supervisors
	Sources of fear and concern	Jobs are hard to get for a man laid off, regardless of the cause of layoff.	Layoff policy
	Extent of one's hopes	Without the right education and social class, advancement is limited.	Incentives, motivation

Table 4-1 (cont'd.)

Differences in these cultural factors—	. . . affect a people's values and habits relating to—	For example, the local employee might feel that—	. . . and this would tend to affect approaches in these (and other) areas of manufacturing management—
III. Interpersonal relationships	The individual vs. society	The individual's wants and needs must be subordinated to the whole group.	Labor relations
	The source of authority	My men don't like the new process. It won't work.	Quality control
	Care or empathy for others	I'd rather give my salary raise to my foreman than have to tell him he is not to receive one.	Merit reviews
	Importance of family obligations	I had to stay home because my father was sick.	Absenteeism
	Objects of loyalty	Friendship is more important than business.	Work-group relationships
	Tolerance for personal differences	If you don't agree with your boss, he will be insulted.	The decision-making process
IV. Social structure	Interclass nobility	I'd refuse to work for a man without a trade school certificate.	Promotion from within

Table 4-1 (cont'd.)

Differences in these cultural factors—	. . . affect a people's values and habits relating to—	For example, the local employee might feel that—	. . . and this would tend to affect approaches in these (and other) areas of manufacturing management—
	Class or caste systems	Men with my standing don't move heavy objects such as typewriters.	Job descriptions—flexibility of job assignments
	Urban-village-farm origins	The company must take the place of the village in caring for its people.	Fringe benefit programs
	Determinants of status	Elderly people have wisdom. They deserve the most important jobs on big machines.	Equipment selection

Source: C. W. Skinner, "Management of International Production," *Harvard Business Review*, Vol. 42, No. 5 (1964), p. 129.

Table 4-2. Differences Between Japanese and American Employees' Cultural Values

Questionnaire items	United States, %	Japan, %
1. *I think of my company as:*		
The central concern in my life and of greater importance than my personal life	1	9
A part of my life at least equal to my personal life	23	57
A place for me to work with management during work hours to accomplish mutual goals	54	26
Strictly a place to work and entirely separate from my personal life	23	6
2. *When a worker wishes to marry, I think his (her) supervisor should:*		
Help select a mate and serve as a possible go-between	2	6
Offer personal advice to the worker if requested	29	70
Merely present a small gift from the company	9	19
Not be involved in such a personal matter	60	5
3. *In regard to housing for workers, management should:*		
Provide company housing at no charge	2	29
Provide company housing at special low rent	8	39
Provide low-interest loans to assist workers in owning their own homes	56	29
Avoid direct financial assistance in housing	34	3
4. *If a worker, although willing, proves to be unqualified on his job, management should feel a responsibility to:*		
Continue his employment until he retires or dies	23	55
Continue his employment for as long as one year so that he may look for another job	19	23
Continue his employment for three months so that he may look for another job	38	18

Table 4-2 (cont'd.)

Questionnaire items	United States, %	Japan, %
Terminate the employment of unqualified workers after giving about two weeks' notice	20	4

Source: A. M. Whitehill, "Cultural Values and Employee Attitudes: United States and Japan," *Journal of Applied Psychology,* Vol. 48 (1964), pp. 70–71.

An examination of the responses indicates that the perceived permanence of the employment relationship, which is so typical in Japan (1), has some very direct implications for personnel practice. Thus, from question 1 it appears that an American firm doing business in Japan would have to give less consideration to matters of company loyalty than in the United States, because feelings of this kind are a basic aspect of the Japanese culture as a whole. This increased proclivity for loyalty appears to come at some cost, however. As questions 2 and 3 demonstrate, the company is expected to assume added roles that are not included in the value expectations of American employees. The Japanese production worker anticipates that the company will take a much more active interest in him and his problems.

In general it would seem that organizational maintenance as a goal would be relatively easy to achieve in a Japanese plant. On the other hand productivity might well present something of a problem. The responses to question 4 suggest that sanctions against ineffective performance, which if not widely accepted in the United States are not widely rejected either, may be almost entirely proscribed in Japan.

Indian Culture

Studies carried out in India provide a picture of the cultural climate in that country that again differs from that found in the United States. In one such investigation a group of 200 Indian factory workers were asked to rate the importance of various job factors (15). These factors were then ranked in terms of their average rated importance and the results were compared with the findings obtained from similar studies conducted in the United States. The most relevant of these comparisons, for our purposes, involves a survey carried out among workers at the General Motors Company (2). The results are presented in Table 4-3.

In spite of the fact that some factors included in the Indian survey were not studied among the General Motors workers and that some ranked at General Motors were not ranked in India, several very interesting differences are identified. The Indian workers show a much greater concern with job security, opportunity for advancement, and comfortable working conditions and emphasize sympathetic supervision much less. In part, these differentials can be accounted for in terms of the very high

Table 4-3. Comparisons of Rankings of Job Factors by Indian and American Workers

Job factor	Ranking among Indian workers	Ranking among American workers
Job security	1	6
Adequate earnings	2	1
Personal benefits	3	2
Opportunity for advancement	4	8
Comfortable working conditions	5	9
Suitable type of work	6	7
Opportunity for increased income	7	
Hours of work	8	
Sympathetic supervision	9	5
Opportunity to learn the job	10	

Source: P. N. Singh and R. J. Wherry, "Ranking of Job Factors by Factory Workers in India," *Personnel Psychology,* Vol. 16 (1963), p. 31.

unemployment rates that have plagued India. It is not surprising that job security is so important. But a very different attitude toward authority in the two cultures is also reflected. Thus, increased consideration and kindness from supervisors would seem to be much less effective as a way of building commitment to the company in India than it is in the United States. Sympathetic supervision is just not that important to Indian workers.

Russian Culture

Russia, with its communist social system, provides an example of a cultural context for business that is almost the direct opposite of that existing in the United States. Although it is unlikely that many American firms will open plants within the USSR in the near future, it is still of interest to contrast the two cultures in view of the current status of world power relationships. Fortunately, information is available on the types of restrictions that serve to limit personnel decisions within the Russian economy (5).

One very clear difference between the two countries is in relation to such factors as work motivation and employee morale. For many years those responsible for the utilization of human resources in the Soviet Union were unconcerned with matters of this kind. Within the communist ideology it was traditionally assumed that workers exert more effort merely because they want to in a noncapitalistic, socialist system. The incentive procedures used in the United States to increase individual productivity have rarely been employed in Russia because such tools have characteristically been perceived as contrary to the prevailing political ideology. There has been a similar lack of interest in programs designed to increase worker morale and thus contribute to organizational maintenance. Recently some emphasis on the use of incentives has appeared under the sponsorship of high government officials, but the process of change in this area has been an extremely slow one.

A similar pattern is present in the area of personnel selection. Traditional communist ideology assumes that there are few important differences between people; consequently the view that some individuals may be more capable workers than others is not acceptable. Because the logic of personnel selection is that within a given framework and for certain purposes some people *are* more capable than others, specialized selection techniques have rarely been used as a management tool in the Soviet Union. It would in fact be unwise for a personnel manager to attempt to use them.

Instead of selection, Russian personnel managers have concentrated primarily on training and skill development, because it is part of the professed ideology that all individuals must be brought to a high level of performance. Thus, training has been the preferred route to the productivity goal. Organizational maintenance, however, has been sought in a different manner. Because all organizations are considered to be arms of the state, it is the state that has been employed as the central unifying point, and the usual approach has been to attempt to build loyalty and faithfulness to the state rather than to the particular business organization.

British Culture

One might expect that differences of this kind would not appear when American culture patterns are contrasted with those of another Western country such as England. Information is available, however, from a comparative study employing insurance clerks in Great Britain and the United States as subjects (3). Among the British, self-reliance, kindness, politeness, obedience, and not creating a nuisance were relatively more important, whereas the Americans placed greater emphasis on respect for parents and on authority, sincerity, honesty, getting along with others, individuality, and being unselfish.

These differences suggest that rather different approaches should be taken to foster organizational maintenance in the two countries. For example, an organization placing considerable stress on rules of procedure and tending to minimize individual spontaneity would be expected to produce higher levels of satisfaction in Great Britain. Perhaps this is why a highly structured and planned incomes policy regulating prices and wages throughout the economy has emerged there since World War II (12). A smaller, more informal type of organizational unit should be preferable in the United States, and the general nature of the economy appears to reflect this.

The Underdeveloped Countries

Although many other examples could be given indicating how cultural constraints can operate to restrict management's freedom of action and to specify acceptable routes for the attainment of company goals within various foreign countries (7), it is probably more appropriate at this point to turn to the difficulties that may be encountered in the underdeveloped countries of the world. These appear to be of two general types—ideological and educational.

In one comparative study of thirty-four nations an attempt was made to relate the level of economic development to the values and motivational patterns of the people (11). A major portion of these findings are of direct relevance here because they indicate that there are certain countries where, because of the value systems, organizational productivity may be relatively easy to achieve and organizational maintenance difficult; there are others where the reverse is true. In those countries that had maintained high levels of economic growth, the people were marked by a strong emphasis on hard work and achievement and, perhaps even more important, by the view that social relationships should occur with some specific purpose in mind, such as a business deal, rather than for purely social reasons. Such a culture pattern should facilitate the productivity goal, but it would appear that special measures would have to be taken so that individuals of this kind could work together in a cooperative manner. It seems less likely that they would spontaneously create the feelings of camaraderie and friendship that are necessary to a stable organization of the kind that will continually resist both internal and external stresses.

On the other hand, in those countries where economic growth was slow, social relationships tended to be valued for their own sake and people did not need particular purposes or goals to engage in them. Here organizational maintenance might be expected to come more easily, but the lower level of achievement motivation would suggest that commitment to a company's productivity and profit objectives might be much more difficult to obtain. Countries where the desire to achieve was low and where economic growth was minimal were by no means all in the category that would be called underdeveloped, however. Many had experienced considerable growth in the past, but not in the last few decades. This low group included such diverse nations as Belgium, Algeria, Denmark, Chile, and Switzerland. In these and other countries the values necessary to productivity and continued economic growth were lacking.

A deficiency in the required values is not the only factor that may serve to limit goal achievement in the underdeveloped areas. An equally important factor is education, at least insofar as productivity is concerned (8). In many countries of the world certain types of personnel programs are out of the question, merely because the labor market does not contain individuals with the necessarv basic education, skills, or professional training. Countries such as Afghanistan, Ethiopia, and Haiti not only have a very limited economic capacity, but they lack the educated personnel needed for advancement.

Removing Constraints

In general, the approach in this section has been one of pointing out some of the constraints within which personnel decisions must be made in foreign countries. Little has been said about the possibility of circumventing these restrictions, largely because this is not easily done. An obvious procedure is to move the business operation to a cultural context where the limitations no longer exist. This may or may not be feasible on other grounds. Personnel considerations are not always paramount. Or it may be possible to staff the organization in large part from outside the culture that imposes the restrictions, perhaps with United States citizens. This may or may not solve the problem.

Another alternative involves inducing change in the culture itself. Because of the widespread support for cultural values within a society, however, these are not easily altered. This is not to suggest that societies and cultures do not change. They most certainly do, and the personnel manager can play a role in this process. For example, there is good reason to believe that rather basic changes are taking place in Japanese society at the present time; the shift is toward a much more Westernized perception of the employment relationship (1,21). And the group responsible seems to be that segment of Japanese management that has had the greatest contact with the West.

A personnel manager may do much to foster change through the development of appropriate training and communications programs within the company. Similarly, he may serve as a public relations agent within the external community by discussing the virtues of the desired change. Although these attempts to modify attitudes may meet with only limited success in and of themselves, they can contribute a great deal to an ongoing change process. Combined with other socioeconomic and political forces in the culture, they can make a very real difference.

In the educational area personnel management can contribute even more markedly. Although it may not be economically feasible to do so, companies can have a rather dramatic impact on the educational systems of foreign countries. The accomplishments of the oil companies in Venezuela provide a case in point (17). Although union and governmental pressures were without question an important factor, it remains true that through their direct investment in schools and hospitals American oil companies have done a great deal to improve the educational level and the health of the Venezuelan populace.

Geographical Characteristics Within the United States

Geographical constraints, as discussed in Chapter 3 and as we shall deal with them here, arise from the fact that national cultures are not homogeneous. Within particular regions and locations various specific aspects of the geography, population, and other factors may serve to produce a relatively unique set of constraints insofar as personnel management is concerned. This chapter will take up a number of these restrictions as they operate within American culture. The coverage cannot be entirely complete, but it should be sufficient to provide a general view of some of the more important aspects of human resources utilization that may be influenced by geographical location.

Continuous-Shift Operation
With the growth of automated technology in many segments of industry, and in view of the heavy monetary outlays that such equipment necessitates, there has been increasing concern with efficient plant utilization. As a result many firms have considered going from a single shift to multiple-shift operations in the hope that a much greater return on the original investment in equipment could be realized in this way.

In many areas of the country this would present no particular problem, especially where the primary mode of transportation is the automobile. However, in those locations such as the urbanized Northeast, where primary reliance is placed on commuting trains, subways, and buses, problems can arise. These public transportation systems are adapted almost entirely to the 8:00-A.M. to 5:00-P.M. workday. Schedules are extremely light in the late night and early morning hours when many people would have to travel to and from work under multiple-shift operations. And yet in many urban areas east of the Mississippi a high percentage of the working population do not even have driving licenses, let alone automobiles that they might use to get to their jobs.

Constraints such as this can be overcome. So can limitations imposed by virtue of the fact that public eating facilities are not likely to be open for those working night shifts in many localities. But overcoming them does require some second thoughts and preplanning. Perhaps the procedures available for removing constraints will in the end prove so costly that certain types of shift schedules will have to be ruled out entirely.

The Employment of Professional Personnel

Many companies have found that to attract qualified technical and professional employees to research and development installations and to other facilities requiring high-talent manpower, it is often necessary to offer an opportunity for continuing education at the undergraduate and particularly at the graduate levels. When university facilities are not available in the area, recruiting can become extremely difficult. It may in fact be impossible to operate certain kinds of installations efficiently in locations where appropriate business, scientific, and technical courses are not available.

Yet there are sizable geographic variations in the extent to which higher education can be readily obtained. In northern New Jersey, for instance, a rather large number of institutions (among them Columbia University, New York University, the City University of New York, Rutgers, Seton Hall, and others) can be utilized by employees seeking advanced training. In the Denver, Colorado area, however, there are very few universities—the University of Colorado some distance away in Boulder, the University of Denver, Regis College, and perhaps a few small others. The variety of programs available is correspondingly reduced; the problems and costs of recruiting at the professional levels are increased.

This type of constraint on the development and recruiting of a high-talent work force tends to increase even more in importance as one moves to the sparsely populated sections of the United States, in the Rocky Mountain region, and in many parts of the South. Certain types of business facilities may not be able to operate at all in some locations, especially in isolated rural communities. The rapid development of community colleges in many parts of the United States has tended to provide a solution insofar as technician and skill training is concerned, but the lack of comprehensive university facilities in many sections remains a major constraint for personnel management throughout much of the country.

Activities in the Civil Rights Area

Reference has already been made to the very marked differences in attitude toward the Negro that characterize various regions of the United States. These differences will inevitably serve to influence personnel procedures in these regions. People in the South tend to react differently to personnel decisions involving Negroes than do people in other sections of the country.

Let us take the matter of a decision to hire a number of Negroes for relatively high-level skilled or technical positions as a case in point. In the North an employer who consistently refuses to hire Negroes in this manner may, of course, find himself exposed to legal pressures, but, perhaps even more important, in many localities he will experience a major boycott of products and services. If the company has a sizable Negro market, this can serve as an important limitation on decisions. On the other hand, hiring individuals of another race is less likely to produce sizable repercussions among the white population in the North, and it should be easier to locate qualified Negroes to fill the skilled and technical positions than in the South.

The forces operating on the same decision in the South, however, can be expected to be quite different. For one thing there are practically no qualified, skilled workers among the Negro population of the South, largely because very few vocational training opportunities have been made available to Negroes there in the past (19). Should satisfactory applicants be located, there would still remain the possibility of considerable difficulty in ironing out hiring arrangements with the unions. However, if hiring should occur, the prospect of retaliation, including boycott, by the local white populace could not be ruled out. Until recently, on the other hand, a decision against hiring would not have elicited any reaction from the Negroes in the area. Now, however, with the advent of civil rights activities in the South, this situation has changed and the civil rights laws have introduced a real possibility of legal constraint.

Operation in Suburban Areas

Some of the problems associated with both rural and urban locations have already been noted, including the fact that educational facilities may be limited in the former and freedom of movement restricted by public transportation schedules in the latter. Another type of geographical constraint occurs *within* the large metropolitan areas. To be specific, there are certain restrictions on personnel decisions that result directly from the fact that a firm has chosen a suburban, rather than a downtown, location for its facilities.

One major constraint arises because placing a facility in a suburb of a major city can be looked on as situating it on the edge or perimeter of a circle. Thus, the distance between the facility and the diametrically opposite side of the circle is twice as great as if the company had located in the center, or in the downtown area. Even more important from a practical viewpoint is the fact that crossing a city in this manner normally takes much longer than traveling the same distance in open country. Whether one uses public transportation or a private car, there are inevitably more stops and slower progress. As a result the labor market available in a suburban area tends to be restricted considerably over that that could be tapped from a downtown location. It may be limited in kind as well as number.

A further restraint is imposed as a result of the normal urban direction of transportation flow. Most public transport routes go inward like the spokes of a wheel. As a result, getting from one suburban point to another, even on the same side of the city, can be difficult if one does not have an automobile. This has not proved to be much of a problem as long as the work force is restricted to male family heads. But if many young female clerical workers are required, it can make for some difficult recruiting problems.

Thus, a suburban location, although it may offer many advantages in terms of land values and other factors, can impose some very definite constraints on a personnel manager. He will not only have a much smaller area to draw from in building the company's labor force, but may find it much harder to recruit certain types of employees. Accordingly, overall labor costs for the same level of accomplishment may be much greater in the suburbs than in downtown areas.

Removing Constraints

It is evident that all these restrictions may be eliminated if operations can be moved to a locale where the specific constraint does not exist. Certainly, factors such as those described should be considered before sites for business installations are decided upon. On many occasions, if past experience is any guide, personnel considerations will not be determining and the personnel manager will have to seek other ways of removing the constraints. This may not be easy.

Yet there are a number of possible courses of action. For example, it may be possible to work out arrangements with a state university to schedule several advanced courses at a location convenient to the company, perhaps at a place where employees of other firms may also participate. Such arrangements have become relatively commonplace at many major defense installations situated some distance from large cities. In some instances the statewide extension courses offered out of the major state universities and some other schools can also help to fill the educational gap.

Overcoming constraints imposed by transportation patterns and schedules is also possible, although it may require considerable community action on the part of the company's management. The same is true of the civil rights area. Company goals will be maximized to the extent that management can contribute to reduced conflict within the community and to an increased respect for law and order. This is because conflict in the community is very likely to spread into the firm itself and result in a reduced commitment to the goal of organizational maintenance.

Actually it is very difficult to offer specific prescriptions for overcoming geographical constraints of the kind discussed, because of the various local conditions that may operate to make one solution appropriate in one instance and another solution appropriate in another. This is one area in which the practice of the personnel profession seems consistently to require a great deal of ingenuity.

Industry Characteristics

The fact that industries differ from one another in many basic characteristics is a fact so obvious that it is practically a truism. Perhaps not so obvious, however, is the fact that such differences set constraints on the policies and practices which management may follow, and thus serve to influence the degree of success that these policies may yield. Industries differ in the geographical locations from which their raw materials derive, in their technologies, in their traditions, in the types of human resources available to them, and in many other respects. All these factors can have considerable significance for practice in the personnel area.

The Potentiality for Strike

Perhaps the most outstanding example of how the characteristics of industries influence the personnel management process comes from a now-famous study of the propensity to strike in different industries (10). In this study the authors obtained information on the history of strikes within eleven different countries over periods of time ranging from twenty to thirty years. The countries were Australia, Czechoslovakia, Germany, Italy, the Netherlands, New Zealand, Norway, Sweden, Switzerland, Great Britain, and the United States. Comparing the strike histories of the various nations, the authors found a consistent tendency for some industries to be much more strike prone than others. Table 4-4 summarizes these results.

In attempting to understand why such consistency across the various countries was present, the authors isolated certain characteristics that distinguished the high-strike from the low-strike industries. Thus, they were able to detail the conditions under which a personnel manager would have to pay particular attention to the strike-provoking potential of a proposed policy or decision—under which he might even have to eliminate certain alternative courses of action because in that particular industry the probability that labor conflict would result was so high.

These conditions that the authors felt distinguished the mining, maritime and longshore, lumber, and textile industries and made them more subject to conflict and strife were (a) a relatively homogeneous work force; (b) considerable isolation from, and lack of integration into, the general community; (c) a capability for cohesive, collective action; and (d) a forceful and somewhat combative labor force. On the other hand, in those industries where the workers were integrated into the community

Table 4-4. General Pattern of Strike Propensities

Propensity to strike	Industry
High	Mining, maritime, and longshore
Medium high	Lumber, textile
Medium	Chemical, printing, leather, manufacturing (general), construction, food, and kindred products
Medium low	Clothing, gas, water, electricity, services (hotels, restaurants, and so on)
Low	Railroad, agriculture, trade

Source: C. Kerr and A. Siegel, "The Inter-Industry Propensity to Strike—An International Comparison," in A. Kornhauser, R. Dubin, and A. M. Ross, *Industrial Conflict*, p. 190. Copyright 1954 by McGraw-Hill Book Company, Inc. Used by permission of McGraw-Hill Book Company.

and were somewhat dispersed, rather than having their homes together and separated from the general populace, the propensity for strike was not as great. Under these latter conditions personnel managers can be less concerned about problems of conflict and organizational maintenance; their decisions need not be made under the constraints imposed by the prospect that any decision with regard to human resource utilization may well provoke labor difficulties.

There is also some additional evidence that the specific technology that characterizes an industry may have implications for the conflict potential inherent in a work group, and thus for union-management re-relationships (14). Unstable, highly demonstrative, volatile behavior of a kind that may produce spontaneous work stoppages, unplanned strikes, frequent grievance filing, and the like appear to be particularly characteristic where the technology requires either crew operations, with all members performing similar tasks, or very short assembly lines. In industries where the production processes must be organized in one of these ways, a personnel manager should be particularly sensitive to the possibility that his decisions may result in spontaneous worker outbursts. On the other hand there is reason to believe conflict will be less acute in declining industries than in those that are stable or expanding. Unions tend not to attack companies that are in trouble (9).

Other Industry Characteristics

Some more general examples of the various ways in which the characteristics of different industries may serve to limit the decisions of personnel managers and focus their activities are given in Table 4-5. These will serve to illustrate further the nature of industry constraints. The table could, of course, be extended to cover a number of other industries (18).

Table 4-5. Examples of Industry Constraints on Personnel Decisions

Industry	Industry characteristic	Implications for personnel management
Automobile	Necessity for periodic layoffs	Concern with seniority questions in recall-layoff situations
	Research and development tradition	Difficulties in recruiting, research-administrative conflicts, and concern with motivating research personnel
Canning	Very small organizational units	Limitations on comprehensiveness of personnel programs
	Geographical dispersion of units	Restrictions on degree of interorganizational cooperation between personnel managers
Cigarette	Very low labor costs, averaging less than 5% of expenditures	Little power in the hands of personnel managers relative to other departments in company
Petroleum	Internationally oriented	Concern with cultural constraints and problems of staffing overseas operations
	Primarily independent, rather than international unions	Conflict and problems of organizational maintenance tend to be local rather than company-wide

However, the material presented is sufficient to provide a general picture of how factors of this kind may operate. Thus, the research and development tradition in the automobile industry, fostered by intense competition, frequent model changes, and perhaps other factors such as the widespread public interest in the industry, produces a number of consequences for personnel management. With current talent shortages in the highly skilled occupations, it means that recruiting will be difficult and for some specialized jobs almost impossible. With the major differences that exist between the ideal conditions for creative work and administrative work, it means almost inevitable conflict between the research and administrative segments of the company and thus a limitation on goal attainment in the maintenance area. With the tremendous importance of the research product to the company and the difficulty associated with creating anything new, it means a constant concern with the problem of motivating research personnel, often to the exclusion of other considerations.

Overcoming Constraints

What can a personnel manager do to circumvent or eliminate industry constraints of this kind? Certainly it is unlikely that, alone, he can move the company into new product lines and thus into another industry, although managers in other areas such as production or marketing may accomplish this when the external constraints on their activities become too severe. Yet there are some other possibilities for action.

In the petroleum industry, job satisfaction surveys can be constructed so as to tap specific local conditions and issues, rather than using the more usual company-wide system. As a result local sources of discontent can be identified and potential labor difficulties headed off before they occur. In the canning industry a special effort might be made to develop a long-distance, intercompany communication system to overcome problems created by dispersed locations. In the automobile industry with its geographical centralization this would seem unnecessary. However, an automobile firm might well turn to a dual promotion system under which scientists are promoted for their ability as researchers, in a research hierarchy, rather than for their administrative and managerial skills. This should serve to overcome some of the problems associated with motivating creative endeavor.

These are some of the possibilities for change that may serve to reduce or remove certain industry constraints. Other possibilities will become apparent as we move on to a discussion of various personnel techniques and procedures in later chapters. Again it is important to emphasize that a good personnel manager cannot afford to be lacking in ingenuity. Perhaps on occasion he may need to be really creative, in the same sense that outstanding research scientists are.

References

1. Chandler, M., *Management Rights and Union Interests*. New York: McGraw-Hill, 1964.
2. Evans, C. F., and V. Laseau, *My Job Contest*. Washington, D.C.: Personnel Psychology, Inc., 1950.
3. Farber, M. L., "English and Americans: Values in the Socialization Process," *Journal of Psychology*, Vol. 36 (1953), 243–250.
4. Farmer, R. N., and B. M. Richman, *Comparative Management and Economic Progress*. Homewood, Ill.: Irwin, 1965.
5. Fleishman, E., "Some Observations of Industrial Psychology in the U.S.S.R.," *Personnel Psychology*, Vol. 16 (1963), 115–126.
6. Haire, M., E. E. Ghiselli, and L. W. Porter, *Managerial Thinking: An International Study*. New York: Wiley, 1966.
7. Harbison, F., and C. A. Myers, *Management in the Industrial World*. New York: McGraw-Hill, 1959.
8. Harbison, F., and C. A. Myers, *Education, Manpower, and Economic Growth*. New York: McGraw-Hill, 1964.
9. Hutchinson, J. G., *Management under Strike Conditions*. New York: Holt, Rinehart and Winston, 1966.
10. Kerr, C., and A. Siegel, "The Inter-Industry Propensity to Strike—An International Comparison," in A. Kornhauser, R. Dubin, and A. M. Ross (eds.), *Industrial Conflict*. New York: McGraw-Hill, 1954, pp. 189–212.
11. McClelland, D. C., *The Achieving Society*. Princeton, N.J.: Van Nostrand, 1961.
12. McKersie, R. B., "Incomes Policy in Great Britain," in G. G. Somers (ed.), *Proceedings of the Nineteenth Annual Winter Meeting*. Madison, Wisc.: Industrial Relations Research Association, 1967, pp. 139–148.
13. Myers, A. S., "Recruiting and Selecting Foreign National Personnel for Overseas Operations," *Personnel Administration*, Vol. 28, No. 4 (1965), 25–30.
14. Sayles, L. R., *Behavior of Industrial Work Groups*. New York: Wiley, 1958.
15. Singh, P. N., and R. J. Wherry, "Ranking of Job Factors in Factory Workers," *Personnel Psychology*, Vol. 16 (1963), 29–33.
16. Skinner, C. W., "Management of International Production," *Harvard Business Review*, Vol. 42, No. 5 (1964), 125–136.
17. Taylor, W. C., and J. Lindeman, *United States Business Performance Abroad—The Creole Petroleum Corporation in Venezuela*. Washington, D.C.: National Planning Association, 1955.
18. Vance, S., *Industrial Structure and Policy*. Englewood Cliffs, N.J.: Prentice-Hall, 1961.
19. Wheeler, J. H., "The Impact of Race Relations on Industrial Relations in the South," in G. G. Somers (ed.), *Proceedings of the 1964 Spring Meeting*. Madison, Wisc.: Industrial Relations Research Association, 1964, pp. 474–481.

20. Whitehill, A. M., "Cultural Values and Employee Attitudes: United States and Japan," *Journal of Applied Psychology*, Vol. 48 (1964), 69–72.
21. Whitehill, A. M., and S. Takezawa, *Cultural Values in Management-Worker Relations. Japan: Gimu in Transition.* Chapel Hill, N.C.: School of Business Administration, Univ. North Carolina, 1961.

Questions

1. Suppose that you were the personnel manager for a large firm that was attempting to decide whether to locate a new department store in Los Angeles, California, or Chicago, Illinois. Discuss the *labor force* characteristics of the two areas that you believe are relevant to this question.
2. Discuss the prevailing attitudes toward work motivation in the United States and the Soviet Union. Why do some people think these differences are narrowing?
3. What are some of the ways in which constraints due to cultural differences may be overcome? What are some of the problems involved?
4. What are some of the characteristics that distinguish high-strike industries from low-strike industries? What are the implications for personnel management?
5. In which industries would you most expect to see the "research-administration" conflict? In what geographic areas have these industries tended to locate?
6. Assume that you are the personnel manager of a firm located in the Washington, D.C. area that has undertaken two major changes: (a) automation of production facilities; (b) expansion into extensive research and development for new products. What would be the implications of these changes for you in terms of new problems, new constraints, new procedures?

5

Legal Constraints on
Labor Relations Decisions

Although the value system of the United States is such that it is a constant source of pride to us that we have been able to build a very prosperous society, while still keeping relatively free of governmental constraints, there can be no doubt that over the past thirty or forty years management's freedom has been eroded substantially by a continued growth in the amount of legislation bearing on the employment relationship. Selection procedures, strikes, collective bargaining, firings, wages, hours of work—these and many other aspects of personnel management have been increasingly influenced by various types of governmental action. Whatever one's own feelings about the need for such legislation, there can be no doubt that from the viewpoint of the business organization there has been a marked increase in the number and restrictiveness of constraining influences.

The purpose of this chapter and the next is to trace the development of these constraints as they operate in different areas of the total personnel function. Because this topic is extensive, it is not possible to treat in a comprehensive manner all the legal statutes that are relevant. The discussion is intended to provide a general coverage only, and even then it will be limited to those legal constraints that specifically restrict managerial decisions. Laws that bear on the activities of union officers, union

WILMINGTON COLLEGE Library WILMINGTON

members, and the general public must be bypassed. Although the latter do have indirect implications for the practice of the personnel profession, they are not of central concern and thus are more appropriately left to an intensive course in the field of labor law. In this chapter the focus will primarily be on legal restrictions that tend to limit management's freedom of action in dealing with labor unions. Laws covering other aspects of the employment relationship will be taken up in Chapter 6.

Overcoming Legal Constraints

The general procedure in this chapter and the next differs somewhat from that employed previously in that little attention will be given to ways of overcoming the various limitations on managerial freedom that are discussed. The reason for this is not difficult to understand. Short of breaking the law, an approach that is not recommended, there are only a limited number of things that can be done to avoid the impact of legal restrictions.

One way, of course, to overcome both state and Federal legal constraints is to take an active interest in the formation of new laws. The management of a company *should* promulgate its point of view in its role as a partner in the democratic processes of the country. Efforts of this kind have achieved some success in the past, and certain constraints have been removed when there has been concerted action on the part of the business community. There is no reason this should not continue to be the case in the future.

A related approach involves challenging existing laws in the courts when they are believed to be at variance with basic constitutional provisions. This method has not proved outstandingly successful over the past thirty years as a means of establishing management's viewpoint relative to legal constraints on personnel decisions, yet it is potentially an important avenue of change.

Another alternative, at least insofar as the restrictions imposed by local and state laws are concerned, is to move to another jurisdiction. This has been done in the past with some success and is still being done. But with the constant increase in the scope of Federal regulation and the spread of essentially comparable state legislation from one state to another, the prospects here are not especially good. It is increasingly becoming a matter of "out of the frying pan into the fire." There is little point in assuming the costs of a move when the new location may very shortly develop the same set of limitations that the move was intended to circumvent.

In this connection there has been some talk about moving manufacturing facilities out of the United States to avoid the high labor costs fostered by legislation passed during the past thirty years or so. No doubt some firms have been influenced to seek foreign locations by this factor.

However, there are so many instances where this alternative is not available that it cannot be considered as a general solution to the problem of overcoming legal constraints.

The Plan of the Discussion

Among the areas of activity with which the personnel manager is typically concerned in his everyday work, there is probably none in which the government takes a greater interest or attempts to exert more control than the labor-management relationship. A company's efforts to achieve the goal of organizational maintenance are circumscribed by a considerably more extensive barrier of legal restraints than are its efforts relative to the productivity objective. In many respects the current legal framework in the labor relations area operates to sustain labor-management conflict through its concern with maintaining a balance of power; thus it inevitably serves to frustrate at least partially, efforts to promote organizational maintenance.

In discussing the nature of these constraints and the reason they have achieved the position they currently have, a historical approach will be used. This should make it possible to gain a better understanding of how laws develop and where they come from. The way in which the legal structure tends, with some lag, to reflect the socioeconomic characteristics and cultural values of a society is best portrayed through a historical analysis. The past can be a helpful guide to the future. A knowledge of what has been done previously and what has succeeded is a valuable asset to the prospective manager.

Federal Legislation

The Pre-1932 Period

As indicated during the discussion of the development of personnel management as a profession in Chapter 2, the United States has some very strong traditions relating to the importance of private property rights and the freedom of the individual. These values and beliefs are deeply embedded in the fabric of our society; they are supported throughout the socioeconomic hierarchy. Thus, it is not surprising that our common law (which is based on the accumulated decisions of the judiciary over a very long period of time) was directly opposed to the idea of imposing constraints on management's freedom to operate a business as it saw fit throughout the early part of the country's history.

Through the first half of the nineteenth century the state judiciary consistently ruled that workers could not act in concert with one another to better wages and working conditions, because to do so would interfere with the free operation of market forces (5). It was, therefore, not until

1842 in the case of *Commonwealth v. Hunt*,[1] which was tried in the state of Massachusetts, that a decision specifically favoring the organization of employees occurred. As noted in Chapter 2, however, this decision was quite limited in scope. Concerted activity in and of itself was not illegal, but the means used to gain the desired ends might well be.

In actual fact *Commonwealth v. Hunt* appears to have had only very limited impact. The basic philosophy of noninterference with the rights of the employer (i.e., private property) remained strong throughout the rest of the nineteenth century and the first third of the twentieth century. This philosophy manifested itself increasingly, however, through the use of the injunction. This is a legal procedure utilizing the courts of equity that provides for relief from an injurious practice, when the damages created by the practice are not compensable in a monetary sense. Thus, if the party asking for relief can demonstrate that irreparable damage would result should the practices of the defendant be permitted to continue, the judge may issue an order or injunction stopping these practices. If this order is disobeyed, the judge may fine the defendant, or even resort to imprisonment, for contempt of court (10).

The typical procedure involved the judge granting an injunction to employers whenever there was a threat of some union action, such as a strike. It was assumed that the union activities would result in irreparable damage to the business. The general pattern in line with the guiding philosophy of the time was to limit by judicial action any attempt to impose constraints upon the right of management to run its business as it saw fit.

Perhaps just as important as the injunction during this period was the judicial support for "yellow-dog" contracts, which for all practical purposes barred a worker from any subsequent union activity at the time he accepted employment. As a result of labor union pressures, a number of states (fourteen in all) did eventually pass laws that made these contracts illegal. Congress did the same thing at the Federal level in the Erdman Act (1898), which dealt with the conditions of railroad employment. However, both the state laws [2] and the pertinent section of the Federal law [3] were declared unconstitutional by the U.S. Supreme Court on the grounds that they were in violation of the Fifth and Fourteenth Amendments to the Constitution, which guarantee freedom of contract as a property right. These decisions served to reinforce even further the prevailing philosophy that there should be as few constraints as possible on the operation of the market place.

This philosophy achieved what would appear to be a highpoint in 1917

---

[1] *Commonwealth v. Hunt*, 4 Metcalf 111 (1842).

[2] *Coppage v. Kansas*, 236 U.S. 1, 35 S. Ct. 240 (1915).

[3] *Adair v. United States*, 208 U.S. 161, 28 S. Ct. 277 (1908).

when the Court ruled that an injunction could be issued forbidding all attempts to organize workers who had signed contracts agreeing not to join labor unions.[4] In this case the principle of governmental support for the doctrine of minimal constraint on the managerial process is clearly evident.

UNIONS IN RESTRAINT OF TRADE. An additional approach to minimizing union power developed shortly after the passage of the Sherman Act in 1890. Although enacted originally to limit *business* combinations in restraint of trade, the law was subsequently invoked against the unions (6). In several instances the courts held that union activities could be viewed as being in violation of antitrust provisions. Sizable monetary damages were assessed against unions and their members.

In 1914, however, the tide appeared to turn in the opposite direction when the Clayton Act was passed. This act exempted the unions from antitrust prosecution and indicated that their actions were not to be viewed as being in restraint of trade. It also attempted to limit the use of injunctions. However, the wording of the act proved imprecise in a number of respects, with the result that court decisions changed very little (12). Overall, the Clayton Act had practically no impact on existing practices. Values stressing the freedom of the business organization remained in control.

1932—The Norris-La Guardia Act

The first step away from this no-constraint philosophy came in 1932 when the depression was at its peak. The disillusionment of the depression years served to stimulate a widespread tendency to question existing values and assumptions. This questioning eventually produced some marked changes in the country's legal position regarding labor unions and union activity. Thus it was that in 1932 Congress passed the Norris-La Guardia Anti-Injunction Act, the product of a Republican Senate and a Democratic House and signed into law by a Republican president. This was to be the first of a number of laws effectively restricting management's freedom in dealing with labor unions.

The logic of the Norris-La Guardia Act, which is still operative today, is very simple, yet the import of the act has been tremendous. It essentially affirms a laissez-faire philosophy in that it specifies that government should not impose constraints upon the conduct of the union-management relationship or interfere with it *in any way*, unless there has been actual violence or damage to tangible property. It thus expressly forbids the enforcement of yellow-dog contracts by the courts and the use of the injunction in cases where damage *might* ensue. In-

---

[4] *Hitchman Coal and Coke Company v. Mitchell,* 245 U.S. 229, 38 S. Ct. 65 (1917).

stead, the injunction can be granted only in cases where there is actual damage or violence, and even then its use is severely limited (15).

The flavor of the Norris-La Guardia Act in directing the judiciary to stay out of the conduct of union-management relations is perhaps best appreciated by reading the relevant section of the act itself. Section 4 is accordingly presented below.

Section 4. No court of the United States shall have jurisdiction to issue any restraining order or temporary or permanent injunction in any case involving or growing out of any labor dispute or prohibit any person or persons participating or interested in such dispute (as these terms are herein defined) from doing, whether singly or in concert, any of the following acts:

(a) Ceasing or refusing to perform any work or to remain in any relation of employment;

(b) Becoming or remaining a member of any labor organization or of any employer organization, regardless of any such undertaking or promise as is described in section 3 of this Act;

(c) Paying or giving to, or withholding from, any person participating or interested in such labor dispute, any strike or unemployment benefits or insurance, or other moneys or things of value;

(d) By all lawful means aiding any person participating or interested in any labor dispute who is being proceeded against in, or is prosecuting, any action or suit in any court of the United States or of any State;

(e) Giving publicity to the existence of, or the facts involved in, any labor dispute, whether by advertising, speaking, patrolling, or by any other method not involving fraud or violence;

(f) Assembling peaceably to act or to organize to act in promotion of their interests in a labor dispute;

(g) Advising or notifying any person of an intention to do any of the acts heretofore specified;

(h) Agreeing with other persons to do or not to do any of the acts heretofore specified; and

(i) Advising, urging, or otherwise causing or inducing without fraud or violence the acts heretofore specified, regardless of any such undertaking or promise as is described in section 3 of this Act.

The major significance of the Norris-La Guardia Act is that it reaffirmed the principle of nonconstraint insofar as the actions of management in labor-management disputes are concerned and also extended this *same* principle to labor. Of secondary, but still considerable, importance is the fact that the act broadened the definition of a labor dispute, and thus the range of occurrences that were defined as out of bounds to governmental intervention. Under the terms of the new law a labor dispute was understood to include such matters as sympathy strikes, boycotts, and other situations where a third party comes to the aid of one of the participants in what was previously a two-party controversy.

1935—The National Labor Relations Act (The Wagner Act)

The passing of the Wagner Act in' 1935 marks the beginning of active *Federal* intervention in labor-management disputes with the express purpose of constraining the activities of one of the participants—in this case, management. The stated purpose of the act was to (a) encourage trade union growth and (b) restrain management from interfering in any way with this growth. Although the Norris-La Guardia Act was pro-labor in spirit, it was essentially laissez-faire in its basic nature. Its intent was to *stop* certain types of governmental intervention.

The Wagner Act went much further. It stated that the government could not remain neutral and that it must take an active role in union-management relationships by constraining the activities of one group (management) in order to advance the fortunes of the other (the unions). The spirit of the act can best be seen by reading the concluding paragraph of its introduction:

It is hereby declared to be the policy of the United States to eliminate the causes of certain substantial obstructions to the free flow of commerce and to mitigate and eliminate these obstructions when they have occurred, by encouraging the practice and procedure of collective bargaining and by protecting the exercise by workers of full freedom of association, self-organization, and designation of representatives of their own choosing, for the purpose of negotiating the terms and conditions of their employment or other mutual aid or protection.

To fulfill this stated purpose, the Wagner Act did two things. It set up machinery to facilitate the choice of a labor union by a group of workers. More important for our purposes, however, it enunciated a list of activities that were forbidden to management. These activities, which in the act are defined as unfair labor practices, were considered to be inimical to the purpose of the act, the encouragement of labor union growth, and hence were specifically proscribed. They comprise the first major set of direct, governmentally imposed constraints on management in the area of union-management relations.

The administrative power inherent in the act was vested in a three-man National Labor Relations Board and a staff of lawyers, investigators, and other personnel, who were responsible to the Board. It was the function of this governmental unit to set up election machinery, upon request, to determine if the majority of a given group of workers wished to have a particular union as a bargaining representative and to investigate complaints regarding unfair labor practices.

Let us now take up the specific restrictions on managerial action that were imposed under the designation—unfair labor practices.

1. *To interfere with, restrain, or coerce employees in the exercise of rights guaranteed in Section 7.* Section 7 of the Wagner Act reads as follows: "Employees shall have the right to self-organization, to form, join, or assist labor organizations, to bargain collectively through representatives of their own choosing, and to engage in concerted activities for the purpose of collective bargaining or other mutual aid or protection."

   This is the most general overall constraint clause of the act, which actually includes all the specific constraints listed later. It did have a particular purpose, however, in that it was designed to end such employer practices as spying and blacklists—practices that the La Follette committee subsequently reported in 1937 had reached alarming proportions. This investigation indicated that in the 1933–1937 period approximately 300 firms had spent over $9 million on strike breaking, espionage, and arms.

   Two major problems arose with regard to this provision, both of which led to amendment in the Taft-Hartley Act of 1947. One difficulty was that by forbidding antiunion speeches with required attendance during working hours the law was in violation of the constitutional guarantees of free speech.[5] Second, the definition of an employer in the Wagner Act was too broad, because it covered any person acting in the *interest* of an employer, directly or indirectly. This definition appeared to make the employer responsible for the unauthorized actions of supervisors or foremen.

2. *To dominate or interfere with the formation or administration of any labor organization or contribute financial or other support to it.* The purpose of this constraint was to prevent the formation and growth of the company unions that were prevalent during the 1920's. These company groups had proved quite effective and were, therefore, a real threat to an independent labor movement (8). In later years, as jurisdictional disputes between the CIO and AFL became more frequent, this clause was also applied in cases where for some reason an employer was clearly assisting one federation to oppose, or organize the members of, the other.

3. *By discrimination in regard to hire or tenure of employment or any term or condition of employment to encourage or discourage membership in any labor organization.* This clause has been called the real heart of the Wagner Act because it had a variety of purposes in mind. Among these were to make the following unlawful:
   a. The use of the yellow-dog contract
   b. To inquire of job applicants if they were union members

---

[5] Clark Brothers Co., Inc., 70 NLRB 802 (1946), 163 F. (2d) 373 CCA (2d).

  c. To inquire of job applicants if they favored unions

  d. To fire employees because of union membership

  The act did permit an employer to require union membership as a condition of employment, however, if the existing union contract so specified. This was the famous *closed shop* provision, which was subsequently amended in the Taft-Hartley Law. Finally, the act did not prevent employers from firing employees who engaged in unlawful activities or who struck in violation of contract provisions.

  A major problem that continually arose in relation to this clause involved the employer's freedom to hire replacements for those workers who had gone out on strike in protest against the discharge of a fellow employee for union activity or against some other unfair labor practice. In response to this obviously crucial question, NLRB policy gradually developed over a number of years to the point where there were two sets of reinstatement rules covering two distinct types of strikes, as follows:

  a. *Unfair Labor Practices Strike.* Those who strike because of or following the employer's unfair labor practices, or who participate in a strike which is prolonged or aggravated by the employer's unfair labor practices, have an absolute right to reinstatement if the strike is for a lawful purpose and lawfully conducted. The employer must reinstate the strikers when they apply for jobs, even if their jobs are filled by replacements. In the case of an unfair labor practice that prolongs what began as a simple economic strike, the strike becomes an unfair practice strike, and the strikers must be reinstated when they request to return to work. Replacements hired after the date that the strike was converted into an unfair labor practices strike must be discharged, if necessary, to make room for the strikers.[6]

  b. *Economic Strike.* Those who strike for higher wages and other improvements in working conditions have a limited right to reinstatement. They can reclaim their jobs if permanent replacements have not been hired.[7]

  The major constraints on management, then, were imposed in the case of unfair labor practices disputes, although it is not always easy to distinguish between these two types of strikes. In ordering

---

 [6] Kohler Company, 46 LRRM 1389.

 [7] *National Labor Relations Board v. Mackay Radio and Telegraph Co.*, 304 U.S. 333, 58 S. Ct. 904 (1938).

reinstatement of strikers, the NLRB usually requires employers to pay them an amount equal to the wages lost. These back-pay awards have on occasion cost companies hundreds of thousands of dollars.

4. *To discharge or otherwise discriminate against an employee because he has filed charges or given testimony under this act.* This provision was included for the protection of employees who attempted to avail themselves of the act's provisions.

5. *To refuse to bargain collectively with the representatives of employees duly chosen pursuant to other provisions of the act.* The purpose of this clause was to ensure that the other provisions of the act were not negated because the employer refused to bargain at all. In general it has served this purpose well, although it is possible to delay the bargaining process through court action for several years if a company has the resources and the inclination to do so. There has, however, been some controversy because a number of personnel managers have felt that the clause implied not only a need for bargaining but for agreement as well. Thus, an additional constraint seems to be imposed on management.

CONSEQUENCES OF THE WAGNER ACT. The provisions of the Wagner Act that were devoted to imposing specific constraints on the practices of management in order to stimulate union growth were important, wide-ranging, and outstandingly successful. During the twelve years when the Wagner Act was the basic law of the land (1935–1947), union membership increased from 3 million to over 15 million, and the trade unions assumed a position among the largest and strongest social institutions in the country (2). In fact, the growth was so phenomenal and the power of the labor movement became so great that strong sentiment began to develop in favor of correcting the inherently one-sided viewpoint of the Wagner Act. Many came to feel that a legal situation in which all constraint was placed on one side and the government took its place with the other was intolerable.

By 1947 public opinion in support of change had become so strong that Congress responded with the Taft-Hartley Act. The nature of the public demand at this time provides a good example of how legal constraints can be altered and even removed by concerted management efforts that are attuned to the values of the society.

1947—The Taft-Hartley Act

On June 23, 1947, the Congress of the United States passed an amendment to the Wagner Act known as the Labor-Management Relations Act, or, as it is more popularly known, the Taft-Hartley Act. With this piece of legislation a new philosophy regarding the proper role of government in the conduct of union-management affairs achieved formal acceptance. This was the concept of the impartial policeman. The explicit pro-union bias of the Wagner Act was repudiated, and the basic position, at least in theory, now was that government should not take sides, but rather should stand aside like a policeman, taking care to observe that the collective bargaining process took place fairly and according to the rules and that the interests of the general public were preserved. The essential neutrality of spirit that characterized this law is exemplified by the following wording:

Employees shall have the right to self-organization . . . for the purpose of collective bargaining or other mutual aid or protection, and shall also have the right to refrain from any or all of such activities.

The Taft-Hartley Act is now the most important labor law in this country. As a result of it the government was officially placed in the middle, neither encouraging nor discouraging union organization. The employee could either seek union representation or reject it, and the government backed this right of free choice.

Administration of the law was left in the hands of the National Labor Relations Board, but the Board was now enlarged from three to five members. A General Counsel was added to aid the Board and an explicit policy of decentralized decision making was stated. At the present time this means that all representation elections are conducted and all representation decisions rendered by the thirty-one regional directors. The Board in Washington will consider appeals only under a limited set of specified conditions. Unfair labor practices cases have not been decentralized and all are decided in Washington.

Since the basic purpose of the Taft-Hartley Act was to loosen the constraints on personnel decisions imposed by the Wagner Act, it is important to note how this was achieved. There are four major areas in which management was given greater freedom to act as it saw fit in pursuit of its goals.

1. *Supervisors.* The law removed supervisors and foremen from coverage. Whereas there had been some question on this matter under the Wagner Act, there was none under Taft-Hartley. The unfair labor practices provisions of the law were deemed not to be applicable when the individuals of concern were supervisors. Thus, no protection was given to the various foremen's and supervisors' unions, with the result that they have now largely disappeared. On

the other hand, in certain industries, such as printing, foremen do retain union membership.

2. *Free Speech.* The law included in Section 8(c) what has been called a free speech amendment. This provides that employers are now free to express their views and opinions without being charged with an unfair labor practice. However, this freedom holds only so long as there are no threats or promises of benefits in return for acting in a desired manner.

As can be imagined, enforcing this free speech amendment over the years has aroused considerable controversy, because the border between an expression of opinion and a promise or threat is tenuous, to say the least. The tendency during the Republican, Eisenhower years was to allow a rather wide range of expression by management. During the Truman years, the NLRB held that employers who addressed employees on company time and property must make equal time and facilities available to the union. However, this was changed in 1953, shortly after President Eisenhower assumed office, to mean that equal time did not have to be provided as long as the employer spoke more than twenty-four hours before the representation election. In recent years under Democratic presidents there has been a swing back in the other direction. It can be assumed that a similar, politically related flexibility of interpretation will continue in the future.

3. *Representation Elections.* The law gave employers the right to seek an election whenever any union made a claim for recognition as a bargaining agent for the company's employees. Under the Wagner Act the employer was constrained from obtaining an election unless the demand for recognition was made by two or more competing unions. This lifting of an employer constraint has made premature claims by unions much less frequent in the years since passage of the Taft-Hartley Act, because if a representation election is lost, another cannot be held for a calendar year.

4. *Court Suits.* The law gave employers the right, at least nominally, under Section 301(a) to sue unions in the courts for breach of contract, a right they had not had previously. This section of the act reads:

Suits for violation of contracts between an employer and a labor organization representing employees in an industry affecting commerce as defined in this Act, or between any such labor organizations, may be brought in any district court of the United States having jurisdiction of the practices without respect to the amount in controversy or without regard to the citizenship of the parties.

At the present time the value of this freedom to management has not become fully apparent. In fact, the constraint appears to be fully operative in spite of Taft-Hartley. The reason for this is that the Supreme Court has held that a suit of this nature to stop, for example, a strike in violation of a no-strike clause in the union-management contract would involve a court order similar to an injunction. This has been interpreted as being in violation of the Norris-La Guardia Act.[8]

NEW CONSTRAINTS ON MANAGEMENT. The preceding are the major areas in which a specific loosening of the limitations on managerial action is indicated in the Taft-Hartley Act. In addition, there were a number of new but relatively minor constraints placed on management by the law. Among these were the requirement that sixty days' notice must be given to the other party prior to any termination or change in a contract, and thirty days' notice must be given to the mediation agency in the state.

INTERPRETATION OF THE ACT. Of much greater consequence than these few added statutory limitations has been the way in which the law has been interpreted and applied since 1947 by the National Labor Relations Board and the courts. These interpretations have been the major source of new constraints on management. This can best be demonstrated by examining the precedents that the NLRB has built up over the years as to (a) the instances under which the NLRB will accept jurisdiction, (b) how collective bargaining will take place, and (c) what areas the collective bargaining process should cover.

Precedent has been explicitly established by the NLRB as to the necessary volume of business a firm must have before the Board will accept jurisdiction. The limited funds with which the Board has always had to operate have made it impossible to regulate all the cases involving interstate commerce, which both the Wagner and the Taft-Hartley Acts specifically delegated to it. Thus, for a number of years employers in interstate commerce, too small to meet the NLRB standards, were not covered by either of these acts. Nor, as a result of a series of Supreme Court decisions, were they covered by the various state labor relations acts (in those states having them) (11). This situation has now been remedied by the Landrum-Griffin Act of 1959, which will be discussed in greater detail in the next section. This act gives the states jurisdiction over those cases that might fall under Federal law but that the NLRB has chosen not to accept primarily because the firm involved does not have the necessary volume of business (9). The standards used by the NLRB in such cases, and now largely frozen by the Landrum-Griffin Act, are set forth in Table 5-1.

---

[8] *Sinclair Refining Company v. Atkinson*, 82 S. Ct. 1328 (1962).

Table 5-1.   NLRB Standards for Asserting Jurisdiction

1. Nonretail: $50,000 outflow and inflow, direct or indirect.
2. Office buildings: Gross revenue of $100,000, of which $25,000 or more is derived from organizations which meet any of the standards except the indirect outflow and indirect inflow standards.
3. Retail concerns: $500,000 gross volume of business.
4. Instrumentalities, links, and channels of interstate commerce: $50,000 from interstate (or linkage) part of enterprise, or from services performed for employers in commerce.
5. Public utilities: $250,000 gross volume, or meet standard 1 (nonretail).
6. Transit systems: $250,000 gross volume. (Except taxicabs, as to which the retail test ($500,000 gross volume of business) applies.)
7. Newspapers and communication systems: Radio, television, telegraph, and telephone: $100,000 gross volume. Newspapers: $200,000 gross volume.
8. National defense: Substantial impact on national defense.
9. Hotel-motel industry: Establishments with gross revenues of $500,000 a year, other than permanent or residential ones.
10. Business in the Territories and District of Columbia: D.C.—Plenary. Territories—Standards apply.
11. Associations: Regarded as single employer.
12. Employers who decline to furnish jurisdictional data if their operations affect interstate commerce to any extent.

Direct outflow refers to goods shipped or services furnished by the employer outside the State. Indirect outflow includes sales within the State to users meeting any standard except solely an indirect inflow or indirect outflow standard. Direct inflow refers to goods or services furnished directly to the employer from outside the State in which the employer is located. Indirect inflow refers to the purchase of goods or services which originated outside the employer's State but which he purchased from a seller within the State. Direct and indirect outflow may be combined and direct and indirect inflow may also be combined to meet the $50,000 requirement. However, outflow and inflow may not be combined.

In secondary boycott cases, jurisdiction is determined by combining the business of the primary employer with the business of the secondary employer at the location affected by the boycott.

Jurisdiction ordinarily is calculated on the business of the employer involved during the most recent calendar year.

In ordinary circumstances, the meeting of those gross dollar volume standards will necessarily entail activities "affecting commerce." But evidence of and a finding that the Board has legal jurisdiction is required in addition to proof that the gross dollar volume test is satisfied.

The Board has declined jurisdiction over racetracks and private hospitals.

Source: National Labor Relations Board, *Summary of the National Labor Relations Act.* Washington, D.C.: The Board, 1967, pp. 25–26.

The question of what constitutes "bargaining in good faith" has also produced numerous NLRB decisions and court rulings with the result that certain precedents have been established. Changing wage structures during the collective bargaining process [9] and failure to provide necessary wage information [10] have been proscribed by NLRB action and these constraints on management have been supported in the courts. However, the Supreme Court has questioned some of these attempts to regulate the bargaining process on the part of the NLRB.[11]

A similar problem has existed over the years in relation to the content of collective bargaining. The original wording of the Wagner Act stated that bargaining should take place with reference to "rates of pay, wages, hours . . . or other conditions of employment." This has gradually been spelled out over the years to include a great variety of things, including pensions, insurance plans, Christmas bonuses, rentals for company housing, and stock purchase plans. These and many other items are now considered to be subject to the constraints of collective bargaining and thus to be covered by the Taft-Hartley Act. But in this area also, the Supreme Court has made some attempts to reduce the growth in the size of the area circumscribed by government regulation.[12]

1959—The Landrum-Griffin Act

During the late 1950's a series of Congressional investigations resulted in some rather sweeping disclosures indicating that union members were being victimized both physically and financially by their elected union officials. There were also some instances in which employers appeared to be guilty of racketeering practices (4,13). The result was the passage of the Labor-Management Reporting and Disclosure Act of 1959, known as the Landrum-Griffin Act.

This act had as its major purpose the regulation of the internal affairs of unions and the relationships between union leaders and members. However, since the investigations had also indicated that employers were in some cases engaging in undesirable practices, the act did contain a number of clauses aimed at regulating managerial activity. It is the most recent major piece of legislation on the Federal level that imposes some constraint on managerial action in the personnel area.

These constraints were of two major types (1). For one thing the

---

[9] General Motors Corp., 81 NLRB 779, enforcement granted 179 F. (2d) 221 (2d Cir. 1950).

[10] *National Labor Relations Board v. F. W. Woolworth Co.*, 352 U.S. 938, 77 S. St. 261 (1956).

[11] *National Labor Relations Board v. Insurance Agents' International Union AFL-CIO*, 361 U.S. 477, 80 S. Ct. 419 (1959).

[12] *National Labor Relations Board v. American National Insurance Co.*, 343 U.S. 395, 72 S. Ct. 824 (1952).

law required employers to report to the Secretary of Labor any payments or loans made to unions, their officials, or members. Excluded from this requirement were payments made for some valid reason such as (a) payments to a union officer because of his services as an employee, (b) payments resulting from some legal action, (c) payments into valid benefit funds, and (d) payments as a result of the purchase of an article at the prevailing market value. The purpose of this provision was to eliminate what have been called *sweetheart contracts,* under which the employer and union agree to terms that maintain substandard working conditions to their mutual advantage.

Another group of limitations imposed under the law required a variety of other reports from employers as to any payments made to employees, if these payments were for reasons that fall generally under the heading of influencing employees concerning their right to organize and bargain collectively. There was also a provision calling for reports on payments made to labor consultants, if the payments were made in order to purchase influence over the behavior of employees.

A final and closely related piece of legislation that imposed some minor constraints on personnel management is the Teller Act, first enacted in 1958 and amended to give it more teeth in 1962. The purpose of this act, also known as the Welfare and Pension Plans Disclosure Act, was to regulate the administration of the employer-financed health and retirement plans that mushroomed in the late 1950's. As currently constituted, the act requires the filing of plan descriptions and annual reports regarding operation with the Secretary of Labor and the bonding of all plan administrators. This requirement holds whether the plan is completely or partially financed by the company and whether it was instituted unilaterally or as a consequence of collective bargaining.

State Legislation

In addition to the Federal laws, there has also been a considerable amount of legislation at the state level, beginning in 1937 (7,14). Relatively few states, however, have enacted labor legislation designed to accomplish on a state level what the Wagner and Taft-Hartley Acts had done on a Federal level. In 1966 Vermont passed the fifteenth state labor relations act, the first such enactment since 1961. At present such laws are in effect in Colorado, Connecticut, Hawaii, Kansas, Massachusetts, Michigan, Minnesota, New York, North Dakota, Pennsylvania, Puerto Rico, Rhode Island, Utah, Vermont, and Wisconsin (3). These acts usually cover those interstate cases where the NLRB has refused to accept jurisdiction (see Table 5-1), and also intrastate commerce.

Even in states that do not have comprehensive labor relations laws, however, many aspects of labor relations activities are covered under more limited laws and regulations. Several of these aspects are listed in Table 5-2.

Table 5-2. Selected List of Labor Relations Activities Covered by State Laws and Regulations

State	Antitrust laws	Deduction of union dues from pay (checkoff)	Injunctions	Public employees	Strikes, picketing, and boycotts
Alabama	. . .	×	. . .	×	×
Alaska	. . .	. . .	. . .	×	×
Arizona	. . .	×	×	. . .	×
Arkansas	×	×	. . .	. . .	×
California	×	×	. . .	×	×
Colorado	. . .	×	×	. . .	×
Connecticut	×	×	×	×	×
Delaware	. . .	. . .	. . .	×	×
D.C.	. . .	×	. . .	. . .	×
Florida	×	×	. . .	×	×
Georgia	. . .	×	. . .	×	×
Hawaii	. . .	×	×	×	×
Idaho	×	. . .	×	×	×
Illinois	×	×	×	×	×
Indiana	×	×	×	×	×
Iowa	×	×	. . .	. . .	×
Kansas	. . .	×	×	. . .	×
Kentucky	. . .	×	. . .	. . .	×
Louisiana	×	×	×	×	×
Maine	×	. . .	×	×	×
Maryland	. . .	×	×	. . .	×
Massachusetts	×	×	×	×	×
Michigan	×	×	. . .	×	×
Minnesota	. . .	×	×	×	×
Mississippi	. . .	×	. . .	. . .	×
Missouri	×	. . .	. . .	×	×
Montana	×	. . .	×	. . .	×
Nebraska	×	×	. . .	. . .	×
Nevada	. . .	×	. . .	. . .	×
New Hampshire	×	. . .	. . .	. . .	×
New Jersey	. . .	. . .	×	. . .	×
New Mexico	×	. . .	×	×	×
New York	×	×	×	×	×

Table 5-2 (cont'd.)

State	Antitrust laws	Deduction of union dues from pay (checkoff)	Injunctions	Public employees	Strikes, picketing, and boycotts
North Carolina	×	×	...	×	×
North Dakota	...	×	×	...	×
Ohio	×	×	...	×	×
Oklahoma	×	...	...	...	×
Oregon	×	...	×	×	×
Pennsylvania	...	×	×	×	×
Puerto Rico	...	...	×	...	×
Rhode Island	...	×	×	×	×
South Carolina	×	×	...	...	×
South Dakota	...	×	...	...	×
Tennessee	×	×	...	...	×
Texas	×	×	×	×	×
Utah	×	×	×	...	×
Vermont	...	...	...	...	×
Virginia	×	×	...	×	×
Washington	...	...	×	×	×
West Virginia	...	...	...	...	...
Wisconsin	×	×	×	×	×
Wyoming	...	×	×	×	×

Source: Compiled from *Labor Relations Reporter*. Washington, D.C.: The Bureau of National Affairs, Inc.

These state laws differ from one another considerably in both coverage and provisions and include constraints on unions as well as on management. Of particular interest are the growing number of state laws regulating labor relations for public employees. In light of recent increases in union activity among such groups as teachers and other employees of state and local governments, these laws may be expected to have considerable significance in years to come.

References

1. Aaron, B. J., "The Labor Management Reporting and Disclosure Act of 1959," *Harvard Law Review*, Vol. 73, Nos. 5 and 6 (1960).
2. Bernstein, I., "The Growth of American Unions," *American Economic Review*, Vol. 44 (1954), 308–317.

3. Bond, D. T., "1967 Changes in State Labor Laws," *Monthly Labor Review,* Vol. 90, No. 12 (1967), 21–28.
4. Chamberlain, E. H., et al., *Labor Unions and Public Policy.* Washington, D.C.: American Enterprise Association, 1958.
5. Chruden, H. J., and A. W. Sherman, *Personnel Management,* 2nd ed. Cincinnati: South-Western Publishing, 1963.
6. Heneman, H. G., and D. Yoder, *Labor Economics,* 2nd ed. Cincinatti: South-Western Publishing, 1965.
7. Katz, H. A., "Two Decades of State Labor Legislation: 1937–1957," *Labor Law Journal,* Vol. 8 (1957), 747–767, 818.
8. Millis, H. A., and E. C. Brown, *From the Wagner Act to Taft-Hartley.* Chicago: Univ. Chicago Press, 1950.
9. National Labor Relations Board, *Summary of the National Labor Relations Act.* Washington, D.C.: The Board, 1967.
10. Northrup, H., and G. F. Bloom, *Government and Labor.* Homewood, Ill.: Irwin, 1963.
11. Purver, J. M., "The Supreme Court and the Federal-State 'No-Mans' Land," *Labor Law Journal,* Vol. 11 (1960), 1031–1037.
12. Randle, C. W., and M. S. Wortman, *Collective Bargaining: Principles and Practice.* Boston, Mass.: Houghton Mifflin, 1966.
13. Saposs, D. J., "Labor Racketeering—Evolution and Solutions," *Social Research,* Vol. 25 (1958), 253–270.
14. United States Department of Labor, Bureau of Labor Standards, *State Labor Relations Acts,* Bulletin No. 224. Washington, D.C.: U.S. Government Printing Office, 1961.
15. Yoder, D., *Personnel Management and Industrial Relations,* 5th ed. Englewood Cliffs, N.J.: Prentice-Hall, 1962.

Questions

1. What were the so-called "heart" provisions of the Wagner Act? What is their current status?
2. Describe an unfair labor practices strike and an economic strike. Why were they differentiated by the National Labor Relations Board?
3. Discuss the varying philosophies underlying the Norris-La Guardia Act, the Wagner Act, and the Taft-Hartley Act. What were their similarities and differences? What is the predominant current philosophy? Do you see any portents of change? If so, what?
4. What were the four explicit differences between the Wagner and Taft-Hartley Acts in the area of managerial constraints? What have been some of the problems in applying these acts over the years?
5. What were the managerial constraints involved in the Landrum-Griffin Act?

6

Legal Constraints on Employment Decisions

The previous chapter discussed at some length the legal restrictions that circumscribe the actions management may take in the area of labor relations. As indicated, however, this is not the only type of limitation that the legal system places on personnel management. A number of aspects of the total employment process such as wages, hours of work, hiring specifications, layoffs, safety practices, and retirement are also affected.

In this chapter the constraint structures associated with these areas are discussed. As has been the practice previously, only those statutory provisions that bear on *managerial* actions are emphasized. Many of the laws refer to other groups in society as well, but these features are not directly relevant for our purposes. It is, however, important to discuss the various types of *state* legislation in the employment area, just as it was when considering the legal aspects of the union-management relationship.

Constraints on the Payment of Wages

Governmental interest in and control of wage rates dates back over half a century to a law passed in Massachusetts in 1912. The logic or rationale for the extensive legal structure that has developed since that time is rather complex, but at least three clearly distinguishable reasons for this growth can be identified. For one thing the laws are designed to assist the marginal employee so that he may maintain at least a minimally satisfactory standard of living. It is also argued that these laws help the employee by protecting him from unfair firms that would pay extremely low wages and drag down the entire wage structure of the community. Third, there is a contention that the laws help the general economy by providing increased purchasing power through increased income.

Despite these arguments in their favor, however, the wage laws have been quite controversial over the years. Opponents contend the increased wage costs result in a loss of jobs, because more employers are forced out of business and others are compelled to mechanize or automate their plants. A second contention is that the increased money put in circulation by the laws has served only to produce inflationary pressures, and thus any resulting increases in the standard of living are largely illusory.

Whatever the merits of these opposing positions, and evidence can be adduced on both sides, it remains true that minimum wage laws are very much a part of the economic structure of the United States right now; also, they are likely to continue as an important legal constraint on personnel management at both the Federal and state levels for some time to come.

Federal Legislation

THE FAIR LABOR STANDARDS ACT. The first of the three major minimum wage laws, at least in terms of its importance, is the Fair Labor Standards Act, which was passed by Congress in 1938 and amended in 1949, 1955, 1961, and 1966. At the time of the original enactment the law (which also has an hours of work provision to be discussed later) set as its goal a national minimum wage of 40 cents per hour by 1945. However, this target was reached considerably before the date specified, as a result of increases during the war years. The 1949 and 1955 amendments then raised this floor to 75 cents per hour and $1.00 per hour, respectively.

Sweeping changes occurred with the 1961 amendments. First, many large retail and service establishments and construction operations, which had not previously been covered, were brought under the act's jurisdiction. As a result some 3½ million new employees became subject to the law's provisions. A second feature of the 1961 amendments was that it raised the minimum rates again. For employees previously covered by the act, the minimum scale was increased to $1.15 per hour for 1961 and 1962, and then to $1.25 for 1963. For those covered for the first time, the rates were set at $1.00 per hour for the first two years, and at $1.25 for 1963.

The most far-reaching amendments to the Fair Labor Standards Act were those passed in 1966, which resulted in the extension of the coverage to 9 million workers previously excluded and brought the total number of employees covered by the Act to nearly 41.5 million (8). Several types of enterprises that had previously been exempt, such as laundry and dry-cleaning establishments, non-Federal hospitals and nursing homes, private and public elementary and secondary schools, and institutions of higher learning were now included. Prior to the 1966 amendments many establishments, particularly in retail trade and the services, were covered only if their gross annual volume of business amounted to $1 million or more. This dollar-volume test was reduced to $500,000 as of February 1, 1967, and to $250,000 as of February 1, 1969. Also covered for the first time were workers on large farms.

**Table 6-1. Federal Minimum Wage Legislation—
Fair Labor Standards Act**

Legislation	*Minimum hourly wage*	*Minimum hourly wage for employees not previously covered*	*Minimum hourly wage for new farm coverage*
Original enactment—1938			
Effective 1938	$.25		
Effective 1940	.30		
Effective 1945	.40		
1949 Amendments	.75		
1955 Amendments	1.00		
1961 Amendments			
Effective September 1961	1.15	$1.00	
Effective September 1963	1.25	—	
Effective September 1964	—	1.15	
Effective September 1965	—	1.25	
1966 Amendments			
Effective February 1967	1.40	1.00	$1.00
Effective February 1968	1.60	1.15	1.15
Effective February 1969	—	1.30	1.30
Effective February 1970	—	1.45	—
Effective February 1971	—	1.60	—

Source: Compiled from S. Kocin, "Basic Provisions of the 1966 FLSA Amendments,"
    Monthly Labor Review, Vol. 90, No. 3 (1967), pp. 1–4.

The increase in the minimum wage under the 1966 amendments was spread over several years, and special rates apply to farm employment, as shown in Table 6-1. By 1971 all nonfarm workers covered by the Act will be subject to a $1.60 per hour minimum, whereas the rate for farm employment will be $1.30 per hour.

With the 1966 amendments, employees of nearly all businesses in interstate commerce, except those with a very small dollar volume, are subject to the Federal minimum wage. The largest groups still exempt from the law's coverage are executive, administrative, and professional employees, outside salesmen, self-employed workers, and government employees (11). Presumably most individuals in these categories are currently at rates above the minimum, and for this reason the exemptions are most meaningful as they relate to the hours and overtime provisions of the Act to be discussed later in this chapter.

THE DAVIS-BACON ACT. A second Federal minimum wage law is the Davis-Bacon Act of 1931, known as the Prevailing Wage Law. Its essential purpose is to require contractors and subcontractors on Federal construction projects to pay the prevailing wage rates for the locality, as determined by the Secretary of Labor. Thus, the law in fact produces considerably more than a minimum wage constraint. The prevailing wage has usually been interpreted to be the average union rate in the area.

The coverage is quite broad. The act applies to all contracts of $2,000 or more and the penalties for violations are severe (4). Furthermore, clauses similar to those of the Davis-Bacon Act have been inserted in the Hospital Survey and Construction Act of 1946, which was designed to provide state agencies with Federal assistance in hospital construction, and in the Housing Act of 1949 in connection with Title I (slum clearance and community development) and Title III (low-rent public housing).

THE WALSH-HEALEY ACT. The third Federal minimum wage law is the Walsh-Healey Public Contracts Act of 1936. This act applies to the employees of companies that have contracts to do work for the national government, when these contracts exceed $10,000 for materials and supplies. The coverage does not apply to office and custodial employees. All workers under the jurisdiction of the act must be paid at least the basic minimum wage for the particular industry, as this has been determined by the Secretary of Labor. The Labor Department may use either regional or nationwide wage rates to make this determination, at its own discretion.

State Legislation

As has been indicated, minimum wage legislation has a considerably longer history on the state level than on the Federal. By the end of 1913 nine states had passed some type of minimum wage act. This was 18 years before the first Federal law. As of 1968 more than half the states, plus the District of Columbia and Puerto Rico, had general minimum wage laws, and several others provided machinery for administrative determination of general wage rates. Only in the southeastern part of the country are such laws uncommon. The intent of these laws is essentially the same as with the Federal legislation, and the arguments pro and con are similar. In most states agricultural and domestic occupations are excluded. Yet the state laws do tend to cover a number of workers who fall outside the jurisdiction of the Federal legislation, in particular those employed by companies not in interstate commerce.

Working Hour Constraints

Closely tied to the growth of legislation dealing with the regulation of wages has been the spread of legal constraints on hours of work. To a large extent legislation that has specified allowable wage structures has also contained certain restrictions on the amount of time certain people can spend at work. As with the wage limitations, working hour laws passed at the Federal level apply to those firms engaged in interstate commerce and those at the state level to companies operating on an intrastate basis.

Federal Legislation

Among the laws discussed in the previous section, both the Fair Labor Standards Act, as amended, and the Walsh-Healey Public Contracts Act have provisions governing the working hours of employees. A major intent of these laws is to limit the length of the workweek indirectly, by requiring premium pay for time worked in excess of a specific standard.

Most important for our purposes is the Fair Labor Standards Act, which requires the payment of time and one half for all work in excess of 40 hours per week in most covered industries. A workweek is defined as a recurring period of 168 hours (seven consecutive 24-hour periods). It need not be the same as the calendar week and it may begin at any hour of the day. The 1966 amendments extended the overtime requirements to a number of groups of employees for the first time. This extension was made with the stipulation that they be paid time and one half for hours worked over 44 per week as of February 1, 1967, over 42 per week on February 1, 1968, and over 40 per week on February 1, 1969.

As noted earlier, several categories of employees are exempt from both the minimum wage and overtime provisions of the Fair Labor Standards Act, notably executive, administrative, and professional employees paid on a salaried rather than an hourly wage basis. In addition, employees in certain specified businesses such as hotels and restaurants are exempt only from the overtime provisions. The number of these exemptions has been narrowed considerably since the initial law was enacted in 1938.

State Legislation

Governmental restraints on working hours have a much longer history in the states than they do at the Federal level; also they are much more direct. The Federal government restricts hours of work primarily through overtime payment provisions. The states specifically limit the amount of time that can be worked.

The reason for this difference is that the state laws have been based much more on humane considerations. State laws controlling hours of work were passed originally for the specific purpose of preventing the exploitation of child and female employees. On the Federal level this type of concern is characteristic only of certain sections of the Fair Labor Standards Act that require a minimum age of sixteen for general employment and of fourteen for jobs outside school hours. The Secretary of Labor may also establish the employment age at eighteen for certain hazardous occupations. There has been some Federal regulation of the working hours of railroaders and other transport workers, but this has been justified primarily on the basis of passenger safety rather than on the basis of humane considerations.

LEGISLATION OF WORKING HOURS FOR CHILDREN. Concern over the number of hours children were required to work goes back as far as 1813 when the state of Connecticut passed a generally ineffective law requiring owners of manufacturing concerns to make provisions so that their child employees would have time to learn how to read and write. In 1836 the first really effective law was passed by the state of Massachusetts. This legislation required that all children employed in manufacturing must attend school at least three months per year if they were under the age of fifteen.

The spread of child labor laws was quite rapid from that time on. Currently all states, Puerto Rico, and the District of Columbia have laws regulating the employment of minors. These characteristically limit the number of hours that can be worked within a given time period and place a restriction, or complete prohibition, on night work for employees under sixteen years of age. In some cases these statutes apply to all employees under eighteen.

LEGISLATION OF WORKING HOURS FOR WOMEN. Governmental interest in safeguarding the health and welfare of women workers has almost as long a history as the interest in child labor. In the year 1852 the state of Ohio passed the first ten-hour law for women. From that time on state legislation controlling the conditions of female employment grew steadily, until today a company that employs women is confronted with a rather extensive set of constraints in practically every state.

Table 6-2 details the growth of such laws on the state level since 1913. An examination of this table provides graphic evidence of the comprehensive nature of the legal constraints within which personnel management must operate in today's society. Yet there has been relatively little change in this area since 1940.

Table 6-2. Chronological Development of State Hour Laws for Women (1913–1960)

| Year | Number of Jurisdictions with Daily Maximum Hour Laws | | |
| | Number of hours per day | | |
	8 or less	Over 8 but less than 10	10 or over
1913	3	5	19
1920	10	14	19
1940	19	15	10
1950	18	14	11
1960	18	14	11

| Year | Number of Jurisdictions with Weekly Maximum Hour Laws | | | |
| | Number of hours per week | | | |
	44–47	48–53	54–57	58–60
1913		1	8	13
1920		9	20	8
1940	4	21	12	5
1950	1	25	10	5
1960	1	26	10	4

| Year | Number of Jurisdictions with Special Laws Regarding Women's Work | | | |
	Day of rest	Lunch period	Rest period	Night work
1913	1	6		7
1920	14	20	4	17
1940	24	27	4	19
1950	23	29	8	18
1960	23	27	12	22

Source: U.S. Department of Labor, *Growth of Labor Law in the United States.* Washington, D.C.: the Department, 1962, p. 79.

LEGISLATION OF WORKING HOURS FOR MEN. State legal constraints on working hours for men do not stem from the humanitarian considerations that provoked the enactment of statutes governing the work of women and children. The laws applicable to men are primarily maximum hour

restrictions covering positions where public safety is a major consideration or where there are extremely hazardous working conditions. Examples of the laws of the former type are those relating to bus drivers and
airline pilots. Hours of work in mining, on the other hand, are controlled
largely out of safety considerations. Legislation of this kind goes back
to 1890 when a law was passed in the state of Ohio. Today almost all
states have some such restrictions.

Constraints on Employment Decisions Arising out of Civil Rights Considerations

Federal Legislation

It is now illegal in this country for employers engaged in interstate
commerce to use race, color, religion, national origin, or sex as a basis
for hiring. It is also unlawful, under the same act, to fire "or otherwise
discriminate against any individual with respect to his compensation,
terms, conditions or privileges of employment" because of that person's
race, color, religion, nationality, or sex. Third, the legislation serves to
proscribe any limitation, segregation, or classification of employees for
these same reasons, if doing so "would deprive or tend to deprive any
individual of employment opportunities or otherwise adversely affect
his status as an employee." These three constraints on employment decisions, along with certain others to be discussed shortly, stem from Title
VII of the Civil Rights Act of 1964.

Although the Act does impose certain limitations on labor unions and
employment agencies, the present discussion, in accordance with our
standard practice, is restricted to those specific features that serve to
constrain managerial decisions. It should be noted in passing that there
is a section that makes it illegal for an employer, either acting alone or
in conjunction with a union, to discriminate against an individual on the
basis of race, color, religion, national origin, or sex in connection with
an apprenticeship or training program.

The Act defines an employer as a person who has 25 or more people
working for him at least 20 weeks of each calendar year. However, the
law affected only those with 100 or more employees beginning July 2,
1965. On July 2, 1966, it covered those employing 75 or more people,
then 50 in 1967, and finally on July 2, 1968, it reached the standard level
of 25 or more employees. Exemptions from employer status as thus defined are granted to religious organizations employing members of the
specific sect for religious purposes and to private clubs if they are exempt from the Federal income tax.

Employers may use religion, sex, or national origin (but not color)
as a hiring requirement, if these seem to be necessary to the operation

of the business. For example, it would seem likely that a cosmetics manufacturer who sold his products through door-to-door sales personnel could legally specify "female sex" as a hiring requirement. Also, employers may legally discriminate against individuals who are members of an organization registered as a communist front by the Subversives Activities Control Board.

The law specifically states [Section 703(j)] that employers are *not* required to match up the racial or religious composition of a work force with that of the community. Thus, if a company facility is situated in a community that is half Negro and half white, there is no requirement that the employee group be similarly distributed. However, it would seem obvious that having only a very few Negroes or whites, or none at all, in such a situation would be suspect.

The enforcement provisions vary depending on whether the firm is located in a state having a Fair Employment Practices Commission (FEPC) that has been established under state law. In those states not having any such law, the complainant files charges with the Equal Employment Opportunity Commission (EEOC), the purely advisory Federal agency created by the Act to help enforce the law. The EEOC has 30 days (60 under certain circumstances) in which to secure voluntary compliance. Failing this, the complainant may go into Federal district court to secure enforcement of his employment rights. The Attorney General may also intervene, if he judges the case to be of sufficient public importance. The courts may assist the complainant by appointing an attorney for him and by hearing the case without requiring the payment of fees and costs. Should the employer be found guilty, the court may (a) enjoin him from discriminating further and (b) order "affirmative" action, such as reemployment of the aggrieved individual.

The procedure differs somewhat in states having FEPC laws. In these cases the state agencies must be used first; they are given 60 days (120 days during a state law's first year). If no solution is found within this period, the complainant may take the case to the EEOC. At this point the state agency is given another 60 (or 120) days to attempt to resolve the problem. After this second period has expired, court proceedings may be instituted.

These are the basic aspects of the Civil Rights Act of 1964 that operate as constraints on management in connection with the employment process (1). In general it seems clear that the Act does have the support of the courts, although specific provisions will no doubt be contested for years to come.

As an example of the type of problem that is likely to arise, it might be worth noting a case involving the Motorola Company (3,12,13). Although the law specifies that testing for selection purposes is legal so long as the test is not specifically designed, intended, or used to discriminate, the particular state commission involved raised a question regarding the use of a standard verbal ability measure when there is evidence that Negroes, on the average, score lower on such measures than whites (see Chapter 3). The question raised, therefore, is whether these verbal tests must of necessity discriminate against Negro applicants irrespective of the purposes of the employer. It is obvious that this is a complex problem that will result in considerable discussion before it is solved. The courts seem destined to face a barrage of questions in the area of testing. Because major constraints on the nature of employment decisions are involved, personnel managers will undoubtedly be concerned with such matters for some time.

State Legislation

As indicated in the preceding discussion, a number of states (and some cities) have passed FEPC laws outlawing discrimination on the basis of race, color, religion, or national origin. These laws vary considerably in enforcement provisions and applicable penalties and have been subject to considerable change over the years. In addition, a number of states have passed legislation barring discrimination on the basis of age or sex, when the job requirements do not appear to have an age- or sex-related basis (see the discussion in Chapter 3). States having statutes constraining employment decisions in these various ways are noted in Table 6-3. This table is complete through 1967.

Table 6-3. State Fair Employment Practice Laws

State	Type of illegal discrimination		
	Racial, religious	Sex	Age
Alabama	...	...	...
Alaska	×	...	×
Arizona	×	×	...
Arkansas	...	...	...
California	×	...	×
Colorado	×	...	×
Connecticut	×	...	×
Delaware	×	...	×
District of Columbia	×	×	...
Florida	...	...	...
Georgia	...	...	...
Hawaii	×	×	×
Idaho	×	×	×
Illinois	×	...	...
Indiana	×	...	×
Iowa	×	...	...
Kansas	×	...	...

Table 6-3 (cont'd.)

State	Racial, religious	Sex	Age
	\multicolumn{3}{|c|}{*Type of illegal discrimination*}		
Kentucky	×	...	...
Louisiana	...	...	×
Maine	×	...	×
Maryland	×	×	×
Massachusetts	×	×	×
Michigan	×	×	×
Minnesota	×	...	...
Mississippi	...	...	...
Missouri	×	×	...
Montana	×	...	×
Nebraska	×	×	×
Nevada	×	×	...
New Hampshire	×	...	...
New Jersey	×	×	×
New Mexico	×	...	...
New York	×	×	×
North Carolina	...	...	...
North Dakota	...	...	×
Ohio	×	...	×
Oklahoma	×	...	...
Oregon	×	...	×
Pennsylvania	×	...	×
Puerto Rico	×	...	×
Rhode Island	×	...	×
South Carolina	...	...	...
South Dakota	...	...	...
Tennessee	...	...	...
Texas	...	...	×
Utah	×	×	...
Vermont	×	...	...
Virginia	...	...	...
Washington	×	×	×
West Virginia	×	×	...
Wisconsin	×	×	×
Wyoming	×	×	...

Source: Compiled from *Labor Relations Reporter*. Washington, D.C.: The Bureau of National Affairs, Inc.

Constraints on Separations

To encourage employers to stabilize their employment policies and keep individual workers on the job, every state in the union today has an unemployment compensation program, which is financed by taxing employers according to the extent to which their companies have contributed to the unemployment rolls. These programs have other objectives as well—to keep purchasing power at a high level and thus assist the economy, and to minimize the impact of unemployment as it may affect the individual and his family. However, it is because unemployment compensation laws operate as a constraint on personnel policy by encouraging employment stabilization and a minimal number of separations that they are included in this chapter.

Although the first law in the United States was on the state level in Wisconsin in 1932, the real impetus to the growth of unemployment insurance came in 1935, in the midst of the depression, when the Social Security Act was passed (9). An important provision of this act was a Federal tax on payrolls, of which 90 per cent was to be refunded to the states if they passed acceptable unemployment compensation programs. By July 1937, all had enacted laws of this kind, including the District of Columbia.

Since that time there have been a number of changes in these programs in the various states, all of which have been directed toward increased coverage. The original Federal requirement for an acceptable state law was that it cover employers with eight or more workers in each of twenty weeks. In 1956 this requirement was reduced to four or more workers. However, many states have gone beyond this in their coverage. By 1968 more than half the states covered firms too small to be included under the Federal requirement. Many of these state laws provide for unemployment insurance regardless of the size of the firm (6).

The common characteristics of the various systems are that:

1. There must usually be a waiting period before unemployment benefits are paid to the worker who has just lost his job (generally one week), although in recent years a few states have abolished the waiting period.
2. The person who receives benefits must establish his eligibility for unemployment payments by virtue of previous employment and earnings; these then determine the amount of the subsequent weekly benefit payments and the number of weeks the payments will continue.
3. The person who receives benefits must be ready, willing, and able to work in his "usual line of work" should a suitable position be located for him.
4. Individuals may be disqualified from benefits for quitting without cause or for being fired with cause (for justified disciplinary reasons).

5. Strikers are usually disqualified from benefits entirely, although in some states unemployment benefits can be paid after a limited period on strike.

It should be noted that the constraint features of the state unemployment insurance laws, which allow a lower tax rate for those employers who minimize their layoffs and firings, are a source of some controversy. Union leaders have argued that the possibility of paying lower taxes by getting a better "rating" has encouraged employers to contest any unemployment insurance claim that might be without merit. These opponents have also objected to the "ratings" on which the individual company's tax is based on the grounds that separations are only rarely determined by a firm's policies and practices. Employment stability, they contend, is primarily a function of the general level of business, and the tightness or looseness of labor markets—factors over which the individual employer has very little control. This point of view appears to be a minority one at the present time, however; and it seems likely that the existing experience-rating procedures will be retained, with the result that the pressures on management not to separate employees will continue (5).

Although the result of governmental intervention in this area might seem to be a contribution to organizational maintenance, this need not invariably be the case. The employees retained may represent a source of considerable dissension within the firm. Also, the maintenance goal may be achieved at great cost in terms of profits, if there is not sufficient work to keep employees busy or if the retained employees are ineffective performers whose deficiencies are beyond the power of management to correct.

Constraints on Safety Policies

The fact of accidents, and their resulting costs both physical and psychological, are a source of continual concern to personnel managers. Although accurate figures are difficult to obtain, there can be no doubt that accidents at work involve very sizable monetary costs, as well as even greater costs in human suffering.

In earlier days an employer was protected from costs associated with accidents by employer liability laws stemming from three major aspects of common law:

1. The doctrine of contributory negligence: Employers were not liable if an accident resulted from an employee's negligence.

2. The doctrine of the assumption of risk: An employee who accepted a job also accepted the risks involved.
3. The doctrine of the fellow-servant rule: If an employee was injured by a fellow employee, the employer was not responsible.

This legal structure proved increasingly unsatisfactory on a number of counts. The employer was constantly harassed with suits to determine liability, and the employee was faced with a major loss of income unless he could win a legal battle that inevitably involved considerable expense. These earlier laws also proved inadequate from the point of view of society as a whole in that they forced many accident victims onto the public relief rolls.

For these reasons a somewhat different way of looking at accidents, and the manner in which their costs should be borne, began to achieve acceptance. Instead of attempting to determine causation and liability, the new idea was that accidents were a cost of production and therefore should be passed on to the consumer. The result was the development of a variety of *workmen's compensation* plans, which are essentially insurance systems with the benefits payable to those employees who are accident victims. Every state in the union, as well as the District of Columbia and Puerto Rico, now has such a plan. In addition the Federal government has a workmen's compensation arrangement for its employees and for longshore and harbor workers.

Because each state has its own plan, details vary greatly and are constantly changing. However, nearly all have as a common feature the provision of benefits as a percentage of wages up to a maximum amount and for a specified period. Allowances are usually provided for hospital expenses and for benefits to survivors in case of death. In the typical plan, also, the employee does not have to initiate a claim; this is done by a state commission at little or no cost to the injured person.

Most significant for our purposes is the fact that nearly all the laws adjust the rates to be paid by the company in terms of the firm's safety record. Thus, strong pressures are put on management to develop policies and procedures that will foster employee safety. It is in this sense that workmen's compensation legislation has served most markedly to impose constraints on personnel decisions. This adjusting of the payment rate in terms of the number and costliness of accidents tends to be the usual practice whether the system used is a state-operated insurance plan or one that utilizes a private insurer.

In addition, most states have encouraged the employment of handicapped workers by passing legislation that specifies that the employer is to have charged against him only those injuries that actually occur within his firm. The reason for this is that if an already handicapped worker were to be injured, the result might well be a total disability. Should such a situation result in a total disability accident being charged against the firm, the impact on the workmen's compensation rate might be sizable, and management would be under some pressure to avoid hiring the handicapped. The laws, as now written, however, indicate that only the specific injury is to be charged. The disabled worker is paid out of a special state fund that is not dependent on employer contributions.

It should be noted that workmen's compensation is not an all-embracing type of legislation and that there are many kinds of employers who do not operate under legal constraints in this area. These include, in the usual case, those who employ agricultural or domestic workers and those who are in charge of religious or charitable institutions (7,15).

Constraints on the Employment of Older Workers

In 1900 the percentage of the total population of the United States 65 years of age and older was 4.1. In 1930 this percentage had risen to 5.4, and in 1960 to 9.2. By 1975 a figure of 9.7 is anticipated, or, in absolute figures, 22 million people. It is unlikely, however, that personnel managers will be drawing on this potential labor pool to any very great extent, because it is the public policy of this country, as first enunciated in the Social Security Act of 1935, that individual workers should be encouraged to retire from the labor market by the age of 65 at the very latest. This statement of intent is manifested in the now-famous program known as social security, which is more correctly designated as Old Age and Survivors Insurance (OASI).

This insurance program is operated entirely at the Federal level with no state participation and is supported by a payroll tax shared equally by employer and employee. There have been numerous revisions of the plan as a result of legislation passed since 1935, but the basic pension program remains much the same. The number of occupations and employees covered has increased and so has the tax rate. In addition, there has been a change in name so that the formal designation is now Old Age, Survivors, Disability, and Health Insurance. This change reflects the fact that disability benefits were added to the plan by amendment in 1956, and health insurance, or Medicare, benefits in 1965.

Although a major factor in the passage of this act was undoubtedly its humanitarian purpose, to help citizens meet the exigencies of old age, it is also true that many people favored it during the depression years because of its anticipated impact on employment. It was hoped that the enactment of public pension legislation would induce older people to leave the labor force and thus would reduce the number of individuals seeking work. As indicated in Table 6-4, this goal, although perhaps not as appropriate to the postwar period as it was during the depression years, is being achieved (10). Whereas the number of men working or available for work decreased by something less than six percentage points from 1947 to 1966, the drop in the proportion of men 65 and over was nearly four times as great. In fact almost all the decline in the male participation rates can be attributed to the reductions in the older age group. Similarly, although female participation in the labor force has been increasing steadily since the war, the net change among women 65 and over has been minimal.

Table 6-4. Labor Force Participation Rates for Persons 16 Years and Over

Year	All males	Males 65 and over	All females	Females 65 and over
1947	86.8	47.8	31.8	8.1
1948	87.0	46.8	32.7	9.1
1949	86.9	46.9	33.2	9.6
1950	86.8	45.8	33.9	9.7
1951	87.3	44.9	34.7	8.9
1952	87.2	42.6	34.8	9.1
1953	86.9	41.6	34.5	10.0
1954	86.4	40.5	34.6	9.3
1955	86.2	39.6	35.7	10.6
1956	86.3	40.0	36.9	10.9
1957	85.5	37.5	36.9	10.5
1958	85.0	35.6	37.1	10.3
1959	84.5	34.2	37.2	10.2
1960	84.0	33.1	37.8	10.8
1961	83.6	31.7	38.1	10.7
1962	82.8	30.3	38.0	9.9
1963	82.2	28.4	38.3	9.6
1964	81.9	28.0	38.7	10.1
1965	81.5	27.9	39.3	10.0
1966	81.4	27.0	40.3	9.6

Source: *Manpower Report of the President.* Washington, D.C.: United States Government Printing Office, 1967, p. 202.

It is this impact on employment policies that represents the major constraint element of the social security legislation. An employer who wants to hire older people is finding it increasingly difficult to do so. Even more important, a company will have a very hard time retaining employees, other than the more highly paid professional and managerial groups, beyond the age of 65—perhaps even beyond age 62, in view of amendments passed in 1956, which reduce the age of eligibility, although with somewhat lower benefits.

Because the general pattern has been for Congress to increase the coverage of this program since its inception and to provide more extensive benefits, an even more pronounced reduction in the employment of older people can be anticipated. Many people will not work for an income when it is automatically available to them at a specified age under a public pension plan. Moreover, contrary to the situation that exists where private, company-operated retirement plans have been instituted, the company has nothing to say about the age at which payments in lieu of wages will begin.

Table 6-5. Federal Social Security (Old Age, Survivors, Disability, and Health Insurance) Provisions. Past and Future Financing Provisions

Period	Maximum taxable earnings, $	Combined employer-employee tax rate, %			Self-employed tax rate, %		
		OASDI	HI	Total	OASDI	HI	Total
1937–1949	3,000	2	—	2	°	—	°
1950	3,000	3	—	3	°	—	°
1951–1953	3,600	3	—	3	2.25	—	2.25
1954	3,600	4	—	4	3	—	3
1955–1956	4,200	4	—	4	3	—	3
1957–1958	4,200	4.5	—	4.5	3.375	—	3.375
1959	4,800	5	—	5	3.75	—	3.75
1960–1961	4,800	6	—	6	4.5	—	4.5
1962	4,800	6.25	—	6.25	4.7	—	4.7
1963–1965	4,800	7.25	—	7.25	5.4	—	5.4
1966	6,600	7.7	.7	8.4	5.8	.35	6.15
1967	6,600	7.8	1.0	8.8	5.9	.50	6.4
1968	7,800	7.6	1.2	8.8	5.8	.60	6.4
1969–1970	7,800	8.4	1.2	9.6	6.3	.60	6.9
1971–1972	7,800	9.2	1.2	10.4	6.9	.60	7.5
1973–1975	7,800	10.0	1.3	11.3	7.0	.65	7.65
1976–1979	7,800	10.0	1.4	11.4	7.0	.70	7.7
1980–1986	7,800	10.0	1.6	11.6	7.0	.80	7.8
1987 and after	7,800	10.0	1.8	11.8	7.0	.90	7.9

° Self-employed not covered in this period.
Source: Social Security Administration.

At the present time some of the distinguishing features of the Act that are of basic relevance for personnel management are the following:

1. The program is financed by a tax, half of which is paid by the employer *and* half by the employee. The amount of this tax has increased steadily over the years, as shown in Table 6-5. As indicated, the self-employed tax rate is three fourths of the total combined rate.

2. Almost all workers are now covered by statute, or can choose to be covered under the program of voluntary coverage developed to apply to employees of nonprofit institutions and of state and local governments.

3. Retirement benefits are paid monthly to workers who have reached the specified age and whose annual earnings are less than a given maximum ($1,680 before age 72; no maximum thereafter); the program is designed for workers who have reached the age of 65, but both they and their wives can take their benefits starting at age 62 at somewhat reduced rates.

4. Benefits may consist of *primary benefits,* consisting of payments to the beneficiary, and *supplemental pension benefits,* which are given to the spouse, if that individual has reached retirement age; *survivors benefits* are available to dependents of the beneficiary and *monthly disability benefits* are payable after age 50; the actual rates of benefit payment vary according to wages paid in, time of retirement, number of dependents, and so on. *Health insurance, or Medicare, benefits* were introduced in 1965 to provide payments for hospital and doctor bills.

5. Eligibility for the program is determined on the basis of the number of quarters worked. To be *fully insured,* one must have been in covered employment for 40 quarters, or one fourth of the quarters since the year 1950, or one fourth of the quarters since the age of 21, with a minimum of six quarters; such a fully insured worker cannot lose his eligibility. To be *currently insured,* one must have worked for six of the thirteen quarters before he either dies or turns 65. Disability benefit eligibility is established after twenty quarters.

Constraints on Research and Development Employment

A problem that has existed for many years, but which has assumed much greater significance since World War II, involves the employment of a man who is currently working for a competitor. Although difficulties may arise in this connection when the man is in one of the regular operating departments of the firm, it is unlikely that legal constraints can be invoked to keep the man from changing employers.

However, this is not necessarily the case if the man is engaged in some type of research and development activity.

It is in the research area that the new ideas and innovations that will determine the future shape of an industry are developed. Since American business is spending millions of dollars on research and development, and has at least tripled this expenditure in the past decade (14), it is easy to understand why this area has come to assume a rather unique position. In essence the employment problem as it relates to these research positions, and perhaps to some other jobs where the individual is likely to have specialized knowledge, is as follows:

Can a company prevent an employee who had had access to the working operations of a firm, to its procedures and plans, to its new product ideas, and so on, from obtaining employment with a competing firm on the grounds that *trade secrets* would be revealed if this were permitted? A trade secret is generally considered to be any formula, pattern, device, or compilation of information that is used in a business and that makes it possible to obtain an advantage over competitors who do not utilize it (2).

To the extent that the answer to this question is "No," a company might well be discouraged from investing in the research and development area, because it would be very difficult to keep new ideas and processes generated out of the research from falling into the hands of competitors. On the other hand, to the extent that the answer is "Yes," the talented researcher might find himself unable to change jobs, at least while continuing to work in the areas for which he is most qualified. He would, thus, be largely at the mercy of his present employer and could be considered to be in a condition that is very close to that of involuntary servitude.

At the present time society has not developed an adequate solution to this dilemma, despite the fact that a number of cases have reached the courts. Perhaps most famous among these is *Goodrich Company v. Wohlgemuth* (14), which involved the employment of Wohlgemuth by a competitor of the Goodrich Company. Wohlgemuth had terminated his work at the Goodrich Company and immediately entered the employ of a competitor, carrying out the same duties in a similar department. The Goodrich Company brought suit to prevent the individual involved from going to work for the competitor, the International Latex Corporation, on the grounds that Wohlgemuth had knowledge that would permit him to pass along the trade secrets of the Goodrich Company. After a bitter and extended court battle Wohlgemuth was allowed to go to work for International Latex but was prohibited from passing on any trade secrets.

Other court decisions in this area have not been as favorable to the original employer,[1] and it is now generally recognized within the legal profession that the question involved here remains largely unanswered. It appears at the present time that within one legal jurisdiction hiring from a competitor to obtain trade secrets will not be proscribed; within another jurisdiction it may well be. Presumably a consistent pattern of judicial thought will develop in years to come, but whether the consequence will be a widespread imposition of constraints on the employment of those holding trade secrets remains an open question. Nevertheless, many employers continue to obtain signed agreements from newly hired scientific personnel, stipulating that trade secrets will remain the property of the company.

References

1. *Administrative Management,* Vol. 25 (1964), 41–45.
2. American Law Institute, *Restatement of the Law of Torts.* New York: the Institute, 1939.
3. French, R. L., "The Motorola Case," *The Industrial Psychologist,* Vol. 2, No. 3 (1965), 29–50.
4. Gitlow, A. L., *Labor and Industrial Society,* rev. ed. Homewood, Ill.: Irwin, 1963.
5. Heneman, H. G., and D. Yoder, *Labor Economics,* 2nd ed. Cincinnati: South-Western Publishing, 1965.
6. Hickey, J. A., "Unemployment Insurance and Employment Security," *Monthly Labor Review,* Vol. 90, No. 12 (1967), 33–39.
7. Katz, H. A., "Workmen's Compensation in the United States," *Labor Law Journal,* Vol. 9 (1958), 866–874.
8. Kocin, S., "Basic Provisions of the 1966 FLSA Amendments," *Monthly Labor Review,* Vol. 90, No. 3 (1967), 1–4.
9. Larson, A., and M. G. Murray, "The Development of Unemployment Insurance in the United States," *Vanderbilt Law Review,* Vol. 8 (1955), 182–217.
10. *Manpower Report of the President.* Washington, D.C.: U.S. Government Printing Office, 1967.
11. Martin, E. C., "Extent of Coverage Under FLSA as Amended in 1966," *Monthly Labor Review,* Vol. 90, No. 4 (1967), 21–24.
12. Motorola, Inc., *Motorola F.E.P.C. Case.* Franklin Park, Ill.: the Company, 1964.
13. Motorola, Inc., *Motorola's Employment Test Procedure.* Franklin Park, Ill.: the Company, 1964.
14. *New Yorker,* Vol. 39, January 11 (1964), 37–64.
15. Turnbull, J., J. C. Williams, and E. F. Cheit, *Economics and Social Security,* 2nd ed. New York: Ronald Press, 1962.

---

[1] *Murray, Arthur, Dance Studios v. Witter,* 105 N.E. 2d 685.

16. United States Department of Labor, *Growth of Labor Law in the United States*. Washington, D.C.: the Department, 1962.

Questions

1. In what ways are the Fair Labor Standards Act, the Walsh-Healey Act, and the Davis-Bacon Act similar to one another? In what ways are they different?
2. Discuss the significance of the Motorola Company case in the light of the research findings mentioned in Chapter 3 dealing with age and sex differences.
3. What are the different philosophies underlying Federal working hour legislation and the same legislation on the state level? How does the age and sex of the individual enter in here?
4. What are some of the conditions under which the unemployment insurance laws serve to minimize organizational maintenance and productivity? Give examples.
5. Why was the "common law" in relation to liability for accidents unsatisfactory? In what ways are the new laws better? poorer?
6. Indicate why, with reference to our current laws, one would recommend the establishment of a research and development department in a company. Then indicate why one would not. Then state your own position and why.

III

Role Prescriptions and Role Behavior: The Evaluation of Individual Outputs

7

Organization Planning

It has become increasingly common in recent years to conceive of business organizations, and in fact all organizations, as behavioral systems, which operate in accordance with the characteristics of the input-output model (26,30). Because this conception will serve as a basis for the discussion of organization planning in this chapter and will also be utilized in a variety of other connections throughout the remainder of the book, it is important to establish a clear understanding of what is meant at the outset.

On the input side we shall be primarily concerned with people, the human resources that become available to an organization as a result of the employment process. As indicated in Chapter 3, people enter the firm with various abilities, skills, personality characteristics, and cultural values that may operate to impose constraints on personnel decisions. But these individual differences are also the raw materials with which productivity and maintenance goals must be attained. Screening and selection, as they will be discussed in Part IV, are techniques for controlling this human input so that insofar as possible the people hired will be those most likely to contribute to organization objectives.

It should be emphasized that human resources are not the only inputs that would have to be considered in a truly comprehensive analysis of organizational functioning. Financial resources, materials, facilities, and technology, among other things, are also important. Because this is a book about personnel management, rather than finance or production or real estate, the discussion here will be restricted to specifically human inputs. It is important to keep in mind that management is faced increasingly with the alternatives of having a variety of tasks performed *either* by a human being *or* by a machine. As new developments in technology and automation occur, decisions must constantly be made as to whether a specific type of work will be assigned to a man or to a machine. Decisions of this kind are strongly influenced by economic considerations: Labor costs are compared against anticipated capital expenditures (28). Thus, a personnel manager may have only a limited amount of influence on the outcome.

On the output side, in an ultimate sense, the major consideration is the degree to which the firm is able to utilize all its resources to attain the goals of organizational productivity, or profitability, and organizational maintenance. Insofar as personnel management is concerned, however, the primary consideration is the behavior of the individual as an organization member. Do the firm's employees do the things required to maximize their contribution to goal attainment?

This means that any discussion of organizational outputs from the personnel viewpoint must be concerned with three factors:

1. The things that the people who work for the company say and do.
2. The things that the people who work for the company are *expected* to say and do.
3. The relationship between these expectations and what actually occurs.

Role Prescriptions

In this chapter and the next, primary attention will be given to the matter of establishing expected patterns of behavior. These expected patterns, which are more appropriately called role prescriptions, may be developed for positions of a managerial nature, in which case we are essentially concerned with organization planning. Or they may be established for positions where actually doing the work is paramount, rather than managing or supervising it. In this case it is more common to speak of job analysis. It is true, nevertheless, that many companies do carry their job analysis procedures well up into the managerial ranks for purposes of salary administration. Thus, this distinction between organization planning and job analysis on the basis of level of position is not entirely clear-cut.

In the remaining two chapters of this section the focus will be on techniques that may be used to determine whether individuals actually do approximate the established role prescriptions for their positions. When a person acts in a way that is highly congruent with the expected pattern, he is normally defined as successful or effective. When he deviates too far from existing role prescriptions, he is likely to be considered unsuccessful or ineffective. The process of establishing role requirements and determining the degree of deviation from them in actual behavior is what is meant when we speak of *The Evaluation of Individual Outputs.*

It may seem strange that a discussion of the output side has been placed ahead of any description of input processes such as recruitment, selection, and placement. There is, in fact, some logical inconsistency in this approach. Yet to do otherwise would be even more confusing. The individuals selected for employment must be those who will most closely approximate in their work behavior the role prescriptions for the positions they will fill. Hiring should be oriented toward obtaining successful people who will contribute the most to the company's goals. But this cannot be done without a full understanding of what kinds of behavioral outputs are desired, of how success is defined in a given job and in a given company. Thus, the discussion of what we select *for* must precede any detailed treatment of *how* we select.

Organization Planning As Establishing Managerial Role Prescriptions

Psychological research provides considerable evidence that there are certain role prescriptions that operate with a rather high degree of consistency across a great variety of managerial positions in the business world (19). Because of their prevalence and their nature, these requirements are not likely to be specifically designated when organization plans are drawn up and managerial job descriptions devised. Yet when people are selected for managerial work, there is a very high probability that an individual's ability and desire to behave in accord with these prescriptions will be an important consideration, irrespective of the specific position to be filled.

The evidence indicates that managers, as managers, are expected to have a relatively favorable attitude to their superiors (those in positions of authority over them). In their relationships with other managers at comparable levels, the role prescriptions call for a generally competitive attitude and thus a desire to do better than the others. Finally, managers are expected to impose their own wishes on subordinates and to exercise power over them. It is the nature of the managerial role that incumbents are supposed to get those who work for them to do what they want.

These are general prescriptions that are very likely to appear no matter what the particular position, as long as it is essentially managerial, and that we shall return to again in connection with the discussion of management appraisal. But there are also specific role requirements that are unique to a given job or a group of jobs. They are the major concern of those involved in the process of structuring and restructuring organizations.

The Organization Planning Group

The actual work of organization planning units can vary considerably depending on the degree to which top management has relinquished its control over decisions in this area. In some instances the planning is carried out by the chief executive himself, perhaps with the help of other corporate officers or an outside consultant. Here the organization planning group, if it exists at all, prepares position guides, policy manuals, organization charts, and the like, which have as their essential purpose the implementation of decisions made at higher levels.

Other companies use their organization units more directly for the specific purpose of restructuring the company. In such cases the units have much greater authority to actually establish role prescriptions for managerial personnel and to decide who is supposed to do what.

Under the latter set of circumstances the organization planning process becomes extremely complex, if the company is large and the types of work performed are varied. There is, first, the necessity of spelling out the task or productivity objective of the company in detail—products, services, markets, and so on. Then a clear picture of existing managerial role prescriptions must be obtained and maintained. This requires extensive interviewing of managers throughout the company, often coupled with the use of written questionnaires. Special attention is given to identifying necessary functions that have not been provided for and to investigating what might be unnecessary duplication of activities. Organization and policy manuals are prepared as a result. These represent a complex amalgam of what is and what should be.

Many firms also develop an ideal plan as a goal for the future. For a variety of reasons this specific organizational structure may not be feasible at present. Yet it is considered to be the most suitable for attaining productivity objectives if organizational maintenance considerations and the limitations of currently available manpower could be ignored. Often the ideal plan includes manpower-planning data such as inventories of existing managerial talent, future skill requirements, and anticipated rates of development for current managers. (These matters will be covered in later chapters.) Phase plans are developed that spell out in detail how and when the ideal structure might be achieved. Theoretically, all that is needed is for the organization planning group to implement changes and issue new organization charts in accord with the phase plans. In actual fact, however, organizational change is a much more complex process than this, a process that is heavily invested with "the art of the possible." In many instances the ideal structure is changed long before it is attained (24).

We have already noted the close relationship between organization planning and management appraisal: The former provides the standard against which the behavioral outputs of individual managers are evaluated. As later discussions will indicate, management development as a device for closing the gap between role prescriptions and role behavior is also closely allied. There is, therefore, an increasing tendency to integrate these three personnel functions under common leadership. Certainly a close tie between organization planning and management appraisal, both of which are integral aspects of the output side of the organizational model, is highly desirable. At the same time it should be recognized that, in spite of the steady growth in the number of such units (9), many successful firms have not formed organization planning groups as yet, relying entirely on top management for this purpose. Furthermore, such groups as do exist are not always found in a personnel department (2). Yet the functions performed are clearly related to the utilization of human resources.

Considerations in Organization Planning

The primary consideration in developing a company structure is that the organization pattern selected be one that will contribute to the attainment of the firm's goals—that will facilitate coping with the uncertainties of the environment, within the restrictions imposed by existing constraints (27). Ideally, the structure in effect at any given time will be the one that can make a maximal contribution. The difficulty is that no one knows exactly what this ideal is. The great diversity of organizational patterns to be found in American industry today reflects in part the diversity of the problems faced by different companies. But even more it reflects the diversity of opinion among those responsible for organization planning. It would appear to be primarily because of these opinion differences that most large firms undergo a major reorganization at least every two years (7).

There are several considerations that can provide some guidance and thus permit an organizational design at least approximating the ideal. One of these is the role that organization structures and the resulting managerial prescriptions play in reducing conflict and thus fostering the maintenance objective. When role prescriptions are unclear and ambiguous, there will inevitably be considerable internal stress generated within an organization as managers fight to gain control over new activities and thus build their empires. This kind of conflict can be minimized if clear role prescriptions, which are accepted widely throughout the firm as being legitimate, can be established.

The important thing is to gain acceptance for areas of jurisdiction or realms of authority before a power conflict has developed and thus before intense emotions are aroused. If this is done, then certain activities will be viewed as within the legitimate domain of certain managers and controversy will be held to a minimum. The existing role prescriptions will have the support of managers throughout the company and personal power plays aimed at extending the authority of a given manager will be discouraged.

This means that an organization planning group has to give particular attention to areas of overlapping jurisdiction. Every effort should be made to have as clear a statement as possible regarding which manager has which set of responsibilities. Without this, the organizational maintenance objective will almost certainly suffer as a consequence of internal disputes. It is also important that the role prescriptions established by the organization planning group be accepted and viewed as legitimate throughout the firm. Far too many companies have moved from a centralized to a decentralized structure only to face chaos rather than increased effectiveness as a result. Old role prescriptions and patterns of authority may not be relinquished, and the new structure may not achieve widespread acceptance. Thus, those responsible for organization planning must take steps to gain support for the new designs they introduce. Some of the difficulties that may arise in doing this will be discussed toward the end of this chapter.

Another major consideration in organization planning involves the constraints imposed by individual differences. There has in the past been some tendency to conceptualize the "good" organizational structure quite apart from any thought about the people who might be available to fill the positions created. As a result the disparity between role prescription and role behavior has on occasion been rather large, and ineffective performance has been the result.

Increasingly the need to design organizational structures and establish role prescriptions that are in accord with existing abilities, skills, and personality characteristics has become apparent. For example, two vice presidents might be equally competent in most spheres, but whereas one is a very sociable individual who functions most effectively when he is surrounded by people, the other is somewhat withdrawn and is really comfortable only with a few individuals whom he has known for many years. In the former instance a relatively wide span of control with a number of people reporting directly to the vice president would seem to be appropriate. But this type of organizational structure would almost guarantee trouble for the second man. In the latter instance an additional level could be introduced so that perhaps two individuals report *directly* to the vice president; the remainder would report only through these two.

This means that organization planning must be done with considerable knowledge of the people who will be filling the various positions and with a full understanding of the various organizational arrangements that are possible. To put these two together in an effective manner requires a high level of ingenuity.

In this connection particular attention must be given to the trained combinations of knowledge that are developed by educational institutions. As the structure of knowledge becomes increasingly complex with each new scientific advance, the universities are forced more and more into making certain rather basic decisions for society. When a specific curriculum is decided upon for a given professional training program or for any other type of occupational preparation, this curriculum serves to predetermine the combinations of knowledge that a company can acquire. Certain fields of specialization will be found regularly in conjunction with one another, but other patterns are very unlikely to emerge at all. Accountants can be expected to do an effective job of determining assets and liabilities, preparing financial statements, establishing taxable income, and obtaining indexes of profitability for various types of activities, but they are rarely trained to obtain organizational measures of another kind: those related to the maintenance objective—to conduct attitude surveys and the like. This type of competence is much more likely to have been developed by an industrial psychologist, who knows very little about measuring profits in any form.

These trained combinations of knowledge, which result from curriculum planning at the university level, have major implications for organization structure. It is pointless to establish role prescriptions for a position that are at variance with the patterns of specialization the universities have created. Certain types of groupings are almost forced on companies as a result of the constraints imposed by the educational process. As a result it is common practice to have physical science research units, accounting units, legal units, and so on, in a manner that parallels the various university curriculums and to have these units headed by men who are trained specialists in these areas. To introduce role prescriptions that require combinations of knowledge that people do not possess will almost inevitably produce a less effective organization.

A final consideration in organization planning relates to the nature of the work to be done. To achieve their goals, various companies must carry out certain tasks in certain ways; the structure of external constraints and pressures is such as to almost demand particular activities and approaches. When this is the case, particular organization structures may be especially appropriate. Thus, the development of complex computers that are extremely expensive and that must be fully utilized to be economically feasible has militated in favor of considerable centralization of accounting functions.

On the other hand, extremely intense price competition at the local level can be most effectively handled through a generally decentralized marketing organization with decision making moved down to relatively low levels. When much of the work is of a project nature, a systems type of structure is particularly appropriate. The evidence available suggests that where the production process is on a single-unit basis the ideal is a rather flat organizational structure. As the technology shifts to batch production, assembly-line mass production, and finally continuous-process production of the kind utilized in much of the chemical industry, the number of hierarchic levels required tends to increase (29). Clearly, as the nature of an industry's technology changes, comparable changes in organization structure may well become necessary.

ORGANIZATION STRUCTURE AS A CONSTRAINT. Until now the discussion of organization planning has been concerned with the process of adopting a structure that, hopefully, will maximize goal attainment. But it is also apparent that company structures and the role prescriptions that are indigenous to them can operate as internal constraints on decision making, after they have been introduced and have won widespread acceptance. Thus individual differences are not the only source of restriction within the firm itself. The way in which an organization has been designed will impose certain patterns of communication and characteristically indicates which managers must be contacted to make and implement particular types of decisions. The constraints imposed by organizational structure can of course be overcome through a change in the existing pattern of managerial role prescriptions, but that takes time and may or may not be feasible.

Variables in Organization Planning

The Bases for Grouping

Characteristically, the major activities to be performed in a company, and thus the managerial role prescriptions, are grouped together on the basis of a variety of different types of similarities. Departments, divisions, sections, and groups are constructed in terms of certain common features. One basis may be used at one level and another basis at another. The diversity across companies and industries in this regard is tremendous: A basis that is superordinate and serves to designate vice-presidential roles in one firm may be used only at the very lowest levels in another.

Clearly there is very little by way of consensus in this regard. Yet it is important to be aware of the bases that are in common use (13,16). Some of the more frequent groupings are designated in Figure 7-1.

SERVICE OR PRODUCT. The prime examples here are the large divisionalized firms in manufacturing industry. Many operate their product

Figure 7-1. Examples of Various Types of Groupings (Based on Top Management Roles)

Service or Product

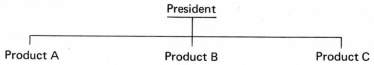

Functional Area

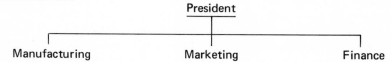

Geographical Location

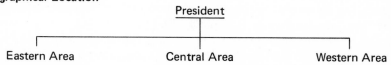

Customer Type

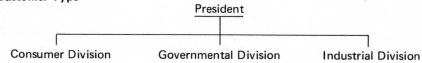

groups as separate companies or subsidiaries. In these extremely large corporations, where problems of coordination among the various activities required to produce and sell a given type of product become extremely complex, the advantages accruing from a product type of grouping at the highest levels are likely to be considerable (17). In smaller firms, where coordination may not be as difficult to attain, some other basis for superordinate grouping may well prove more appropriate. In any event managerial roles may still be specified in terms of certain product categories within such major designations as manufacturing or sales. Service groupings are particularly likely to occur within a marketing framework—licensing, product repair and maintenance, and so on.

FUNCTIONAL AREA. At the very highest levels this type of organization is most likely to appear in the refining and extractive industries and in the smaller manufacturing companies. It has the advantage that it most closely parallels the typical university curriculums, and therefore role prescriptions that are distinctly at variance with the knowledge combinations possessed by single individuals are least likely to emerge. As the physical and social sciences contribute more and more to our fund of knowledge, this consideration can be expected to become increasingly important.

Practically every firm uses some type of functional grouping at one level or another. The designations differ from industry to industry, but major functional departments may have titles such as manufacturing, marketing, finance, personnel, research and development, legal, purchasing, operations, and accounting. At lower levels the variety of managerial role prescriptions is extremely large: quality control, budgeting, warehousing, sales promotion, management development, credit, chemical research, medical, assembly, organization planning, and many others.

GEOGRAPHICAL LOCATION. Regional groupings are particularly characteristic in service-type industries and within sales organizations. With continuing advances in the case of communications, one rationale for this type of structuring is rapidly disappearing. Yet where there are unique problems that occur within a given area, it makes considerable sense to organize the work along geographical lines. It is for this reason that most companies group their foreign or overseas operations separately, often by individual country. Variations in cultural characteristics, governmental constraints, and languages make such an approach almost essential.

There are other times when a regional or geographical grouping is employed simply because some breakdown must be introduced into a very large and homogeneous component. Thus, many of the railroads split up their operations on a geographical basis. Similarly, large national marketers are often organized on a district and regional basis, although the superordinate grouping may be along product lines.

CUSTOMER TYPE. This basis for differentiation is rare at the higher levels of large manufacturing firms but may well be utilized by wholesalers or other kinds of merchandisers. In general, its use indicates a strong marketing orientation within the company. At lower levels it is a relatively common practice in all types of companies to set up separate units to deal with major customer groups. Thus, there may be such designations as industrial, Federal, and local governmental sales. Department stores characteristically have separate managers for men's and women's clothes. The primary considerations are that the customer group be at least potentially a relatively large one, that it be clearly differentiated, and that the specific type of customer require a particular kind of service.

OTHER BASES. There are a number of additional ways in which activities may be grouped, although these are normally found at levels below the vice-presidential. Perhaps most frequent is some degree of specialization by technical process or equipment, a relatively common occurrence within manufacturing departments. In a sense this is a subtype within the general concept of functional area grouping, but it is widely used to designate managerial roles at the foreman level.

Another basis is the time at which the work is performed. Different shifts usually have separate first-line supervisors and on occasion there are separate managerial hierarchies above the first level as well. The skill level of the workers may also serve to determine groupings. Within a given functional unit separate groupings may exist for unskilled laborers and the more highly skilled, or for technicians and professionals. Particular industry characteristics may introduce other requirements for managerial specialization.

Centralization and Decentralization

It is important at the outset to understand that centralization and decentralization have reference to the point or level at which decisions are to be made regarding various matters. Thus, the concern is with a set of managerial role prescriptions that bear no necessary relation to the way in which a company's activities have been grouped. It is true that decentralization of a kind has in recent years been practiced rather widely among firms that are divisionalized on a product basis. But a similar type of decentralization has also existed for years in some companies that are organized in terms of functional areas. Certainly either of these types of organization can be operated in a highly centralized manner. So, too, can companies designed on a geographical, customer, or any other basis.

A further point concerns the level to which decision making is decentralized: the depth of delegation. In many of the divisionalized firms decentralization means only that the role prescriptions of certain division managers now include decision making of a kind that was previously reserved only to the president. Below this point renewed centralization is often characteristic. This need not be the case, however. Decentralization can be carried down to much lower managers, and important decisions can be made well below the general manager or vice-presidential level. There are three major considerations involved (25).

First, decentralization of decision making must be related to the judged competence of a given individual to make effective decisions. This means that even at the division manager level there may be major differences in role prescriptions depending on the experience and ability of various men. Second, decision making requires information. If there are certain relevant types of information that are more readily available at higher levels, or if particular kinds of information cannot be made available to a given manager, then decentralization is not to be recommended. Third, an individual manager cannot be permitted to make decisions that will have considerable impact on the activities of other managers who are not subordinate to him. Put somewhat differently, decision making in a given area cannot be decentralized if to do so would mean that one manager would frequently infringe upon the role prescriptions of another. Thus, for instance, decisions that involve very sizable expenditures cannot be decentralized because the resulting depletion of the corporation's capital resources would work undue hardships on managers who would gain no benefit from the expenditures.

Inherent in the idea of decentralization is the view that any consistent and major differences between expected behavior and actual behavior should result in removal. A manager is supposed to be given the means to make effective decisions and to implement them. If after this he fails to meet the role prescriptions, then some other manager, who will, should replace him. Such a philosophy is much less likely to apply in centralized organizations where individual accountability is much harder to establish, at least below the presidential level.

Among companies that are decentralized and divisionalized along product lines, it is typical to establish profit centers at the division level. Thus, the role prescriptions can be stated directly in profit terms. The manager in charge is expected to behave in ways that will yield a given level of profit for his division. When functional divisions are used, this type of direct evaluation in monetary terms becomes much more difficult. Here the profit on a given product is a consequence of the way in which the contributions of the various functional units are integrated, as well as of performance within the specific divisions. This integration occurs at the very highest level, and it is therefore difficult to expect lower managers to meet role requirements stated *directly* in terms of profitability.

TOP MANAGEMENT UNDER DECENTRALIZATION. Under a decentralized type of organization it is characteristic that a rather sizable top management or corporate superstructure is superimposed above the various operating divisions. This group carries out activities that have remained centralized. It contains managers whose role prescriptions require them to determine specific corporate objectives in terms of products and markets, to create the ethical and value climate of the company, to establish organizational structures and select managers for positions at the higher levels, to evaluate individual managers in terms of their success in fulfilling role prescriptions, and to allocate funds as appropriate to stockholders, employees, governments, and units within the company itself (25).

This corporate component includes the chairman of the board, the president, and one or more group executives. These group executives are placed over two or more operating or staff divisions and are often given the title of executive vice president or senior vice president. The units that are grouped together in this manner vary tremendously from company to company, depending in part on the specific needs for coordination and in part on the areas of knowledge and competencies of the particular group executive. Finally, there are a rather large number of staff executives who contribute to corporate planning in their various areas of specialization, who develop and operate various evaluation and control procedures as they apply to the decentralized division, and who may on occasion provide technical services and advice to the divisions.

The functions represented in these staff units at this corporate level are by no means standardized. Among those found rather frequently are the controller, systems planning, finance, auditing, legal, marketing research, engineering, advanced projects research, public relations, purchasing, and traffic. Within the personnel area organization planning, management development, manpower planning, management appraisal, and industrial relations are particularly likely to be carried out at the corporate level. It should be emphasized, however, that any of these staff designations may also appear within the various operating divisions. These lower-level groups provide services to the specific division only. The fact that a corporate unit exists to assist in planning and control for the company as a whole does not mean that similar units cannot contribute in the same functional areas within the divisions.

AN EXAMPLE OF DECENTRALIZATION—GENESCO (10). This corporation has a large number of plants and retail outlets manufacturing and selling footwear, clothing, and jewelry throughout the United States. In 1963, when the organization structure to be described was in effect, there were 33,000 employees and the sales volume was over $400 million. Headquarters are in Nashville, Tennessee, and the profit margin on sales runs at about 2 per cent, which was slightly below the industry median in 1963.

The organization structure consists of over sixty operating companies that have been grouped together into a number of operating units containing from three to six companies. Sometimes the companies have been formed on a product basis, sometimes on a geographical basis, sometimes on a customer-type basis, and sometimes on a functional basis (manufacturing or sales). This is not surprising in view of the fact that the corporation has been put together largely through acquisition.

The operating companies make their own decisions on many matters, including new store locations. There are also a variety of decision-making committees in which operating company executives participate. Decisions regarding the marketing scope of the individual companies, finance, legal matters, insurance, taxes, accounting policies, top management selection, and compensation are centralized in a nine-man corporate executive committee. The corporate staff is broken down as follows:

Control responsibility	*Advisory*
Finance	Industrial Relations
Accounting	Marketing
Legal	Administrative Services
Insurance	Public Relations
Taxes	Research
Top Management Selection	Real Estate
Compensation	Product Development
Retirement Fund Investment	Systems and Procedures
Central Purchasing	
Organization Planning	

AN EXAMPLE OF CENTRALIZATION—MAYTAG (23). The Maytag Company has its headquarters in Newton, Iowa, and in 1963 employed approximately 3,500 people. At that time it had an 11.9 per cent profit on sales of just over $117 million. This puts it well above the industry average. There are three appliance manufacturing plants located in Iowa, ten sales branches spread throughout the United States, and six wholly owned distributing companies.

The firm has no major committees, nor does it invest in management development. Functional area organization is employed under six categories: manufacturing, marketing, research and development, finance, personnel, and legal. Within manufacturing and marketing there are plant and geographical differentiations, respectively. These two departments constitute the major line units of the company, all others being staff and advisory to them. Industrial engineering, production engineering, and inspection are advisory within manufacturing, and market research, advertising, field education, and market planning are advisory within marketing. The number of managerial levels is kept to a minimum and decision making is on an individual basis rather than participative. The primary source of decisions is the president, who delegates only to the vice presidents in charge of manufacturing and marketing.

Line-Staff and the Allocation of Decision Making

Although the line-staff concept has become rather confused over the years, it is probably most appropriate to think of it in terms of horizontal differences in the allocation of decision-making authority. Staff managers have role prescriptions that tend to severely limit the types of decisions they can make; line managers do not.

There has been a concentration of decision making in the hands of line managers in much the same way that authority is concentrated at the top under centralization. Thus, in moving from the previous section to this one, we move from an analysis of vertical differentials within organizations to an analysis of horizontal differentials. Line managers are in the direct chain of command and have role prescriptions that call for decisions concerning the main operations of the firm. Staff managers, although they may be expected to make decisions regarding those subordinate to them in the staff unit, are primarily concerned with providing advice and assistance to the line. They function outside the direct chain of command. This definition of the staff role will require some modification later to embrace the control concept, but in essence it is correct.

THE UNIVERSITY OF CALIFORNIA STUDIES. Support for this view, that staff managers experience a deficiency in decision making, relative to line managers, which is in many ways comparable to the differential between the lower and top organizational levels, comes from research conducted at the University of California (20). Almost two thousand managers from firms throughout the country completed a questionnaire that yields an index of the extent to which various needs or motives are felt to be satisfied on the job. The results presented in Figure 7-2 are broken down by position level within management and line or staff designation.

It is apparent that irrespective of the need area there is a rather marked tendency for dissatisfaction to be more pronounced in the lower-level positions. This is true of both line and staff. If we add the 114 presidents and board chairmen to the table, this conclusion gains even more support. At this very top level there is considerably more satisfaction in all areas than in any other group, with one exception. On social needs the top executives have an average score of .34 (21). Apparently men in these positions experience some relative deprivation insofar as opportunities for social interaction are concerned.

With the exception of the social area, a tendency similar to that associated with hierarchic position is in evidence when line and staff are compared, although in the case of the desire for security only the lower

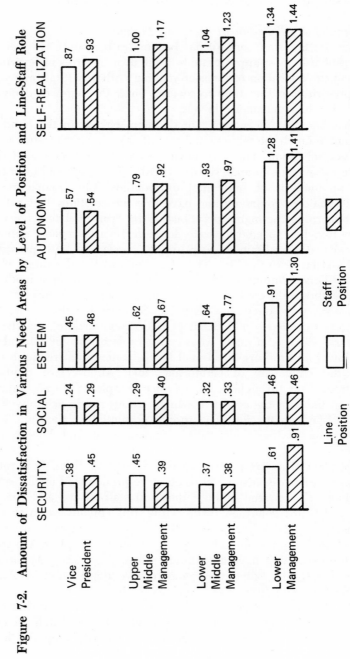

Figure 7-2. Amount of Dissatisfaction in Various Need Areas by Level of Position and Line-Staff Role

Source: Adapted from L. W. Porter, "Job Attitudes in Management: III. Perceived Deficiencies in Need Fulfillment as a Function of Line Versus Staff Type of Job," *Journal of Applied Psychology, Vol. 47* (1963), p. 270.

management staff positions produce a real difference in the sense of deprivation. Apparently satisfaction with the opportunities for social interaction is essentially comparable in staff and line and so is the feeling of security, except at the very lowest managerial levels. When we move to autonomy and self-realization, both of which are clearly related to decision making, however, there is no question but that the staff role yields a greater sense of deficiency, unless one holds a position as vice president.

The evidence is clear in indicating that the staff-line differential is a real and meaningful aspect of most industrial organizations, although it may become blurred in certain research-based firms such as those in the electronics industry (6). Role prescriptions for staff positions characteristically produce a sense of lack or deficiency, insofar as freedom to make decisions relative to the job is concerned, that is much more pronounced than in line work. Yet this line-staff differential is not as pronounced as that between upper and lower management. The vertical disparity in role prescriptions seems to be greater than the horizontal.

ASPECTS OF THE STAFF ROLE. As noted previously, the staff role is not really homogeneous in terms of expected behavior. There appear to be at least three major components, all of which can be present in a single role prescription. First, a staff member is often expected to deal with the line organization in an advisory manner. This was the characteristic pattern at Maytag. Information is collected and interpreted to line managers; conclusions may be drawn and preferred patterns of action recommended, but the final decision is not made within the staff unit.

Second, staff groups may assume a service role in their relationships with the line. A personnel manager may take on the task of recruiting and screening job applicants for manufacturing or marketing; a member of the company's legal staff may develop a contract to cover a particular purchase being made by a line unit. These services may be merely a matter of handling routine chores on a more centralized and thus more economical basis, or they may be of a highly skilled, professional nature requiring knowledge that is not available elsewhere in the company. Here the degree to which the staff unit is actually expected to make decisions for the line varies considerably. In most instances final authority is *said* to reside with the line manager, but this may be more of a myth than an actuality. Probably, more frequently than not, however, the staff member does find that some degree of control is exercised over him in the performance of his service function.

Finally, certain staff units impose their control on other segments of the company, be they line or staff. Thus, personnel policies, budgets, standard procedures, and so on, are characteristically enforced by staff units. In connection with these activities staff managers are expected to carry out continuing measurements on other components of the firm, to evaluate performance against standards, and to correct deviations. In Genesco a number of corporate staff units are designated as having this role. Here the staff actually makes decisions vis à vis the line.

It should be apparent that when this third control role is combined with the advisory in a single position, the latter may suffer. Inevitably managers will be somewhat defensive toward another manager who is evaluating them, whether he is a superior or a staff specialist. When the same man returns with his "advising hat," he is likely to be suspect. Managers may feel that he is not really interested in helping them, but only in "snooping around" and getting more information on the performance of their units. Certainly any weaknesses will not be revealed if at all possible and such advice as is offered may well be rejected.

One solution to this problem is to allocate the control and advisory roles to two distinctly separate staff managers. This may mean in some instances that there will be two units in the same specialized functional area, although the total number of specialists employed by the company need not be increased. Thus, a number of companies have organized what amount to internal consulting services (12). In such instances the title Consultant is frequently used, and the staff man, who is usually assigned for administrative purposes at the headquarters or corporate level, does nothing but advise and counsel.

THE UTILIZATION OF PROFESSIONALS. In administrative organizations of the kind that are characteristic in the business world, the problem of absorbing professionals has created some difficulties. And yet the knowledge of people such as lawyers, physicians, research chemists and physicists, economists, and industrial psychologists is so desperately needed that a solution must be found.

One problem is that many professionals have a strong commitment to the profession itself and may look to this group rather than to their company for rewards. Thus, there may be questions regarding the loyalty of these people and their devotion to company goals. Because of this, professionals are normally placed in staff positions, at least initially, where they cannot exercise too much influence (8). This does not mean that professionals cannot eventually move into line management positions as they demonstrate a sense of commitment to the firm. Many become very effective, sometimes as chief executives. But there is a strong tendency to utilize professionals in a staff capacity initially, so that their decisions and recommendations can be reviewed for relevance to the company's objectives.

The major exception to this policy within the business world is the professional organization itself—the law firm, the research organization, psychological and management consulting groups, accounting firms, some construction corporations, brokerage companies, and so on. There are an increasing number of these organizations that are dominated by professionals, while offering their services almost entirely to business. In these instances the professionals themselves assume a central decision-making role and the administrative units are allocated considerably less control.

One of the major problems in organization planning for professional groups arises because, outside of the specifically professional firms, there is very little opportunity for such people to move upward without assuming a primarily administrative role. To circumvent this, a number of research and development groups have resorted to a dual system of promotion. There is the normal managerial hierarchy and in addition a second hierarchy in which promotion is based entirely on professional or research competence. The pattern is very similar to that employed in the universities, where a man can move from assistant professor to associate professor to professor with practically no change in duties and no increase in managerial responsibilities.

This technique permits the company to provide an outstanding researcher with increased salary and status while still retaining him in the type of work in which he can contribute the most. In all likelihood this dual basis for organization will emerge in other specialized units and departments as time goes on. Marketing is one area where it would appear to have particular appeal. Many companies find themselves losing their best salesmen year after year because the only promotional route available is essentially managerial in nature. A dual type of organization could contribute much to the solution of this problem. Increases in salary and status could be provided without a move from selling into administrative channels.

Span of Control and Group Size

The evidence from a rather sizable body of research indicates that all other things being equal there are distinct advantages associated with the relatively small work group (3). Thus, as we move up through the organization, a structure that makes it possible to minimize the number of managers reporting to a single individual at the next higher level would seem highly desirable. Small group size seems to produce somewhat greater output as well as better morale.

Probably the ideal would be to keep this span of control rather consistently in the range 5 through 10 throughout the organization. The specific number of people reporting to a given manager must take into account the inherent nature of the work itself, the personality of the superior as it relates to the desire for social interaction, and the level of effectiveness of the subordinates. The importance of keeping the group small increases when the men are inexperienced, when turnover is high, and when conditions are such that a high incidence of performance failure that will require supervisory attention is likely to be present (18). This would suggest that in the upper echelons of management, where highly selected and experienced men are characteristically found, somewhat larger spans of control can be employed without negative effects.

It is apparent that keeping the size of groups small all the way up through the hierarchy can produce a very tall organization with a large number of managerial levels. This has generally been assumed to be an undesirable state of affairs, partly because communication will inevitably be more difficult and partly because the impersonality associated with such a structure might produce low morale and dissatisfaction.

At least on the latter count it now seems clear that the negative consequences of the tall organizational form are not as pronounced as often feared. In connection with the University of California studies, information was obtained on the number of managerial levels and company size for each firm, as well as on line-staff status. Overall, there was no evidence of any greater amount of dissatisfaction in the tall as opposed to the flat organizations (22). However, this statement needs some qualification. In companies with less than 5,000 employees there was a tendency for managers to be somewhat less satisfied in the tall structure; in particular they experienced some deprivation in self-realization. Over 5,000 employees, just the reverse was true, the tall structure producing somewhat greater satisfaction. In these larger companies the tall organization form seemed to be particularly advantageous in yielding satisfaction with the degree of security a manager experienced.

It seems that in the larger companies a tall structure with relatively small groups is desirable, at least insofar as achieving organizational maintenance goals is concerned. In smaller firms it would seem wise to keep the number of managerial levels to a minimum, if at all possible.

The Systems Design

The newest major development in organization planning involves the systems concept, which was noted briefly in Chapter 1. An example of a company organized along these lines is presented in Figure 7-3.

When a firm utilizes the systems approach, the allocation of role prescriptions differs considerably from what would be the case under more conventional procedures (11). The master planning council serves primarily to formulate policy with regard to products and services. These policy decisions are made in the light of recommendations from the top-level financial, research and development, and market research managers. Once a new product has been decided upon, responsibility moves to the resource allocation committee, which puts together the technology and the human resources needed to operate the system. Finally, the new system having been designed, authority shifts to the operations committee.

Facilitating systems are constructed to provide a special service, or

Figure 7-3. The Systems Model: Top Management

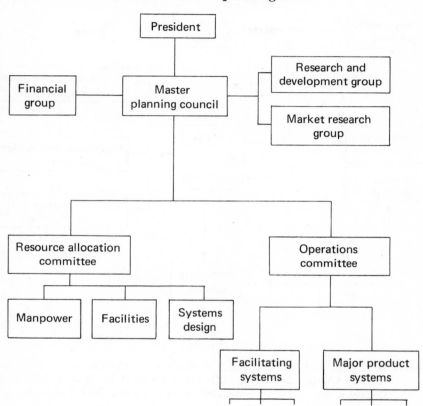

Source: R. A. Johnson, F. E. Kast, and J. E. Rosenzweig, *The Theory and Management of Systems*. 2nd ed., p. 119. Copyright 1967 by McGraw-Hill Book Company, Inc. Used by permission of McGraw-Hill Book Company.

perhaps a major component, for the project systems, although every effort is characteristically made to have each system as self-sufficient as possible. Typically the individual systems are highly automated and make use of a variety of different and rather specialized personnel components. Very precise planning is an essential requirement.

A specific system design is detailed in Figure 7-4. Inputs are of three major kinds. First, there is technical information that serves to determine the nature of the system and its capacities. Then, there is processing information that specifies more precisely how the system will operate. Finally, there is the material that is to be processed. Process control

Figure 7-4. An Operating-system Model

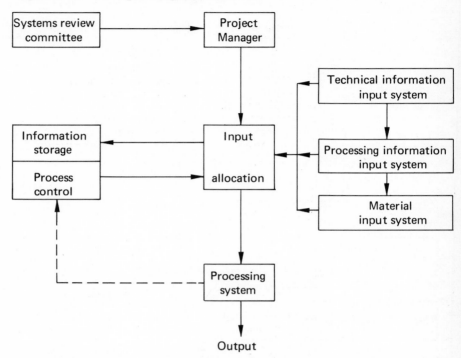

Output

Source: R. A. Johnson, F. E. Kast, and J. E. Rosenzweig, *The Theory and Management of Systems.* 2nd ed., p. 121. Copyright 1967 by McGraw-Hill Book Company, Inc. Used by permission of McGraw-Hill Book Company.

serves to measure these inputs and the product or service outputs. When corrections must be made in either, this is accomplished by the input allocation component.

It should be apparent that this type of organization is particularly suited to the demands of companies with heavy commitments to research and development and to the introduction of new products. Its value is in the flexibility that it permits. Companies organized on a system basis can move rapidly from the idea stage to full-scale production on a number of products at once by rotating men and, on occasion, equipment from one project to another.

The systems concept has been utilized most effectively within the space, defense, and electronics industries where rapid product change is characteristic, but even there it is rare to find an entire firm constituted on this basis. The concept requires a specific goal toward which planning is directed, plus a tremendous amount of engineering precision in the design. For these reasons, as well as the financial resources required, it is very doubtful that it can be utilized on a large scale in industries such as steel or automobiles (4).

The Size of Middle Management

With the advent of high-speed computers, operations research, and simulation techniques there has been much speculation regarding the future organization of managerial roles. Some writers have contended that much of the decision making currently done at the middle management level will be taken over by the new technology (15). As a result they anticipate that the organization of the future will be highly centralized with a clear-cut break between top management, where the really creative, innovative planning will be done, and lower management, which will carry out relatively routine functions. Middle management as such will largely disappear. Its decision-making roles will be taken over by the new computer techniques and top management. Its decision-implementation roles will be taken over by lower management.

This conception attributes capabilities to the computers of the future and to operations research techniques that are well beyond what is currently possible. Thus, there is some reason to believe that the new technology cannot, or will not, be used in the manner described, and that consequently the organization of middle management roles will not change drastically. According to this latter view, the decision-making structure will remain much the same, although many routine decisions will be handled increasingly by computers, and some degree of recentralization can be anticipated (1). Few managers will be displaced, although some change in role prescriptions can be anticipated.

The argument in support of minimal change runs as follows. Decisions are basically of two types: programmed and nonprogrammed. The former are routine in nature and occur frequently in essentially the same form. They can be made in terms of tested rules. Nonprogrammed decisions, on the other hand, are complex and occur only rarely. There is no history of essentially comparable situations to rely on and thus rules are difficult to formulate. Decisions of the first type will probably move increasingly into the realm of the new technology, but there is little reason at present to believe that computers will be able to handle the more unique decisions in the second category.

To this argument is added another of an economic nature. Not only will nonprogrammed decisions remain the responsibility of middle and top management, but the utilization of computers in areas where they can contribute will be limited by the costs involved. In many instances, especially in smaller firms, it will prove considerably less expensive to utilize humans for decision-making purposes than the complex computers that might substitute for them.

Clearly the future role of the middle management structure is a debatable question at the present time. As of now no clear trend toward diminution in size is in evidence.

Organizational Change

As noted previously, changing organizational role prescriptions is not likely to be accomplished easily. Especially where the change is of a rather drastic nature, as when there is a shift from a highly centralized functional area structure to a decentralized product grouping, a considerable amount of resistance can be anticipated. Conflict may become rampant, and dissatisfaction can rise to high levels, resulting in considerable turnover among key people. What was intended as a move toward greater effectiveness in achieving the productivity goal, and thus increased profits, may well accomplish as a final result only a sizable loss in the organizational maintenance area. In view of this fact it is important for a personnel manager to be thoroughly conversant with the phenomenon known as *resistance to change* and with the factors that may have an influence on it (5,31).

For one thing, resistance is almost inevitable if those who will be affected are not given a clear indication of the exact nature of the anticipated shifts and the reasons behind them. Incomplete and ambiguous information is likely to be reinterpreted as a threat by nearly everyone involved. As a consequence, people who might be affected can be expected to band together in a close-knit unit to fight the change in any way they can. It is particularly undesirable to permit word to get around long before the change occurs that some type of major reorganization is in the offing. Such rumors, even though true, are very likely to be viewed with alarm when the exact impact on each individual has not been spelled out.

Second, people will interpret an organizational change in different ways depending on their particular motives and other personality characteristics. Thus, resistance may derive from a variety of causes. Yet in the ranks of management, especially at the highest levels, power considerations are very likely to be primary (19), and accordingly any resistance may well stem from a perceived threat to a manager's power position. One can assume that those who do not have power will favor change, largely because they can only gain—they have nothing to lose. Similarly, those who have every reason to anticipate increased decision making and thus greater power as a consequence of the organizational shift will also offer their support. Resistance will predominate among those who have some basis for believing their power within the company will be diminished, either through demotion or movement to a staff role or in some other manner. Reorganization almost always involves some alteration in the power balance.

Third, resistance is a common consequence when strong pressure for change, e.g., from the organization planning group and perhaps higher management, is coupled with strong pressure against it, e.g., from the group of managers at the same level. At such times a manager may exert considerable effort to maintain the status quo, even after a new set of role prescriptions have been allocated. There may as a result be no real change in role *behavior*.

Fourth, to the extent a manager can participate in the decision to make a change and exert some influence in determining what the new allocation of role prescriptions will be, to that extent he is likely to support the change and any potential resistance will in all probability be dissipated. When he has been given a chance to participate, a person will normally feel that he has had an opportunity to protect his power position and that any loss in this regard has occurred voluntarily. Under pressure he can only assume, even if his decision-making authority is extended by the reorganization, that he is not in fact a very important person in the firm, because he was not consulted on an action of direct significance to him.

Fifth, if an organizational change is promulgated as the personal action of some one individual or as an attempt to achieve the ends desired by a single manager, it is particularly likely to arouse resistance. If, on the other hand, the change is closely and logically tied to organizational goals, so that it can be viewed by many as a sensible means to achieve productivity and/or maintenance objectives, then support can be expected to be at a maximum.

Sixth, resistance will be at a high level when the change is carried out in a way that ignores the established customs, values, and institutions. A shift in role prescriptions is ideally achieved by paying strict attention to other role prescriptions—by consulting those who can expect to be consulted, by having the change announced by the man who should announce it, by taking action at the time when such actions are supposed to be taken, and by relating the change to existing organizational values. Thus, the change must be viewed as legitimate.

Finally, organizational change will be easier where there is a readiness for change—where people are set for this type of thing and accept it as a fact of life. This is one of the advantages of the systems design. The whole structure is established to phase out one system and establish another as appropriate. Under these circumstances resistance is difficult to justify on any rational grounds and even a person who wants desperately to fight a change may not do so largely because he knows others will not go along with him. Here, organizational restructuring is viewed as inevitable and entirely legitimate. Managerial role prescriptions are in fact constructed to include a proviso that all managers must expect major alterations in their roles at uncertain intervals. If this is a part of the pattern of expectations, it is difficult for a particular manager to obtain much group support for any resistance when his role does change. Thus, any opposition to reorganization will probably be short-lived.

In view of these considerations it should be apparent that carrying out a successful reorganization, even on a small scale, is no easy task. The matter of gaining acceptance for the new structure and keeping repercussions in the organizational maintenance area to a minimum can be just as difficult and time-consuming a task as settling upon the exact design that is to be instituted. Yet studies indicate that very sizable improvements in productivity and profits can be achieved without any major long-term loss insofar as other company goals are concerned (14). It is clear that a change in managerial role prescriptions need not create a greater disparity between expected and actual behavior and thus less effective managers. An adequately planned and implemented reorganization will produce major shifts in *behavior*, in the direction of the new role requirements.

References

1. Anshen, M., "Managerial Decisions," in J. T. Dunlop (ed.), *Automation and Technological Change*. Englewood Cliffs, N.J.: Prentice-Hall, 1962, pp. 66–83.
2. Bailey, J. K., "Organization Planning: Whose Responsibility?," *Academy of Management Journal*, Vol. 7 (1964), 95–108.
3. Bass, B. M., *Organizational Psychology*. Boston: Allyn and Bacon, 1965.
4. Bello, F., "The Technology Behind Productivity," in J. T. Dunlop (ed.), *Automation and Technological Change*. Englewood Cliffs, N.J.: Prentice-Hall, 1962, pp. 153–168.
5. Coch, L., and J. R. P. French, "Overcoming Resistance to Change," *Human Relations*, Vol. 1 (1948), 512–532.
6. Dalton, M., "Changing Staff-Line Relationships," *Personnel Administration*, Vol. 29, No. 2 (1966), 3–5, 40–48.
7. Daniel, D. R., "Reorganizing for Results," *Harvard Business Review*, Vol. 44, No. 6 (1966), 96–104.
8. Etzioni, A., *Modern Organizations*. Englewood Cliffs, N.J.: Prentice-Hall, 1964.
9. Glueck, W. F., "Applied Organization Analysis," *Academy of Management Journal*, Vol. 10 (1967), 223–234.
10. Jarman, W. M., and B. H. Willingham, "The Decentralized Organization of a Diversified Manufacturer and Retailer—Genesco," in M. Haire (ed.), *Organization Theory in Industrial Practice*. New York: Wiley, 1962, pp. 56–67.

11. Johnson, R. A., F. E. Kast, and J. E. Rosenzweig, *The Theory and Management of Systems*, 2nd ed. New York: McGraw-Hill, 1967.

12. Kolb, H. D., "The Headquarters Staff Man in the Role of a Consultant," in M. Haire (ed.), *Organization Theory in Industrial Practice*. New York: Wiley, 1962, pp. 143–152.

13. Koontz, H., and C. O'Donnell, *Principles of Management*, 3rd ed. New York: McGraw-Hill, 1964.

14. Lawrence, P. R., *The Changing of Organizational Behavior Patterns*. Boston: Graduate School of Business Administration, Harvard Univ., 1958.

15. Leavitt, H. J., and T. L. Whisler, "Management in the 1980's," *Harvard Business Review*, Vol. 36, No. 6 (1958), 41–48.

16. Litterer, J. A., *The Analysis of Organizations*. New York: Wiley, 1965.

17. March, J. G., and H. A. Simon, *Organizations*. New York: Wiley, 1958.

18. Miner, J. B., *The Management of Ineffective Performance*. New York: McGraw-Hill, 1963.

19. Miner, J. B., *Studies in Management Education*. New York: Springer, 1965.

20. Porter, L. W., "Job Attitudes in Management: III. Perceived Deficiencies in Need Fulfillment as a Function of Line versus Staff Types of Job," *Journal of Applied Psychology*, Vol. 47 (1963), 267–275.

21. Porter, L. W., *Organizational Patterns of Managerial Job Attitudes*. New York: American Foundation for Management Research, 1964.

22. Porter, L. W., and E. E. Lawler, "The Effects of Tall Versus Flat Organization Structures on Managerial Job Satisfaction," *Personnel Psychology*, Vol. 17 (1964), 135–148.

23. Scoutten, E. F., "Application at the Maytag Company," in M. Haire (ed.), *Organization Theory in Industrial Practice*. New York: Wiley, 1962, pp. 76–87.

24. Stieglitz, H., *Corporate Organization Structures*, Studies in Personnel Policy, No. 183. New York: National Industrial Conference Board, 1961.

25. Stieglitz, H., and A. R. Janger, *Top Management Organization in Divisionalized Companies*, Personnel Policy Study No. 195. New York: National Industrial Conference Board, 1965.

26. Stogdill, R., *Individual Behavior and Group Achievement*. New York: Oxford, 1959.

27. Thompson, J. D., *Organizations in Action*. New York: McGraw-Hill, 1967.

28. Wallis, W. A., "Some Economic Considerations," in J. T. Dunlop (ed.), *Automation and Technological Change*. Englewood Cliffs, N.J.: Prentice-Hall, 1962, pp. 103–13.

29. Woodward, J., *Management and Technology*, Problems of Progress in Industry, No. 3. London: Department of Scientific and Industrial Research, Charles House, 1958.

30. Young, S., "Designing a Behavioral System," in P. J. Gordon (ed.), *Proceedings of the Annual Meeting, 1963*. Boston: Academy of Management, 1964, pp. 76–83.

31. Zander, A., "Resistance to Change: Its Analysis and Prevention," *Advanced Management*, Vol. 15, No. 1 (1950), 9–11.

Questions

1. What are the different ways in which the organization planning function may be carried out in a company? What are the things that organization planning groups do?
2. There are those who believe that the best possible organization structure should be established and then the people selected who will fill these positions. Others contend that the organization should be designed to fit the capabilities of available personnel. What are the arguments on either side?
3. What are the major considerations that would argue for and against decentralization? Would it be easier to move from a centralized to a decentralized form than to recentralize? Why?
4. What possible applications of the dual line of promotion procedure can you imagine? Are there any particular difficulties associated with this technique that occur to you?
5. What are the implications of the systems concept for organization planning? What are the advantages of this approach?

8

Job Analysis

A personnel manager must rely heavily on a knowledge of the existing job structure in developing and administering programs designed to provide effective utilization of human resources within a company. In part, as indicated in the preceding chapter, this knowledge is developed through the process of organization planning; in part it is a product of job analysis.

Organization planning is concerned basically with role prescriptions at the upper levels and with defining expected behavior within the managerial hierarchy. Job analysis carries this process down through the rest of the organization, usually with a much greater degree of specificity and detail than is provided by organization planning. Because this type of detail is often helpful in the case of managerial jobs as well, a number of companies utilize job analysis techniques to establish role prescriptions for many positions at the managerial level also. Thus, some degree of overlap between the two techniques can develop. When this happens, it is important that the managerial role prescriptions derived from the two sources be closely coordinated, so that disparities do not emerge.

In any event job analysis, like organization planning, is a method of establishing a base against which the actual behavior of a firm's employees may be evaluated. It helps to provide a picture of each job and of the interrelationships between jobs. The results of organization planning and job analysis taken together yield a comprehensive and detailed view of how a company has structured itself to achieve its objectives.

The Terminology of Occupational Study

Before turning to a discussion of the methods and procedures employed in performing a job analysis, it is essential that we establish an understanding of some of the terms that will be used. This will help to prevent considerable confusion later on. The definitions that follow constitute what has come to be the generally accepted terminology among personnel managers. They are in line with the terminology used by the Occupational Research Program of the U.S. Employment Service (11).

A *task* is a distinct work activity carried out for a distinct purpose. An example would be a retail clerk in a department store dusting merchandise. Another example would be the same clerk setting up the same merchandise in an attractive display. When there are enough such related activities, a position is created.

A *position* is a specific set of tasks and duties performed by a given individual in a given firm at a given time. The number of positions in a company at one time is equal to the number of employees at the same time.

A *job* is normally made up of a number of similar positions in a given company. However, a job may involve only one such position at a given time. For example, a store may have one retail hardware clerk or many, depending on the size of the store and the scope of its business.

An *occupation* is a number of similar jobs existing in different companies and at different times. Examples of occupations are carpenters, civil engineers, and so on.

A *job description* is a written statement of the tasks, duties, and behaviors required in a given job, plus the personal qualifications that all candidates for the job must of necessity possess. (The latter aspect is often referred to separately as the *job specification*.)

A *job family* is a collection of two or more jobs that either require similar worker characteristics or contain parallel tasks, as determined by the job analysis.

When a study is made of the tasks performed by a single person, the term *position analysis* is usually employed. When the scope is broadened to include two or more positions that are similar enough to be considered one job, it is more characteristic to speak of *job analysis*. Because in the business world, at least at lower levels, there are usually two or more similar positions within a firm, the designation job analysis is typically used (12). This analysis provides information about the job, the necessary activities and personal requirements involved, and its relationship to other jobs.

It is important to understand that although the job analysis frequently *utilizes* the actual behavior of incumbents, the job description, nevertheless provides a statement of what *should* be; it is a set of role prescriptions or requirements. Job analysts develop their descriptions based on information that is usually derived from people actually doing the work, just as organization analysts do, but this does not mean that the final result is necessarily a specific statement of what any individual is actually doing. It is instead an idealized statement of what he and others holding the position are expected to do.

It is also true that on occasion job descriptions are written well before the company has actually employed anyone in positions of a particular type. In such instances the role prescriptions cannot be based in any way on the actual behavior of incumbents. Perhaps the most striking example of this derives from the field of space travel. Before each astronaut starts out on his flight, a detailed job description is developed specifying exactly what he is expected to do and when. Because of the physical and psychological stresses involved, a great variety of factors must be considered in constructing these role prescriptions. In many instances simulated conditions are devised to determine which behaviors will contribute most effectively to goal attainment (5). Here, there can be no question but that an *ideal* behavior pattern is being developed.

The Uses of Job Analysis

As noted previously, the data derived from job analyses are of considerable value in evaluating the behavior of individual organization members as this behavior contributes to the attainment of company goals. Jobs are structured in a way that is intended to contribute maximally to productivity and maintenance goals; then individual behaviors are compared against these expected patterns. In this way an evaluation of the individual outputs of the organization is obtained.

This contribution to the appraisal and evaluation process is an important function of job analysis, but it is by no means the only use to which this information may be put. There are, in fact, many ways in which job descriptions may be utilized by a company (10). Some of these are noted below:

JOB EVALUATION. Job evaluation is perhaps the most widespread application to which the data of job analysis are put. Job descriptions are used to evaluate jobs in terms of their worth to the company. Wage and salary differentials are then established to reflect the existing differences in job requirements. In this connection it is important to make a clear distinction between job analysis, job evaluation, and individual evaluation. The first refers to the establishment of role prescriptions, the second to the rating of *jobs* for payment purposes, and the third to the rating of *people* in relation to role prescriptions.

SELECTION AND PLACEMENT. Job descriptions are of considerable value as guides to hiring and placement practices. People who will be most successful, who will most closely approximate role requirements, should be selected for employment and assigned to appropriate kinds of work. Therefore, selection procedures must be developed based on a detailed knowledge of position requirements. This is the consideration that led us to take up the evaluation of individual outputs prior to discussing the evaluation of inputs into the organization.

TRAINING AND DEVELOPMENT. Job analysis provides an indication of the needs that training and management development must fulfill. Training programs should be devised to provide skills, knowledge, and motives that are lacking but that are required for effective or outstanding performance and adequate morale. Training should be along the lines required to generate a closer match between actual and expected behavior.

SAFETY. The safety director can utilize the data of job analysis to identify job hazards and dangerous working conditions. In fact many job descriptions include this information as an integral aspect. With this information steps can be taken to minimize the possibility that an accident will actually occur.

LABOR RELATIONS. By providing a means to common understanding between management and the labor unions with regard to the duties of each position, job analysis eliminates, or at least reduces, one type of employee grievance. Suspicion of favoritism is considerably reduced to the extent pay differentials are based on clear differences in job duties. Thus, job analysis contributes to reduced internal conflict once the program is well established and widely accepted; the organizational maintenance goal is thereby fostered.

METHODS IMPROVEMENT. The data of job analysis provide an index of what are presumed to be the most appropriate work procedures, given the existing equipment. But after a job has been studied in this amount of detail, it may become apparent that certain changes in the man-machine balance are economically feasible and desirable. Automatic equipment may be introduced, or on occasion human actions may be substituted for machinery. Thus, job analysis can provide a basis for reengineering the positions involved.

WAGE AND SALARY SURVEYS. Job descriptions from different companies provide a method of comparing rates of pay within occupations. With such information it is possible to be reasonably certain that the jobs compared are in fact similar. A company may determine how its pay scales jibe with others for comparable work in the community and adjust its rates to a desired level.

COUNSELING. Counseling, of course, is primarily an application outside the company itself. Yet job descriptions such as those developed by the U.S. Employment Service, and occupational information based on extensive job analyses, can have considerable value in areas such as vocational guidance and rehabilitation counseling. With this type of data it is possible to guide the inexperienced and the disabled into occupations where they are most likely to succeed.

The Scope of the Job Analysis

What are the kinds of information that must be obtained in connection with a job analysis? There is no simple answer to this question, because the specific job under consideration, the company, and the purpose to which the data are to be put all exert an influence. Different jobs have quite different salient aspects, and companies develop varying procedures for a number of reasons. If the primary purpose is to prepare a set of training guidelines, the information sought may well differ considerably from that desired should the objective be to construct a wage system. Yet there are certain types of data that are included in most analyses, although in by no means all, and it is these that have been singled out for discussion here. Exactly where a particular type of information may appear within a given job description is subject to considerable variation: A specific item may well initiate one job description and come at the end of another. There are almost as many variants as there are companies with job analysis programs.

Elements of the Job Description

JOB TITLE. All job descriptions should contain a specific job title or name, because this is needed for bookkeeping purposes within the firm and to facilitate reporting of the firm's activities to the government and to other data-collection agencies. In many cases alternative or slang titles are also noted.

WORK ACTIVITIES AND PROCEDURES. The segment of the job description covering work activities and procedures should be devoted to describing, in whatever detail is necessary, the tasks and duties to be performed on the job, the materials used in carrying out these tasks, the machinery operated if any, the kinds of formal interactions with other workers required, and the nature and extent of the supervision given or received.

PHYSICAL ENVIRONMENT. The section on physical environment should contain a complete description of the physical working conditions where the work is to be performed. Among the factors that should be noted are the normal heat, lighting, noise levels, and ventilation in the work situation. In addition, it is sometimes desirable to indicate the location of the work in terms of a rural-urban or some other geographical designation, because this may be of relevance in recruiting and for other purposes. Any particular accident hazards are also described.

SOCIAL ENVIRONMENT. An increasingly common part of the job description is a section devoted to specifying the social conditions under which the work will be carried out. This is a relatively new component, and as a result the types of information included tend to vary considerably from company to company. Often there is a statement regarding the number of individuals in the working environment of the particular job. There may also be considerable information on the age, sex, and other characteristics of these work associates. Thus, some idea may be gained regarding the homogeneity or heterogeneity of the individuals who will be employed together.

Physical aspects of the job that have a bearing on the social aspects may also be noted—time of work hours (night or day), work location (city, suburban, or rural), availability of noncompany facilities (stores, restaurants, and so on), and availability of recreation (company-sponsored or not). These and other features of the social environment are significant in relation to the organizational maintenance goal. Role prescriptions in the areas of conflict minimization, cooperation with superiors, maintaining continued employment uninterrupted by excessive absenteeism, and the like always exist, even though these requirements may not be explicitly stated in the job description. Knowledge of the social environment can be extremely helpful in minimizing disparities between prescriptions of this kind and actual behavior.

CONDITIONS OF EMPLOYMENT. The aspect of the job description dealing with conditions of employment is concerned with the place of the job in the formal organization, in such terms as the wage structure, working hours, method of payment, permanency of the positions, seasonal or part-time nature of work, allowable fringe benefits, relation to other jobs, and opportunities for promotion or transfer. Although every effort should be made to have statements in a job description as clear and precise as possible, this is particularly important when the conditions of employment are being described, because of the possible legal implications of many of the items. A number of the constraints on company actions discussed in Chapters 5 and 6 relate to these matters.

In Tables 8-1 and 8-2 two rather different types of job descriptions are presented. The first is much more generalized and contains the type of information that might be used by a vocational guidance counselor in advising young men with regard to a career (1). Thus, the description has been written to cover role prescriptions that might be found in a variety of employing organizations. For instance, constructing trade tests that cover the specific knowledge required for job performance may or may not be an aspect of such a position depending on whether such tests are actually used by a particular company.

By way of contrast, the dealer-sales supervisor description is much more specific as to what is required in this particular company. Here the exact role prescriptions are spelled out in considerable detail. Considerable attention is given to differentiating between what the sales supervisor is expected to do and what is expected of his superior, the district manager. In this sense the job description has clearly been coordinated with the organization planning function.

Table 8-1. A Typical Generalized Job Description: Job Analyst °

A. TITLE: Occupational Analyst.

B. ALTERNATE TITLES: Job Analyst, Personnel Studies Assistant, Employment Service Analyst, Personnel Technician.

C. DUTIES: Analyzes jobs and prepares descriptions and specifications; prepares or revises trade tests; supervises subordinates in compiling material; performs other functions. (Occupational analysts sometimes specialize in job analysis or in aptitude or job performance testing work.)
Details of above:

   1. Analyzes jobs and prepares descriptions and specifications. Studies jobs in plants, describes work performed, analyzes abilities and training required and writes descriptions largely in form of specifications for the use of employment interviewers, counselors, and other personnel workers for use in employment, in-service training, transfer, and job evaluation.

   2. Prepares or revises trade tests. Prepares trade test questions and administers them to workers for standardization purposes. May analyze results and select questions which show highest validity.

   3. Supervises subordinates in compiling material. May direct others in making job analyses, developing trade questions, and in related work.

   4. Performs other functions. May be required to contact employers and workers to obtain their cooperation and to explain the value of the techniques developed. May assist in one or more phases in the development of aptitude test batteries or in the preparation of surveys of jobs in plants using the *Dictionary of Occupational Titles*. May assist or train other staff members in the use of the techniques developed.

D. QUALIFICATIONS:

   1. Educational—College graduation or substitution of experience year-for-year is generally required as a minimum. However, in specialized fields, such as test-development, an M.A. may be required. Courses in industrial psychology, tests, and measurements statistics are most often required. Persons with a year or more of graduate training sometimes enter this work without previous experience.

   2. Training—

Table 8-1 (cont'd.)

---

    a. On-the-job: Knowledge of the industry if employed in private in-
dustry or familiarity with the practices of public employment offices
if so employed. This varies from two weeks to six months.

    b. Prior: Some experience in job analysis, employment interviewing,
or use of testing techniques in industry is usually required. Amount
necessary depends on amount of college training. Generally four or
five years or its equivalent in college training is required.

  3. Personal—Ability to meet and get along with others is essential. Must
write clearly and concisely and have ability to supervise others.

E. PROMOTIONS: From Employment Interviewer to Senior Analyst or Section Chief in charge of test development.

F. RELATION TO OTHER POSITIONS: Related to positions of Employment Counselor or Interviewer and Industrial Psychologist.

---

* Adapted from Carroll L. Shartle, "Occupational Description for Positions in Psychology." A Report submitted to Division of Anthropology and Psychology, National
Research Council, Columbus, Ohio.

Source: R. Bellows, *Psychology of Personnel in Business and Industry*, 3rd ed., p.
      198. Copyright 1961. Reprinted by permission of Prentice-Hall, Inc., Engle-
      wood Cliffs, New Jersey.

**Table 8-2. A Typical Job Description for a Specific Position
in a Specific Firm: Dealer Sales Supervisor
for a Petroleum Company**

TITLE: Dealer Sales Supervisor
SALARY GRADE: 12
DEPARTMENT: Domestic Marketing
TITLE OF IMMEDIATE SUPERVISOR: District Manager
DUTIES: Under direction, supervises 6–15 salesmen engaged in selling and
    stimulating resale of company products to and/or by assigned accounts,
    acquiring new business, and in developing stations. Plans and supervises
    direct marketing activities within district or assigned territory in order to
    acquire and maintain maximum amount of profitable business by securing
    and retaining superior operation of service stations, developing dealers,
    acquisition of new direct marketing accounts, etc.

  1. Performs supervisory duties; assigns work, answers questions, etc.; follows current activities by review of reports, discussions with subordinates, etc. Interviews job applicants, and makes selection subject to
District Manager's approval. Handles minor disciplinary matters. Is
consulted relative to promotions, transfers, salary treatment, etc. En-
dorses expense and mileage accounts.

  2. Plans and supervises direct marketing activities within the district or
territory in order to acquire and maintain maximum amount of profit-

Table 8-2 (cont'd.)

able business by securing and retaining superior operation of service stations, developing dealers, acquisition of new direct marketing accounts, etc. Receives occasional special assignments from District Manager, consults him as necessary on policy problems, and keeps him advised as to direct marketing activities; otherwise, works independently in accordance with established policies. Keeps currently informed of current activities by field observations, advice of subordinates, etc.

a. Recruits new dealers through personal contacts, newspaper ads, etc.; interviews candidates in conjunction with salesmen and recommends selection to District Manager. Gathers necessary credit information and personal references. Schedules trainees in training school, and reviews periodic progress reports. Attempts to place graduate trainees awaiting station with established dealer for further training. Indoctrinates and motivates new dealers; makes in-station inspections to check on training, answer questions, etc. Upon request, arranges for dealer employee clinics to be held within the district and assigns service salesmen as instructors; acts as faculty member of Dealer Training Schools.

b. Reviews monthly profit and loss statement and housekeeping reports prepared by salesmen on each financed dealer; looks for possible trouble spots such as excessive personal accounts receivable, expenses, personal loans, unbalanced sales, etc.; discusses weak points with salesmen, recommends remedial measures, and follows for correction. Participates in annual district reviews of dealers for purpose of discussing past performance, planning future programs and goals, pointing out weak spots in operation and offering advice relative to elimination. Prepares dealer lease analysis forms recommending future rental treatment, and discusses with District Manager.

c. Trains, coaches and assists salesmen in selling and acquiring accounts, training their dealers, investigating and settling complaints, overcoming problems, negotiating contracts, planning and executing sales promotions, etc. by double teaming with them in the field. Requests assistance from regional staff personnel and supplier's representatives, and handles necessary liaison duties.

d. Inspects stations in conjunction with District Manager; checks on appearance, service rendered, personnel's working knowledge, customer contacts, etc.; prepares written report, and follows for correction of noted deficiencies. In daily travels around territory makes casual inspections of stations, and advises others of items needing correction. Follows closely, and handles non-routine matters in connection with dealer changeovers.

e. Performs sundry related duties; plans and may conduct periodic sales meetings. Attends districts staff meetings. Handles correspondence with regional and home office personnel, dealers, etc. relative to matters supervised. Contributes to district's monthly marketing

Table 8-2 (cont'd.)

letter. Assists District Manager in preparation of service station site justifications, budgets, quotas, performance reports, etc. Speaks at local service organizations, and may serve as member of various industry and trade associations and committees.

3. As individually assigned, substitutes partially for District Manager during vacations and other absences to the extent of signing forms, reports, etc. normally signed by District Manager, and handling familiar matters according to District Manager's known views or his handling of similar problems in past; refers questionable matters to Regional Office for advice or decisions; advises District Manager of matters handled.

EDUCATIONAL REQUIREMENTS: High school graduate.

SPECIFIC KNOWLEDGE TO START: General knowledge of dealer marketing; company products; district organization and facilities; company marketing policies and procedures; service station operation. Supervisory experience.

WHERE EXPERIENCE REQUIRED: 4–5 years' experience in dealer marketing with at least 1–2 years as Dealer Salesman.

KNOWLEDGE ACQUIRED ON JOB: Experience in motivating, training, and supervising salesmen; learn to develop and apply effective selling programs; familiarity with company and competitive direct marketing activities in district; learn responsibility limits of positions. (6–9 months to acquire.)

PHYSICAL EFFORT: Semi-active; drives car approximately 1,100 to 2,000 miles/month.

RESPONSIBILITY:

Men—Supervision of 6–15 salesmen.

Materials—Economical use of office supplies.

Equipment—Care and use of office machines; inspection of service stations.

Markets—Acquiring and efficient servicing of accounts; occasional public relations contacts.

Money—Economical use of company expense funds by self and subordinates.

Methods—Execution, selection and control of methods used in direct marketing.

Records—Preparation, analysis and endorsement of records, reports and forms relative to direct marketing activities.

WORKING CONDITIONS:

Regular working hours 8:30 to 5:00 five days a week.

Surroundings and hazards:

10–60% normal office conditions.

40–90% field and travel conditions, with related hazards.

The Job Specification

The job specification part of the job description may not be labeled separately or, if it is, it may well appear under the heading of qualifications. It contains information on the personal characteristics that are believed necessary for the performance of the job. Included are such factors as educational background, experience, and personal qualifications.

Although the job specification is not universally treated as a separate entity within the job description, there are strong arguments for doing so. The reason is that it performs an entirely different function from the other components. The job specification neither states role prescriptions nor describes the conditions of work. Instead it attempts to indicate what kind of people can be expected to most closely approximate the role requirements. Thus, it is basically concerned with matters of selection, screening, and placement.

A detailed discussion of problems in the selection area will have to await Part IV. Nevertheless, it is important to note here that job specifications are often written with little real knowledge as to their actual relationship to work performance. Thus, it has become common practice to require high school graduation for a great variety of positions. Yet this is often done without trying out individuals who have not graduated from high school in the particular type of work to determine if they are capable of effective performance. In most jobs it seems likely that a reasonably intelligent and emotionally mature person who has not finished high school will do as well as the graduate who lacks one or both of these characteristics.

Numerous other examples could be given. The point is that job specifications can serve to artificially restrict the labor market, so that it is very difficult to find anyone who meets all the requirements. This sort of thing is fine—if the specifications must in fact be met to assume satisfactory performance. But all too often the information that would indicate whether this is true or not has not been obtained. Specifications are often written without the intensive study that should precede the introduction of any selection procedure.

The Methods of Job Analysis

The methods used to gather information about a job vary greatly in comprehensiveness and systematic rigor. In the discussions that follow, an effort will be made to explain some of the more commonly used techniques. Emphasis will be placed on the advantages and disadvantages of each approach and an attempt will be made to cite typical occupations for which the particular procedure is most useful.

Observation of the Job Occupant

Observation of the job occupant is a frequently used method of identifying the tasks and duties actually involved in fulfilling the demands of a particular job. It requires merely that the job analyst observe a number of job occupants, as they perform the job in a normal, workaday manner, and then that he record these observations in some systematic manner. This may be done either by writing down what was done in narrative form or by selecting what is relevant from among alternatives on some sort of checklist. The checklist approach, of course, requires some prior knowledge of the particular job and those closely related to it. The job description is then written to include any new role prescriptions that may be desired. It is important that more than one job occupant be watched at work, because to do otherwise might result in the highly idiosyncratic and unique behaviors of a specific individual being written into the description.

Unfortunately the simplicity of this approach is somewhat misleading. There are certain related problems that can be very significant in the business situation. First, the use of this method requires the assumption that the act of observing an individual at work does not have an impact on the work behavior itself. For the method to be of value the worker must do the same things in the same way when he is being watched as when he is not. In many instances this is clearly not the case.

Many people have a tendency to show off under circumstances such as this; others become anxious. Activities that are expected to yield approval are often exaggerated. If the worker feels he is being observed in order to set his wage rate (as may well be the case), it is very likely that he will pattern his activities so as to obtain as favorable a rate as possible. These difficulties can, of course, be avoided by setting up a procedure whereby the worker may be observed without his knowledge. This is not easily accomplished, however. If the subterfuge is found out, labor relations problems can be anticipated, and considerable damage to morale is almost inevitable. All in all it would seem that some distortion of normal behavior as a function of observation is very likely in most instances.

A second difficulty with the direct observation method of job analysis is that it becomes almost meaningless in the case of work that is primarily mental in nature. Thus, there are many positions ranging from private secretary to chairman of the board that are not really subject to this type of study. Observation alone will not yield a clear and meaningful picture of what the individual is doing. It should be noted, also, that this particular objection will become increasingly significant as automation spreads into new areas, because the general trend with the introduction of new technology is for the amount of physical behavior to decrease, whereas mental activities increase as a factor in job performance.

A final problem with observation is that it is not very practical when the *job cycle* is rather long, that is, when the time from the beginning to the end of a specific task extends over a considerable period of time. For example, the individual who has only to punch holes in some material with the aid of a machine may have a cycle of only ten or twenty seconds. But the skilled machinist who is making up an extremely complex and sensitive die may have a cycle of three to six months. In any instance where a specific action occurs only infrequently, it is very uneconomical to attempt a complete job description based on observation alone.

For the reasons stated it appears that the observation technique should be employed only when the work is largely automatically controlled (such as a conveyor belt system), is primarily physical, and the job cycle is rather short (as with certain lower-level clerical jobs and many unskilled and semiskilled factory jobs).

Interview of the Job Occupant

Many of the objections to observation as a method of establishing the tasks, duties, and responsibilities of a job can be overcome by utilizing the interview as a source of information. The job cycle problem is largely eliminated, because the worker can observe himself and briefly summarize, in words, behaviors that were spread over a long time span. Similarly, an individual can monitor his own mental processes even though an observer cannot. As a result the difficulty with nonphysical tasks is minimized; mental and behavioral activities can both be described. Furthermore, the employee is made an active participant in the information-gathering process, with the result that negative attitudes and resistances are much less likely to develop. Finally, this procedure utilizes the often considerable information the worker has about his job, information that may not be available to the job analyst from any other source.

It is desirable that this procedure be utilized only after considerable preplanning and forethought. The individual doing the interviewing, the job analyst, must be thoroughly trained in the techniques of interviewing. Questions should be worked out in advance and there should be a clear concept of exactly what information is desired.

The job analyst needs to be able to gain *rapport* with the worker whose job is being studied. Confidence must be elicited and the worker must be induced to accept the usefulness of the job analysis procedure. This is not easily done. Sometimes it is impossible. But the difficulties are compounded when, for instance, a college-trained job analyst goes into a plant to interview a blue-collar worker with only a minimum of formal schooling and uses a vocabulary that is well above the level that the worker can adequately comprehend. In such cases misunderstanding is inevitable and resentment very likely. The information-gathering function will probably not be adequately served.

A second possible source of difficulty is that the person being interviewed may, consciously or unconsciously, present a distorted picture of his position. He may, for example, attempt to portray his work as more difficult and important than it really is, in the hope that his pay and status will be increased accordingly. Interview data derived from a number of individuals performing the same or very similar tasks can be used to correct this tendency in part, but it is sometimes difficult to fit several disparate interviews together to form a comprehensive picture. The important thing is that the job analyst retain a clear conception of his own role—that he keep constantly in mind the fact that he is supposed to establish a set of role prescriptions. These will only rarely be identical with any one incumbent's statements regarding his work behavior. Thus, job descriptions must go beyond mere interview data to effectively structure the whole pattern of work within the organization.

Job Occupant Description

Job occupant description is similar in intent and procedure to the interview, except that the occupant either writes a narrative description or fills out a questionnaire, rather than giving the information orally. Usually he is expected to go into considerable detail regarding the tasks performed, the conditions of work, and the materials and equipment employed.

As might be expected, this technique has many of the advantages and disadvantages of the interview. It is, however, somewhat more economical of time and effort, because the services of an interviewer are not required. On the other hand there is a loss in flexibility, which means that mistaken impressions can go uncorrected or require considerable time to correct. Also, the benefits of a face-to-face discussion, as they may contribute to rapport and consequently to the correctness of the information obtained, are lost.

Yet evidence from several studies indicates that job occupants are quite consistent in describing their work, even when the jobs are as complex as those of aircraft control and warning operator, aircraft control and warning radar repairman, and jet fighter crew chief (8). People holding these military jobs note much the same tasks at one time as they do at another. An equally high degree of consistency was obtained with the checklist for various engineering occupations presented in Table 8-3 (2).

Both the interview and the written description suffer from the fact

Table 8-3. Job Description Checklist for Research, Development, Production, and Sales Engineers (Occupants are to rank the items in terms of importance.)

A. Evaluating ideas.

B. Conducting negotiations.

C. Planning the best use of equipment and materials.

D. Investigating problems of a basic and fundamental nature which may not be undertaken for specific practical application.

E. Keeping informed about competitive products and activities.

F. Simplifying production methods.

G. Developing a working model of a new instrument or process.

H. Developing and testing useful hypotheses or generalizations.

I. Preparing initial specifications for equipment installation.

J. Completing experimental or pilot projects.

K. Performing liaison work with departments and personnel to maintain overall efficiency of process or equipment production.

L. Applying theoretical and empirical principles to develop an economically feasible instrument or process.

M. Developing a fund of basic research knowledge.

N. Evaluating performance of present materials, designs, methods, processes, products, equipment.

O. Selling ideas to people.

P. Planning best use of personnel.

Q. Working with customers' representatives to suggest equipment and/or process modification.

R. Originating technical ideas.

S. Controlling expenses.

T. Preparing and making technical recommendations and proposals.

U. Attending seminars, symposia, and colloquia to keep abreast of current developments.

V. Trouble shooting and/or meeting emergencies.

W. Setting up pilot projects to develop and test new process and equipment designs.

X. Writing technical articles, correspondence, instructions, manuals, patent disclosures, reports, specifications.

Source: M. D. Dunnette and G. W. England, "A Checklist for Differentiating Engineering Jobs," *Personnel Psychology,* Vol. 10 (1957), pp. 194–195.

that job occupants may report incorrectly regarding their work. Probably the most effective way to compensate for any such bias is to have the data obtained from the incumbent reviewed by his immediate superior. If the superior has actually performed the work in the past, he is likely to be particularly helpful. Even without such personal experience, however, he can be presumed to possess considerable knowledge, merely because of the nature of his relationship to the incumbent and to the job. Because the objectives of the worker himself and those of his superior are likely to be somewhat different, this review may well provide a valuable antidote to the worker's statements in certain areas.

In general the methods involving the securing of information directly from the job occupant have a considerable advantage when the job analyses cover positions at middle or relatively high levels, where the work is not very repetitive. Individuals in these types of jobs are also those with whom the typical job analyst is likely to be most capable of gaining rapport.

Examination of Previous Job Descriptions

Another way of gathering information about a job is to determine what is already known about it. This cuts down on duplication of effort and can provide a substantial base for subsequent study. Thus, for those companies that have them, previous job descriptions can be of real benefit. Before utilizing such information, however, or any job descriptions that may be available from other firms either, it is important to look into the analysis procedures employed. A poorly prepared job description may well do more harm than good. Also, the possibility that technological and other changes may have altered the job considerably should be considered. Many job descriptions prepared in the past are in fact obsolete, insofar as present day activities are concerned, even though the job titles may have remained the same.

There are several other sources of occupational information that can be of help. Perhaps most important among these is the *Dictionary of Occupational Titles,* published by the U.S. Employment Service (14). This contains very brief job descriptions of over 20,000 jobs. Almost any job title in normal usage can be found there. The job descriptions, however, are quite short and are based on multicompany studies. Thus, they may well not be appropriate for establishing role prescriptions in connection with a specific job in a specific company.

Two other sources are the *Alphabetical Index of Occupations and Industries* put out by the Bureau of the Census (13) and the *International Standard Classification of Occupations* (6). Both are intended primarily for use in connection with a census of population and thus provide only minimal information about each job in the job description sense. However, by providing classification information, they do indicate the general type of work to which each job title refers.

Examination of Work Materials

In some cases it is possible to gain important information concerning the tasks and duties of a particular job by examining the materials typically used during work performance. A good example would be the tools of a carpenter, or perhaps the typewriter used by a secretary.

The usefulness of this method is, of course, quite limited, but it can be of considerable supplementary value in certain instances.

Performance of Work Activities

It has long been said that the best way to learn about something is to do it. More recently this assumption has received considerable support from laboratory research in the field of psychology. Thus, it seems apparent that one of the best ways for a job analyst to obtain information about a job is to take on its duties himself.

In many cases this is entirely feasible. Such jobs as retail clerk and truck driver can be learned rather rapidly, as can many others requiring relatively limited skills. However, it is obvious that this is a technique of rather restricted usefulness and generality, because many jobs take years of training. For positions of the latter type the procedure is obviously of little value. Probably as the complexity of our knowledge increases, there will be fewer and fewer jobs that can be studied by actually performing them, but the advantages of the approach where it can be used are considerable.

Developing Job Families

One of the primary goals of a job analysis program is to develop systematic knowledge of how the jobs in a given company are related to one another in terms of either the required tasks or the necessary personal characteristics, or both. Such information can be of considerable value in planning training programs, selection, transfer, promotion, and other personnel activities. If certain jobs can be shown to group together, the occupants of these similar positions can be treated as a unit for a number of purposes. Groupings of this kind are particularly valuable as a guide in the placement of employees.

A useful way of constructing such job families has been developed based on the differing aptitudes presumed to be required by each job (9). This technique will form the basis of the ensuing discussion. It has considerable practical value and can be employed by any company, utilizing the total pool of jobs identified within the firm as a starting point.

In the particular research under consideration the jobs to be studied were drawn at random from the *Dictionary of Occupational Titles*. The analysis as a whole was based on over 300 jobs. Each of these was rated from the brief job descriptions in the dictionary by six specifically trained raters, who were to indicate the degree of aptitude required for satisfactory, not maximum, performance. The aptitudes employed were the nine described in Table 8-4. The scale for the ratings is contained in Table 8-5. The scale values assigned by each

Table 8-4. Aptitudes Used in Rating Jobs

Code	*Aptitude*
G	*Intelligence:* General learning ability: the ability to "catch on" or understand instructions and underlying principles; ability to reason and make judgments.
V	*Verbal:* Ability to understand meanings of words and ideas associated with them, and to use them effectively; to comprehend language and understand relationships between words and to understand meanings of whole sentences and paragraphs.
N	*Numerical:* Ability to perform arithmetic operations quickly and accurately.
S	*Spatial:* Ability to comprehend forms in space and understand relationships of plane and solid objects: may be used in such tasks as blueprint reading and in solving geometry problems; frequently described as the ability to "visualize" objects of two or three dimensions.
P	*Form Perception:* Ability to perceive pertinent detail in objects or in pictorial or graphic material; to make visual comparisons and discriminations and see slight differences in shapes and lengths.
Q	*Clerical Perception:* Ability to perceive pertinent detail in verbal or tabular material; to observe differences in copy, to proofread words and numbers, and to avoid perceptual errors in arithmetic computation.
K	*Motor Coordination:* Ability to coordinate eyes and hands or fingers rapidly and accurately in making precise movements with speed; ability to make a movement response accurately and quickly.
F	*Finger Dexterity:* Ability to move the fingers, and manipulate small objects with the fingers, rapidly or accurately.
M	*Manual Dexterity:* Ability to move the hands easily and skillfully; ability to work with the hands in placing and turning motions.

Source: D. B. Orr, "A New Method for Clustering Jobs," *Journal of Applied Psychology,* Vol. 44 (1960), p. 45.

Table 8-5. Definitions of Rating Scale Values

Level 1—An amount possessed only by the top 10% of the working population.

Level 2—An amount possessed by the highest third, exclusive of the top 10%.

Level 3—An amount possessed by the middle third of the working population.

Level 4—An amount possessed by the lowest third, exclusive of the lowest 10%.

Level 5—An amount possessed by the lowest 10% of the working population.

Source: D. B. Orr, "A New Method of Clustering Jobs," *Journal of Applied Psychology,* Vol. 44 (1960), p. 45.

of the six raters were averaged and thus an aptitude requirement was established in all nine areas. Profiles over the nine aptitude dimensions were developed for all the jobs studied. The total distance or difference between each job profile was then computed ignoring the sign of the difference. Let us take as an example three hypothetical jobs, A, B, and C. The aptitude profiles obtained from the raters might have been as follows:

Aptitude code	Job A	Job B	Job C
G	3	1	5
V	2	1	5
N	1	4	4
S	4	3	3
P	5	3	3
Q	5	2	1
K	1	1	1
F	3	5	4
M	2	1	1

The difference or distance between job A and job B is

$$(3-1) + (2-1) + (4-1) + (4-3) + (5-3) + (5-2) + (1-1) + (5-3) + (2-1) = 15$$

The difference or distance between job A and job C is

$$(5-3) + (5-2) + (4-1) + (4-3) + (5-3) + (5-1) + (1-1) + (4-3) + (2-1) = 17$$

The difference or distance between job B and job C is

$$(5-1) + (5-1) + (4-4) + (3-3) + (3-3) + (2-1) + (1-1) + (5-4) + (1-1) = 10$$

It is apparent that jobs B and C are much more alike in their requirements than are A and B or A and C. Thus, jobs B and C would probably be classified together in a single job family. Job A, on the other hand, would clearly be left out of this particular grouping, although it could be assigned to some other family with which it showed greater similarity.

Thus, those jobs that demonstrate a small difference or distance from each other are clustered together. In the study using jobs from the *Dictionary of Occupational Titles*, six job families were found. These seemed to account for all of the more than 300 jobs studied. The characteristics of these six families are presented in Table 8-6, along with a number of typical jobs. Within each of the groupings the aptitude patterns of the component jobs appear to be much more similar than when jobs from different families are compared. Transferring individuals from job to job within families should be more successful than transferring them across families.

Table 8-6. Job Families Based on Similarity of Aptitude Patterns

Job family characteristics	*Typical jobs*
I. High level technical, supervisory, and mechanical jobs. The aptitudes required are Intelligence, Verbal, Numerical, Spatial, and Form Perception. Clerical is rated low.	Meter Engineer X-Ray Technician Engineering Specification Writer Pattern and Foundry Inspector
II. Extremely low level jobs, primarily unskilled.	Cement Finisher Helper Hydraulic Riveter Helper Cameraman Assistant Cooky Mixer Helper
III. Fairly high level skilled jobs, mostly mechanical and artisan types. The emphasis is on Spatial, Form Perception, Manual Dexterity, and Finger Dexterity.	Transformer Tester Steam Fitter Tubular Furniture Maker Rock Cutter
IV. Jobs at a very high level with respect to their requirements of Intelligence and Verbal. Supervisory jobs are contained in this cluster, and there is some emphasis on clerical abilities.	Rate Analysis Clerk Public Accountant Law Examiner Actor
V. Clerical jobs and supervisory jobs at a lower level than those in I. The aptitudes required in the greatest amounts are Intelligence, Verbal, Numerical, and Clerical.	Coal Inspector Service Establishment Attendant Beef Weighing Clerk Depot Master
VI. Mechanical-manual jobs of a medium grade of skill. Intelligence, Finger Dexterity, and Form Perception are required, but no aptitude is needed in more than an average amount.	Machine Driller Steam Table Attendant Thermite Welder Cable Splicer

Source: D. B. Orr, "A New Method of Clustering Jobs," *Journal of Applied Psychology*, Vol. 44 (1960), pp. 46–48.

Criticisms of Job Analysis

In concluding this chapter the reader should be made aware that this entire matter of job analysis is surrounded by some controversy. There are those who believe that such analyses are too restrictive in nature—that they are not desirable because the job is largely what an individual makes of it. According to this viewpoint, job descriptions, and the role prescriptions that they contain, impose undue limitations on the development or growth of the individual in his job.

Although it is true that these criticisms have some validity, this does not mean that companies should dispense with job analysis. It is important that areas of work specialization and concentration be spelled out, both as an aid to the productivity objective and to minimize internal conflict and stress, thereby contributing to organizational maintenance. To eliminate all types of job description would be tantamount to eliminating any attempt at planning in the utilization of human resources.

A more appropriate answer would seem to be the development of better, more realistic job descriptions, perhaps utilizing several methods of gathering information. It may well prove desirable to write job descriptions at a somewhat higher level of generality, especially in the more skilled, professional, and managerial occupations. Thus, an individual would have more latitude to fulfill himself in his job and to utilize his own unique talents and skills.

The amount of research being done on problems in the area of job design is increasing steadily. Engineering psychology, in particular, has made important contributions aimed at achieving a better fit between the requirements of the work and its technology, as they influence role prescriptions, and the characteristics or competencies of human beings (4,7). Job specifications are increasingly being established on the basis of sound investigations into the factors that do in fact predetermine success in a given job. Finally, there has been a trend recently toward linking jobs together vertically into career ladders, as well as into the largely horizontal groupings of the job families. Training requirements for movements up a ladder are specified, and different ladders are established for different entry occupations (3). These developments suggest that the job descriptions of the future will, in fact, be far superior to many of those that have raised the critics' ire.

References

1. Bellows, R., *Psychology of Personnel in Business and Industry,* 3rd ed. Englewood Cliffs, N.J.: Prentice-Hall, 1961.
2. Dunnette, M. D., and G. W. England, "A Checklist for Differentiating Engineering Jobs," *Personnel Psychology,* Vol. 10 (1957), 191–198.
3. Fine, S. A., *Guidelines for the Design of New Careers.* Kalamazoo, Mich.: W. E. Upjohn Institute for Employment Research, 1967.

4. Gagné, R. M., *Psychological Principles in System Development*. New York: Holt, Rinehart and Winston, 1962.
5. Grether, W. F., "Psychology and the Space Frontier," *American Psychologist*, Vol. 17 (1962), 92–101.
6. *International Standard Classification of Occupations*. Geneva, Switzerland: International Labour Office, 1958.
7. McCormick, E. J., *Human Factors Engineering*, 2nd ed. New York: McGraw-Hill, 1964.
8. McCormick, E. J., and H. L. Ammerman, *Development of Worker Activity Check Lists for Use in Occupational Analysis*, Technical Report WADD-TR-60-77. Lackland AFB, San Antonio, Texas: Personnel Laboratory, Wright Air Development Division, Air Research and Development Command, USAF, 1960.
9. Orr, D. B., "A New Method of Clustering Jobs," *Journal of Applied Psychology*, Vol. 44 (1960), 44–49.
10. Otis, J. L., and R. H. Leukart, *Job Evaluation*, 2nd ed. Englewood Cliffs, N.J.: Prentice-Hall, 1954.
11. Shartle, C. L., *Occupational Information*, 3rd ed. Englewood Cliffs, N.J.: Prentice-Hall, 1959.
12. Shartle, C. L., "Occupational Analysis, Worker Characteristics, and Occupational Classification Systems," in H. Borow (ed.), *Man in a World at Work*. Boston: Houghton Mifflin Company, 1964, pp. 285–309.
13. United States Department of Commerce, Bureau of the Census, *Alphabetical Index of Occupations and Industries*. Washington: Government Printing Office, 1960.
14. United States Department of Labor, *Dictionary of Occupational Titles*, 3rd ed. Washington: Government Printing Office, 1965.

Questions

1. In talking about occupations, it is important to be aware of the distinctions between terms that are a part of the vocabulary of this field of study. What are the major characteristics that distinguish the following:

   a task and a position
   a job and an occupation
   the job description and the job specification
   position analysis and job analysis
   a job family and an occupation
   job analysis and job evaluation

2. What are the uses to which job analysis information may be put? Can you think of any possible uses not discussed in the text?

3. What are the disadvantages of observation of the job occupant as a method of obtaining job analysis information? To what extent do

the interview procedure and job occupant description serve to overcome these disadvantages?

4. Take four jobs with which you are reasonably familiar and assign aptitude ratings to them using the aptitudes of Table 8-4 and the scale of Table 8-5. Determine the distance between each pair of jobs. Which would you group together in the same job family?

9

Management Appraisal

In the two preceding chapters some of the methods used to establish and formalize role prescriptions have been discussed at length. Let us now turn to the various methods that have been developed to evaluate individuals relative to these role prescriptions—more especially, in this chapter, to the evaluation of managerial personnel.

It should be understood at the outset that the fact of evaluation in some form is inevitable. All organizations make some effort to determine whether individual members are contributing to the attainment of objectives. This may be done in an offhand way by the top person or through the use of a complex, formal appraisal and evaluation system. The evaluations may be precise and accurate or vague and almost entirely in error. But whether we like it or not, we can almost certainly expect to be judged in some way when we join an organization, especially if it is an employing organization that rewards its members with money for their efforts in its behalf.

There are a great variety of techniques and procedures that have been devised to aid in this process of evaluation and appraisal. All have in common the fact that they attempt to provide some indication of the extent to which an individual's behavior matches a conception of what he is expected to do. The basic consideration in appraisal is whether the behavior of a person is so integrated with established role requirements that he is considered a success or so much at variance with them that he is considered a failure.

Because any given position is likely to have a number of different role prescriptions, we can expect that job-related behavior will be evaluated in a number of different aspects. Particularly in the case of managers, it is not a matter of doing one or even a few things correctly, but of doing a great variety of different things, all designed to meet one role prescription or another. Accordingly, an individual may be considered a great success in one regard only to fall down badly in some other area, relative to some other requirement (25).

It is characteristic to evaluate people in terms of various aspects of their behavior, or dimensions of performance. Generally the major concern is with actual behavior, with the things a person does or says. But on occasion evaluation systems move one step back into the individual and attempt to deal with the abilities, motives, and emotional patterns that cause or determine the behavior. The most general approach is to establish the extent of the match to a role prescription, or the degree of success. But often *standards* are introduced so that behavioral output is considered only as it relates to some minimal acceptable level. Either the person is above standard in a particular regard or below it.

Individual appraisal is carried out to determine what actions should be taken with regard to a person, in the present instance a manager. The result may be a decision to increase his pay, or decrease it, or leave it the same. Or the evaluation may be used as a basis for a placement decision: promotion, demotion, transfer, retention in the same job, or even separation. Management-appraisal data are also used to guide management-development activities, either directly, through a feedback of the conclusions to the person evaluated, or indirectly, as an indicator of future educational needs. Finally, the evaluations may be used to provide *criterion* data when selection procedures are being developed. This topic will be a primary concern in Part IV. It is sufficient to note here that a company normally tries to select from among job applicants those who have characteristics similar to the characteristics of its more successful employees and to screen out applicants who appear to be like unsuccessful workers of the past.

The Behavior of Effective and Ineffective Managers

Before discussing the numerous techniques and procedures used in management appraisal, it seems advisable to review in a general way what we know about the behavior of managers who have consistently been judged successful in their companies. In large part, managing is characterized by the attempt to elicit high levels of productivity and a maximal contribution to organizational maintenance from others. The manager is assigned much more work than he can do alone, and so he must get others to help in the performance of his role. Thus, managerial behavior is consistently evaluated in terms of its effects on others, that is, in terms of its supervisory aspects: Does the manager facilitate the work efforts of his subordinates or does he act in such a way as to actually make them less effective than they might otherwise be?

Research on Effective Supervision

The most extensive studies of supervisory behavior have been carried out by psychologists at the University of Michigan. This work has been done in a great many different types of firms, from insurance companies to heavy manufacturing. As a result a rather consistent picture has been obtained of how the typical effective supervisor acts (13).

For one thing, the ideal manager should devote his efforts primarily to supervisory and leadership tasks and not become deeply involved in actually doing the work of his subordinates. The factory foreman who spends long periods operating a machine beside his men and the sales supervisor who is primarily engaged in direct selling are not likely to be considered effective. They do not have the time to plan the work of their groups, perform any required special technical tasks, provide materials as necessary, observe the group's performance, motivate their subordinates, and deal with less effective workers. The whole process of supervision is left largely undone.

A second type of behavior found among less successful managers is extremely close supervision. Some delegation, which permits subordinates a degree of freedom, is apparently essential. The manager who continually hovers over his men, giving them frequent and detailed instructions on all phases of their work, seems to have a primarily negative impact rather than the positive effect he presumably intends.

Third, more effective supervisors tend to be relatively employee-centered and to exhibit considerable concern for their subordinates as human beings. On the other hand, the less effective maintain an unreasonable pressure for production with very little indication of human kindness. They take a punitive attitude whenever a mistake occurs, make no effort to develop their subordinates, rarely talk things over with their men, do not give praise, and usually neglect such special requests as their subordinates may make of them.

A fourth finding from the University of Michigan research indicates that the manager who exhibits none of the three negative behavior patterns just discussed may nevertheless remain relatively ineffective if he cannot exert influence on his own superiors. He must try and succeed in getting support for his actions up the line. Thus, it is not enough to appear employee-centered if the results cannot be made to stick. A promised change in work schedules that is never put into effect or a salary increase that is turned down at higher levels indicates only that in actual fact the manager does not matter very much. Repeated occurrences of this type tend to produce a work group that largely ignores most efforts at supervision.

The fifth type of behavior found to be associated with success is for the manager to assume an active leadership role in his relations with his men. It is essential that the group be led and that the members be given some understanding of their role prescriptions. A laissez-faire approach is characteristically unsuccessful.

These findings, as well as others of more recent origin, have been interpreted as providing support for a participative or democratic managerial style almost to the exclusion of other approaches (14,30). However, the evidence is not entirely consistent with this interpretation. There is good reason to believe that the permissive manager is more effective in certain situations, but not all (7).

THE OHIO STATE UNIVERSITY STUDIES. A similar series of investigations has been carried out by psychologists at Ohio State University. After conducting a number of detailed statistical analyses, these researchers conclude that behavior toward subordinates can be described adequately in terms of only two groupings, rather than five. In general, managers who exhibit both consideration and what was called initiating structure toward their subordinates appear to be most successful (26,29).

The studies indicate that a major factor contributing to failure is inconsiderate behavior toward subordinates. Being overdemanding and critical, "riding" one's workers, failing to consult the men on actions of concern to them, refusing to accept suggestions or to listen to problems, never doing a favor for a subordinate—these and similar behaviors were found to predominate among managers who were not meeting the requirements of their jobs.

The second factor deals more directly with the work output of the group. Those managers who initiated structure for their men, who established standards and specified role prescriptions, were consistently found to be more successful. Managers at the other pole who placed little emphasis on following rules, who gave the impression of being "one of the boys," who rarely assigned work duties or took a position on anything, and who neglected planning and organizing activities were identified as generally ineffective.

There is considerable similarity between the findings of the Ohio

State studies and those of the Michigan studies. The first type of be-havior noted by the Michigan psychologists, doing the work of sub-ordinates, seems very much like a failure to initiate structure. The second factor, too close supervision, and the third, a lack of employee-centeredness, are presumably comparable to the Ohio State conception of a deficiency in consideration and kindness. The fourth and fifth factors, which involve the exercise of influence both upward and down-ward in the organization, seem to fall in the general category of initiat-ing structure and exercising control. Thus, it seems that the successful manager is normally the one who acts to enforce role requirements and standards, but with a degree of consideration and human kindness toward his subordinates. This appears to be the approach that will elicit the greatest contributions in both the maintenance and the productivity areas from a group. Yet it must also be recognized that there are sizable variations from organization to organization in the types of individuals who will be viewed as successful in a leadership role (21).

Additional Aspects of Managerial Behavior

Successful managing is not, of course, defined entirely in terms of behavior directed toward subordinates, although this may be extremely important. A manager, especially one at the upper levels or in some specialized aspect of the company's total operations, may also be called upon to make decisions that have a direct impact on company profits and productivity. Decisions on new plant locations or converting to automated production processes or entering new markets are of this kind. If these decisions later prove to be incorrect, then the manager responsible for making them is likely to be considered unsuccessful, at least in the particular regard. Furthermore, any unwarranted wastage of company assets or deliberate reduction of company productivity and profits, either through theft or for purposes of stock manipulation or for any other reason, can be assumed to produce a judgment of sizable departure from role requirements.

In addition, a manager may be evaluated in terms of his impact on internal stresses within the company. Does he act to reduce conflict and dissension, to negotiate peaceful solutions to conflicts with other managers? Does he attempt to head off labor difficulties? Or does he foment discord, antagonize others, and provoke union representatives? The answers to these questions can well exert considerable influence on judgments as to whether a manager is effective or not.

Decisions and actions of much the same kind are also required of many managers in relation to external threats to organizational main-tenance. Thus, an acquisition involving the company in a costly anti-trust suit, which is finally lost, may eventuate in an extremely negative opinion of the managers involved. A highly articulate and successful lobbying effort that results in the defeat of a law unfavorable to the firm, on the other hand, can yield a very favorable evaluation.

These are the kinds of activities that are unique to managerial occupations and thus of particular concern in management appraisal. When added to such more frequent considerations as the quantity and quality of work output, and the matter of being physically present on the job—absenteeism, tardiness, and so on—they largely cover the gamut of behaviors that are considered in connection with the management evaluation process. It should be recognized, however, that a number of personnel managers and writers employ methods of classifying managerial behaviors that differ in a number of respects from those used here.

Judgmental Appraisal

Probably the most widespread method of evaluating managers is to obtain some type of judgment regarding their effectiveness. This may be done as required whenever a manager is being considered in connection with some personnel action, such as promotion or a proposed development activity. Or the appraisals may be conducted at regular intervals, so that all managers are considered within a specified time span. Ideally this would be done once a year, or at most at two-year intervals. Anything longer than that is likely to produce considerable error, because managers do change and consequently evaluations that are badly outdated may be employed to guide personnel actions.

It is probably most common in the business world to have managers appraised by other managers who are above them in the hierarchy. However, there are a number of other techniques that require discussion, some of which are gaining increasing acceptance. Among these are evaluations by peers, i.e., managers at the same level, or by subordinates; evaluations by, or with the assistance of, personnel managers and industrial psychologists; and self-appraisal.

In this chapter little attention will be given to the specific rating procedures and the types of judgmental errors that may occur. It is sufficient here to cover the different sources of appraisal data and the relative merits of each. The details of rating scale construction and use will be taken up in Chapter 10. It is important to recognize, however, that what is said there regarding the techniques used with lower-level employees is equally applicable to judgments regarding managers. Many management-appraisal systems utilize rating systems that are identical in format to those discussed in the next chapter, although the variables or dimensions measured may be different (because managerial work is different).

Appraisal by Superiors

One of the first questions that arises in constructing any management appraisal system is whether to use the judgments of a single superior or several. On this point the evidence is clear (3). The average of several evaluations made by equally competent raters is far superior to a single rating. This means that if at all possible several levels of supervision should be tapped, provided of course that all the individuals involved are in a good position to observe the work behavior of the man being appraised. Sometimes it is possible to utilize managers at higher levels who are not in the direct chain of command above the man—an individual who works in close spatial proximity, a staff manager with whom he often deals, or similar people. Multiple ratings appear to be preferable, even if the immediate superior is the only person who is really knowledgeable regarding the man. Thus, the average of several successive evaluations made by the same superior over a period of perhaps six months is generally superior to a single report.

The difficulty with using managers at various higher levels to obtain multiple ratings is that the condition of equal competence is frequently not met. A manager several levels above the individual being appraised may well not have a really adequate opportunity to observe. Thus, his conclusions may be based on a limited number of isolated incidents, plus hearsay.

Table 9-1. Correlations Between Supervisory Ratings at Three Different Levels and an Independent Index of Job Proficiency ($N = 100$)

	Supervisory level		
Rating scale question	Commissioned officers	NCO flight chiefs	Immediate NCO superiors
How much does he know about his job?	.24	.19	.42
How well does he do his job?	.25	.18	.40

Source: D. K. Whitla and J. E. Tirrell, "The Validity of Ratings of Several Levels of Supervisors," *Personnel Psychology*, Vol. 6 (1953), p. 464.

This is clearly demonstrated in Table 9-1. In this particular study 100 lower-level noncommissioned officers were rated first by their immediate superiors, then by the next higher level of NCO's, and finally by the commissioned officers responsible for their work (32). Thus, each man was rated three times. These ratings were then correlated with scores obtained by the men being appraised on a special written test of job knowledge and proficiency. Ideally the correlations could go as higher as 1.00 (which would indicate a perfect relationship between the ratings and the test scores), the best ratings matching the highest scores and so on down the line, until the lowest rating was obtained by the man with the worst test performance.

This degree of precision was not obtained (it never is in studies of this kind). There was, however, a tendency for the ratings and test scores to correlate (all values in Table 9-1 are well above .00). More important for our purposes is the superiority of the immediate NCO superiors, as revealed by their higher correlation coefficients. These men apparently had picked up information that was also reflected in the test scores but that was not available to those at higher levels. Clearly the immediate superiors, because of a greater amount of acquaintance, were in a better position to make evaluations of their men than were those above them. In any averaging of the three ratings one would want to give their opinions much greater weight.

This raises an additional problem with regard to multiple ratings by superiors. Many companies conduct what they call appraisal sessions, where several of the manager's superiors meet and discuss his work in detail. They then make what amounts to a group rating, which is the particular composite of their individual opinions that they can agree on or that the majority favors. This composite is likely to be heavily weighted with the views of the highest-level individual present, or the highest-level person who clearly states his opinions. Yet, as we have seen, this person may not be in the best position to appraise the manager. As a result the degree of error can be considerable.

To overcome this difficulty it is generally considered desirable to have the evaluations made separately and to record all of them in the personnel office before any group appraisal session is conducted. If a composite rating is then made by the group, it can be checked against the average of the independent ratings to see if it represents a shift in the direction of the highest level person, who unfortunately may not be in a position to keep himself as well informed as he believes.

THE APPRAISAL SUMMARY. In companies that maintain an ongoing appraisal system with periodic evaluations, the typical procedure is for a member of the personnel department to write up the findings in an appraisal summary. This summary may be merely a brief synopsis, but more frequently it takes the form of an extensive and detailed description of the individual. An outline for an appraisal summary of this latter type is presented in Table 9-2.

The data used to write the appraisal summary on a specific individual are derived in large part from his superiors. But, in addition, the typical program utilizes psychological tests, a personal history form to be filled out by the manager himself, and in many cases a personal interview with the manager conducted by a personnel representative.

**Table 9-2. Outline Covering Items Included in a
Typical Appraisal Summary**

---

1. Personal Background
   Age
   Family background
     Marital status
     Children
   Education
     Types of specialization and degrees
     Extracurricular activities and offices
   Military experience
     Period of service
     Rank at start and end
     Nature of chief assignments
     Campaigns and decorations
   Work history
     Employers
     Position titles and duties
   Special accomplishments
     Honors and awards
     Professional or trade organization memberships and offices
     Community and church activities and offices
     Publications
   Special limitations
     Health
     Family problems
   Hobbies and recreational activities
2. Nature of Work
   Generalized statement based on organization planning and job analysis
       data
   Committee assignments
   Number and titles of people supervised
3. Job Performance and Personal Qualifications
   General statement of value to company and probable future contribution
   Technical performance
     Evaluation against expectations in each of the key areas noted in job
         description
     Specific achievements in each of key duties
   Motivation in current position
     Attitude toward superiors, company, and job
     Acceptance of and desire for responsibility
     Personal desire for accomplishment and drive
     Self-reliance in making decisions
     Degree and fairness of competition
     Loyalty to company and general managerial orientation
   Intelligence as manifested on the job
     Selection of realistic goals and methods of goal attainment

Table 9-2 (cont'd.)

Ability to learn new techniques
Resourcefulness in new and trying situations
Quality and speed of thinking
Organizational and planning ability
Judgment
Thoroughness and accuracy
Ability to sell ideas
Flexibility in dealing with ideas of others
Creativity
Emotional stability
Adjustment to frustrations and constraints
Capacity to take calculated risks
Ability to get along with others
Reaction to criticism and pressure
Objectivity and freedom from prejudice
Excessive emotionality
Impairments caused by off the job problems
Leadership skills
Ability to elicit cooperation from subordinates
Ability to criticize and give orders if necessary
Skill as a team worker with other organizational units
Development of subordinates
Delegation and use of controls
Capacity to establish and publicize performance standards
Type of subordinates sought and ability to appraise
Three accomplishments in present job that indicate what he is capable of
Summarizing snapshot covering major strengths and weaknesses
4. Overall Performance Rating
Individual rating relative to what is expected
Ranking among others at same level doing similar work
5. Potentiality
Promotability and expected rate (or timetable) of progress
Actual jobs or job types (job families) qualified for
Long-range potential
6. Recommended Actions
Changes in placement
Ideal duration of current placement
Development needs and plans based on comparison against following list
   of management knowledges and skills
   Knowledge of: Technical information bearing on job
                 Related specialties and jobs
                 Labor relations and labor law
                 Business economics
                 Company and departmental objectives
                 Job evaluation and payment policies
                 Safety

Table 9-2 (cont'd.)

	Employee benefits and privileges

Employee benefits and privileges
Company organizational structure
Legal constraints
Industry practices and competitive picture

Skill in: Delegation to subordinates
Coaching subordinates
Setting performance standards
Establishing controls and follow-up
Long-range planning
Decision making
Selling ideas
Negotiation
Evaluation of individuals and groups
Taking disciplinary action
Maintaining morale
Communications
Analyzing accounting reports and other data
Cost control
Discussion leadership
Report and letter writing
Public speaking
Interviewing and meeting people
Developing budgets
Reading (speed and comprehension)

The summary itself is characteristically considered confidential and is made available only to the manager's direct-line superiors and to appropriate personnel managers.

When all these appraisal summaries have been completed in a given company unit, it is common practice to prepare a management personnel inventory indicating future replacement needs and listing the candidates who may qualify for anticipated vacancies, immediately or after further development. Anticipated needs for at least five years are usually considered, based on performance, expected promotions, retirement schedules, health, and projected organizational changes.

Replacement candidates are obtained not only from the specific unit but from other segments of the company as well. It is entirely possible that an individual may appear as a candidate on inventory lists for several units, depending on the breadth of his training and experience. The lists are maintained on a continuing basis and are reviewed and updated frequently. On occasion the management inventory is developed in chart form along the lines of Figure 9-1.

Figure 9-1. Management Inventory Chart

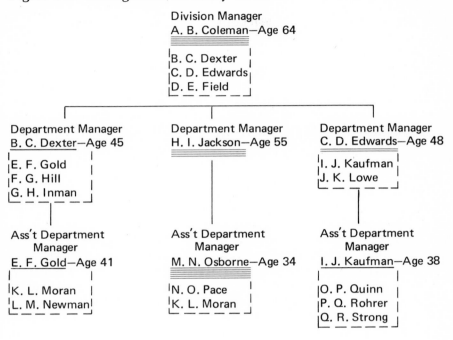

Code for Underlining of Incumbents

———————— Outstanding potential. Ready for job above. High promise for unit head.

════════ Good potential. Fair promise for unit head.

════════ Potential for some growth. Not likely to make unit head.

════════ Not likely to advance beyond present position.

════════ Age or health make replacement necessary within 5 years.

════════ Unsatisfactory performance. Replacement needed.

Appraisal by Peers or Subordinates

During World War II a technique known as *buddy rating* was developed by Navy psychologists. This procedure requires that each member of a group rate all other members on certain aspects of their work performance. The ratings on each individual are then averaged to provide an index of the man's competence.

In the years since these initial applications much has been written about the advantages of this technique, especially as an aid in the evaluation of managers. Either all managers at a comparable level in a given unit, perhaps all first-line foremen in a small manufacturing plant, rate each other, or as a variant each manager is rated by his subordinates. In this way it is possible to obtain evaluations from those who are likely to be well acquainted with the man being appraised, to have observed his work closely over a long period, and thus to be capable of making extremely accurate ratings.

Despite these apparent advantages, however, buddy-rating procedures have not achieved widespread acceptance in the business world. There are a number of reasons for this. For one thing, men at the same level in the managerial hierarchy are apt to be either friends or rivals. In the former instance the ratings may be elevated inappropriately; in the latter, they may be depressed. Also, where there is mutual rating, there is always the possibility of a deal, such that both parties agree to do well by each other.

Other problems arise where subordinates are asked to evaluate their superiors. There is, for one thing, the anticipation of reprisal, whether justified or not. As a result only the reckless or those who are on the verge of quitting may be willing to express a negative opinion. Furthermore, subordinates are likely to have personal objectives that differ from corporate objectives and that may exert an undue influence on the ratings. This is a problem in any rating system, but its impact tends to be increased when evaluations are made by people far removed from the policy-making level in the organization. Subordinates may well view a superior in terms of the degree to which he has served to satisfy or frustrate their own personal motives, rather than in terms of his contribution to company goals.

Table 9-3. Correlations Obtained when Candidates for Promotion are Rated by Co-Workers and Superiors ($N = 100$)

	Ratings compared	
Item rated	Co-workers and superiors	Pairs of superiors
Job knowledge	.15	.63
Cooperation	.29	.67
Job performance—quality	.25	.61
Job performance—quantity	.33	.66
General fitness for promotion	.39	.71

Source: D. Springer, "Ratings of Candidates for Promotion by Co-Workers and Supervisors," *Journal of Applied Psychology,* Vol. 37 (1953), pp. 348–349.

Certainly, as Table 9-3 indicates, the ratings made by peers or subordinates do tend to differ considerably from those made by superiors. In this particular study 100 candidates for promotion at North American Aviation were evaluated by their co-workers and also by both their foreman and assistant foreman (27). Although the two levels of supervision agreed reasonably well, as indicated by correlations in the .60's, the co-workers apparently were taking somewhat different factors into account: The correlations between co-worker and superior ratings on the same men are considerably lower. In addition, the co-workers gave more favorable ratings. These findings are consistent with the view that co-workers may be influenced to some degree by personal considerations, whereas superiors tend to hold to a managerial orientation.

Appraisal Systems Involving Personnel Managers and Psychologists

One variant on the standard methods of evaluation by superiors involves much more active participation on the part of the personnel department. In this approach the appraisal data are collected orally rather than through the use of written forms (9). Normally a personnel representative will go to the office of the man's superior with a specific list of questions. Answers to these questions are obtained in conversation and recorded in note form. The notes are then converted to a written description after the personnel man returns to his own office. A draft of this written description is reviewed by the superior and then it is put in final form.

The advantages of this approach are inherent in the fact that an oral procedure is more likely to elicit specific information regarding the man being appraised. Superiors will say things about a person in a free discussion of this kind that they will not put in writing. In addition, the fact that a personnel representative will actually spend an hour or more conducting the interview conveys the impression that the appraisal process is considered quite important. Thus, the kind of superficial, hurried response that written rating forms sometimes produce is much less common. The man being interviewed tends to feel that if the personnel people are willing to go to this much trouble to obtain his opinions he should at least try to provide as considered a judgment as possible.

Finally, this technique has the advantage that the personnel representative can maintain similar standards of evaluation across a large number of interviews. He can establish what amounts to a set of ground rules, which are held constant for all managers appraised. He can introduce the conditions necessary for true comparability among ratings. This control over the general level of ratings and of the factors to be considered is much more difficult to exercise when written forms are used or when appraisal sessions are conducted by differing groups of managers each constituted to judge a particular individual.

In the latter instance it has become common practice to have a management-appraisal specialist from the personnel department sit in

on the group meetings for just this reason. Usually this person writes
the appraisal summary also. Such an individual can establish common
standards for the ratings within a department or division or across
the company as a whole. If he feels a particular group of superiors is
being excessively lenient, or harsh, as compared with other such groups,
he can take steps to correct this variation in standards, either by inducing the group to change its views or by introducing compensating
statements into the final appraisal summary.

PSYCHOLOGICAL APPRAISAL. A markedly different type of appraisal
is typically carried out by industrial psychologists who have had some
training in the techniques of personality assessment. These appraisals
usually involve extensive interviewing coupled with individual psychological testing (2,8,17). They are often employed in conjunction
with other evaluation procedures. But even if this is not the case, efforts are made to integrate the test and interview data with information available from personnel files and other sources. The psychologist
attempts to get as clear an understanding as he can of the underlying
intellectual, emotional, and motivational characteristics of the man, and
then converts this into a picture of how such a person might be expected to behave. The resulting psychological description, as the example of Table 9-4 indicates, is not so much a summary of actual
behavior as a prediction of anticipated behavior under certain specified circumstances.

**Table 9-4. Example of a Psychological Description
on a Candidate for Promotion**

Albert W. Woodworth, sales training representative

Mr. Woodworth appears to be the outstanding man among the four candidates for District Marketing Manager evaluated. The evidence suggests that
Mr. Woodworth would not only make a major contribution in the position
for which he is currently being considered, but that he also has the potential to perform very effectively at higher levels in the company. The following strengths are apparent:

1. Mr. Woodworth's general verbal intelligence level is very high. He
   has a Wechsler Verbal IQ of 136. This is the top score obtained among
   the 31 members of marketing management who have been evaluated
   to date. This showing is particularly surprising in view of the fact
   that Mr. Woodworth has no formal college education. Reasoning and
   problem-solving ability are also at a high level, as indicated by the
   results of the Terman Concept Mastery Test. Apparently Mr. Woodworth has not only accumulated a great deal of knowledge: He is
   capable of bringing his intellectual abilities to bear in the solution of
   complex problems.

Table 9-4 (cont'd.)

2. Mr. Woodworth is very strong on problem solving in the numerical area, being particularly adept in quickly grasping a problem and coming up with a solution. He should be outstanding in drawing references from an analysis of sales figures and in the accounting aspects of his work.

3. Mr. Woodworth's mechanical ability is at a very high level. In fact, his ability in this area is actually quite outstanding.

4. Mr. Woodworth has very wide interests and keeps himself informed in a great variety of fields. This breadth of interest plus his capacity for very rapid learning should permit Mr. Woodworth to adapt readily to new situations. It is unlikely that he will require a very long training period if promoted.

5. From the Picture Arrangement Test it is apparent that Mr. Woodworth has very strong work motivation. He can be counted on to push himself hard. He has the capacity to get things done and will keep at a problem until he has it licked. He appears to be happiest when he is working hard and effectively.

6. Mr. Woodworth is a rather independent person. He is unlikely to lean on others and is quite capable of reaching his own decisions. He would much prefer to figure out problems himself and do things his own way. Although he will on occasion follow the advice of others, he tends to distrust it. However, he can be counted on to follow directions and company policy meticulously when this is necessary. There is little question but that Mr. Woodworth will do his best work when given a free hand.

7. It is evident from the Thematic Apperception Test stories that Mr. Woodworth is an extremely competent planner and organizer. He will take risks but prefers to do so only after he has made a careful analysis of the alternatives. He has his own ideas about how things should be done and these ideas are likely to be both original and practical.

Although these strengths taken as a whole seem to argue very strongly for Mr. Woodworth's selection as District Marketing Manager, there are two problems which should be mentioned:

1. At the present time Mr. Woodworth is somewhat uncertain about his own ability. Although he seems to enjoy management responsibilities and likes to participate in the solution of complex marketing problems, he has no clear conception of his own capacities and tends to underestimate them. He realizes that he has never held a job that has really challenged him, but, on the other hand, perhaps because of this lack of challenge, he has no idea of the level at which he might be able to function. It seems probable that Mr. Woodworth is the type of person who will perform more effectively the higher he rises in the organization. He needs to find out how good he really is, and only by facing greater challenges is he likely to gain confidence in his own

Table 9-4 (cont'd.)

---

ability. He needs to prove himself to himself and only after he has done this is he likely to realize his full potential. This entire problem came out quite clearly during the course of the interview.

2. Mr. Woodworth tends to be rather impatient with mediocrity. He holds himself to very high standards and expects others to perform at the same high level. He may find it hard to delegate to people whom he feels are not as competent as he would wish. As a result he may try to do too much himself and thereby fail to develop his subordinates to the full. He is also unlikely to establish warm relationships with his men, tending to remain somewhat at a distance from people. Mr. Woodworth is well aware of these problems but appears to be incapable of solving them at the present time. As Mr. Woodworth becomes more confident of his own abilities, he may well feel freer to let subordinates learn through an occasional failure and become capable of greater freedom in his own emotional relationships. This problem, like the other, should largely solve itself if Mr. Woodworth rises to higher levels of management responsibility. Nevertheless, it should be recognized that Mr. Woodworth will probably never be as effective in his handling of people as he is in problem-solving and organizing efforts.

Evaluations of this kind are particularly helpful when decisions must be made regarding promotion or transfer, because they provide information regarding how the man might be expected to act in the new position relative to revised role prescriptions. However, psychological procedures are also used by many companies in connection with a regular, periodic appraisal program. Although some companies do maintain an internal staff of industrial psychologists to conduct assessments of this type, a large proportion of the work is done by outside consultants. Because the actual techniques and procedures used are in many respects comparable to those of performance control, any further discussion will be delayed until we take up the latter approach in Chapter 18.

Self Appraisal

In some companies it has become standard practice for the superior to conduct an appraisal interview with his subordinate manager after the appraisal summary has been prepared. This interview represents an attempt to induce the man to overcome his deficiencies and improve his performance. Thus, the feedback of appraisal results in this manner has as its primary objective the *development* of a more effective manager.

Unfortunately the accumulated evidence indicates increasingly that these interviews often do not achieve their purpose. As development tools they are not very effective. Furthermore, the introduction of a feedback requirement tends to have some unanticipated effects on the ratings that may vitiate them for other purposes.

Intensive studies of appraisal interviews conducted at General Electric indicate that any criticism by a superior is usually rejected as incorrect (12,20). Defensiveness was the characteristic attitude among the subordinates and indications of a desire to actually improve performance occurred less than once per interview. Yet without the development of carefully stated goals for improvement, criticism was unlikely to produce an increase in effectiveness. Clearly, feedback procedures may well yield a considerable loss insofar as the organizational maintenance goal is concerned and very little if any improvement in productivity.

In addition, the experience of many companies has been that it is very difficult to get managers to conduct appraisal interviews with their subordinates. Because the situation is perceived as an unpleasant one, managers avoid it, and the interviews are held only after considerable pressure and dissension. Many are never held in any real sense at all.

Another response to the anticipated unpleasantness of feeding back negative evaluations is a distortion of the ratings. In one study the average rating on 485 supervisors moved from a score of 60, under normal nonfeedback conditions, to 84 when a rerating to be combined with appraisal interviews was obtained two weeks later (28). One way of making the ratings easier to report to others is to make them more favorable. Obviously, evaluations that are to be used for development purposes in an appraisal interview should not be used for other purposes such as pay or promotion.

Because of these deficiencies in the feedback approach, several writers have suggested that the development goal can be better served if managers appraise themselves (15,16). Although the various advocates differ somewhat on the specifics, the usual approach is for the man to sit down with his immediate superior and establish a series of targets or objectives for the next six months or for some other appropriate time period. Then, at the end of the specified interval the two have a second discussion during which the man evaluates his performance relative to his objectives, attempts to solve any problems that he now recognizes, and sets new objectives for the next period. Throughout this process the superior assumes the role of a listener, and on occasion a guide, but never that of a critic. Because there is no external criticism, there is no defensiveness. To the extent the man criticizes himself, the basis for a change in his behavior has presumably been established. Recent research raises some question as to whether goal setting of this kind does contribute either to increased job understanding or increased managerial effectiveness (18).

It should be emphasized that self-appraisal cannot be a substitute for other approaches, except possibly insofar as the self-development goal is concerned. If appraisal data are desired for other purposes, they should not be obtained from the man himself. The evidence on this is quite strong.

Table 9-5. Mean Ratings Given by Immediate Superiors and by Self ($N = 117$)

Scale	Superior rating	Self-rating
Ability to work with others	8.9	10.7
Amount of work done	9.4	10.5
Quality of work done	9.5	10.4
Leadership potential	5.9	8.9
Ability to do complicated jobs	8.5	10.4
Ability to work with minimum supervision	9.2	11.6
Conscientiousness	8.9	10.4
Overall performance	9.8	10.5
Average of 8 scales	8.8	10.4

Source: J. W. Parker, E. K. Taylor, R. S. Barrett, and L. Martens, "Rating Scale Content: III. Relationships Between Supervisory and Self-Ratings," *Personnel Psychology,* Vol. 12 (1959), p. 51.

For one thing, self-appraisals tend to be considerably more favorable than ratings by superiors, as Table 9-5 indicates. In this particular study the men rated themselves on the various characteristics and at the same time similar ratings were obtained from their superiors (22). In no instance were the superiors' ratings lower; on leadership potential and the ability to work with minimum supervision the differences are sizable. Other studies in which self-ratings and supervisory ratings were correlated indicate that the two measure quite different things. In one instance ratings by the two levels of supervision immediately above the men correlated .60 on 96 individuals. The self-ratings yielded values of only .25 and .13 when correlated with the two superior ratings (23). Clearly these individuals were not evaluating themselves in terms of the same type of standards their superiors employed with considerable consistency.

Objective Measures of Productivity and Profit

Although subjective rating procedures are probably the most widely used in evaluating managers, at least in connection with formal appraisal programs, a variety of hard or objective indexes may also be employed. These characteristically are based on the behavior of the unit under the manager being appraised. If productivity and contribution to profit of a unit is high, then the manager is considered effective. If the average level of stress originating within a unit is low and the capacity to reduce external stresses high, the manager is also evaluated favorably.

At the present time, various productivity and profit indexes are more frequently obtained than are measures of organizational maintenance. This is particularly true at the higher levels of management. There seems to be a tendency to assume that maintenance considerations are primarily a matter of concern for lower-level supervisors and that profitability should weigh more heavily in the role prescriptions of managers toward the top of the hierarchy. This situation may well change in the future, but currently it does appear to be a fact of business life.

Productivity Measures

Largely because of the central interests of the industrial engineers who have made major contributions in this area, objective indexes of manufacturing output are available in the greatest number. Some of these measures of group productivity that can be used to evaluate the effectiveness of a manager are the following:

> Units produced
> Number of rejects
> Training time to reach standard production
> Meeting of production schedules
> Machine down time
> Scrappage

Many of these indexes when computed on an individual basis and attributed to a single worker are more relevant to the considerations of the next chapter than to management appraisal. Only when such individual measures are combined to provide a group statistic can they be used to evaluate the competence of supervision.

The same holds for the evaluation of managers in areas of work other than the direct production of a product. Thus, the total sales figures, or gains and losses over a prior period, for a group of salesmen can be used to evaluate sales managers and so, too, can the number of customer complaints. Research and development managers may be appraised using variables such as the number of patents resulting from the efforts of their subordinates or the number of assigned projects that move to actual completion. Office managers may be considered in terms of subordinate activities such as words typed, filing errors, and IBM cards punched.

The important thing is that these indexes must be relevant to the role prescriptions for the specific position and that measures of some kind must be developed for all important role prescriptions. It is unfortunately easier to establish objective, numerical measures in some areas than others. The result is that these areas may receive undue emphasis, purely because of their measurability, whereas other factors included in the job description are entirely neglected in the appraisal. If this happens, a manager can easily learn to direct his efforts toward those requirements of his job that can form a basis for evaluation. The consequence may be a major imbalance in the distribution of work, especially if a number of managerial jobs have similar role prescriptions and are evaluated in the same manner. This is why it is crucial that appraisal systems be developed by working back from a knowledge of the total job and its requirements, rather than by utilizing a few easily obtained measures that appear to have some relevance. It is also absolutely essential that the factors selected be subject to the influence and control of the manager.

Some companies have gone to considerable lengths to establish comprehensive evaluation systems of this kind for managerial jobs, introducing very specific criteria to indicate what are to be considered acceptable levels of performance. Thus, one may find such standards as the following:

Warehouse turnover is greater than 200 per cent per year.

Frequency of vehicle accidents is less than .35 per hundred thousand miles.

Operating overtime hours are less than 2.5 per cent of scheduled hours worked.

Training sessions are held once each month.

Accounting Measures

In recent years some major developments in the field of accounting, especially cost accounting, have made it increasingly feasible to evaluate managers in terms of their contributions to profits. It has long been common practice to establish budgets for various groups and to consider managers who unnecessarily exceed these budgetary allocations as unsatisfactory in this particular regard. Similarly, many companies have evaluated wastage, equipment maintenance, and labor, in terms of the costs involved.

Much more sophisticated procedures are being introduced now in an effort to deal with the entire gamut of factors influencing profitability in a single comprehensive analysis. Thus, cost centers may be established to coincide with the divisional boundaries of a company that has decentralized along product lines (6). The division is then treated as a separate firm and the manager is evaluated in terms of share of the market, net sales, profit as per cent of sales or invested capital, and the like. If in such cases the divisional unit utilizes services, materials, or components from other segments of the company outside the manager's jurisdiction, transfer prices are negotiated in terms of market value.

Increasingly these procedures are being moved down through the managerial hierarchy so that the contributions to profit achieved by lower-level managers, especially those within the line organization, can be determined. Standard costs are established for labor, materials, and overhead on the basis of prior experience and judgment. Cost variances are then computed by comparing actual figures with these standards (1,4), and managers are evaluated in accordance with the direction and amount of these variances. The technique requires a detailed organization plan with clear-cut designation of areas of responsibility. Also, there is a very considerable element of subjectivity inherent in setting the standard costs. Yet variance analysis of this kind does appear to provide an extremely valuable tool in appraising managers.

Objective Indexes in the Maintenance Area

As with productivity, organizational maintenance measures taken within the group or unit that is a particular manager's responsibility may also be used for purposes of appraisal. This assumes that a major factor contributing to any lack of job satisfaction, or sense of attachment to the work organization, can be the behavior of the manager in charge. If the various indexes suggest that a certain manager has a highly dissatisfied group, the undesirable situation can be attributed to him and an unfavorable evaluation result.

Unfortunately the use of this type of information in evaluating individual managers has not been developed to the level of sophistication achieved in the productivity and profit areas. Although studies such as those conducted by the University of Michigan and the Ohio State University researchers do emphasize the importance of supervisory consideration and kindness, other evidence is consistent in indicating that a number of additional factors may also operate to influence the level of satisfaction (31). Immediate supervision is not the only factor that must be considered.

Clearly policies and decisions made at a variety of managerial levels can have an impact. Yet very few companies have worked out their role prescriptions and allocations of responsibility among the various levels of management with the same precision in the organizational maintenance area that they have achieved when dealing with productivity and profits. There appears to be a tendency at the present time to exaggerate the role of immediate supervision, when higher-level management may actually be exerting greater influence. Therefore the various maintenance indexes should be used with caution when appraising individual managers. It is important to know who or what actually is responsible for the existing state of affairs. Yet some measures of this kind are essential because of their relationship to an important company goal.

Measures of Withdrawal from the Job

There are a number of indexes that seem to reflect the tendency of people to avoid or escape from that which they experience as unpleasant. In units where dissatisfaction is marked and there is little sense of belongingness or cohesion pulling them to the group, employees may be expected to seek out various ways of leaving the specific work situation, either temporarily or permanently.

SEPARATIONS AND TURNOVER. Research indicates that employees who experience a sense of deprivation on the job insofar as important motives are concerned are particularly likely to leave the firm (24). Turnover has been demonstrated to bear a close relationship to the level of satisfaction at work and to the degree to which work interferes with other satisfactions. Whether or not, however, the sources of frustration involved are under the control of any particular manager must be ascertained separately in each individual case.

A variety of different procedures are used to compute turnover. For purposes of evaluating managers, it is generally desirable to eliminate involuntary separations such as those caused by death, illness, and mandatory retirement from the statistics, because these causes are not normally subject to managerial influence. Often a ratio such as the following is computed for each unit:

$$\text{Turnover} = \frac{\text{Number of separations}}{\text{Midmonth employment}} \times 100$$

It is important in evaluating statistics of this kind to utilize data collected over a period of time to eliminate the effects of seasonal and other temporary fluctuations. Only when a manager has consistently high turnover figures month after month should the possibility that he is ineffective be actively considered. Also, it is important to hold the general type of occupation and certain employee characteristics relatively constant in evaluating these figures. Turnover among young female clerical employees, for instance, is almost invariably high due to marriage, family moves, returning to school, pregnancy, and other factors that are less likely to operate in other groups.

ABSENTEEISM. Although it is by no means universal practice to keep absence statistics for the various individual work units, these data can be of considerable value in appraising managers. One way of avoiding an unpleasant work environment is to stay away from the job as much as possible. There are a variety of types of excused absences—sick leaves, military leaves, and the like—that normally do not reflect a desire to withdraw from a disturbing situation. Nevertheless, much that passes for sickness is probably not, and many illnesses are emotionally caused. It does seem appropriate to consider a manager unsatisfactory in the maintenance area if his group has a continuing, disproportionately high absenteeism rate.

As with turnover, a variety of formulas are used to indicate absence rates. A common approach is the following:

$$\text{Absenteeism} = \frac{\begin{array}{c}\text{Number of man-days lost through}\\ \text{job absence during period}\end{array}}{\begin{array}{c}\text{Average number of employees} \times\\ \text{number of work days}\end{array}} \times 100$$

Some firms keep records covering not only the number of days lost, but the number of times also. Usually older work groups will have a higher number of days lost from work than those containing largely younger employees, but the actual frequency of separate incidents of absenteeism may not be as great.

Closely related is the use of tardiness statistics, which may well reflect a similar withdrawal tendency and which are easily obtained for any group that punches time cards. However, measures of lateness are probably much less frequently maintained on a regular basis than absenteeism data. Certainly they are less commonly used to evaluate managers.

INJURIES AND DISPENSARY VISITS. Although the use of accident statistics as indexes of managerial competence is probably more appropriately explained in terms of the direct relationship to profits and out of humane considerations, it is nevertheless true that people who are more upset and disturbed at work are particularly susceptible to injury. Thus, maintenance considerations can be involved. In the case of dispensary visits the relationship is still clearer. A common method of escaping an unpleasant work environment is to seek medical attention. At the most one might be sent home; at the least one will be away from the work place for a period.

In many cases injuries that involve lost time are recorded separately from those that do not require that the man be sent home. Both lost time and minor injuries are expressed as a frequency per man-hours worked in the unit. Although statistics on dispensary visits are only rarely maintained as a basis for evaluating managers, there is reason to believe that a count of the number of initial visits for a new complaint within some specified time span can be an effective method of identifying a widespread desire to avoid a particular work situation (19).

Measures of Resistance Against Management

Another way in which internal stress may manifest itself within a work unit is through direct resistance and conflict. Group members who are dissatisfied may not avoid the situation that disturbs them; rather they may attack the management that they see as causing their difficulties. Such resistance may be covert or overt. In any event the manager who heads up a unit where signs of resistance are numerous can find himself judged less competent; whether this is justified or not must depend on the degree of influence he has over the situation.

DISCIPLINARY ACTIONS. One way in which dissatisfaction may appear is through overt flouting of work rules and intentional deviation from role prescriptions. Such behavior characteristically results in either a warning, suspension, or discharge, after a formal disciplinary hearing. When such formal disciplinary actions occur frequently within a given unit, it may well be that the manager has provoked considerable resentment by his actions. Among the behaviors that may elicit formal action of this kind by the company are:

> Unauthorized absence
> Insubordination or impertinence
> Loafing or sleeping
> Misrepresentation such as tampering with time
>   cards or records
> Smoking when forbidden
> Drinking or carrying liquor
> Dishonesty or stealing
> Fighting on the job
> Gambling
> Willful breach of safety rules
> Repeated lateness
> Leaving the job without permission
> Immoral conduct

GRIEVANCES. Another commonly used index is the number of grievances filed by employees within a given time period. Although complaints of any kind can theoretically be used, the usual procedure is to count the number of separate, formal grievances filed in writing under the terms of the union contract.

By filing a grievance, an employee is taking on action that he is well aware management does not wish him to take. Furthermore, in most cases the grievance statement is directly critical of some managerial behavior. The union may make this particular outlet for dissatisfaction readily available and may even ask the employee to take the action. Yet it is doubtful that many grievances occur in the complete absence of some measure of discontent. Thus, a manager with a high grievance rate can be presumed to have a group that represents some threat to the integrity of the firm.

OTHER INDICATIONS OF RESISTANCE. There are several other possible measures that may or may not be appropriate, depending on the company and situation. Among these are the number of man-hours lost from work due to work stoppages, strikes, slowdowns, and the like—or the total number of separate incidents of this kind. The manager who experiences a high incidence of such occurrences is not likely to be fulfilling the requirements of his job, whether or not the resistance behavior is union-inspired—provided that he is in a position to exert some influence over such events.

Actually any failure to behave in ways that management is widely known to desire, if it is prevalent enough in a group, may yield evidence regarding the extent of dissatisfaction. Thus, a consistent refusal to join the company retirement system or to participate in group insurance plans might be used as an index in evaluating managers. So, too, may the extent of participation in suggestion systems and in company-sponsored recreational programs. Obviously the more relatively independent indexes that are developed, the more certain one can be in describing a particular manager as successful or unsuccessful in his efforts to foster organizational maintenance.

Attitude or Morale Surveys

A final procedure for evaluating managers is the attitude survey. In general the results of these surveys tend to be closely related to other measures, such as turnover and absenteeism, discussed previously in this section, although they do not necessarily yield a high correlation with measures of productivity and profits (5).

When used to evaluate managers, or to predict labor relations problems, attitude surveys are normally handled on a group basis. That is to say, it is not so much the feelings of a particular individual that are of concern, but the overall level of morale in a given unit. For this reason the surveys are usually conducted on an anonymous basis, and on occasion only a sample of the employees in a group is measured. In the latter instance it is important that the sample be truly representative. The usual procedure is to select the sample at random so that each individual in the unit has an equal chance of showing up in the survey group.

Although a detailed discussion of attitude measurement techniques must await the next chapter, several points should be made here. For one thing, surveys of this kind normally contain questions dealing with working conditions, supervisory behavior, attitude toward the job itself, loyalty to the company as a whole, company policies, and other considerations. If the questionnaire is this broad in scope, it is inappropriate to use the total result to evaluate immediate supervision. The various sections of the survey form must be sorted out in terms of the particular level of management with the appropriate responsibility. One cannot expect a manager whose role prescriptions do not call for action in a given area to exert influence over attitudes in that area.

Second, a decision as to whether a particular unit is satisfied or dissatisfied should be based on information that can be presumed to be valid and that is characteristic of the group as a whole. To do otherwise can only produce a biased evaluation of the unit's management. Thus, there must be reason to believe that the people surveyed have in fact given evidence of their true feelings, a topic that we shall cover in greater detail later. And the survey should include all, or nearly all, members of the unit. If a sample is used, the respondents should not be permitted to select themselves. Replies obtained from the 30 or 40 per cent who may take the trouble to return a mailed questionnaire can well reflect only the attitudes of those who are relatively satisfied. It is essential to obtain evidence regarding the attitudes of those who did not reply originally, in such instances, and correct the results accordingly. This is a difficult and time-consuming process, but only after it has been done can a manager be appraised correctly through the use of attitude survey findings.

Career Appraisal

Although management appraisal is normally concerned with determining how well a man is doing on his present job relative to a given set of role prescriptions, there are instances where a measure of overall career success to date is desired. This is a particularly important consideration when evaluation data are being used to provide a criterion for use in developing selection procedures. Usually it is more desirable to select management trainees who will achieve continuing success in a variety of positions, rather than those who will do an outstanding job as trainees or perhaps in their first subsequent assignment.

Perhaps the most frequently used career index is the managerial level attained. Most firms maintain a system of salary grades, with each job from assistant foreman to president assigned to some point on the scale. The particular grade for the position held by an individual then becomes a measure of his success.

Because these grade levels may be closely related to age or seniority and because they are strongly influenced by the level at which a man started with the company, it is more desirable to employ some index of grade progression than the absolute level. Thus, one can use a promotion rate measure such as the following:

$$\text{Success} = \frac{\text{Present grade—starting grade}}{\text{Total years of employment}}$$

In recent years there has been considerable interest in the use of salary data as a basis for evaluation (10,11). Certainly such a measure is consistent with popular sentiment. It appears to offer a number of advantages when employed within a single company that awards salary increases on grounds of merit and that maintains a stable salary scale utilizing comparable standards for all managers. Usually when salary is employed as a success index, some correction for age or tenure is introduced to produce a change rate rather than an absolute amount. On occasion more complex statistical procedures are developed to provide data on the degree to which each man's salary deviates from the figure to be expected for people of his age and experience.

Rating procedures may also be used to evaluate career success as well as success on the current job. The most commonly used technique is some kind of promotability index of the type noted in Figure 9-1. When a man is said to have outstanding potential for advancement, a major determinant of this evaluation is likely to be a pattern of consistent accomplishment in prior positions. Thus, predictions of future progress are in large part predicated on past successes. Of course, potential ratings are conditioned to some degree by age, and thus should not be used to evaluate career success among individuals over 50. A man of 55 may have little prospect of progressing further in his remaining ten years with the company and yet have had a very outstanding career.

References

1. Axelson, K. S., *Responsibility Reporting*. New York: Peat, Marwick, Mitchell, 1961.
2. Balinsky, B., "Some Experiences and Problems in Appraising Executive Personnel," *Personnel Psychology*, Vol. 17 (1964), 107–114.
3. Bayroff, A. G., H. R. Haggerty, and E. A. Rundquist, "Validity of Ratings

as Related to Rating Techniques and Conditions," *Personnel Psychology*, Vol. 7 (1954), 93–113.

4. Bierman, H., *Financial and Managerial Accounting*. New York: Macmillan, 1963.

5. Brayfield, A. H., and W. H. Crockett, "Employee Attitudes and Employee Performance," *Psychological Bulletin*, Vol. 52 (1955), 396–424.

6. Dean, J., "Profit Performance Measurement of Division Managers," *The Controller*, Vol. 25 (1957), 423–426, 449.

7. Fiedler, F. E., *A Theory of Leadership Effectiveness*. New York: McGraw-Hill, 1967.

8. Glaser, E. M., "Psychological Consultation with Executives: A Clinical Approach," *American Psychologist*, Vol. 13 (1958), 486–489.

9. Habbe, S., "Merit Rating—Plus," *Management Record*, Vol. 15 (1953), 323–324.

10. Hilton, T. L., and W. R. Dill, "Salary Growth as a Criterion of Career Progress," *Journal of Applied Psychology*, Vol. 46 (1962), 153–158.

11. Hulin, C. L., "The Measurement of Executive Success," *Journal of Applied Psychology*, Vol. 46 (1962), 303–306.

12. Kay, E., H. Meyer, and J. R. P. French, "The Effects of Appraisal Interviews Upon Attitudes and Performance: An Experimental Study in General Electric," in A. F. Zander (ed.), *Performance Appraisals—Effects on Employees and their Performance*. Ann Arbor, Mich.: The Foundation for Research on Human Behavior, 1963.

13. Likert, R., *New Patterns of Management*. New York: McGraw-Hill, 1961.

14. Likert, R., *The Human Organization: Its Management and Value*. New York: McGraw-Hill, 1967.

15. Maier, N. R. F., *The Appraisal Interview*. New York: Wiley, 1958.

16. McGregor, D., "An Uneasy Look at Performance Appraisal," *Harvard Business Review*, Vol. 35, No. 3 (1957), 89–94.

17. Megargee, E. I., *Research in Clinical Assessment*. New York: Harper & Row, 1966.

18. Mendleson, J. L., *Manager Goal Setting: An Exploration into Its Meaning and Measurement*, DBA Thesis. East Lansing, Mich.: Michigan State Univ., 1967.

19. Merrihue, W. V., and R. A. Katzell, "ERI-Yardstick of Employee Relations," *Harvard Business Review*, Vol. 33, No. 6 (1955), 91–99.

20. Meyer, H. H., E. Kay, and J. R. P. French, "Split Roles in Performance Appraisal," *Harvard Business Review*, Vol. 43, No. 1 (1965), 123–129.

21. Miner, J. B., *The School Administrator and Organizational Character*. Eugene, Oregon: Univ. of Oregon Press, 1967.

22. Parker J. W., E. K. Taylor, R. S. Barrett, and L. Martens, "Rating Scale Content: III. Relationships Between Supervisory- and Self-Ratings," *Personnel Psychology*, Vol. 12 (1959), 49–63.

23. Prien, E. P., and R. E. Liske, "Assessments of Higher-Level Personnel: III. Rating Criteria: A Comparative Analysis of Supervisor Ratings and Incumbent Self-ratings of Job Performance," *Personnel Psychology*, Vol. 15 (1962), 187–194.

24. Ross, I. C., and A. F. Zander, "Need Satisfactions and Employee Turn-over," *Personnel Psychology,* Vol. 10 (1957), 327–338.
25. Seashore, S. E., B. P. Indik, and B. S. Georgopoulos, "Relationships among Criteria of Job Performance," *Journal of Applied Psychology,* Vol. 44 (1960), 195–202.
26. Shartle, C. L., *Executive Performance and Leadership.* Englewood Cliffs, N.J.: Prentice-Hall, 1956.
27. Springer, D., "Ratings of Candidates for Promotion by Co-workers and Supervisors," *Journal of Applied Psychology,* Vol. 37 (1953), 347–351.
28. Stockford, L., and H. W. Bissell, "Factors Involved in Establishing a Merit-Rating Scale," *Personnel,* Vol. 26 (1949), 94–116.
29. Stogdill, R. M., and A. E. Coons, *Leader Behavior: Its Description and Measurement.* Columbus: Bureau of Business Research, Ohio State Univ., 1957.
30. Tannenbaum, A. S., *Social Psychology of the Work Organization.* Belmont, Calif.: Wadsworth, 1966.
31. Vroom, V. H., *Work and Motivation.* New York: Wiley, 1964.
32. Whitla, D. K., and J. E. Tirrell, "The Validity of Ratings of Several Levels of Supervisors," *Personnel Psychology,* Vol. 6 (1953), 461–466.

Questions

1. What are the findings of the Michigan and Ohio State studies regarding effective managerial behavior? How do the two sets of findings relate to each other and to our conception of organizational goals?
2. Suppose that you were asked to design a management appraisal system for a company based primarily on judgmental procedures. What would your recommendations be? Cover the various aspects in detail. Why do you prefer these specific approaches over other available alternatives?
3. In what ways does psychological appraisal differ from the other techniques? What are some of the problems that may arise if this type of approach to management appraisal is introduced in a company? When would it seem particularly desirable to use an outside consultant for this purpose?
4. Formulas have been presented to measure turnover and absenteeism in a group. Can you think of any variants of these formulas, perhaps including additional variables, that might prove useful?
5. What kinds of behaviors among work group members are likely to reflect problems in the organizational maintenance area? Note as many as you can think of.

10

Employee Evaluation:
Rating Systems and
Attitude Surveys

Because the preceding chapter devoted considerable space to the so-called hard or objective measures of productivity and maintenance, there is little need to recapitulate here what has been said already. It is important to remember, however, that in evaluating managers, at least insofar as their supervisory skills are concerned, we were interested primarily in average or total measures for the subordinate group as a whole. Now, as we move to nonmanagerial employees, we are concerned with the number of units produced or the number of absences or the number of disciplinary actions for each individual.

Although the preceding discussion covered the hard measures in some detail, it did not deal with the specifics of rating scale construction and the techniques of judgmental evaluation. These will be of primary concern in this chapter. One of the tasks that nearly every personnel manager must perform at one time or another is to construct a new rating form, or to revise an old one that is not working properly. At first glance this may seem to be a relatively simple task, but there are a number of pitfalls. It is extremely helpful to have some familiarity with the relevant research and with the experience of others.

A second emphasis of this chapter will be in the area of attitude measurement. One method of evaluating the attitudes of employees, usually relative to the organizational maintenance goal, is to obtain ratings from superiors and others who are in a good position to observe job behavior. Another approach involves the actual measurement of employee attitudes on the assumption that these attitudes determine employee behavior. The techniques of conducting surveys of this kind were touched on briefly in Chapter 9. They will be considered in much greater detail here.

Finally, a section will be devoted to the various obstacles and resistances that may obstruct the effective utilization of these techniques. For various reasons the systematic evaluation of employee behavior relative to role prescriptions may face a number of difficulties and become a source of considerable internal conflict itself. It is important that a personnel manager be sensitive to these problems, especially as they relate to seniority provisions in union contracts.

Rating Systems

There are, unfortunately, a number of presumed biases or errors that may creep into any rating process. Because most of the newer developments in the field of rating scale construction represent attempts to reduce one or another of these, it seems desirable to become conversant with the problems that may arise at the outset (1).

HALO. There is, for one thing, a tendency for people to judge others almost entirely with reference to some one factor that they consider important. A man who is easy to get along with may be evaluated favorably in all other areas quite independent of his actual behavior. When a halo of this kind is operative, and it nearly always is to some degree, rather sizable correlations between the different scales of a measuring instrument—quantity, quality, cooperativeness, and so on—will emerge: Those who are high on one scale tend to be high on others, and those who are low tend to be low consistently. As a consequence the value of ratings in different areas, relative to different role requirements, can be dissipated.

CONSTANT ERROR. The tendency of superiors to use somewhat different sets of standards in judging subordinates has already been noted. The situation is essentially the same as that existing in colleges and universities where every student is familiar with the existence of difficult and easy graders. When evaluations made by different managers are compared, as they must be, this tendency can introduce considerable error. All the men rated by one manager may score below those rated by another, even though the two groups are in actual fact very similar. The differences obtained are due to a difference in managerial standards, not in performance.

RECENCY ERROR. Most ratings are intended to cover a preceding period of time, perhaps six months or a year. Ideally they should represent the average or typical behavior for this period. There is a tendency, however, to base ratings on what is most easily remembered, i.e., the most recent behavior. This may well not be characteristic of the total period, especially if the man is aware of the approximate date when he will be evaluated.

ERROR OF CENTRAL TENDENCY. Whatever the level of the standards employed by a given superior, there is a possibility that he will rate all his subordinates within a narrow range. For one reason or another the difference between the best and the worst employee on a particular scale often turns out to be minimal, even though much larger differences do in fact exist. In small units it is not unheard of to find the whole group clustered at one point on the scale. Errors of this kind tend in large part to obviate the value of the evaluations.

PERSONAL BIAS. Perhaps the most important error of all arises from the fact that none of us is capable of carrying out judgments entirely independent of his values, prejudices, and stereotypes. All kinds of inappropriate criteria and standards may be introduced into the evaluation process with the result that, on occasion, ratings relate not so much to company goals as to the personal goals of a particular manager (18). Thus, evaluations can be influenced by factors such as an employee's racial or ethnic background, physical attractiveness, religion, manner of dress, alcoholic consumption, social standing, treatment of wife and children, and ancestry, which are normally of little significance in the meeting of occupational role requirements.

Rating Scales

One method of classifying judgmental procedures utilizes the categories of rating scales, employee comparison systems, checklists, and critical incident techniques (23). The free-written or essay approach should probably be added to this list. Let us take these up in order.

Rating scales may take various forms, but the primary characteristic is the requirement that a check be placed at some point along a scale of value. There may be a line along which a manager is to place a mark (the graphic scale) or numbers may be used, one of which is to be circled, or the approach may be that of Figure 10-1. The high and low ends are identified as such and intermediate points may be defined through the use of appropriate adjectives.

Scales of this kind are widely used, primarily because they are so simple to construct. Yet in contrast to other techniques they make no provision for reducing halo, constant error, and errors of central tendency, all of which can have a considerable impact.

Figure 10-1. A Typical Rating Scale

```
Name:                             Date:
Department:                       Seniority Date:
Job Title:

        Quantity                  Quality                   Cooperation
Output of satisfactory    Accuracy, thoroughness &   Ability to get along
work                      effectiveness of work      with supervisors and
                                                     other employees

Quantity far below typical;   Quality far below typical;   Cooperation far below typical;
requires improvement          requires improvement         requires improvement
                    [ ]                         [ ]                           [ ]

Quantity below                Quality below                Cooperation below
typical performance           typical performance          typical performance
                    [ ]                         [ ]                           [ ]

Quantity within               Quality within               Cooperation within
typical performance           typical performance          typical performance
                    [ ]                         [ ]                           [ ]

Quantity above                Quality above                Cooperation above
typical performance           typical performance          typical performance
                    [ ]                         [ ]                           [ ]

Quantity outstanding,         Quality outstanding,         Cooperation outstanding,
far above typical per-        far above typical per-       far above typical per-
formance                      formance                     formance
                    [ ]                         [ ]                           [ ]

Comments:
```

Studies indicate, however, that the central tendency problem can be overcome through training and discussion with the raters (13). Probably other sources of error can be similarly reduced. With an adequate awareness of the factors that introduce bias and a desire to overcome them, rating scales apparently can be employed effectively by managers in evaluating their subordinates. In actual practice this degree of freedom from error may not be too common. This is particularly true if the rater is asked to mark a great variety of scales, which appear frequently to be overlapping, on each man. When the number of dimensions is over ten, at most, the prospect of appropriate motivation in the rater becomes rather low.

Figure 10-2 presents a rating scale that has been constructed for a slightly different purpose than the scale of Figure 10-1. This particular measure is designed to obtain information regarding whether or not an employee should be retained at the end of the initial probationary period, usually from two to six months. It has a strong negative orientation because the major concern is to identify those who will not be capable of effective performance. Perhaps the greatest value of scales of this kind is that they help to remind a manager of the great variety of behaviors that must be compared against role requirements in reaching a decision on retention. Notice that this decision is not actually requested until the end of the scale, after all the various aspects of the employee's behavior have been considered.

Employee Comparison Systems

Employee comparison systems do not require the use of an absolute standard, as do the rating scales. Instead of comparing each man against some generalized concept of acceptable behavior, the rater makes comparisons among the various individuals being evaluated. Thus, other workers provide reference points for the ratings and the result is a relative evaluation.

RANKING. With ranking the manager merely orders his subordinates on as many dimensions or characteristics as are required. Each dimension is treated separately. Various aids have been developed for this purpose, because ranking may not be an easy task when a relatively large number of employees are involved.

One of these, called the alternation-ranking method, represents an attempt to get the easier discriminations, those involving the poorer and better individuals, out of the way first, so that the rater can concentrate on the middle range where decisions are more difficult (7). Thus, the best person is selected first, then the worst, then the next best, the next worst, and so on, working inward, until the last person noted is the one in the median position.

An alternative approach involves having the manager assume a hypothetical role as the head of a newly formed firm. He is then asked to select the one individual from among his present subordinates whom, on the basis of performance and potential, he would like to have as his vice president. This name is recorded. Next the manager is asked to assume this particular individual has refused the appointment, and to select a second person from among his current group. This procedure is repeated until all members have been ranked. Although this technique provides only a single measure, on an overall effectiveness

Figure 10-2. Typical Probationary Employee Evaluation

Name: Current Date:

Department: Date Probationary Period Ends:

Job Title:

Please check the appropriate statement or statements in each area to indicate extent of employee's progress.

Quantity of Work

    Slow to learn _____

    Has to be pushed on occasion _____

    Consistently meets requirements _____

    Does more than required _____

Quality of Work

    Not really very good _____

    Sometimes drops below acceptable level _____

    Acceptable _____

    An accurate worker _____

Personal Characteristics

    Does not cooperate with other workers _____ Cooperates _____

    Is absent frequently _____ Rarely absent _____

    Wastes time _____ Does not waste time _____

    Is not a safe worker _____ A safe worker _____

    Demands frequent supervision _____ Can work alone _____

    A troublemaker _____ Does not stir up trouble _____

Are you satisfied to have the employee remain working for you? _____

If not suitable for retention in present job, would you recommend another job? _____

Comments:

scale, the approach does appear to meet most criteria for a satisfactory rating system (24).

The major advantage of any type of ranking is that it spreads individuals out over the whole range of performance. The error of central tendency is eliminated and constant errors cannot occur as such. In addition, halo appears to be minimized, because the dimensions are ranked separately and person-to-person comparisons must be made on each. The biggest problems arise when there is a need to combine ratings made by different supervisors on different groups. It is always possible, although not probable, that the best man in one group is actually below the poorest in another. This difficulty will be discussed in more detail shortly.

PAIRED COMPARISONS. A second method of employee comparison produces a ranking as a final result, but requires only that the superiority of one individual over another be established by judgment. From a series of such comparisons of pairs, a rank ordering may be constructed. The nature of the technique is illustrated in Figures 10-3 and 10-4, which are derived from a study in which ratings of office tabulating machine operators were used to establish criteria for use in setting up a selection testing program (16,17).

In Figure 10-4 a group of five operators are rated on one dimension by their superior. If the number of "better" evaluations is totaled for each man, the results are as follows:

Cooper	4
Adams	3
Dalton	2
Baker	1
Emory	0

These data provide a ranking within this particular group, with Cooper the most effective man and Emory the least. The actual study involved the combining of similar information on four different tabulating units, most of them considerably larger than this one.

Table 10-1 provides information on the similarity between the paired comparison ranking of the same individuals by pairs of superiors and on the similarity between ratings made by the same superior at an interval of one year. The results suggest that the procedure is generally effective but that the cooperation ratings, at least relatively, are defective. This may well be due to certain inadequacies of the instructions to raters (Figure 10-3) in this particular area. Placing cooperation with fellow workers and with superiors together in one dimension may produce some ambiguity, with the raters emphasizing one aspect at one time, another aspect at another. If fellow workers and superiors

Figure 10-3. Instructions to Raters Used in the Tabulating Machine Operator Study

The purpose of these rating forms is to see how the various members of the group you supervise compare with each other in important aspects of tabulating machine operation.

In making the ratings, compare the employees under you on the following aspects of tabulating machine operation:

1. *Application*—Which employee is stronger in his application to the job? Which shows more interest in the work and strives to do well in it?
2. *Accuracy*—Which employee produces more consistently accurate work? Which do you feel you do not have to check on as much?
3. *Speed*—Which employee gets his assigned jobs done faster? Which one can produce more in a given time?
4. *Cooperation*—Which employee demonstrates a greater spirit of cooperation with his fellow workers and his supervisor? Which gets along better with people on the job?
5. *Overall effectiveness*—Considering the four factors above, and others not mentioned, which are important in tabulating work, which employee would you say is a more effective tabulating machine operator?

A separate form for each of these aspects on which you will rate your employees is attached. In completing these forms, you are to compare each employee with every other employee once on each of the five aspects.

1. In the column running down the left side of each form are the names of employees in your group who do the tabulating work. The same names in the same order appear in the row running across the top of the form.
2. No ratings are required in the blanks below the diagonal line running from the top left to the bottom right corner of the sheet. Obviously you cannot compare any man with himself.
3. Beginning with the name of the first employee in the left column, you are to compare him with each of the other employees whose names appear in the upper row. If, in your opinion the employee whose name is to the left is better in the aspect of the job which is being judged, place a "1" in the square made by the intersection of the column and the row. If you feel the employee whose name is in the upper row is better, place a "0" in the square.
4. Repeat the process for the succeeding names in the left column until the form is finished.
5. Even though two employees may be nearly equal on any characteristic, you must decide who is better and assign a "1" or "0"
6. Leave no blank spaces and use only "1's" or "0's."

Figure 10-4. A Typical Completed Paired Comparison Rating Form from the Tabulating Machine Operator Study

Aspect: *Overall effectiveness*—Considering application, accuracy, speed, cooperation, and any other aspects which are important in tabulating work, which employee would you say is a more effective tabulating machine operator?

Mark "0" if the man is better

	Adams	Baker	Cooper	Dalton	Emory
Adams		/	O	/	/
Baker			O	O	/
Cooper				/	/
Dalton					/
Emory					

(Mark "1" if the man is better)

had been separated by setting up two different dimensions, this would probably have produced more satisfactory results.

FORCED DISTRIBUTION. One of the difficulties with ranking, and particularly paired comparisons, is that when the unit to be evaluated is large, e.g., over twenty-five, it is often necessary to break down the

Table 10-1. Correlations Between Paired Comparison Ratings Made by Two Superiors and Between Ratings Made at a One-Year Interval (tabulating machine operators)

Aspects rated	Average correlations between ratings of two superiors (average N = 16)	Correlations between ratings separated by one-year interval (N = 35)
Application	.85	.75
Accuracy	.79	.72
Speed	.81	.78
Cooperation	.67	.64
Overall effectiveness	.79	.75

total group into subgroups for purposes of rating. An alternative to this is a forced distribution.

In a sense this is a variant of the rating scale procedure, with a provision eliminating constant errors and errors of central tendency. Managers are to place their men in categories on each dimension according to certain predesignated proportions. The common distribution is:

Low 10%   Next 20%   Middle 40%   Next 20%   High 10%

Thus, for a unit of forty-five men the foreman would be asked to sort his men as follows:

Low 5   Next 9   Middle 18   Next 9   High 5

Notice that no assumption is made regarding the absolute level of performance. The lowest five are not necessarily unsatisfactory, only relatively less effective.

COMBINING EMPLOYEE COMPARISON DATA. The major difficulty with all the techniques discussed in this section is that although the relative position of each *man* within a group is established, there is no provision for determining the relative status of various *groups*. Two rankings on separate work units by their separate supervisors do not reflect any existing differences between the groups. One unit may have many more outstanding performers than the other, yet the ranking data will not indicate this fact.

The most common approach has been to assume that the groups to be compared or combined do not differ appreciably. If the groups are of different size, the ranks obtained from ranking or paired comparisons are translated into *standard scores,* through the use of appropriate conversion tables (9), and then combined into a single list. Sometimes rating scale data are obtained along with the employee comparisons as a check on the assumption of equality of groups. If an average on a rating scale for one group should closely approximate that for another group, it is considered appropriate to combine the two.

Where there is good reason to believe real group differences exist, the employee comparison approaches have only limited application. The major exception is where a few individuals can be included in the evaluations of more than one rater. These key individuals serve to provide reference points around which the data for the various groups in which they have been included may be combined (10). It is important, however, that all who rate these key men be well acquainted with their work.

Checklists

The major characteristic of the checklist procedures is that they deal with specific on-the-job behaviors rather than with the more abstract generalities of the rating scales. Thus, the manager actually reports on or describes the behavior of his subordinates rather than evaluating it. This means that separate checklists must be developed for each position that differs to any sizable degree in role prescriptions from other positions. Although job descriptions can be of considerable assistance in constructing these checklists, it remains a time-consuming and expensive task to apply these techniques on a widespread basis within a company. On the positive side is the fact that all types of error, including personal bias, tend to be reduced when the rating process moves to the level of differences in specific behaviors.

Because the manager provides only a number of checked behaviors that serve to describe a particular man, the actual evaluation process must be carried out elsewhere. The behavior descriptions included in the checklist must be categorized in terms of the degree to which they match role prescriptions. This is normally done by people who are familiar with the specific type of work—various levels of supervision, job analysts, personnel specialists, and perhaps industrial engineers or others who serve in a staff capacity relative to the positions under consideration.

These evaluations of checklist items may be carried out in a rough manner or by using the more precise techniques of attitude scaling to be described later in this chapter. In any event the result is a designation of certain behaviors as good or desirable and others as less so. If the good behaviors are consistently checked by the superior of a particular employee and the less desirable behaviors are not, then he is considered to have been given an outstanding rating. The weights or evaluations attached to items are not normally known to the supervisors doing the rating.

FORCED-CHOICE PROCEDURES. A variant of the checklist technique has been developed that appears to almost completely eliminate the personal bias problem. Unfortunately it accomplishes this result while at the same time introducing a situation where those doing the rating have no idea as to whether they are evaluating a man favorably or not. The consequence has been that many managers have developed considerable resistance to this approach—so much so that very few firms are now using it. Yet it is desirable to have some familiarity with the forced-choice procedure, if only because of the extensive discussions it has provoked within personnel management.

The basic elements of the measure are a series of blocks of two or more behavior descriptions. The descriptions within each block are selected so as to be approximately equal in their degree of favorableness or unfavorableness, but markedly different in the degree to which they have been found in prior studies to be associated with effective or ineffective performance, as defined by some other, external criterion.

Thus, a block of items used for rating training skills and containing favorable descriptions is:

a. Patient with slow learners
b. Lectures with confidence
c. Keeps interest and attention of class
d. Acquaints classes with objective for each lesson in advance

A block of unfavorable items is:

a. Does not answer all questions to the satisfaction of students
b. Does not use proper voice volume
c. Supporting details are not relevant

Within each of these blocks certain items have been found to discriminate between poor and good teachers, whereas others have little relation to success (3).

Critical Incident Technique

This approach is best described by reference to a specific system developed for evaluating salesmen at the Minnesota Mining and Manufacturing Company (12). Initially, sales managers in the various divisions were asked to submit short stories or anecdotes, called critical incidents, that illustrated what they considered particularly effective or ineffective salesman behavior. The result was sixty-one instances of effective performance, and thirty-five instances of ineffective performance. Analysis of these data revealed that fifteen basic types of behavior were involved, such as following up, carrying out promises, and communicating all necessary information to sales managers.

A rating sheet was then constructed covering these fifteen areas, based on items as closely allied to the original critical incidents as possible. The rater was asked to indicate the degree of his agreement or disagreement should he hear a particular statement used to describe the salesman being evaluated. Examples of these statements based on critical selling incidents are:

a. Follows up quickly on requests from customers
b. Promises too much to customers
c. Writes poor sales reports

The major advantages of this technique are in establishing comprehensive definitions of role requirements, if these are not available from other sources, and in providing items that, because they are close to on-the-job behavior, can serve to reduce personal bias. Other sources of error may well remain, however, and the basic procedures have been criticized as fostering excessively close supervision and blame finding (21).

Essay Evaluations

Here the superior merely writes out what he thinks of the subordinate, usually with very little by way of guidelines as to what points he should cover. An example is presented in Figure 10-5.

Figure 10-5. A Typical Essay Evaluation

Name: Date:

Department: Seniority Date:

Job Title:

                                    Type of Review

New Employee _____   Annual _____

Special _____   Separation _____

Transfer _____   Promotion _____

Employee's Strong Points:

Employee's Weak Points—Areas Where Improvement is Needed:

Comments with Regard to any Contemplated Separation, Transfer or Promotion:

This approach does little to reduce the various types of error that may influence the evaluation process. Personal bias in particular may be marked, because the manager selects his own grounds for judging his subordinate. Comparisons between individuals become difficult, because one man may be evaluated in one regard and another man on a completely different basis.

Specific role prescriptions may be introduced and free-written statements requested in each area. If this is done, however, a rating scale is normally much easier to employ.

Attitude Measurement

When we move to the matter of attitude measurement, the primary focus is on factors related to a company's organizational maintenance objective. The major techniques are management estimation, interviews, questionnaires, attitude scales, and indirect measures (2). The techniques of sociometry should probably be added to this list, although they are based on somewhat different considerations.

Management Estimation

As previously noted, rating procedures can be employed to obtain information regarding a man's attitudes and the behavior that is a consequence of these attitudes. Under most work arrangements immediate superiors are in a good position to observe their subordinates. There is no reason they cannot do as well in judging people relative to maintenance considerations as they do in the productivity area. Actually, almost all rating forms contain some items having to do with cooperation; such questions deal directly with behavior that is a consequence of job attitudes and job satisfaction.

On the other hand, many supervisors may not wish to inform higher management regarding any widespread dissatisfaction within their groups for fear this condition will reflect on their own competence, or they may not actually be aware of the degree of discontent. Yet such trouble spots are exactly what higher management wants and needs to know about, primarily because of their implications for labor relations trouble. As a consequence various techniques have been developed which involve obtaining information directly from the employees themselves.

Interviews

One obvious approach is to ask employees how they feel. The difficulty is that many will not feel free to express negative attitudes because of fear of retaliation. Various techniques have been devised to deal with this problem, but it still remains the major barrier to effective attitude measurement.

Many companies have found it desirable to have interviews conducted either by a consulting firm or representatives of a university. In this way they hope to reassure the employees that responses will not serve as a basis for retaliation against individuals.

In addition, efforts are usually made to ensure anonymity insofar as management is concerned. Thus, only the outside organization receives information on the names of those interviewed. The company's management is given a report in terms of group frequencies, rather than individuals' attitudes. This represents a major loss insofar as the process of comparing employees against role prescriptions is concerned. Certainly any management would much prefer to know the feelings of individual employees and thus the type of behavior it can expect. However, it is widely believed, probably correctly in many cases, that to attempt this would invalidate the survey entirely. Thus, companies tend to accept what from their viewpoint is the less desirable practice of comparing groups against role prescriptions in the maintenance area in order to improve their chances of obtaining information that can be trusted as predictive of behavior (19).

Interviews may be *guided* or *unguided*. In the latter instance the interviewer encourages the employee to express himself in various areas but does not follow a definite format. Questions may be worded quite differently when asked of different men. Attitudes are assessed by the interviewer based on what happens in the interview as a whole.

The problems here are maintaining comparability across interviews and minimizing the effects of interviewer bias. A talkative worker provides information differing in many ways from that derived from a reticent man. Questions will inevitably be worded differently and the interviewer may well react much more favorably toward an employee who is willing to talk, thus making the interview easier to conduct.

Because unguided interviews are difficult to quantify, the tendency has been to resort primarily to the guided approach. This approach tends to approximate the questionnaire procedure to be discussed in the next section, but the questions are asked orally. Administering such a standard questionnaire in an interview situation is costly, but it has the advantage of ensuring a high response rate within a group. Employees are much more likely to give answers to an interviewer than to return a mailed questionnaire. Thus, the bias that results when a nonrepresentative set of responses is obtained from a particular work unit tends to be reduced.

EXIT INTERVIEWS. Some firms make it a regular practice to conduct exit interviews with employees who are leaving the company voluntarily in order to assess attitudes in the groups where they worked. The assumption is that these people will talk freely because they have nothing to lose and that, therefore, the information obtained from them is more valid.

Although this assumption may be correct in some instances, it must be accepted with caution. Many employees will want references later and to ensure a good report will avoid any criticism of the company. Others may feel guilty about leaving their jobs and to justify doing so will tend to exaggerate negative factors in the work situation. Thus, the blame for the separation is shifted from the individual to the company. Both these considerations make the exit interview a somewhat questionable source of attitude data.

Questionnaires

In the past it has been a common practice to enclose attitude questionnaires with paychecks, to mail them to the employee's home, or even to hand them out at quitting time. These procedures rarely elicit a response from more than 50 per cent of a group, usually considerably less, and it is difficult to know what the results mean. Because anonymity is usually protected in order to foster valid answers, it is not possible to follow up on those who do not return completed forms. A more desirable procedure, now widely adopted, is to assemble the employees in groups and have them complete the forms on company time. In this way response rates comparable to those obtained with personal interviews can be obtained.

The topics covered in an attitude questionnaire vary with the particular needs of a company at a given time. Thus, firms may carry out surveys because they are concerned about labor relations problems, attitudes toward fringe benefits, and so on. In these cases the questionnaires should be constructed to fit the specific problem.

Where more general coverage is desired, some of the standardized forms that are available commercially may be preferable. These have the advantage that information on response frequencies in other companies are available for comparison purposes. Among these standardized measures is the Triple Audit Employee Attitude Questionnaire, which contains fifty-four items dealing with the following topics (6):

Working conditions
Company
Pay
Hours
Co-workers
Type of work
Supervision
Promotions
Communications
Recognition
Security

Another widely used measure is the SRA Employee Inventory (11), which covers:

> Job demands
> Working conditions
> Pay
> Employee benefits
> Friendliness, cooperation of employees
> Supervisory-employee relations
> Confidence in management
> Technical competence of supervision
> Effectiveness of administration
> Adequacy of communication
> Status and recognition
> Security of job and work relations
> Identification with the company
> Chances for growth and advancement

Attitude questionnaire items are of two basic types: fixed-alternative and open-ended. In the former category are questions with simple Yes or No alternatives as well as those of a multiple-choice nature. Open-ended questions either ask for a free-written answer or require that blanks be filled in. In either case the responses must be categorized after the answers have been obtained.

Open-ended questions can be expensive to use because of the need to construct categories (similar to multiple-choice alternatives) afterward and to code responses into these categories. On the other hand, if one is not sure what alternatives should be included in a fixed-alternative measure, the open-ended approach may be preferable. Often it takes as much time and money to conduct preliminary studies aimed at setting up appropriate multiple-choice alternatives as it does to categorize free responses.

Attitude Scales

Attitude scales are frequently utilized in instances where a more precise and reliable measure is desired than can be obtained from a few questionnaire items. Measures of this kind have been developed for a great variety of purposes (20). There are several procedures, but all have in common the fact that various scores or weights are attached to different alternatives to indicate the degree of feeling that characterizes a person who responds in a particular manner.

Perhaps the most frequently used approach is that developed by Thurstone (22), or some variant of it. The first step is to write out a great many statements bearing on the attitude to be measured; let us say satisfaction with one's present job. A number of people are then asked to serve as judges and to classify these statements in terms of their favorableness. Traditionally, eleven categories are used ranging from 1, indicating the least favorable viewpoint, to 11, the most favorable.

The *scale value* of each statement is the average of the category numbers assigned by the various judges. Not all the statements are normally used in the final attitude scale, however. It is important to select items indicating all variants of opinion. Thus, those finally used should be spread evenly throughout the range, from a scale value close to 1 to a scale value close to 11. Also, statements on which the judges cannot agree must be discarded. If several indicate that a statement should be in category 2 and the others have it in various categories up to 9, then agreement is clearly minimal and the item should not be used. The scale of Figure 10-6 represents what remains from an original 246 statements (5).

If the Brayfield-Rothe scale were administered without the five multiple-choice alternatives for each item and employees were asked merely to check those of the eighteen items that applied to them, then we would have a typical Thurstone scale. The score for an individual would be the sum of the scale values for the statements he checked. Items like 5 and 12 carry high-scale values, whereas items like 4 and 18 carry low values.

In this particular instance a modification of the standard Thurstone procedure has been introduced that allows employees to express the degree of agreement (14). Statements with scale values above 6 (positive statements) were scored 5 for a "strongly agree" response, 4 for "agree," and so on down to 1 for "strongly disagree." Statements with scale values below 6 (negative) are scored in the reverse direction with a 5 given for "strongly disagree." Thus, total scores range from 18 to 90.

As indicated previously, these same approaches may also be used to scale items descriptive of some dimension of job performance and thus to develop a weighted checklist of job behaviors for rating purposes.

Indirect Measures

Most of the approaches to attitude measurement discussed to this point attempt to deal with the tendency of employees to suppress unfavorable feelings by protecting the anonymity of respondents. Thus, groups rather than individuals must be compared against existing role prescriptions.

Figure 10-6. Brayfield-Rothe Job Satisfaction Questionnaire

Some jobs are more interesting and satisfying than others. We want to know how people feel about different jobs. You are to cross out the phrase below each statement which best describes how you feel about your present job. There are no right or wrong answers. We should like your honest opinion on each one of the statements. Work out the sample item numbered (0).

0. There are some conditions concerning my job that could be improved.
    Strongly Agree   Agree   Undecided   Disagree   Strongly Disagree
1. My job is like a hobby to me.
    Strongly Agree   Agree   Undecided   Disagree   Strongly Disagree
2. My job is usually interesting enough to keep me from getting bored.
    Strongly Agree   Agree   Undecided   Disagree   Strongly Disagree
3. It seems that my friends are more interested in their jobs.
    Strongly Agree   Agree   Undecided   Disagree   Strongly Disagree
4. I consider my job rather unpleasant.
    Strongly Agree   Agree   Undecided   Disagree   Strongly Disagree
5. I enjoy my work more than my leisure time.
    Strongly Agree   Agree   Undecided   Disagree   Strongly Disagree
6. I am often bored with my job.
    Strongly Agree   Agree   Undecided   Disagree   Strongly Disagree
7. I feel fairly well satisfied with my present job.
    Strongly Agree   Agree   Undecided   Disagree   Strongly Disagree
8. Most of the time I have to force myself to go to work.
    Strongly Agree   Agree   Undecided   Disagree   Strongly Disagree
9. I am satisfied with my job for the time being.
    Strongly Agree   Agree   Undecided   Disagree   Strongly Disagree
10. I feel that my job is no more interesting than any other I could get.
    Strongly Agree   Agree   Undecided   Disagree   Strongly Disagree
11. I definitely dislike my work.
    Strongly Agree   Agree   Undecided   Disagree   Strongly Disagree
12. I feel that I am happier in my work than most other people.
    Strongly Agree   Agree   Undecided   Disagree   Strongly Disagree
13. Most days I am enthusiastic about my work.
    Strongly Agree   Agree   Undecided   Disagree   Strongly Disagree
14. Each day of work seems like it will never end.
    Strongly Agree   Agree   Undecided   Disagree   Strongly Disagree
15. I like my job better than the average worker does.
    Strongly Agree   Agree   Undecided   Disagree   Strongly Disagree
16. My job is pretty uninteresting.
    Strongly Agree   Agree   Undecided   Disagree   Strongly Disagree
17. I find real enjoyment in my work.
    Strongly Agree   Agree   Undecided   Disagree   Strongly Disagree
18. I am disappointed that I ever took this job.
    Strongly Agree   Agree   Undecided   Disagree   Strongly Disagree

Source: A. H. Brayfield and H. F. Rothe, "An Index of Job Satisfaction," *Journal of Applied Psychology*, Vol. 35 (1951), p. 309.

The indirect measures attempt to solve the problem of suppressed attitudes in a different manner: one which does permit individual evaluation. The approach is comparable in certain respects to that employed in forced-choice rating. The employee does not know what he is revealing about his attitudes. As a consequence he cannot withhold that which he might not wish to say.

PROJECTIVE METHODS. Here the essential element is that the employee "projects" himself into a situation portrayed by a picture or by a written statement and in responding to this situation reveals his attitudes. He may be required to describe a picture or to tell a story or complete a statement of some kind. In any event he tends to ascribe to the situation and the people in it characteristics that belong to himself.

In general these techniques are administered in an interview situation, but measures can be devised to fit the questionnaire format. The major problem is to be absolutely certain that the attitude measured is what one wants to measure. Devising a good projective attitude index requires considerable training and experience, and unfortunately little in the way of standardized measures related to job problems is available commercially.

STRUCTURED DISGUISED MEASURES. A second approach requires the employee to respond to a series of questions that appear to constitute a test of general information or intelligence. However, the questions are so constructed that there either are no correct answers or the employee could not possibly be aware of the answers. Thus, any choice between alternatives must be based on attitudes. Employees are encouraged to guess.

One such measure of general morale makes extensive reference to the results of scientific research and pronouncements by unidentified well-known people (4). For instance, one question asks about the proportion of the workers in a group such as the respondent's who have been found in prior research to be particularly susceptible to discouragement when things go badly. Another question refers to statements by a social scientist and then asks what proportion of workers, this man believes, considers their jobs boring.

The major difficulty with the use of these techniques in industrial situations is that, unlike the other approaches discussed, they are often deliberately misleading. Considerable resentment may result should employees become aware of the fact that management is not being entirely honest. Especially in unionized firms, the losses can be greater than the gains. For this reason a personnel manager should give considerable thought to the pros and cons before undertaking an attitude survey with a structured disguised measure.

Sociometry

Although sociometric procedures have not been widely utilized in the business world, they appear to have considerable potential, especially as an aid in establishing the degree of attachment to a work group or organization—what has been called the cohesiveness of the group. They should provide particularly valuable information regarding a tendency to resort to escape behavior as a solution to discontent.

The sociometric questionnaire, in its most common form, merely asks each member of a group to indicate which among the other members he would like to have as a companion in some activity, such as teaming up on a job or eating lunch. Usually negative choices are also requested. Thus, each employee also indicates those he would not want as a companion. These choices provide valuable information regarding an individual's ties to his group, whether he is accepted by others, and whether he feels close to certain group members. An index of the pull of the group vis à vis external social forces may be obtained if the questionnaire is designed so as to permit choices both within and outside the specific work unit.

Resistance to Evaluation

In spite of the obvious significance of employee evaluation for the attainment of company goals, there are a number of sources of resistance that make it extremely difficult to install and maintain systems of this kind. As a result there has been a clear-cut trend away from formal evaluation systems for blue-collar workers, at the same time that management appraisal has been on the increase (25). Although rating systems are still widely used, a number of firms have phased out their programs in the face of individual and union resistance.

One major difficulty is that employees who do not anticipate a favorable rating are likely to be opposed to the whole evaluation process, which is perceived as a personal threat. Because only a very limited number can have a feeling of certainty that their rating will be a favorable appraisal, the great majority of employees are likely to exhibit resistance in one form or another. Managers and supervisors may well experience considerable group pressure in this regard with the result that many of them, especially those who are particularly sensitive about such matters, may find it very difficult to actually do the ratings. Thus, there may be delays and other difficulties that, although probably not intentional, do reflect the conflicting pressures to which lower-level managers are exposed. Finally, the entire system may well collapse as these individual considerations are added to the long-standing union position on such matters.

There is reason to believe that problems of this kind are not unique in the area of rating programs. A number of companies have also found it difficult to maintain a system of periodic attitude measurement (8). Many firms have at one time or another instituted continuing procedures aimed at obtaining data relative to the organizational maintenance goal. For various reasons a number of these have discontinued the procedures after a relatively brief trial.

Part of the difficulty seems to be that, historically, organizational maintenance has never attained quite the same stature as productivity. Thus, a number of managers have considered attitude survey results relatively unimportant. Although appreciation of the significance of this goal is now on the upswing, attitude measurement in the past has not had the support that other evaluation techniques have enjoyed.

Perhaps related to this consideration is the fact that if attitude surveys are to be of real value they must be tied to action. When a number of employees in a unit are discontented, and a survey identifies the source of the difficulty, an effort should be made to improve the situation and thus to improve attitudes. Unfortunately this has not always been done. Accordingly, periodic surveys have often yielded almost identical results, time after time, to the point where measurement was finally discontinued because no new information was obtained.

Finally, and perhaps this is the underlying difficulty, what management typically wants from attitude measurement is individual employee evaluation of the kind produced by rating procedures. Yet many of the commonly used procedures yield group results only. Although these group data do have considerable value in appraising managers and in pinpointing labor problems, the return on the investment may be insufficient to convince some managers that continuing measurement is warranted.

This does not mean that employee evaluation should be eliminated. Rating procedures and attitude measurement, as well as the various objective indexes discussed in the last chapter, are an important aspect of personnel management. But it would be misleading to suggest that these techniques can be utilized without provoking some resistance.

Seniority and Union Resistance

Perhaps the greatest present source of difficulty in the area of employee evaluation stems from the unions. Attitude surveys are frequently opposed because they are viewed as an attempt to undermine the union. Rating procedures are almost universally condemned as being inconsistent with a long-standing labor union commitment to the seniority principle.

When seniority holds for purposes of layoff, promotion, shift selection, eligibility for overtime, work assignment, and the like, it is the senior employee in terms of service with the company, or in the seniority unit, who gets the preferred treatment. This tends to eliminate most, if not all, need for a merit rating system.

Union contracts contain a variety of provisions insofar as seniority is concerned. In the most extreme case seniority only is mentioned. Other contracts say that seniority governs provided the senior employee is minimally capable of doing the work. Still others indicate that seniority shall be the deciding factor where ability is equal. This of course places the burden of proof on management. Evidence must be presented that a person with less seniority is the more capable if, for instance, he is to be promoted. Even in the latter case close inspection of actual practices often reveals that merit characteristically takes a position secondary to seniority. This may be because of expediency, the belief that adherence to seniority will foster labor peace, a lack of adequate criteria of ability, or the feeling that the existing evidence of merit differences would not convince an arbitrator should the union file a grievance (15). In any event there is a strong tendency for seniority to govern if it is mentioned at all in the labor agreement.

Union contracts contain widely varying provisions regarding the date that seniority starts to accumulate, loss of seniority, individuals who are exempt from the standard seniority provisions, and so on. It is almost impossible to generalize on these matters. There are also wide differences in the way the seniority unit is defined. Seniority may be company-wide or plant-wide. It may hold only within certain occupations or occupational groups or departments or even pay ranges.

In general, managements prefer to keep the seniority unit as small as possible. The reason for this is that when layoffs must occur and higher-level positions are eliminated, it is common practice to permit *bumping* within the unit; i.e., an employee with seniority may demand the job of another employee with less seniority. This can extend down through the unit until the person with the least seniority, in the lowest-level job, is the one laid off. Where seniority is company-wide and a highly skilled position is eliminated, the amount of dislocation occasioned by successive bumping can be considerable. Where the seniority unit is small, changes in the job structure are much more easily accomplished.

One final point should be made regarding the union and rating procedures. Even where seniority provisions have not obviated the need for employee evaluation, the union may exercise a certain degree of control over an existing rating system. Thus, some contracts call for a review procedure under which a combined union-management committee reconsiders certain supervisory evaluations and may in fact change them. Normally such reviews are restricted to a certain percentage of the bargaining unit, perhaps 1 per cent.

It is apparent, therefore, that when employee evaluation systems are installed, the personnel manager will have to be sensitive not only to possible sources of individual resistance, but to union attitudes as well.

References

1. Barrett, R. S., *Performance Rating*. Chicago: Science Research Associates, 1966.
2. Bass, B. M., *Organizational Psychology*. Boston: Allyn and Bacon, 1965.

3. Berkshire, J. R., and R. W. Highland, "Forced-Choice Performance Rating: A Methodological Study," *Personnel Psychology,* Vol. 6 (1953), 355–378.
4. Bernberg, R. E., "The Direction of Perception Technique of Attitude Measurement," *International Journal of Opinion and Attitude Research,* Vol. 5 (1951), 397–406.
5. Brayfield, A. H., and H. F. Rothe, "An Index of Job Satisfaction," *Journal of Applied Psychology,* Vol. 35 (1951), 307–311.
6. England, G. W., and C. I. Stein, "The Occupational Reference Group— A Neglected Concept in Employee Attitude Studies," *Personnel Psychology,* Vol. 14 (1961), 299–304.
7. Foundation for Research on Human Behavior, *Assessing Managerial Potential.* Ann Arbor, Mich.: the Foundation, 1958.
8. Foundation for Research on Human Behavior, *Assessing Organization Performance with Behavioral Measurements.* Ann Arbor, Mich.: the Foundation, 1964.
9. Guilford, J. P., *Psychometric Methods,* 2nd ed. New York: McGraw-Hill, 1954.
10. Guion, R. M., *Personnel Testing.* New York: McGraw-Hill, 1965.
11. Industrial Relations Center, Univ. Chicago, *SRA Employee Inventory.* Chicago: Science Research Associates, 1951.
12. Kirchner, W. K., and M. D. Dunnette, "Identifying the Critical Factors in Successful Salesmanship," *Personnel,* Vol. 34, No. 2 (1957), 54–59.
13. Levine, J., and J. Butler, "Lecture vs. Group Decision in Changing Behavior," *Journal of Applied Psychology,* Vol. 36 (1952), 29–33.
14. Likert, R., S. Roslow, and G. Murphy, "A Simple and Reliable Method of Scoring the Thurstone Scales," *Journal of Social Psychology,* Vol. 5 (1934), 228–238.
15. McConkey, D. D., "Ability vs. Seniority in Promotion and Layoff," *Personnel,* Vol. 37, No. 3 (1960), 51–57.
16. Miner, J. B., "The Concurrent Validity of the Picture Arrangement Test in the Selection of Tabulating Machine Operators," *Journal of Projective Techniques,* Vol. 24 (1960), 409–418.
17. Miner, J. B., "The Validity of the Picture Arrangement Test in the Selection of Tabulating Machine Operators: An Analysis of Predictive Power," *Journal of Projective Techniques,* Vol. 25 (1961), 330–333.
18. Miner, J. B., *The Management of Ineffective Performance.* New York: McGraw-Hill, 1963.
19. Selltiz, C., M. Jahoda, M. Deutsch, and S. W. Cook, *Research Methods in Social Relations,* rev. ed. New York: Holt, Rinehart & Winston, 1960.
20. Shaw, M. E., and J. M. Wright, *Scales for the Measurement of Attitudes.* New York: McGraw-Hill, 1967.
21. Strauss, G., and L. R. Sayles, *Personnel: The Human Problems of Management,* 2nd ed. Englewood Cliffs, N.J.: Prentice-Hall, 1967.
22. Thurstone, L. L., and E. J. Chave, *The Measurement of Attitude.* Chicago: Univ. Chicago Press, 1929.
23. Tiffin, J., and E. J. McCormick, *Industrial Psychology,* 5th ed. Englewood Cliffs, N.J.: Prentice-Hall, 1965.

24. Ward, W. H., "The 'It's Your Business' Approach to Ratings," *Personnel Psychology*, Vol. 14 (1961), 183–191.
25. Whisler, T. L., and S. F. Harper, *Performance Appraisal—Research and Practice*. New York: Holt, Rinehart & Winston, 1962.

Questions

1. Describe the different types of error or bias that may appear when rating procedures are used. What effect does each have on the ratings?
2. What particular difficulties must be considered when the following techniques are used?
      Paired comparison rating
      Exit interviews
      Essay evaluation
      Structured disguised measures
3. Describe how a Thurstone scale might be constructed to provide a checklist type of rating system.
4. What are the various techniques or procedures that may be used to ensure that valid information is obtained from an employee attitude survey?
5. What are the various ways in which the seniority—merit problem may be handled in the union contract? Why do you suppose the unions have tended to place so much emphasis on the seniority principle?

IV

Screening and Selection: The Evaluation of Individual Inputs

11

The Logic of Selection
and the Process
of Recruitment

The matter of dealing with the individual human inputs to a company is basically a personnel function. First, a pool of applicants or potential employees (perhaps candidates is the best word) must be recruited. Information must then be collected on these individuals, in terms of which some will be selected for employment and others screened out. The primary consideration in reaching such a decision on employment is whether or not the individual is likely to achieve success in the organization, that is, whether he can be expected to make a sizable contribution to the attainment of organizational objectives.

Part III discussed at some length the various ways in which the behavioral outputs of managers and other employees can be measured and evaluated. Thus, a man could be rated high or low on the quality of his work, he could have a good absenteeism record or a poor one, and so on. Part IV will take up the techniques—interviews, psychological tests, reference checks, physical examinations, application blanks—that are used to select people who will obtain favorable evaluations on these various indexes of success.

The first part of this chapter will be devoted to a general treatment of the logic of selection. Much of our knowledge in this area was originally developed with reference to psychological testing. However, these approaches have much wider applicability, and the considerations involved are just as relevant for interviews, application blanks, and the other selection procedures as they are for psychological tests. Basically we shall be concerned with the various methods used to relate the pre-employment, or preplacement, data on an individual to indexes of the degree of matching between role behaviors and role prescriptions. The latter measures are usually referred to as *criteria* in the selection context.

The second part of the chapter will take up the initial step in the selection process: the recruitment of a group of candidates from which selection can occur. Here the concern will be with such matters as college recruiting, the "pirating" of executives, employment agencies, and promotion from within.

The Longitudinal Prediction Model

The logic of the selection process has been most completely developed in what is called the longitudinal prediction model. When a selection measure meets the requirements of this model, it is said to possess *predictive validity*. There are two major variants or cases involved.

Case 1—Single Predictor

STEP 1. Study the job, or group of related jobs, for which selection is to occur in order to identify characteristics that might be related to success. These may be intellectual abilities, personality factors, types of prior experience, physical attributes, or anything else that can be measured prior to actual job placement.

STEP 2. Decide on the specific measures of these characteristics to be used. If verbal ability is a potential predictor, is it to be estimated from an interview or measured by a test? If a test, which particular one?

STEP 3. Obtain these predictor measures on a relatively large group of job applicants or candidates. Then hire from this group without reference to the predictor data. That is, select the individuals to be employed without looking at the measures obtained and without taking this information into account in any way. This normally means that employment decisions should be made by a person other than the one conducting the study. If, on the other hand, the measures are used to select those who will be hired at this initial stage, and these predictors do have some validity, only relatively good performers will be found on the job and the possibility of identifying predictors that differentiate between good and poor performers will be to that degree lost. The sample may be accumulated over time as hirings occur, but there should be a bare minimum of thirty individuals in the hired group and preferably many more.

STEP 4. Gather criterion data on the individuals hired, after such information becomes available. The measure used may be any of those discussed in Chapters 9 and 10. Usually these data are not suitable for use as criteria until after the man has been on the job long enough for his performance level to stabilize.

STEP 5. Determine the degree of relationship between the predictor values and the criterion values. Usually a correlation coefficient is used to indicate the degree of this relationship. The specific statistical index may vary depending on the distribution of predictor and criterion values in the group, but in any event the result will be a coefficient ranging from −1.00 through 0 to +1.00 with the larger values, both negative and positive, indicating a closer relationship between predictor and criterion. The larger the coefficient, the greater the predictive validity of the measure taken before hiring.

A simple chart of the relationship may be established if a summary statement of the kind a correlation coefficient provides is not needed. Thus, at each level on the predictor index the number of people falling at each point on the criterion would be indicated as follows, assuming a sample of 50:

Predictor values	Criterion values				
	1	*2*	*3*	*4*	*5*
5			1	2	2
4		2	1	4	3
3	2	2	12	4	
2	1	5	4		
1	2	1	2		

It is not necessary to compute a correlation coefficient from this chart to ascertain that a predictor is rather closely and positively related to a criterion.

STEP 6. If the results of step 5 indicate a relatively good predictive validity, then under most circumstances a second study should be carried out on the same job using the same predictor and criterion measures. This is called the *cross-validation* and is undertaken because any relationship established in the first group might have been due to a mere chance fluctuation. A second study is done to be sure the relationship is there and that it can be relied on subsequently when people who obtain high values on the predictor are actually selected for employment.

Obtaining a cross-validation sample is not always easy, especially if there is some urgency about getting the selection procedure into use as soon as possible. Under these circumstances it is relatively common practice to collect data on both groups at once. Thus, if 100 men are hired for a job, the total group may be split in half, with the initial validation done on one subsample and the cross-validation on the other. In any event step 6 should be carried out. It is particularly crucial when a number of different predictor measures have been tested for a relation to the criterion, and only one or two have produced significant results. Under these circumstances chance may well be operative, and the one or two predictors that seemed to work in the first group may not work in the second (5).

Case 2—Multiple Predictors

Most jobs are not so simple that a single measure of a single predictor is sufficient to yield maximum results. Normally the best predictions are obtained when a number of predictors measuring a variety of characteristics are combined in some manner.

Steps 1 through 4 are essentially the same under multiple prediction as they are when predictors are validated separately. The major difference emerges in step 5. Some solution must be developed to the problem of combining the various factors in such a way as to maximally predict job success. There are four basic approaches to this problem.

MULTIPLE CORRELATION. In multiple correlation the correlations between the predictors are computed, as well as the correlations between various predictors and the criterion. A multiple-correlation coefficient is then derived that represents a maximal index of the relationship, one that automatically weights the separate predictors so as to yield the best prediction of the criterion. So-called *regression weights* may then be developed. The values obtained by an individual on the various measures may be multiplied by these weights and then combined to produce a maximum estimate of the chances for job success. Because this procedure is particularly sensitive to chance fluctuations, it is essential that step 6, cross-validation, be carried out.

ADDITIVE CORRELATION. Additive correlation is essentially an approximation procedure for the multiple-correlation coefficient. It involves adding the values obtained by an individual on all the predictors together and then computing the correlation between this composite index and the criterion. Rather surprisingly this technique does yield a close approximation to the results obtained from the multiple-correlation approach.

MULTIPLE-STAGE PREDICTION. In multiple-stage prediction the predictors are utilized one at a time rather than in combination. Thus, correlations are computed as in case 1 for each of the predictors with the cross-validation step included. Then the predictor that consistently produces the highest relationship with the criterion is identified, and some value is established as minimally satisfactory for employment. All candidates who fall below this value are screened out; all others continue as candidates. These remaining individuals must then meet a similar test based on the predictor having the second highest correlation with the criterion. This process of successive screening out is continued until all predictors exhibiting a consistent relationship to the criterion are exhausted. Those who at least equal the minimum satisfactory value on all predictors are hired. Normally three or four such hurdles are all that are required. Beyond that very little predictive power is added.

CLINICAL PREDICTION. With clinical prediction the combining of predictors is accomplished by the personnel manager or psychologist based on his own experience and without resort to statistical aids. The result is a decision that takes into account all the information available, but weights the different measures and factors on a largely intuitive basis. Selection decisions of this kind have been successfully simulated on a computer (16).

The Concurrent Model

The concurrent approach is identical to that of longitudinal prediction with one very important exception: the predictor and criterion measures are obtained at roughly the same point in time, usually on individuals who have been employed for a considerable period in the job to be studied. Thus, there is no long wait after the predictor data have been obtained to collect the criterion information. Either case 1 or case 2 may be applied, and the cross-validation is done on a second sample of employees selected from the current group.

This procedure is admittedly a shortcut, and as such has certain rather marked deficiencies. For one thing the motivation of present employees in taking a test or filling out a questionnaire or even in an interview situation may be quite different from that of job applicants: They may not try as hard. Yet the results are to be applied to an applicant group. This can introduce considerable error into the selection process, especially when measures of interests and certain kinds of personality tests are used. With physical examinations, intelligence tests, application blank data, and the like, it probably matters very little.

Second, the results obtained from certain measures may be largely a function of job tenure. Thus, indexes of job knowledge may yield higher scores the longer the person has been on the job. This can produce rather misleading results when the job knowledge measure is used as a predictor in an applicant group, none of whom have had prior experience in that particular type of work. If, however, one is aware of this problem, appropriate statistical procedures can be used to take the effects of job tenure out of the results. Thus, this potential source of error can be eliminated.

Finally, it is possible with some predictors that success or failure on the job may serve to determine the values obtained, rather than the reverse. For instance, in one study decreases in self-confidence as measured by a psychological test were found repeatedly over eight years of employment among less successful managers, but this same trend did not appear among the more successful (8). Clearly any predictor-criterion relationship involving self-confidence established from a concurrent study would not necessarily appear under the more exacting conditions of a longitudinal prediction study. This problem of "what causes what" is particularly common when measures of certain attitudes, interests, and personality characteristics are used as predictors. Often a review of the relevant research literature will reveal whether or not a particular predictor should be trusted, based on evidence of concurrent validity.

An Example of the Concurrent Model with Multiple Predictors

A good example of the concurrent method as applied to the selection of lower-level factory managers is a study carried out at IBM (17). The first task of the personnel researchers was to study thoroughly the managerial role requirements of these particular jobs through interviews with a number of incumbents. These interviews suggested that knowledge of the work done was not as important as such factors as supervisory interest, decision-making skill, and employee orientation. Accordingly a number of predictors in these areas were selected for trial and administered to the managers.

Those predictors that gave any hint of possessing value are described in generalized terms in Table 11-1. Several other measures were used but have not been noted because of the consistently negative results. The criteria were, first, the average of the performance ratings made by a number of fellow managers. This index proved to be of only limited value because the peer ratings on the same manager were not generally in very close agreement. Second was a corrected salary figure that was constructed to eliminate the influence of seniority with the company and as a manager. Finally, there were ratings by superiors, which, like the peer ratings, suffered from considerable unreliability.

In the first sample of forty-two managers, as Table 11-1 indicates, a number of predictors yielded some evidence of concurrent validity. Six measures produced coefficients above .20. The corrected salary criterion proved the most predictable, as might be expected in view of the deficiencies in the other indexes.

As so often happens, however, cross-validation washed out a number of these initial findings—the relationships were not consistently present

Table 11-1. Correlation Coefficients Showing Relationships Between Predictors and Criteria. First Sample ($N = 42$)

Predictors	Criteria		
	Peer rating	Corrected salary	Superior rating
Intelligence test	.26	.40	.13
Personality test			
Ascendancy	.29	.28	.22
Responsibility	.02	.25	.09
Emotional stability	−.03	.08	−.07
Sociability	.08	.07	.07
Total score	.19	.39	.22
Supervisory test	.11	.04	.12
Biographical questionnaire	.03	.23	.19
Age	−.16	−.47	−.16

Source: Adapted from M. E. Spitzer and W. J. McNamara, "A Managerial Selection Study," *Personnel Psychology*, Vol. 17 (1964), p. 32.

in these managerial positions and thus the predictors could not be relied upon in a selection system. (See Table 11-2.) As a consequence the measures of ascendancy, responsibility, personality test total score, and age had to be abandoned. Emotional stability and the supervisory test showed some new strength as predictors, but because both were totally ineffective in the first sample, these later findings had to be discounted.

Table 11-2. Correlation Coefficients Showing Relationships Between Predictors and Criteria. Cross-Validation Sample ($N = 42$)

Predictors	Criteria		
	Peer rating	Corrected salary	Superior rating
Intelligence test	.14	.36	.11
Personality test			
Ascendancy	−.02	.16	.11
Responsibility	−.17	.09	.07
Emotional stability	−.06	.23	.17
Sociability	−.06	−.14	−.12
Total score	−.09	.12	.04
Supervisory test	.13	.17	.33
Biographical questionnaire	.34	.35	.24
Age	.13	−.03	.25

Source: Adapted from M. E. Spitzer and W. J. McNamara, "A Managerial Selection Study," *Personnel Psychology*, Vol. 17 (1964), p. 32.

Only the intelligence measure and the biographical questionnaire, which resembled an application blank and contained questions dealing with personal experiences and interests, held up in cross-validation, primarily in relation to the salary criterion.

When these two predictors were combined to yield a multiple correlation coefficient, the value obtained in the first managerial sample was .43. In the cross-validation group it was .41. If the top 25 per cent of the managers, based on the weighted combination of intelligence and biographical measures, had been selected for these positions, 68 per cent of them would have proved to be above-average performers. Thus, the new selection system yields an improvement of 36 per cent over existing procedures. In view of the nature of the predictors identified, there is little reason to believe a longitudinal study would have produced differing results.

Newer Approaches to Selection

Although the methods described are the most widely used in personnel selection, there are certain other approaches to validation that require mention. The latter are not currently in widespread use, but they offer potential solutions to important problems and there is reason to believe that they may see much more extensive application in the future. It is important, therefore, to be at least generally familiar with them.

Synthetic Validity

One of the major disadvantages of the longitudinal and predictive models is that both require a relatively large number of employees doing similar work. They are thus of limited value in small companies, and in larger firms wherever the number of people employed in a given type of activity is small. The synthetic validity model was developed for application in such situations (9,10). The approach is analogous to that of the methods engineer who, when developing a standard time for a specific job, combines the various estimated times for separate elements of the operation.

First, various work elements or job requirements must be identified using job analysis procedures. Then the predictor measures must be validated on a number of jobs having a particular work element or job requirement in common. If a sizable relationship between the values on a given predictor and those on some criterion index can be established for these jobs having a common characteristic, then the predictor can be used in selecting individuals for other jobs with the same work elements or requirements. The essence of the approach is that a high level of accomplishment on a predictor is almost invariably associated with a high level of a certain type of job behavior. If this can be established, the predictor can be used for any job where the behavior is required and important.

The Decision Model in Selection

A second approach that has fostered considerable discussion, even though because of certain practical difficulties it has not been widely applied, derives from mathematical decision theory (3,6). According to this view, the ultimate purpose of any predictor is to assist in making a *decision* as to what should be done with a given applicant or candidate, and therefore the soundest approach to evaluating a measure is through determining the benefits that accrue to the total organization as a result of a particular decision. The utility concept is used to provide an index of value. Utility is defined in terms of the benefits that accrue from a given set of decisions, less the total costs incurred in the decision-making process.

Although a detailed mathematical treatment is not contemplated here, it is possible to describe the basic elements of this approach. There is, first, certain information regarding the individual—interview data, a completed application blank, test scores, and the like. Second, there are various treatments that may be utilized depending on the decision made— hire the man, reject him, collect further information. Third, the outcomes of decisions are expressed in terms of various criterion values, which may be based on ratings and objective indexes. Finally, there are the utilities attached to the various outcomes: the benefits, less the costs, derived from having an individual perform effectively in a given type of work or the net benefit derived from rejecting an individual with somewhat different characteristics.

Probabilities are attached to these factors and a matrix constructed so that it is possible to evaluate each applicant in terms of his expected value to the firm should he be hired for a particular position. The difficulty with this approach, and the reason for its limited use, is that good measures of the utilities associated with various decision outcomes have not been available. Recently some solutions to this problem have been developed, based on psychological scaling methods analogous to the Thurstone procedure (4). It may well be that the future will see a much wider application of the decision model in personnel selection.

The Limitations of Selection

It should be apparent from the correlations between predictors and criteria noted previously, such as those in Tables 11-1 and 11-2, that available selection techniques are not a panacea for all ills. Effectively utilized, they can increase the level of goal attainment in a company, but instances of performance failure and individual discontent will inevitably remain. There are certain inherent limitations in selection models and technology that may never be completely overcome.

One major problem, and this will become increasingly apparent after the discussions in Chapters 12 and 13, is that the available predictors are far from perfect. They do not always reveal a characteristic that is important in determining job behavior, nor do they consistently specify correctly the degree to which it may be present. Interviews, psychological tests, physical examinations, and all the other techniques may not yield the information they should, and on occasion they may produce erroneous information.

Another difficulty is associated not so much with the techniques themselves as with the people who use them. Human error is almost inevitable, even though it can be reduced through effective selection and training of personnel managers and workers. In one instance the author had a sample of several hundred answer sheets for the psychological tests used in a company's selection battery rescored at a later date. Although in most cases the divergence was not large, there were some tests that had clearly been scored with considerable error—sufficiently so to produce an inappropriate selection decision. Similar errors, because of the misunderstanding of an interview statement or the misreading of some physical measure, occur more often than is generally recognized.

Considerations of economy are also relevant. The physical exam is a good example. Increasingly, medical science is developing complex procedures for the detection of various diseases. Many of these diagnostic aids are extremely costly and require highly trained personnel to use them; some necessitate hospitalization during the period that tests are carried out. There can be no question that these techniques have considerable value in predicting subsequent events. Yet companies rarely use them in connection with the preemployment physical examination. They are too costly in time and money, and the disorders they identify are frequently rather rare. As a result a decision has been made in many instances to risk future absenteeism and perhaps ineffective job behavior rather than invest in the available selection techniques.

The investment decision here is analogous to that involved in a deferred maintenance policy as applied to equipment and machinery. Instead of attempting to spot potential breakdowns before they occur and correcting the situation, one allows the breakdown to develop, on the assumption that the resulting costs will be less than those that preventive maintenance would necessitate. Many companies have not adopted psychological testing programs and other selection procedures for much the same type of reason. They assume that a sizable investment in selection procedures is not warranted because any difficulties that develop can be handled later. Thus, emphasis is concentrated on the output processes rather than on organizational inputs. As firing becomes more difficult due to union pressures and other factors, a number of these firms may attempt a recalculation of the relative costs and come to a somewhat different conclusion regarding investment in the selection process (14).

In addition to these limitations associated with the selection procedures themselves, there are other problems. One of the major reasons for the failure of selection predictions is that people change in unexpected ways. A physical disorder may develop, personality changes may occur, and so on. Marital difficulties may produce discontent that is subsequently transferred to the job. Or financial problems may arise that could not have been anticipated but that leave the employee preoccupied and upset. The list of possibilities is endless. The point is that things happen to people over the years of employment that leave them changed individuals. When these are added to the normal alterations associated with aging (see Chapter 3), it is obvious that selection procedures have a potential that to be realistic must be considered somewhat limited. Certainly prediction in the short run is much better than it is over a long period.

This problem of change is not restricted to the individual himself, however. Jobs change, too. A man who was quite effective on an assembly line may not do so well when his job is automated more fully. A salesman who can sell one type of product in one market may run into difficulty when competitive pressures force the company to shift to a somewhat different consumer market or product. It is difficult if not impossible to select for the jobs of the future, especially when at the same time one must select for the still existing jobs of the present.

Change may also occur across jobs rather than within them. That is to say, a man may shift from job to job within the company rather than be faced with a change in the role prescriptions of a given position. Some amount of career change is the general rule rather than the exception. Certainly this is the case among college-educated employees and within the ranks of management. This matter of career prediction is one of the most difficult in the entire field of personnel selection. It requires that predictors be validated against career criteria and that longitudinal studies extend over long time periods. It is not too difficult to successfully predict whether a man will do well during his training period or in his initial placement with the company. It is quite another matter to predict that he will perform effectively twenty years hence in a position whose level and nature are something of a mystery. Yet there is no question that career selection of this kind is what most companies need, at least for a sizable proportion of the people they hire.

A final source of error has already been mentioned in a different context. Two managers may not evaluate their subordinates in exactly the same way, using the same criteria and standards. This is particularly true when organization planning and job analysis have had only minimal application, with the result that role prescriptions are ambiguous and uncertain. A man who is considered satisfactory by one superior may be rated considerably lower by another, even though his behavior has not changed. Two workers whose role behavior is almost identical can be evaluated quite differently. Obviously when criteria are unstable and unreliable in this manner, selection techniques will not come out looking very effective.

All these limitations are superimposed on the constraints imposed by the available manpower pool and the restrictions created by the nature and extent of the recruiting process. No selection procedure can yield an effective work force if the recruitment procedures cannot, or do not, provide an adequate group of candidates from which selection can occur. Recruitment, then, becomes the *sine qua non* for selection. If the number of possible hires equals the number of jobs to be filled, there is no selection. Therefore it is crucial to develop recruiting procedures that will provide a sufficiently large and varied candidate manpower pool so that the selection techniques can at least achieve their maximum potential. Actually, any valid selection technique will perform quite effectively if it can be used to skim the cream off a very large candidate group.

College, Professional, and Executive Recruitment

College Recruiting

As Table 11-3 indicates, recruiting on college campuses has become a very extensive operation for many companies. Almost all colleges have at least one placement office to coordinate the visits of company representatives and arrange interviews with students. Some have created specialized facilities within various professional schools as well. In most instances these placement offices are operated by the colleges themselves, but in a minority of cases they are branches of the state employment service (7).

From the company viewpoint this type of recruiting endeavor has many disadvantages. Representatives of the firm spend many unproductive hours in traveling from one campus to another. The competition among companies for the better candidates is extremely intense, and during recent years the graduate schools have been siphoning off a large proportion of the top students, often into nonbusiness occupations. One survey indicated that the larger corporations were conducting about ten campus interviews for each man hired. In smaller companies the number of interviews per hire was even greater (15). Such an effort can become extremely costly, both in time and money. Yet for many firms it represents the major source of managerial, professional, and sales manpower.

Table 11-3. How Many Vacancies Will Your Company Have this Year for College Graduates To Be Obtained from the Spring 1960 Interviews? (Based on responses from 88 companies recruiting at the University of Michigan, School of Business Administration.)

Number of vacancies	Number of companies
1–25	39
26–50	9
51–75	9
76–100	7
101–150	4
151–200	6
201–250	4
251–300	3
400	2
450	1
500	1
Over 1,000 (to maximum of 3,000)	3

Source: G. S. Odiorne and A. S. Hann, *Effective College Recruiting.* Ann Arbor, Mich.: Bureau of Industrial Relations, Univ. of Michigan, 1961, p. 92.

Although few studies that would indicate the specific techniques most likely to yield a sizable return on an investment in this area have been conducted, certain guidelines have achieved widespread acceptance (1,12). Most firms prepare brochures describing the organization and its jobs and distribute these to college placement offices before the interviewer arrives. In general, companies attempt to maintain continuing contact with college placement officials and to recruit regularly each year. When a company is a steady recruiter on a particular campus, it is more likely to be offered desirable interview dates by the placement office and to obtain assistance in other forms.

Most campus interviews are conducted only for the purpose of initial screening and to provide the candidate with information regarding the job and/or training program for which he is being considered. Normally a visit to some company facility follows, and it is there that the selection decision is actually made. In some instances job offers are made on the basis of the campus contact alone, although rarely at the actual time of the interview.

Increasingly, companies have attempted to go beyond the placement office contact in their search for candidates. Many utilize summer or part-time employment opportunities to attract college students who might later be considered for permanent positions. There is a widespread effort to get through to the professors directly to solicit information on students with outstanding potential. On occasion professors are retained as consultants with this as the primary objective.

Most firms maintain detailed statistics with regard to the campus recruiting process. Comparisons are usually made from year to year and, where possible, with other companies. Some of the more common ratios are:

$$\frac{\text{Number of invitations to visit company}}{\text{Number of campus interviews}}$$

$$\frac{\text{Number of invitation acceptances}}{\text{Number of invitations to visit company}}$$

$$\frac{\text{Number of job offers}}{\text{Number of company visits}}$$

$$\frac{\text{Number of job acceptances}}{\text{Number of decisions to hire}}$$

Probably the major factor contributing to an unsatisfactory result when statistics of this kind are computed is some type of deficiency in the campus contact process itself. College recruiting is often a grueling and, for some people, a boring process. The result is that a man who is potentially a very effective interviewer may not actually live up to his potentialities out in the campus placement office. What is needed is an individual who is interested in working with college students and who is enthusiastic about the company. Given these requirements, it probably matters very little whether he is a representative of a line unit, temporarily detached to recruit in his area of expertise, or a personnel man assigned regularly to this type of work. Most large companies appear to utilize individuals of both types.

Professional Manpower

The average company secures a large proportion of its professional employees—engineers, accountants, scientists, and the like—as a result of campus recruiting. In recent years, however, limited supplies of talent and rapid growth have forced a number of firms into the open market. This source may well have the disadvantage that outstanding employees will not be available, because they have been recognized by their current employers and rewarded sufficiently to keep them from changing jobs. On the other hand, the open market, in contrast to the college placement office, can be turned on and off as needed. It is not the type of recruiting source that requires extensive and precise manpower planning in advance and constant attention.

The approaches used to recruit professional employees from other companies vary considerably. The engineering shortages that have prevailed over the past fifteen years have produced considerable ingenuity, with the result that recruiting innovations have been widespread. Newspaper advertisements are no longer limited to the fine print of the classified columns. Large notices, prepared by company advertising departments or agencies, appear in the financial and sports sections of many papers. *The New York Times* carries hundreds of these notices every Sunday. Increasingly, professional society meetings are becoming as important in their role of employment market as they are for the communication of knowledge.

When shortages become particularly acute, there is a tendency for the recruiting to be carried even closer to the employee. Thus, a company may advertise in the newspapers of a city where large numbers of the desired type of professionals are known to work, indicating that a personnel representative will be in a given hotel suite for a specified period. In such instances hiring may well occur on the spot. Or intensive recruiting may be carried on at university-sponsored management-development conferences. Some firms pay particular attention to canceled government contracts and other indications of declining business activity. Where a reduction in the professional work force of another company is suspected, a telephone call is made and, if the original hunch is confirmed, a recruiter will very shortly be on the premises interviewing displaced employees.

This type of very active recruiting need not be restricted to professional employees. However, it is in this area that it has been most commonplace in recent years, largely because of the existence of continuing shortages of professional manpower.

Executive Search: The Practice of Pirating

In the years since World War II there has been what appears to be an increasing tendency to hire managers, especially manager-specialists, away from other firms (19). In some instances these candidates come to a company's attention as a result of contacts initiated by the candidates themselves, either in response to advertising or unsolicited. More commonly they are sought out directly by the firm or by its representatives.

There are a number of companies that fill the majority of their managerial positions through outside pirating. The more common practice is to rely primarily on promotion from within and to resort to recruiting from other firms only in unusual instances. In the latter cases companies may carry out the recruiting largely on their own. But where hiring on the outside is frequent, the usual practice is to utilize employment agencies, consulting organizations, and search firms to keep the company name out of the picture until a man is clearly a strong candidate.

General employment agencies are probably the least frequently used of these three outside intermediaries when it comes to hiring managerial and professional personnel. In part this is because agencies of this kind rarely conduct extensive searches designed to locate the most promising candidates, but rather rely on advertising and unsolicited contacts; in part it is because employment agencies do little initial screening, and as a result refer many obviously unqualified applicants to a company; in part it is because managers, especially those at higher levels, rarely contact such agencies when seeking a new employer. Yet employment agencies are utilized as a source of executive recruiting, primarily at the lower levels, and when they are used the fee is characteristically paid by the company.

Another source is the various management-consulting firms. These usually charge on a fee basis by the day for the time spent on a search. This can be a relatively lucrative business, but it can also be a source of considerable anxiety to clients who are afraid they will be raided by their own consultants. As a result a number of the larger consulting organizations have either moved out of this type of business or have established subsidiaries for the purpose.

In recent years the prime source for outside hiring has been the search organization, which devotes all of its energies to management recruiting. The largest of these firms are those based in New York City, but there are others spread throughout the country. These organizations guarantee to produce at least three qualified candidates in return for a fee consisting of 10 to 20 per cent of the first year's salary, which must be paid in many instances whether a man is actually hired or not (18). Normally these firms make their initial contact with a prospective candidate through a letter that describes the job in some detail and asks for recommended candidates. If the man recommends himself, then he places himself in a position to be seriously considered for the job.

Recruiting at the Lower Levels

At levels below those just discussed, a large range of recruiting sources are typically employed. These include unions, employers' or trade associations, public employment services, private employment agencies, friends and relatives, advertisements in newspapers or magazines, high schools and trade schools, other firms, and the company's own employment office. In many instances the last is the major approach—candidates either come in directly seeking work or they are developed from within the company by the personnel department. When an outside source is used, the particular one called upon appears to depend in large part on the tightness of the labor market, as indicated in Table 11-4.

Table 11-4.   Recruiting Practices and the Firm's Position in the Labor Market

Degree of tightness in the labor market	Sources used in recruiting	Area covered in recruiting
1. Most loose	Direct hiring	Immediate vicinity
2. Intermediate	Unions Friends and relatives Private and public agencies	Part of the metropolitan industrial area
3. Tight	Advertising Nearby special sources (business colleges, private agencies with employer paying fee)	All the metropolitan area
4. Most tight	Labor scouting	Regional and national

Source: F. T. Malm, "Recruiting Patterns and the Functioning of Labor Markets," *Industrial and Labor Relations Review*, Vol. 7 (1954), p. 518.

Manual Workers

The major mechanisms for recruiting production, maintenance, warehousing, and similar workers are direct contacts in the company's employment office, public employment agencies, and labor unions. In addition, friends and newspaper advertisements are rather widely used, although not as frequently as the three first mentioned (11). In general, the labor market for manual workers tends to be a local one.

Whether or not a firm can rely heavily on individuals who come in seeking work or who call in depends in large part on the extent to which the company is widely known in an area and on its reputation as an employer. Normally the smaller company will not be in as good a position to utilize this source as the larger one, although in some instances the effects of size on visibility can be overcome through product advertising and the introduction of unusually attractive employment practices.

The use of unions as an aid in recruiting varies considerably. Although the Taft-Hartley Act specifically forbids the *closed shop,* which requires that employers hire only union members, there are numerous cases where in fact recruiting for manual jobs is restricted almost entirely to the unions. In the maritime industry, union hiring halls represent practically the only labor source. Similarly, union control of the labor pool is characteristic in construction, printing, and the operating aspects of wholesale trade. In other industries the union is only rarely contacted for recruiting purposes.

Clerical Workers

In seeking office workers, most companies utilize a variety of practices depending on the nature and extent of their manpower requirements. Direct hiring is frequent in the larger firms. Recommendations by friends and current employees are perhaps a more common source among smaller businesses. Private employment agencies are normally more extensively involved in recruiting clerical employees than with any other group. Yet the public employment services operate in this area on a broad scale also.

Newspaper advertising is widely used, but there are certain drawbacks that should be recognized. After the ad appears, there is no way of controlling the number of applicants. As a result firms have been literally flooded with people seeking advertised positions, to the point where personnel resources were not adequate to cope with the influx. Yet it is very poor public relations policy to turn people away at such times without at least a brief interview. For this reason many of the larger companies place primary emphasis on techniques other than advertising in recruiting clerical and manual workers, especially when a labor surplus is known to exist in the employment area.

Sales Workers

It is a frequent practice in a number of companies to fill sales positions from within, either through transfer from nonsales positions or promotion. When this is not done, the more commonly utilized approaches are direct hiring, advertising in newspapers, contacts with friends and relatives, and employment agencies. Unions are of major significance as a source only in retail trade (11).

In recruiting sales employees, it appears to be particularly important to provide applicants with a detailed picture of the work they will be doing. Otherwise turnover is likely to be high. This may be true of other occupational areas also, but the relevant research has been done in the sales field.

One such study compared termination rates for two groups of
newly hired insurance salesmen (20). One group contained salesmen
hired in regions where a specially prepared job description brochure
was introduced for all sales applicants. The comparison group contained
salesmen hired in regions having similar turnover rates prior to the
introduction of the brochure. But these men were never given the
brochure and thus had to make the decision to accept employment with
only rather limited information regarding the job.

As Table 11-5 indicates, prior knowledge of job duties, which will
permit those who are not interested in the particular kind of work
to withdraw on their own prior to hiring, can serve to consistently
reduce turnover. Information such as that contained in the brochure
should be provided to permit knowledgeable self-selection to occur.
Recruiting that ignores this caution can put an inordinate strain on
the company's selection procedures.

**Table 11-5. Termination Rates over a Six-Month Period for
Life Insurance Agents Who Did and Did Not Receive
a Special Recruiting Brochure**

Month when hired	Receiving brochure (N = 226) Per cent terminating May–October	Not receiving brochure (N = 248) Per cent terminating May–October
May	32	47
June	34	49
July	25	31
August	18	22
September	5	10
October	3	9
All months	19	27

Source: J. Weitz, "Job Expectancy and Survival," *Journal of Applied Psychology,*
Vol. 40 (1956), p. 246.

The United States Employment Service

A word should be added about the public employment agencies that
operate in the various states under the general guidance of the U.S.
Employment Service (USES). There are over 1,900 such offices that
are staffed with state employees, although funds are provided by the
Federal government (7).

These offices make a variety of services available to employers.
These include the referral of candidates for employment, of course, but
also the conduct of intensive recruitment campaigns, psychological
testing, the furnishing of occupational information, and advice on

turnover and absenteeism problems. In addition, the public agencies administer the unemployment compensation system.

It is this latter aspect that creates the major difference between the state services and the private employment agencies. Under existing law the USES is required to make every effort to find work for the unemployed before insurance claims are paid. The result is that, although the public service does attempt to refer people for those jobs that are most appropriate in terms of whatever skills may be present, they may well send men to a company's personnel office even though these men are not strong candidates for employment. Probably in some instances those referred are not particularly interested in obtaining work at all, preferring to collect unemployment insurance payments for the period of their eligibility.

Private agencies, on the other hand, being under no compulsion to attempt to find a job for everyone, can carry out an initial screening and thus relieve the pressure on a company's personnel office. Because of the dual function of the USES, employment and insurance administration, many companies tend to tap other sources first, utilizing the state agencies only when forced to do so. On the other hand, some firms have made arrangements to fill all hourly personnel vacancies from the state employment service rolls. Clearly, attitudes toward USES activities differ from company to company.

Recruitment from Within

When a vacancy is identified, the normal practice, of course, is to carry out a search within the company to identify possible candidates before turning to the various outside sources. Individuals may be considered for *promotion* into the position or for *lateral transfer* or in some cases for *demotion,* although the latter is relatively rare.

Recruitment from within of this kind appears to be the primary method of obtaining candidates at the management level (11). There are, however, some firms, as previously noted, that place considerable reliance on outside sources in filling managerial vacancies. Management inventory charts of the kind discussed in Chapter 9 are particularly helpful when an effort is being made to recruit within the company. If an up-to-date IBM card system containing personnel data is maintained, this can be of considerable assistance in rapidly identifying men with the necessary qualifications. In fact a number of firms appear to be making rather extensive use of computers for this purpose. Data on skills, training, prior experience, and so on, may be stored in the computer and subsequently brought forth in desired combinations. With the increased memory capacity of such systems it is now possible to extend the management inventory approach to much lower organizational levels (2).

At these lower levels, however, seniority lists may well exercise considerable control over the internal recruiting process. As indicated in Chapter 10, many companies are required by the terms of their contract with the union to obtain candidates from among the longest service employees within the particular seniority unit where the vacancy exists.

It is also common practice below the management level to post vacancies by advertising them widely throughout the firm. A candidate pool is then constructed out of those who bid on the advertised position. This procedure has the disadvantage that many well-qualified individuals may fail to volunteer for consideration because they fear reprisal on the part of their superiors. This is a particular problem where the change in position would represent a lateral transfer. Many supervisors do, in fact, consider such an attempt to leave their unit as a slap in the face on the part of the subordinate. In spite of this drawback many firms have bound themselves to the posting and bidding procedure under terms of the union contract.

A closely related procedure is the talent search. Usually this is used when a company anticipates a number of future vacancies at the highly skilled and lower management levels and wishes to recruit candidates for promotion from within the firm. The search is widely advertised and employees are asked to notify the personnel office if they wish to be considered for various training programs that will qualify them for promotion. Those who indicate interest are administered an extensive battery of psychological tests and evaluated in various other ways. The men finally selected are given appropriate training and then placed in a reserve talent pool, while continuing on in their regular jobs until selected for promotion. A variant of this procedure involves the use of a short battery of psychological tests emphasizing verbal ability, which is given to all lower level employees. Candidates for the more refined screening are then identified on the basis of test scores rather than through a bidding process (13). The success of these talent search procedures is of course constrained by existing individual differences, as discussed in Chapter 3.

References

1. Allen, L. A., "An Effective Program of Campus Recruiting," in M. J. Dooher and E. Marting (eds.), *Selection of Management Personnel*, Vol. I. New York: American Management Association, 1957, pp. 391–403.
2. Austin, B., "The Role of EDP in Industrial Relations," *Management of Personnel Quarterly*, Vol. 3, No. 4 (1965), 24–30.

258 Screening and Selection: The Evaluation of Individual Inputs

3. Cronbach, L. J., and G. C. Gleser, *Psychological Tests and Personnel Decisions*. Urbana, Ill.: Univ. of Illinois Press, 1965.
4. Curtis, E. W., *The Application of Decision Theory and Scaling Methods to Selection Test Evaluation*, Ph.D. Dissertation. Eugene, Oregon: Univ. of Oregon, 1965.
5. Dunnette M. D., *Personnel Selection and Placement*. Belmont, Calif.: Wadsworth, 1966.
6. Forehand, G. A., "A Note on Executive Selection and the Decision Model," in R. Tagiuri (ed.), *Research Needs in Executive Selection*. Boston: Graduate School of Business Administration, Harvard Univ., 1961, pp. 99–104.
7. Haber, W., and D. H. Kruger, *The Role of the United States Employment Service in a Changing Economy*. Kalamazoo, Mich.: The W. E. Upjohn Institute for Employment Research, 1964.
8. Katkovsky, W., "Personality and Ability Changes over Eight Years," in D. W. Bray (ed.), *The Young Business Manager*. New York: Personnel Research Division, American Telephone and Telegraph Company, 1965, pp. 24–36.
9. Lawshe, C. H., "Employee Selection," *Personnel Psychology*, Vol. 5 (1952), 31–34.
10. Lawshe, C. H., and M. D. Steinberg, "Studies in Synthetic Validity, I. An Exploratory Investigation of Clerical Jobs," *Personnel Psychology*, Vol. 8 (1955), 291–301.
11. Malm, F. T., "Recruiting Patterns and the Functioning of Labor Markets," *Industrial and Labor Relations Review*, Vol. 7 (1954), 507–525.
12. Maloney, P. W., *Management's Talent Search: Recruiting Professional Personnel*. New York: American Management Association, 1961.
13. Miner, J. B., *Intelligence in the United States*. New York: Springer, 1957.
14. Miner, J. B., *The Management of Ineffective Performance*. New York: McGraw-Hill, 1963.
15. Odiorne, G. S., and A. S. Hann, *Effective College Recruiting*. Ann Arbor, Mich.: Bureau of Industrial Relations, Univ. of Michigan, 1961.
16. Smith, R. D., and P. S. Greenlaw, "Simulation of a Psychological Decision Process in Personnel Selection," *Management Science*, Vol. 13 (1967), 409–419.
17. Spitzer, M. E., and W. J. McNamara, "A Managerial Selection Study," *Personnel Psychology*, Vol. 17 (1964), 19–40.
18. Strong, L., "Recruiting at Middle and Upper Executive Levels," in M. J. Dooher and E. Marting (eds.), *Selection of Management Personnel*, Vol. I. New York: American Management Association, 1957, pp. 404–417.
19. Stryker, P., "The Pirates of Management," in W. M. Fox (ed.), *Readings in Personnel Management from Fortune*, rev. ed. New York: Holt, Rinehart & Winston, 1963, pp. 38–43.
20. Weitz, J., "Job Expectancy and Survival," *Journal of Applied Psychology*, Vol. 40 (1956), 245–247.

Questions

1. What are the differences between concurrent and predictive validity? Under what specific circumstances can the concurrent model lead to erroneous selection decisions?
2. What is cross-validation? Why is it an essential ingredient of the selection process? Does cross-validation become increasingly important as the number of predictors tried out is expanded?
3. How would you evaluate the use of predictors in personnel selection? What are their shortcomings and their strengths? Under what conditions are they most effective?
4. What appear to be the advantages and disadvantages associated with using private employment agencies? Contrast them with other available recruiting sources, especially in obtaining managerial personnel and hourly manual workers.
5. What are the pros and cons of recruiting from within versus going to outside sources to build up a candidate pool?

12

The Employment Interview and Related Techniques

There are two approaches that characteristically provide a basis for selection decisions. One relies heavily on the assumption that a candidate's behavior in the past can serve as a guide for predicting his future. Accordingly, extensive information is collected regarding the person's previous behavior in various educational, occupational, and perhaps other situations. Then this information is evaluated relative to the role requirements of the position to be filled—or of several positions, if career considerations are involved. The expectation is that the individual will remain much the same person in the future that he was in the past; that he will retain the same or similar characteristics and will behave in accordance with the previous pattern.

This rationale underlies many of the procedures regularly employed in the selection interview. It also underlies most biographical inventories, application blanks, medical history forms, and reference-checking techniques. In all these instances the primary, although not exclusive, emphasis is on accumulating valid information about the past to provide a basis for selecting the particular human inputs to the organization that will maximize future effectiveness.

A very different rationale underlies most psychological testing, the physical examination, and certain adaptations of the interview and the application blank. As we shall see, these adaptations make the particular interviews and application blanks very similar to psychological tests. This second approach relies heavily on the sampling of present behavior as a basis for prediction. Relatively standardized situations, which presumably have some relation to the job or jobs, are established and candidates are asked to behave within these contexts. It is assumed that their behavior in these limited situations is typical of their total present behavior and that they will remain sufficiently unchanged in the future to permit effective prediction.

The present chapter will take up those selection procedures that have their primary roots in an evaluation of the candidate's past: the interview, the various adaptations of the application blank procedure, and reference checks. In the next chapter attention will be focused on techniques of sampling current behavior to obtain information on intellectual and physical functioning and on personality characteristics.

The Interview

Although it should be evident that interview procedures are widely used for a variety of purposes, the primary concern here is with specific applications in the evaluation of human inputs to a business organization. Therefore applications in such areas as marketing research, employee counseling, management appraisal, and attitude surveys will receive very little attention.

Even within the input context, the interview serves a number of purposes: It is much more than a selection device. This is probably why it has survived and even thrived in the face of extended attacks by industrial psychologists and others and in the face of considerable evidence that, as commonly used, it is often not a very effective selection technique.

There are, in fact, a number of requirements connected with the input process that at present cannot be accomplished in any other way, although telephone and written communication might be substituted in certain instances. One of these roles has already been noted in the preceding chapter. Interviews are used as often to sell the company and thus recruit candidates for employment as to select. A single interview frequently involves both selection and recruiting aspects. Furthermore, terms of employment are characteristically negotiated in the interview situation, and an important public relations function is performed. Applicants who must be rejected are particularly likely to leave with very negative attitudes toward the company if they have not had an opportunity to talk with a responsible representative.

Even when the focus is directly on the selection process, the interview appears to possess certain unique values, which may account for its continued widespread use. For one thing, the great flexibility of the technique, which can contribute to limited validity in some selection situations, may represent a major asset in other situations. The interview is the method *par excellence* for filling in the gaps between other selection techniques—gaps that could not have been foreseen until the other techniques were actually applied. Responses on the application blank may make it clear that further information regarding the circumstances surrounding certain previous employment and separation decisions is needed. An interview can be of considerable help in providing such information.

It is also clear that the interview is widely used to determine whether an applicant is the type of person who can be expected to fit in and get along in the particular firm. Its use with reference to such organizational maintenance considerations is probably much more widespread than in predicting productivity. This is not to imply that other selection techniques cannot be used to predict maintenance criteria, but for various reasons they often are not given the same emphasis as the interview. There is something about the process of personal judgment that produces a strong feeling of validity, even when validity is not present. It is not surprising, therefore, that many companies place heavy emphasis on interviewing when attempting to predict whether a man will be a source of conflict, will have a negative impact on others, or will be an extremely unhappy employee.

Finally, there are situations, especially when managerial and professional positions are involved, where the interview is the only major selection technique that realistically *can* be used. When a man who already has a good job, who gives every evidence of being a good prospect, and who does not have a strong initial incentive to make a move is faced with extensive psychological testing, a physical exam, and an application blank (above and beyond the résumé he has already submitted), he may shy away. If this seems likely, it is often wiser to rely on the interview, reference checks, and the like in spite of their shortcomings, rather than face the prospect of losing the man entirely.

What is Known About the Selection Interview

A great deal has been written regarding the techniques of interviewing for various purposes (1,5,11,12). Much of this, however, derives from the expertise and opinion of specific individuals. What is really known, in the sense that it is based on studies using selection models of the kind discussed in the previous chapter and on other scientific research procedures, is considerably less.

The discussion here will be restricted to what is known in this scientific sense. Unfortunately, when this is done, a great deal is left to the discretion of the individual interviewer. Yet there is little point in continuing to perpetuate much of the existing lore, which in many instances has been developed out of situations far removed from the company employment office and which may therefore be quite erroneous when applied to a selection interview in the business world.

CONSISTENCY OF INTERVIEWER JUDGMENTS. There is considerable evidence to indicate that, although an interviewer will himself exhibit consistency in successive evaluations of the same individual, different interviewers are likely to come to quite disparate conclusions (13). Thus, when two employment interviewers utilize their own idiosyncratic interview procedures on the same applicant, the probability is that they will come to differing decisions. They will normally elicit information on different matters, and even when the topics covered do overlap, one man will weight the applicant's responses in a way that varies considerably from that employed by another.

These problems can be overcome. Interviewers can be trained to follow similar patterns in their questioning and to evaluate responses using the same standards. When more structured interview techniques are used, when the questions asked are standardized and responses are recorded in some systematic manner, the consistency of the judgmental process increases markedly. Within limits it does not matter which interviewer is used; the results tend to be similar. Unfortunately, however, structuring of a kind that will increase the consistency of judgments appears to be the exception rather than the rule in most personnel offices. Thus, where strong reliance is placed on the interview, the final selection decision often depends as much on which interviewer is used as on the characteristics of the applicant. On the other hand, agreement does not guarantee accuracy of prediction; there can be great consistency in picking the wrong people.

ACCURACY OF INTERVIEW INFORMATION. Studies aimed at determining the accuracy of statements regarding work history made in the interview indicate that reporting errors may occur. Thus, in one instance when a check was made with employers, information given by the interviewees regarding job titles was found to be invalid in 24 per cent of the cases. Job duties were incorrectly reported by 10 per cent and pay by 22 per cent (26). In general, the tendency was to upgrade rather than downgrade prior work experience.

Other research suggests that in most employment situations interview distortion is probably not as prevalent as the preceding figures suggest (23). Yet in any given instance an interviewer may be faced with an applicant who deliberately, or perhaps unconsciously, falsifies his report. In such cases the usual tendency is for the man to make his record look better than it is. It can be assumed, also, that many applicants will attempt to avoid discussing previous instances of ineffective work performance. Where valid data are essential, it is usually desirable to check interview statements against outside sources.

ACCURACY OF INTERVIEWER JUDGMENTS. The inevitable conclusion derived from a number of investigations is that interview judgments, as they are usually made in the employment situation, are not closely related to independent measures of the characteristics judged. Nor are they closely related to measures of success on the job. In an overall sense the evidence regarding the validity of the selection interview yields a distinctly disappointing picture (13).

Yet there are conditions under which the interview exhibits considerable strength as a selection device, and there are some characteristics that are capable of being judged more effectively than others. Studies dealing with the relationship between interview estimates of intelligence and test scores indicate that the interview can be quite valid in this area. The interview would also appear to have good potential as a predictor of self-confidence, the effectiveness with which a man can express himself, certain types of attitudes, sociability, and a variety of mental abilities. Such characteristics as dependability, creativity, honesty, and loyalty would seem to be much more difficult to estimate correctly in the normal interview situation.

Table 12-1. Correlations Between Attitude Evaluations from Interviews and Supervisors' Performance Ratings

Attitudes	*Group 1* (N = 12)	*Group 2* (N = 14)
Formulation of goal	.14	.60
Strength of job interest	−.13	.40
Strength of general interests	.42	.85
Self-regard	.67	.63
Acquisitive perseverance	−.13	−.30
All five attitudes combined	.45	.71
Formulation of goal, strength of general interests, and self-regard combined	.54	.66

Source: Adapted from K. A. Yonge, "The Value of the Interview: An Orientation and a Pilot Study," *Journal of Applied Psychology*, Vol. 40 (1956), p. 29.

The evidence regarding the value of the interview as a selection procedure is certainly not all negative. Where the interview approach is planned in advance and a relatively structured format is followed, so that much the same questions are asked of all interviewees, relatively good validities have been obtained against job performance criteria (6,27). The results of one such study, which utilized the concurrent model, are presented in Table 12-1. Clearly these interview judgments constitute quite adequate predictors in certain instances. Others among the attitude estimates are considerably less effective.

In another series of studies rather sizable predictive validities were reported for overall interviewer estimates of suitability for employment when a highly structured, patterned interview approach was followed (14). When validated against duration of employment for the 587 people who left the company within an eighteen-month period, the interviews yielded a correlation of .43. The men rated higher initially in the employment interview stayed longer. The 407 employees who were still on the job eighteen months after hiring were rated for performance effectiveness by their superiors and the results compared with the earlier interview judgments. A predictive validity coefficient of .68 was obtained. Subsequent studies using the same patterned interview format produced correlations with success criteria that were consistently in the range of the .60's.

It is evident that the interview can be quite effective when used in a relatively standardized manner and when individualized interviewer approaches and biases are controlled. Under such standardized conditions the interview takes on certain characteristics of the application blank or a psychological test. It becomes in many respects an oral version of the common written selection procedures, although still with greater flexibility. There is nothing in what has been said to imply that less structured (and less directive) interviews may not yield equally good validities under certain circumstances and with certain interviewers, but without further research it is not possible to specify exactly what these requisite conditions are.

THE MCGILL UNIVERSITY STUDIES. Certain other conclusions regarding the decision-making process in the interview are derived from a series of studies carried out at McGill University over a ten-year period (25). As a result of this research it is now clear that in the actual employment situation most interviewers tend to make an accept-reject decision early in the interview. They do not wait until all the information is in. Rather a bias is developed and stabilized shortly after the discussion starts. This bias serves to color the remainder of the interview and is not usually reversed.

Second, interviewers are much more influenced by unfavorable than by favorable data. If any shift in viewpoint occurs during the interview, it is much more likely to be in the direction of rejection. Apparently selection interviewers tend to maintain rather clear-cut conceptions regarding the role requirements of the jobs for which they are interviewing. They compare candidates against these stereotypes in the sense of looking for deviant characteristics and thus for negative evidence with regard to hiring. Positive evidence is given much less weight.

These findings suggest certain guidelines for maximizing the effectiveness of employment interviewing. For one thing, if it is intended that the interview should make a *unique* contribution to the selection process, the interviewing ought to be done with relatively little foreknowledge of the candidate. Thus, contrary to common practice, application blanks, test scores, and the like should be withheld until after the initial selection interview. Personal history data should be obtained directly from the candidate in oral form even if written versions are available. This approach will serve to delay decision making in the interview, with the result that information obtained during the latter part of the discussion can be effectively utilized in reaching a judgment. If data are needed to fill in the gaps between the various selection techniques, these can be obtained from a second interview. Thus, the interview as an independent selection tool should be clearly differentiated from the interview as a means of following up on leads provided by other devices. The interviewer should be clear in his own mind as to which objective he is seeking.

When the interview is used as an independent procedure, information obtained from the various sources should be combined and evaluated subsequently to reach a final selection decision, rather than during the interview proper. When the interview is used to supplement application blank, medical history, and psychological test data, it should be considered as an information-gathering device only, not as an ideally constituted selection procedure. In neither case should it assume the proportions of a final arbiter, superseding all other techniques and sources of information.

Types of Employment Interviews

It is evident that the content of the selection interview may be varied. Different interviewers may ask different questions, concentrate on different parts of the man's prior experience, and attempt to develop estimates of different characteristics. It is also true that the basic technique or procedure may be varied.

PATTERNED OR STRUCTURED INTERVIEWS. This approach has already been noted in connection with the discussions of the consistency and accuracy of interviewer judgments. Often a detailed form is used with the specific questions to be asked noted and space provided for the answers. The form is completed either during the interview or from memory immediately afterward. In other cases only the areas to be covered are established in advance, the order of coverage and actual question wording being left to the interviewer. Either way the more structured approach offers distinct advantages over the usual procedure, where different interviewers may go off in completely different directions, depending on their own and the candidate's predilections. On the other hand, it should be recognized that information loss may occur because of a lack of flexibility.

NONDIRECTIVE PROCEDURES. The nondirective approach derives originally from psychotherapy and counseling. It permits the person being interviewed considerable leeway in determining the topics to be covered. The basic role of the interviewer is to reflect the feelings of the other person and to restate or repeat key words and phrases. This tends to elicit more detailed information from the interviewee, especially with reference to his emotional reactions, attitudes, and opinions. Because the candidate actually controls the content of the interview, this procedure may take the discussion far afield from what the interviewer might wish to treat. It frequently yields a great deal of information about the prior experiences, early family life, and interpersonal relationships of the individual, but much of this often has no clear relationship to the employment decision. For this reason the nondirective technique is usually mixed with a more directive, questioning approach when it is used in the selection interview.

MULTIPLE AND GROUP INTERVIEWS. Another procedure, which has proved to yield very good validity (13), involves the use of more than one interviewer. Either the candidate spends time talking to several different people separately or he meets with a panel or board whose members alternate in asking him questions. The latter approach can easily be integrated into a patterned or structured format, and when this is done, the resulting decisions and evaluations appear to maximize prediction of subsequent performance. Normally the group evaluation is derived after discussion among the various interviewers, but independent estimates can be obtained from each man and these then averaged to achieve a final decision. The major disadvantage of any multiple interviewer procedure is that it can become very costly in terms of the total number of man-hours required. For this reason it is usually reserved for use in selecting people for the higher-level positions in a company.

STRESS INTERVIEWS. The stress approach achieved some acceptance in the business world after World War II as a result of its use during the war to select men for espionage work with the Office of Strategic Services. As used in industry, this procedure usually involves the induction of failure stress. The interviewer rather suddenly becomes quite aggressive, belittles the candidate, and throws him on the defensive. Reactions to this type of treatment are then observed.

Because it utilizes a sample of present behavior to formulate predictions, rather than focusing on past behavior, the stress interview is in many ways more like a situational test than a selection interview. It has the disadvantage that rejected candidates who are subjected to this process can leave with a very negative image of the company, and even those whom the company may wish to hire can become so embittered that they will not accept an offer. This does not happen often, and usually a subsequent explanation can serve to eradicate any bad feelings. Yet when the fact that there is little positive evidence on the predictive power of the stress interview is added to these considerations, it seems very difficult to justify its use under normal circumstances. The selection situation appears to be anxiety-provoking enough already for most people.

The Interview and Selection Models

It seems absolutely essential that the interviewer receive some systematic feedback on the validity of his decisions if a company is to make effective use of the selection interview. To accomplish this, written evaluations of each candidate must be recorded at the conclusion of the interview. These interview ratings can then be compared at a later date, with criterion information provided by the man's immediate superior or derived from some other source. In this way the interviewer can modify his technique over time to maximize his predictive validity (4).

This approach suffers from the fact that no follow-up can be made on those applicants who are not hired. Yet in most companies personnel recommendations are not followed religiously. For various reasons those recommended for rejection are hired on occasion. In addition, other selection procedures may outweigh an original negative interview impression. Thus, there will be individuals in the follow-up group who have received rather low ratings, although the preponderant number will have had generally favorable evaluations in the interview.

One should not expect perfect success from these studies. Yet an interview should contribute something above what might be obtained by chance alone and from the use of other techniques. Also, if a standardized interview form is used, individual questions can be analyzed to see if they discriminate between effective and ineffective employees. If certain questions appear not to be contributing to the predictive process, others can be substituted and evaluated in a similar manner.

Application Blanks and Biographical Inventories

Probably the most widely used selection device is some type of written statement regarding the applicant's prior experiences and behavior. This may take the form of the conventional application blank, or an extended biographical inventory utilizing a great variety of multiple-choice questions may be employed. On occasion the form and content of the statement are determined by the applicant rather than the company. Such *résumés* are particularly likely to be used when the applicant is at the professional or managerial level.

Application Blanks

The actual items included on the application blank vary considerably from company to company (17). Many firms maintain several different versions for various positions. It is particularly common to have a separate blank for professional and technical employees, but it may be expedient to develop special forms for any group of jobs that are similar in their requirements and for which applications are received frequently.

In addition to such routine matters as name, address, telephone number, date of birth, social security number, marital status, children, and citizenship, most forms request information on arrest history, education, and previous employment. Although many applicants will not report arrests and convictions when requested to do so, it is nevertheless desirable to include a question in this area, merely because important information is sometimes obtained. Items dealing with education normally emphasize the extent of training rather than the quality of the work done. Information on grades, if it is desired, is better obtained from the educational institution itself.

Work history data may be requested in a variety of forms. Usually it is desirable to determine not only job title, but duties and also the level of the position within the employing organization. Salary data can be helpful in negotiating a salary figure with those who will be entering positions that do not have a set starting rate. Questions regarding the reasons for leaving previous employers are often unrevealing, but on occasion they do yield valuable information.

It is important in constructing an application blank to obtain only data that will be used. There is a tendency for these forms to grow in length over the years, to the point where they can well serve to discourage applicants who, at least initially, are not strongly motivated for employment. It is also important to be sure that the information requested is not in violation of Federal and state fair employment practices legislation. In general it is desirable to avoid any questions dealing with race, nationality, and religion.

Weighting Application Blank Items

The scoring of application blanks in accord with the demands of the selection model dates back to the early 1920's. The basic requirement is that responses to the various items on the blank be related to some criterion of job success. Studies have been done using job tenure, success ratings, salary increases, and a variety of other indexes. Application blank data appear particularly useful in predicting turnover (20). One advantage of this approach is that, because application blanks are almost universally filled out by all applicants, it is possible to carry out weighting studies at any time. All that is required is a search of the files for the application blanks of people hired for a given type of work during a specified period. These blanks may then be related to available measures of success or turnover.

Figure 12-1. Form for Weighting Application Blank Responses by Horizontal Percent Method (Hypothetical Data)

Response Categories	Low Group	High Group	Total Number	Percent High	Weight
Marital Status					
Single	35	19	54	35	4
Married	52	97	149	65	7
Divorced	25	8	33	24	2
Separated	15	6	21	29	3
Widowed	13	10	23	43	4
	140	140	280		
Education					
Grade School	13	14	27	52	5
High School Incomplete	28	23	51	45	5
High School Graduate	56	46	102	45	5
College Incomplete	18	16	34	47	5
College Graduate	16	25	41	61	6
Graduate Work	9	16	25	64	6
	140	140	280		
Most Recent Work Experience					
None	18	5	23	22	2
Production	40	30	70	43	4
Clerical	38	28	66	42	4
Sales	8	35	43	81	8
Managerial	5	17	22	77	8
Professional	13	16	29	55	6
Other	18	9	27	33	3
	140	140	280		
Military Service					
Yes	77	86	163	53	5
No	63	54	117	46	5
	140	140	280		

A variety of techniques for weighting application blank items have been developed, some of them quite statistically complex (9). In general, however, the more involved procedures do not add a great deal as long as the number of cases used in the analysis is sufficiently large. The much simpler horizontal per cent method, as illustrated in Figure 12-1, appears to be perfectly adequate for most purposes. All that is needed is a sample of employees that may be divided, usually at the median, into a high and low group on some criterion index. Application blanks filled out previously, at the time of employment, are then checked to determine how many in the low and high groups selected each alternative on a given item. The per cent of those responding in a particular way who also fall in the high group on the criterion is then computed. This percentage is converted to a weight by rounding to a single number. High values are associated with the desired performance and low values with that which is not desired. A total score for the blank is obtained by adding up the weights on the individual items.

In the hypothetical example of Figure 12-1, it is clear that the married group tends to produce more than its share of effective employees. Accordingly this response on the application blank receives a high score. The divorced and separated responses, being associated with less effective performance, receive a low score, whereas those who report themselves as single or widowed receive only a slightly negative weight. Education does not serve to discriminate very well between the high and low groups, although there is some slight advantage associated with the very highest levels of educational accomplishment. A sales or managerial background, on the other hand, appears to be highly desirable, whereas no previous work experience, or employment in areas other than those listed, perhaps farming, yield low weights. Military service does not matter one way or the other. Using these four questions only, a married man with college education, immediately preceding experience as a salesman, and military service would have a total score of 26. This is well above the 14 obtained by a divorced high school graduate with no previous work experience and no military service.

After weights have been developed in this manner, it is important that the scoring be cross-validated on another sample drawn from the same employee group. This is essential in constructing a weighted application blank, because many of the differences in weights may not reflect real differences but only chance fluctuations. When a large number of items are weighted in this manner, cross-validation may yield validity coefficients well below what the analysis of the original sample seemed to suggest.

Additional cross-validations should also be conducted at periodic intervals after the weighting procedure has actually been introduced into the selection process, especially if any major changes in the jobs involved or in the labor market have occurred in the interim since the weights were originally established. Continuing studies of the relationship between weighted scores and job performance should also be made when the weights used are widely known in the company. In at least one instance an initially entirely satisfactory validity shrank to zero over a three-year period, because field managers, who were anxious to find replacements and familiar with the weights, tended to guide applicants into the desired responses (10). This sort of situation can develop with any selection instrument if there are acute shortages in the labor market or if recruiting is very difficult.

It should be emphasized that studies done to date do not yield support for the view that certain responses on an application blank are universally predictive of future success, irrespective of the job and the situation. In fact the responses that contribute the most to the relationship with a criterion are often difficult to explain in any manner. Thus, in one study the factors found to be predictive were an average of at least ten months' service with all previous employers, no unfavorable employment references, leaving the last job to seek advancement, living on the north side of the city, living in the city rather than the suburbs, and over twenty-four years of age (21). Other studies on different groups produce very different results.

Biographical Inventories

The distinction between a weighted application blank and a biographical inventory is by no means clear-cut. However, the typical biographical inventory contains a somewhat larger number of items, utilizes a multiple-choice format exclusively, and deals with matters that would not normally be covered in an application form. Often there are questions dealing with early life experiences, hobbies, health, social relations, and so on, that go well beyond the application blank in their detailed coverage of prior experiences. In some instances questions on attitudes, interests, values, opinions, and self-impressions are included. When this occurs, the biographical inventory begins to approximate a test. Thus, selection instruments of this kind, although they tend to place primary emphasis on the past as a predictor of the future, can also serve to sample present behavior and functioning to achieve their predictive purpose. Examples of the various kinds of items currently in use are presented in Figure 12-2.

Biographical inventories are usually constructed for the specific purpose of predicting success in a given type of work. The items included are those that the person conducting the analysis believes have some potential as predictors. The mechanics of weighting are essentially the same as those described for the weighted application blank. Usually, however, items that do not discriminate between high and low performers are dropped from the final measure. Thus, the validation and cross-validation process serves as a means of item selection.

Although biographical inventories have been developed for a great variety of purposes, some of the most interesting recent applications have been in the prediction of scientific accomplishments, especially in the

Figure 12-2. Typical Biographical Inventory Questions

Classification Data
   What is your present marital status?
      1. Single
      2. Married, no children
      3. Married, one or more children.
      4. Widowed.
      5. Separated or divorced.

Habits and Attitudes
   How often do you tell jokes?
      1. Very frequently.
      2. Frequently.
      3. Occasionally.
      4. Seldom.
      5. Can't remember jokes.

Health
   Have you ever suffered from:
      1. Allergies
      2. Asthma
      3. High blood pressure
      4. Ulcers
      5. Headaches
      6. None of these

Human Relations
   How do you regard your neighbors?
      1. Not interested in your neighbors.
      2. Like them but seldom see them.
      3. Visit in each others' homes occasionally.
      4. Spend a lot of time together.

Money
   How much life insurance, other than company group insurance, do you carry on your
   own life?
      1. None
      2. $1,000 to $7,500
      3. $7,500 to $12,500
      4. $12,500 to $25,000
      5. Over $25,000

Parental Home, Childhood, Teens
   During most of the time before you were 18, with whom did you live?
      1. Both parents.
      2. One parent.
      3. A relative.
      4. Foster parents or non-relatives.
      5. In a home or institution.

Personal Attributes
   How creative do you feel you are?
      1. Highly creative.
      2. Somewhat more creative than most in your field.
      3 Moderately creative.
      4. Somewhat less creative than most in your field.

Figure 12-2 (cont'd.)

Present Home, Spouse, and Children
  Regarding moving from location to location, my wife:
    1. Would go willingly wherever my job takes me.
    2. Would not move under any circumstances.
    3. Would move only if it were absolutely necessary.
    4. I don't know how she feels about moving.
    5. Not married.

Recreation, Hobbies, and Interests
  Have you ever belonged to:
    1. A high school fraternity or its equivalent.
    2. A college fraternity.
    3. Both a high school and a college fraternity.
    4. None of the above.

School and Education
  How old were you when you graduated from high school?
    1. Younger than 15.
    2. 15 to 16.
    3. 17 to 18.
    4. 19 or older.
    5. Did not graduate from high school.

Self Impressions
  Do you generally do your best:
    1. At whatever job you are doing.
    2. Only in what you are interested.
    3. Only when it is demanded of you.

Values, Opinions, and Preferences
  Which one of the following seems most important to you?
    1. A pleasant home and family life.
    2. A challenging and exciting job.
    3. Getting ahead in the world.
    4. Being active and accepted in community affairs.
    5. Making the most of your particular ability.

Work
  How do your feel about traveling in your work?
    1. Would enjoy it tremendously.
    2. Would like to do some traveling.
    3. Would travel if it were necessary.
    4. Definitely dislike traveling.

Source: J. R. Glennon, L. E. Albright, and W. A. Owens, *A Catalog of Life History Items.* Washington, D.C.: Division 14, American Psychological Association.

pharmaceutical industry. In one such study carried out with the research staff of G. D. Searle and Company, a correlation between biographical inventory responses and ratings of research competence of .57 was obtained. The more creative researchers had a positive self-image, a need for independence, broad interests, a background of parental permissiveness, a tendency to become overinvolved in their work, a positive reaction to challenge, a desire for unstructured work situations, and an interest in contemplative pursuits (2). Similar results were obtained from a study carried out at Richardson-Merrell, Inc. (3,24). The latter study suggests that items dealing with the early years and with the parental family have much less value in predicting creativity than do those in such areas as academic background, adult life, and adult interests. There is also evidence that the biographical inventory responses that work for pharmaceutical company scientists are very similar to those that will predict the accomplishments of physical scientists engaged in space research.

Projective Personality Analysis of Application Blanks

A final variation on the application blank theme involves the collection of information on previous experience and behavior, but this information is analyzed for the leads it may provide on present personality functioning. The basic rationale is that an applicant will reveal much of his personality by the unique way in which he answers the questions— whether he writes out his full name or uses initials, the specific type of vocation he would prefer, and so on.

This approach to personality assessment has been most fully developed by the authors of the Worthington Personal History Blank. This is a four-page questionnaire to be filled out in pencil, which contains items dealing with family, physical condition, education, activities, U.S. service experience, business experience, and aims. The questions allow for a variety of forms of response and are interpreted in accordance with the dictates of personality theory. The result is a personality description, which may be used as a basis for predicting success on the job. These descriptions appear to be relatively accurate (18). In addition, they have exhibited some validity in predicting the job tenure of salesmen, a constantly recurring selection problem (22). Yet the universal validity of the technique has not been demonstrated. In certain situations it does not appear to be a very effective selection tool.

References and Background Checks

A final method of obtaining information on an applicant's prior behavior utilizes not the individual himself, but those who have associated with him and been in a position to observe him. Usually a written evaluation is obtained, but sometimes telephone or even face-to-face interviews with informants are conducted.

Although the use of references, usually individuals named by the applicant, is widespread in the business world, the available research does not provide much basis for optimism insofar as this approach to the selection problem is concerned. One study related scores obtained from a standardized recommendation questionnaire to subsequent supervisory ratings of performance (15). The questionnaire contained items on occupational ability, character and reputation, and employability. On the average two completed questionnaires were returned on each individual included in the study, and the scores on these were averaged for the purpose of computing validity coefficients. The recommendations come from previous employers, supervisors, personnel managers, co-workers, and acquaintances. The men evaluated were all civil service employees working in various skilled trades. Results are presented in Table 12-2.

Table 12-2. Correlation of Employee Recommendation Scores with Supervisors' Ratings

Trade	N	r
Carpenter	51	.01
Equipment repairman	40	.23
Machinist	100	.24
Machine operator	108	−.10
Ordnanceman (torpedo)	125	−.01
Radio mechanic	107	.29
Aviation metalsmith	94	.24
Highlift fork operator	108	.21
Auto mechanic	98	.09
Painter	70	.07
Ordnanceman	100	.10
Printer	116	.11

Source: J. N. Mosel and H. W. Goheen, "The Validity of the Employment Recommendation Questionnaire in Personnel Selection," *Personnel Psychology*, Vol. 11 (1958), p. 484.

Only the correlations in the .20's have any predictive significance and these are still low. Since only five of the twelve values reach even this level, the findings cannot be interpreted as providing much support for the use of recommendations. The major difficulty is that the responses were almost without exception very positive. Thus, the range of scores was narrow and discrimination among applicants minimal. This appears to be a typical difficulty with recommendations. However, there is some evidence that when references are obtained in letter form, rather than by standardized questionnaire, different types of positive statements can have differential significance (19). When only positive statements regarding such characteristics as cooperation, consideration, and urbanity appear in the letter, there is a good chance the person writing the reference has some doubts regarding the man's qualifications. If, on the other hand, there are positive statements in the areas of mental agility, vigor, dependability, and reliability, then it can be assumed that a favorable opinion regarding performance potential really exists.

A question may arise concerning the source of the recommendations.

Is it possible that certain types of people, having had particular kinds of relationships with an applicant, will provide more valid information than other types? A study to check on this hypothesis has been conducted, again with civil service employees in various skilled trades (16). Employment recommendation scores of the kind previously described were correlated with performance ratings given by superiors subsequent to employment. The results are given in Table 12-3.

Table 12-3. Correlation of Employee Recommendation Scores for Different Respondent Types with Supervisors' Ratings

Respondent type	N	r
Personnel officers	102	.02
Supervisors	188	.19
Co-workers	311	.09
Acquaintances	182	.20
Relatives	12	−.16

Source: J. N. Mosel and H. W. Goheen, "The Employment Recommendation Questionnaire: III. Validity of Different Types of References," *Personnel Psychology*, Vol. 12 (1959), p. 474.

The correlations for supervisors and acquaintances are reliably different from zero and therefore meaningful. The others are not. In general, friends tend to be the most lenient, previous subordinates are next, previous co-workers next, and previous employers and superiors the most critical. This would suggest that if one does use letters of recommendation as a selection tool, the letters will discriminate most effectively and yield the highest validity when they are obtained from previous supervisors.

A final question involves the relationship between written recommendations and more intensive field investigations, which attempt to develop a picture of a man's background from personal interviews with a variety of people who have known him. A study in this area dealt with government employees hired to fill positions as economists, budget examiners, and training officers (8). Field interviews were conducted with from three to six people who knew the applicant, and the results of these interviews were combined into an overall field evaluation. The latter investigation report ratings were then correlated with previously obtained ratings on a standardized recommendation questionnaire dealing with the applicants' personality, skill, knowledge, human relations competence, and occupational development.

As Table 12-4 indicates, there was a positive relationship between the written recommendations and the more intensive field investigations. What the table does not indicate is the amount of information that came out in the interviews but not in the letters. Such matters as gross incompetence, alcoholism, and homosexuality were practically never mentioned in writing. Yet the field interviews often led to the identification of such factors. It seems clear, therefore, that the more effort one puts into an investigation of an applicant's background, the greater the probability that meangingful results will be obtained. Letters to friends identified by the applicant are in all probability not even worth the cost of mailing. Intensive interviews with former superiors, and others who know the man well, may be worth the effort.

Table 12-4. Correlation of Employee Recommendation Scores and Investigation Report Ratings

Position	N	r
Economist	41	.22
Budget examiner	21	.54
Training officer	47	.45

Source: H. W. Goheen and J. N. Mosel, "Validity of Employment Recommendation Questionnaire: II. Comparison with Field Investigations," *Personnel Psychology,* Vol. 12 (1959), p. 300.

It should be emphasized that field investigations of the type described are not restricted to government employees. Bonding and security clearance investigations are frequently carried out on industrial employees. Many firms regularly obtain credit evaluations on applicants, and the credit agencies often provide detailed information on other matters as well. For a rather nominal price, checks are carried out on court records, educational credentials, prior work experiences, and places of residence. On occasion detective agencies are used to investigate managerial candidates. It is common practice to speak either on the telephone or in person with mutual acquaintances, especially those with occupational skills similar to the applicant's. Although the evidence on the matter is sparse, it seems likely that all these techniques, if they are used in a systematic manner with cross-checks between sources, will be more valuable and valid than written references. Nevertheless, it is important to maintain an ongoing validation effort to determine whether all types of preemployment information are related to subsequent success.

References

1. Bellows, R. M., and M. F. Estep, *Employment Psychology: The Interview.* New York: Holt, Rinehart & Winston, 1961.
2. Buel, W. D., "Biographical Data and the Identification of Creative Re-

search Personnel," *Journal of Applied Psychology,* Vol. 49 (1965), 318–321.

3. Cline, V. B., and M. F. Tucker, *The Prediction of Creativity and Other Performance Measures Among Pharmaceutical Scientists.* Salt Lake City, Utah: Univ. of Utah, 1965.

4. England, G. W., and D. G. Paterson, "Selection and Placement—The Past Ten Years," in H. G. Heneman et al. (eds.), *Employment Relations Research.* New York: Harper & Row, 1960, pp. 43–72.

5. Fear, R. A., *The Evaluation Interview.* New York: McGraw-Hill, 1958.

6. Ghiselli, E. E., "The Validity of a Personnel Interview," *Personnel Psychology,* Vol. 19 (1966), 389–394.

7. Glennon, J. R., L. E. Albright, and W. A. Owens, *A Catalog of Life History Items.* Washington, D.C.: Division 14, American Psychological Association (undated).

8. Goheen, H. W., and J. N. Mosel, "Validity of the Employment Recommendation Questionnaire: II. Comparison with Field Investigations," *Personnel Psychology,* Vol. 12 (1959), 297–301.

9. Guion, R. M., *Personnel Testing.* New York: McGraw-Hill, 1965.

10. Hughes, J. F., J. F. Dunn, and B. Baxter, "The Validity of Selection Instruments under Operating Conditions," *Personnel Psychology,* Vol. 9 (1956), 321–324.

11. Kahn, R. L., and C. F. Cannell, *The Dynamics of Interviewing.* New York: Wiley, 1957.

12. Lopez, F. M., *Personnel Interviewing—Theory and Practice.* New York: McGraw-Hill, 1965.

13. Mayfield, E. C., "The Selection Interview—A Re-evaluation of Published Research," *Personnel Psychology,* Vol. 17 (1964), 239–260.

14. McMurry, R. N., "Validating the Patterned Interview," *Personnel,* Vol. 23 (1947), 263–272.

15. Mosel, J. N., and H. W. Goheen, "The Validity of the Employment Recommendation Questionnaire in Personnel Selection," *Personnel Psychology,* Vol. 11 (1958), 481–490.

16. Mosel, J. N., and H. W. Goheen, "The Employment Recommendation Questionnaire: III. Validity of Different Types of References," *Personnel Psychology,* Vol. 12 (1959), 469–477.

17. National Industrial Conference Board, *Forms and Records in Personnnel Administration,* Studies in Personnel Policy, No. 175. New York: the Board, 1960.

18. Peck, R. F., and R. E. Worthington, "New Techniques for Personnel Assessment," *Journal of Personnel Administration and Industrial Relations,* Vol. 1 (1954), 23–30.

19. Peres, S. H., and J. R. Garcia, "Validity and Dimensions of Descriptive Adjectives Used in Reference Letters for Engineering Applicants," *Personnel Psychology,* Vol. 15 (1962), 279–286.

20. Schuh, A. J., "The Predictability of Employee Tenure: A Review of the Literature," *Personnel Psychology,* Vol. 20 (1967), 133–152.

21. Shott, G. L., L. E. Albright, and J. R. Glennon, "Predicting Turnover in

an Automated Office Situation," *Personnel Psychology,* Vol. 16 (1963), 213–219.

22. Spencer, G., and R. E. Worthington, "Validity of a Projective Technique in Predicting Sales Effectiveness," *Personnel Psychology,* Vol. 5 (1952), 125–144.

23. Tiffin, J., and E. J. McCormick, *Industrial Psychology,* 5th ed. Englewood Cliffs, N.J.: Prentice-Hall, 1965.

24. Tucker, M. F., V. B. Cline, and J. R. Schmitt, "Prediction of Creativity and Other Performance Measures from Biographical Information among Pharmaceutical Scientists," *Journal of Applied Psychology,* Vol. 51 (1967), 131–138.

25. Webster, E. C., *Decision Making in the Employment Interview.* Montreal, Canada: Industrial Relations Centre, McGill Univ., 1964.

26. Weiss, D. J., and R. V. Dawis, "An Objective Validation of Factual Interview Data," *Journal of Applied Psychology,* Vol. 44 (1960), 381–385.

27. Yonge, K. A., "The Value of the Interview: An Orientation and a Pilot Study," *Journal of Applied Psychology,* Vol. 40 (1956), 25–31.

Questions

1. Discuss the various uses of the interview both within and outside the selection situation. What do you feel will be the future of the technique in the selection context? Why?

2. What do stress interviews, biographical inventories containing items asking for self-impressions, and projective questions in application blanks have in common?

3. How might you construct a biographical inventory using the horizontal per cent method to weight and select items? Write five biographical inventory items and carry out the weighting process using hypothetical data.

4. What do we know about the value of recommendation questionnaires and letters of reference in the selection process?

13

The Physical Examination and Psychological Testing

In this final chapter on the selection process the coverage will be restricted to methods of regulating the human inputs to an organization, which place primary stress on samples of current activity. Both the physical examination and psychological testing attempt to develop an estimate of future effectiveness from an analysis of present functioning in a particular sphere.

The parallel between the two does not end there, however. Both techniques normally require the services of a specialist, medical or psychological, although certain types of psychological testing can be carried out by individuals without the professional degree, as can certain aspects of the physical exam. Both have also become embroiled in a certain amount of controversy of an ethical nature: Is it proper to obtain information on a person's physical or emotional functioning and then report this information to a third party rather than the person examined? Is it proper at such times to obtain information that the individual is not aware he is giving and that he might not wish to make available?

The arguments pro and con on these questions will be discussed at some length in a later section. For the moment it is sufficient to emphasize that some rather complex procedures will be under consideration and that only a cursory treatment is possible here. Advanced training at the graduate level is required before one can become adept in the use of many of the techniques to be discussed.

The Pre-employment Physical Examination

As with a number of other selection tools, the pre-employment physical examination is characteristically utilized with more than a single purpose in mind. True, these procedures are normally intended as a method of eliminating individuals who might not be physically capable of performing effectively. Thus, the selection goal is an important one. But there are a number of other objectives that no doubt would induce many firms to continue using physical examinations for job candidates, even if the examination procedures were known to have very limited predictive validity.

For one thing, information on physical functioning can be helpful in determining the specific type of position in which a man might perform most effectively and with the least likelihood of injury. Thus, a placement as well as a selection role may be involved. Many industrial physicians appear to believe that the physical examination should rarely be used for purposes of rejection, but primarily to establish a suitable placement. This, however, does not appear to be the dominant viewpoint (23).

On the other hand, rejections on medical grounds do not normally run as high as for other reasons. The data of Table 13-1 are probably typical. In this instance the physical examination clearly served to guide a placement decision in 10 per cent of the cases and to bar employment in 12 per cent. The latter were largely applicants for work in oil fields and refineries, who exhibited abnormalities in back X rays.

Table 13-1. Classification Based on 7,500 Preplacement Physical Examinations Conducted by Mobil Oil Company from 1948 to 1962

Class		Per cent
A	Physically fit for any work	20
B	Defect negligible or correctable: otherwise fit for any work	58
C	Defect limits fitness for certain work and/or requires medical control	10
D	Defect requires medical control or attention and disqualifies for employment	12

Source: E. P. Luongo, "The Preplacement Physical Examination in Industry—Its Value," *Archives of Environmental Health*, Vol. 5 (1962), p. 359.

Another goal has to do entirely with safety. Data from the physical examination can be used to sensitize a man to his limitations. Thus, he may be in a better position to protect himself against accident and injury. Closely related is the fact that a physical examination given just prior to employment can provide a base against which to evaluate any subsequent workmen's compensation claims. From a management viewpoint it is important to know whether any injuries, defects, or diseases that may appear in an employee were present before the man started working for the company or whether they could be a direct result of the conditions of employment. The existence of accurate pre-employment data can serve to limit the company's liability for a subsequent disability.

Finally, there are circumstances under which a physical examination must be given to applicants. For example, the Interstate Commerce Commission requires such an examination for truck drivers and states specific physical criteria for employment in this type of work. Visual defects in particular are likely to lead to rejection.

The physical examination does not take an identical form in all companies and for all jobs. Where the nature of the work is such that a specific type of disability will almost inevitably restrict effectiveness, this particular sphere tends to receive greater attention, and more detailed medical tests are normally carried out. Thus, the pre-employment physical examination is in reality a battery of tests, which should be selected with a view to maximizing predictive effectiveness in the particular situation while at the same time keeping related costs to a minimum. Some of the measures that may be used are a serological test, blood counts, roentgenograms of the chest, electrocardiograms, a metabolism test, measures of sensory functioning, a urinalysis, the electroencephalogram, and tests of neuromuscular reactions.

Consistency and Validity of Physical Tests

Research carried out some years ago dealing with the consistency of pre-employment physical examinations given applicants for positions as airline pilots was rather discouraging (26). Repeated examinations did not yield the same results. In one instance, even when comparisons were restricted to items on which the same tests were used, and items, such as weight, that might have changed between the two examinations were eliminated, only 16 per cent of the total number of defects noted were listed as similar by two different medical examiners. In another case, 43 per cent of a group of pilot applicants who had already passed a Civil Aeronautics Administration physical exam were subsequently found to have disqualifying defects. A major problem seems to be the tendency of physicians to be very strict with regard to their own specialties and considerably less so in other areas.

There have been a number of improvements in the objectivity and standardization of the various medical tests in recent years, and greater consistency than that found in the studies just described can now be expected. Yet it is still possible in some instances to memorize an eye chart with glasses on before being asked to read the chart without glasses. If the results of such a test are compared with those obtained when a man is required to remove his glasses before entering the test room, the conclusions derived from the two measurements are not likely to be similar. Clearly the consistency of results obtained in actual practice from various medical tests is far from perfect.

In addition to consistency, it is also important to demonstrate validity —the actual contribution of the selection physical examination to lowered workmen's compensation costs, improved performance, and reduced accident rates and absenteeism. A series of studies that permit a comparison of accident rates among airplane pilots who did and did not possess certain physical defects at the time of employment is relevant to this issue (26).

The first investigation was carried out on a group of Pan American World Airways ferry pilots during World War II. Because of shortages of available personnel, only 9 of 281 applicants were rejected. Of those accepted, 75 had one or more defects that would normally be disqualifying—poor visual acuity, defective color vision, overweight or underweight, high blood pressure or pulse rate, hay fever, hearing loss, and structural defect. In spite of these physical inadequacies, there were only five fatal accidents in the ensuing operations. Of the 10 pilots killed, only 5 had physical defects at the time of employment, and none of these defects appeared to be causally related to the accident.

In another case a group of 114 Lockheed test pilots was studied. On the average these men had three separate physical defects. Over a five-year period, however, there were only 19 accidents causing destruction of aircraft. The physical condition of the pilot did not appear to be a causative factor in any of these instances.

Finally, the RAF conducted a comparison between a group of 106 pilot applicants with known physical defects and a matched group who met all screening standards. At the end of ten years almost exactly half of each group were still flying. There were no reliable differences in the number of accidents while flying.

It should be emphasized that in none of these cases were the "physically unfit" men totally unselected. Extreme disabilities were disqualifying in all instances. Yet it does appear that standards may often be set much higher than is necessary and that many tests having no relation to job performance are used. Under such circumstances the predictive validity of the physical examination does not appear to be very high.

This situation has led some to the conclusion that in the majority of cases physical examinations should be abandoned and health questionnaires substituted. Under such circumstances little effort would be made to improve the predictive power of physical tests, to establish validities and minimum standards on an empirical basis. Rather, physical examinations would be played down in the selection process and given only in certain special cases or when required by law (18).

HEALTH QUESTIONNAIRES. The available evidence on the use of health questionnaires in the selection situation is rather encouraging. Considerable research has been conducted with the Cornell Medical Index-Health Questionnaire, which contains 195 Yes-No items dealing with disorders of the eyes and ears, respiratory system, cardiovascular system, digestive tract, musculoskeletal system, skin, nervous system, and genitourinary system, as well as fatigability, frequency of illness, miscellaneous diseases, habits, and mood patterns. The questions cover both present physical functioning and the past medical history. They are very similar to those a physician would ask in an interview situation.

When this questionnaire was used as a selection device in a factory of the Benson and Hedges Tobacco Company, it was found that the applicants indicated considerably fewer complaints than are normally noted on the measure (11). Presumably many were attempting to hide disorders that they felt might be disqualifying. Yet, when physical examinations were given to the applicants and the rejected group were compared with those who surmounted this last hurdle and were hired, the ones who failed to pass the physical exam did indicate significantly more complaints on the health questionnaire. Furthermore, among those hired, correlations of .40 for men and .26 for women were found between the number of complaints and the frequency of absenteeism after employment.

It is apparent that medical questionnaires can provide a useful adjunct to the selection process. On the other hand, total elimination of the physical examination does not seem wise. Perhaps appropriate research based on selection models will reveal that the examination can be shortened in many cases and testing restricted to those particular measures that are known to possess predictive validity for the particular job under consideration. This could mean putting together a very markedly different set of medical tests to constitute the total examination in one situation as opposed to another. Such an approach is, of course, widely used in psychological testing.

Psychological Testing: Abilities

In this and the following sections a variety of psychological tests will be discussed. An attempt will be made to provide an understanding of the various types of tests in common use. The general approach will be to note a number of measures of each kind, which have had considerable application in industry, and then to describe one or two of these in some detail. The latter tests have been selected to illustrate some particular point rather than because they are presumed to be the most outstanding. At the end of each section a general review will be attempted of the validities obtained with each type of test in various business positions. More detailed information on the tests noted can be found in *The Sixth Mental Measurements Yearbook* (4).

General Intelligence Tests

Tests of general intelligence are heavily weighted with material of the kind that is normally learned in school. Thus, the majority of the items tend to be verbal in nature and to deal with learning in subjects such as reading, spelling, English, literature, and the like. A secondary emphasis is in the numerical and arithmetic area and a few of these tests stress symbolic reasoning. The more widely used measures in industry are the Wechsler Adult Intelligence Scale, Otis Self-Administering Test of Mental Ability, Wonderlic Personnel Test, Adaptability Test, Miller Analogies Test, Thurstone Test of Mental Alertness, Wesman Personnel Classification Test, and Concept Mastery Test.

WECHSLER ADULT INTELLIGENCE SCALE. This is an individually administered test, with questions asked orally by the psychologist of the person tested and answers recorded on a special test form. Because it is time-consuming and costly to administer, the Wechsler is not widely used for personnel selection except at the higher levels. It has, however, been shown to have satisfactory validity within management, especially the strictly verbal subtests (1). There are eleven subtests in all:

Verbal

1. Information. A series of open-ended questions dealing with the kinds of factual data people normally pick up in their ordinary contacts.
2. Comprehension. Another series of open-ended questions covering the individual's understanding of the need for social rules.
3. Arithmetic. All the questions are of the story or problem type. Scoring is for the correctness of solutions and the time to respond.
4. Digit span. Here a group of numbers is read off and the subject repeats them from memory, sometimes backward.
5. Similarities. Pairs of terms are read off and a common property or characteristic must be abstracted.
6. Vocabulary. A series of words that must be defined in the subject's own terms.

Performance

7. Picture completion. A number of pictures are presented in which the subject must identify the missing component.
8. Picture arrangement. Items require that a series of pictures be arranged in the order that makes the most sense as rapidly as possible.
9. Object assembly. Jigsaw puzzles that must be put together within a given time limit.
10. Block design. Working with a set of small blocks having red, white, or red and white faces, the subject attempts to duplicate various printed designs as quickly as possible.
11. Digit symbol. The subject is given a series of paired symbols and numbers as a code. He is then to write as many correct numbers as he can for each of a whole series of scrambled symbols within a set time period.

WESMAN PERSONNEL CLASSIFICATION TEST. A test devised specifically for industrial use, the Wesman is completed by the subject himself but has a strict time limit. The total score is the number of correct answers written down in the period allowed. There are two types of items that may be scored separately to provide indexes of verbal and numerical abilities, if desired. The verbal items are of the analogy type (_____ is to _____ as _____ is to _____), with both the first and last components left blank. The correct words must be selected from among a number of choices that are presented. The numerical items are varied, but all require a certain amount of computation. There is less emphasis on the story or problem format than in the Wechsler Arithmetic subtest. Because the speed with which a person works has a very marked influence on his score, tests of this kind characteristically yield relatively low scores among older people. Where rapid thinking is not required in the job itself, an untimed test is probably more appropriately used, especially if many applicants are in the mid-40's or older.

CONCEPT MASTERY TEST. This is a specially devised test that is intended to discriminate between individuals at the very highest intellectual levels. It was developed for use in connection with a continuing research study of a large group of individuals, originally selected because of their extremely high intelligence in grade school (37). The hope was that by concentrating on very difficult items it would be possible to identify differences among members of this group in adulthood. As Table 13-2 indicates, this goal was achieved. The highest possible score is 190. Very few, even among the Ph.D.'s, come close to this level.

The test contains two types of items. The majority are pairs of words that must be identified as either the same or opposite in meaning. In addition, there are a number of analogies, primarily of a verbal nature.

Generally a considerable background of information is required to do very well on the test. For this reason it should be used as a selection device only when the job specification calls for a bachelor's or higher degree.

Table 13-2.   Concept Mastery Test Scores According to Educational Level for Gifted Group

Educational level	N	Mean score
Ph.D.	51	159.0
M.D.	35	143.6
LL.B.	73	149.4
Master's degree	151	144.3
Graduate study without degree	122	143.0
Bachelor's degree only	263	135.7
College study without degree	163	128.7
No college	146	118.4

Source: L. M. Terman and M. H. Oden, *The Gifted Group at Mid-Life.* Stanford, Calif.: Stanford Univ. Press, 1959, p. 58.

SHORT VOCABULARY TESTS. Where time is available it is desirable to use longer tests of the type just described, but there are situations where a quick, rough screening is desired. Under such circumstances a short vocabulary test appears to give results that approximate very closely those obtained with the longer measures. Evidence on this point is given in Table 13-3.

Table 13-3.   Correlations Between General Intelligence Tests in a Sample of 108 Sales Employees

Test	Mean score	Vocabulary Test G-T		Concept Mastery	WAIS Verbal Score
		Form A	Form B		
Vocabulary Test G-T, Forms A & B (40 items)	27.64	.89	.89	.73	.56
Vocabulary Test G-T, Form A (20 items)	13.03		.59	.64	.47
Vocabulary Test G-T, Form B (20 items)	14.61			.67	.54
Concept Mastery Test	61.50				.54
WAIS Verbal Score	67.22				.54

Source: J. B. Miner, "On the Use of a Short Vocabulary Test to Measure General Intelligence," *Journal of Educational Psychology,* Vol. 52 (1961), p. 158.

The test used in this study contains a series of multiple-choice items that are scaled from very easy to quite difficult. The test appears to meet all requirements for a satisfactory measure, in spite of the fact that it can be completed in less than ten minutes. It correlates with the Concept Mastery Test better than the Wechsler Verbal Score does. The particular group of men studied were all of above-average intelligence. When a correction is made for this restriction of range, both 20-item tests yield correlations with the more extensive general intelligence measures of at least .75 (28).

Tests of Special Intellectual Abilities

These measures tap a variety of special abilities. Among the more widely known are the Minnesota Clerical Test, Bennett Test of Mechanical Comprehension, Revised Minnesota Paper Form Board, AC Test of Creative Ability, Watson-Glaser Critical Thinking Appraisal, Miller Survey of Mechanical Insight, and Miller Survey of Object Visualization. In addition there are several multiability test batteries that provide separate measures of a number of abilities. In this category are the Differential Aptitude Tests, Flanagan Aptitude Classification Tests, General Aptitude Test Battery, and Employee Aptitude Survey. The following treatment will concentrate on these multiability measures because they provide the best opportunity to illustrate the various item types.

DIFFERENTIAL APTITUDE TESTS. One of the most carefully constructed sets of tests currently available, the DAT, takes about four hours to administer. There are eight separate aptitude measures included. With the exception of the clerical test, all have liberal time limits, with the result that older applicants are not unduly penalized. For most purposes it would probably not be necessary to administer the entire battery, but rather only those tests that have proved to have relevance for the particular position under consideration. The aptitudes measured are:

1. Verbal Reasoning. These are a series of verbal analogies of the same type as those employed in the verbal part of the Wesman Personnel Classification Test. A good background of general information is required.
2. Numerical Ability. Arithmetic computations with a multiple-choice format. The choices are structured in such a way that the answers must actually be computed.
3. Abstract Reasoning. The items are made up of sets of four "problem figures" that constitute a logical sequence of some kind. A fifth figure must then be selected from among five "answer figures" to complete the sequence.
4. Space Relations. A series of items requiring visualization of forms

in space. A key pattern must be matched in some way with one or more of five multiple-choice forms.

5. Mechanical Reasoning. Pictures are shown depicting various mechanical problems. A number of questions are then asked to determine if the subject understands the mechanical processes involved. This is the typical item type in mechanical ability measures.
6. Clerical Speed and Accuracy. Five pairs of numbers and/or letters are shown, one of which is underlined. On an answer sheet the same pairs are shown, but in a different order. The task is to pick out the underlined pair on the answer sheet. The test is timed, and the score is based on the number of items completed correctly.
7. Language Usage, Spelling. A series of words, some spelled correctly and some not. The subject must indicate which are right.
8. Language Usage, Sentences. A measure of the degree to which an individual understands the formal rules of grammar.

GENERAL APTITUDE TEST BATTERY. This battery, constructed by the USES, has had wide distribution because of its use in the state employment offices. It is aimed primarily at the lower job levels and contains twelve separately timed tests. Scores from these tests are combined to yield measures of nine aptitudes, plus an index of general intelligence.

Table 13-4. Correlations Between General Aptitude Test Battery Scores and Piece-Rate Earnings for 65 Radio Tube Mounters

Aptitude	Mean score	r
G—Intelligence	106.9	−.08
V—Verbal Aptitude	102.2	−.06
N—Numerical Aptitude	105.8	.06
S—Spatial Aptitude	109.3	−.01
P—Form Perception	111.8	.02
Q—Clerical Perception	106.2	.10
A—Aiming	107.1	.23
T—Motor Speed	103.6	.19
F—Finger Dexterity	109.5	.44
M—Manual Dexterity	98.7	.35

Source: U.S. Department of Labor, *General Aptitude Test Battery Manual*, Washington, D.C.: the Department, 1958, Section III.

The tests have been used extensively in occupational research conducted by the USES. The results of one such study are presented in Table 13-4. In this instance the aptitude scores were validated against piece-rate earnings. The highest validities on this type of assembly task were obtained with the measures of finger and manual dexterity. In addition, aiming, or perhaps better, motor coordination, and motor speed come close to significance. These are all measures of so-called *psychomotor* abilities, i.e., abilities that depend upon muscular speed, strength, and coordination. Interestingly, the various measures of special intellectual abilities do not yield significant validities for this type of work—nor does G, the general intelligence index.

In another study of fifty file clerks, using supervisory ratings of work output as a criterion, the measures producing significant validities were Verbal, Clerical, Perception, and the comprehensive score—G (10). It is clear that the aptitudes that are related to success in one type of work are not always the same as those that are associated with success in another. Furthermore, evidence from other sources indicates that special abilities are more effective in predicting quality and quantity of work output, i.e., productivity criteria, than in predicting contributions to organizational maintenance.

Psychomotor Tests

The psychomotor tests of the General Aptitude Test Battery have already been mentioned. Other measures of a similar type are the MacQuarrie Test for Mechanical Ability, O'Connor Finger and Tweezer Dexterity Tests, Purdue Pegboard, Minnesota Rate of Manipulation Tests, and the Crawford Small Parts Dexterity Test. In addition, there are a number of special coordination measures and apparatus tests that tap muscular skills of a grosser nature.

MACQUARRIE TEST FOR MECHANICAL ABILITY. Although most psychomotor tests require some kind of special equipment, the MacQuarrie utilizes only pencil and paper. There are seven subtests:

1. *Tracing.* The subject draws a continuous line from a start through gaps in a series of vertical lines to a finish point.
2. *Tapping.* The subject makes dots on a paper as quickly as possible.
3. *Dotting.* Dots are made within small irregularly placed circles.
4. *Copying.* Simple designs are copied by connecting the appropriate dots from among a much larger number.
5. *Location.* The subject is required to locate specific points in a smaller version of a large stimulus.
6. *Blocks.* Piled blocks are shown in two dimensions and the total number in the pile must be determined.
7. *Pursuit.* The subject visually traces lines through a maze.

This type of test appears to measure something rather different than the psychomotor tests utilizing special equipment. There is also reason to believe that the latter are more likely to yield adequate predictions in the selection situation (16). Yet tests such as those in the MacQuarrie have proved valid for occupations such as aviation mechanic and stenographer.

O'CONNOR FINGER AND TWEEZER DEXTERITY TESTS. These tests require a board with 100 small holes in rows of 10 and a shallow tray in which a number of pins are placed. The subject's job is to fill the holes with the pins using either his fingers or, in some instances, tweezers. The score is the amount of time required to complete the task. This is the traditional type of measure used to obtain an index of finger dexterity. Similar pegboards with screws, nuts and bolts, and so on, provide a measure of more comprehensive psychomotor skills of the kind subsumed under the title manual dexterity.

The O'Connor measures have been found valid as predictors of success among power sewing-machine operators and also for dental students, as well as for a variety of other manipulative tasks. The pegboard format is the most widely used among the psychomotor tests. It has in general proved to be a highly effective one in the selection situation.

COORDINATION MEASURES. In the coordination area, the most typical measure probably is the pursuit rotor, which establishes aiming skill, or, perhaps more appropriately, motor coordination. The task here is to follow a dot on a rotating disk, using a stylus. The best measures electronically record the number of seconds the stylus is actually on the moving point.

Much more complex apparatus tests requiring a subject to pull certain levers, push certain pedals, and so on, when a given pattern of lights appear, were developed for use in selecting pilots during World War II (5). Such apparatus techniques, although they have not been widely used in industry, do appear to possess considerable potential. Unfortunately, separate procedures must be developed for each job, or perhaps on occasion for a job family. This is costly and requires considerable research. In fact, further research seems to be needed in the area of psychomotor abilities generally. The various tests are not closely related, and a measure that will predict for one job often does not do so for another that on the surface would seem to be very similar. Therefore specific psychomotor predictors must be established separately in each instance.

General Pattern of Validities: Abilities

The most comprehensive and up-to-date summary of previous research available at the present time breaks the ability measures into intelligence, spatial and mechanical, clerical, and psychomotor types (14). Under intelligence are placed not only all the studies involving the use of general intelligence tests, but also those employing specific measures of numerical and verbal abilities. This seems appropriate in view of the fact that the more general tests are heavily weighted with arithmetic problems, verbal analogies, and vocabulary.

In general the various measures of intelligence, spatial, and mechanical abilities seem to achieve their greatest predictive effectiveness when used to select individuals for training programs. Used in this capacity, they far excel other types of ability measures. However, when prediction goes beyond the training period and moves to actual on-the-job performance, tests of intelligence, spatial, and mechanical abilities appear to do only as well as the clerical and psychomotor measures. This would suggest that generally, where there is particular concern about selecting people who will be able to get through a training period, emphasis can best be placed on intelligence, spatial, or mechanical measures, as appropriate to the particular jobs under consideration. Tests of this kind deal with the capacity to learn and thus are particularly suited to predicting success in training or educational programs. Job effectiveness, on the other hand, requires these "learning" abilities no more than abilities of other kinds.

When attention is focused on specific types of occupations and the tests that will predict success in training for these occupations, the differential significance of the various abilities begins to appear. Success in training for clerical positions is best predicted with the intelligence measures and with the job-specific clerical ability tests. In addition, the indexes of spatial and mechanical abilities also yield good validities.

In selecting people for training in the service occupations, it seems best, in view of the validities obtained, to concentrate on intelligence, spatial, and mechanical tests. These measures are also effective in predicting training success for the skilled industrial occupations, as are measures of clerical ability. At the semiskilled level this picture shifts drastically. The highest validities against training criteria have been obtained with the psychomotor ability tests. The superiority of these measures is so great that there seems little point in using anything else. Yet training success for the unskilled occupations is again best predicted with the old standbys—intelligence, spatial, and mechanical tests.

JOB PERFORMANCE. When we shift from success in training to effectiveness on the job, a greater number of studies are available and more occupations have been investigated. At the managerial level measures of intelligence and also those of a clerical nature appear to work well. With industrial foremen, however, the clerical tests lose their effectiveness, whereas measures of spatial and mechanical abilities have proved to be valuable selection techniques.

Success in clerical work is predicted about equally well by intelligence and clerical indexes. Because spatial and mechanical measures are also effective with clerical employees, it appears that in this area a test battery constructed to select people for training should carry its validity over into the actual job situation.

In the sales occupations, abilities are not generally very important. An exception to this generalization can be made, however, in the case of the highest-level jobs, such as industrial and insurance sales, where intelligence, and to a lesser degree clerical ability, are important. In the lower-level positions, especially among sales clerks, ability tests do not seem to carry any validity at all.

Effective performance in the protective service occupations, such as policeman and fireman, is about equally well predicted by all types of ability measures, with some slight superiority accruing to the intelligence tests. Performance in the personal service occupations, however, appears to be almost totally unrelated to the abilities. None of the tests discussed have consistently produced satisfactory validities for these jobs.

Success in the various industrial positions at the skilled, semiskilled, and unskilled levels can be predicted with ability measures, although generally the validity coefficients tend to be lower than those obtained with managers, foremen, clerical workers, and higher-level salesmen. Spatial and mechanical measures are of increasing significance as the skill level ascends. Tests of this kind have very little validity for unskilled jobs, but are the most effective at the skilled level, although clerical indexes take a close second. Among semiskilled workers all the abilities have much the same significance. Clerical tests have the highest validities among the ability measures in the unskilled occupations. Generally, the intelligence measures are not the most helpful in selecting for performance effectiveness in these industrial occupations. Also, a battery of tests that will predict training success for these jobs may have to be expanded, if predictions of on-the-job success are desired as well.

Psychological Testing: Personality

This discussion of personality measures will develop more fully some of the distinctions made in Chapter 10, where the various methods of attitude measurement were presented. The available tests appear to fall into two categories, depending on the measurement rationale employed. The majority of the personality tests currently on the market ask the respondent to describe himself in some way, and these self-reports are either taken at face value or related to some group with known characteristics to obtain a score. A second approach utilizes the projective rationale. Tests of this kind obtain descriptions or reactions, not with reference to the self in the here and now, but to some far-removed situation or stimulus. Inferences are then made back to the individual's personality pattern.

As with attitude measurement the major problem in personality testing is the tendency to portray oneself in the most favorable light. This problem becomes acute in the selection situation. Although the desire to make a good impression may represent a positive contribution when abilities are measured, because it ensures that the applicant will do his best on the tests, such a desire may produce only a distorted and atypical picture in the personality area. Much of the work that has been done in the field of personality testing over the past twenty years has been concerned with the effort to find a solution to this problem.

Self-Report Techniques

Perhaps the most widely used self-report measures are those that provide information on the degree of interest in various types of activities, primarily those of an occupational nature. The major titles are the Strong Vocational Interest Blank and the Kuder Preference Record-Vocational. There are, in addition, a number of tests that yield scores on several personality characteristics, usually at least four and in some instances as many as eighteen. Among these self-report tests are the Minnesota Multiphasic Personality Inventory, Bernreuter Personality Inventory, Guilford-Zimmerman Temperament Survey, California Psychological Inventory, Activity Vector Analysis, Thurstone Temperament Schedule, Gordon Personal Profile and Personal Inventory, Edwards Personal Preference Schedule, and the Study of Values. All have seen considerable use in the industrial situation and a number have produced at least adequate validities for managerial selection (39).

KUDER PREFERENCE RECORD-VOCATIONAL. The Kuder contains groups of three statements descriptive of various types of activities. The subject indicates which of the three he would most like to do and which least. These choices are then totaled to obtain various interest area scores, based on the particular activity described. The ten regular scores obtained from the test are listed in Table 13-5. Also noted is a special supervisory interest score developed for the specific purpose of predicting success in managerial work (27).

As the table suggests, the Kuder does not generally achieve very impressive validities when used to select people for initial hiring or promotion. The Scientific and Supervisory scores do yield values significantly different from zero when correlated with the managerial performance ratings; the Outdoor, Persuasive, Artistic, Literary, Clerical, and Supervisory indexes do the same when validated against potential ratings. Yet the correlations are not high. Even the Supervisory measure has not always proved effective in subsequent studies (36).

The major difficulty seems to be that an applicant, or a manager seeking promotion, can, and often does, make his choices in accordance with what he feels would be expected in the desired position, rather than on the basis of his real feelings. Thus, job applicants tend to obtain different scores on the test than would be obtained under less stressful, research conditions (15). A tendency of this kind may very well account for the low scores obtained by the managers of Table 13-5 on the Outdoor (or agricultural), Mechanical, and Clerical measures. The managers in all probability consider these to be rather low-status activities in which as managers they *should not* have much interest.

Table 13-5.   Correlations Between Kuder Preference Record-Vocational and Management Appraisal Ratings for 420 Managers

Interest area	Mean score	Ratings	
		Present performance	Potential
Outdoor	34	.02	−.12
Mechanical	40	−.01	−.01
Computational	62	.05	.04
Scientific	65	−.15	−.08
Persuasive	64	.09	.20
Artistic	48	−.05	−.12
Literary	69	.04	.11
Musical	59	.04	−.01
Social Service	46	.02	.02
Clerical	35	−.03	−.10
Supervisory		.14	.24

Source: J. B. Miner, "The Kuder Preference Record in Management Appraisal," *Personnel Psychology*, Vol. 13 (1960), pp. 191–192.

More recently the Kuder Preference Record-Occupational has been developed, which, although it uses an item format similar to the Vocational, is scored in a different manner. Keys for a variety of occupations have been constructed based on the specific choices made by people working in the occupations. Thus, it is the response pattern characteristic of actual job performers, rather than the particular type of activity described, that determines scoring. This is the approach used in the Strong Vocational Interest Blank as well. Validities should be higher under these circumstances, although as long as the applicant is in a position to guess how those in an occupation might respond, there would appear to be a chance of bias in the selection situation.

EDWARDS PERSONAL PREFERENCE SCHEDULE. Another approach to the elimination of bias is reflected in the Edwards. This is a forced-choice procedure (see Chapter 10) requiring the subject to choose between paired alternatives, the majority of which have been selected so as to be matched in terms of their social desirability. Thus, on most items the subject cannot respond so as to present a "good" image, because he must choose between two equally "good" alternatives. The test measures some fifteen motives: the need or desire for achievement, deference, order, exhibition, autonomy, affiliation, intraception, succorance, dominance, abasement, nurturance, change, endurance, heterosexuality, and aggression. It takes approximately forty minutes to administer.

The Edwards has rather consistently yielded reliable correlations when studied in relation to various indexes of occupational success (17). Yet there is reason to believe that the use of forced-choice alternatives equated for general social desirability does not entirely overcome bias (38). In the selection situation it seems to be the case that applicants bring with them certain specific conceptions of what answers will be valued. Although these preconceived answers are influenced by social desirability considerations, there is more to it than that. There is also the matter of specific desirability for the job under consideration. Two alternatives may be entirely equal in their social acceptability, but one may be clearly more desirable in relation to a given position. The result can well be a response that looks good when compared against the job but that is not truly descriptive of the individual.

ACTIVITY VECTOR ANALYSIS. This is a unique measure, not in its technique of measurement or in its approach to bias, but in the way in which it is merchandised. The test is available only to those who have completed a special training course given by the consulting firm that publishes it. This means that independent validity studies conducted by individuals other than members of the consulting firm are few and far between, especially in proportion to the widespread use the test has had in industry.

The measure itself consists of a list of eighty-one adjectives, all generally favorable in nature. The subject is to check those that he believes have ever been used by others to describe him, and also those that he truthfully feels are descriptive of him. The words thus checked are then scored to yield indexes of aggressiveness, sociability, emotional control, social adaptability, and activity. This is, of course, a self-report technique *par excellence*. Unfortunately it is also one that does little to control job-related bias. In the selection situation the applicant can easily emphasize those adjectives that appear to be associated with success in the particular job under consideration. If he is right, he will be hired; if not, he will not be. In either case very little information is obtained about the kind of person he really is.

AVA has failed to correlate with performance criteria in a number of instances, but there have also been some very good validities reported. The research underlying these validities has, however, been severely questioned (9,21). Yet these studies are no more deficient relative to the longitudinal prediction model than are those carried out with several other widely used tests, ability as well as personality. The fact is that perfectly controlled, predictive validity studies are not easy to conduct in industry and AVA has not really proved itself one way or the other.

Thus, it is not possible to say whether AVA can be a valuable selection tool, although on the surface it would appear to be rather bias-prone. Unfortunately this sense of uncertainty is unlikely to be lifted as long as the test and the research on it continue to be rigidly controlled by a single consulting firm.

Projective Techniques

The projective procedures approach the problem of bias in a very different manner than the self-report techniques. A projective test is constructed so that the uninformed person cannot determine what is being measured. The subject simply does not know what he is revealing about himself when he responds to a test item. As a consequence he cannot bias his response so as to present a socially desirable picture or a picture that seems to be congruent with job expectations.

In theory, at least, this would appear to be the ideal solution to the bias problem. The subject does not describe himself; he reacts, and by reacting in a particular manner reveals what type of person he is. In practice this approach has encountered sizable difficulties. The problem is that the very procedures that keep the subject from understanding his own responses also make it difficult for the test administrator to understand them. Thus, the projective approach in conquering the bias problem introduces the new problem of interpretation. Work with techniques such as the Rorschach Test, the Thematic Apperception Test, the Rosenzweig Picture-Frustration Study, the various sentence completion measures, the Tomkins-Horn Picture Arrangement Test, and the Worthington Personal History has recently resulted in some real progress in this area. Yet there can be no question that much more must be learned about the various ways in which people reveal themselves through their test responses before the projective tests can achieve their full potential as personnel selection techniques.

THE THEMATIC APPERCEPTION TECHNIQUE. The TAT, as originally developed, contained twenty pictures, many of them quite ambiguous. In many instances, however, fewer pictures are employed, especially in the industrial situation. Furthermore, a number of special versions of the TAT have been conceived, often using pictures of a much clearer and more structured nature than those originally utilized in the test. In all instances the subject is asked to tell a story using the picture as a starting point. He is to describe the people, tell what is happening, and develop both the past and the future of the scene depicted. Because he must go beyond the picture itself, his own personal imaginative and fantasy processes are brought into play.

Very little evidence is available regarding the relationship between the TAT in its original form and job performance. Furthermore, although the test may be given in a group situation with the subjects writing their stories, analysis remains a time-consuming process. For these reasons the original TAT cannot be recommended as a selection technique under most circumstances.

On the other hand, research has been done with certain special versions of the technique, and relatively simple and objective scoring systems have been developed. Thus, a set of pictures selected to measure a desire for achievement has been found to produce responses that can be scored rapidly, with minimal error. This achievement motivation measure has been shown to yield consistent relationships with various indexes of managerial success in this country and abroad. On the other hand, it does not appear to be a valid predictor of sales performance (24).

Another approach that is closely related to the TAT is the Tomkins-Horn Picture Arrangement Test (PAT). In this instance the subject is presented with three pictures at a time, which he must arrange to produce a sequence that makes a logical story. Then the brief story describing this pattern of events is written below the pictures. There are twenty-five such items.

Table 13-6. Validity Data for the Tomkins-Horn Picture Arrangement Test

Criterion measures	Concurrent validity (65 petroleum product salesmen)	Predictive validity (58 tabulating machine operators)
Sales figures		
Gasoline	.56	
Motor oil	.46	
Tires, batteries, and so on	.33	
All products	.58	
Supervisory ratings		
Cooperation		.43
Application		.50
Accuracy		.69
Speed		.40
Overall effectiveness		.61

Source: J. B. Miner, "The Validity of the PAT in the Selection of Tabulating Machine Operators: An Analysis of Predictive Power," *Journal of Projective Techniques*, Vol. 25 (1961), p. 331; and J. B. Miner, "Personality and Ability Factors in Sales Performance," *Journal of Applied Psychology*, Vol. 46 (1962), p. 10.

As indicated in Table 13-6, the PAT can yield very satisfactory validities. In the case of the petroleum product salesmen, success was found to be associated with such characteristics as perennial happiness, dependence, self-confidence, and a desire for social interaction (30). Among the tabulating machine operators, whose performance was measured by paired comparison ratings made some nine months after testing, the major predictors were measures of conformity and strong work motivation (29).

THE RORSCHACH TECHNIQUE. Like the TAT, the Rorschach has emerged in a variety of forms over the years while still retaining its essential character (the ink blot). In its original version it contained ten cards, each with a single ink blot either in black, white, and gray or with various colors. The subject describes what he sees in the blot, and as many responses as produced are recorded. Normally, testing is done individually and a so-called inquiry is appended, during which the subject goes back over his responses and indicates his reasons for selecting the particular descriptions, i.e., what it was about the blot that led him to a given conclusion. The test may also be administered on a group basis with the subjects writing their responses.

Because of the ambiguous nature of the stimulus forms, an almost infinite variety of descriptions is possible, depending on what the subject projects into the blots from his own personality. Bias, in the sense of consciously predetermining the personality portrait that will emerge, is almost impossible. Yet because of the ambiguity of the blots, interpretation is also extremely difficult. For this reason it is easy for the inexperienced person to reach incorrect conclusions about an applicant from his Rorschach responses. The individual making the interpretations has only a limited amount to go on.

With lower level employees the Rorschach technique has not proved very effective, but some recent studies involving managers suggest that validity can be quite good. In one instance a number of company officers who had continued to progress in their careers were compared with a similar group who had been demoted or fired (34). The successful executives were found to possess strong power motivation, foresight, self-confidence, a desire to cooperate and compete within the rules, the ability to integrate their activities toward a specific goal, a capacity for rapid mental productivity, and controlled aggressiveness. Research conducted with managers at lower levels suggests that many of these characteristics are associated with success there also (19).

THE SENTENCE-COMPLETION TECHNIQUE. These tests, of which there are a number available, present a series of verbal stems, or beginnings of sentences, that the subject is asked to complete. Usually there is an additional request that in finishing the sentences he express his real feelings. Although some of the items may elicit completions of a self-report nature, the tests are usually constructed so that inferences regarding personality characteristics can be made in terms of the symbolic significance of the responses. Thus, the self-reports are not accepted at face value.

Although validity studies are not extensive, there is reason to believe this technique may prove valuable as a selection device. Unlike the other projectives discussed, it is both easy to administer and to score. In one instance, as indicated in Table 13-7, a sentence completion measure has been found to yield very good concurrent validity when related to accident rates. The industrial workers with frequent accidents were significantly less optimistic, trusting, and sociable. They also had a more negative employment attitude (7). Studies with the Miner Sentence Completion Scale, which has been devised specifically for use with management personnel, have consistently indicated that this instrument has both predictive and concurrent validity when used with managerial groups (31,32). This test, like a number of other projective measures, may be scored so as to eliminate any tendency to give socially desirable responses.

Table 13-7. Relationships Between Sentence-Completion Indexes and Accident Rates ($N = 34$)

Sentence-completion variable	r
Optimism	−.34
Trust	−.51
Sociocentricity	−.76
Pessimism	−.19
Distrust	.02
Anxiety	.09
Egocentricity	.19
Resentment	.29
Negative employment attitude	.70

Source: A. Davids and J. T. Mahoney, "Personality Dynamics and Accident-Proneness in an Industrial Setting," *Journal of Applied Psychology*, Vol. 41 (1957), p. 304.

General Pattern of Validities: Personality

Studies relating personality measures, whether self-report or projective, to indexes of success during the training period have almost uniformly yielded disappointing results (14). In those groups where any sizable amount of research has been done, which includes clerical, protective service, skilled, and semiskilled occupations, the reported validities have consistently been well below those obtained with certain types of ability measures.

When the focus shifts to on-the-job performance, this picture changes. Managerial success is best predicted by clerical and general intelligence tests, but personality measures are nearly as effective. With foremen, however, the personality measures do not do as well as those tapping various abilities.

Among clerical employees the personality measures again come right behind the intelligence and clerical tests. Although personality factors appear to make little difference, relatively, in clerical training, they do contribute to actual job performance in almost as great proportion as the most relevant abilities. It is in the sales area, however, that personality tests have proved most useful, primarily because here their contribution is almost unique. Ability measures appear to have little relationship to sales success, except for the intelligence measures among those in higher-level sales positions. Personality measures, on the other hand, have consistently turned out to be good predictors at all levels of sales employment. Among sales clerks they are the only kind of test that yields positive relationships at all.

Within the various service occupations, personality tests, although not nearly as effective as in the sales area, achieve validities that are generally superior to those reported for ability measures. Thus, they offer the best prospects as selection instruments, with the exception of intelligence tests for the protective service occupations, although still failing to achieve the predictive levels one would desire, especially in the personal service area.

Job performance in the industrial occupations generally is no better predicted by personality measures than ability measures, with one major exception. At the unskilled level, personality tests are by far the most valid selection techniques. This is probably because emotionally disturbed individuals tend to gravitate to unskilled jobs, if they remain in the labor force at all (33). The personality tests presumably pick out those who have little prospect of continued employment within this group, i.e., those who are the most severely disturbed.

In general the evidence indicates that personality measures can make a valuable contribution to the selection process. When ranked in terms of validity levels, along with the four types of ability measures, across the ten occupational groups compared, they emerge in what amounts to a tie with the intelligence tests for first place (14). Among sales clerks, personal service workers, and the unskilled they are the best predictors; the validities obtained with managers and salesmen generally are such as to recommend their use there as well.

Psychological Testing: Skills and Achievements

Measures of this kind are derived directly from the job and thus tend to be specific to the occupation for which selection is to occur. Either a job sample is developed as with the various typing and stenographic tests, or a series of questions are asked regarding the job. In some instances tests of this type are available on a commercial basis, but it is also common practice to construct home-grown measures that are specifically suited to the needs of a particular company.

Job-Sampling Procedures

Job-sampling tests are feasible only where the role prescriptions for a job form a rather homogeneous unit. If the job is complex, requiring many different types of activities, all of which are equally important to success, any truly inclusive job sample test would be so lengthy and cumbersome that its use in a selection battery would not normally be expedient. Even with the more homogeneous jobs most such tests tend to be only similar to the actual work situation and not exact duplicates of it (20).

The use of job-sample testing also must be restricted to positions that have been designed with rather simple role requirements or for which only previously trained or experienced applicants are hired. Testing a group of inexperienced individuals on a complex job sample is of little value, because all will obtain low scores. Under such circumstances ability measures are much more likely to discriminate within the group and predict which individuals will learn rapidly and achieve job success.

A number of firms have developed job-sample tests for skilled and semiskilled positions. In some instances special equipment simulating that used on the job has been constructed. In other cases a standardized test situation utilizing actual equipment is employed. In any event it is crucial that all people tested be required to perform the same tasks under the same conditions in the same period of time. Job samples of this kind have been developed for a variety of positions in such areas as punch press operation, inspection, packaging, fork-lift operation, truck driving, and certain kinds of special machine operation (38).

Job-sampling procedures have also had widespread use in the clerical field. Here, where jobs tend to be highly standardized across a great many firms, regular commercial tests are much more common than for blue-collar workers. Among those available are the Blackstone Stenographic Proficiency Tests, the Thurstone Examination in Typing, and the Seashore-Bennett Stenographic Proficiency Tests. These require that applicants take dictation and/or type, using materials that are the same for everybody. Scoring procedures have been worked out, and the scores obtained by a given applicant can be compared with those for a large number of clerical workers who have taken the test.

Although managerial work is generally less suitable for job sampling, certain aspects of the job have been simulated with some success. Typical is the In-Basket Test, which requires that various items in an in-basket be handled under controlled conditions. Scores derived from the test are positively correlated with overall managerial effectiveness (2,22).

Although the job-sampling approach is probably most widely used to screen initial applicants, especially those who have gone through apprenticeship, vocational, or secretarial training programs prior to applying for a job, it is also used in connection with promotions. Job-sample tests have proved particularly valuable in those instances where the union contract placed limitations on the promotion process. If, for instance, the contract says seniority shall govern, provided the senior man is qualified to perform the higher level job, it is important to determine whether he is qualified. Job samples can be very helpful in this regard. In other cases management has more freedom of action and can promote the most qualified man, provided that where capability is equal the senior man will be moved up. Here also, the level of qualification can best be demonstrated with a job-sample test. The advantage of using job samples in these situations is that they do tend to be predictive of subsequent performance *and* they are usually acceptable to the union. An equally valid projective personality measure would normally be of much less value for this purpose because of the *apparent* disparity between the test and the job.

Achievement Tests

Achievement tests differ from job samples in that they deal with the knowledge or information required to perform a job. Instead of demonstrating his skill, the applicant answers written or oral questions about the work. There is considerable overlap between the two procedures.

Measures of this kind have proved particularly useful in discriminating between those who are and are not qualified to perform a given type of work. Because they are relatively easy to construct and administer, they are usually more appropriate for this purpose than job samples. It is not at all uncommon for a job applicant to claim prior work experience, as a carpenter, machinist, engineer, or accountant, when he has actually performed in a less skilled capacity. Either the man intends to bluff his way into a higher-level position or there is some ambiguity in the true meaning of the occupational title. In any event a test of job knowledge can be very helpful.

So-called trade tests have been developed along these lines by the United States Employment Service for a number of skilled occupations. These are oral tests, usually containing fifteen questions. The questions are selected by administering a much larger number of questions to three groups of workers: journeymen, apprentices and helpers in the trade, and individuals employed outside the trade in positions that are part of the same job family. A good question, one that is retained in the final test, should yield consistently correct responses in the first group and practically no correct responses in the third group. When a number of questions of this kind are put together in a test, experienced journeymen can easily be identified, because they will obtain total scores at a level almost never obtained by those in the other two groups.

Tests of this type have also demonstrated considerable validity as predictors of the degree to which an individual's role behavior actually matches the role prescriptions for a job. In one such study a test containing twenty-one questions, selected from an original pool of ninety-five as the most discriminative, was found to yield good predictions against supervisory ratings of machinists in a shipyard (25). Among those rated above average, 75 per cent had thirteen or more questions right. Among those rated below average, only 10 per cent achieved this score.

Achievement testing need not be restricted to short oral tests. Written tests have been developed by a number of firms for a whole range of positions. Tests of accounting knowledge, policies and procedures, human relations, business law, and economics, which cover segments of a job rather than the totality of information required, have also been constructed.

Although, in general, achievement measures are constructed by the company to fit its own specific needs, some commercial tests are available. The Occupational Research Center at Purdue University has developed a number of these for the skilled trades. These are measures of information regarding such occupations as electrician, lathe operator, carpenter, sheet-metal worker, and welder. More specific tests also deal with industrial mathematics, blueprint reading, and scale reading.

Ethical Considerations in Human Measurement

Throughout this chapter a considerable amount of evidence regarding the validity of various measurement procedures has been presented. There can be little doubt that selection tools of the type described offer an opportunity to regulate the human input to an organization in such a way as to make a very sizable contribution to goal attainment. A recent review of the literature indicates that validity coefficients on the order of .60 for training criteria and .45 for job performance criteria can be anticipated when an appropriate fit between some test and job requirements is established. These figures apply when a single measure is used. If multiple predictors are employed and combined to yield a multiple-correlation coefficient, values of a considerably higher order can be obtained (14). Thus, given adequate research both in the area of test construction and in test selection, it is possible for management to contribute a great deal toward both productivity and organizational maintenance through the use of psychological tests. The tests do work; not perfectly, but they work.

Further evidence on this point, in dollars and cents terms, comes from a study carried out on the selection of telephone operators in the San Francisco area (35). A test battery containing numerical and clerical ability measures was used as a predictor. The savings attributable to the fact that many operators who would have failed if hired did not have to be trained were calculated. The following figures correct these training savings for the additional recruiting costs the tests introduce. Scores on the test battery may range from 0 to 80, and the minimum score for hiring could, of course, be set at any point between, depending on the availability of applicants in the labor market and the degree of selectivity desired. This study was published in 1956, and it can be assumed that the savings would be greater today.

Minimum score for hiring	Net saving, $
30	8,000
40	35,000
50	47,000
60	50,000

It is apparent from these data that good selection procedures developed with reference to organizationally meaningful criteria can yield very sizable savings. The real strength of human measurement techniques in selection is that when correctly validated they place primary emphasis on merit rather than on the biases and moods of the person doing the selection (8).

It is true, as some people have contended, that measurement may contribute to a selection process that emphasizes conformity. Whether or not this is the case depends on the role prescriptions for the job under consideration. In some instances, perhaps among such people as inspectors, typists, and certain kinds of machine operators, conformity may well be a valued quality contributing to success. In other cases it is clear that it is not. There are, in fact, studies providing clear evidence that nonconformity can be valued in certain occupations— within certain managerial groups (12,31) and among research scientists (6). The point is that psychological tests, correctly used, predict success and contribution to company goals. If success in certain jobs requires conformity, then the tests may well select conformists. If success requires nonconformity, they will select nonconformists.

The Invasion of Privacy Question

In spite of these obvious contributions to profitability, industry generally has been under considerable pressure to give up selection testing. Several major companies have actually done so, usually as a result of policy decisions made outside the personnel function. Several congressional investigations have been conducted with a view to imposing constraints on the use of psychological tests, although no legislation has been passed. In recent years there have also been a number of books and articles written that attack the use of tests.

A major concern in all these instances is that selection testing, especially personality testing, represents an invasion of privacy: that individuals are called upon to reveal things that they might not wish to reveal; that they often do not even know what they are revealing about themselves; that information obtained through selection testing is not held to a confidential psychologist-applicant relationship, but imparted to a third party, the company's management. These actions are felt to be unethical. Those who attack testing and who feel that perhaps legal constraints should be imposed in this area believe that individual freedoms are being violated.

On the other side is the fact that employers do need information about applicants. We would certainly not expect companies to hire at random from among those in an applicant pool. We consider it proper that those who will contribute the most to an organization should be selected for membership. To do this, information must be collected so that these potential contributors can be identified.

In some ways it is surprising that psychological testing has aroused such heated controversy when other selection tools, often with much less evidence of validity, have been accepted with very little question. The interview, application blanks, reference checks, and the physical examination all are potentially subject to the invasion of privacy criticism, yet only the physical examination has been questioned, and that only on the grounds that there is in the pre-employment physical examination situation a violation of the confidential physician-patient relationship because the results are given to management.

What seems to be not clearly understood in all this is that the selection situation is not synonymous with the physician-patient relationship or that of lawyer to client. It is not the applicant who wants information or assistance, but the company. Furthermore, the applicant is aware of the purpose of the various selection procedures. If he takes a test, he recognizes that this experience is germane to his being considered for employment. In this sense selection testing is a far cry from such activities as wire-tapping, searching a home without a warrant, or opening personal mail, with which it has been compared (13). The applicant presumably wants something from the potential employer and understands quite clearly that he must provide certain information to have a chance of obtaining what he wants. Thus, he trades information about himself for the opportunity of being hired. This is a long way from coercion, and it is coerced invasion of privacy, where the individual has no choice, that is normally considered unethical.

This is not to say that information obtained from psychological tests, or physical examinations, or other selection tools, cannot be misused by unscrupulous individuals. There are important security problems here, and there can be a major ethical problem as well, if information is used for some purpose other than that anticipated by the applicant, i.e., the evaluation of his qualifications for employment. To protect the public against such misuse of tests, psychologists have devoted considerable time and energy to the formulation and the enforcement of appropriate ethical controls (3). There is reason to believe that these efforts have achieved a considerable measure of success.

References

1. Balinsky, B., and H. W. Shaw, "The Contribution of the WAIS to a Management Appraisal Program," *Personnel Psychology*, Vol. 9 (1956), 207–209.
2. Bray, D. W., and D. L. Grant, "The Assessment Center in the Measurement of Potential for Business Management," *Psychological Monographs*, Vol. 80, No. 17 (1966), 1–27.
3. Brayfield, A. H., "Testimony Before the Senate Subcommittee on Constitutional Rights of the Committee on the Judiciary," *American Psychologist*, Vol. 20 (1965), 888–898.
4. Buros, O. K. (ed.), *The Sixth Mental Measurements Yearbook*. Highland Park, N.J.: Gryphon Press, 1965.
5. Cronbach, L. J., *Essentials of Psychological Testing*. New York: Harper & Row, 1960.
6. Crutchfield, R. S., "Conformity and Creative Thinking," in H. E. Gruber, G. Terrell, and M. Wertheimer (eds.), *Contemporary Approaches to Creative Thinking*. New York: Atherton Press, 1962, pp. 120–140.
7. Davids, A., and J. T. Mahoney, "Personality Dynamics and Accident-Proneness in an Industrial Setting," *Journal of Applied Psychology*, Vol. 41 (1957), 303–306.
8. Dunnette, M. D., "Critics of Psychological Tests: Basic Assumptions: How Good?," *Psychology in the Schools*, Vol. 1 (1964), 63–69.
9. Dunnette, M. D., and W. K. Kirchner, "Validities, Vectors, and Verities," *Journal of Applied Psychology*, Vol. 46 (1962), 296–299.
10. Dvorak, B. J., "Development of Occupational Norms," in W. L. Barnette (ed.), *Readings in Psychological Tests and Measurements*. Homewood, Ill.: Dorsey Press, 1964, pp. 132–144.

11. Erdmann, A. J., K. Brodman, J. Deutschberger, and H. G. Wolff, "Health Questionnaire Use in an Industrial Medical Department," *Industrial Medicine and Surgery,* Vol. 22 (1953), 355–357.
12. Fleishman, E. A., and D. R. Peters, "Interpersonal Values, Leadership Attitudes, and Managerial Success," *Personnel Psychology,* Vol. 15 (1962), 127–143.
13. Gallagher, C. E., "Why House Hearings on Invasion of Privacy," *American Psychologist,* Vol. 20 (1965), 881–882.
14. Ghiselli, E. E., *The Validity of Occupational Aptitude Tests.* New York: Wiley, 1966.
15. Green, R. F., "Does a Selection Situation Induce Testees to Bias Their Answers on Interest and Temperament Tests?" *Educational and Psychological Measurement,* Vol. 11 (1951), 503–515.
16. Guion, R. M., *Personnel Testing.* New York: McGraw-Hill, 1965.
17. Guion, R. M., and R. F. Gottier, "Validity of Personality Measures in Personnel Selection," *Personnel Psychology,* Vol. 18 (1965), 135–164.
18. Hanks, T. G., "The Physical Examination in Industry: A Critique," *Archives of Environmental Health,* Vol. 5 (1962), 365–374.
19. Hicks, J. A., and J. B. Stone, "The Identification of Traits Related to Managerial Success," *Journal of Applied Psychology,* Vol. 46 (1962), 428–432.
20. Lawshe, C. H., and M. J. Balma, *Principles of Personnel Testing,* 2nd ed. New York: McGraw-Hill, 1966.
21. Locke, E. A., and C. L. Hulin, "A Review and Evaluation of the Validity Studies of Activity Vector Analysis," *Personnel Psychology,* Vol. 15 (1962), 25–42.
22. Lopez, F. M., *Evaluating Executive Decision Making: The In-Basket Technique.* New York: American Management Association Research Study No. 75, 1966.
23. Luongo, E. P., "The Preplacement Physical Examination in Industry—Its Values," *Archives of Environmental Health,* Vol. 5 (1962), 358–364.
24. McClelland, D. C., *The Achieving Society.* Princeton, N.J.: Van Nostrand, 1961.
25. McCormick, E. J., and N. B. Winstanley, "A Fifteen-Minute Oral Trade Test," *Personnel,* Vol. 27 (1950), 144–146.
26. McFarland, R. A., *Human Factors in Air Transportation.* New York: McGraw-Hill, 1953.
27. Miner, J. B., "The Kuder Preference Record in Management Appraisal," *Personnel Psychology,* Vol. 13 (1960), 187–196.
28. Miner, J. B., "On the Use of a Short Vocabulary Test to Measure General Intelligence," *Journal of Educational Psychology,* Vol. 52 (1961), 157–160.
29. Miner, J. B., "The Validity of the PAT in the Selection of Tabulating Machine Operators: An Analysis of Predictive Power," *Journal of Projective Techniques,* Vol. 25 (1961), 330–333.
30. Miner, J. B., "Personality and Ability Factors in Sales Performance," *Journal of Applied Psychology,* Vol. 46 (1962), 6–13.
31. Miner, J. B., *Studies in Management Education.* New York: Springer, 1965.

32. Miner, J. B., "The Prediction of Managerial and Research Success," *Personnel Administration*, Vol. 28, No. 5 (1965), 12–16.
33. Miner, J. B., and J. K. Anderson, "The Postwar Occupational Adjustment of Emotionally Disturbed Soldiers," *Journal of Applied Psychology*, Vol. 42 (1958), 317–322.
34. Piotrowski, Z. A., and M. R. Rock, *The Perceptanalytic Executive Scale*. New York: Grune and Stratton, 1963.
35. Rusmore, J. T., and G. J. Toorenaar, "Reducing Training Costs by Employment Testing," *Personnel Psychology*, Vol. 9 (1956), 39–44.
36. Spitzer, M. E., and W. J. McNamara, "A Managerial Selection Study," *Personnel Psychology*, Vol. 17 (1964), 19–40.
37. Terman, L. M., and M. H. Oden, *The Gifted Group at Mid-Life*. Stanford, Cal.: Stanford Univ. Press, 1959.
38. Tiffin, J., and E. J. McCormick, *Industrial Psychology*, 5th ed. Englewood Cliffs, N.J.: Prentice-Hall, 1965.
39. Wickert, F. R., and D. E. McFarland, *Measuring Executive Effectiveness*. New York: Appleton-Century-Crofts, 1967.

Questions

1. What are the arguments pro and con on the use of the physical examination in the selection situation? Are there alternative procedures that can be relied upon to yield as good results?
2. You have been asked to develop selection test batteries for the occupations listed below. What specific tests would you try out initially in each instance in your search for valid predictors of on-the-job performance? Explain why you would select each test in each battery.
   a. File clerk
   b. Insurance salesman
   c. Plant manager
   d. Retail sales clerk
   e. Plant guard
   f. Laborer
3. What are the strengths and weaknesses, the advantages and disadvantages, of the following as selection tests?
   a. Wechsler Adult Intelligence Scale
   b. A short vocabulary test
   c. MacQuarrie Test of Mechanical Ability
   d. Activity Vector Analysis
   e. Thematic Apperception Test
   f. Thurstone Examination in Typing
4. Are psychological tests a "good thing" insofar as personnel selection is concerned?

V

Input-Output Mediators: Techniques Fostering Productivity and Profit

14

Management Development

In Parts V and VI we shall take up the various personnel techniques that have been developed to mediate between the human inputs to a firm and the behavioral outputs that contribute to goal attainment. The primary intention in utilizing these techniques is to change, modify, and improve the input so as to maximize the amount of productivity and profit and at the same time ensure the continued stability of the organization itself. In some instances, however, mediators are used merely to sustain the effective functioning of the input against forces that might otherwise drastically reduce the level of output. Thus, the most efficient company is viewed as the one that selects the best applicants and then introduces mediating techniques that at least maintain, and ideally improve upon, the quality of this input, while also inducing members to devote their greatest efforts toward achieving the organization's goals. Mediators can be, along with selection procedures, a means of at least partially overcoming the constraints imposed by individual differences.

Chapters 7 and 8, in dealing with organization planning and job analysis, were concerned with mediators just as much as the chapters that follow in this part and the next. Organization structures and job descriptions provide definitions of role requirements. These requirements are constituted in a manner intended to produce a maximal total effort for the organization by its members. Role prescriptions are established with a view to improving or maximizing the manner in which those who are selected for employment contribute. This is what any mediating technique is expected to do.

The only difference between organization planning or job analysis and the mediators to be discussed now is that the former two are basically *structural* in nature. They deal with the way in which the organization is put together. In Parts V and VI, on the other hand, we shall be concerned with what might best be called *functional* mediators. The latter are processes or subfunctions within the total personnel function that are carried out on a continuing basis to ensure that role behaviors actually do match the role prescriptions established by organization planning and job analysis to the maximum degree possible.

The five chapters of this part discuss those functional mediators that are oriented primarily toward the productivity goal. The following part will take up functional mediators oriented toward organizational maintenance. Although the classification in terms of the type of company goal served is generally appropriate, there are instances where the categorization must be considered somewhat arbitrary. Thus, although management development activities are in most cases intended as methods of increasing the overall productivity of the organization, there are certain types of management development procedures that appear to be directed primarily toward the reduction of conflict within managerial ranks, and that thus ameliorate internal stresses. Yet it seems undesirable to split the discussion of educational processes in the way that strict adherence to this goal dichotomy would require. Rather than do this, instances where particular procedures contribute to an alternative goal will be noted as they occur.

Chapters 14 and 15 are concerned with the various educational techniques used to raise the level of performance of organization members. This may be achieved either by providing new knowledge and information relevant to a job; by teaching new skills of a psychomotor nature; or by imbuing an individual with new attitudes, values, motives, and other personality characteristics. Often these techniques are utilized with segments of a work force irrespective of the existing performance level. Thus, a given work group or managerial component may be given a particular course with a view to improving the role behavior of all members, the outstanding as well as the less effective. On occasion training is focused on those who, either because they are new to the type of work or for other reasons, are not immediately in a position to achieve a successful level of performance.

As has been the custom previously with discussions of procedures for developing role prescriptions and of methods used to evaluate organization members, a split will be made in terms of the company hierarchy. Thus, this chapter will deal with training techniques normally used with managerial and other employees in the upper segment of the organization. Chapter 15 directs itself to employees at lower levels.

Evaluation of Change Models

Just as when a new selection procedure is introduced it should be validated against existing criteria of success in the organization, so when a new training program is introduced, it should be studied to determine whether it really is contributing to improved performance. There is a strong temptation to avoid this step on the part of many personnel managers, because the evaluation of a program always raises the possibility that it will turn out to have been worthless and thus a good deal of time and money wasted. Yet from an overall company viewpoint evaluation is essential if there is any prospect that the same or a similar course might be repeated in the future. As with validity studies in selection, however, there are cost considerations. Validation makes sense only if enough people are to be hired for the particular type of work to justify the expense of the research. Similarly, training evaluation is warranted only when a sufficient number of people are to be trained in a particular way.

It is important that a personnel manager be capable of carrying out change evaluation studies on his own programs when appropriate and that he be familiar with the studies that have been done by others on the various types of courses that he may be considering. This necessitates a sufficient knowledge of the logic of evaluation to permit discrimination between a good study and a poor one. The discussion that follows should provide this knowledge. In addition, it will introduce a basis for determining the effectiveness of the various development techniques to be considered later in this chapter.

The Before-After Model

The basic question that may be asked with regard to any training effort is whether it does in fact yield a change in the people exposed to it. Normally an experimental design for answering this question would involve a pretest, then exposure to training, and then a posttest. The pre- and postmeasurements are made using indexes that are closely related to what the course is expected to accomplish. Thus, an attempt to improve understanding of company policies would presumably be evaluated by using a test of knowledge regarding policy before the course started and the same or a very similar test afterward. Should there be a statistically reliable increase in score for the group as a whole from pretest to posttest, this would provide the type of evidence for change that permits generalization to other applications of the same course.

It would still remain to be demonstrated, however, that such a change had been caused by the course itself, and not by some external factor. For instance, it might be that the change in knowledge of policy identified actually resulted not so much from the training as from the fact that a revised policy manual was issued to all management personnel shortly after the course started. To check on this possibility, one would have to carry out the same pretest–posttest procedure on a *control group,* consisting of managers like those exposed to training but differing in that they did not take the course in company policy. Should this control group increase in knowledge of policy as much as the *experimental group,* who had had the course, this would support the view that some extratraining factor such as the new manual was the major cause of change. On the other hand, a statistically reliable increase in knowledge in the experimental group coupled with a complete lack of change in the control group would provide evidence that the training was in fact achieving its objective.

In selecting such a control group, it is important to use people as similar to those in the experimental group as possible and to make certain that the two groups have much the same types of experiences over the period of training. The only difference should be that one group is exposed to the course and the other is not. To demonstrate that the training has been effective, one must show that the addition of this single factor to one of two otherwise similar groups is sufficient to create a real difference at some later point in time. This before-after model is outlined in Figure 14-1.

Figure 14-1

Group	Time 1	Intervening Period	Time 2
Experimental	Pretest ⟶	Course ⟶	Posttest
Control	Pretest ⟶		Posttest

The After-Only Model

An alternative approach that offers certain advantages, as well as disadvantages, is outlined in Figure 14-2. Here the experimental and control groups are selected as with the before-after approach, but only posttests are administered. Change is presumed to have occurred if there is a statistically significant difference between the two groups at the time the measurement occurs. This assumes that the two groups were identical originally.

Figure 14-2

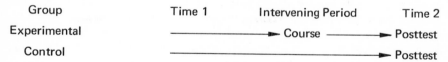

Group	Time 1	Intervening Period	Time 2
Experimental		→ Course →	Posttest
Control			Posttest

The problem is that in most ongoing business situations it is extremely difficult to determine whether identical groups have been selected without employing a pretest to be sure. Thus, there is always the possibility, when the after-only model is used, that any differences between the two groups established after training might have been present before. What appears to be change might only be a long-standing group difference.

Yet the simplicity of the after-only design is appealing, and there are circumstances under which one can feel reasonably confident that relatively good initial matching has occurred. Thus, this approach is used on occasion, although probably not as frequently as the before-after model. It has the additional advantage that there is no possibility of a pretest sensitizing those who take the course to certain specific aspects of the training. Managers may learn certain things only because they get the impression from a pretest that they should learn these particular things. The posttest then reveals a change. But in subsequent administrations of the course, without a pretest (or posttest either for that matter), this learning does not occur and the change can well be negligible. The after-only design avoids this source of error.

This pretest sensitizing effect seems to be a real problem primarily when knowledge changes are being evaluated (20) and when the measures used contain items practically identical to material covered in training. In such cases the ideal evaluation design is a combination of the before-after and after-only approaches, using at least three groups. This permits the identification of any pseudo-changes, resulting from the sensitizing effects of a pretest, through a comparison of the two experimental groups taking the course. Unfortunately studies of this kind that eliminate practically all sources of error are rarely conducted. They are too complex and require more subjects for inclusion in the various experimental and control conditions than are normally available.

The Retention and Organizational Relevance Factors

Although the demonstration of a change caused by the educational process is the first step in any evaluation study, this is not all that is required. To be of much value to a company, the change must be retained, and it must be clearly of a kind that contributes to goal attainment.

Retention is normally determined by taking a third measurement at some point in time well after training has been completed, perhaps as long as a year later. Or the posttest itself may be delayed so that retention and change are measured at one and the same time. In the latter instance, if a pretest-posttest change is not found, there is no way of knowing whether the course was totally ineffective or a real change was vitiated by events occurring subsequent to training.

It is clear that such vitiation of change does occur. The consequence is what has been termed *encapsulated training* (13). Within the education situation itself considerable change occurs, but none of this is actually carried back to the job. Because the training process is eventually terminated, all change will inevitably disappear also.

This type of encapsulation seems to be particularly frequent when there is a disparity between the actual role prescriptions for the job and those taught in the course. Management development may emphasize being kind and considerate toward subordinates, whereas the established role prescriptions for a manager, which are enforced by his superiors, emphasize pressure for production and the frequent use of negative sanctions. One solution to the dilemma thus produced is to accept the training values, but only for purposes of training—not back on the job. Because the entire reward structure built around the job is calculated to obtain a close match between role behavior and the established role prescriptions, and because the training emphasis if incorporated in behavior would tend to widen this gap and thus reduce the chances of being considered a success, the manager is careful not to let any training effects manifest themselves in the actual work situation.

Another type of reaction may also occur when the role requirements presented in the training situation are distinctly different from those characterizing the job situation. On occasion the two sets of expectations are carried into the work environment together, with the result that the manager does not know what he is supposed to do and what kind of behavior will be considered as evidence of success. The result is what is known as *role conflict* (17). Under such circumstances the changes produced by training are retained, but at considerable cost to the individual in terms of anxiety and confusion. The consequence for the organization is likely to be internal conflict and in many cases the eventual loss of a potentially valuable manager.

The solution to problems of encapsulated training and training-produced role conflict is to be sure that the role requirements taught in the course and those existing in the job situation are not divergent.

This can be accomplished by synchronizing the course with existing role prescriptions. When this is done, it can be assumed that the training will be reinforced by subsequent work experiences and changes will be retained. On the other hand, if the training is intended as a procedure for introducing alternative role prescriptions and thus moving managerial behavior toward a new pattern of expectations, the new role prescriptions should be made part of the job context as well. Thus, the changes should be organizational in nature and not restricted to a given management-development experience. It is for this reason that most training directors first attempt to expose the company's top management to any course emphasizing new role prescriptions. Then they work down through the successive levels of the hierarchy. In this way a climate favorable to the new behaviors is created from the outset and retention of change is fostered.

MEASURING ORGANIZATIONAL RELEVANCE. The final step in the evaluation model, and one that is far too often neglected, involves tying the change to organizational goals or to the role prescriptions that mediate goal attainment. Thus, if a knowledge change is produced, it must be demonstrated that the knowledge actually helps those who possess it to perform more effectively. If a change in attitudes occurs, there must be reason to believe these attitudes are associated with success on the job.

Methods of accomplishing this final step vary considerably. The ideal procedure is to use various judgmental or objective appraisal measures at pretest and posttest. Thus, the profit performance of cost centers or the turnover rate in work groups pre and post training might be compared, or ratings might be obtained from superiors at the two points in time. Unfortunately, obtaining comparable objective measures for all members of both experimental and control groups is often difficult. And when ratings are obtained from superiors who know the composition of experimental and control groups, the possibility of bias is pronounced. The wish, even though entirely unconscious, to justify the decision to invest in a training program may well distort the posttest evaluations in favor of the experimental group.

For these reasons it has become common practice to use various tests, attitude measures, and the like as pretest and posttest measures. However, these must be shown to have a positive relationship with success on the job. Thus, validity studies, in many cases predictive validity studies, must be carried out. The models discussed in Chapter 11 are the appropriate ones for this purpose. The point is that there must be good reason to believe that the development procedure has moved a number of individuals along some dimension that is known to yield role behavior that is positively valued within the organization.

Classroom-Type Development Techniques

The designation classroom-type has reference to all the great variety of training procedures that require that the participants leave their jobs and engage in some kind of group learning effort. These techniques should be contrasted with the more individualized approaches that involve building the developmental aspect directly into the job itself—job rotation, special committee assignments, and so on. The latter procedures will be taken up in the following section.

Among the various classroom procedures in common use are human relations training, lectures, group discussions, T-Group or laboratory techniques, conference leadership and coaching training, creativity and problem solution training, role-motivation training, film presentations, university management-development programs, case analysis, business games and other types of simulation techniques, and role playing. Obviously many of these designations are overlapping.

Human Relations Training

Although the human relations programs had their origins in the Hawthorne studies of the post-World War I period, it was the advent of research in the area of democratic leadership during and immediately after World War II that actually sparked their widespread application. Since these beginnings the programs have consistently operated within the welfare tradition of personnel management, emphasizing as they do the crucial significance of consideration and kindness as part of the supervisory process.

Originally the view was that through human relations training a more satisfied employee group could be achieved, with the result that productivity would increase. Thus, in basic conception the programs were intended to foster productivity and profit. In all probability they do contribute to this goal indirectly through a reduction in strikes, slowdowns, and the like. Yet it is also true that there is no necessary direct relationship between job satisfaction and productive output. The recognition of this fact has gradually led to a reconceptualization of the role of human relations training. Increasingly, such programs are viewed as valuable for the specific contribution they make to reduced conflict within the organization and thus to the maintenance objective alone. At the same time, however, other more productivity-oriented subject matter has been included with the specifically human relations content.

Thus, the "human relations package" now may include such topics as safety, production control, union contract administration, company policies, cost control, economics, company organization, job evaluation, methods improvement, and incentive payment, as well as the more typical material on employee motivation and attitudes, group dynamics, communications, counseling, and democratic leadership. In this comprehensive form the human relations program is clearly directed toward both productivity and maintenance considerations.

THE RESULTS OF EVALUATION. Rather consistently, training of this kind has been found effective in producing change—in knowledge, in attitudes, and in leadership behaviors (28). Yet such research as has been done suggests that there is a very considerable risk involved. There is no question but that human relations training can become encapsulated, or that it can produce role conflict. The emphasis on consideration and democratic procedures may be inconsistent with existing role prescriptions.

Table 14-1. Pretest-Posttest Changes for Groups that Did (Experimental) and Did Not (Control) Take a Human Relations Course

Measure		Experimental group means (N = 94)	Control group means (N = 24)
Personnel Relations	Pretest:	21.2	24.1
Test	Posttest:	25.0	25.3
How Supervise?	Pretest:	58.5	62.5
Test	Posttest:	64.4	61.9
Leadership Opinion Questionnaire			
Initiating Structure	Pretest:	54.8	52.0
	Posttest:	52.0	48.5
Consideration	Pretest:	56.3	58.0
	Posttest:	60.0	56.5
Prediction of Human Reactions	Pretest:	47.7	48.6
Test	Posttest:	50.0	47.2

Source: F. J. DiVesta, "Instructor-Centered and Student-Centered Approaches in Teaching a Human Relations Course," *Journal of Applied Psychology*, Vol. 38 (1954), p. 331.

Evidence of the change-producing potential of these courses is contained in Table 14-1. On both the knowledge measures, the Personnel Relations Test and How Supervise?, the experimental group showed a statistically reliable increase, whereas the control group did not. On the Leadership Opinion Questionnaire both groups decreased in Initiating Structure. Presumably this indicates that the school environment, to which both the experimental and the control subjects were exposed, served to produce a less favorable attitude toward a directive approach in supervision. But there was nothing unique about the human relations course per se in this regard. On the other hand, the course did serve to induce more favorable attitudes toward kindness and consideration in the handling of subordinates. Also, on the Prediction of Human Reactions Test, which is primarily oriented toward judging how an individual would react given certain characteristics of individuals and circumstances in a supervisor-subordinate relationship, the experimental group experienced a reliable increase, whereas the controls did not.

This particular study contained one other aspect that is of considerable significance (10). Part of those who took the human relations course were taught by the lecture method and part through group discussions. The various measures noted in Table 14-1 indicated that almost identical changes occurred under both conditions. The two methods were equally effective. Other research suggests that under certain circumstances discussion techniques can be somewhat more effective in producing personality change but that this superiority is likely to be achieved at some cost to learning. In the particular study referred to, those taught by the discussion method did not do as well on a knowledge test as those taught by lecture (3).

In spite of this possible deficiency, discussion techniques are widely employed in industry. The method uses a small group who work with a leader to develop discussion about human relations problems. Usually there are ten to twenty people in each group. Members must have practical experience with the subject being considered to be able to participate actively.

Actual practice differs considerably insofar as the role of the discussion leader is concerned (9). In some instances the leader has the conference content outlined in advance and the major conclusions to be reached already clearly established in his mind. He then guides the group by questions and comments so that the preestablished points are covered. In other cases the approach is much more nondirective, with the group developing its own framework for discussion. Here the leader serves primarily to encourage members to participate and as a resource person. Which procedure is best depends on the goal of the training and on the skill of the leader. The effective guidance of a discussion to a predetermined conclusion is a difficult art.

Changes resulting from a week-long course in the human relations tradition taught by line managers from the company involved are presented in Table 14-2. The approach was primarily discussion, although there were a few lectures and some reading assignments. It is interesting to note that although significant attitude shifts were produced and the managers did improve in their ability to solve human relations problems as reflected in cases, there was no training-produced change in knowledge. Both experimental and control groups increased their performance on the management practices quiz to an almost equal degree. Apparently this increase was a result of practice with the test; certainly it was not specifically due to learning in the course (23).

Table 14-2. Pretest-Posttest Changes for Groups that Did (Experimental) and Did Not (Control) Take a Human Relations Course

Measure		Experimental group means (N = 44)	Control group means (N = 13)
Management Practices	Pretest:	33.8	34.9
Quiz	Posttest:	37.9	40.2
Case Analysis	Pretest:	.8	1.0
	Posttest:	1.9	.4
Attitude Scale	Pretest:	91.9	90.2
	Posttest:	98.9	91.1

Source: T. A. Mahoney, T. H. Jerdee, and A. Korman, "An Experimental Evaluation of Management Development," *Personnel Psychology*, Vol. 13 (1960), p. 94.

This lack of knowledge change occurs sufficiently often with management-development programs to constitute a problem. In this particular case it turned out that the line managers who did the teaching were very poorly informed regarding the subject matter and that the reading assignments were rarely completed by participants. This finding seems to argue for the use of training specialists to conduct human relations programs, specialists who are qualified in the subject matter area and who can teach effectively. It also suggests that management-development programs should be presented as an important aspect of the total job with rewards for good performance, rather than as a semi-vacation from work. Unfortunately the latter view does prevail in some companies.

THE PREDICTION OF CHANGE. Although little work has been done in an effort to predict which managers will change with human relations training, this appears to be a fruitful area for study. If those most likely to change can be identified prior to training, a company will be in a position to save itself considerable money. It is possible to maximize the return on investments in this area by selecting men who exhibit change potential and letting only these individuals undergo management development.

One study of this kind has been completed in Switzerland with favorable results (30). The data are contained in Table 14-3. The

Maudsley Personality Inventory, a self-report measure, was administered to the managers before human relations training. Change on an attitude measure did occur for the group as a whole; the results were statistically reliable. But when the group was split up on the basis of personality test scores, it became clear that this change had been largely restricted to those men who had above-average scores on the indexes of normality-neuroticism *and* extroversion-introversion. Had all efforts been concentrated on this particular group, a maximum return on the investment in training would have been achieved.

Table 14-3. Attitude Change with a Human Relations Course Related to Initial Scores on a Personality Test

Groupings based on Maudsley Personality Inventory scores	N	Mean attitude change
Neurotic-introverted	18	+2.89
Neurotic-extroverted	18	−.89
Normal-introverted	23	+1.57
Normal-extroverted	28	+5.32

Source: A. Papaloïzos, "Personality and Success of Training in Human Relations," *Personnel Psychology*, Vol. 15 (1962), p. 426.

Laboratory, Sensitivity, or T-Group Training

These three terms tend to be used interchangeably, although in a technical sense the T-Group is a special technique within the broader context of a laboratory or sensitivity program. The approach is closely allied to human relations training, but has increasingly taken on certain specific objectives and procedures that have come to distinguish it from other types of training.

Laboratory training originated with a workshop conducted at the New Britain, Connecticut, State Teachers College in 1946 by staff members from the Research Center for Group Dynamics, then located at the Massachusetts Institute of Technology (5). In this early period the major focus was on group discussions of various job-related problems brought in by the participants. These discussions were supplemented with some lectures, demonstrations, and role playing.

Very soon the emphasis shifted from back-home problems to the processes occurring in the here-and-now group situation. It is this technique of learning about oneself and others through observing and participating in an ongoing group situation that is properly designated as T-Group training. Programs of laboratory training containing this element have been conducted at Bethel, Maine, under the auspices of the National Education Association since 1947. Similar training is now offered at a number of universities and in other locations. Increasingly, individual companies have set up what are called family-group programs. These contain only individuals from that firm's managerial ranks, often managers who are closely associated in their everyday work. Such efforts have been directed at the top management group of a company (2) and at the total managerial component of a large refinery (7). The more typical approach, however, is to put together groups of ten or twelve individuals from a variety of occupations and organizations.

Although lectures, role playing, problem-centered discussions, special projects, and the like have remained a part of the total laboratory experience, the major aspect is the T-Group. These groups meet for two or three hours daily over a period of a week, or in most cases longer. Although there is a leader, he does not impose a structure on the group and its activities; there is no specified task to be performed. At first the members tend to be frustrated and embarrassed. They cannot see why they are there and want someone to tell them what to do. Gradually, however, the conversation turns to the group itself and its members. The leader tends to encourage frankness in the expression of feelings and reactions to others. Such matters as the effects of authority, the motives of others, and the need to be understood are discussed. The participants gradually open up and show themselves for what they are. Frequently the ties between them become quite strong, and the group eventually develops its own structure (37). At points during this process certain participants may become quite anxious. Whether there is likely to be a real threat to psychological adjustment remains a matter of some controversy (15,26).

THE RESULTS OF EVALUATION. A number of studies have now been conducted to identify the impact of laboratory training. These have consistently indicated that change does occur. The findings presented in Table 14-4 are typical.

In this particular instance individuals who had attended the Bethel program were compared with co-workers who had not some eight to ten months after returning to their jobs (8). A special questionnaire was administered to people who were in a position to observe both the experimental and control subjects in their work. The questionnaires were designed to elicit information on observed changes in behavior and attitude. The approach is an after-only one with a delayed posttest. The variables noted in Table 14-4 are those that revealed a statistically significant difference between experimental and control groups in the proportion of individuals exhibiting change. An additional four variables did not yield reliable results. Overall, approximately two-thirds of the experimental subjects changed in some respect, whereas only one-third of those who did not attend the Bethel sessions changed.

OBJECTIVES OF TRAINING. The stated goals of the laboratory procedures are to make the manager more sensitive to emotional reaction and expression in others, to produce greater skill in perceiving the consequences of actions through attention to one's own feelings and those of other people, to develop in a manager values of a primarily democratic and scientific nature, to provide information about interpersonal and group situations, and to foster behavioral effectiveness in dealing with others (6). The approach deliberately attempts to make those exposed to training value science, democracy, and helping others more than they have in the past. These are exactly the kinds of changes noted in Table 14-4 and in other similar evaluation studies.

Table 14-4.   Proportions of Experimental and Control Subjects Reported as Changed Subsequent to Laboratory Training

| | Proportions changed | |
Area of change	Experimentals, N = 229	Controls, N = 112
Receiving Communication—more effort to understand, attentive listening, understands	.34	.16
Relational Facility—cooperative, tactful, less irritating, easier to deal with, able to negotiate	.36	.21
Increased Interdependence—encourages participation, involves others, greater leeway to subordinates, less dominating, lets others think	.38	.27
Self-Control—more self-discipline, less quick with judgment, checks temper	.26	.15
Awareness of Human Behavior—more conscious of why people act, more analytic of others' actions, clear perceptions of people	.34	.16
Sensitivity to Group Behavior—more conscious of group process, aware of subcurrents in groups	.24	.09
Sensitivity to Others' Feelings—more capacity for understanding feelings, more sensitive to needs of others	.34	.10
Acceptance of Other People—able to tolerate shortcomings, considerate of individual differences, patient	.49	.29
Tolerance of New Information—willing to accept suggestions, considers new points of view, less dogmatic, less arbitrary	.42	.23
Comfort—relaxed, at ease	.36	.23
Insight into Self and Role—understands job demands, more aware of own behavior, better adjusted to job	.36	.24

Source: D. R. Bunker, "The Effect of Laboratory Education Upon Individual Behavior," in G. G. Somers (ed.), *Proceedings of the Sixteenth Annual Meeting.* Madison, Wisc.: Industrial Relations Research Association, 1964, pp. 225 and 231.

Several writers have raised questions as to whether changes of this kind do foster the objectives of business organizations (14,25). Is laboratory training really an effective input-output mediator? Or does it contribute primarily to individual and societal goals rather than those of an organizational nature? Unfortunately there is little available evidence on this point. Few satisfactory studies that relate training changes to productivity and organizational maintenance objectives have been conducted. The nature of the changes identified suggests, however, that when encapsulation and role conflict are effectively avoided the maintenance goal may well be fostered. What the impact on productivity is remains a matter for conjecture. It seems apparent that a number of those actively engaged in leading laboratory training groups are somewhat more concerned with making a contribution to a better society than they are with the goals of a specific company. This does not mean, on the other hand, that the company is not inadvertently served also.

Performance Appraisal, Coaching, and Conference Leadership Training

These techniques are widely used to enable managers more effectively to evaluate and utilize their subordinates. They are primarily directed at the productivity goal, although other considerations may be involved as well.

Performance appraisal training is intended to teach the various methods of rating and evaluating employees used by the company. It is the basic method for installing many of the procedures discussed in Chapters 9 and 10. Particular emphasis is usually placed on the elimination of various sources of error that may creep into the rating process. There is evidence that when the training utilizes discussions that eventuate in a group decision to minimize certain types of rater bias, this objective is most likely to be achieved (22).

Closely related are the various coaching training programs that attempt to make a manager more effective in feeding back and utilizing appraisal data for the purpose of developing subordinates. These programs have gradually shifted in recent years from a primary concern with methods of telling a man how his work is perceived by his superiors to a concern with self-evaluation. Coaching training now often involves teaching a manager how to guide a subordinate in setting his own objectives or targets for future performance. The subordinate is then subsequently expected to evaluate himself against these previously established goals with the help of his superior. Thus, coaching training has become a basic part of the *management by objectives* approach with its emphasis on individual and group planning and target setting.

Another method a manager may use to develop and more effectively utilize his subordinates is to conduct problem-solving conferences with them (24). This is part of the *participative management* approach that argues in favor of group decision making and group involvement in the managerial process rather than unilateral command. The essence of this view is that in many instances decisions are never implemented because the subordinates who would have to actually do the work are for one reason or another resistant. To overcome this resistance, it is necessary only to have the subordinates become involved in making the decision so that they will perceive it as their own. It is recognized that this may result in a somewhat lower quality decision, but in many instances this is preferable to not having a decision implemented at all.

To use the participative approach effectively and conduct conferences that lead to meaningful results is very difficult for many managers, especially those who believe strongly that decisions should be made individually by the person in charge. A number of firms have instituted training programs for their managers to change attitudes and develop skills in conference and discussion leadership. Just as coaching training has come to have a close association with the management by objectives approach, conference leadership training is an integral part of participative management. The two training procedures, and managerial approaches, can of course be used together.

Problem Solving and Creativity Training

A variety of different training programs have been developed to help managers become more original and effective in thinking of solutions to business problems (27). The emphasis tends to be on upgrading decision-making skills so that the manager will be able to reach more rational conclusions and thus make a greater contribution to a firm's profitability. In some instances the training is intended to provide an impetus in the area of research and invention as well.

One such course is offered through a specialized consulting firm (18). The training contains three aspects. First, there is instruction of a more or less conventional type, using lecture and discussion methods, aimed at providing a general understanding of the concepts and sequential steps in the problem-solving process. Then the participants work together on a simulated problem drawn from the business world. The conferences and conversations that form a part of this practice exercise are recorded. The final aspect of training, and perhaps the most important, is the feedback process. Here the recordings are played back and the efforts at problem solution critiqued. Thus, the manager has an opportunity to see where he may be going wrong and to learn new approaches.

Another course that has been much more extensively evaluated has been developed at the University of Buffalo (31). The participants are taught to defer judgment both at the problem definition and at the problem solution stages until they have a clear picture of the many alternatives. The approach emphasizes a listing of all possible ways in which a problem may be stated, and only then a selection of *the* problem. The latter is broken down into as many aspects as possible and alternative solutions developed for each aspect. Thus, the manager learns a technique that stresses selecting from among a large number of known possibilities. Evaluation studies that meet all criteria for adequacy of design indicate that training of this kind does increase an individual's ability to develop original problem solutions of high quality. Furthermore, these changes are retained.

Role-Motivation Training

Role-motivation training, although it has not had as widespread application as some of the other techniques discussed, has been rather extensively evaluated with consistently favorable results (28). Training is conducted by the lecture method, plus a certain amount of directed discussion. Emphasis is placed on the various factors in the individual, his work group, his family, the organizational milieu, the society as a whole, and the physical work situation that may contribute to ineffective performance in a subordinate. In this way the manager's responsibility for maintaining satisfactory productivity levels among his men is stressed. In addition, the manager's own motivation to meet certain of the role requirements for his own job is increased.

Table 14-5. Pretest, Posttest, and Follow-up Scores on the Miner Sentence Completion Scale for Groups that Did (Experimental) and Did Not (Control) Take Role-Motivation Training

Group	Mean score at pretest	Mean score at posttest	Mean score at follow-up
Research and development managers			
Experimental $(N = 56)$	4.66	6.77	
Control $(N = 30)$	5.60	4.47	
Business school students			
Experimental $(N = 129)$	3.40	6.67	5.90
Control $(N = 54)$	3.67	3.24	

Source: J. B. Miner, *Studies in Management Education.* New York: Springer, 1965, pp. 98, 115, 122, and 127.

Evaluation data on this course are presented in Table 14-5. The research and development managers exhibited a highly reliable increase in motivation to manage after training. The control group actually decreased in this regard. Although it was not possible to carry out a third follow-up testing on these groups, a follow-up was conducted over the subsequent five years using personnel records as a source of information. Experimental and control managers were compared in terms of the number who achieved success in the company after the training was completed. Success was defined as having at least one promotion in the five-year period or, if the man left the company in the interim, a favorable separation rating in his file. Experimental and control groups were at the same average grade level at the time of training and were considered to have the same potential for advancement. Thus, the two groups started the race at essentially the same point. Yet those who underwent role-motivation training were much more likely to win out, as the following data on the per cent achieving success indicate:

Experimentals	81%
Controls	51%

These findings suggest that in this instance the training was congruent with existing managerial role requirements and that encapsulation did not occur. The results for business school students are similar. Although there was some dropoff in motivation within the follow-up period, which averaged about a year, a reliable 70 per cent of the initial pretest–posttest change was retained. Unfortunately the control subjects could not be tested a third time. As indicated in the preceding chapter, the change measure employed is a valid predictor of managerial success. Thus, this particular mediator does appear to contribute to company goals.

Case Study, Role Playing, Business Games, and Other Simulations

Case study, role playing, and business games have in common that the manager is required to think and/or act in terms of a set of role prescriptions differing in some degree from those applying to his own job in the here and now. Thus, he is forced out of his current mold and exposed to new ways of thinking and acting. The result can be a considerable amount of new learning and attitude change. Simulations of this kind can be very close to the present job, dealing with role behaviors that are to be added to the existing patterns; they can also be quite distant, dealing with the role prescriptions for a position for which the trainee may some day qualify.

There are also major differences in the degree of reality inherent in the simulation. In case study, information is presented in written terms and the participant must imagine the situation. At no point does he do any more than think his way through the role. In certain more complex types of simulations considerable effort is devoted to reproducing the salient aspects of the situation, and the individual actually acts out his solution to the problem presented.

CASE STUDY. The case approach is one in which a problem is given in written form to a group for solution. The usual procedure is for the group members individually to assume the role of the manager who is faced with the problem situation. The written statement stops short of a solution, and the participants in the training must then think through to the role behavior they feel to be desirable. The leader does not impose a specific solution. The emphasis is on individual or team problem solving, group discussion, and group critique.

The method is clearly more appropriate for certain purposes than others (35). It is helpful in teaching managers to identify and analyze complex problems and to make their own decisions. It permits coverage of a great deal of ground very rapidly in terms of diverse approaches, interpretations, and personalities. Making snap judgments and applying pat solutions to problems are discouraged at the same time that learning is fostered. When the participants are sufficiently sophisticated and knowledgeable in the subject areas involved, it can serve as a basis for the development of general principles that may then be used in solving actual on-the-job problems. If the trainees do not have the background knowledge to come up with meaningful case solutions, or they lack any real understanding of the role the case requires them to assume, none of these objectives are likely to be achieved and the use of the method should probably be avoided.

THE INCIDENT PROCESS. The incident process is a modification of the basic case study procedure; it attempts to move the training somewhat closer to reality (33). The class is initially given a very brief written incident and a statement of the role to be assumed in viewing this incident. The total case is then developed by means of a question-and-answer process, with the leader supplying information as the trainees ask for it. After the problem to be solved has been established, each trainee writes his own particular solution down on a piece of paper. These solutions are then sorted by the leader and their authors are assigned to discussion groups on the basis of similarity of opinion. These groups develop the strongest statement of their members' mutual opinion that they can. The statements may then be presented in the form of a debate or the groups may role-play their solutions.

Finally, and here the incident process goes beyond traditional case study, the leader presents what actually was done in the particular instance and, where possible, the consequences. A general discussion follows with the focus on such matters as the factors accounting for accomplishments and difficulties, the possibilities of accomplishing more, methods of surmounting difficulties, and what can be learned from the case for transfer to on-the-job situations.

ROLE PLAYING. Basically the role-playing approach may be considered as a type of case study in which actual individuals play the various roles of the persons in the case. All participants do not assume the same role, the role of the responsible manager, as with the typical written case. The fact that participants *behave* in roles rather than merely think in them tends to create a more realistic learning situation.

Usually role playing is done in groups of ten to twenty with members taking turns acting and serving as analysts. The leader assigns individuals to roles. An oral or written briefing is given to put the audience and actors into the situation. Sometimes rather detailed role instructions are given; sometimes the actors actually read a skit up to a certain point; sometimes there is practically no structuring of this kind and the participants largely develop their own roles. In any event the actors eventually take over on their own, behaving as they see fit in the situation. The leader terminates the session when the audience has been emotionally involved and either the problem is analyzed or an impasse has been reached. A lengthy discussion that attempts to point up the objectives of training normally follows.

There are a great many variants in technique used by different trainers, even to the point of employing professional actors to take certain parts in a skit. In addition, the approach has been used in a number of different contexts, although the training of managers in leadership behaviors is most common, usually in conjunction with a human relations program. Specific applications have been made in connection with the handling of discharges, layoffs, merit ratings, and grievances, as well as in sales training.

Role playing can be very helpful in practicing role behaviors, provided a sufficient illusion of reality can be produced. Learning by doing is known to be an effective method of developing new skills, although it does not necessarily guarantee against encapsulation. Research evidence is available, indicating that when there is adequate discussion and critique of each role-playing episode, rather sizable changes in sensitivity to others and in employee orientation can be achieved (21). These changes are similar to those produced by laboratory training, and, in fact, role playing is often used as part of the total laboratory experience. It seems apparent, however, that role playing need not be oriented toward organizational maintenance considerations only. Roles can be constructed to emphasize factors directly related to productivity.

BUSINESS GAMES. Another method of obtaining high levels of participant involvement is the business game, which may be viewed as a case spread out over time with the consequences of decisions made apparent. The usual procedure is to first inform the trainees regarding the business objectives to be sought, the decisions to be made, and the rules that apply. This may be done orally, but it is common practice to provide written instructions as well. Each competing team organizes itself, studies the available information on operations to date, and makes its initial set of decisions. Each decision period is set equal to a unit of time—a day, week, month, or even a quarter or longer. After the first decisions are turned in, the trainers calculate the operating results, either manually or with the aid of an electronic computer, and feed them back to the teams, often with further environmental and competitive data added. This cycle is repeated several times and the results are then discussed and critiqued at length.

Some of the available games deal with top-level decisions affecting the total enterprise. Others have been constructed with reference to specific functions and problems—personnel assignment, materials management, stock transactions, sales management, production scheduling, collective bargaining, inventory control, and bank management (11,19). The list is constantly increasing. Although the tendency is to deal with generalized and hypothetical business situations, there are a number of games constructed with specific reference to a particular firm or industry. In some instances the decisions made by one team are *interactive* with the results obtained by other teams in that constant mathematical probabilities have been built into the game as concomitants of particular types of decisions. This is not always done, however.

Table 14-6. Relationships Between Business Game Performance and Management Appraisal Ratings for 63 Department Store Supervisors

Management appraisal dimension	Mean ratings for supervisors in various final game positions			Correlation values (for significant first-third differences)
	First	Second	Third	
Advancement potential	3.3	3.1	3.0	
Overall performance	9.7	9.0	8.5	.42
Job knowledge	4.2	4.1	3.9	.35
Judgment	2.9	2.9	2.2	.38
Initiative	3.8	3.5	3.4	.17
Cooperation	4.4	4.2	4.2	
Responsibility	4.0	3.9	3.7	
Leadership	3.4	3.4	3.1	
Personality	4.3	4.4	4.3	
Health	4.7	4.6	4.2	.58
Customer service	4.3	4.3	4.4	

Source: H. P. Teich, *Validity of a Business Game.* M.S. Thesis. Eugene, Oregon: Univ. of Oregon, 1964, pp. 56–57.

In spite of the fact that business games have won widespread acceptance, both in the universities and in connection with company management development programs, there is practically no evaluative information available. It may well be that playing these games does change a participant and that in doing so it makes him a better manager; in all likelihood this is the case. But the kind of evidence demanded by the evaluation of change models is lacking.

There is reason to believe that those managers who do well in the game situation will be more effective on the job, whether or not they change during training (38). The data are presented in Table 14-6. The game used in this study (39) requires three companies to compete for industry leadership. For research purposes, individuals rather than teams were set equal to companies so that each player could be ranked as first, second, or third in his group of three competitors, on the basis of his average score on the various company success indexes. The data of Table 14-6 are the average appraisal ratings, made by the store manager, for the twenty-one supervisors who were first in their respective industries, the twenty-one who were second, and the twenty-one who were last. In the five instances where correlations have been computed, the supervisors coming in last on the game have a reliably lower performance rating than those coming in first. On four additional dimensions a similar trend is present in the data. Only the personality and customer service ratings, which would appear on the surface to be far removed from decision-making skills, are clearly unrelated to game performance.

University and University-Type Programs

Although much management development is carried out in classrooms located on company premises near the workplace, there is also widespread utilization of university facilities. In part this involves enrollment in regular courses carrying degree credit. Many universities offer a large number of evening courses for the specific purpose of meeting the demand created by business firms and their employees. Some companies even give time off during the day so that individuals may attend classes. Increasingly, policies are being developed that permit a man to take a leave to pursue graduate study on a full-time basis. This is a particularly common practice within research and development departments.

In some instances the initiative behind this return to school comes from the employee and in some cases from the company. Many firms pay a large proportion or even all of the costs. Policies in this regard vary tremendously, depending in large part on the company's need for individuals with various kinds of university training.

In addition, most universities are engaged in some type of management development effort on a noncredit basis (16,32). These are programs specifically structured to meet the needs of the business community. They vary from one-day conferences to year-long programs of the kind originated at the Massachusetts Institute of Technology in the early 1930's, and since emulated by a number of other schools. In most instances a company will send only one manager, or at most several, to a given university course, with the result that the groups tend to be quite heterogeneous in company representation. Occasionally, however, a university will offer a program specifically for the managers of a single company.

The subjects taught vary a great deal. One recent survey noted the following as frequently included in live-in university programs (34). The listing is in order of preference among participants.

> Business policy
> Human relations
> Social, economic, or political responsibility
> Business economics
> Labor relations
> Finance, accounting
> Public speaking
> Production
> Marketing

Very little information is available regarding the change-producing effects of these programs. Most are intended either to impart new knowledge, in an area related to career objectives and of a kind that the managers do not currently possess, or to update existing knowledge. There is reason to believe that such learning does occur, but it may not be achieved as efficiently as in the regular university classroom. The reason for this is that in most instances examinations are not given, and no report on the managers' level of accomplishment is sent back to the company. A manager who really wants to learn will no doubt do so, but without question some individuals attend these programs with very little gain to either themselves or the firms that send them.

LIBERAL ARTS PROGRAMS. Some mention should be made of the various general liberal arts programs offered by universities specifically for management personnel. These are not widespread, but they have engendered considerable discussion because of their emphasis on general personal broadening rather than directly career-related learning.

One such program, which has been extensively evaluated, was conducted for executives of the Bell Telephone System at the University of Pennsylvania for a number of years (40). The course, which lasted ten months, included such subjects as practical logic, business history, world art, history and aesthetics of music, analytical reading, world literature, social science, philosophy of ethics, history and meaning of science, modern architecture, American civilization, political science, and international relations. Comparison of control and experimental groups indicated that a certain amount of knowledge change did occur in the subject matter areas covered.

There was also a reduction in the value placed on economic considerations and an increase in aesthetic interests as reflected on the Allport-Vernon-Lindsey Study of Values. Various attitude measures indicated that a rather marked shift away from conservative views to radical and liberal positions occurred. Although no attempt was made to conduct follow-up studies and to relate these changes to success indexes, there is reason to believe that some of these changes may have been associated with either encapsulation or role conflict. The nature of the attitude changes induced suggests that the training may not have been organizationally relevant. A similar question can be raised regarding other liberal arts programs of this type. Is the company's investment appropriate in the sense that the changes produced actually contribute to organizational goals? It is interesting to note in this connection that when the participants pay part of the costs, they tend to be more satisfied with this type of training (12).

UNIVERSITY-TYPE PROGRAMS. There are a number of programs in existence that closely parallel those offered by the universities but that are made available under other auspices. The American Management Association conducts a great many such courses, as do a number of other professional and managerial societies and consulting firms. Most of these are very similar to university offerings, but they more frequently utilize business managers themselves as trainers (1). Often, instruction is given in hotel meeting rooms, at country clubs, or at special facilities maintained by the organization.

Another approach that is being utilized by a number of the larger firms is for the company to establish what amounts to a "college" of its own. These are generally located on former private estates or on similar properties. The teaching may be done by the company's own managers, by a special training staff, or by university professors hired as consultants. A group of managers may spend ten weeks or more on the premises and a new group comes in shortly after the last has finished. Perhaps the extreme in terms of this kind of company investment in education is represented by the degree-granting institutions, such as General Motors Institute. The latter is run by the company for its own employees, who attend on a cooperative work-study basis. Degrees are given in mechanical, industrial, and electrical engineering. The average number of students enrolled is 2,500 (29).

Development Outside the Classroom

Management development is not entirely a matter of classroom training. There are a number of other techniques that are utilized by companies with a view to improving the effectiveness of their members. Among these input-output mediators are job rotation, understudy assignments, committee participation, special reading assignments, and correspondence courses.

Job Rotation and Understudy Assignments

In this instance placements are made not so much with a view to selecting those individuals who will perform most effectively on the job as with the idea of exposing an individual who is thought to have good prospects of moving to higher levels of responsibility to new learning experiences. The extent to which these assignments carry full operating responsibilities varies considerably (36). In some cases the man is rotated from one department to another, perhaps at yearly intervals, and takes over each job with all its role requirements. It is not uncommon for this sort of thing to occur at relatively high levels in the managerial hierarchy. The usual practice is to exercise rather close supervision over individuals who are being rotated for purposes of development and to give them a good deal of coaching. At the other extreme is an approach, used mostly with new management trainees, whereby the individual is assigned for varying periods to different types of work primarily for the purpose of observing and perhaps of carrying out special projects of a largely training nature. Here the development emphasis is primary, and there is only a very limited direct contribution to organizational goal attainment in the work the man does.

Understudy assignments are normally used not so much for general broadening as to prepare a man for a specific position that he is expected to assume. Thus, the emphasis is not on obtaining a general understanding of the total company operation or of several important segments of it, as in rotation. Understudies may be in a direct line relationship, serving as assistant managers, or they may hold positions as administrative assistants or assistants to a particular manager. In many cases these jobs are created specifically for the purpose of training a successor to an incumbent manager and are abolished after promotion occurs.

In evaluating the various developmental techniques involving the use of placement procedures, it is important to remember that training that seriously hampers present operations is not really of much value. The ideal is to be able to carry out the training process with a minimum of disruption on the job. This means that throwing a man into a job that he knows nothing about, purely to gain the advantage of rotation, is normally to be avoided. Even if the man does eventually survive and begin to grow, the loss in present efficiency may well be too great.

Also, rotations and understudy assignments in and of themselves have little worth. It is because they can offer opportunities for new learning and change that these procedures are considered to be of value. If, however, because of the way an immediate superior handles men in such positions, or for some other reason, very little learning is possible, then techniques of this kind are likely to do more harm than good. Thus, such placements are probably best restricted to certain groups and departments where there is known to be a high probability that development will in fact occur. Furthermore, the kind of individuals selected for rotation should be those who can be counted on to benefit from the experience. It is clear from what we know about individual differences that placement procedures of this kind will contribute little if applied on a universal basis.

Committee Assignments

Another means of exposing managers to new experiences, and thus opportunities to learn, is through the judicious use of committee assignments. Work on salary and grievance committees, and in groups set up to study special problems, can be of considerable value if these committees are made up of representatives with varied backgrounds.

A related approach is *multiple management,* as originally developed at McCormick and Company (4). This involves establishing what amounts to a junior board of directors, made up of from ten to twenty members of middle management. Such a board deals with problems from the viewpoint of the overall company and makes recommendations directly to the board of directors in a variety of areas. Membership is rotated to a degree by virtue of the fact that the three least effective managers, as determined by peer ratings, are dropped off the board at regular intervals and replaced by new members. Recommendations to the board of directors must be unanimous, and if they are not accepted, the reasons for rejection must be stated in writing by the senior board.

Many firms that have adopted this technique have added factory boards, sales boards, and the like to deal with problems in particular functional areas. Subcommittees to handle such matters as executive actions, new products, human relations, training, and suggestions are often appointed. All this is done primarily for the purpose of development, although other objectives may be fostered as well.

Reading and Correspondence Courses

A number of training departments, although having primary responsibility in the area of classroom training, also assume the role of guide or counselor to management with regard to learning generally. This may well be done on a formal basis. The management-appraisal statement, as indicated in Table 9-2, normally ends with a series of development recommendations that may have reference to special reading assignments, as well as to certain correspondence courses sponsored by a university extension division, a private source, or by the training department itself. Libraries are on occasion maintained on the premises to facilitate these activities. Sometimes companies will buy large quantities of a particular book or journal article and distribute these to management as required reading.

In addition to these more formal programs, training departments normally serve as a source of information regarding self-development. In some instances various department members are assigned responsibility for keeping abreast of knowledge changes in the various subject matter areas relevant to the company's operations. These individuals recommend reading materials to appropriate members of management and in some cases provide synopses of new publications. The latter role, as knowledge broker, represents one of the important recent developments in the training field. It requires, however, that the personnel manager who specializes in the training area be a highly educated and well-informed person.

References

1. American Management Association, *Guide to Intensive Courses and Seminars for Executives*. New York: the Association.
2. Argyris, C., *Interpersonal Competence and Organizational Effectiveness*. Homewood, Ill.: Irwin, 1962.
3. Asch, M. J., "Nondirective Teaching in Psychology: An Experimental Study," *Psychological Monographs*, Vol. 65, No. 4 (1951).
4. Bell, F. J., "Highlights of Multiple Management," in H. F. Merrill, and E. Marting (eds.), *Developing Executive Skills*. New York: American Management Association, 1958, pp. 141–147.
5. Benne, K. D., "History of the T Group in the Laboratory Setting," in L. P. Bradford, J. R. Gibb, and K. D. Benne (eds.), *T-Group Theory and Laboratory Method*. New York: Wiley, 1964, pp. 80–135.
6. Benne, K. D., L. P. Bradford, and R. Lippitt, "The Laboratory Method," in L. P. Bradford, J. R. Gibb, and K. D. Benne (eds), *T-Group Theory and Laboratory Method*. New York: Wiley, 1964, pp. 15–44.
7. Blake, R. R., and J. S. Mouton, *The Managerial Grid*. Houston, Texas: Gulf, 1964.

8. Bunker, D. R., "The Effect of Laboratory Education upon Individual Behavior," in G. G. Somers (ed.), *Proceedings of the Sixteenth Annual Meeting.* Madison, Wisc.: Industrial Relations Research Association, 1964, pp. 220–232.

9. Davis, K., *Human Relations at Work,* 3rd ed. New York: McGraw-Hill, 1967.

10. DiVesta, F. J., "Instructor-Centered and Student-Centered Approaches in Teaching a Human Relations Course," *Journal of Applied Psychology,* Vol. 38 (1954), 329–335.

11. Greenlaw, P. S., L. W. Herron, and R. H. Rawdon, *Business Simulation in Industrial and University Education.* Englewood Cliffs, N.J.: Prentice-Hall, 1962.

12. Gruenfeld, L. W., "The Effects of Tuition Payment and Involvement on Benefit from a Management Development Program," *Journal of Applied Psychology,* Vol. 50 (1966), 396–399.

13. Haire, M., *Psychology in Management,* 2nd ed. New York: McGraw-Hill, 1964.

14. House, R. J., "T Group Training—Some Important Considerations for the Practicing Manager," *New York Personnel Management Association Bulletin,* Vol. 21, No. 9 (1965), 4–9.

15. House, R. J., "T-Group Education and Leadership Effectiveness: A Review of the Empiric Literature and a Critical Evaluation," *Personnel Psychology,* Vol. 20 (1967), 1–32.

16. Houston, G. C., *Manager Development.* Homewood, Ill.: Irwin, 1961.

17. Kahn, R. L., D. M. Wolfe, R. P. Quinn, J. D. Snoek, and R. A. Rosenthal, *Organizational Stress: Studies in Role Conflict and Ambiguity.* New York: Wiley, 1964.

18. Kepner, C. H., and B. B. Tregoe, *The Rational Manager.* New York: McGraw-Hill, 1965.

19. Kibbee, J. M., C. J. Craft, and B. Nanus, *Management Games.* New York: Reinhold, 1961.

20. Lana, R. E., "Pretest-Treatment Interaction Effects in Attitudinal Studies," *Psychological Bulletin,* Vol. 56 (1959), 293–300.

21. Lawshe, C. H., R. A. Bolda, and R. L. Brune, "Studies in Management Training Evaluation: II. The Effects of Exposure in Role Playing," *Journal of Applied Psychology,* Vol. 43 (1959), 287–292.

22. Levine, J., and J. Butler, "Lecture vs. Group Decision in Changing Behavior," *Journal of Applied Psychology,* Vol. 36 (1952), 29–33.

23. Mahoney, T. A., T. H. Jerdee, and A. Korman, "An Experimental Evaluation of Management Development," *Personnel Psychology,* Vol. 13 (1960), 81–98.

24. Maier, N. R. F., *Problem-Solving Discussions and Conferences.* New York: McGraw-Hill, 1963.

25. McGehee, W., and P. W. Thayer, *Training in Business and Industry.* New York: Wiley, 1961.

26. McGregor, D., *The Professional Manager.* New York: McGraw-Hill, 1967.

27. McPherson, J. H., "Environment and Training for Creativity," in C. W.

Taylor (ed.), *Creativity: Progress and Potential*. New York: McGraw-Hill, 1964, pp. 129–153.

28. Miner, J. B., *Studies in Management Education*. New York: Springer, 1965.
29. Osborn, C. R., "The Company-Owned Cooperative College: General Motors Institute," in *Making the Most of Training Opportunities*, Management Bulletin 73. New York: American Management Association, 1965, pp. 35–37.
30. Papaloïzos, A., "Personality and Success of Training in Human Relations," *Personnel Psychology*, Vol. 15 (1962), 423–428.
31. Parnes, S. J., "Research on Developing Creative Behavior," in C. W. Taylor (ed.), *Widening Horizons in Creativity*. New York: Wiley, 1964, pp. 145–169.
32. Pierson, F. C., *The Education of American Businessmen*. New York: McGraw-Hill, 1959.
33. Pigors, P., and F. Pigors, *Case Method in Human Relations: The Incident Process*. New York: McGraw-Hill, 1961.
34. Powell, R. M., "Managers' Needs and University Executive Development," in D. E. McFarland (ed.), *Proceedings of the Annual Meeting, 1962*. University Park, Penn.: Academy of Management, 1963, pp. 50–66.
35. Proctor, J. H., and W. M. Thornton, *Training: A Handbook for Line Managers*. New York: American Management Association, 1961.
36. Schein, E. H., "How to Break in the College Graduate," *Harvard Business Review*, Vol. 42, No. 6 (1964), 68–76.
37. Tannenbaum, R., I. R. Weschler, and F. Massarik, *Leadership and Organization: A Behavioral Science Approach*. New York: McGraw-Hill, 1961.
38. Teich, H. P., *Validity of a Business Game*, M.S. Thesis. Eugene, Oregon: Univ. of Oregon, 1964.
39. Vance, S. C., *Management Decision Simulation: A Non-Computer Business Game*. New York: McGraw-Hill, 1960.
40. Viteles, M. S., "Human Relations and the Humanities in the Education of Business Leaders: Evaluation of a Program of Humanistic Studies for Executives," *Personnel Psychology*, Vol. 12 (1959), 1–28.

Questions

1. Design a complete study to evaluate a special management development course intended to produce knowledge changes in the field of economics. Describe all the steps you would go through.
2. What is meant by the term input-output mediator? Why do companies invest in these techniques? How do they relate to the internal constraints imposed by individual differences? How do structural and functional mediators differ? Give examples of each.
3. Discuss the specific nature of the relationship between each of the various management development techniques and the company goals of productivity and organizational maintenance.

4. What do we know about the change-producing potential of the following:
   a. Human relations courses
   b. T-groups
   c. Creativity training
   d. Role-motivation training
   e. Business games
5. Under what circumstances is job rotation likely to be a worthwhile training procedure?

15

Skill Training and Retraining

At this point it is desirable to differentiate between *training* and *education*. This is not an easy task. Both certainly are concerned with human change and learning, but they differ considerably in purpose (5, 10). Training is basically role specific. It attempts to help those who are or will be performing a certain job achieve successful role behavior. On the other hand, education is tied to the goals of the individual more than to those of the organization, although some overlapping between the two sets of goals can be anticipated. Thus, education tends to take the individual, his growth, and the multiple roles that he may play in society as its starting point. Training starts with the requirements of a particular employing organization and, within that, of a given job.

Where the student is expected to pay tuition to obtain a learning experience he himself desires, as in the universities, we tend to speak of an educational process. Training normally is paid for by the employing organization, although both the individual and the company may benefit.

These distinctions leave the various management development procedures discussed in the preceding chapter in a realm of considerable uncertainty. Clearly they are intended to be training, or at least they should be. But managerial jobs tend to have rather broad role prescriptions, especially at the very top levels where the demand for the generalist is greatest. Furthermore, there are companies that do not place very clear delimitations on the scope of various managerial positions. The result is that management development can easily become transformed into education, even when paid for by the company. That is, it becomes more individual than company oriented.

Such problems of definition do not characteristically arise at lower levels in the organization. In this chapter the focus will be directly on training as a role-specific process. We shall be concerned with learning that in the ideal situation is (a) specifically applicable to the job; (b) complete in its coverage of job requirements; and (c) efficient in terms of the time, money, and resources utilized. The latter requirement implies that the training should not be continued beyond the point where perfectly adequate on-the-job performance is possible.

Because training of this kind must be commensurate with what is known about the processes of human learning, a brief treatment of the implications from learning theory must preface the discussion. A second section will take up methods of identifying training needs. Finally, a number of the techniques, procedures, and applications of industrial training will be covered.

Learning Theory and Industrial Training

This section contains a synopsis of what have been called the *principles of learning*. These principles presumably are as applicable to the management development programs discussed in Chapter 14 as to the training procedures to be considered later in this chapter (1). Unfortunately, however, knowledge regarding specific applications of these principles is far from complete.

Most of these principles were developed originally within the psychological laboratory, often as a result of work with animals. Although subsequent studies have almost without exception extended into the human sphere, research has not always been conducted in an industrial setting. Thus, what follows must be considered a best estimate of how the principles apply in business organizations as of this point in time. Yet as a best estimate it is important for those who, because of operating necessity, must make decisions regarding the content and format of various training programs.

Motivation

Although there is some question whether all learning requires some motive that can be directly satisfied through the learning experience, it does appear certain that greater efficiency is achieved under these circumstances. Thus, if a training program represents a means to achieve some strong personal goal of the trainee, maximal learning is more likely to occur.

This means that training should be directly tied to the various motives known to characterize those who will be exposed to it. Among the motives that seem most frequently to foster learning in the business world are a desire for security, for acceptable working conditions, for social interaction with others, for personal recognition, for intrinsically interesting work, for a sense of accomplishment, for freedom in the workplace (6), and for achievement. To the extent a learning experience can be related to one or more of these motives, as when retraining on a new piece of equipment is presented as a means to increased job security, the overall goals of training will be fostered. Motivation is more likely to operate in the desired fashion if the material to be learned is meaningful to the trainee and if it has some relationship to things he has experienced previously—also, if it is sufficiently varied to maintain motivation rather than produce satiation and boredom.

Reinforcement

Closely related to the matter of motivation is what has been called the *Law of Effect*. According to this law, behavior that is viewed as leading to reward, or that satisfies a motive, tends to be learned and repeated; behavior that seems not to produce a reward, or that yields punishment, tends not to be repeated. Any event that operates in this way, so as to change the probability of a particular behavior, is said to be *reinforcing*.

In general, rewards (positive reinforcers) appear to be more effective in producing learning than punishments (negative reinforcers). In fact, it may be more desirable merely to fail to reward a behavior that is incorrect in a particular situation than to punish it. This is because punishment, at least in its more extreme forms, can lead to a mere suppression of the undesired behavior, with the result that the behavior appears again when the punishment is removed. Punishment can also produce so much anxiety and anger that it disrupts all learning. Yet somewhat less intense punishment can have a favorable effect, especially if it follows closely on the behavior that is to be eliminated.

In this connection it is important to remember that the law of effect applies within the context of a particular person's motivational system and what he considers rewarding or punishing. Thus, although praise is generally a positive reinforcer, it may not always act in this manner (20). If a trainer is frequently an object of contempt, praise from him for a particular type of behavior may produce only ostracism and ridicule from the group in training. The result can be that desired behavior is suppressed rather than positively reinforced by the praise, with the consequence that learning follows a course differing considerably from that originally anticipated.

Knowledge of Results

Learning is not only more efficient when appropriate motivation is present and when adequate reinforcement is given, but also when the trainee has a clear picture of how well he is doing. This process of feeding back information on the effectiveness of responses is what is called *knowledge of results*. It appears to help in part because the trainee can use the knowledge to sort out behavior that he should learn from behavior that he should not. Without knowledge of results a person may well spend long periods of time learning to do things that appear at first to be appropriate but that subsequently turn out not to be (22).

It is also true that knowledge of results affects motivation. When an individual knows whether a given response was right or wrong, whether he is improving or not, he can set goals for himself, thus making a game out of the learning process and maintaining motivation at a high level. There is reason to believe that explicit goal setting in conjunction with knowledge of results can be particularly helpful where the material to be learned is rather difficult and the goals are set at a high level (8,14).

Table 15-1. Waste Ratios for Textile Workers Over a 145-Week Period Which Included Training with Knowledge of Results

Period	Mean waste ratio for period
Pretraining (10 weeks)	2.50
Training (3 weeks)	1.50
Reinforcement (12 weeks)	.87
Posttraining I (14 weeks)	.94
Posttraining II (20 weeks)	1.05
Posttraining III (20 weeks)	1.03
Posttraining IV (20 weeks)	1.01
Posttraining V (20 weeks)	.71
Retraining (26 weeks)	.52

Source: W. McGehee and D. H. Livingstone, "Persistence of the Effects of Training Employees to Reduce Waste," *Personnel Psychology*, Vol. 7 (1954), p. 36.

A demonstration of how knowledge of results can facilitate learning is contained in Table 15-1. In this study textile workers were given considerable training, aimed at reducing material wastage, over a three-week period (19). The knowledge of results aspect of this training was extended for twelve more weeks through on-the-job reinforcement of the original learning: The men were told what their waste rates were. There was a sizable reduction in the amount of waste from pretraining to training and a further reduction with reinforcement. These training effects were maintained over a long period of time. Yet subsequently, when a second training program similar to the first was introduced, the amount of waste was even further reduced.

Active Practice

It is almost axiomatic that learning requires repetition and practice. To the extent possible this practice should be active and overt. The man should do and say what he is expected to learn, rather than merely listen to repetitions of instructions. Active practice of this kind maintains attention and concentration. Thus, job skills are most effectively developed by repeatedly performing the task to be learned, and knowledge is best acquired by writing down the material or reciting it orally.

At least in the early stages of learning it is desirable to guide this practice closely, rather than let a trainee find out by trial and error which are appropriate behaviors and which are not. A great deal of time can be saved if the trainer directs the practice in this manner so that desired responses are produced almost immediately. Because eventually the individual will have to perform the new tasks alone on the job, it is important not to carry close guidance too far into the learning process. Training should include considerable independent practice of the newly acquired role behaviors at some point before it is terminated.

Massed versus Distributed Practice

In general the available evidence indicates that spacing out training sessions is desirable, especially as an aid to retention. This assumes, of course, that there is a good deal to be learned. Short lists of instructions and the like are probably best learned in a single intensive session.

This principle of distributed practice is one of the most widely violated in industrial training. The reason for this is that when a decision is made to place a man on a particular job, every effort is normally made to move him to effective performance in as short a total time span as possible. This means that all his time is devoted to training in the new role behaviors. Where the job is quite simple, the result is repeated practice of essentially the same activities and relatively inefficient learning.

In many such instances it is possible to obtain the advantages of distributed practice if an effort is made to do so. There are a number of approaches that can be used (16). Job training can be alternated with some useful activity that requires minimal skill, such as filing, cleaning, loading, and so on. When men are being retrained to operate some new, possibly automated, equipment, the retraining can sometimes be alternated with continued work performance on the old equipment. Another approach involves grouping the various aspects of the total training into separate packages and alternating among these. This is particularly appropriate if the job is complex and contains a variety of tasks to be performed at different times. Finally, some firms employ high school and college students on a part-time basis and use the work periods for training in activities that will be carried out subsequently when full-time employment occurs.

Whole versus Part Learning

Another principle, which is unfortunately somewhat "shaky" in terms of the evidence supporting it, states that whole learning is preferable to part learning. This refers to the size of the units of content employed. According to this principle, it is desirable to have the trainees deal with large and meaningful wholes, rather than small bits and pieces, which may not be very meaningful in and of themselves and which still must be combined eventually before effective job performance is possible.

Unfortunately, for those making decisions regarding training content, there is evidence that under certain conditions part learning is preferable. Thus, the guidelines for action are not entirely clear in this area. Yet some statements can be made (12). More intelligent trainees tend to handle large, self-contained units of content well, whereas the less intelligent may require a more segmented approach. After an individual has become accustomed to the whole method and has become practiced in its use, its advantages become more marked. Whole learning combined with distributed practice represents a particularly advantageous combination. The whole method is desirable only if the material to be learned does in fact form a meaningful, unified grouping. A job made up of a series of disparate activities without logical connection might best be learned in parts. Finally, because of the nature of most job-related learning, there will almost inevitably be aspects of the material that must be handled on a part basis, even if the initial approach is in terms of the whole. When a particular aspect of the total learning is very difficult, training must focus on this aspect even if some segmentation does result.

Transfer of Training

In Chapter 13 evidence was presented that indicated that psychological tests having considerable validity for the initial training situation often did not predict as effectively when an on-the-job criterion measure was employed. The reverse was also true. Such findings suggest that transfer from the training to the actual work situation may not be perfect in many instances—that what is learned during training, although it may be considered important there, may have very little relevance for job performance. This is the *transfer of training* problem: Under what conditions will information that has been learned in order to do the old job be most relevant for the new job, should the position be redesigned and retraining carried out?

The principle that seems to work most effectively as an answer to these questions is that of identical elements. If the behavior required and the characteristics of a training situation (or of an existing job) have many elements identical to those on the job (or on the redesigned job), a person who performs effectively in the one instance should do so in the other. Thus, to maximize *positive transfer* of the kind that is normally desired, there should be a close resemblance in the behaviors produced and the meaning content of the relevant stimuli in the two situations. This does not necessitate perfect physical identity, as is evident from what has been said about simulation techniques, but it does require psychological identity in terms of the thoughts and emotions aroused in the two situations.

It is also possible, however, for *negative transfer* to occur. What has been learned on one job can be detrimental for another. What has been learned in training can actually hamper job performance if the training is not effectively designed, or if it is designed with reference to goals that differ sharply from those characterizing the job situation. Thus, what one learns during a college education *could* lead to less effective performance in a particular subsequent business position. Negative transfer of this kind tends to be most pronounced when the new job requires behavior that is just the opposite of that a man has learned to apply in comparable situations. The old behaviors seem to keep forcing their way back and thus disturbing performance. This means that in redesigning jobs and equipment one should make every effort to avoid situations where workers must make opposite or nearly opposite responses to familiar situations (20).

Intelligence and Learning

A final guide for the industrial trainer derives from what is known about individual differences and the nature of mental abilities. There is good reason to believe that those with higher ability levels will learn more rapidly than those with less ability, when the ability involved is closely related to the material to be learned (21).

This means that training will be most efficient to the extent that the teaching process can be adapted to the mental ability level of the individual. A very intelligent person can absorb new things very rapidly, and thus the materials to be learned should be presented at an accelerated pace. The less intelligent are likely to require much longer exposure to the same materials before achieving a comparable degree of learning. Ideally, therefore, training experiences should be individualized for maximum efficiency. This is one of the advantages of the teaching machines to be described later in this chapter. If individualized instruction is not possible and large job-related individual differences are known to be present in a trainee group, it is generally desirable to group the trainees into "fast" and "slow" classes. In this way it is possible to avoid the wasteful overlearning that may occur among high-ability individuals who are forced to continue practice while waiting for those of lower ability to catch up. In addition, motivation is more easily maintained where *ability grouping* of this kind is carried out.

Establishing Training Needs

For training to operate efficiently as an input-output mediator, it must be focused on those individuals and situations where the need is greatest. This means that large gaps between role prescriptions and existing role behaviors must be identified. Then a decision must be made as to whether a significant reduction in the size of the gap might be achieved through training. Establishing training needs thus requires an answer to two questions: Is there a problem in terms of the level or type of performance? Can training be of any value in correcting such a situation?

In terms of sheer numbers the training needs problem is usually most pronounced among individuals just starting out on a new job. Thus, new employees, employees who have been shifted into a new position, and employees being retrained because the role prescriptions for a position have been changed, all can normally be assumed to have rather acute training requirements. Fortunately, requirements of this kind tend to be rather easy to identify and the level of motivation to learn quite high.

A much more difficult problem arises in the case of existing employees who have been working on the current job for some time. Here persistent deviations from role prescriptions must be identified on an individual basis. There is no single categorization, such as that of "new man on the job," to make employees with marked training needs highly visible. Furthermore, motivation for new learning may well be minimal. To be singled out for special training and to accept the need for this training represents a tacit admission that one has not been performing with maximum effectiveness in the past. Thus, the "experienced" employee may go to great lengths to cover up any training needs and may resist such training as he does receive to prove that he has been performing his job correctly all along. This is not a universal occurrence, but it is well for a personnel manager to be sensitive to the possibility.

Whether the training needs analysis is directed toward individuals who are just starting on a job or to those who have been there for some time, it remains a very important factor in a firm's total effort to utilize human resources effectively, and it may well become even more important in the future. Union pressure has produced many job assignment systems based in large part on seniority. Furthermore, a number of companies are firmly committed to the concept of promotion from within. These plus other factors mean that job security is much greater today than it has been in the past, and training is often the only available procedure for correcting deficiencies in selection and placement (11). If this training is to be applied in an efficient manner, it must be directed into areas where clearly identified training needs exist.

Specific Techniques in Training Needs Analysis

Because the process of identifying training needs depends at least in part on establishing disparities between role prescriptions and role behavior, any of the various appraisal and evaluation techniques discussed in Part III can be of value. In addition, achievement tests and job samples can provide information regarding the extent to which knowledge and skill are below expected levels. Yet, historically, training needs have been identified largely as a result of requests for training from line management, or through more protracted discussions with those responsible for the performance of the men considered for training, or through direct observation of actual job performance (15). Probably the latter techniques remain the most common ones today, although group production records, turnover statistics, and the like are also widely used to pinpoint areas of difficulty.

The important thing, irrespective of the approach employed, is to develop some conception not only as to whether performance deficiencies are present, but regarding the extent to which training can remedy such deficiencies, and also the type of training that might be most appropriate for this purpose. Thus, a training needs analysis should come before any attempt at establishing the method or content of training.

In attempting to develop a preliminary estimate of training needs in a particular group, it is very helpful to utilize some type of checklist along the lines of the one presented in Table 15-2. Answers to the questions posed can be obtained using data and information from the various sources already noted. After possible training needs are established, the training specialist can then gradually narrow his analysis until he is able to deal with the specific needs of specific individuals in specific jobs. The content of training is then developed from job analysis data, either that contained in company job descriptions or that collected as a result of a limited job analysis carried out for training purposes only. The latter approach may prove necessary where a job analysis conducted for other purposes is outdated or inadequate (7).

Table 15-2. Checklist for Needed Training

Items recorded by training specialist	Is item seen in this production unit?		Possible training need
	Yes	No	
Downward communications to supervisor slow	×		×
Frequent gripes by supervisors about tools		×	
Supervisors use suggestions from workers		×	×
Many rejects returned to production		×	
Customer's complaints from sales ignored		×	
Turnover in shop higher than seems necessary	×		×
Many lost time accidents		×	
Paper work up to date		×	×
Raw material delays		×	
Supervisors use specialists of company		×	×

Source: D. H. Fryer, M. R. Feinberg, and S. S. Zalkind, *Developing People in Industry.* New York: Harper & Row, 1956, p. 41.

Methods and Approaches in Training

With the discussions of learning principles and training needs as a background it is now feasible to consider some of the methods and approaches used in industrial training and to attempt an evaluation of relative merit. Thus, this section will be concerned with such matters as on-the-job training, vestibule schools, apprenticeships, system or team training, teaching machines, and programmed instruction, and finally with job retraining, which has become as much a societal function as a company one.

On- and Off-the-Job Training

The most common procedure is for training to be carried out on the job, particularly for new employees. The individual becomes accustomed to the machinery and materials that he will use in his subsequent work, and he learns in the same physical and social environment in which he will carry out his job duties later on. Usually the training is done by an experienced employee or by a supervisor. On occasion, however, trained instructors are assigned for the specific purpose of teaching job skills.

Much on-the-job training still utilizes procedures similar to those developed for use in connection with the Job Instruction Training sessions conducted by the Training Within Industry Division of the War Manpower Commission during World War II (see Chapter 2). The JIT guidelines are given below.

A. Pretraining Steps
1. Have a timetable developed in terms of which skills are to be attained. Indicate the speed at which the various levels of attainment may be expected.
2. Break down the job into its basic components.
3. Have all materials and supplies necessary for the training process available and ready.
4. Have the workplace arranged in the same way that the worker will be expected to keep it.

B. Training Steps
1. Prepare the worker by putting him at ease, i.e., find out what he already knows and show him the relationship of his job to other jobs.
2. Tell, show, and illustrate the job to be performed.
3. Have the worker try to perform the job and have him tell and explain why he performs each specific operation of the job. This tends to clarify the key aspects.
4. Follow up on the trainee after he has been put on his own by checking him often and encouraging further questions.

On-the-job training of this kind is very attractive in a number of respects. It requires relatively little special attention, no extra equipment is needed, and the man can do some productive work while he learns. Furthermore, it is consistent with several principles of learning. There is active practice, motivation should be maximal due to the more meaningful nature of the learning materials, and the problem of transfer of training from the learning to the job situation is almost nonexistent.

Yet there are major difficulties. There is a risk that expensive equipment will be damaged by inexperienced employees, and the accident rate among on-the-job trainees tends to be high. In the absence of specially assigned trainers the instruction is often haphazard or neglected entirely. The pressures of the workplace may in fact leave little time for effective training. Some activities may actually be more difficult to learn on the job because of their complexity or as a result of the regulated speed at which the machinery operates.

For these reasons it seems desirable, in many cases, to carry out a large portion of the training process away from the job. This is a widespread practice in the management development area, but it is considerably less common insofar as skill training is concerned. Only in the case of relatively simple production, clerical, and sales jobs does the use of on-the-job training alone seem appropriate. If it is necessary to restrict the learning process to the actual work situation, it is usually desirable to have specific individuals designated as training specialists and to relieve them of other job duties, at least on a temporary basis. This permits a systematic training effort comparable to those obtained with many of the Training Within Industry programs of World War II.

VESTIBULE TRAINING. An approach that is in a sense intermediate between on- and off-the-job training utilizes the vestibule school. Here the trainee uses equipment and procedures similar to those he would use in on-the-job training, but the equipment is set up in an area separate from the regular work place. The intent of this special installation is to facilitate learning, not to obtain productive output. A skilled trainer is in charge and new workers receive detailed instruction while practicing their new skills at a rate appropriate to each individual.

From the learning viewpoint this appears to represent an ideal approach. There is evidence that it does reduce training time and yield more skilled work performance (20). But it is also expensive, especially if the number of men to be trained on a particular type of equipment is small. Then, too, it is not suitable for many jobs. Unfortunately, some companies have placed obsolete or even broken machinery in vestibule schools in an effort to avoid the expense of purchasing duplicate equipment. This tends to limit severely the value of the training. It may even yield negative transfer effects.

ORIENTATION TRAINING. Orientation programs are established to provide new employees with information on such matters as company organization, the history of the firm, policies and procedures, pay and benefit plans, conditions of employment, safety practices, names of top executives, locations of various departments and facilities, manufacturing processes, and work rules. On occasion brief orientation programs are offered for experienced employees to bring them up to date on current procedures.

In many companies this kind of orientation training is conducted by the personnel department during the first few days of employment. Handbooks, films, and other materials may play an important part in this initial effort to provide the employee with knowledge regarding the salient features of his new environment. In those cases where immediate supervision has primary responsibility for these matters the training tends to become more individualized, more variable, and on occasion more superficial. For most purposes a standardized program including classroom sessions and group tours of facilities appears to offer major advantages, but these can frequently be integrated with further training by supervision.

Apprenticeship

Apprentice training offers an integration of on- and off-the-job learning that under ideal conditions appears to be extremely effective. It is used to prepare employees for a variety of skilled occupations of the kind noted in Table 15-3. The apprentice agrees to work for a company, at a rate averaging somewhat above half of that paid to fully qualified workers, in return for a specified number of hours of training. In many instances the conditions of training have been negotiated with the relevant union and are specified in the union contract. Most of the programs are registered with the Federal Department of Labor, which has responsibility for promoting apprenticeship training throughout the United States, and with appropriate state agencies.

Table 15-3. Selected Apprenticeable Occupations Classified by Length of Apprenticeship

Two years	Four years	Six years
Baker	Carpenter	Compositor
Barber	Draftsman	Electrotyper
Iron worker	Locksmith	Stereotyper
	Millwright	
Two to three years	Tailor	Seven years
Jewelry engraver		Engraver (bank note)
Meat cutter	Four to five years	
	Electrician	Eight years
Three years	Instrument maker	Die sinker
Commercial photographer	Tool and die maker	
Granite cutter		Five to ten years
Painter and decorator	Five years	Picture engraver
	Plumber	(steel plate
Three to four years	Pottery presser	engraver)
Bricklayer, mason		
Cook, chef	Five to six years	
Roofer	Job pressman	
	Photoengraver	

Source: New York State Apprenticeship Council, 1968.

The actual content of the training is usually established by a local apprenticeship committee that specifies the number of hours of experience for each machine or kind of work. The classroom part of the apprenticeship is conducted at a vocational school, with an experienced journeyman in the trade acting as instructor. These courses emphasize applied mathematics, the physical sciences, and the techniques of the occupation. The classroom instruction may be offered during the work day or after hours. It may also be by correspondence. The on-the-job training is also given by a skilled journeyman, and insofar as possible it is integrated with the classroom material. Thus, the apprentice is given an immediate opportunity to practice what he has been taught.

EVALUATION. Apprenticeships can be extremely effective where complex skills must be learned. Yet there is some reason to believe that many apprenticeship programs are unnecessarily long, with the result that a good deal of inefficient overlearning occurs. A number of the trades represented are not as complex and difficult to learn as their members would like to believe. Yet largely as a result of union pressure, extended training periods of the kind noted in Table 15-3 have become accepted. Evidence for the view that overlearning is widespread in apprentice programs comes from the fact that many individuals attain the same skilled positions through considerably less lengthy on-the-job experience. Also a number of dropouts from apprentice programs nevertheless go on to enter the same trade, in spite of the abbreviated learning period (24).

It is also true that apprentice training is on occasion subverted by a desire among certain management representatives to obtain as much productive labor as possible at the reduced apprentice rate. On-the-job learning is deemphasized and there is little concern as to whether the man attends classes or not. The major stress is on the amount of work produced, with the result that the training objective is lost.

Perhaps the most difficult problem is that apprenticeships tend to take on a rigidity that is unsuited to the advent of automation and a shifting technology. Occupations are changing constantly as skills must be combined and recombined to meet the demands of new working environments. There is some question under these circumstances as to whether the traditional skilled trade categories are any longer appropriate. This questioning has extended to the apprenticeships that prepare individuals for these trades. Many personnel managers would prefer to avoid formal apprentice training programs entirely and utilize a more flexible approach that could yield individuals with the specific combinations of skills needed to do a given job in the most efficient manner. Yet changes are gradually being introduced into the formal apprenticeship programs. And there is still widespread agreement that carefully integrated classroom and on-the-job training can be very effective, given a satisfactory method of keying learning materials to existing job requirements.

Teaching Machines and Programmed Instruction

The principles of learning described earlier in this chapter find their clearest manifestations in the field of programmed instruction. This is an individualized procedure that utilizes training materials organized into a series of frames, usually of increasing difficulty and with each successive frame building on those that precede. Information, questions, and problems are presented to the learner with the requirement that he either write in his answer or select the answer from multiple-choice alternatives. Then feedback is provided on the correctness of the answer. The material is developed in such a way that a high proportion of the questions will elicit the desired response and thus result in positive reinforcement. The frames are frequently presented in a teaching machine that utilizes film or sound tapes. Some such machines are tied in with computers; almost all have electronic features. There are also a variety of programmed books and other printed materials in which the trainee uncovers the successive frames manually (18).

Inherent in all programmed instruction, irrespective of the way in which materials are presented, are such features as active practice, a gradual increase in difficulty levels over a series of small steps, immediate feedback, learning at the individual's own rate, and minimization of error. Thus, a variety of learning principles are explicitly built into the technique. There is reinforcement, knowledge of results, active practice, and guidance. There can be distributed practice and the material may be learned in a time period suited to the ability level of the trainee. If the material is selected from the job in an appropriate manner, there should be positive transfer. The only factor that seems to be missing is whole learning, and that may not be essential. Also, the routine nature of the training may on occasion serve to dampen motivation.

EVALUATION. Given this degree of synchronization with learning theory, one would expect that programmed instruction would provide an extremely efficient method of training. Such evidence as is available certainly confirms this expectation (23). Selected data are presented in Table 15-4.

Yet there are certain cautions. The approach is more suitable for knowledge than for skill training. As a result it is currently of rather limited value in the case of many production jobs, although some applications have been developed in this area. It is also extremely costly if a new program must be written. A single frame takes up to an hour to write and a total program can contain hundreds or even thousands of frames, depending on the complexity of the material and the desired size of the learning steps. This means that the approach is feasible only when a large number of employees must be trained for a given job.

In spite of these considerations industry is making increasing use of the technique. Programs are being written for new jobs and job components at a rapidly expanding rate. Some of these are noted in Table 15-4. Others are telephone operator procedures, company benefit plan characteristics, computer language, fundamentals of life insurance, telephone relay adjustment, and product characteristics. To date there has been little application at the management level.

Table 15-4. Examples of Improved Performance and Training Time Savings Associated with the Use of Programmed Instruction

Course and company	Average performance score		Average length of time (hours)	
	Conventional instruction	Programmed instruction	Conventional instruction	Programmed instruction
7070 computer nomenclature (IBM)	86.2	95.1	15	11
Reading engineering drawings (du Pont)	81.2	91.2	17	13
Dermatology and mycology (Schering)	60.1	91.9	No information	
Basic electricity (Bell Labs)				
Facts	64.9	76.8	No information	
Concepts	47.5	66.4		
Analog computation (du Pont)	No information		40	11
Package billing (Spiegel)	No information		40	26

Source: J. R. Murphy and I. A. Goldberg, "Strategies for Using Programmed Instruction," *Harvard Business Review*, Vol. 42, No. 3 (1964), pp. 118–119.

System and Team Training

The training of groups of individuals whose work tasks interact has developed primarily within the armed services. However, various types of work unit training are gradually finding their way into industry, especially in the field of air transportation (3).

In general, when the systems concept is applied as a basis for organizing work, the terms system or subsystem training are applied. In other instances one hears of team or crew training. In either case complex man-machine interactions may be involved.

Training of this kind is normally introduced relatively late in the overall learning sequence, when individual workers are reasonably knowledgeable and proficient on their own individual jobs. A task is developed that requires role behavior from a number of employees in interaction. Usually the task is selected to focus on special problem areas within the total work effort. The training may be conducted in the real-life work situation or in a simulated environment with the salient features built in. At the end of the exercise knowledge of results on total team performance is provided insofar as this is possible, and the team members discuss their own performance. It is generally considered undesirable to introduce any type of evaluation or criticism from outside the team at this point (25).

The intent in all this is to develop a cooperative effort and thus overall levels of effectiveness beyond those that can be obtained from individual learning alone. As training progresses through successive trials on various tasks, the individual becomes increasingly aware of how his role behaviors may help and hinder his co-workers. He also begins to view his own work in terms of its place in the total team effort. Thus, team training can permit a group to develop solutions to various problems, such as the overloading of a single member, with the consequent formation of a bottleneck in production. Solutions of this kind are rarely learned when the training program relies entirely on individual instruction.

Especially when simulations are used, and simulations can be of considerable value in focusing on specific work problems, training of this type tends to have much in common with the business games discussed in the preceding chapter. This parallelism even extends to the situation in which employees are trained in a simulated situation to subsequently take over the operation of a man-machine system, the machine components of which are still under construction. Business games also are often used prior to any assumption of actual job duties.

There are several major differences as well. For one thing, business games characteristically operate in fast time: Events occur much more rapidly than in the actual business situation. System training on simulators occurs in real time. Second, business games are normally played with peers. Either all those engaged are students or, if management groups are involved, the tendency is to select individuals from approximately equal levels. Under system concepts all those engaged in the operation of the system as it relates to the specific problem simulated must participate in the training, irrespective of the level in the organization.

EVALUATION. Several strong arguments have been advanced against the use of this type of team training in the industrial situation (9,27). No doubt these are the major reasons the approach has not been adopted outside the military more rapidly than it has.

For one thing it is extremely wasteful of time and money. Team training exercises almost invariably require role behavior from only a few members at a given point in time. The others act as observers or await their turn for participation. It is difficult to maintain alertness and motivation among these nonactive members. Thus, their time is often wasted and labor costs increase with little return on the investment. In addition, there are the costs associated either with the use of machinery for nonproductive purposes or with the construction of adequate simulations.

Second, there are problems related to the identification of individual errors and the overall evaluation of results. It is often almost impossible to determine exactly what went wrong when difficulties arise. Thus, immediate feedback and knowledge of results may be hard to achieve, and the specific source of an error may not be identified. Also, suitable criteria of team performance must be established so that an effective effort can be clearly differentiated from an ineffective one. This can be done, but an adequate backlog of information does not yet exist in this area, with the result that team standard-setting can become a major problem. Thus, the knowledge of results requirement tends to run into difficulties both at the level of the individual team member and at the level of the total team.

On the positive side is the fact that where cooperative effort represents a major aspect of the work, clear gains in efficiency above those obtainable with individual training do appear to result from the team approach. There are factors in any actual work situation with its flow of work activities and its patterning of social interactions that cannot be adequately handled through individual training. When considerations of this kind are marked, some group training seems to be a desirable adjunct to other procedures.

Automation and Retraining

One consequence of the accelerated rate of technological change that has characterized the past few decades is that skill training obtained before a worker enters the labor force, or shortly thereafter on the job, no longer provides a guarantee of continued lifetime employment. There is a very real risk that one's entire occupation will become outmoded, and it is almost certain that the skills required in an occupation will change considerably before a man reaches retirement age.

Given this increasing need for retraining, both for entirely new jobs and to develop new skills within a current occupation, a considerable controversy has arisen with regard to sources of control and payment. The parties involved are the employing company, the union, government, and the specific individual whose job has acquired new role prescriptions or has been deleted entirely. In general the solutions developed over the past few years have tended to follow a pattern whereby those who remain with a company to take on changed jobs have been retrained at company expense and those who become unemployed have been retrained at governmental expense. In both instances the unions have tended to exert a strong influence on the content and scope of the retraining. In a few instances they have forced all retraining into the company sphere.

COMPANY RETRAINING. It is a rare company today, among those with sizable manufacturing components, that has not had some experience with the retraining of large numbers of employees to operate new equipment. Such efforts have been particularly extensive in the automobile industry. All the procedures discussed in preceding sections of this chapter appear to have been utilized, but there is almost invariably a considerable amount of classroom training. This means that acceptable levels of literacy must be assumed as well as some competence in arithmetic.

Although one might expect that these factors would not create problems in the America of today, this has not turned out to be the case. Many companies have run into major difficulties with current employees, whose schooling has proved insufficient or inadequate—especially when it becomes necessary to carry out very rapid retraining to get new machinery operative as quickly as possible. In most instances companies have not been in a position to provide the basic schooling required, with the result that the less literate employees are the ones most likely to be displaced by automated equipment. A number of firms use brief tests of reading, vocabulary, and arithmetic skills to select employees for retraining.

Although the content of retraining tends to vary with the shifting currents of technological change, certain subject matter areas and skills have become increasingly important in recent years. Hydraulics, lubrication, electricity, electronics, control circuits, and similar subjects appear frequently in company retraining programs, along with classes dealing with the specifics of automated equipment operation and maintenance.

In addition to activity aimed at preparing workers for new jobs within the company, there has been some pressure from unions to have companies take on the expense of retraining workers that are slated for layoff to prepare them for new jobs in the community. This pressure has been successful in a few instances (26). However, in view of strong management resistance to this practice and the increasing sums of money being made available by the Federal government for the retraining of displaced workers, it seems unlikely that companies will be forced to assume the entire burden of preparing workers for new or revised jobs, or for the more conventional types of employment.

GOVERNMENTAL RETRAINING. Governmental support of vocational education was initiated with the Smith-Hughes Act of 1917. Until the present decade this support generally was concentrated at the high school and vocational school level, especially in the fields of agriculture and home economics. With the Area Redevelopment Act of 1961 and the Manpower Development and Training Act of 1962, government began to assume direct responsibilities for the training and retraining of individuals who were already in the labor force, although often as unemployed job seekers rather than as employed workers (13,17).

These acts provided not only training opportunities, but also subsistence payments, transportation allowances, and vocational counseling. The Area Redevelopment Act programs were geared to prepare underemployed and unemployed workers in depressed areas for immediate employment. They were usually oriented toward entry jobs within the labor force and were an integral part of a total area redevelopment effort. The Manpower Development and Training Act programs, which now represent the major Federal effort in this area, are generally longer in duration and take a greater variety of forms. Selection for training is carried out by the state employment agencies.

The emphasis in all programs is on preparing individuals for occupations in which there is a high probability of employment. To date the largest numbers of retrained workers have been in such occupations as stenographer, typist, office clerk, machine operator, practical nurse, automobile mechanic, and welder. Basic literacy training has been provided for a number of individuals who needed this type of schooling prior to any strictly vocational learning. The major concerns in connection with basic literacy and other recent training efforts have been to locate the so-called "hard-core unemployed," to prepare them for employment, and to equip them for continued employment after a job has been obtained (4).

As originally planned, the Manpower Development and Training Act programs were to stress on-the-job training conducted on the premises of employing firms. For a number of reasons this aspect of the total effort failed for some time to achieve the emphasis originally intended (2). Some unions opposed governmental retraining generally, and on-the-job programs in particular, on the grounds that the supply of trained workers within their jurisdictions might become excessive, with a resulting negative impact on wages. In addition, governmental administrators were cautious lest their money be used to support company programs that would have existed in any event. Cooperative efforts involving unions, companies, and the government are becoming increasingly widespread, however, and the original intent of the legislation is now being more fully achieved (17).

References

1. Bass, B. M., and J. A. Vaughan, *Training in Industry: The Management of Learning.* Belmont, Calif.: Wadsworth, 1966.
2. Becker, J. M., W. Haber, and S. A. Levitan, *Programs to Aid the Unemployed in the 1960's.* Kalamazoo, Mich.: The W. E. Upjohn Institute for Employment Research, 1965.
3. Biel, W. C., "Training Programs and Devices," in R. M. Gagné (ed.), *Psychological Principles in System Development.* New York: Holt, Rinehart and Winston, 1962, pp. 343–384.
4. Cassell, F. H., "Manpower Program Implications of Skill Imbalances," in G. G. Somers (ed.), *Proceedings of the Nineteenth Annual Winter Meeting.* Madison, Wisc.: Industrial Relations Research Association, 1967, pp. 230–239.
5. Crawford, M. P., "Concepts of Training," in R. M. Gagné (ed.), *Psychological Principles in System Development.* New York: Holt, Rinehart and Winston, 1962, pp. 301–341.
6. Dunnette, M. D., and W. K. Kirchner, *Psychology Applied to Industry.* New York: Appleton-Century-Crofts, 1965.
7. Fryer, D. H., M. R. Feinberg, and S. S. Zalkind, *Developing People in Industry.* New York: Harper & Row, 1956.
8. Fryer, F. W., *An Evaluation of Level of Aspiration as a Training Procedure.* Englewood Cliffs, N.J.: Prentice-Hall, 1964.
9. Glanzer, M., "Experimental Study of Team Training and Team Functioning," in R. Glaser (ed.), *Training Research and Education.* Pittsburgh, Penn.: Univ. of Pittsburgh Press, 1962, pp. 379–407.
10. Glaser, R., "Psychology and Instructional Technology," in R. Glaser (ed.), *Training Research and Education.* Pittsburgh: Univ. of Pittsburgh Press, 1962, pp. 1–30.
11. Haire, M., *Psychology in Management,* 2nd ed. New York: McGraw-Hill, 1964.
12. Hilgard, E. R., *Introduction to Psychology,* 3rd ed. New York: Harcourt, Brace, and World, 1962.
13. Levitan, S. A., *Federal Manpower Policies and Programs to Combat Unemployment.* Kalamazoo, Mich.: The W. E. Upjohn Institute for Employment Research, 1964.
14. Locke, E. A., "A Closer Look at Level of Aspiration as a Training Procedure: A Reanalysis of Fryer's Data," *Journal of Applied Psychology,* Vol. 50 (1966), 417–420.
15. Mahler, W. R., and W. H. Monroe, *How Industry Determines the Need for and Effectiveness of Training.* New York: The Psychological Corporation, 1952.
16. Maier, N. R. F., *Psychology in Industry,* 3rd ed. Boston: Houghton-Mifflin, 1965.
17. *Manpower Report of the President.* Washington, D.C.: U.S. Government Printing Office, 1967.

18. Margulies, S., and L. D. Eigen, *Applied Programmed Instruction*. New York: Wiley, 1961.

19. McGehee, W., and D. H. Livingstone, "Persistence of the Effects of Training Employees to Reduce Waste," *Personnel Psychology*, Vol. 7 (1954), 33–39.

20. McGehee, W., and P. W. Thayer, *Training in Business and Industry*. New York: Wiley, 1961.

21. Miner, J. B., *Intelligence in the United States*. New York: Springer, 1957.

22. Mosel, J. N., "How to Feed Back Performance Results to Trainees," *Journal of the American Society of Training Directors*, Vol. 12 (1958).

23. Murphy, J. R., and I. A. Goldberg, "Strategies for Using Programmed Instruction," *Harvard Business Review*, Vol. 42, No. 3 (1964), 115–132.

24. National Manpower Council, *A Policy for Skilled Manpower*. New York: Columbia Univ. Press, 1954.

25. Porter, E. H., *Manpower Development*. New York: Harper & Row, 1964.

26. Shils, E. B., *Automation and Industrial Relations*. New York: Holt, Rinehart and Winston, 1963.

27. Smode, A. F., "Recent Developments in Training Problems, and Training Research Methodology," in R. Glaser (ed.), *Training Research and Education*. Pittsburgh: Univ. of Pittsburgh Press, 1962, pp. 429–495.

Questions

1. Differentiate training and education. Should companies engage in education? Should universities engage in training?

2. Describe the various procedures you might employ in carrying out a training needs analysis among the hourly work force of a large manufacturing plant.

3. Which principles of learning appear to operate most consistently when the following training procedures are used? Which are lacking?
   a. Programmed instruction
   b. Vestibule school
   c. System training
   d. On-the-job training

4. Who should assume the responsibility for retraining? What are the arguments for and against
   a. Leaving retraining to the individual
   b. Requiring the company to do the job
   c. The programs supported by the government
   d. Union-supported retraining efforts

16

Wage, Salary, and Incentive
Payment Programs

The primary intent in developing different types of monetary payment programs for employees is to introduce an input-output mediator that will serve to maximize motivation to contribute to company goals. Whereas training is directed toward *changing* people to make them more effective, payment programs are instituted to provide inducements so that individuals will try to make the best use of their *existing* capabilities. Pay is also used as an aid in recruiting, to induce people to join a firm and to contribute to its goal attainment.

It is clear that money has reward value in a purely economic sense and when made available in appropriate relationship to job behavior can influence the level of motivation, but its impact can also be largely symbolic (6). People will work harder and in a manner more consistent with role prescriptions not only to gain the things that money can buy, but also to obtain the esteem and status that money represents. Thus, one study of a managerial group found that greater pay did produce more satisfaction insofar as the desire for security was concerned. However, its reward value in the areas of esteem and autonomy was even more pronounced. Money clearly provided a feeling of importance and a sense of freedom (13).

Whatever the specific meaning of money to the individual, it seems safe to assume that it will normally be desired, and that as a result it can be used to induce a maximal contribution to the company. There is considerable research evidence indicating that people can achieve higher levels of task performance when there is the prospect of achieving a greater monetary reward commensurate with their efforts (27). Unfortunately this evidence derives from somewhat artificial laboratory situations. Research on the effectiveness of existing monetary compensation programs in the business world is almost entirely lacking. Although we know that potentially money can be an effective input-output mediator, we are much less certain that it does in fact achieve this result. Nor are we at all certain that if money does achieve an increase in employee motivation, it does so to the extent of its full potential.

What is needed are studies evaluating the various types of payment programs currently in use. Research of this kind would utilize the evaluation models discussed in Chapter 14 to determine whether shifts in motivation and role behavior do in fact occur as a consequence of the use of a given compensation procedure. Because such studies are a rarity, the present discussion will have to rely on what is known about the subject of motivation generally whenever the different approaches are compared. Even from this limited perspective it appears that many people are paid in a way that does little to arouse motivation, and that as a result the potential value of the payment process as a mediator is often lost (7).

Wage Levels and Wage Surveys

Before taking up specific wage, salary, and incentive payment programs, it is necessary to devote some time to the various procedures used to establish (a) the general level of a company's payments to its employees relative to the payments made by *other* companies and (b) the relative grading or positioning of the jobs *within* a company in terms of pay. In the first instance the concern is with the *wage level* of the firm, which is usually expressed either as an average figure for all jobs or through a gross comparison of job rates for various key jobs with rates for comparable jobs in other companies. In the second instance the concern is with the internal *wage structure*, which is characteristically established in terms of various job grades or levels. Information used in determining a company's wage level is often obtained from *wage surveys* conducted within the industry or in the geographical locality. Information used in setting up a wage structure is usually derived from some kind of *job evaluation* procedure.

Considerations Related to the Company Wage Level

One might expect that traditional economic theory, or wage theory, with its emphasis on competition in the marketplace and conscious profit maximization would provide a sure guide for establishing the company wage level. This does not appear to be the case, however. Economic wage theory is helpful in understanding long-term shifts in wages within a particular country or to explain wage differences between countries or regions. It has very little usefulness as a basis for short-term decisions where a single company is concerned. In actual fact such decisions regarding the company wage level seem to be much better predicted from a knowledge of various social, political, ethical, and union pressures than from the competitive hypothesis of economic theory. Profit maximization appears to operate primarily to the extent that it establishes certain broad limits within which a wage level must be set (23).

Among the specific factors that appear to have some relationship to existing wage levels are union pressures, what other employers in the area or industry are paying, the average skill level of positions in the firm, minimum wage legislation, the ease with which potential employees may be recruited, the number of positions that must be filled, the level of employee satisfaction, the degree to which product market competition exists, prospects for future profits, and company size. Which of these will exert the most influence depends on the particular circumstance, although it seems clear that the wage level is rarely a product of a single factor. Various studies at different times based on different samples of firms have served to emphasize community wage levels, competition in the product market, union demands, and area labor supply as major considerations (2). Yet under certain circumstances other determinants may assume a paramount role.

When economic conditions are favorable the general pattern has been for unions to press for increasingly higher wage levels. Yet on occasion in the process of collective bargaining unions will trade off wage increases for greater job control in the form of seniority provisions, the elimination of merit rating procedures, and so on. Under less prosperous circumstances, during a recession or when a firm is in financial difficulty, the primary union stress is likely to be on maintaining employment, including even the least effective workers. Thus, a company that is unable to pay may well find itself exempt from industry or community wage patterns. Because financial problems are more likely to develop in smaller firms, wage levels tend to be consistently higher among the large corporations.

Even in unionized firms, however, there are other factors that influence wage levels besides the demands of the union itself. If employees are dissatisfied, either with their pay or with other job-related factors, a sizable pressure for wage increases frequently develops. If there are a number of positions to be filled, as a result of turnover or because of expansion, and the labor market has little to offer, wages may well go up. Or a similar rise may occur when a company is experiencing recruiting difficulties as a consequence of low prestige or because it is unknown in the labor market area. Also, if competition for sales and profits is extremely sharp, companies tend to pare their labor costs to a bare minimum by such devices as the assignment of apprentices to full-time work. If profits are good, the wage level is likely to rise even without the advent of union pressures.

WAGE CRITERIA. For purposes of establishing a company wage level, it is important not only to understand the various considerations and influences that may operate, but also to have some kind of yardstick that will indicate just how much of an increase (or decrease) is appropriate. This is what the various *wage criteria* attempt to provide. As measures they are often deficient, but they do have the advantage that they exist in numerical form and thus can serve to focus and in a sense arbitrate disagreements between management and union. It is also true that a number of the criteria commonly used represent rationalizations more than basic causes of company and union wage positions. As such their introduction into the wage negotiation process may serve to divert the parties from more basic issues. Furthermore, the wage guideline provided tends to depend strongly on the specific criterion invoked. Conflicting implications as between criteria are the rule rather than the exception.

In spite of these drawbacks, wage criteria do influence managerial decisions regarding wage levels in varying degrees and governmental conceptions of an appropriate national wage level to an even greater extent. Thus, they have become deeply engrained in the collective bargaining process. Among the commonly noted criteria are:

1. The results of wage surveys conducted either in the geographical area or in the industry. Industry data are more commonly used by the larger corporations.
2. The Consumer Price Index put out by the Federal government. Some companies have built this measure directly into their labor contracts through the use of *escalator clauses* that adjust wage levels to cost of living changes over the period of a two- or three-year agreement.
3. Various ideal family budgets that serve to specify the living wage required to maintain a standard of living judged to be adequate. The City Workers' Family Budget prepared by the Federal government is an example.

4. Company profit figures for the immediately preceding period, which are considered indicative of ability to pay.
5. Indexes of physical productivity for certain industries and for the economy as a whole developed by the U.S. Bureau of Labor Statistics. These specify a percentage improvement factor attributable to the combined effects of labor, management, tools, and materials.
6. Company turnover statistics, position vacancy data, and unemployment rates in the area that in combination provide information relative to recruiting difficulties and labor shortages.

Among these criteria, the results of wage surveys appear to be the most widely used (4). There is ample evidence that satisfaction with pay is dependent on relative rather than absolute wage levels (19). Although comparisons with other individuals in the same firm have a strong impact on feelings of equity as regards pay, outside comparisons are also made—either with individual and average rates in the local area or with information regarding the industry or profession. There are research data to indicate that such outside comparisons are particularly prevalent among lower middle management, those with more education, and the youngest employees (1). In view of this strong tendency on the part of individual employees to use outside comparisons as a basis for determining whether pay is equitable, it is not surprising that such considerations would have a strong impact at the level of management decision making and union-management negotiation. Wage surveys are the means to obtaining objective data in this area.

Wage Surveys

Wage survey data both from the local labor market and for the industry can be derived from a number of sources. Such surveys are conducted by individual companies, groups of companies formed specifically for this reason, employer associations created primarily for collective bargaining purposes, unions, consulting firms, professional survey companies, the Federal government, and various professional societies.

When groups of companies are involved, an intercompany committee is usually formed to plan and conduct the studies. The grouping is usually of a relatively permanent nature and as a result survey procedures tend to become standardized over time. Under such circumstances mailed questionnaires are by far the most common data-gathering devices. This is in contrast to the Occupational Wage Surveys conducted at periodic intervals in a number of local labor markets by the Federal Department of Labor. These latter derive their data from personal interviews made by special field workers on the company premises (5).

In either case it is important that the companies included be typical of the local area or industry and that enough such companies be included to provide stable results.

DATA COLLECTION. Surveying all jobs in all companies would represent an almost impossible task, and the usual practice is to select a number of key jobs. These should cover the full range of positions, should contain sizable numbers of employees, should be clearly defined in terms of content, and should include all jobs likely to be discussed in connection with union negotiations. The survey form should contain in each instance not only the job title, or job titles if more than one designation is in common use, but also at least a brief job description. This will help to ensure against the possibility that jobs that actually differ to a considerable degree might be grouped together because of similarities in their titles.

The information obtained on each job tends to vary considerably depending on the needs of the companies involved. Perhaps most important is the *base rate* of pay for the job. This is defined for hourly workers as the wage per hour stripped of all overtime, shift differentials, and fringe benefits, but before deductions for taxes, social security, and the like. Salaries may also be changed into such an hourly base rate to permit comparability of all jobs under study. Incentive payments based on the actual amount of work produced may similarly be converted to a per-hour equivalent.

Other important figures are *hiring rates*—the amount paid to beginners who are just starting out in a given job; *earnings*—the total amount paid a worker per standard period of time including overtime, incentives, shift differentials, and the like; *rate ranges*—the minimum and maximum amounts paid to workers on the particular job; *wage changes* —recent shifts in either the amount or kind of payments made to various employee groups. In all these instances it is essential that the number of employees at each payment level on each job be specified.

Beyond these facts, information may be obtained on policies and practices related to incentive and bonus plans, shift work, overtime, vacations, holidays, seniority, travel time, call-in pay, sick leave, rest periods, cleanup time, severance pay, guaranteed annual wages, work clothing, group insurance, retirement plans, hours of work, escalator clauses, paid lunch periods, and perhaps other factors. Many of these are fringe benefits and will be discussed in Chapter 20.

REPORTING RESULTS. The findings from a wage survey may be reported in a variety of forms. In general a company will prefer to compare its own internal wage structure with that of various other firms. Figure 16-1 provides an abbreviated example of a format used for this purpose. An actual survey would involve many more companies and many more jobs.

Figure 16-1. Example of Wage Survey Summary Report Form

Job	Company A				Company B				Company C				Company D				Company E				Averages for all Companies (Weighted by No. of Employees)			
	Average	Minimum	Maximum	Employees	Average	Minimum	Maximum	Employees	Average	Minimum	Maximum	Employees	Average	Minimum	Maximum	Employees	Average	Minimum	Maximum	Employees	Average	Minimum	Maximum	Employees
Office Jobs																								
File Clerk																								
Sorter																								
Operator																								
Typist																								
Factory Jobs																								
Loader																								
Welder																								
Drillpress																								
Operator																								
Sales Jobs																								
Sales																								
Trainee																								
Industrial																								
Salesman																								
Sales Clerk																								

In this instance anyone who knows the code designation for his own company can compare it individually with other companies included in the survey. One of the major disadvantages of the Occupational Wage Surveys conducted by the Department of Labor has traditionally been that they deal with averages and distributions of rates for each occupation but are not broken down by individual companies. This, plus the need for industry as well as geographical data, has tended to foster the use of private surveys.

When averages are used, it is often helpful to present the findings graphically, as in Figure 16-2. In this instance the various jobs surveyed have been grouped into grade levels in accord with the specific company's job evaluation system. Then weighted averages were computed for each of the job grades such that those jobs containing the largest number of employees received proportionately greater emphasis. It is apparent that although this particular company is relatively close to the industry average insofar as its lower level jobs are concerned, it lags rather markedly in the higher job grades.

Figure 16-2. Comparison of Company and Area Average Rates

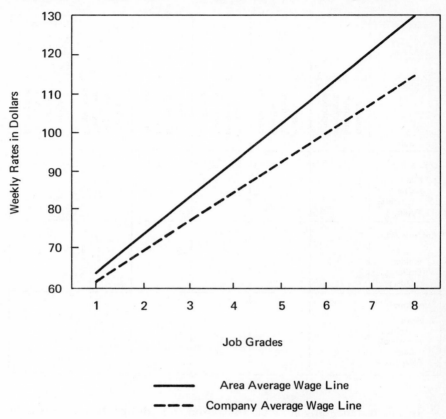

Job Grades

—————— Area Average Wage Line

– – – – Company Average Wage Line

Job Evaluation and Wage Structures

It is possible to establish the internal wage structure of a firm entirely on the basis of wage surveys or even some less precise index of wage levels in the area labor market. There are a number of companies that do just this. The major difficulty is that the pay for any given job tends to vary considerably from company to company, depending in large part on the significance of the job for the operations of that particular organization. Thus, the market often provides an imperfect guideline at the level of the individual job. Furthermore, wage surveys must inevitably focus on a limited number of key jobs. As a result the majority of positions in a company will have to be priced without adequate knowledge of market conditions.

The consequence of these considerations is that those companies that attempt to use the market as the only criterion for an internal wage structure are likely to find themselves without any real criterion at all. It is one thing to use market conditions as a guide to the overall wage level of the firm; it is quite another to use the market in determining the pay for each specific job. When this is attempted, there will almost inevitably be continuing dissension over pay scales—frequently with the union as a major participant. Thus, the inherent ambiguity of market considerations combines with insufficient knowledge to create internal stress, and organizational maintenance suffers.

Given the fact that pay can clearly be an important source of employee satisfaction and dissatisfaction (8), it seems desirable to structure the relationships among the amounts paid for various jobs within a firm so that conflict is minimized. If the maintenance goal is to be adequately served, a system for relating jobs must be introduced that will be perceived as generally equitable by all parties and that will provide reasonably stable criteria for placing jobs in the structure.

This is what the various methods of job evaluation attempt to provide. Their major role is in obtaining agreement in the area of wage and salary payments (15). After such a system of job evaluation is introduced, it provides a readily available basis for arbitrating disputes. Thus, just as wage surveys make it possible to reduce feelings of inequity when a worker compares his earnings with others outside the firm, job evaluation can serve to reduce such feelings when internal comparisons are made.

The conditions for introducing a job evaluation system in the first place, and getting widespread agreement on its essential features, appear to vary considerably from one firm to the next. In some instances real acceptance of the plan is never achieved, with the result that it is almost valueless as a means of arbitrating disputes. Under such circumstances job evaluation itself may become a major source of controversy. Usually, however, where initial acceptance appears to represent a major problem, management has tended to move in the direction of sharing the administration of the system. Thus, many companies have a great variety of wage and salary committees. It is not uncommon to find the job evaluation system administered on a joint union-management basis. These sharing procedures appear to be very effective as a means to acceptance and thus must be recommended under certain circumstances. Yet there are firms, where acceptance has not proved a problem, that administer the entire job evaluation system out of the personnel department with little or no resort to involving individuals and groups throughout the organization in the process.

Methods of Job Evaluation

As indicated in Chapter 8, job analysis provides the essential information on which job evaluation is based. Job evaluation takes the data set forth in the job description, and sometimes in the job specifications as well, and appraises these role prescriptions in terms of their degree of relationship to company goals. Thus, a rating of the job relative to productivity and maintenance goals is obtained that is in many ways similar to the rating an individual might receive relative to the role requirements of his specific position. As will become evident, the methods of job evaluation have much in common with the employee-rating systems discussed in Chapter 10.

In part because of space limitations and in part because it is common practice to offer advanced courses in this area, no effort will be made to present a detailed treatment of the many different job evaluation methods in current use. Only enough information to permit a general understanding of the four basic approaches will be provided along with some appraisal of these methods. Those who may wish to move from this to a more extended discussion of a specific method can find the appropriate information in the advanced texts in the area (3, 5,22).

JOB RANKING. In job ranking the various jobs are arranged in order of merit according to their worth as a whole. No attempt is made to separate out different factors within the jobs, although certain aspects such as difficulty level may be specified as criteria for the ranking. Usually separate ranks are developed, using the job descriptions for each department and raters who know the work done in that department.

Either of two approaches may be used in developing ranks. The job descriptions may be sorted directly so that a continuous ordering results, or the paired comparison technique may be applied and a ranking developed out of the various individual comparisons between pairs of jobs (see Chapter 10). In either case the ratings made by several individuals must be combined by averaging to produce the final ranking for the department. Then the data from all departments are dovetailed either on the basis of the knowledge of a single individual who is well informed regarding role prescriptions for the company as a whole or through committee action. The result is an ordering of all jobs in the organization.

JOB CLASSIFICATION. Grouping of jobs into various grades or levels may of course follow the use of the ranking approach. It is, in fact, common practice to do this. A similar assignment of jobs to categories of worth is also frequently used with the other methods to be discussed shortly. But in the job classification method proper, grades are established first, and then jobs are fitted into the appropriate classes, using preestablished grade descriptions or grading rules. Thus, the various groupings are not developed after some type of ordering process has already been carried out, but at the very outset.

Usually separate classification systems are established for office, factory, sales, and managerial positions. Within each of these, descriptions are written that establish the bounds for the various grades. The number of grades so established will vary with the total range of job difficulty or complexity represented in the company, as well as with the fineness of differentiation desired. In general between seven and fifteen classes will be required. The number of sales grades may, however, differ from those in the factory area, for instance. The very crucial task of writing the grade descriptions or grading rules, against which individual job descriptions are subsequently compared, may be assigned to an individual or to a committee.

FACTOR COMPARISON. Factor comparison is in reality a complex variant of the ranking approach, because jobs are compared with each other rather than against category descriptions. The rankings are not done on a global basis, taking the whole job into account but individually in terms of various component factors—usually skill, mental effort, physical effort, responsibility, and working conditions.

The initial step is to select some fifteen to twenty-five key jobs that seem to be generally in the correct relationship to each other insofar as wage rates are concerned. Usually these will be jobs that are widely distributed in level and that have not been a subject of controversy regarding payment rates. These key jobs are then rank ordered on each of the five factors. Thus, in the case of the sixteen jobs noted in Table 16-1, the jobs rated highest are:

> Mental effort—pattern maker
> Physical effort—common laborer
> Skill—pattern maker
> Responsibility—pattern maker
> Working conditions—common laborer

The jobs rated lowest are:

> Mental effort—common laborer
> Physical effort—tool crib attendant
> Skill—common laborer
> Responsibility—common laborer
> Working conditions—pattern maker

Next, the present wage being paid on each of the key jobs is divided among the five factors, with the greatest proportion being given to the most important factor. This is as much a judgmental process as is the ranking. In both instances averages of a number of independent ratings by different individuals should be obtained. With reference to the backup data for Table 16-1, given a present wage for gager of $3.08, this might be distributed among the factors as follows:

Mental effort	$.72
Physical effort	.38
Skill	1.02
Responsibility	.51
Working conditions	.45
	$3.08

For pattern maker the average of the judgments might be:

Mental effort	$.90
Physical effort	.39
Skill	1.13
Responsibility	.60
Working conditions	.23
	$3.25

The money amounts thus established may then be used to set up a second ranking on each of the five factors. The two rankings, on difficulty and money, are then compared as in Table 16-1. Where sizable disparities exist, as with gager (working conditions) and blacksmith (skill and working conditions), these jobs are eliminated from the list of key jobs.

The remaining jobs are then put into a job comparison scale. This scale indicates the money amounts associated with each job for each of the five factors. Thus, the key jobs become bench marks against which other jobs may be compared. The appropriate pay for each non-key job is determined by establishing which jobs it falls between on each of the five factors. The five money amounts thus identified are added to obtain the wage rate for the job. Each job in the company is related to the job comparison scale one factor at a time in this way, using the job descriptions for key and nonkey jobs. The result is not only an evaluation, but an actual pricing of the firm's job structure.

POINT SYSTEM. The point system is an extension of the job classification approach that utilizes a variety of factors as a basis for classification rather than a single dimension. In one variant or another it appears to be the most widely used of the job evaluation methods. Factor comparison comes next and job classification proper third, although some type of classification procedure is usually superimposed on the other methods. The ranking approach is used only infrequently (12).

Table 16-1. Difficulty Rank vs. Money Rank for 16 Tentative Key Jobs

Jobs	Mental effort		Physical effort		Factors Skill		Responsibility		Working conditions	
	Difficulty	Money	Difficulty	Money	Difficulty	Money	Difficulty	Money	Difficulty	Money
Gager	2	2	13	13	2	2	3	3	15	4
Pattern maker	1	1	12	12	1	1	1	1	16	16
Common laborer	16	16	1	1	16	16	16	16	1	1
Power shear operator	11	11	11	11	9	9	5	5	4	6
Plater	10	10	6	6	6	7	12	12	9	10
Riveter	12	12	3	3	12	12	14	14	8	9
Blacksmith	13	13	2	2	8	5	13	13	7	2
Punch press operator	14	14	4	4	13	13	15	15	5	7
Screw machine operator	4	4	8	8	3	3	2	2	13	14
Casting inspector	3	3	7	7	4	6	4	4	10	11
Millwright	9	9	10	10	5	4	6	6	11	12
Tool crib attendant	7	7	16	16	14	14	10	10	14	15
Arc welder	8	8	9	9	7	8	9	9	3	5
Electrical truck operator	6	6	15	15	11	11	8	8	12	13
Crane operator	5	5	14	14	10	10	7	7	6	8
Watchman	15	15	5	5	15	15	11	11	2	3

Source: D. W. Belcher, Wage and Salary Administration, 2nd ed. p. 266. Copyright 1962. Reprinted by permission of Prentice-Hall, Inc., Englewood Cliffs, New Jersey.

377

As with job classification, point systems are usually developed separately for different categories of jobs—factory, clerical, sales, and the like. The reason is that the relevant factors may differ considerably from one category of job to another. Thus, a single system for the whole organization could be extremely cumbersome, and at the same time yield some rather incongruous results. The number and type of factors on which ratings are made tend to vary considerably between companies and even within companies between job categories. Among the factors that often occur are education, job knowledge, mental demand, effect of error, personal contact skill, initiative and ingenuity, physical demand, responsibility (in various areas such as safety, work of others, equipment and materials), working conditions, hazards, and level to which the job reports. It is not uncommon to use as many as ten or even more factors in a single system.

When the factors have been established and defined, degrees are determined for each factor so that those who subsequently rate jobs using the point manual may identify the amount or level of a factor in the particular job under consideration. Different numbers of degree differentiations may be used on the various factors, but in any case the definitions for each degree should be stated in considerable detail and should include if possible the titles of several key jobs falling at that particular level.

Table 16-2. Hypothetical Point Values for Job Factors

Factors	Lowest degree	Next degree	Next degree	Next degree	Highest degree
Mental demand	15	30	45	60	75
Experience	20	40	60	80	100
Physical demand	15	35	55		75
Hazards	10	20	30	40	50
Education	10	20	30	40	50
Personal contact	10	30			50
Equipment responsibility	10	20	30	40	50
Initiative	10	23	37		50

Table 16-2 provides an example of how points might be assigned after the appropriate factor and degree descriptions have been written. Judgments must be made either by individuals or committees as to how the total number of points should be allocated among factors. The most common procedure is to start with 500 points and split this up in accordance with the importance of the various factors to set the point values for the highest degrees. Then the lowest degrees are set equal to one fifth of the number of points used at the highest levels.

Intermediate degree points are allocated in terms of arithmetically equal intervals. This interval varies in size depending on the number of separate degrees identified on the factor.

Once a manual is developed describing factors and degrees and indicating points for each degree on each factor, jobs may be evaluated by comparing their descriptions against those in the manual. The points obtained on each factor are summed to yield a point total that indicates the value of the job. Usually these point totals are then grouped to yield a series of job grades within each of which a single pay scale applies.

As previously indicated, a variety of point systems have been developed. Some use a few factors, some many. Some use more than 500 total points, some less. Some use statistical procedures for weighting the various factors. Some assign points to the degrees, using a geometric rather than an arithmetic progression. Although it seems generally desirable to develop a point manual that is adapted to a specific company situation, there are many general systems that have achieved rather widespread use. Among these are the National Electrical Manufacturers Association and the National Metal Trades Association systems for factory jobs, the National Electrical Manufacturers Association system for salaried jobs, and the National Office Management Association system. In any case it should be emphasized that no matter how great the statistical elaboration of the data, the point system like other job evaluation procedures remains primarily a judgmental process.

The Selection of a Job Evaluation Method

The most crucial consideration in selecting among the various methods described is that the plan actually yield a stable job structure, which is capable of winning acceptance and therefore minimizes controversy in the area of monetary payments. In all probability the approach that will accomplish this in one company is not the one that will yield the same result in another. Employees in one firm may be conditioned to expect intensive study of each job along the lines of the factor comparison and point systems. In other instances the major requirement may be that the procedures employed be simple and easy to understand, as with the job ranking and job comparison procedures. Where there is a strong need to recapitulate the current situation in any newly established job structure, the factor comparison method appears to offer some advantages, because it is directly tied to existing wage rates. In a small company with a limited number of positions, job ranking may be all that is needed to achieve a sense of equity.

Given these situational differences that may overrule all other considerations, the results of a number of studies bearing on the job evaluation process can provide certain guidelines. For one thing it is now clear that a single-factor, overall value, accounts for the majority of the results obtained with the factor comparison and point methods (17). Thus, the single-factor approaches, such as job ranking and job classification, do not produce any great loss in precision. Yet, where a work force is convinced that a variety of factors should be explicitly considered in setting wage rates, it may be desirable to use the more complex approaches merely to gain acceptance.

If a factor approach is used there seems little reason to go beyond three factors under any but the most unusual conditions (26). Experience, or time to learn the job, seems to be of the greatest importance in almost all situations. Hazards, education, initiative, safety responsibility, complexity of duties, and character of supervision may be added, depending on the company and the type of job covered.

Studies dealing with the degree of agreement obtained with different judges or raters suggest that this is not a major problem. Independent ratings of the same jobs by different individuals tend to yield similar results. Thus a large number of judgments need not be averaged. Three or four raters should be entirely adequate. Furthermore, the raters need not be experienced in the field of job evaluation. Studies indicate that inexperienced raters can achieve at least as high a level of agreement as the experienced (26).

Job Pricing and Rate Ranges

In shifting from job evaluation to job pricing and the establishment of the minimum and maximum pay for each job, we move from considerations of equity, conflict, and organizational maintenance to matters of motivation, reward, and productivity. To the extent it is possible for an individual through his own efforts on the job to achieve a pay level above that of other people with whom he compares himself, both outside and within the company, a true incentive exists. Thus, pay schedules must be established in such a way as to make this possible if money is in fact to serve as an input-output mediator fostering productivity. In this section the focus will be on increasing motivation through the use of wage and salary procedures. In the following section the more direct pay-for-work incentive plans will be considered.

Pricing the Job Structure

It is in the pricing process that wage structures and wage levels merge. The wage structure relates to the average pay assigned to each job. The wage level is the average pay for the firm, or the overall level of the wage structure. When the job structure is priced, this results not only in a wage structure but in the wage level as well.

Of the job evaluation methods discussed, only the factor comparison approach can yield a priced job structure directly. And even with this method it has become a frequent practice to convert the dollar amounts into percentages or some type of point equivalents to avoid the possible biasing effects of using existing wage rates in making the judgments.

PAY GRADES. When job evaluation is carried out using any but the job comparison method, it is possible to assign different money amounts to each individual job. This, however, produces an extremely complex pay structure in any but the smallest firms and for this reason is not a widely accepted approach. Normally jobs are grouped, and all jobs in the same group or grade level have the same pay schedule.

The number of pay grades in a given job structure will vary with the nature of the structure. In actual fact one can find as few as four and as many as sixty. Generally, however, something in the range ten to sixteen should be adequate. Pay differentials between grades for factory jobs tend to run at 5 to 7 per cent; for office work they are higher, in the 8- to 12-per-cent range (3). Usually the grades are of equal width in terms of point spread, but on occasion a gradually increasing spread is introduced as one moves up the scale.

PRICING. Jobs may be priced in accordance with the existing wage level. If this is done, the average pay for all individuals working on jobs falling in a given grade category is determined; then adjustments are made so that this average is roughly applicable to each individual job.

In other cases an average wage line of the kind shown in Figure 16-2 is used. Such a line may be established by connecting the high and low points directly, by drawing a freehand line that seems to come closest to the largest number of points on the dollar versus job grade scatterplot, or by actually fitting a line statistically using a least-squares solution. The result can be a straight line or a curve. After this smoothed line has been established, it may be used to read off average rates for pay grades and the jobs within grades, rather than using the actual averages for the grades.

When adjustments are made either to actual averages or to a smoothed line, with a view to establishing a logically consistent and equitable wage structure, the usual practice is to raise individual pay to the extent required by the new structure, but not to decrease the earnings of any individual who is performing adequately. New employees come in at the pay rates established under the new schedule. The result of this policy is that introducing a job evaluation system almost inevitably raises the overall company wage level, while at the same time leaving some employees whose pay is out of line with the rest of the system in the sense that it is too high. Yet to do otherwise might have a negative effect rather than a positive one, because the motivation of a number of entirely satisfactory individuals would suffer. Furthermore, as a result of retirements, separations, promotions, and subsequent general rate raises that the overpaid individuals do not receive, these out-of-line situations do tend to correct themselves over time. Those rates that become out of line with the introduction of a job evaluation system are commonly referred to as *red circle rates.*

In certain instances as a result of union pressures, recruiting difficulties, or other considerations, a company may wish to raise its wage level, rather than maintain an approximation to the existing level. At such times wage survey data become of crucial significance in pricing. Ideally a company should pay at or above the going level for the area and industry if it is to obtain maximum motivational value out of its payment system. This assumes, of course, that the company's employees are at least as competent as those of other employers.

Many companies adopt a policy of maintaining a wage line very close to the industry or area average. In such cases indexes derived from wage surveys, as, for instance, the area average wage line of Figure 16-2, provide a basis for establishing average pay rates for grades and jobs within grades. Or a third line may be drawn on such a graph establishing a new basis for pricing. Normally, under the economic conditions that have existed since World War II, any shift to a new wage line has involved an upward movement of the company wage level. Downward changes have been rare indeed in recent years. Thus, overpayment situations caused by a policy barring wage reductions have not in general represented a widespread problem. All that is required is that general pay increases be withheld from such individuals until their rates are back in line.

Rate Ranges

Although there are circumstances, notably in the basic steel and automobile industries, where single rates exist for all employees on a given job, this is definitely the exception. The usual practice is to move a man through a range of rates as he gains experience and competence in his work. Certainly to the extent this is done, the potential incentive value of the payment process increases, because the average individual will devote his efforts, at least to a degree, toward doing that which he believes will increase his earnings.

When a single rate is in effect, the motivational value of money is vested entirely in the promotion process. For many this means that money cannot function as a motivator, either because promotion is not anticipated at all or because it is viewed as a very distant event. When, however, a man can look forward to raises within his present job and knows exactly what rate he can achieve, an added motivational potential is introduced, one that normally yields rewards in a much shorter period of time than would be possible with the promotional pay increase alone.

Unfortunately, although rate ranges are widely used in the business world for both hourly and salaried workers, the potential incentive value of the approach is often lost. The reason is that there has been a marked tendency to move individuals through ranges on the basis of seniority and experience rather than on the basis of merit, as determined by evaluation techniques of the kind discussed in Chapters 9 and 10. In addition, progression to the top pay level is often accelerated so that at any given point in time a high proportion of a company's employees are likely to be at the maximum pay for the job. The result is that the incentive value of the rate range disappears (25). When a man can expect to reach the top pay level as a result of average rather than outstanding work, and when he can anticipate raises merely as a consequence of maintaining employment rather than through consistently reducing the gap between role behavior and role prescriptions, there is very little to be gained from a productivity viewpoint in having rate ranges at all.

The fact that the incentive value of the rate range is frequently eroded may often be attributed to union pressures. In attempting to maintain job control, foster seniority at the expense of merit considerations, and push all employees to the highest payment level possible without regard for performance effectiveness, the unions have tended to deprive management of one of its most potentially effective input-output mediators.

There is an additional sense in which the unions have reduced the motivational value of pay that should also be noted. Many collective bargaining agreements have resulted in rather sizable yearly increases. These are frequently labeled as cost-of-living or productivity raises and given on an across-the-board basis to all employees, union and nonunion, to maintain existing pay differentials. When this is done, the increase in earnings attributable to union efforts tends to dwarf any merit increase attributable to employee performance. Consequently, even for many nonunion members, the union may be viewed as contributing more than individual effort ever could to the size of the paycheck.

ESTABLISHING RATE RANGES. The usual practice is to establish a range from minimum to maximum pay that represents from 10 to 20 per cent of the minimum for hourly wage jobs, from 15 to 35 per cent for salaried office jobs, and from 25 per cent on up for management jobs. In some instances the range is held constant at a set dollar amount; more usually it increases in amount as a given percentage of the minimum.

An example of rate ranges for clerical jobs is contained in Table

16-3. In this instance, as is often the case, considerable overlap exists: A man in grade 1 can make as much as a grade 4 employee; at grade 11 one can make as much in grade 14. This raises an important question regarding job worth: Is even a perfect worker in grade 1 worth as much to the company as someone doing grade 4 work? There is no categorical answer to this. However, balancing equity and incentive considerations, it seems desirable to minimize overlap while at the same time keeping the rate range for each grade as large as possible, even if this means reducing the number of job grade levels. Such an approach permits greater flexibility in administering payment increases than is possible when one must rely heavily on promotional raises as a method of reward. Ideally, this approach would be coupled with sufficient wage and salary control so that an average, entirely satisfactory employee would not move above the middle of the rate range for his job, irrespective of the extent of his seniority.

Table 16-3.   Examples of Rate Ranges for Clerical Jobs

Grade	Weekly minimum	Weekly maximum
1	$69.80	$85.21
2	73.68	90.31
3	77.90	95.87
4	82.47	101.97
5	87.43	108.63
6	92.82	115.92
7	98.67	123.87
8	105.03	132.59
9	111.92	142.68
10	119.42	153.71
11	127.55	165.77
12	136.38	178.96
13	145.96	193.36
14	156.36	209.11

STEPS. In some firms it is normal practice to divide the range between minimum and maximum pay into a series of equal intervals or steps—usually three or more. To the extent a single-step raise tends to become associated in the minds of employees with the concept of a normal yearly increase, this procedure may have major disadvantages from a motivational viewpoint. There is strong pressure on managers to move everyone up at least one step a year, with the result that constant movement to the maximum is likely to occur, quite irrespective of performance evaluations. This is not inevitable, but it is common. Where seniority progression has become established practice, steps are in fact always indicated and regular movement through them occurs. Given these considerations, it seems desirable to maintain the flexibility that a nonstep approach permits in the hope that the payment process can retain its incentive value.

Wages versus Salaries

In the discussion to this point the term *wage* has been used in a general sense to include all monetary payment based on time worked, but there is a more limited definition that equates wages with an hourly rate. Such hourly wages have been the tradition in factory employment, in contrast to the weekly or monthly salary that has been characteristic in the office situation. Where employment is intermittent and layoffs are frequent, there is probably good reason to maintain the hourly rate. But under more stable conditions, the use of a regular salary seems to offer a number of advantages.

Because of its association with certain high-status managerial and professional positions, the salary approach has considerable appeal to employees at all levels. Research studies indicate that factory employees consistently prefer a weekly salary to an hourly wage (10). In addition, there is evidence that the introduction of salary payment for factory workers does not yield an increase in absenteeism and tardiness. If anything, the trend is in the reverse direction, and at the same time the costs associated with administering the payment process are reduced (11). Taken together, these considerations yield a strong case in favor of salaried payment, rather than an hourly rate, in situations where a choice can be made between the two approaches.

Incentive Payment

The essential characteristic of incentive payment is that earnings are directly related to output. A standard of performance is established for each job in the case of individual incentives, or an interlocking group of jobs in the case of group incentives. The employee's earnings are then promptly and automatically varied in accordance with some established formula that relates either individual or group performance to the standard (30).

Because reward is achieved in a relatively short time span and is closely tied to work output, incentive payment may be presumed to possess greater potential as an input-output mediator than the wage and salary approaches just discussed. This is true even when rate ranges and merit increases are used effectively to foster productivity. It is this motivational potential that has led many companies to adopt incentive payment systems on a widespread basis, wherever it is possible to do so.

Individual Incentive Systems

Over the past seventy years or so many different types of individual incentive plans have been developed. Most have been created by industrial engineers and are closely tied to time study procedures. The listing that follows covers only the more widely known approaches. Many individual companies have developed their own special variants. As with job evaluation, the reader interested in more detailed information on these techniques should consult the more specialized texts.

DIFFERENTIAL DAYWORK. The differential daywork approach involves the use of an hourly rate, but the rate applied varies depending on whether the employee makes standard or not. Generally, workers who maintain output above the standard level are paid at an hourly rate 20 per cent higher than that given those who are below standard.

PIECEWORK. Under straight piecework an employee is paid a given amount for each unit produced. The rate is determined through time study by relating the standard time to produce the unit, e.g., fifteen minutes, to the regular hourly rate, e.g., $2.00. In this instance the unit rate would be $.50. In many cases the basic hourly rate, $2.00, in this instance, is guaranteed. Thus, for any hour in which an individual produces four or less units, he would be paid $2.00; for any hour in which he produces five or more, the $.50 per unit rate would apply.

THE STANDARD HOUR PLAN. The standard hour plan is a piecework variant that expresses the standard in time per unit of output rather than in money values. Thus, if an employee produces a unit in less than the standard time, he gets paid the full rate for the standard time. A man who produces a unit more rapidly has time left over to make additional units, all of which are counted as if they had taken the full standard time. At the end of the day this means that a worker may be paid for a ten-hour day even though actually he has been on the job for only eight hours.

THE TAYLOR PLAN. In the Taylor plan a standard is first determined using time and motion study. Above this standard a relatively high piece rate is applied; below standard the rate is very low. The normal consequence is that individuals who consistently fail to make standard are encouraged to quit.

THE MERRICK PLAN. The Taylor approach tends to maintain a sizable pay differential between acceptable and unacceptable workers. The Merrick plan modifies this differential by introducing two steps rather than a single step. The result is that the individual who is only slightly below standard output can still achieve a rate above the worker who is well below standard.

THE GANTT PLAN. The Gantt plan, a modification of the Taylor procedure, guarantees the worker his regular hourly rate for all output below standard. Above standard a 20 per cent step bonus is introduced. As with the Taylor and Merrick procedures standard is established by time and motion study. However, in this instance the strong pressure on less effective workers to seek employment elsewhere is diluted because of the guaranteed hourly rate.

THE HALSEY PLAN. Under the Halsey plan standards are established on the basis of production records for past years, rather than as a result of time study. The consequence is that they are considerably lower than those used under the Taylor, Merrick, and Gantt plans. In view of the low standards, which can be met without a great deal of employee effort, it is assumed that the gains associated with above-standard output should not accrue entirely to the worker. Thus, if the man spends the standard time or more on a job, he is paid his regular hourly rate. If the job is completed in less than standard time, he receives his hourly rate for the time actually worked plus a percentage, usually 50 per cent, of the additional money he would have received if he had gone to the full standard time. The other 50 per cent of money saved goes to the company. It is important to remember here that the standard time in this instance tends to be much longer than under time study.

THE ROWAN PLAN. With the Rowan plan the basic procedure is identical to that of the Halsey plan except that the percentages on money saved going to the individual and to the company are computed in a different way. According to the Rowan procedure, the proportional bonus is determined by dividing the time saved by the standard time. Thus, if the standard time is two hours and thirty minutes and the worker produces a unit in two hours, he gets two times his basic pay per hour plus a bonus of 20 per cent of his pay for the two hours.

THE BEDAUX PLAN. The Bedaux plan in its current application tends to closely approximate the standard hour plan, although in earlier years savings were shared among employee and management as in the Halsey and Rowan plans. The standard times are established by time and motion study, but are expressed in units of "points" or "B's." The standards tend to be set somewhere between the low standards of the Halsey and Rowan plans and the high standards of the approaches based on time study. The Bedaux plan, although complex in application because of the methods used to compute the standard B's, has the advantage that it allows production control and efficiency comparisons between departments.

SALES COMMISSION PLANS. The approaches just discussed were originally developed to apply to direct production workers. In recent years they have been extended to maintenance jobs, inspection, janitorial work, clerical jobs, and many other types of positions. In the sales field the approach has been to pay commissions based on either the number of units sold, the total dollar volume of sales, or the gains and losses over the previous year's record in the same location—or perhaps even on number of new accounts secured.

In some sales occupations these commission payments are set on top of a guaranteed base salary. It is also common practice to establish a drawing account, so that when a salesman's commissions are down, he can draw out an amount sufficient to bring his earnings up to a guaranteed base level. This money must be repaid later when commission earnings are up. Such an approach is most applicable when wide fluctuations in sales are common, due to economic or seasonal factors.

Group Incentive Systems

Group procedures offer the advantage that payroll and industrial engineering costs tend to be lower than with the individual plans. In addition, the group approach appears to permit more flexibility in that resistance to technological changes seems to be less. On the negative side is the fact that paying members of a group, either equally or in proportion to job level, out of a pool determined by comparing group output with a group standard serves to reduce the motivational impact on the individual. Too much of what a man makes depends on the work of others rather than on his own efforts. In very small groups some direct motivational impact may remain; in large groups this seems quite unlikely. It is also true, however, that under certain circumstances a group will establish higher productivity aspirations and push its laggard members more under group than under individual incentives. Thus, the motivating effects of group pressure may be substituted for individual reward.

WORK GROUP PLANS. A number of the individual incentive plans can be adapted for group use. The standard hour plan in particular has received widespread application. Regular hourly rates are paid up to group standard output. Above this point group efficiency is calculated by dividing the standard hours for the job by the actual hours worked. This yields an efficiency figure above 100 per cent, which is multiplied by each individual group member's hourly rate to get his actual hourly earnings.

For this approach to operate effectively as a motivational force, the work of the various group members must be interlocking, membership must be stable with little turnover, and the group must possess a certain cohesiveness. Given these factors, a work group incentive can be effective with as many as forty people (3).

THE SCANLON PLAN. The Scanlon plan is much more than a group incentive system. It operates at the plant or company level as a means of gaining union-management cooperation toward the goal of increased productivity. The incentive feature, however, is a bonus that is calculated from savings in labor costs. A standard ratio of payroll costs to sales value of production is developed from past records. Each month current data are compared against this ratio to determine savings. Of the resulting amount, 80 per cent goes into a direct bonus and 20 per cent is held to cover deficit periods. The latter fund is closed at the end of the year.

A major feature of the plan is its emphasis on suggestions for increased efficiency. These are evaluated by a complex committee structure that gives the union and management equal representation. Thus, management shares much of its normal control over the production process with the employees and with the union. The result can be a widespread concern with improved efficiency and increased output. This, however, has not always been the case. There are also instances where the Scanlon plan has been tried and has failed. It seems to work best where the company is in financial difficulty, and management is willing to give up some of its prerogatives to salvage the firm.

THE LINCOLN PLAN. For many years the Lincoln Electric Company of Cleveland has utilized a cooperative plan that has not only received considerable publicity, but has also apparently proved extremely effective. Actual compensation is in terms of an individual standard hour plan, which has been extended to cover all jobs that can possibly be standardized. There are, nevertheless, so many cooperative features in the total plan that it must be considered as basically a group approach. Among these features are extensive employee stock ownership, a sizable profit-sharing bonus at year end, an employee advisory board that has considerable influence on company policies and procedures, and a suggestion plan that yields sizable monetary awards. The bonus is distributed from year-end profits on the basis of a merit rating system that emphasizes cooperation, job knowledge, quality of work, and quantity of work. Thus, those who are seen as contributing most effectively to company goals receive the greatest rewards.

Problems Associated with Incentive Payment

The weight of the available evidence suggests that taken as a whole incentive plans have resulted in increased output and reduced costs (18). Thus, such plans can operate effectively as input-output mediators, above and beyond what the usual time payment procedures achieve. Apparently, however, they do so less frequently when the work is extremely repetitive, or boring, and definitely disliked.

There are certainly many instances in which the full motivational potential of the incentive is not obtained. This occurs largely as a result of a quite conscious restriction of output by the workers themselves. Many work groups establish a group production norm that serves to set a very effective lid on output (28). Any worker who produces above this norm is likely to become the object of considerable group pressure and as a result will in most cases hold back on his output. The desire to maintain the respect and acceptance of the group appears to be a stronger motive for most workers than the desire for increased earnings.

Five different types of motivation have been identified behind this restriction of output phenomenon, which effectively hamstrings many incentive plans (9). For one thing there may be a widespread belief that if incentive earnings and production were allowed to move up to the level possible, the job would be restudied and the standard set higher. Thus, earnings would not increase for long, and all employees would have to work much harder to maintain the same income level. Second, workers assume that if the more competent individuals went all out in accord with the intent of the incentive system a number of less capable workers would then stand out for all to see and be fired. In this sense restriction serves to protect the ineffective members of the group. Third, if members started to compete for earnings as the incentive approach implies, the whole social structure of the group would be disrupted. Restriction maintains the social ties. Competitive striving would break this down, leading to distrust and individual isolation.

The other two types of motivation are of a more positive nature. The very process of establishing restrictive norms produces a sense of "groupness" with its consequent social satisfactions. In addition, restriction provides a feeling of control over one's own behavior, a sense of freedom from the manipulations of management. This final point may be particularly important in explaining why a group norm is often maintained long after any real threat of revised standards has disappeared.

Difficulties in the use of incentive plans are not limited to group output restriction. Another major problem is that workers generally will devote considerable effort to getting a low standard established, if this seems at all possible. Thus, when time and motion studies are conducted, the workers may well do the job in a way that makes it appear more difficult and time-consuming than it is. The lower standards are not only a means to increased earnings, they are also viewed as a protection against layoffs. Under such conditions it is very difficult to set truly appropriate standards, and controversy between management and industrial engineers on the one side and workers and the union on the other may well become intense.

In fact, it seems to be inherent in the very nature of incentive payment that although the approach does contribute to the goal it is directed to, namely productivity, it does so at some cost to organizational maintenance. Disputes and grievances related to inequitable standards are common in nearly every case in which incentive systems have been installed.

Perhaps if a system could be devised that would reward an appropriate balance between productivity and maintenance consideration, this problem could be overcome. To date, however, little has been done in this area.

Incentives and Automation

It has been widely assumed that the advent of automated technology would sound the death knell for incentive payment. As control over output rates shifts from the individual to the machine, it seems logical to expect that time will be substituted for productivity as a basis for payment. Yet the evidence to date does not support this conclusion (16,24).

What appears to be happening now is that group incentives are often being substituted for those of an individual nature. In addition, new approaches to both individual and group standard setting are being developed. The role of the worker in automated and semiautomated installations is largely one of maintaining maximal equipment utilization, of keeping the machinery operating. Given this requirement, a number of companies have developed standards of an entirely new kind that are more suited to an automated technology. It may be that eventually automation will result in the abolition of incentive payment, but this day appears to be a long way off.

Payments to Management

Top Management

At the very uppermost levels of the management hierarchy salaries appear to be influenced in part by company size, in part by the specific industry, and in part by the contribution of the incumbent to the process of making decisions (21). Surveys have repeatedly indicated that the larger the firm (as defined by sales volume), the greater the payment to the top-level group.

It is also true, however, that there are sizable industry differences. The major differentiating factor appears to be the competitive environment that is characteristic. Thus, those industries that are more highly constrained by governmental regulation (banks, life insurance, air transport, meat packing, railroads, public utilities) pay relatively low salaries and those that are more free to engage in unfettered competition (chemicals, department stores, automobiles, steel, textiles, appliances) pay well. The high-pay industries generally demand more decisions of top management and the alternative courses of action available tend to be greater in number. At the other extreme, decisions are often so limited by external constraints that little if any discretion is left.

Although job evaluation is not employed at the upper levels by many companies that use it at lower levels, it still remains relatively common. The factors used, however, are different, emphasizing such things as accountability, decision making, organizing, planning, responsibility, and supervision. In general the chief executive's salary serves to limit the pay of those below him. Thus, the second man may receive 50 to 60 per cent of what his superior receives. Characteristically, staff managers receive somewhat less, all things being equal, than line managers at the same level (14).

BONUSES. A large proportion of companies pay bonuses averaging from 30 to 50 per cent of base salary to their top executives. These bonuses operate most effectively in increasing motivation when the following circumstances exist:

1. The amount paid is closely related to the level of individual performance.
2. The amount paid after taxes represents a clearly noticeable rise above the base salary level.
3. The amount paid is closely related to the level of company performance.
4. The amount paid is tied into base salary in such a way that combined earnings are equitable both in relation to internal and to external standards.
5. The amount paid is reduced drastically whenever an individual experiences a real and continuing decrease in performance effectiveness.
6. The amount paid is based on an easily understandable system of allocation and the individual is provided with complete information on the relationship between bonus and performance (29).

The usual procedure is to discount the normal salary structure to some extent if a bonus system is in effect. Thus, the bonuses are not entirely in addition to equitable salaries. The potential amount payable is usually a percentage of the base salary. However, within the range thus established, there can be a variation from zero to the maximum allowable, depending on level of performance and company profits. Most plans pay in cash, although some include stock. In some instances the payment is deferred until retirement so that the individual will not have to pay taxes on this income during a high-earnings period. This approach, however, removes the current reward value of the bonus and thus dilutes its impact as an input-output mediator. Payment may also be in the form of options to buy company stock at some later date. Such purchases may be made at a specified current rate. If the stock goes up in value, the option may be exercised. The gain from resale is taxed at a somewhat lower rate than a regular bonus would be, but there is always the risk that the stock will not rise and the option remain worthless.

Table 16-4. Comparison of Success Over a Ten-year Period for 100 Bonus-Paying Companies and 100 Nonbonus Payers

Success index	Bonus payers, %	Nonbonus payers, %
Profit increase	104	52
Return on invested capital increase	21	14

Source: Adapted from A. Patton, *Men, Money and Motivation*, p. 77. Copyright 1961 by McGraw-Hill Book Company, Inc. Used by permission of McGraw-Hill Book Company.

The evidence for an association between bonuses and company success is convincing, although it is impossible to establish the extent to which a bonus system can serve as a direct *cause* of an improved profit picture. In the study noted in Table 16-4, two groups of companies of approximately equal size and representing similar industries were compared (20). The superior performance of the bonus payers is clearly evident.

Middle Management

Below the top management level the major influence on salaries appears to derive from the national labor market. Many of these managers have special skills that have applications not only within the specific company or industry but on a much more widespread basis. This is particularly true of those with a professional background—personnel managers, accountants, lawyers, engineers, and the like. Sales skills are also widely transferable.

Middle management positions are usually subjected to job evaluation, using techniques that represent modifications of the basic procedures discussed previously. At this level and above, rate ranges are almost universal, and increases are granted at least in theory on the basis of merit. In actual practice, however, the man's previous history, cost of living factors, raises at lower levels, and internal equity considerations exert a strong influence.

Incentive payments above and beyond base salary take two forms at the middle management level. On occasion the type of bonus system described for top executives is extended down to considerably lower managerial levels. In other instances incentive payments are made in terms of definite standards dealing with such matters as sales volume, production capacity achieved, budgetary attainment, and so on. Generally this latter type of system operates quite independently of company profit considerations. It pays in relation to the preestablished standard no matter how well or poorly the firm is doing.

First-Line Supervision

At the very lowest supervisory level, especially among production foremen and similar individuals whose training is not of a professional nature, the local rather than the national labor market exerts the greatest influence. In addition, pay levels at the next lower, nonsupervisory level have considerable impact, with the supervisor usually being paid roughly 25 per cent above his highest paid subordinate. Often supervisory positions are included in area and industry wage surveys.

Formal job evaluation systems for lower grades are sometimes merely extended upward to include the first level of supervision. Even if this is not done, managers at this level are more likely to be covered by some type of job evaluation plan than middle management. To the extent that flat rates rather than ranges occur at all in the ranks of management, they do so at this point. In many cases, even where ranges are used, a commitment to the merit principle seems to be totally lacking. Thus, in general, first-line supervisors are paid in ways that more closely resemble the procedures used with their subordinates than those used with managers higher in the hierarchy.

Incentive payments for supervisors are sometimes based entirely on the incentive earnings of subordinates. Under these circumstances the supervisor is relatively easily integrated into the existing plan established for his men. There is, however, the risk that in an effort to increase his own earnings, a supervisor may exert what influence he can to obtain low standards and thus a higher incentive payment to subordinates. To circumvent this problem, a number of companies have resorted to multifactor systems emphasizing labor costs, quality of production, safety, absenteeism, and similar considerations. This method of divorcing incentives for first-line supervisors from incentive payments to subordinates, although costly in time and money, appears to be quite effective.

References

1. Andrews, I. R., and M. M. Henry, "Management Attitudes Toward Pay," *Industrial Relations,* Vol. 3 (1963), 29–39.
2. Belcher, D. W., "Employee and Executive Compensation," in H. G. Heneman et al. (eds.), *Employment Relations Research.* New York: Harper & Row, 1960, pp. 73–131.
3. Belcher, D. W., *Wage and Salary Administration,* 2nd ed. Englewood Cliffs, N.J.: Prentice-Hall, 1962.
4. Bernstein, I., *The Arbitration of Wages.* Berkeley, Calif.: Univ. of California Press, 1954.

5. Brennan, C. W., *Wage Administration*. Homewood, Ill.: Irwin, 1963.
6. Gellerman, S. W., *Motivation and Productivity*. New York: American Management Association, 1963.
7. Haire, M., E. E. Ghiselli, and M. E. Gordon, "A Psychological Study of Pay," *Journal of Applied Psychology Monograph*, Vol. 51, No. 4 (1967), 1–24.
8. Herzberg, F., B. Mausner, and B. B. Snyderman, *The Motivation to Work*, 2nd ed. New York: Wiley, 1959.
9. Hickson, D. J., "Motives of People Who Restrict Their Output," *Occupational Psychology*, Vol. 35 (1961), 110–121.
10. Jones, L. V., and T. E. Jeffrey, "A Quantitative Analysis of Expressed Preferences for Compensation Plans," *Journal of Applied Psychology*, Vol. 48 (1964), 201–210.
11. Kaponya, P. G., "Salaries for All Workers," *Harvard Business Review*, Vol. 40, No. 3 (1962), 49–57.
12. Lanham, E., *Job Evaluation*. New York: McGraw-Hill, 1955.
13. Lawler, E. E., and L. W. Porter, "Perceptions Regarding Management Compensation," *Industrial Relations*, Vol. 3 (1963), 41–49.
14. Lawler, E. E., and L. W. Porter, "Predicting Managers' Pay and Their Satisfaction with Their Pay," *Personnel Psychology*, Vol. 19 (1966), 363–373.
15. Livernash, E. R., "Wage Administration and Production Standards," in A. Kornhauser, R. Dubin, and A. M. Ross (eds.), *Industrial Conflict*. New York: McGraw-Hill, 1954, pp. 330–344.
16. Mangum, G. L., "Are Wage Incentives Becoming Obsolete?" *Industrial Relations*, Vol. 2 (1962), 73–96.
17. Myers, J. H., "An Experimental Investigation of Point Job Evaluation Systems," *Journal of Applied Psychology*, Vol. 42 (1958), 357–361.
18. Opsahl, R. L., and M. D. Dunnette, "The Role of Financial Compensation in Industrial Motivation," *Psychological Bulletin*, Vol. 63 (1966), 94–118.
19. Patchen, M., *The Choice of Wage Comparisons*. Englewood Cliffs, N.J.: Prentice-Hall, 1961.
20. Patton, A., *Men, Money and Motivation*. New York: McGraw-Hill, 1961.
21. Patton, A., "What is an Executive Worth?" *Harvard Business Review*, Vol. 39, No. 2 (1961), 65–73.
22. Patton, J. A., C. L. Littlefield, and S. A. Self, *Job Evaluation*, 3rd ed. Homewood, Ill.: Irwin, 1964.
23. Reder, M. W., "Wage Determination in Theory and Practice," in N. W. Chamberlain, et al. (eds.), *A Decade of Industrial Relations Research 1946–1956*. New York: Harper & Row, 1958, pp. 64–97.
24. Shultz, G. P., and A. R. Weber, "Technological Change and Industrial Relations," in H. G. Heneman, et al. (eds.), *Employment Relations Research*. New York: Harper & Row, 1960, pp. 190–221.
25. Slichter, S. H., J. J. Healy, and E. R. Livernash, *Impact of Collective Bargaining on Management*. Washington, D.C.: The Brookings Institution, 1960.

26. Tiffin, J., and E. J. McCormick, *Industrial Psychology*, 5th ed. Englewood Cliffs, N.J.: Prentice-Hall, 1965.
27. Vroom, V. H., *Work and Motivation*. New York: Wiley, 1964.
28. Whyte, W. F., et al., *Money and Motivation*. New York: Harper & Row, 1955.
29. Winstanley, N. B., "Keeping Executive Compensation in Balance," *Personnel*, Vol. 42, No. 2 (1965), 24–33.
30. Wolf, W. B., *Wage Incentives as a Managerial Tool*. New York: Columbia Univ. Press, 1957.

Questions

1. Define and describe the following:
    a. Occupational Wage Surveys
    b. Base rate of pay
    c. Escalator clause
    d. Wage level
    e. Wage structure
2. In what ways does the job evaluation process relate to the organizational goals of productivity and maintenance?
3. Under what conditions are promotional increases, rate ranges, incentive systems, and bonuses likely to operate effectively as input-output mediators?
4. What are the advantages and disadvantages of group incentives? Under what circumstances are they most attractive?
5. What types of factors serve to exert the greatest influence on the earnings of managers at the various levels?

17

Safety Management and
Preventive Medicine

The preceding chapters have dealt with input-output mediators that contribute to the productivity or profit goal either by changing the human input in some way or by increasing motivation to work toward the company's objectives. In this chapter the focus shifts away from such maximizing processes to the somewhat more prosaic goal of maintaining organization members in good status as active contributors.

To keep employees producing at least at the level indicated by their potential when hired, it is necessary to prevent anything from happening to them that might result in a temporary or permanent reduction in output. The major sources of such "happenings" are injuries and illnesses. Thus, it becomes extremely important for business firms to take any steps possible to reduce accident frequency and severity and to eliminate anything that might contribute to the onset or prolongation of an illness. This is a humanitarian responsibility of any management, but it is also a factor in company goal attainment. Injuries and illnesses disrupt output and carry with them sizable monetary costs.

The current chapter will focus first on the various techniques that have been developed to prevent accidents, either by changing the environment to make it safer or by influencing the individual to make him less likely to fall prey to the potential danger around him. A second major topic will be the peculiar proclivity some individuals exhibit to have accidents and incur injury. A final section will then take up preventive approaches in the health area and the role of the medical profession in this regard. The various legal constraints on safety policies inherent in the workmen's compensation laws have been discussed in Chapter 6.

Safety Management Procedures

Although it is common practice to administer an accident prevention program out of a safety division, usually located within the personnel structure, committees have become an important adjunct in this area, as they have in wage and salary administration. The primary reason for this development appears to be that widespread acceptance and cooperation is essential to the success of any safety effort. To the extent a large number of individuals distributed throughout the company can be involved in the program and made to feel a part of it, actual implementation of decisions related to safety is likely to be facilitated. It is particularly important that those at the higher levels of management feel this sense of involvement.

Under normal circumstances the highest-level safety committee is established on an interdepartmental basis and is concerned primarily with policy matters. This committee has primary responsibility for establishing safety rules, for investigating particularly hazardous situations, for making expenditures related to accident prevention, and for resolving disputes.

In addition, there usually are a number of departmental committees to deal with inspection and the correction of unsafe conditions. Unlike the policy committee, the latter groups are not restricted to managerial personnel. In fact they appear to function more smoothly and effectively if there is a heavy representation from below the managerial level.

The departmental committees may also handle safety training and publicity, although frequently a separate committee structure is devoted to the specific purposes of developing and implementing programs to promote interest in safety, to obtain compliance with safety rules, and to disseminate safety knowledge. In some companies safety training committees and those concerned with inspection have taken on a joint union-management character. Less frequently the higher-level policy group also has union representation. In some instances this joint approach is necessary and even helpful, especially if the union leadership is strongly concerned about safety matters, but it does tend to introduce a number of extraneous considerations into a group decision-making process that is often rather slow-moving and cumbersome even without this additional obstacle. The result is that the joint union-management committees can become so bound up in conflict that they are incapable of action.

Accident Statistics and Reports

Accident statistics are a valuable aspect of a total safety effort for two reasons. When calculated for the company as a whole, they permit comparison against the national and industry figures provided by such organizations as the National Safety Council and the U.S. Bureau of Labor Statistics. Thus, a company can determine its position relative to other firms and set its accident prevention goals accordingly. Where the comparative statistics suggest that a major problem exists, a sizable total investment in safety procedures may be warranted. Second, when rates are determined separately for the various work units within a firm, it is possible to pinpoint trouble spots and concentrate preventive efforts with these in mind. In this way, the accident prevention process may be focused where it will do the most good.

Most accident statistics are developed using two rate formulas:

$$\text{Injury frequency rate} = \frac{\text{Number of disabling injuries} \times 1{,}000{,}000}{\text{Number of man-hours worked}}$$

$$\text{Injury severity rate} = \frac{\text{Number of days lost} \times 1{,}000{,}000}{\text{Number of man-hours worked}}$$

The usual practice is to use disabling or *lost time injuries* only in these calculations, although rates for *minor injuries* may be determined separately. Lost time injuries include deaths, permanent disabilities whether partial or total, and injuries that render a person unable to do his job for at least an entire work shift subsequent to the accident. Minor injuries are those that do not meet the above criteria but that do require treatment in a dispensary or physician's office or first aid. Because they may be used for workmen's compensation claims and reflected in absenteeism statistics, lost time injury data tend generally to be valid. Minor injuries, however, may go unreported. In calculating severity rates, standard time charges are used in the case of deaths and disabilities and actual days lost for temporary conditions.

Over the years frequency and severity rates have tended to be high or low in a particular industry. Thus, communications, electrical equipment, aircraft manufacturing, automobile, rubber, and storage and warehousing are generally low on both indexes; mining, marine transportation, construction, lumber, quarry, and transit are high. Yet there are some marked exceptions to this generalization. Steel and cement have low-frequency rates, but are well up among the various industries in severity. Wholesale and retail trade have a very low severity index, but are above the average in frequency. The electric utilities are high in terms of the severity of injuries but do not have a particularly high frequency rate. Meat packing is just the reverse, being a high-frequency industry with relatively low severity (14).

Motor vehicle accident rates are normally recorded on a separate basis for all company-owned cars or trucks. For purposes of motor safety an accident is defined as any contact with the company vehicle causing either personal injury or property damage. The rate formula is

$$\text{Motor vehicle accident frequency rate} = \frac{\text{Number of accidents} \times 100{,}000}{\text{Number of vehicle-miles operated}}$$

An attempt is usually made to compute separate rates for accidents that are chargeable against the company employee who was driving and those that do not appear to be his fault. There is some question, however, whether such efforts at differentiation are ever entirely successful. Obtaining the required information is often difficult and almost always time-consuming.

ACCIDENT REPORTS. Statistics of the type discussed are developed from accident reports that are normally prepared by the immediate superior of the man involved. The requirement that supervisors must fill out reports in this manner has the advantage that it makes the particular person who can do the most to promote safety aware of accidents occurring under his jurisdiction. Thus, it not only provides necessary information, but serves a useful educational purpose as well.

Many of the questions asked on an accident report form are noted in Figure 17-1. Several of these require explanation. For example, the accident is referred to as "alleged." This is done to protect the company against damage claims. Any report signed by a supervisor that refers in an unqualified manner to a specific accident can serve as evidence in court that the employer acknowledges responsibility in the case, whether or not the employer actually wishes to do so. And, of course, all such records can be subpoenaed. Thus, the use of "alleged" on a standard basis provides a defense against false claims.

The *agency* is the thing most closely associated with the injury. Examples are animals, boilers, chemicals, conveyors, dusts, electric apparatus, elevators, hand tools, flammable substances, hoisting apparatus, machines, radiations, and working surfaces. The *agency part* is that specific part or aspect of the agency most closely associated with the injury. The *unsafe mechanical or physical condition of the agency* refers to the aspect of the agency that could have been guarded or corrected. The categories normally used are inadequate mechanical guarding, defective condition of the agency, unsafe design of the agency, hazardous processes or procedures, incorrect illumination, incorrect ventilation, and unsafe apparel.

Figure 17-1. Typical Accident Report Form

Name of Employee _____ Location _____

Address _____ Division _____

Sex _____ Age _____ Occupation _____

Married _____ Children _____ Wage Rate _____

Date and Time of Alleged Accident _____

Place of Alleged Accident _____

Description of Alleged Accident _____

_____

_____

_____

_____

_____

_____

Working on Regular Job? _____

Agency Involved _____

Part of Agency _____

Unsafe Mechanical or Physical Condition of Agency _____

_____

Accident Type _____

Unsafe Act _____

Unsafe Personal Factor _____

Safeguards Provided _____

Safeguards in Use _____

Nature and Extent of Injury _____

_____

_____

Days Lost _____ Attending Physician _____

Recommendations to Prevent Similar Accidents _____

_____

_____

Prepared by _____ Date _____

The *accident type* refers to the type of contact of the injured person with the agency. Examples are caught in or between, struck by, struck against, fall of person, scratched, overexertion, and contact with either electricity, extreme temperatures, or noxious substances. The *unsafe act* is the type of behavior leading to the accident, such as working unsafely, performing unauthorized operations, removing safety devices, operating at unsafe speeds, use of improper equipment, using equipment unsafely, horseplay, and failure to use safe attire. The *unsafe personal factor* is the characteristic of the individual responsible for the unsafe act—unsafe attitudes, lack of knowledge, bodily defect, or disturbed emotional state (17).

Unfortunately, reports of this kind do not always yield completely valid information. Those involved in an accident, including the supervisor in charge, may well be strongly motivated to cover up certain aspects of the case to protect themselves against anticipated criticism from higher management. Thus, it is often difficult to obtain objective data. Nevertheless, experience indicates that tabulations based on questions of the kind illustrated in Figure 17-1 can yield information that is at least sufficiently valid so that major sources of difficulty can be identified.

Safety Training

There is evidence that, where the work situation is relatively hazardous, injuries are particularly likely to occur during the first few months of employment when the man has not yet learned how to protect himself against the dangers in his environment (20). Under such circumstances it becomes apparent that any kind of training, whether directed toward orientation, skills, attitudes, or anything else connected with the job, can serve a preventive purpose insofar as accidents are concerned. To the extent such early training makes a new employee more capable of coping with his work environment, it will inevitably contribute to the safety goal.

In actual practice training programs for new employees do characteristically contain considerable safety content. Items covered are special hazards in the work situation, examples of previous accidents, nature and use of safety equipment, availability of medical services, accident reporting, and safety rules. Where the work is particularly hazardous, first-aid procedures are often included.

Some firms introduce more general discussions of safety off the job into the training process. This is done because most companies, as a result of their safety efforts, have produced a situation where injuries at work are less frequent than during the rest of the day. Factories are often safer than the home. Time lost due to off-the-job injuries may well be greater than for those that are work-connected. Under such circumstances the tendency has been to include a rather broad treatment of accident prevention within the training context.

RETRAINING. Another type of safety training is directed to specific situations where there has been a deterioration in accident rates. It is not uncommon for experienced employees to develop group norms that sanction the breaking of safety rules and a failure to use protective devices. When this happens, safety training becomes an important antidote. The usual procedure is to review safety rules in a series of discussions conducted by a safety specialist. Considerable opportunity is given for open criticism of existing rules and procedures and on occasion changes are introduced in response to group decisions. Every effort is made not only to impart safety information, but to get employees personally involved in the safety effort. Some companies carry out this type of retraining on a periodic basis with all workers, irrespective of the accident rate in the group. The techniques used include lectures, reading assignments, films, television, discussions, and programmed instruction (2).

Publicity and Contests

Safety publicity can take a variety of forms. Among those commonly used are posters, booklets, special memoranda, and articles in company publications. In many instances these media are used to advertise contests that pit various work groups against each other in an effort to minimize the number of lost time accidents.

A major source of posters for industry is the National Safety Council, which provides new material monthly for a special fee in addition to membership. Many companies also print their own posters and notices. Insofar as possible these should concentrate on reminding employees of safe practices without arousing too much anxiety. Gruesome and disturbing material is simply avoided by many people; they do not look at it at all. The main function of a good poster is to attract attention and keep employees thinking about safety, not to scare them.

There is some scientific evidence that safety posters of this kind are effective as a means of reducing accidents. In one such study the introduction of posters into seven steel mills was found to produce a sizable increase in safety behavior over a six-week test period (9). Yet it remains true that many personnel managers have serious doubts regarding the value of posters.

Company publications can be used to provide information on accidents that have occurred or on hazardous situations that have been corrected. Running accounts of the results of safety contests are often provided. All these serve to promote safety consciousness, and to the extent the average employee is kept aware of the possibility of injury, he is likely to exhibit safer behavior.

Safety rules and regulations are usually printed in a separate booklet that is given wide distribution. Unfortunately these booklets rarely achieve a readership even approximating their distribution. Furthermore, some of them actually create disrespect for safety procedures rather than promote them. The reason is that there is a strong temptation for management to absolve itself of responsibility in connection with accidents by proscribing all behaviors that might conceivably prove unsafe. As a result many of the rules turn out to be entirely unrealistic and employees break them without thinking, often with the tacit approval of their supervisors. When this happens, the whole system of safety regulation tends to become denigrated, with little differentiation being made between realistic and unrealistic rules. The only way to protect against this eventuality is to keep safety restrictions to a minimum and to recognize that a rule that no one will obey and that cannot be enforced is of little value to anyone. In fact it can have a negative impact because of its influence on more appropriate regulations.

CONTESTS. All manner of contests are conducted in the safety area, in most cases with considerable success. In general the emphasis is on internal comparisons within a company, but there are some industry-wide contests such as those conducted by the National Safety Council. Perhaps most common is a competition between departments with similar accident potentials as indicated by national rates. These contests may stress maintaining a low-frequency rate or they may be concerned with the number of days without an injury. Sometimes only lost time injuries are counted; sometimes minor injuries as well. Departments may also compete against their own records for certain periods in the past. Awards are often given to individual employees working in high-accident occupations, such as truck drivers, for remaining accident-free over an extended time span.

Although contests do appear to have a generally salutary effect on injuries, there are certain negative aspects that should be recognized. One is the tendency to let down when a long accident-free period finally comes to an end. A rash of injuries can occur at such a time, if something is not done to divert interest to some new contest or record. Second, there is some tendency to cover up injuries when they occur in the context of a contest, especially if minor injuries are included. The result can be a failure to obtain needed first-aid and dispensary treatment. In addition, accident reports may not be filed when they should be, with a resulting distortion of statistics.

Control of the Working Environment

Design of the workplace, and of equipment used in it, is probably the major approach to accident prevention and the most effective. Safety devices and the like have the advantage that they not only reduce accidents but give employees a sense of confidence and security in the workplace. Anxiety levels are reduced accordingly, and a potential source of performance disruption and failure is eliminated. This is a particularly important consideration in situations that would be extremely dangerous without accident prevention devices.

Although an extended discussion of safety engineering techniques would take us well beyond the field of personnel management as it is usually defined, several points can be made. More detailed information may be obtained from the advanced texts (7,17).

The most crucial consideration is that equipment be constructed so as to introduce barriers that make it very difficult, if not impossible, for the individual to expose himself to danger. Protective clothing, guards, covers, and the like can often isolate a person from a danger source so that irrespective of what he does there is little chance of injury. In addition, controls should be designed and placed so that opportunities for erroneous use are kept to a minimum. Devices that will yield information regarding any malfunctioning or breakdown of equipment should be installed wherever possible, and they should be readily visible. Self-correcting mechanisms and automatic shutoffs are, of course, the ideal, because then danger is eliminated without the need of human intervention. But if these cannot be installed, all controls, releases, gauges, and the like should be built so as to mesh to a maximal degree with the capabilities and characteristics of the human operator.

Equipment design considerations probably constitute the major aspect of environmental control insofar as safety management is concerned, but there are other factors. Floors, stairs, ramps, elevators, and many other features must be constructed initially with safety in mind and they must be inspected continually. Fire prevention and protection is also a normal safety division function, as is protection against catastrophes such as floods, windstorms, and nuclear attack. As previously noted, automobile accidents represent a safety management concern even when only property damage is involved. Safety considerations in the design of new products and such matters as air and water pollution may also contribute to the role prescriptions of a safety manager or engineer. In all these areas plans must be developed, inspections or tests carried out, and corrective actions taken.

Safety Management and Automation

In general, automation seems to have resulted in a decreased injury rate and it should produce even more impressive results in the future. Ventilation, temperature, humidity, and noise can easily be controlled and kept at an optimal level. Materials need not be handled by the worker and thus toxic effects are minimized. Also, contact with machinery is almost nonexistent, as is most lifting and loading. Hernia cases decreased by 85 per cent at the Ford Motor Company after the introduction of automated equipment (16).

One result should be that handicapped workers will increasingly find opportunities for employment in automated industries. Yet there is reason to believe that during the period of transition to automated equipment injury rates may rise. Workers are not used to the new procedures and, unless training is extensive, feelings of nervousness and anxiety in the face of the complex electronic and mechanical systems can become acute—so acute, in fact, that the distracted workers may fall prey to accident hazards that they would otherwise avoid (11).

Maintenance work on automated equipment may prove to be the most resistant to accident prevention efforts. Electrical hazards are considerable and so is the possibility of falls. Although operating conditions can be largely standardized and the operator isolated from danger, maintenance and repair will invariably introduce unanticipated circumstances. Thus, it is here that injuries are, and will probably continue to be, most frequent and also most serious.

Accident Proneness

Accidents are most frequent in the age range from seventeen to twenty-eight and decline steadily after that to reach a low point in the late fifties and the sixties (15). Other evidence indicates that those individuals who have high injury rates in one year are the ones who are most likely to have high rates the following year (18). The data of Figure 17-2 are typical. In this instance there is a steady increase in the number of accidents experienced during the second year as a function of the first-year frequencies. Those who had no accidents the first year had an average of only .69 the second year. Those who had nine accidents the first year averaged 5.14 the second year. The same trend appears in all of the eleven separate departments represented in the combined data of Figure 17-2. Additional studies conducted to determine whether the hazards associated with specific jobs could account for these results produced negative results. When differences in job danger were controlled, the same pattern was still present in the data.

Findings of this kind are consistent with the widely held opinion that injuries are not merely a direct function of the degree to which the working environment contains hazardous features. It is true that training deficiencies and the fact that younger workers are more likely to be new on the job could account for part of the injury-age relationship. But these cannot explain all the findings. For one thing, the increase during the early years is far too marked. For another, the injury rates do not reach their highest level until age twenty-one or twenty-two, even though skill deficiencies are most pronounced among those who are younger.

Figure 17-2. Frequency of Hospital Visits in Second Year for Steel Mill Workers with Various Rates in First Year

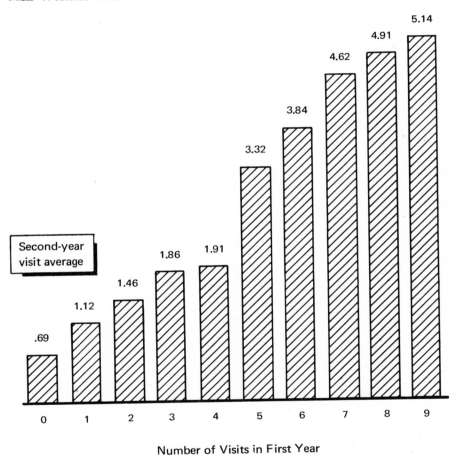

Number of Visits in First Year

Source: J. Tiffin and E. J. McCormick, *Industrial Psychology*, 5th Ed., p. 558. Copyright 1965. Used by permission of Prentice-Hall, Inc., Englewood Cliffs, N.J.

It seems, then, that contrary to the earlier view that differences in accident frequencies could be accounted for in terms of chance fluctuations (13), there are certain individuals who are consistently more susceptible to injuries than others. This tendency may well be more pronounced during a specific period of a man's life, however. Research into the personality characteristics of individuals with high-injury-frequency rates tends to support this conclusion. There do appear to be some consistent differences between these accident repeaters and those who do not have such a high injury potential.

Table 17-1. Relationships Between Sentence Completion Indexes and Accident Rates (N = 34)

Sentence completion variable	
Optimism	−.34
Trust	−.51
Sociocentricity	−.76
Pessimism	−.19
Distrust	.02
Anxiety	.09
Egocentricity	.19
Resentment	.29
Negative employment attitude	.70

Source: A. Davids and J. T. Mahoney, "Personality Dynamics and Accident-Proneness in an Industrial Setting," *Journal of Applied Psychology*, Vol. 41 (1957), p. 304.

One such study has already been discussed in Chapter 13. The results noted in Table 13-7 are reproduced in Table 17-1. The *accident-prone* individuals are clearly very negative in their attitudes. They dislike their superiors, their jobs, and work generally. Furthermore, they tend to be almost devoid of optimism and trust, and, in fact, have little positive feeling toward people at all (4).

Another investigation involved the testing of fifty-four individuals with extremely high injury-frequency rates (10). The lack of warm emotional relationships with others was again apparent. Most had a number of acquaintances, but they were not really close to these people. In addition, the negative attitudes toward those in positions of authority noted in the study just mentioned were once again present. These accident-prone individuals exhibited a marked, and often unreasonable, hatred of their superiors at work as well as of other authority figures.

There were certain other findings. The high-accident group was characterized by a great deal of concern about health matters, even though actual illness tended to be rare. There was a strong desire for increased social status coupled with very little accomplishment in this regard. Emotionally disturbing situations were often handled by misperceiving and distorting the world around them so as to make it less threatening. As a result these people made bad mistakes in judgment rather frequently. Planning for the future was apparently minimal. They preferred to live from day to day and were, in fact, quite impulsive. The latter finding fits well with data from another study that indicates that people with high injury-frequency and -severity rates are likely to act with a high degree of muscular speed even though they lack the visual capacity to comprehend a situation with equal rapidity (5). Thus, action often precedes perception and thought, which is a good description of what is meant by impulsiveness. This particular study was carried out in the metal-working department of a large factory.

Taken together, these investigations and others of a similar nature (1,19) yield a rather consistent picture of the accident-prone person, although it must be understood that a great many work injuries, perhaps the majority, involve people who do not have frequent accidents and who do not possess the characteristics found among these accident repeaters. The accident-prone seem to be rather socially irresponsible and immature, although not really emotionally ill in most cases. Because their high injury rates are not normally maintained throughout life, but only over periods of a few years, it seems most appropriate to view accident-proneness as a transient personality maladjustment that is most likely to develop in the years before age thirty.

The major motivation behind the repeated accidents themselves would appear to be a desire to impress others by resorting to sudden and very risky decisions and behavior. Research has repeatedly demonstrated the very marked "adventuresomeness" of those with high accident frequencies (8). This impulsiveness is usually combined with a strong hatred of people at higher levels in the organization and a consequent defiance of the rules and policies established by these people. Thus, safety regulations are deliberately flouted, not only as a way of impressing others with one's skill or bravery, but as a means of attacking and resisting management. Under such circumstances exposure to danger becomes unusually frequent for these employees. With an exposure level this high it is not surprising that they are in fact injured on a number of occasions. By their own actions they repeatedly place themselves in an extremely hazardous work environment, even though their jobs might not, under normal circumstances, be considered dangerous at all.

In some instances this pattern may be supplemented as a result of certain additional personality processes. Hatred toward one's superiors can on occasion generate considerable guilt, and a wish, whether conscious or unconscious, to escape this guilt by being punished. To the extent punishment is viewed as a means of atoning for one's sins, it may well be desired. For people such as this an accident may be equated with punishment, and a real desire to suffer injury may develop at periodic intervals when guilt becomes too pronounced. Here the accident is not merely a chance event in a personally created hazardous environment, but a specific outcome that is desired and directly caused. The need for self-preservation gives way before the need to expiate guilt, just as it often does in suicide cases.

Dealing with Accident-Proneness

The question remains—What can be done to reduce the frequency of personally created accidents of this kind? To some extent selection procedures may be used to screen the input on this basis, although this has not been widely done. Such an approach seems particularly desirable in high-accident-rate industries such as mining and lumber. It seems less appropriate in safer industries, where it may not be economically feasible to invest heavily in selection—to screen out a limited number of accident-prone individuals who in all likelihood would not have an extremely high rate of injury in any event because of the lower danger level.

Given the fact, then, that because of a lack of, or the imperfections of, input screening, accident-prone people are likely to be employed by any company at least in limited numbers, what can be done to deal with the problem? As the age-accident frequency relationship suggests, accident proneness tends to correct itself eventually, but not until a number of injuries have occurred, large sums have been disbursed in disability payments, and in many instances sizable output and equipment losses have accrued.

Thus, some kind of direct action does seem to be called for. One approach is to reduce the danger in the work environment as much as possible. This will have only limited impact on those who really want to injure themselves to reduce guilt, but it will yield results among the high risk-takers because there will be less chance for an accident to occur. In part, danger reduction can be achieved through equipment design and in part through transferring the accident-prone individual to low-hazard work. Equipment design is of value, however, only to the extent it takes control of the safety factor out of the hands of the employee. Protective clothing and warning devices are of little help with the accident-prone. Automatic shutoffs and fixed barriers, on the other hand, can be much more effective.

The second point relates to the hatred of people in positions of authority, which is known to characterize the accident-prone. It is when they are forced into continuing close relationships with their superiors that these individuals are most likely to be injured. In view of this, managers should, insofar as possible, keep at a distance from those who have had high accident rates. Everything possible should be done to minimize conflict and resentment. To the extent the man can work on his own with only limited restriction, control, and discipline, the chances of injury will inevitably be reduced. Appropriate supervisory techniques for use with the accident-prone can be taught as part of various management development programs (12).

Preventive Medicine

Industrial medicine involves three major aspects. The first of these, the use of the physical examination in selection and placement, has been discussed in Chapter 13. A second, the elimination of health hazards and the prevention of illness, will concern us here. The third aspect, having to do with the diagnosis and cure of existing maladies, will be covered briefly in the next chapter.

Actually treatment is not a major concern of most industrial physicians. Generally firms do not offer continuing assistance of this kind to their employees. The normal procedure is to refer an individual who becomes ill to his own personal physician, after short-term, immediate treatment is provided as required. The exceptions to this occur primarily in those instances where the work is carried out in an isolated situation. Under such circumstances, when adequate medical services are not available in the community, they are often furnished by the company. In addition, there are a few firms that make it a policy to provide extensive treatment facilities for employees. Usually, though, preventive considerations remain paramount over those of a therapeutic nature.

The Development of Industrial Medicine

In an earlier period the primary duty of the industrial physician was to give prompt treatment in connection with accident cases (3). Gradually, however, the records of such treatments, which the physician maintained, became important as a source of information on specific situations that were particularly hazardous. At the same time workmen's compensation cases involving phosphorous and lead poisoning began to appear frequently, and the industrial physician assumed an important preventive role in this area. Subsequently, management came to recognize the potential value of the physical examination both for selection purposes and, when utilized on a periodic basis, in the early identification of disorders among current employees. Periodic physical examinations of this kind are the more likely the greater the importance of the individual's work to the organization.

In recent years the preventive role of the industrial physician has spread to many other areas. He normally decides whether an employee can safely return to his job after an injury or illness. The work a handicapped person may perform is characteristically determined after a physical examination directed to this specific purpose. Recommendations regarding the shutdown or modification of hazardous situations often emanate from this source. So do company-wide programs of inoculation and similar preventive efforts. Industrial physicians and hygienists are also concerned with calculations regarding gas, dust, fume, and smoke concentrations that may prove to be noxious. They make tests on chemical compounds and atmospheric conditions to determine toxicity. They deal with situations where noise levels may be such as to produce damage to the ear. Finally, in the last few years they have become increasingly concerned with problems of radiation and with the detection of radiation hazards.

There is considerable evidence that preventive efforts of this kind do have a positive effect (6). Silicosis has been entirely eliminated in the granite sheds of the East. Lead poisoning has virtually disappeared in the paint, printing, and storage battery industries. Sick leaves have been materially shortened in many instances, with a comparable reduction in workmen's compensation payments. It seems clear that preventive medicine has contributed to employee welfare and continued productivity in much the same manner as safety management.

The Organization of Medical Services

There has been considerable discussion regarding the advantages of providing medical services through full-time professional employees who are on the company payroll, as against retaining outside specialists for this purpose. There are strong arguments pro and con. The inside physician is clearly at a disadvantage in dealing with representatives of higher management because he is entirely dependent on them for his employment. The result can be some loss of effectiveness in this area. At lower levels there may be problems in maintaining the traditional physician-patient confidential relationship because of the presence of a third party, the company.

On the other hand, it can be assumed that physicians who have accepted regular employment with a firm will not deliberately do things that are detrimental to that firm, even if on occasion because of professional considerations they do not contribute maximally to it. Private physicians, however, will normally feel a much greater commitment to the patient than to the company. Furthermore, they are not usually in a position to contribute a great deal to the prevention of illness and injury. They may or may not be able to offer prompt treatment of injuries at the time they occur. For these reasons most large corporations with sufficient demand for medical services at a single installation hire a professional staff and set up a dispensary. Smaller firms and installations of limited size within a much larger company are normally serviced by private physicians in the community, either on retainer or on a fee basis.

Even where a full-time physician is not employed, a dispensary may be operated. A local physician may be retained part-time, or a nurse may be put in charge. In larger dispensaries a number of physicians and nurses as well as various medical technicians and clerical workers may be on the staff. In some cases, especially in foreign countries, companies operate full-scale hospitals for employees, and on occasion for their dependents as well.

Such facilities can provide for a great variety of medical services. At the very minimum, however, when a physician is in residence, these include physical examinations, immediate care of injuries and illnesses, elimination and control of health hazards, maintaining medical records, and referrals to outside physicians and hospitals when appropriate.

References

1. Alexander, F., *Psychosomatic Medicine*. New York: Norton, 1950.
2. Bass, B. M., and J. A. Vaughan, *Training in Industry: The Management of Learning*. Belmont, Calif.: Wadsworth, 1966.
3. Burling, T., "Medical Ethics Versus Needs of Personnel Officers," *ILR Research*, Vol. 3, No. 1 (1956), 9–10.
4. Davids, A., and J. T. Mahoney, "Personality Dynamics and Accident-proneness in an Industrial Setting," *Journal of Applied Psychology*, Vol. 41 (1957), 303–306.
5. Drake, C. A., "Accident-proneness: A Hypothesis," *Character and Personality*, Vol. 8 (1940), 335–341.
6. French, W., *The Personnel Management Process*. Boston: Houghton Mifflin, 1964.
7. Heinrich, H. W., *Industrial Accident Prevention*, 4th ed. New York: McGraw-Hill, 1959.
8. Kunce, J. T., "Vocational Interests and Accident Proneness," *Journal of Applied Psychology*, Vol. 51 (1967), 223–225.
9. Laner, S., and R. G. Sell, "An Experiment on the Effect of Specially Designed Safety Posters," *Occupational Psychology*, Vol. 34 (1960), 153–169.
10. LeShan, L. L., "Dynamics of Accident-prone Behavior," *Psychiatry*, Vol. 15 (1952), 73–80.
11. Mann, F. C., and L. R. Hoffman, *Automation and the Worker*. New York: Holt, Rinehart and Winston, 1960.
12. Miner, J. B., *The Management of Ineffective Performance*. New York: McGraw-Hill, 1963.
13. Mintz, A., and M. L. Blum, "A Re-examination of the Accident Proneness Concept," *Journal of Applied Psychology*, Vol. 33 (1949), 195–211.
14. National Safety Council, *Accident Facts*. Chicago, Ill.: the Council.

15. Schulzinger, M. S., *The Accident Syndrome*. Springfield, Ill.: Thomas, 1956.
16. Shils, E. B., *Automation and Industrial Relations*. New York: Holt, Rinehart and Winston, 1963.
17. Simonds, R. H., and J. V. Grimaldi, *Safety Management*, rev. ed. Homewood, Ill.: Irwin, 1963.
18. Tiffin, J., and E. J. McCormick, *Industrial Psychology*, 5th ed. Englewood Cliffs, N.J.: Prentice-Hall, 1965.
19. Tillmann, W. A., and G. E. Hobbs, "The Accident-prone Automobile Driver," *American Journal of Psychiatry*, Vol. 106 (1949), 321–331.
20. Van Zelst, R. H., "The Effect of Age and Experience upon Accident Rate," *Journal of Applied Psychology*, Vol. 38 (1954), 313–317.

Questions

1. Differentiate the following:
    a. Injury frequency rate versus injury severity rate
    b. Lost time injuries versus minor injuries
    c. Unsafe act versus unsafe personal factor
2. What are the various negative features associated with each of the safety management approaches to accident reduction?
3. What is accident-proneness and how might it be minimized as a factor in company injury rates?
4. What is the role of the industrial medical department?

18

Performance Control

The preceding chapters of this part have dealt with a variety of functional input-output mediators, all of which are directed primarily toward the achievement of productivity and profit goals. These have been classified to differentiate between mediators that attempt to improve upon the quality of the original human input, mediators that are intended to maximize motivation relative to role requirements, and mediators that work toward an essentially hygienic function in that they serve to prevent output disruption from occurring. One further type of mediator remains to be discussed. An individual may in fact perform below the level of his initial promise, even to the point where a sizable disparity between role behavior and role prescriptions exists; he may fail to perform satisfactorily in one or more respects. At this point concern tends to focus on the process of performance control and on mediators that may serve a corrective function.

The discussion that follows will first take up certain details of this control model in its application to human performance. A subsequent section will deal with the factors that may cause an individual to perform in an ineffective manner. Finally, the various mediators that may be used for corrective purposes will be considered. Special attention will be given to such approaches as moving the man to another job, modifying existing personnel policy, discipline, counseling, and medical treatment.

The Control Model and Human Performance

Procedures used to correct performance deficiencies are best understood when viewed in the context of the control model. This model serves to focus attention on those cases where some deviation from an established standard occurs. With regard to performance this refers to the employee whose work behavior departs from role prescriptions so markedly that it falls below a minimum acceptable level. In specific instances of clear-cut ineffective performance, some type of corrective procedure is needed if the employee is to make any sizable contribution to company goal attainment. Thus, the process of performance control involves identifying individuals whose work is consistently below standard and taking action to restore performance to an acceptable level. In its major characteristics it is essentially comparable to production control, quality control, inventory control, and cost control.

Establishing Standards

Minimum acceptable standards are established using a variety of performance indexes of the kind discussed in Chapters 9 and 10. Any type of appraisal or evaluation variable may be used, with the single proviso that all should be related to organizational goal attainment.

The minimum acceptable level on each of these performance indexes or criteria may be established in either of two ways. The most common practice is for the immediate superior to set standards in his own mind on a judgmental basis. Under such circumstances the minimum acceptable level of performance may vary somewhat from manager to manager and even at different points in time with the same manager. A second approach that avoids this difficulty involves a more objective standard-setting process carried out by some group such as industrial engineering on a company-wide basis. Unfortunately, however, suitable objective measures of the latter kind are not always available.

Performance standards, whether established judgmentally or in a more objective manner, relate to both the productivity and the organizational maintenance goals, although it is common practice for the former to be stressed. Thus, the greatest concern tends to be with the quantity and quality of output. Other important considerations are the extent of absenteeism, impact on the work of others, contribution to internal stress and conflict, and dishonest behavior.

Performance Analysis

In areas other than personnel management the control concept has often been applied without giving detailed attention to determining the specific cause of the deviation from standard. The major concerns have tended to be with (a) establishing the standard, (b) measuring the deviation, and (c) setting up a feedback mechanism or some similar procedure to correct the deviation.

When the control model is applied in the personnel area, however, it becomes clear that corrective procedures cannot be effective unless information is available regarding the *causal* factors that have operated to produce the performance failure. The situation is essentially comparable to that which exists in medicine. A physician must make a suitable diagnosis, which identifies the *cause* of the failure to meet acceptable health standards, before he can select from among the numerous available treatments. He needs to know what specific disease entity he is dealing with. Otherwise his treatment will be on a trial and error basis and the chances for cure will be small.

Performance analysis is the name given to this process of identifying contributory causes, of diagnosing the factors that have combined to produce a given instance of performance failure (17). Basically what is involved is that a series of hypotheses are formulated regarding the possible strategic factors. Each hypothesis is then checked against what is known about the individual and either accepted or rejected. The result is a list of contributory causes that can serve to guide the selection of an appropriate corrective procedure.

Firing as an All-Purpose Solution

As indicated in Chapter 11, selection procedures cannot achieve perfection. There will inevitably be some individuals hired who either immediately or at some subsequent date will fail to perform effectively. Thus, although a judicious use of selection techniques can reduce the incidence of performance failure, the problem will still remain. Performance control cannot be entirely circumvented by concentrating on achieving a high quality of input to the organization.

One other possibility does remain, however. Could not all those who become ineffective be immediately fired, thus eliminating any need for time-consuming and costly procedures such as performance analyses and corrective actions? The answer is that although firing is always a possibility, it has become hedged with so many constraints, both internal and external to the organization, that it is often not really feasible. In addition, it can well be as costly as taking corrective action. Thus, it must be considered a last resort in most cases.

The fact that company payments toward unemployment compensation are based on an experience-rating procedure that penalizes a firm for high involuntary turnover rates tends to exert pressure against firing. Furthermore, a number of companies have policies requiring severance payments to individuals who are separated against their will subsequent to an initial probationary period. Although these may not always be paid in discipline cases, a unionized firm that utilizes firing extensively as a solution to performance failure can expect to make severance payments in a relatively large number of instances.

This is only one of the pressures related to unionization. If there is a possibility that the dismissal represents an unfair labor practice in that the firing occurred because of union activity, a firm may have to reinstate with back pay. This can be ordered by a Labor Relations Board or by the courts. Even if the company wins such a case, the investment in time and money is likely to be sizable. In any event formal grievances are nearly always filed in discharge cases and in many instances these require outside arbitration. In one series of over 300 discharges appealed to an arbitrator, only 46 per cent were sustained. In 19 per cent of the cases the man was reinstated with full back pay; the remainder were reinstated but with some pay loss (1).

Strikes in response to a firing that is considered unfair are frequent in firms that do not have a clause incorporated in the union contract that bars such work stoppages. Even where a no-strike agreement does apply over the period of the agreement, slowdowns and other types of retaliatory action may occur. The only solution to these varied union pressures may be eventual reinstatement.

Internal pressures against firing need not, of course, be mediated through the union. Individuals or groups of employees may consider a discharge inequitable and take action to make things difficult for the responsible manager or retaliate against the company in some way. Even where a manager does not view such an eventuality as likely, he may hesitate to fire because of the enmity his action might create or because he himself would feel guilty were he to discharge the man. Especially in the case of long-service employees, strong social pressures against firing are characteristic in the business world generally.

Externally there is always the possibility that a company that frequently resorts to discharge may create an image for itself in the community that severely restricts the available labor market. The number and quality of applicants may be sharply curtailed, and recruiting costs may rise considerably. In some instances, too, antagonism toward the company resulting from a high discharge rate may influence the sale of products and other types of business dealings. Thus, both the product and the labor markets may suffer.

Finally there are all the costs associated with personnel turnover of any kind:

1. The cost of recruiting and selecting a replacement
2. The cost of training a replacement
3. The costs associated with overpayment of the replacement during the period of learning when he cannot produce at full capacity
4. The cost of breakage and waste during the learning period and of any accidents that may occur
5. The cost of any overtime work put in by others during the period between firing one man and the achievement of full capacity by another
6. The cost of production losses due to the lack of a man to perform the job between firing and replacement, plus the similar costs attributable to the process of achieving an adjustment between the work group and its new member
7. The costs resulting from a failure to fully utilize equipment during the replacement's training period (21)

Taken as a whole, this rather imposing array of factors exerts a strong pressure for performance control rather than discharge. Certainly, firing is not an impossibility, but it is often a last resort. As an all-purpose solution to ineffective performance it is clearly inappropriate. As a solution when corrective action is known to be either impossible or inexpedient, it seems preferable to letting the employee stay on indefinitely while remaining entirely unsatisfactory.

A Schema for Performance Analysis

Intensive study of a large number of cases where performance failures have occurred has resulted in the development of a schema that appears to cover at least the great majority of the factors that may prove strategic (7,17). The elements of the schema may be treated as hypotheses that should be considered either implicitly or explicitly in the process of performance analysis or, to use the medical term, diagnosis. Each hypothesis is checked against all available information and either confirmed or rejected.

The number of confirmed hypotheses or strategic factors that will emerge from this process varies considerably from case to case. Job failure is rarely a result of a single cause. Usually the number of contributory factors runs to something like four, but in an occasional instance it can be as high as seven or eight. People fail because they, with their own particular pattern of abilities and personality characteristics, become enmeshed in a specific constellation of circumstances. The problem is to spell out exactly which among these individual and environmental factors have in fact played a causal role.

Intelligence and Job Knowledge

INSUFFICIENT VERBAL ABILITY. As noted in Chapter 3, the higher up in the job hierarchy a position is located, the greater its demand in terms of verbal ability or general intelligence. Given this circumstance, it is not surprising that on occasion people attain a level where the role requirements are intellectually beyond them. At such times failure is likely to be reflected in a high incidence of errors and incorrect decisions.

The available evidence suggests that underplacement on the basis of verbal ability is not generally a problem. At least it seems clear that a great many people are working in jobs that demand much less intellectually than they could give (15). Yet under certain circumstances, especially where advancement opportunities are severely restricted, underplacement can be a source of difficulty, although usually in interaction with certain personality factors.

INSUFFICIENT SPECIAL ABILITY OTHER THAN VERBAL. Various jobs, irrespective of their level in the hierarchy, require widely differing types of intellectual abilities. Numerical, spatial, mechanical, clerical, and other abilities are relevant for some types of work and not for others. To the extent an individual lacks whatever such abilities may be required, he is likely to fail through an inability to think effectively and learn rapidly. Having abilities that are not utilized in a job constitutes less of a problem, unless the desire to use the ability is particularly strong.

INSUFFICIENT JOB KNOWLEDGE. Insufficient job knowledge cannot be attributed to lack of ability. The individual has the intellectual capacity to learn the job, but either because of inadequate training or for some other reason, he has not done so. In some instances the difficulty stems from a lack of any real desire to take advantage of learning opportunities or from emotional blocks to learning.

DEFECT OF JUDGMENT OR MEMORY. In most cases defects of judgment or memory reflect the interference of emotional factors with intellectual processes. On standard intelligence tests the individual may score quite high, but when it comes to applying his intelligence on the job, the results are not as good. Defects of this kind are particularly frequent among those suffering from some type of emotional disorder, but they can also result from a disturbance in brain functioning, such as might occur as a result of a head injury.

Emotions and Emotional Illness

CONTINUING DISRUPTIVE EMOTION. As noted, emotions can serve to disrupt intellectual functioning to produce defects of judgment and memory. They can also, if intense enough and frequent enough, have a detrimental impact on many other aspects of job behavior. This is particularly true of negative emotional states such as anxiety and fear, depression, shame, and guilt. But failure can also occur as a result of persistent anger, jealousy, and excitement. The individual need not be emotionally ill for a severe impact on the level of work performance to manifest itself. The result may be a number of errors, an inability to concentrate so that output is slowed, a tendency to be constantly immersed in controversy, or, and this is perhaps most frequent, a continuing avoidance of many required job behaviors.

PSYCHOSIS. Psychoses, like the neuroses to be discussed next, manifest themselves in a variety of symptoms that take on an inflexible character and serve to disrupt many of the ongoing processes of life. In a psychosis the preoccupation with symptoms, emotions, and the warding off of unpleasant feelings becomes so intense that a real break with reality occurs, at least at certain times and under certain circumstances. Symptoms vary from incessant emotional states to disorders of physical functioning, to pathological behavior and speech, and even to extreme distortions of perception and belief. Although the various psychotic conditions represent relatively rare phenomena insofar as the work environment is concerned, their impact on performance is generally marked. Often the man cannot continue work at all while in the psychotic state.

NEUROSIS. The neuroses, although milder in their impact on the personality, may on occasion have just as detrimental an effect on work performance as psychoses. This appears to depend to a considerable extent on the job level, however.

As Table 18-1 demonstrates, true emotional health is found much more frequently at the higher occupational levels. In lower-level positions of a repetitive nature, symptoms of emotional disorder, primarily those associated with neuroses, are much more common, and in these particular jobs the detrimental effects appear to be minimal (13). Thus, in such positions it cannot be presumed that if a neurosis is present, it will account for any ineffective performance that may appear. At higher levels, on the other hand, neuroses are typically quite disruptive. Whether the high incidence of poor mental health in low-level factory positions is primarily attributable to the impact of the routine work on the individual (11) or to the fact that the emotionally ill gravitate to such jobs (18) remains an open question. There is evidence for both views. In any event it seems clear that people *can* be overplaced emotionally, as well as intellectually.

Individual Motivation to Work

STRONG MOTIVES FRUSTRATED AT WORK. Probably the most common type of motivationally caused performance failure is the case where an individual wants something very much from his job and is unable to attain it. Among the things desired that seem to be important in this sense are success, the avoidance of all failure, domination of others, popularity, social interaction, attention, emotional support, and freedom from any anxiety that may have become associated with certain job aspects. When such motives are frustrated, the individual may leave his job, may stay on but make practically no effort, may become sullen and angry, or may attempt to achieve what he wants through behavior that is antithetical to effective job performance.

Table 18-1. Mental Health Differences Beween Factory Occupational Groups

Occupational category	Young (20–29)		Middle-aged (40–49)	
	Proportion with high mental health, %	Number of workers	Proportion with high mental health, %	Number of workers
Skilled			56	45
	58	33		
High semiskilled			41	98
Ordinary semiskilled	35	46	38	82
Repetitive semiskilled	10	30	26	73
Total workers		109		298

Source: A. Kornhauser, *Mental Health of the Industrial Worker.* New York: Wiley, 1965, p. 57.

UNINTEGRATED MEANS TO SATISFY MOTIVES. Workers who resort to behavior that is not job-integrated may not actually experience any frustration of a strong motive at work. Many people almost immediately develop an approach to a new job that permits motive satisfaction, but at the expense of fulfilling role requirements. A secretary who desires social interaction may make friends rapidly and spend most of her time talking to others, to the detriment of their performance and her own. Similarly, theft and other forms of dishonesty may represent a rapid route to the goal of success.

EXCESSIVELY LOW PERSONAL WORK STANDARDS. Another possibility in the area of motivation involves the individual who sets very low work standards for himself, standards well below those considered minimally acceptable either by his superior or in the company as a whole. There is evidence that individuals who have such low standards, as well as those with unrealistically high standards, do tend to be poor workers (9). Apparently they achieve a sense of personal success and accomplishment with a degree of effort far below that actually required.

GENERALIZED LOW WORK MOTIVATION. These are individuals whose motivational systems are so structured that their important desires tend to be satisfied outside the work situation, or at least through behavior that is not included within the role prescriptions for any job. In such cases there is practically no mesh between the individual and the world of work at all, and as a consequence the quantity, and perhaps quality also, of the man's output will be low, quite irrespective of the position held.

Physical Characteristics and Disorders

PHYSICAL ILLNESS OR HANDICAP. The major avenue through which physical disorders contribute to ineffective performance is absence from the job, although quantity and quality of output may also be affected. And there may even be an increase in uncooperative, conflict-producing behavior, such as occurs with certain kinds of brain disorder. Handicapped employees have generally proved as competent as other workers, if their handicaps do not bar working at all (2), but in some instances certain disabilities may contribute to failure in specific jobs. There are things that the deaf, the blind, those with heart conditions, epileptics, and other handicapped people just cannot do effectively.

PHYSICAL DISORDERS OF EMOTIONAL ORIGIN. A number of physical symptoms such as headaches, fainting, ulcers, high blood pressure, hay fever, backache, and skin disorders may be caused by emotional factors. When this is the case, the symptoms and the work disruption are identical to that which would exist if no emotional element were present; only the causation is different. Yet, to select an appropriate corrective action, disorders of this kind must be differentiated from those due entirely to physical illness or handicap.

INAPPROPRIATE PHYSICAL CHARACTERISTICS. Inappropriate physical characteristics are the features of bodily proportion and aesthetics that although not widely significant may become strategic in certain jobs. A large man may have difficulty working in a cramped space, as may a small man in a truck cab with the seat far removed from the controls, or an unattractive woman in a modeling position. Many physical characteristics are less important today, what with the advent of human engineering and the consequent emphasis on designing equipment to fit the human operator, but these factors can become crucial at times.

INSUFFICIENT MUSCULAR OR SENSORY ABILITY. As noted in Chapter 3, a variety of muscular dexterities and abilities, as well as the purely intellectual abilities, may influence job performance. Where there is a deficiency in some ability of this kind that is required by the job, ineffectiveness can result. Strength and physical dexterities do appear to have decreasing relevance as automation advances, but they still can be a factor in failure on some jobs. Defects and deficiencies of vision and hearing also remain a significant source of problems in many cases. Competence in driving a truck, for instance, is strongly influenced by such sensory abilities.

Family Ties

FAMILY CRISES. There are a number of significant events occurring in the home environment that can have an impact on the personality of certain individuals that is sufficient to disturb work performance. Among these are desertion, divorce, threatened divorce, illness of a family member, death, or criminal prosecution. Normally these effects are transitory, but on occasion the performance decrement is maintained for a considerable period. Unfortunately, such crises do not always come to the attention of a personnel manager and as a result the frequency with which they are strategic may be markedly underestimated.

SEPARATION FROM THE FAMILY. The mere fact of extended separation from either the parental family or a wife and children can produce a very intense homesickness in some individuals. Business trips, temporary assignments out of town, management development programs at universities, and the like can induce considerable anxiety in some people, especially those who have rarely been away from home before. The result can be a severe disruption of performance during the period of absence, with frequent errors, poor decisions, and difficult interpersonal relationships.

PREDOMINANCE OF FAMILY CONSIDERATIONS OVER WORK DEMANDS. In contrast to the family crises, there are factors that do not represent a threat to the family's unity or survival. Yet they can, and frequently do, have a considerable impact on performance. A demanding wife can require so much of her husband's time that he has little left for work. Or a wife may become disturbed at leaving her home town, or going to a foreign country, and impose a severe burden on her husband as a result. Certain family situations are little short of chaos, and some carryover into the work situation is inevitable. Competition between father and son or wife and husband may well produce emotional reactions that permeate the job.

The Groups at Work

NEGATIVE CONSEQUENCES ASSOCIATED WITH GROUP COHESION. Chapter 16 contained an extended discussion of how restriction of output within a cohesive group can yield a low level of production that is, nevertheless, socially sanctioned. Although it is common to observe a generally centralizing tendency among group members when restriction occurs, it is also true that some individuals may be forced below the minimum acceptable level of output by the restricted standard. These are typically low producers who are incapable of gauging their work sufficiently well to remain above the unacceptable level when a low group standard is established.

Also, groups with a marked sense of cohesiveness or belongingness can reject members whom they believe to be deviant. Although such ostracism may have no effect on some people, it is extremely threatening to others. The result can be intense anxiety or anger that constantly disrupts work.

INEFFECTIVE MANAGEMENT. The discussion of management appraisal techniques in Chapter 9 was preceded by a review of studies dealing with the behavior of effective and ineffective managers. Using the terminology of the Ohio State research, it was found that managers who were inconsiderate of subordinates and those who failed to initiate structure were particularly likely to have low-producing groups (27). It is also apparent that a similar lack of consideration or a failure to establish and enforce standards can contribute to the ineffective performance of specific subordinates. It is not at all uncommon for supervisory action to conflict with subordinate personality patterns and as a result actually produce failure, even where just the opposite result is desired.

INAPPROPRIATE MANAGERIAL STANDARDS OR CRITERIA. As previously indicated, the criteria on which subordinates are judged are usually set by their superiors, as are the performance standards used to determine effectiveness. In certain cases these may be established without any reference to organizational goals. Thus, failure may be embedded in the evaluative process rather than in the individual. Because of supervisory biases, standards may be set at an unrealistically high level. Or the criteria employed may be totally irrelevant to role prescriptions and the company's goals. In such instances the failure may be by definition only. This is one of the few cases where only one factor may be strategic.

The Company

INSUFFICIENT ORGANIZATIONAL ACTION. Job failure may occur or be perpetuated because the company does not take the kind of corrective action required. Medical treatment, training, and the like simply may not be provided, either intentionally or through some oversight. In either case the lack of action on the part of the company or its representatives in the personnel area can become strategic.

The decision not to invest in corrective action may be based on various considerations. The cost may be too high. The time required to restore effective performance may be too long, as with certain kinds of education and training. The chances of success, if the best available type of corrective action is applied, may be far from good. This is true, for instance, of psychotherapy with certain kinds of emotional disorders. Finally, potentially effective replacements may be readily available so that any sizable investment in correction that may be required seems to be unwise.

PLACEMENT ERROR. Placement error probably appears in more cases than any other. It is particularly prevalent where random assignment policies, seniority, or union pressures govern the placement process and where there is accordingly little effort to put individuals with known characteristics in appropriate jobs. If intellectual, emotional, motivational, or physical factors are strategic, there is nearly always a placement error.

ORGANIZATIONAL OVERPERMISSIVENESS. On occasion a company will operate under such lax and permissive personnel policies and procedures that employees are actually encouraged not to work. When circumstances of this kind exist, individuals with certain types of motivational patterns may become ineffective as a result.

A company may, for instance, encourage insubordination through a lack of discipline. Excessive training, far beyond that required for complete learning, can foster a feeling that actual on-the-job production is unimportant. Liberal sick-leave policies can result in excessive absenteeism. In all these cases there is a deficiency in organizational action of a kind that interacts with individual motives to produce job failure in specific employees.

EXCESSIVE SPAN OF CONTROL. In some cases a manager may fail to deal effectively with a particular subordinate and thus contribute to a performance failure, not because of any inadequacy in himself as a manager, but because there simply is not sufficient time. The number of individuals supervised, the span of control, may be so great that the manager cannot deal with his subordinates as individuals, carrying out performance analyses and the like. Here the deficiency is not in the manager, and thus a group factor is not strategic. Rather, the organizational structure has been established in such a way as to preclude effective action by a superior aimed at preventing performance failure.

INAPPROPRIATE ORGANIZATIONAL STANDARDS OR CRITERIA. Inappropriate organizational standards or criteria is the counterpart of the inappropriate managerial standards or criteria category discussed under the work group heading. In this instance, however, the focus is on standards set as a result of organizational policy or high-level decisions, rather than on those established by individual superiors.

Society and Its Values

APPLICATION OF LEGAL SANCTIONS. "Application of legal sanctions" is introduced to cover those cases in which an individual is unable to perform his job duties because he has committed a crime and been sent to jail. Under such circumstances societal values are strategic in the sense that they form the base on which the legal structure is erected.

ENFORCEMENT OF SOCIETAL VALUES BY MEANS NOT CONNECTED WITH THE ADMINISTRATION OF THE LAW. Although society obtains compliance with its values in large part through the agency of the legal process and police action, it is also true that pressure may be exerted outside the law. Thus, a salesman may fail because no one will buy from him after he has committed some act that his potential customers consider unethical or immoral. In cases of this kind it is the enforcement of the societal value structure that produces the ineffective performance, but the source of enforcement is not connected with the legal process.

CONFLICT BETWEEN JOB DEMANDS AND CULTURAL VALUES. The most frequent type of strategic factor involving societal values is the situation in which an individual holds strong convictions that are in conflict with the role prescriptions for his job. Intense commitments to equity and fair play, to individual freedom, and to morality can contribute to job failure, even though all are highly valued in the society as a whole. It is not uncommon for industrial scientists, for instance, with a strong belief in freedom of inquiry, to become incensed at the restrictions of a bureaucratic organization. Similarly, salesmen with a particularly strong sense of honesty are very likely to fail because they view the behavior required of them on the job as basically dishonest (16).

Situational Forces

NEGATIVE CONSEQUENCES OF ECONOMIC FORCES. Negative consequences of economic forces usually occur in conjunction with an emotional or motivational factor. Competing firms, or economic conditions generally, operate to produce a situation in which an employee cannot achieve at a level consistent with his standards. As a result he becomes emotionally distressed and eventually his performance does not even come up to what could realistically be expected under the existing circumstances. Problems of this kind are particularly common among salesmen who are assigned to economically depressed territories or who face sharp price cutting by competitors.

NEGATIVE CONSEQUENCES OF GEOGRAPHICAL LOCATIONS. A similar type of reaction may occur as a result of being forced to work in an inappropriate geographical location. Being sent to a foreign country is very disturbing to some individuals because of the strangeness of the world and people around them. This reaction may be totally unrelated to the fact of separation from loved ones at home. Some people experience debilitating physical symptoms in certain climates, and a sailor who is prone to seasickness may well never achieve a satisfactory performance level when he is at sea. In all such cases something associated with the geographical location of the work makes effective performance impossible.

DETRIMENTAL CONDITIONS OF WORK. Many of the environmental forces impinging on an individual on the job derive from the various groups of which he is a member—his family, the work group, the company, society. Others derive from the aspects of the situational context already noted—other economic organizations and the geographical location. Equally effective as situational forces are the physical characteristics of the actual working environment—the noise level, the amount and type of illumination, the temperature, and various aspects of the design of the work place or the equipment in it. To the extent this working environment contains features that do not mesh with the physical capacities and characteristics of the individual, or on occasion with his intellectual, emotional, or motivational makeup, it can contribute markedly to employee performance failure.

EXCESSIVE DANGER. One aspect of the physical work context that appears to be sufficiently important to warrant separate attention is the danger level. The preceding chapter dealt with this topic at some length. A work environment with a high built-in accident potential can contribute to excessive absenteeism. It can elicit anxiety, too, and thus interfere with output.

SUBJECTIVE DANGER. It is also true that an individual may read much more danger into a situation than actually exists. Fears associated with heights, airplanes, closed places, and the like are common. Almost any aspect of the work context can serve to produce such reactions in certain people. And when this happens, the individual experiences emotions comparable to those aroused under really dangerous conditions. Subjective danger situations of this kind stimulate sufficient anxiety in some instances to make any work effort impossible. In other cases the emotion serves only to distract, producing errors and reduced output.

The Role of the Industrial Clinical Psychologist in Performance Analysis
   It should be apparent that precise answers to the questions noted can be obtained only when there is considerable information available regarding the individual. The more that is known about an employee, the better the performance analysis. In large part the required information can be obtained by observing behavior on the job and by talking to the employee himself and others who know him. This any competent manager can do.

   There is, however, another source of data that normally requires extensive psychological training to utilize effectively. A battery of psychological tests combined with an intensive clinical interview can provide much information. However, to use these tools well requires a background in personality theory and considerable knowledge of various psychological tests. Projective measures are particularly helpful, but using them effectively in connection with a performance analysis is a complex task (22,26). Normally, work at the graduate level in personnel management, industrial psychology, and clinical psychology is required. Such an industrial clinical psychologist can make a major contribution in carrying out difficult performance analyses, where the strategic factors are numerous and complexly interrelated. Even in somewhat simpler cases a psychological evaluation can expedite the finding of a solution.

Corrective Procedures

A number of the input-output mediators discussed in preceding chapters may be used as corrective procedures to restore effective performance in a man who has failed. Because applications of these mediators in the area of performance control were not noted previously, it seems appropriate to do so now. Subsequent sections will then take up corrective techniques that have a more specific connection with the performance control process.

One obvious approach is to redesign the job so that it more closely approximates the individual's capabilities. Thus, through the processes of organization planning and job analysis new role prescriptions may be established to fit the intellectual, physical, or personality characteristics of a specific person. Behaviors that the individual finds difficult or impossible are no longer required; new behaviors that are within his repertoire are introduced. This is feasible, of course, only within certain limits. Beyond these, transfer to a new position is usually more appropriate.

In addition to this application of structural mediators, a number of the functional mediators discussed previously may be used as corrective procedures. Thus, management development and training may serve to overcome knowledge lacks, to change an individual's motivation relative to job requirements, and to introduce new skills of a physical nature. Furthermore, management development as applied to the ineffective individual's immediate superior may so change the superior that he becomes capable of restoring effective performance in his subordinate. In this way management development is used to improve the leadership environment.

When motivation is strategic, alterations in the payment process may prove useful. Shifting an employee from salary to a partial or total incentive may arouse appropriate motivation. In other instances the security of a guaranteed salary may be what is needed. In general, where motivational problems are present and pay is known to be a relevant factor, providing an opportunity to earn more money in return for effective job-integrated behavior appears to be an appropriate solution.

Transfer, Promotion, and Demotion

The changing of an employee from one position to another may occur for a number of reasons. It may be that, owing to shifts in technology, new product lines, or a reorganization, certain jobs must be eliminated. Expanded or contracted operations almost always involve numerous job changes. The process of *bumping*, whereby men with greater seniority move down to lower-level positions when layoffs are required, is commonly provided for in union contracts. Reassignments for training and development purposes are also widespread. Thus, moving a man into a new position is not merely a way of correcting performance deficiencies, although this is a common consideration.

When such a change of job is carried out, it may be done to overcome the impact of almost any type of strategic factor. The important thing is that the new position have role prescriptions that the individual can meet. Thus, in the intellectual area a demotion is usually required if the employee has been overplaced on verbal ability, but a lateral transfer will normally be sufficient to overcome deficiencies in other abilities. Jobs with emotional, motivational, and physical requirements that are more appropriate to the individual can often be located. When separation from the family is a problem, this can be corrected by transferring the employee to a job in which separation is not necessary. A more suitable work group or type of supervision can be achieved through reassignment. So, too, can a value climate better fitted to the individual, or a more appropriate working situation.

The only strategic factors that cannot under any circumstances be overcome by placement changes are some in the company or organizational category. In these cases the causal process continues to operate irrespective of the particular job, because it reflects company-wide policies or philosophies as applied to all positions.

In actual practice, however, placement change is not the all-purpose corrective action it appears to be. Most firms, especially the smaller ones, do not have enough kinds of positions available to permit the transfer of all their ineffective workers to more appropriate jobs. Thus, the potential value of reassignment as a corrective procedure is limited by the kinds of openings that can be found in any given company.

TRANSFER. Strictly speaking, a transfer involves shifting an individual to another job at the same grade level, as determined by job evaluation. In some companies such shifts are relatively easy to accomplish, if they appear to provide an adequate means of improving performance. In other cases they are so restricted by seniority provisions, supervisory prerogatives, and craft demarcations that there is little a personnel manager can do, even when he is sure he has a potential solution to a particular failure situation. In any event it is important that supervisors not be permitted to foist their unsatisfactory workers on unsuspecting colleagues without reference to performance considerations. A transfer will achieve a corrective purpose only if there is good reason to believe the man will succeed in the new position.

Where transfers (or promotions) involve moving the employee's family, help is often provided by the company. Management employees nearly always get monetary assistance of this kind. At lower levels moving expenses may or may not be paid, but they are much more likely to be covered if the transfer is initiated by the company than if it is employee-requested (19). Some firms also assist in the sale of a home.

PROMOTION. It may seem strange to consider promotion as a solution to problems of performance failure, yet in clear-cut cases of underplacement, where an employee is strongly motivated to do the things a higher position requires and perhaps also to achieve the status that goes with such a job, promotion can work. On the other hand, where the employee seems hesitant about moving up in the job hierarchy, promotion is normally not a good solution.

In handling any promotion there is always the problem of the unsuccessful candidates. This difficulty is accentuated in cases in which an employee who is failing in his current job is to be the one selected. Organizational maintenance considerations may, in fact, weigh so heavily that promotion cannot be applied as a solution even though it is clearly appropriate on all other grounds. If the employee can be promoted into a different work unit, this may help to minimize conflict somewhat. Certainly the crucial consideration is that he actually make good. Promoting a poor performer who then merely continues to fail will inevitably create long-term dissension and feelings of inequity.

DEMOTION. Moving an employee to a lower-level position is a more common solution to performance deficiency than promotion. It is most appropriate when there has been overplacement either on intellectual or emotional grounds. At such times resistance to the change is likely to be minimal, if the employee has actually experienced failure in his current position over a continuing period. In fact, in the writer's experience actual requests for demotion under such circumstances are not at all uncommon. Even when the employee does resist, this reaction is normally short-lived, if he is able to perform satisfactorily on the new job and achieves a sense of freedom from the anxieties associated with failure. Should this not be the case, however, continued and often vociferous resistance can be expected. The demotion solution must achieve its goal.

Personnel Policy Modification

Policies are formulated to apply to all employees of a company or, on occasion, to certain clearly defined groups. They limit the discretion of individual managers by serving as commands when certain indicated circumstances arise. They provide decision-making criteria so that consistency of action can be maintained across the company, and thus they obviate the need for frequent repetition of an extended decision-making process. In this sense they foster economy of time and effort. In some cases they represent abstractions or generalizations that are in fact retrospective recognitions of existing decision guides. But in other cases policies are a means to establishing new role prescriptions and thus a source of organizational change (10).

Yet a policy can contribute to ineffective performance, either because it is poorly thought out and formulated or because in a given instance it happens to have a negative impact on a specific individual. In the former case policy modification means changing the policy or perhaps eliminating it entirely. When this is done, it may be possible to carry out actions with regard to an employee in areas such as placement, discipline, payment, training, and the like that were not previously possible. In those company-caused instances of failure where transfer, promotion, or demotion are inappropriate as solutions because all jobs are affected equally by a policy, modification of this kind may be the only answer.

Changing or eliminating a policy is not an easy task, and at times it is clearly not desirable. An appropriate alternative may be to modify the policy only in the sense of permitting an exception. Such an exception can allow for the solution of a relatively unique instance of ineffective performance while leaving the overall policy structure intact. In general, exceptions to policy should be kept to a minimum and sanctioned only at the highest levels. They should be recorded in writing, so that if a number of exceptions are required in the same area, this fact can be ascertained and a basis for policy revision provided (14).

The sources from which personnel policies emerge, and thus the points at which modifications can be made, vary considerably (20). Many firms have high-level personnel policy committees; others subsume this function under a general management committee. In some cases policy emerges from the decisions of individual executives, usually those with specific responsibilities in a particular policy area. The result of this approach can be a lack of integration among the policies applied to different personnel problems. Some chief executives attempt to overcome this failure of coordination by making the personnel policies themselves, or at least by exerting a strong influence on the policy-making process. In some instances an *ad hoc* approach predominates. Companies that operate in this manner attempt to distill policy out of the decisions of the past, using various records, minutes of meetings, and memoranda. Whatever the approach, it is important that procedures for obtaining feedback on the effects of a policy at lower levels be introduced and that provision be made for modification either through permanent revision or special exception.

Threat, Punishment, and Disciplinary Action

One type of corrective action that may be applied in instances where motivational factors are strategic is the use of managerial power to either threaten or actually invoke sanctions against an individual. In this way motivation appropriate to job role prescriptions may be aroused and effective behavior restored. This approach is particularly useful when standards of conduct or productivity are low and new standards must be introduced. Unfortunately, however, threat and discipline are often applied in cases where the failure is not due to motivational causes that can be corrected in this manner. At such times, where the performance analysis has been faulty or nonexistent, the use of punishment may do more harm than good.

A resort to negative sanctions in an effort to restore effective performance may take one of two courses, although in any given case both may be invoked eventually. One approach is for a supervisor or personnel representative to demand improved performance and couple this demand with a threat of future managerial action if improvement does not occur. The threat may be implicit or explicit, but the entire process is relatively informal and does not usually involve any written statement or record.

FORMAL DISCIPLINARY ACTION. The alternative to this is a formal disciplinary action carried out in the manner specified by company rules or in the union contract. In many instances this results in an appeal through the grievance machinery. Actions of this kind are normally recorded in writing and become a part of the man's personnel file. The entire approach is strongly legalistic.

Disciplinary actions take varying forms depending on the nature and frequency of the behavior defined as ineffective. The kinds of penalties that can be expected to withstand union attack, should such an action be subjected to review by an outside arbitrator, are reflected in Table 18-2 (27). Other students of arbitration decisions reach somewhat different conclusions with regard to specific violations (23), although the general sequence of warning, suspension, and discharge for successive infractions appears to be widely accepted.

At one time it was common practice to insert a table similar to Table 18-2 directly into the union contract, specifying the required penalty for each type of violation. At present the tendency is to vary the penalty somewhat depending on circumstances and to leave the basic contract open on these matters; supplementary agreements at the local level are common and plant or shop rules normally go into the specifics of disciplinary action. Usually there is at least a reference to management's right to apply discipline for *just cause* in the master contract. The implication is that there must be grounds for the action in the employee's

Table 18-2. Examples of Work Rule Violations and Penalties

Violation	Penalties for single violation and repetitions in a 12-month period *		
	First	Second	Third
Unexcused absenteeism	Warning	5-Day suspension	Discharge
Unexcused, excessive lateness	Warning	3-Day suspension	5-Day suspension
Leaving without permission	Warning	3-Day suspension	Discharge
Loafing and loitering	Warning	3-Day suspension	Discharge
Sleeping and reading	3-Day suspension	Discharge	
Soliciting and selling	Warning	3-Day suspension	5-Day suspension
Creating unsanitary conditions	Warning	3-Day suspension	5-Day suspension
Disorderly conduct, fighting	3-Day suspension	Discharge	
Intent to harm people or property	Discharge		
Drinking	Warning	5-Day suspension	Discharge
Drunkenness	5-Day suspension	Discharge	
Gambling	3-Day suspension	Discharge	
Possession of narcotics	Discharge		
Possession of firearms	Discharge		
Violation of safety rules	Warning	3-Day suspension	Discharge
Unauthorized smoking	Warning	Discharge	
Negligence causing injury or expense	5-Day suspension	Discharge	
Stealing	Discharge		
Falsification of records	Discharge		
Performing other than company work	Warning	Discharge	
Insubordination, refusal to work	Discharge		
Slowdown of production	Warning	Discharge	

* For violations where discharge is not recommended by the third offense in a 12-month period, it is recommended for a fourth offense.

Source: Adapted from J. B. Wollenberger, "Acceptable Work Rules and Penalties: A Company Guide," *Personnel*, Vol. 40, No. 4 (1963), pp. 24–28.

behavior and that the punishment should be appropriate to the violation. In actual practice supervisors do not resort to disciplinary actions nearly as often as they could in terms of the actual infractions that occur (12). This may be due to a recognition that discipline is not an appropriate corrective procedure in many cases, but it may also reflect a fear of employee retaliation and the anticipation that support for the action will not be forthcoming at higher managerial levels.

The mildest of the formal disciplinary actions is an official warning. This is prepared in writing and signed by the employee, usually in the presence of a union representative. If the employee does not sign, the case goes immediately into the grievance procedure.

Disciplinary layoff, or suspension without pay, for varying periods is a common practice. Most companies do not normally suspend in this manner for more than a week, but longer periods are utilized on occasion. This is the most extreme type of discipline available to management short of discharge. And discharge is not a corrective action, but an admission of failure.

Demotion may also be used in a disciplinary sense, although this is relatively rare. The question of whether the employee will do any better on the new lower-level job than he did on the old one must be considered, and the answer is often negative. Temporary demotions with an understanding that good performance would result in the employee being restored to his old position could be used, but these are difficult to administer in the legalistic context that has come to surround the disciplinary process.

Personnel and Psychological Counseling

The history of counseling in industry began with a department established in the Ford Motor Company in 1914 to advise employees on personal affairs and to assist them with health, legal, and family problems (3). The approach was strongly directive and permeated with Henry Ford's own personal philosophies. The result was considerable employee resistance and an eventual abandoning of the program. Similar large-scale efforts have been initiated in a number of firms, most notably the Western Electric Company, where counseling was introduced as an aspect of the Hawthorne studies (4). In almost every instance these comprehensive programs have failed to survive over an extended period.

In recent years industrial counseling has tended to focus more on specific types of employee problems, has involved the industrial clinical psychologist to a much greater extent, and has been more widely viewed as a corrective procedure for ineffective performance rather than as a means of increasing employee satisfaction. Under these conditions, limited-scale programs have prospered and appear to have made sizable contributions to the productivity goal. It is now recognized that the needs of an individual and the goals of an organization may well be in conflict and that for this reason certain kinds of counseling activities involving such matters as career planning and general emotional adjustment should usually be performed outside the employment context.

COUNSELING TECHNIQUE. Although in dealing with some types of problems a counselor must of necessity be somewhat directive, in that questions must be answered and information conveyed, the general approach in industry where emotional or motivational factors are strategic has been to stress so-called *nondirective counseling*. This emphasis is particularly prevalent where the counselor has had extensive psychological training. Under the nondirective approach the employee is encouraged to express his feelings, to gain an understanding of himself, and eventually to solve his own problems. The counselor listens and occasionally reformulates what the employee has said to permit greater understanding of the true emotional meaning of certain words. The counselor may also repeat certain phrases or sentences to stimulate the employee to continue and to lead him to concentrate on certain topics.

In the business context counseling of this kind tends to focus on matters of performance and on social relationships at work, although family and other considerations may be treated if they subsequently prove relevant. Often the counselor serves as an upward communication channel between the employee and his organization, correcting distorted communications and misunderstandings (25). The emphasis is on working out relatively mild adjustment problems that may be blocking performance effectiveness. More severe emotional disorders are normally referred to a psychotherapist working outside the company. If the problem appears to require more than perhaps ten or fifteen one-hour sessions, the employee is almost invariably advised to seek help on a private basis. Some firms, in fact, reject all internal adjustment counseling of this type, on the grounds that such matters are the sole responsibility of the individual (5).

EXECUTIVE COUNSELING. At the higher managerial levels counseling is usually carried out by an outside psychological consultant rather than a professional on the regular company staff (6, 8). Although in some instances this counseling represents an attempt to cope with a performance failure, it is also true that many top-level men are emotionally alone and thus in real need of someone with whom they can discuss problems. Under these circumstances an industrial clinical psychologist may continue to counsel an executive at intervals over an extended period of time. The approach, in contrast to that of a regular management consultant, tends to be nondirective, with the executive increasingly learning to understand himself and the motives behind his actions.

RETIREMENT COUNSELING. In general, counseling of this kind is intended to prepare employees for retirement, although on occasion it may be directed toward the rehabilitation of older workers whose performance has fallen off sharply with the approach of retirement. The counseling tends to be rather directive, emphasizing information on pension plans and other benefits. The counselors usually do not have psychological training. Counseling of this kind may be initiated as much as five years before the anticipated date of separation, although the total number of meetings with the counselor is not likely to be large.

Medical and Psychiatric Treatment

As indicated in the preceding chapter, medical treatment is not likely to be a major aspect of the industrial physician's job. Companies are much more prone to invest in selection through the physical examination and in preventive measures. Thus, although medical treatment is the major corrective procedure in cases where physical illness disrupts performance, this treatment does not represent a specific personnel management function. It is performed outside the company.

Similarly, psychiatric treatment for psychoses and neuroses is usually not provided by the company, although some firms do have psychiatrists on the regular staff. In certain instances, however, a company will take an active role in arranging for the treatment of a high-level executive and will pay all bills incurred. Also, there are companies that maintain special facilities for the treatment of alcoholics or contribute to the support of such facilities. It is not at all uncommon for a firm to maintain a close liaison with a local Alcoholics Anonymous chapter and to arrange for a representative of that organization to be constantly available to assist employees.

References

1. American Arbitration Association, *Procedural and Substantive Aspects of Labor-Management Arbitration: An AAA Research Report*. New York: the Association, 1957.
2. Barker, R. G., *Adjustment to Physical Handicap and Illness: A Survey of the Social Psychology of Physique and Disability*. New York: Social Science Research Council, 1963.
3. Bellows, R., *Psychology of Personnel in Business and Industry*, 3rd ed. Englewood Cliffs, N.J.: Prentice-Hall, 1961.
4. Dickson, W. J., "The Hawthorne Plan of Personnel Counseling," in S. D. Hoslett (ed.), *Human Factors in Management*. New York: Harper & Row, 1946, pp. 228–250.
5. Dunnette, M. D., and W. K. Kirchner, *Psychology Applied to Industry*. New York: Appleton-Century-Crofts, 1965.
6. Flory, C. D. (ed.), *Managers for Tomorrow*. New York: New American Library, 1965.

7. Ginzberg, E., J. B. Miner, J. K. Anderson, S. W. Ginsburg, and J. L. Herma, *The Ineffective Soldier: Vol. II, Breakdown and Recovery.* New York: Columbia Univ. Press, 1959.

8. Glaser, E. M., "Psychological Consultation with Executives: A Clinical Approach," *The American Psychologist,* Vol. 13 (1958), 486–489.

9. Heller, F. A., "Measuring Motivation in Industry," *Occupational Psychology,* Vol. 26 (1952), 86–95.

10. Katz, D., and R. L. Kahn, *The Social Psychology of Organizations.* New York: Wiley, 1966.

11. Kornhauser, A., *Mental Health of the Industrial Worker.* New York: Wiley, 1965.

12. Maier, N. R. F., and L. E. Danielson, "An Evaluation of Two Approaches to Discipline in Industry," *Journal of Applied Psychology,* Vol. 40 (1956), 319–323.

13. Markowe, M., "Occupational Psychiatry: An Historical Survey and Some Recent Researches," *Journal of Mental Science,* Vol. 99 (1953), 92–101.

14. Miller, E. C., "Personnel Policies—Framework for Management Decisions," *The Management Review,* Vol. 49, No. 1 (1960), 20–26.

15. Miner, J. B., *Intelligence in the United States.* New York: Springer, 1957.

16. Miner, J. B., "Personality and Ability Factors in Sales Performance," *Journal of Applied Psychology,* Vol. 46 (1962), 6–13.

17. Miner, J. B., *The Management of Ineffective Performance.* New York: McGraw-Hill, 1963.

18. Miner, J. B., and J. K. Anderson, "The Postwar Occupational Adjustment of Emotionally Disturbed Soldiers," *Journal of Applied Psychology,* Vol. 42 (1958), 317–322.

19. National Industrial Conference Board, *Company Payment of Employees' Moving Expenses,* Studies in Personnel Policy, No. 154. New York: the Board, 1956.

20. Odiorne, G. S., *Personnel Policy: Issues and Practices.* Columbus, Ohio: Charles E. Merrill, 1963.

21. Pigors, P., and C. A. Myers, *Personnel Administration,* 5th ed. New York: McGraw-Hill, 1965.

22. Piotrowski, Z. A., and M. R. Rock, *The Perceptanalytic Executive Scale.* New York: Grune and Stratton, 1963.

23. Stessin, L., *Employee Discipline.* Washington, D.C.: BNA Incorporated, 1960.

24. Stogdill, R. M., and A. E. Coons, *Leader Behavior: Its Description and Measurement.* Columbus: Bureau of Business Research, Ohio State Univ., 1957.

25. Tannenbaum, A. S., *Social Psychology of the Work Organization,* Belmont, Calif.: Wadsworth, 1966.

26. Tomkins, S. S., and J. B. Miner, *PAT Interpretation—Scope and Technique.* New York: Springer, 1959.

27. Wollenberger, J. B., "Acceptable Work Rules and Penalties: A Company Guide," *Personnel,* Vol. 40, No. 4 (1963), 23–29.

Questions

1. What is meant by performance control? How does it differ from other types of control? To what extent does performance control appear to be an important function in a firm? Can it be ignored?
2. How is a performance analysis carried out? Can you analyze an instance of job failure that you yourself have observed in the past?
3. What difficulties do you see associated with the introduction of an employee counseling program in a company? Why do you think a number of these programs have failed?
4. Take each of the possible strategic factors noted in the schema for performance analysis and indicate for each whether a placement change might provide a solution, and, if so, what specific characteristics should be present in the new position.
5. Why might a foreman fail to take disciplinary action when faced with a clear instance of work rule violation? Should a foreman have the authority to fire a man if he wishes, when such an infraction occurs?

VI

Input-Output Mediators: Techniques Fostering Organizational Maintenance

19

Approaches in Labor Relations

The area with the greatest potential for stress and conflict within business organizations is that of labor relations. Since the 1930's when, with the assistance of favorable legislation, unions first achieved a stable foothold in American industry, personnel management has had a continuing concern with the development of policies and approaches calculated to reduce labor-management conflict. In some instances these efforts have been devoted to creating a relatively conflict-free relationship with unions already representing groups of employees and in other cases to thwarting the organizing attempts of unions desiring to achieve such representation.

The use of the various approaches that attempt to foster organizational maintenance is conditioned by several considerations that should be specified at the outset. For one thing the goal in this area has normally been not so much to maximize maintenance aspects as to achieve a suitable level, while pursuing productivity and profit to the maximum degree possible. This means that companies do not normally devote their energies to conflict reduction at all costs. It is important, for instance, that management not sign a contract with a union that would impose internal constraints making it impossible to remain competitive in the industry, even if by doing so, continuing labor peace and high levels of employee satisfaction could be guaranteed. The primary objective, then, in using the approaches to be discussed in Part VI, is to attain the least internal conflict and stress possible while at the same time maintaining maximum control over all aspects of human relations utilization and productivity. Firms that have devoted themselves to internal conflict reduction almost exclusively, without adequate concern for the external realities of the marketplace and a competitive economy, have often committed themselves to give away so much as to make continued survival impossible.

In this chapter the major focus will be on approaches that have been developed to deal with unions. In subsequent chapters fringe benefits, such as retirement and health insurance plans, will be discussed, as well as the various employee communications procedures that companies have introduced. All these have as their goal the reduction of employee dissatisfaction and the minimization of conflict within the organization. Only rarely are they directly concerned with increasing productivity and profit.

As it has developed over the past thirty or forty years, the field of labor relations is far too extensive to cover in detail in a text such as this. Almost all universities offer more specialized courses in the area, which concentrate on various aspects of labor relations exclusively. For this reason the coverage here will be restricted to major problems and concepts, with particular emphasis on some of the more recent developments.

Two important aspects of labor relations have been treated in earlier chapters. The history of the union movement in relation to the evolution of personnel management has been discussed in Chapter 2. Legal constraints on labor relations decisions and the current status of labor legislation were the subject of Chapter 5. Because, however, management's conduct in dealing with a union is constantly conditioned by legal considerations, specific points of law will also be noted as appropriate in this chapter.

The Extent of Unionization

As noted in Chapter 1, a personnel manager should be thoroughly familiar with the field of labor relations whether the firm's employees are unionized or not. Although less than a quarter of the nation's total labor force is represented by a union at the present time, a high percentage of the production workers in nearly all the larger and more consequential manufacturing operations are organized. Furthermore, wage rates, working conditions, and fringe benefits gained by the unions at the bargaining table tend to have considerable influence on personnel practices throughout an industry or area of influence—in union and nonunion firms alike.

Then, too, there is the continuing prospect that a union may attempt to organize a segment of a firm or even the total work force. Since the end of World War II, during which the labor movement experienced its most pronounced expansion, many personnel managers have increasingly concentrated on approaches that might improve employee satisfaction and consequently keep the unions at a distance. The effectiveness of these efforts may well account in large part for the slowdown in union growth since the mid-1950's.

Figure 19-1. Trends in Union Membership

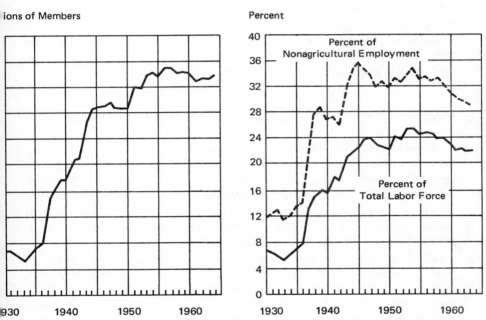

Membership of National Unions

Membership as a Percent of
Total Labor Force and of Employees
Outside Agriculture

Source: Bureau of Labor Statistics, United States Department of Labor *Directory of National and International Labor Unions in the United States, 1965.* Bulletin No. 1493, Washington, D.C.: The Bureau, 1966, p. 51.

As shown in Figure 19-1, union membership increased steadily from the mid-1930's to the mid-1950's, the only major exception being the 1948–1950 recession period. In 1956 union membership in the United States reached 17.5 million, or 24.8 per cent of the total labor force of 70.4 million. By 1963, however, membership had dropped to 16.5 million, or 21.8 per cent of the total labor force of 75.7 million. The first significant increase in the number of union members in recent years occurred between 1963 and 1964 when 300,000 were added. According to the

Bureau of Labor Statistics, much of the gain in manufacturing industry occurred as a result of expanded operations in plants where a union shop provision in the labor contract required new workers to join an existing union. Only in government employment and certain other white-collar groups did the increase reflect successful membership drives by union organizers (7).

Aside from more effective personnel management, there undoubtedly are a number of other reasons for the relative ineffectiveness of union organizing efforts and the general slowdown in the growth rate (15). There has, for instance, been a shift away from production employment involving males to white-collar workers and women. Both these groups have traditionally resisted union membership. Second, a number of firms have moved from heavily unionized areas to locations that have characteristically been more opposed to union membership. Finally, a number of unions have had to concentrate almost exclusively on internal problems, some of them resulting from the corrupt practices and scandals that were highly publicized in the late 1950's (2).

Factors Related to a Union's Conflict Potential

There seems little question that the preferred approach to organizational maintenance insofar as labor relations are concerned has been to keep the unions out, if at all possible. And personnel managers have devoted, and still are devoting, considerable effort toward just this end. The reason is that any situation involving a union represents a potential source of internal conflict. The mere presence of the union restricts management's freedom of action in many areas.

Although American labor unions have traditionally shown little interest in assuming a managerial role in the firms with which they deal, their goals are clearly antithetical in many ways to those of the companies. Not only do the unions seek to win higher wages and fringe benefits, thus cutting into profits, but they also attempt to ensure that all employees are treated on the same basis in such matters as work scheduling, promotions, discipline, and the like. In the absence of a union these matters can be handled in terms of the individual and his particular capabilities. The unions argue, however, that the individual has relatively little power, if he has any at all, in dealing with the business firm when management acts in an arbitrary or inequitable manner. Thus, an employee will fare much better with the collective power of the union membership behind him.

It is, in fact, this collective power of the membership that provides the unions with their real strength in dealing with the management of a single firm; it is also the basis for the political strength of the labor movement as a whole. But there are other factors contributing to the strength, and thus to the conflict potential, inherent in a specific union in a particular situation. These factors are closely related to the nature of the union itself.

The Nature of the Union and Its Power

In what follows, an attempt will be made to identify some of the ways in which unions may be categorized, especially as these relate to matters of union power. Thus, the discussion will take up the various types of unions, the matter of affiliation, and certain other aspects of union membership, as well as differences in style of union leadership.

TYPES OF UNIONS. Most unions may be classified as *craft* or *industrial,* depending largely on the kind of workers making up the membership. The earliest labor organizations were of the craft type, with the members almost entirely restricted to workmen within a single job skill such as carpentry or bricklaying. The original American Federation of Labor (AFL) was an affiliation of these craft groups.

Industrial unions, such as the United Auto Workers and the United Steelworkers, tend to include in their memberships only workers of a given industry and do so whether the employees are skilled, semiskilled, or unskilled. These are the unions that disaffiliated from the AFL in the mid-1930's and formed the Congress of Industrial Organizations (CIO). Actually, however, some of the traditional craft unions have organized plants on an industrial basis also; the Machinists Union, for instance, represents all workers in a number of factories, particularly in the aircraft industry.

It is primarily in the building trades that the craft unions still operate in their original form. Because they often work for many employers for relatively short periods of time, the members of these crafts tend to look to their unions for assurances that they will be hired for the specific skill required, that skills will be acquired through appropriate apprentice training, and that high wage rates plus fringe benefits will be maintained. Industrial unions, on the other hand, are more likely to be as concerned about matters related to job security, such as seniority and grievance procedures, as they are about wages and fringe benefits. This is not surprising in view of the more stable nature of their members' employment relationships and the lower average skill levels, which makes unemployment a realistic threat.

A third type of union that has emerged in recent years is the *professional union,* which encompasses groups such as scientists, engineers, and teachers. These groups tend to be particularly concerned with preserving professional status as related to such matters as salary and the special privileges of the profession.

AFFILIATION. The majority of all local unions are associated with a national or international union, which is in turn affiliated with the AFL-CIO. The latter organization was formed when the two major components of the labor movement merged in 1955. Of the nearly 17 million union members in the United States in 1964, more than 14 million belonged to AFL-CIO affiliates. Another 2.7 million belonged to national unions not affiliated with the AFL-CIO. These latter include several that were expelled from the AFL-CIO for various reasons—notably the Teamsters, whose membership of 1.5 million is the largest of any single union in the United States. Other unions with sizable memberships include the United Auto Workers with 1.2 million, the Steelworkers with 965,000, the Machinists with 808,000, the International Brotherhood of Electrical Workers with 806,000, and the Carpenters with 760,000. Together these six unions account for roughly one third of the union membership in the United States (7).

A very small proportion of union members belong to unaffiliated local unions, usually an independent group limited to the employees of a single company. In a number of cases these unions began as company-sponsored employee associations. This pattern is particularly prevalent in the petroleum industry. The Bureau of Labor Statistics does not include these unions in its standard estimates of union membership and for this reason these groups are not represented in the statistics cited previously. At most there are some 450,000 workers in these independent unions, representing less than 3 per cent of the total U.S. labor movement.

The affiliation of an employee group can have a sizable effect on its strength. Nearly all the national unions have large funds available for strike benefits, and they can provide a variety of full-time staff members to aid in organizing efforts, in negotiating contracts, and in handling grievance or arbitration procedures. At the same time a national organization can exert considerable control through the threat of withholding these benefits and services, if the local membership acts in a manner inconsistent with its desires.

ADDITIONAL FACTORS. Although the type and affiliation of the union are perhaps the most significant factors contributing to conflict potential, and influencing the issues over which conflict is likely to be joined, there are other factors more closely tied to the local plant situation. A newly organized union often has considerable power in dealing with management, especially if the workers have given the union overwhelming support in the representation election. Where the union has been in the plant for some time and has gained much of its membership through a union shop agreement, which forces new employees to join, the potentiality for concerted action may be less. Workers who become union members and pay dues voluntarily may give their leaders greater support than those who are required to join as a condition of employment.

A second factor is whether the union represents all or only a segment of the firm's nonmanagement employees. If all the production, maintenance, and perhaps white-collar workers are represented, this gives a union considerable power, because the threat of a strike implies a total shutdown. For the same reason, representing the employees in several plants of a multiplant company also tends to buttress union power. The total potential impact on the firm is greater.

On the other hand, there are situations in which a relatively small union group within a plant can achieve a degree of strength entirely out of proportion to its size. This happens if the location of the group in relation to the production process is particularly strategic, as with a small maintenance unit represented by a craft union, or if the group is able to utilize the allegiances of other workers in support of its demands.

DIFFERENCES IN UNION LEADERSHIP. The conflict potential, and the power, inherent in a given union is also influenced by the nature and the position of its leadership. In some cases a labor leader will have the rank and file solidly behind him—in which case he may have considerable power, but little need to exhibit it. In other cases the leadership may be less secure in its position. At such times a militant membership can force a union leader into actions that are clearly inappropriate, but that he must take to maintain his position in the union. Or a leader may take a belligerent attitude toward management merely to demonstrate to the rank and file that he is standing up for their rights. At such times he may be well aware that his position is untenable on economic or other grounds. Under such circumstances it is often difficult for management to assess the true strength of the leadership in relation to the internal "political" situation in the union itself. Yet there is reason to believe that in recent years such divisiveness within the labor movement as a whole has contributed to a decrease in the real power of many unions. Thus, management has been able to reassert its authority in the personnel area in a number of instances (39).

Environmental Factors and Industrial Conflict

The potential for conflict varies considerably from firm to firm, from area to area, and from one point in time to another. Although the relative strength of company and union do represent important determining factors, there are other considerations. Some of these are set forth in Table 19-1, which is based on an extensive study of collective bargaining relationships involving parties of relatively equal strength (24).

Clearly, many of the circumstances that have been isolated as sources of conflict are beyond the control of personnel management. A number have been discussed at length in Chapter 4 as external constraints on personnel decisions.

Figures on union membership provide some indication of where "union towns," as noted in Table 19-1, would be likely to predominate. Nearly half of all the union members in the United States reside in five states— New York, California, Pennsylvania, Illinois, and Ohio. Unionized work

Table 19-1.   Environmental Factors * and Industrial Peace †

Factors	Frequently favorable circumstances	Frequently unfavorable circumstances
Industrial environment		
1. Size of plant and company	Medium-sized company	Industrial giant
2. Production pattern	Steady	Seasonal; intermittent; production crises
3. Technological advance	Moderate	Severe
4. Nature of the jobs	Skilled; responsible	Assemblyline type
5. Cost factors	Inframarginal plant	Marginal plant
6. Market factors	Expanding; cyclically insensitive; inelastic demand	Contracting; sensitive to cycle; elastic demand
7. Locational factors	Relatively immobile plant	Relatively mobile plant
Community environment		
1. The work force	Steady; tractable	Inconstant; combative
2. The plant and the labor	Metropolitan area	One-industry town
3. Local wage levels	Low-wage community and high-wage industry	Low-wage industry and high-wage community
4. Industrial climate	"Union town"	"Open shop town"

* The full range of environmental conditions is not set forth in this table, but only those conditions that appear to relate to the prospects for industrial peace.
† Reference is made here to "industrial peace" developed by parties of relatively equal strength, not arrived at because of domination by one side or government.

Source: C. Kerr, "The Collective Bargaining Environment," in C. S. Golden and V. D. Parker (eds.), *Causes of Industrial Peace Under Collective Bargaining.* New York: Harper & Row, 1955, p. 22.

forces are most characteristic in the Northeast, the Great Lakes region, and the Far West. In the Southeast and the Great Plains areas a relatively small proportion of the labor force is represented by a labor organization.

In addition to these geographical differentials there are others associated with the particular industry. In 1964 about one half of manufacturing employment was unionized, one fourth of nonmanufacturing, and one seventh of government. More than 40 per cent of the union members were in three industry groups—metals and machinery, trans-

Table 19-1 (cont'd.)

Factors	Frequently favorable circumstances	Frequently unfavorable circumstances
"Political" environment of the parties		
1. The union	Secure union; secure leaders; homogeneous membership; local autonomy; pattern following	Insecure union; insecure leaders; heterogeneous membership; external domination; pattern setting
2. The employer	Pattern following; in employers' association; local autonomy in non-contractual matters	Pattern setting; lone bargainer; strong central domination of local plant
Time as an environmental factor	Origins in peaceful period; old relationship	Origins in warlike period; new relationship

portation, and construction. At the other extreme are trade, finance and insurance, and agriculture and fishing (7).

The Unionization Process

Historically, labor-management conflict has been most acute during union organizing efforts. Management typically has used every available weapon to avoid the necessity of bargaining over wages, conditions of employment, and the like. With the passage of the Wagner Act in 1935, however, many antiunion tactics were barred, and as a result it became increasingly difficult to deal with this threat to organizational maintenance through exclusion.

Yet there are many companies that have been able to avoid unionization entirely, or at least in some of their facilities. Most of these firms have faced repeated organizing attempts, and in spite of the slowdown in such union efforts during the 1960's, they can no doubt anticipate many more. A number of the unions representing production workers are seeking to extend their influence to white-collar groups, and there have been some concerted drives aimed at certain traditionally nonunion areas and industries. A related type of conflict involves the situation in which an established local union is either weak or considered to be weak and another union attempts to establish its jurisdiction over the same employee unit. There are also cases where two or more unions may attempt to organize the same group. In these latter instances, where interunion conflict is added to that between labor and management, the internal stress on an organization may become considerable.

Motives in Union Membership

A large proportion of new members presently join unions automatically because it is required under a union shop contract as a condition of employment. Undoubtedly many of these workers give relatively little thought to this action, especially if they were raised in a pro-union environment. In the past, however, such automatic membership was uncommon and it is not always the case today, especially where employees select a new union as their bargaining agent. Under such voluntary conditions it seems apparent that union membership can provide for the satisfaction of important motives.

Over the years scholars have advanced numerous theories of union membership. The earlier theories were predicated primarily on economic grounds. The assumption was that, as individuals, workers are at the mercy of their employers, particularly in times of job scarcity. Only by joining forces and forming a union can workers achieve the power to force an employer to provide fair wages and adequate working conditions. Furthermore, under prosperous economic conditions, when profits are high, the union's power in collective bargaining can give the workers a means of obtaining what they consider to be a fair share.

More recently, however, investigators have found that the desire for economic gain may not be the primary factor in union membership. A variety of social and psychological needs are satisfied as well. The union can provide a worker with a sense of security, perhaps some status, a feeling of independence in relation to his employer, and the satisfactions of group membership. Even in a well-managed firm that pays good wages and offers ideal working conditions, union membership may have considerable appeal solely because it frees the employees from a sense of being dependent on their employer. This is particularly likely to be the case when the union is well established and has achieved some status in the community (1).

Furthermore, the fact that employees join a union does not necessarily mean that they dislike the company or intend in any sense to be disloyal to it. A survey of attitudes in the meat-packing industry indicated that nearly three fourths of the workers were favorably disposed to both the company *and* the union. Thus, a real dual allegiance was demonstrated among the rank-and-file union members (31).

It is generally conceded that the employees most likely to be susceptible to union organizing appeals are those who are dissatisfied. This dissatisfaction may relate to wage rates, to the lack of available channels for complaints regarding unfair treatment, and to many other things (14). Thus, dissatisfaction may be primarily economic in nature, but it may also be associated with a variety of social or psychological considerations. In many instances employees are not really aware of the true sources of their dissatisfaction.

In any event, if through appropriate personnel policies and procedures a company can keep its employees satisfied with their jobs and with management's actions, a union will find it much more difficult to become established. On the other hand, union leaders will almost certainly attempt to capitalize on any signs of dissatisfaction within an employee group they are attempting to organize. It is for this reason that many companies conduct attitude surveys to ascertain the extent and sources of employee discontent, whenever they believe a threat of unionization exists. With such knowledge it is often possible to blunt the appeals of the union.

White-Collar Unionization

Many factors involved in the unionization process may be illustrated with reference to the current situation within the white-collar group, which is understood to include office workers, technical and professional employees, and government employees. Until the mid-1950's the white-collar workers were consistently a minority of the nation's labor force; since that time they have outnumbered blue-collar workers. In fact, the gap has been continually widening as automation has reduced the demand for factory employees.

Recognizing this shift in labor force composition as a basic threat to the strength of the labor movement, a number of unions have initiated extensive organizing campaigns within the white-collar sector. Some of these unions are composed entirely of white-collar employees—the Office and Professional Employees, the Retail Clerks, and the Government Employees, for example. In other instances office workers are represented by an industrial union, such as the United Auto Workers, that also represents the production workers of the same company. Finally, certain unions, whose membership was originally restricted to a quite different group, have turned their efforts in this direction. Among these, the Teamsters, initially a union of truck drivers, has been especially active.

To date these white-collar organizing drives have not been spectacularly successful. From 1956 to 1960 there was, in fact, a decline in the number of white-collar union members from 2.5 to 2.2 million, but by 1964 the total had increased again to 2.6 million (7). As of the latter date, 11 per cent of the appropriate labor force was organized as contrasted with something between 50 and 60 per cent of all manual and service workers (23).

Much of the growth in the early 1960's was in retail trade, communications, and public service. One of the fastest growing unions is the American Federation of Government Employees, which achieved much of its impetus from an executive order issued by President Kennedy in 1962. At that time the right of governmental employees to be represented by unions in collective bargaining was restated, with the result that union membership was encouraged. On the other hand, these employees are legally barred from the use of the strike weapon, and bargaining on wages and benefits is not feasible, because these are established by law.

There appear to be several reasons for the frequent failures among organizing efforts in the white-collar sector. One factor would appear to be the structure of the labor movement, with its stress on craft differentiations. Even the industrial unions may need to make some internal structural changes to have a major appeal for white-collar employees (2,27).

At a more basic level, however, the problem for the unions appears to be the attitudes that have traditionally prevailed in the white-collar group. In part this situation is attributable to the large percentage of women engaged in this type of employment. The majority of these women view their work as a short-term matter. They are not career-oriented and thus expect little benefit from the dues they must pay a union. Furthermore, they tend to view unions as essentially male organizations, a conception that has probably been fostered by the unions themselves, because little was done to recruit female members in earlier years.

A second cause of antiunion attitudes among white-collar workers is the higher status these employees have enjoyed. Many have felt much closer to management than to the production workers. Working conditions have generally been good, and opportunities for advancement and reward on an individual basis have been frequent. Why should a person join a union when he or she can achieve as much or more without resort to collective action?

As white-collar units in the business world increase in size, however, much of this may change. Groups of office workers as large as those on the production line are emerging, and in many cases these groups are as far removed from management as their blue-collar counterparts. Much of the differential in wages and benefits has been eliminated by union gains, so that many firms now treat their unionized and non-unionized employees alike (5). In one case, where a union was successful in organizing a group of office workers, the two major reasons for dissatisfaction were the fact that white-collar employees were not given the same pay raises as unionized production workers and the lack of a satisfactory method of handling complaints, such as the grievance procedure provided for union members (22). If the status of the office worker cannot be protected, opportunities for promotion maintained, and provision made for upward communication, the appeal of the union for white-collar employees may increase sharply.

The Union Organizing Drive

The impetus for a union organizing campaign may derive from a group of employees within the company, especially if there has been considerable discontent. Far more frequently, however, the campaign is initiated by a national union as part of an overall effort in the particular industry, or by a union that already represents one segment of the company's work force and desires to extend its jurisdiction into other areas. Usually a union will attempt to contact individual employees first, emphasizing any known sources of dissatisfaction such as wage rates or working conditions. After sufficient interest is aroused, the union will hold a mass meeting to discuss the advantages of membership and to solicit signatures in support of union representation.

In most cases management becomes aware of the organizing effort at an early point, either through the rumor transmission process or because of the appearance of union literature. As noted in Chapter 5, the actions of management at this point are subject to a number of constraints of a legal nature. The company cannot discriminate on the basis of union activity and cannot interfere with the formation of a labor organization among employees. Under the *free speech* provisions of the Taft-Hartley Act, however, management can communicate with employees regarding an organizing drive, as long as threats are not used and rewards are not offered for rejecting the union. A further deterrent to management action was introduced by the Landrum-Griffin Act of 1959, which requires employers to report to the Secretary of Labor all expenditures for outside labor relations consultants who aid management at the time of an organizing drive.

After a union has obtained signed authorization cards from 30 per cent or more of the employees in the company unit it seeks to represent, it can petition the National Labor Relations Board for a representation election. If such an election is held and the union wins a majority of the votes, it is certified as the bargaining agent. It is entirely permissible for the company to recognize a union without such an election if it chooses, but as a practical matter most employers prefer the election, to be certain that the union does have a majority and because after one NLRB election has been held another cannot be scheduled in the same bargaining unit for at least a year.

Besides supervising the election, the NLRB also determines the appropriateness of the bargaining unit, should there be a dispute on the matter. This can be a very important consideration. If a particular group of employees is known to be strongly pro-union, it is to management's advantage to have them excluded. Similarly, the inclusion of an antiunion segment of the work force may swing the election, so that the organizing effort fails. Thus, attempts to have the bargaining unit defined in favorable terms often represent an important aspect of management strategy in dealing with a union threat to organizational maintenance.

Because similar efforts normally characterize the union approach also, the early stages of an organizing drive may involve numerous petitions and counterpetitions to the NLRB, aimed at obtaining a favorable ruling in this regard. Yet the judgments rendered by the NLRB in such matters are far from arbitrary. Decisions are reached in accordance with certain very definite guidelines related to common employment interests and any previous bargaining history.

Thus, governmental constraints in connection with an organizing effort do not operate entirely on management. Unions are also restricted. This is particularly true with regard to picketing. If a union initiates picketing as part of an organizing campaign, it must petition for an NLRB election within thirty days or cease picketing. After an election has been held, *organizational picketing* is illegal for a year, whether the union has won or lost. When one union has been certified as bargaining representative, other unions may not engage in organizational picketing.

JURISDICTIONAL DISPUTES. Rivalry between two or more unions attempting to represent a group of employees can produce one of the most difficult labor relations problems for management. When jurisdictional disputes of this kind develop, a serious threat to organizational maintenance is posed without management being in any sense a party to the controversy. Even when an employer clearly prefers to have the employees represented by a particular union, it is illegal to overtly proclaim this preference or to provide support to a particular union.

Jurisdictional problems have plagued the labor movement for decades. When the AFL and CIO merged in 1955, there was some hope that this particular type of difficulty would diminish. Yet it was not until 1962 that a workable plan for handling internal disputes evolved. Since that time most controversies between affiliated unions have been resolved, although not always before the company involved has experienced considerable internal stress. Disputes with independent unions, particularly the Teamsters, have, however, become increasingly frequent.

Managerial Attitudes During an Organizing Drive

In terms of organizational maintenance a union organizing drive can be a devastating experience for a firm. Few companies welcome the presence of a union. After a union wins the right to represent a group of employees, management's authority is challenged and its freedom to act is restricted in many areas (34).

Thus, when faced with a union representation election most managements will do everything possible to keep the union out. In this connection it is important to refrain from any actions that might be interpreted as interference with a union's rights under the law. If the union loses the election and can claim management interference, the company may be faced with an NLRB unfair labor practices charge and another election may be ordered. The period of internal strife will be prolonged accordingly, and management may lose employee goodwill to the point where the second election goes against it.

In attempting to avoid legal difficulties and minimize internal stress in the firm, management normally relies upon its own labor relations experts or, in the case of smaller companies, outside consultants. It is important for these individuals to keep all levels of management, from first-line supervision up, fully informed as to what can and cannot be done or said during the organizing drive. There have been many instances when, at such times, uninformed and overzealous managers have done their companies irreparable damage.

It is almost always difficult to remain unemotional in the organizing situation. Managers often feel that employees are being ungrateful or disloyal if they even consider a union, especially if the firm is already providing good wages and fringe benefits. Many firms have succeeded in avoiding unionization through effective personnel management, but successes have been most notable in those industries and geographical areas that were the least heavily unionized initially. Thus, there are instances in which the union will almost inevitably achieve its goal. At such times a personnel manager may find himself shifting from mere personal involvement, which is quite natural under the circumstances, to highly defensive behavior, as the campaign progresses. A union victory may become in his mind clear-cut evidence of his own personal failure to perform effectively.

Yet by doing all it can to minimize tension and avoid feelings of bitterness, management will be in a far better position subsequent to an election. If the union should win, and be certified as a bargaining agent, the company is legally bound to negotiate on the terms of employment. This process of collective bargaining is considerably easier if hostile relations and personal animosities built up in the past do not provide a backdrop for the negotiations.

Collective Bargaining

Assuming that excluding the union has either failed as a strategy or has not been attempted in the first place, the next approach to labor-management conflict reduction must be collective bargaining. Although the form such bargaining actually takes is highly variable from situation to situation, its use in some form is required by law, given the fact that a union has been certified as a bargaining agent. Because of this legal constraint, collective bargaining is now the major approach to organizational maintenance in the labor relations area, at least in the United States. Thus, management is required as a matter of public policy to bargain with the union and to do so in "good faith."

This does not mean that management must relinquish its right to direct the company or that it must accede to union demands. The extent to which a union can persuade a firm to grant its demands depends in large part on the relative power balance between the two parties. After this has been established and an agreement is reached, a contract outlining terms of employment for a specified period of time is prepared and signed.

Approaches to Bargaining

The particular individual or individuals who deal with the union, either in collective bargaining or in day-to-day administration of the contract, vary considerably depending on the size and complexity of the firm and the extent to which it is unionized. Labor relations may be handled by the personnel manager, the plant manager, or even the company president, in the case of a small company dealing with a single union. On the other hand, a large multiplant corporation bargaining with many unions in several locations may have an entire department staffed with experts in wage and salary administration, insurance and pension planning, contract negotiation, labor law, and the like. A number of these individuals will be located at corporate headquarters, but others may be distributed throughout the firm. In some areas employer associations staffed in a similar manner handle relations with unions for groups of firms.

THE NEGOTIATING COMMITTEE. A company bargaining committee normally contains anywhere from two to six people, including at least one personnel representative and at least one representative from the line organization. The company president usually retains final authority to accept or reject the agreement reached by his negotiating committee, but does not sit in on the bargaining itself. It is common practice for the president to indicate to the committee exactly how far they can go in making concessions. Within the limits thus established, the committee, in effect, has full authority to negotiate a final agreement. Although it is by no means a universal practice, some firms include first-line supervisors and other managers in negotiations on a rotating basis to provide these individuals with a better understanding of union and management viewpoints.

The union bargaining committee tends to be larger and includes some or all of the officers of the local union, one or more shop stewards or specially elected committeemen, and a representative of the national union. Local craft unions employ a full-time *business agent* who acts as the chief negotiator in all bargaining conducted by the local.

Unlike the company bargaining committee, the union negotiators do not have authority to accept a final agreement. When bargaining is initiated, the union committee presents a set of demands originally prepared by the executive board or some similar group in the local. These demands must have the approval of the membership. Similarly, any final agreement must also be ratified by a vote of the membership. In most cases the union bargaining committee is well aware of what the membership will accept. Thus, the ratification requirement does not constitute a major barrier to settlement. In recent years, however, there have been an increasing number of instances in which the membership has rejected a proposed agreement. This has occurred primarily in situations involving multiplant or industry-wide bargaining, and the negotiators have usually been top officials of national unions. Apparently these individuals do have difficulty keeping attuned to the sentiments of the rank and file.

The current trend appears to be for larger and larger units to be subsumed under the same bargaining process, either on an area or on an industry basis. In the past the usual union tactic was to concentrate on obtaining a settlement with an industry leader and then to attempt to obtain essentially the same agreement from other firms in the industry. In most cases these other firms accepted the original pattern rather than suffer a strike and a loss of market position to the leader, who already had a contract. Although such *pattern bargaining* is still common, there are a number of industries in which the leading firms have banded together and now bargain as a single unit. In most such cases some provision is made for negotiation on local issues. Nevertheless, industry bargaining of this kind does serve to reduce the power of the individual company and of local plant management. It also tends to increase the probability of some kind of governmental intervention in the bargaining process, because a major segment of the economy is often involved.

PREPARATIONS FOR BARGAINING. For many years the typical approach was for the union to present a series of demands, which the company would subsequently either accept, attempt to modify, or reject outright. Often a company would await these demands and then formulate a response. In recent years it has become common practice for a company to spend considerable time and effort preparing for negotiations, and even to take the initiative by presenting proposals for contract changes that would be beneficial to management.

In determining what, if any, changes might be warranted with regard to wages and fringe benefits, companies tend to utilize survey data on competitive practices in the industry and area. This information may be readily available within the company (see Chapter 16) or special surveys may be conducted for bargaining purposes. To pinpoint sections of the existing contract that may represent sources of difficulty, grievances and arbitration awards are studied; supervisors are polled for suggested changes. Company negotiators are usually provided with information on the company's financial position, on the cost to the company of various changes in wages and fringe benefits, and on the power position of the union.

The union, too, will study wage and other information before entering upon negotiations. All the major unions maintain staffs at national and regional headquarters for the sole purpose of collecting information on recent wage settlements and on changes in the cost of living. In the case of the larger unions that bargain with major segments of an industry, the union demands may be announced publicly well in advance of actual negotiations to gain public support, if possible, or at least to determine the trend of public sentiment.

Legal Considerations

The major legal consideration in collective bargaining revolves around the Federal labor law's requirement that both parties bargain in "good faith." As noted in Chapter 5, what constitutes bargaining in good faith has been subject to a variety of interpretations at different points in time. Accordingly the constraint structure is unclear. Although the NLRB has consistently contended that certain specific actions are unlawful, it has generally viewed a great many charges of refusal to bargain on an *ad hoc* basis, taking into account characteristics of the specific situation. Thus, in a recent case involving General Electric,[1] the NLRB declared that it was the "totality" of the company's bargaining conduct that constituted refusal to bargain in good faith, rather than any specific aspect of its behavior. In this particular instance the union objected to the company's presenting an initial offer on a "take it or leave it" basis and refusing to change this offer subsequently. It also objected to the fact that the company tried to communicate with the employees directly regarding the equity of this offer. The NLRB decision upholding the union on both these counts has now been appealed to the courts. The ultimate decision will without question have major implications for collective bargaining in the future.

Specific items for which the NLRB has established definite guidelines include the issues that are subject to bargaining. Here there are three categories—unlawful issues, mandatory issues, and nonmandatory issues. Because the parties are forbidden to agree on unlawful issues, such as the closed shop, and cannot legally include them in a contract, insistence on bargaining on such issues is considered an unfair labor practice. Mandatory issues include matters relating to wages, hours, and working conditions. Both parties are required to negotiate regarding any such bargainable issue proposed by either one, and each party is within its rights when it makes a demand involving a mandatory issue and refuses to sign a contract that does not grant its demand. Neither party is required to bargain on nonmandatory issues, but if both agree to bargain on such matters any agreement reached voluntarily is lawful (3).

Although the NLRB has laid down these guidelines, their interpreta-

---

[1] *General Electric Co.*, 150 NLRB No. 36 (1964).

tion often leads to difficulty. Most items involving payments have been categorized as mandatory, bargainable issues. These include pensions, insurance, Christmas bonuses, and the like. So, too, are issues involving union membership requirements and no-strike provisions. Included in the voluntary, nonmandatory category would be issues such as a demand by a union that the company discharge a certain supervisor (presumably for antiunion behavior) before an agreement could be signed, or a demand by a company that a union withdraw unfair labor practice charges. Unfortunately, there are a number of issues that do not fall clearly into one category or another. However, the trend has been for more and more of these to be considered mandatory.

Thus, the NLRB has been upheld by the courts in a decision that a company must bargain on the subcontracting of work formerly performed by a union-represented company unit.[2] The NLRB was reversed in another decision, however, where the U.S. Supreme Court ruled that a company does not have to bargain regarding a decision to go out of business, even if antipathy toward the union was the major reason behind the decision.[3]

In an extension of the "good faith" concept the NLRB has held that employers who refuse to furnish data that have been requested by a union, and that are relevant and necessary for bargaining, are guilty of unfair labor practices. Such data may include information on wage rates and earnings of individual employees, on payments under fringe benefit programs, and on the company's financial position. In effect, whenever the company refers to its own records to support its arguments, these records must be made fully available to the union negotiators.

The Bargaining Relationship

A number of studies have been conducted dealing with various bargaining relationships (11, 12, 13, 26). In general the emphasis has been on the identification of those types of relationships that are and are not conducive to industrial peace. Several of the more frequently noted types are discussed below.

OPEN CONFLICT. Open conflict arises when management does not in fact accept the union and refuses to deal with it on other than a "minimal compliance" basis. Relationships of this kind are unlikely to be effective from a management viewpoint after a union has been certified. Not only do legal difficulties frequently result, but pro-union employees often become so disruptive that there is a major threat to both organizational maintenance and productivity.

CONTAINMENT. Containment has also been referred to as the "armed

---

[2] *Fibreboard Paper Products Corp. v. NLRB*, 379 US203 (1964).
[3] *Textile Workers Union v. Darlington Manufacturing Co.*, 380 US263 (1965).

truce" relationship and is probably the most common type. It is based on the premise that management and the union have inherently conflicting interests. Thus, the company deals with the union only to the extent required by legal constraints, although it is careful not to violate the law. Every effort is made to contain the union's power and preserve the rights of management.

ACCOMMODATION. In accommodation the parties recognize some common goals and therefore work together through information-sharing, problem-solving, and other techniques to achieve joint solutions to bargaining problems. The result is likely to be a minimum of conflict, but other consequences may not always be as desirable. The Studebaker Company, for example, apparently had an extremely harmonious relationship involving considerable discussion of problems with the union. Nevertheless, very few real solutions evolved. In general, management acquiesced to the union arguments, with the result that little was done to control excess manpower. The consequent rise in production costs was a major factor in the company being forced out of the automobile business (41).

COOPERATION. Cooperation usually involves an extension of the bargaining relationship under a formal plan for joint consultation and action on matters ordinarily handled by management alone. It tends to emerge because of some major problem facing the firm, or the entire industry; a new approach is clearly needed. There have been several dramatic examples of such cooperative efforts in recent years resulting from problems created by automation. These will be discussed in a separate section later in the chapter, because they represent some of the newest and most interesting approaches in the collective bargaining field.

THE DEAL. One further relationship that has existed in the past and that no doubt still exists in some localities is one in which management makes certain special arrangements with the union leaders, usually without membership knowledge or approval. The leaders may agree to forego a wage increase in return for a union shop. Where racketeering elements are present, a small employer may agree to sign a contract under threat of being forced out of business. In many of these situations the union leaders have an inordinate amount of power. It was to correct such abuses that the Landrum-Griffin Act was passed in 1959.

This type of bargaining relationship does not always remain stable. Often feelings of resentment created during an organizing drive are difficult to erase, and an open conflict relationship may persist for years. Then, with a change in union leadership or management personnel, a more effective approach may evolve. In other cases a firm may prefer a policy of containment, but on occasion work with the union on an accommodation basis for a particular purpose. Joint safety committees established to deal with a sharply rising accident rate represent a case in point. Factors influencing the union may also produce a change in the character of the bargaining relationship. In bad times, when jobs are scarce or when the company is in a precarious competitive position, a union may utilize accommodating or cooperative procedures. In good times, when profits are high and there is full employment, the same union may engage in open conflict (40).

Irrespective of the overall relationship between a company and a union, it is almost inevitable that conflict will arise during the collective bargaining process itself, simply because the parties have different desires and expectations as regards the final solution. This concept is illustrated in Figure 19-2.

Figure 19-2. Desires, Expectations, and Tolerance Limits That Determine the Bargaining Zone

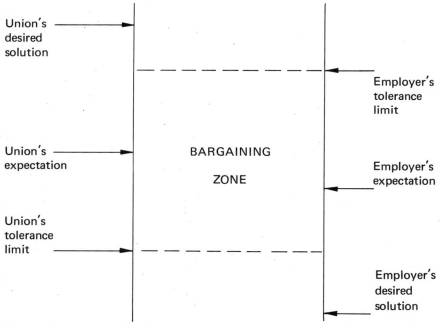

Source: R. Stagner and H. Rosen. *Psychology of Union-Management Relations*, p. 96. Copyright 1965 by Wadsworth Publishing Company, Inc., Belmont, California. Used by permission.

In most negotiations each party begins by listing its demands for contract changes. These constitute the desired solution. The demands are normally accompanied by supporting facts and figures. The primary task then becomes one of determining the tolerance limits of the respective parties, thus establishing the bargaining zone (37).

There are a number of problems that characteristically arise and contribute to conflict. Primarily these are communications problems resulting from faulty perceptions and differences in the personalities, backgrounds, and motives of the management and union negotiators. Other sources of difficulty are the ritualistic formality of the bargaining situation (which tends to thwart new approaches), the needs of both sets of negotiators to convey a favorable impression to their respective constituencies, and the lack of appropriate support (which may arise on either the management or the union side) (14,41).

A number of approaches have been suggested and used to minimize bargaining conflicts. Sometimes training programs designed to produce awareness of communications problems can have a positive effect. For example, if company negotiators can recognize when the union leaders are pressing a demand merely to placate the national officers, the vehemence of their counterresponse may well be reduced considerably. In several cases in which outside consultants have had an opportunity to work with both parties along these lines, the incidence of conflict has been markedly reduced (4,29).

The Settlement Process

On occasion the bargaining relationship is influenced by the intervention of a third, outside, party, either at the request of the other two parties or as a result of direct governmental action. This usually occurs when the negotiations have seemingly failed and a strike deadline is near. It is common practice for union members to vote a strike authorization to become effective should there be no settlement by a certain date, usually the expiration of the current contract. As the deadline approaches the union may extend this date should a settlement appear imminent. If this is not the case, the contesting parties may ask for outside help before moving into a strike situation. In actuality the majority of settlements are achieved without resort to either strike action or outside intervention, but cases of bargaining failure are most likely to achieve mention in the press.

The usual process through which an impartial outside party helps to break a deadlock in negotiations is *mediation* or *conciliation* by a governmental representative. Such a mediator has no power to force a settlement, but he can work with the parties separately to determine their respective positions, explain a position more fully to the opposition, point out bases for agreement that may not have been apparent previously, help in the search for solutions, and generally facilitate the reaching of an agreement. In effect, the mediator acts as a communications catalyst, and his effectiveness depends on his impartiality and on his capacity to win the trust of both parties.

Another related process is *arbitration,* under which unresolved bargaining issues are submitted to an impartial arbitrator or board of arbitrators whose decision is binding on both parties. In practice, arbitration is used primarily in settling grievances that arise under an existing contract, rather than to determine the terms of the contract itself. Less than 1 per cent of all labor contracts provide for arbitration of contract issues, although in a few states arbitration of such issues is compulsory in areas of public interest, *i.e.*, government employment, hospitals, and so on.

Although a number of states have mediation services, the majority of mediators are provided by the Federal Mediation and Conciliation Service, which was established as an independent agency by the Taft-Hartley Act in 1947. Either or both parties can seek the assistance of the FMCS, or the Service can offer help should it feel the situation warrants it. Federal law requires that sixty days prior to the expiration of a contract any party wishing to change the contract must give notice of this intention to the other party. If no agreement has been reached thirty days prior to the expiration date, the FMCS must be notified. Thus, the FMCS is informed in cases in which strike action seems imminent and is likely to take action on its own if not asked to do so. This is particularly common when large numbers of employees are involved or when the public interest is clearly at stake.

NATIONAL EMERGENCY DISPUTES. Further government intervention in the bargaining process with a view to facilitating a settlement may be initiated by the President in cases in which a threatened strike would "imperil the national health or safety." When this occurs, the Taft-Hartley Act provides for an eighty-day postponement of any strike action, during which time a fact-finding board must investigate the dispute and report to the President. The NLRB is to poll the employees as to their willingness to accept the company's last offer. If a majority reject this offer, the President may approach Congress for further authority to deal with the situation.

In the first fifteen years of the Taft-Hartley Act, emergency dispute provisions were invoked twenty-three times, most commonly in the longshoring and defense industries. None of the parties involved appear to have been satisfied with the procedure and there is almost inevitably a controversy as to whether a particular strike would actually "imperil the national health and safety." To date, however, no acceptable alternative approaches have been advanced (30).

Actually, government intervention in collective bargaining has occurred most commonly in the transportation industry, much of which is governed by the terms of the National Railway Labor Act rather than the Taft-Hartley Act. The situation there has developed to the point where it is now almost automatically assumed that the government will have to intervene before a settlement can be reached. Thus, free collective bargaining has to a large degree lost its value as a method of conflict reduction in this industry.

EFFECTS OF GOVERNMENT INTERVENTION. Although the segment of the economy that is covered by the National Railway Labor Act represents an extreme case, there is no question that mediation and other forms of governmental intervention can thwart the normal processes of collective bargaining. Often agreement is delayed in anticipation of governmental action. There are a number of reasons for this.

Union leaders may believe it will be easier to gain the support of their membership after the mediation process has been invoked. In times when the political climate is favorable to labor, unions have delayed a settlement on the assumption that governmental intervention will produce results not readily available otherwise. On the other hand, management has used the same tactic when there is widespread concern about inflation and the undesirable effects of wage increases on the economy. At such times government pressures may serve to limit the union severely.

As industry-wide bargaining becomes more prevalent and different unions combine to negotiate on a company-wide basis with many of the larger firms, the public appears to be increasingly concerned about the threat of large-scale strike activity. At the moment, therefore, the prospects appear to be for more widespread intervention by government. Many firms will undoubtedly find that governmental action, rather than free collective bargaining, has actually become their primary method of conflict resolution and organizational maintenance in the labor relations field. The choice between these two approaches is unlikely to be one that a company can make for itself. Outside the United States direct governmental intervention in one form or another is a more common method of dealing with labor-management conflict than is free collective bargaining. There is reason to believe that a comparable situation could develop in the United States as a result of shifts in public policy.

The Labor-Management Agreement

The settlement reached in collective bargaining is incorporated in a legal document, a contract. In an earlier period these contracts were relatively short and dealt almost entirely with hours of work and rates of pay. Over the years the size of the bargaining arena has expanded. More issues have been included and more complex settlements reached. Contracts now sometimes run to fifty pages or more, and many companies issue supplementary guides to explain the various provisions.

DURATION OF THE CONTRACT. Another noticeable trend is for contracts to apply over a longer period of time. The standard used to be one year, but a study of 1965 agreements indicates that almost half run for two. Nearly all these more extended contracts provide for a second wage increase at some date during the term of the agreement, usually a year after the initial effective date, or for a reopening of negotiations on wage issues only at a specified time (8).

These longer-term contracts have both pros and cons from the management viewpoint. On the one hand, management can avoid the internal stress of repeated strike threats and can save the time and money associated with yearly negotiating sessions. On the other hand, the buildup of change proposals over several years can be considerable. Thus, the re-negotiation process may be much more difficult and the chances of a strike increased disproportionately. Various approaches have been developed to alleviate this situation and still maintain the longer contract duration. In the basic steel industry a joint union-management study committee has been established to make recommendations regarding provisions that are known to be potentially troublesome prior to the start of negotiations on a new contract.

Management Rights

The question of whether to include a provision in the contract aimed at protecting the basic rights of management has long been a subject for debate. Some companies take the position that because certain rights and responsibilities are inherent in the very process of management, there is no need to spell these out in the agreement. To attempt to do so might actually be restrictive, in that anything not mentioned could be interpreted as outside the exclusive domain of management.

However, more and more companies are insisting on the inclusion of a management rights clause in the contract. Nearly three-fourths of all union agreements contain some such statement (8). Some of these are very general in nature on the theory that a more detailed treatment might be restrictive; others list specific areas (sometimes as many as fifteen or twenty) in which management retains its freedom to act; some even contain such a listing plus a proviso that the items noted are not all-inclusive. The more frequently noted rights in contracts with a detailed statement are those concerning the closing or relocating of facilities, framing company rules, instituting technological changes, and determining employee duties.

On the other hand, most contracts also include a statement to the effect that management has no rights that are in conflict with the terms of the agreement. Thus, there may be explicit restrictions limiting management's freedom to act in such areas as subcontracting, carrying out technological changes, and (in a small percentage of contracts) shutting down or relocating plants. Although most of these provisions do not actually prohibit management from taking action in these areas, they do require prior discussion with the union, the retraining of affected employees, and job guarantees.

In practice, what the contract specifies in the way of management rights may be a moot point. Whether the contract requires it or not, companies frequently do notify the union of job changes, make special arrangements for affected workers when operations are moved or equipment is changed, and otherwise act in accordance with many union expectations. They do so on the theory that these actions will minimize disruptive effects and contribute to organizational maintenance.

Actually the trend in arbitration awards and court decisions has been to reinforce the view that any management decision affecting the employment relationship should be discussed with the union unless such discussion has previously been waived by both parties. The current assumption is that in exercising its rights management must take into account the rights that workers have built up over the years as employees. It is in situations in which management has ignored these considerations, usually in connection with subcontracting, plant relocation, or technological change, that union protests have been supported (17).

Union Security

Just as provisions relating to management rights may be critical from the employer viewpoint, those relating to union security are of paramount importance to the union. After a union has been successful in organizing a group of employees and gaining recognition, union security stipulations in the contract, requiring union membership of all employees in the bargaining unit, provide the best assurance of continued strength. Management generally is opposed to such provisions, because they force employees to join or pay dues to the union whether they wish to or not. However, for many years union security was the major noneconomic issue advocated by the unions. Under the threat of strikes and other stresses many firms agreed to some type of union security. Where compulsory membership is not excluded by law, nine out of ten contracts provide some form of union security (8).

RIGHT-TO-WORK LAWS. One approach management has used to avoid compulsory union membership is to influence state legislatures to enact "right-to-work" laws that forbid union shop agreements. Such laws are explicitly condoned in the Taft-Hartley Act. They exist in twenty states at the present time, although most of these are not heavily industrialized. The South and Great Plains are the major areas of the country represented.

TYPES OF UNION SECURITY PROVISIONS. The most common form of union security is the *union shop*, under which all employees in the bargaining unit are required to join the union and to maintain membership as a condition of employment. Some agreements permit certain exceptions. Thus, employees who were not members as of the contract's effective date may be allowed to stay out, but all persons hired after the agreement goes into effect are required to join. Provisions of the latter kind are referred to as a *modified union shop.*

Another approach is known as *maintenance-of-membership.* Employees who choose to join the union are required to maintain membership as a condition of employment, but joining the union is not essential. Furthermore, there is usually some provision for an escape period at the time of contract negotiations. At this time anyone who wishes to resign can do so without losing his job.

The *agency shop* requires employees who do not join the union to pay the union a fee equal to union dues. This type of arrangement came about as a result of union objections to "free riders" who benefited from negotiations without paying dues to support the union. A number of states that forbid compulsory union membership nevertheless permit agency shop arrangements.

Other hiring arrangements, including the *closed shop,* requiring that only union members be employed, and the *preferential shop,* requiring that union members be given preference in filling job openings, were outlawed by the Taft-Hartley Act and thus no longer appear in collective bargaining agreements. Nevertheless, some contracts still contain references to union hiring halls and to certain requirements involving apprenticeships, which in effect do give preference to union members.

Most union security provisions are accompanied by the *checkoff,* an arrangement whereby the company agrees to deduct union dues, and sometimes initiation fees and assessments, from the member's paycheck, and submit this money to the union. For such provisions to become operative members must sign an authorization form, which is usually irrevocable for the term of the contract.

REGULATION OF UNION ACTIVITY. Although not classified specifically as union security, many provisions of a related nature may be scattered throughout the contract. These are aimed at regulating various activities of the union on company premises, or at providing special status for union representatives in carrying out the terms of the agreement. Among the former are provisions guaranteeing access to the plant by union representatives who are not company employees (sometimes with the stipulation that there be no interference with production), restrictions on the use of union bulletin boards, bans on membership solicitation or dues collection on company time, and limitations on the number of union representatives who may function within a company facility.

Provisions relating to union representatives may include such things as superseniority in matters of layoff, overtime, transfer, and holiday assignments; leaves of absence for union business; pay for time spent in processing grievances; and in some cases the use of company telephones or office space to conduct union affairs. Increasingly such provisions are being included in labor contracts. Presumably, companies consider them to be worthwhile in terms of improved union relations and conflict minimization (35).

Job Security

A matter of increasing importance for the unions as automation continues to threaten a variety of production jobs is job security. In the past, provisions relating to discipline and discharge were of primary significance to the union insofar as job security was concerned. Almost all contracts listed grounds for action in this sphere, and they still do. There are also provisions for such procedures as warnings, notice to the employee and the union, hearings, and appeals (see Chapter 18).

But at the present time, from the union viewpoint, seniority appears to be the most important aspect of job security. Under most agreements employees in the bargaining unit are ranked on the basis of seniority for purposes of preferences in promotion, transfer, choice of shift, layoff, and recall from layoff. In some instances the seniority unit may be limited to a single department, particularly where special skills are involved, but there are plant-wide units as well. As noted in Chapter 10, seniority and merit may carry varying weights in various types of employment decisions.

In the face of loss of jobs through technological displacement unions have pushed for a considerable broadening of seniority rights. Thus in some cases where a company has decided to shut down one of its operations, the union has insisted that employees have an option to transfer to another plant on the basis of overall company seniority. If a company decides to transfer an operation to a new location, the union position has often been that the new jobs should be offered to those previously employed at the old plant in terms of seniority. Also in this category are provisions for retraining employees whose jobs are eliminated by automation (see Chapter 15); for early retirement with full benefits, when the jobs of older employees are affected by plant shutdowns; and for maintaining full or partial income during periods of layoff (33).

Wages and Hours

Although wage increases have traditionally been the major economic goal of unions in collective bargaining, most agreements do not include detailed rates and ranges (see Chapter 16). Generally any increase negotiated by a union is added to the existing rates on the basis of either a cents-per-hour, across-the-board raise for all, or a percentage raise, with a larger total amount going to the higher-rated job classifications. For many years the former approach was followed almost exclusively, with the result that pay differentials for skilled work diminished markedly in percentage terms. This became a major source of conflict within the union movement, especially within the industrial unions. Under pressure from the more skilled groups there has been a gradual shift, so that percentage increases are now more common.

Most contracts that run for more than a year provide for certain automatic wage adjustments. These are called *improvement factors* or *productivity increases,* and usually become effective at yearly intervals. *Escalator clauses,* requiring automatic wage adjustments at quarterly intervals on the basis of changes in the cost of living, are found in a small percentage of all agreements, primarily in the automobile industry.

SUPPLEMENTARY WAGE PRACTICES. Most contracts contain provisions on various payments that extend beyond the base wage. The most common of these are *shift differentials,* providing extra pay for work on a night shift; *reporting pay* guarantees, which require a minimum payment (usually for four hours' work) when employees report in as scheduled and find work is not available; and *call-back* or *call-in* guarantees, which usually specify a minimum of four hours' pay for employees called in to work at some time other than a regularly scheduled shift. Other practices related to payment that are sometimes mentioned in the contract include hiring rates, job evaluation, progression through the rate range, incentive plans, time study procedures, and rates to be paid on temporary transfer from one job to another.

HOURS AND OVERTIME. Nearly all contracts include provisions regulating hours of work. This is accomplished as in the Federal law (see Chapter 6) by requiring overtime or premium pay for hours worked in excess of a normal schedule. The overtime rate is usually one-and-one-half times the regular rate, although occasionally double time is paid, or even triple time in cases where the work day extends beyond ten hours.

Premium pay for weekend or holiday work is included in most contracts, usually at the rates of time and a half for Saturdays, and double time for Sundays and holidays. There are often extensive stipulations regarding the scheduling of this overtime and premium work.

Employee Benefits and Services

Any so-called *fringe benefit* that can be considered of economic worth to employees or that influences working conditions is bargainable in a legal sense. Consequently, contracts normally deal at great length with paid vacations, holidays, insurance plans, pensions, and the like. These and other employee benefits will be considered in detail in Chapter 20.

Strikes and Lockouts

More than half of all union contracts contain unconditional no-strike clauses banning work stoppages during the term of the agreement. Another 40 per cent provide that the union will not strike except under specified conditions, such as exhaustion of the grievance procedure, violation of the contract terms, or failure to enforce an arbitration award. No-strike provisions often include statements to the effect that the union must take positive action against any unauthorized strikes if it is to avoid liability. Also, there are likely to be penalties for individual employees who participate in such unauthorized strikes. Nearly all no-strike clauses are accompanied by a comparable ban against lockouts by the company (8).

Grievances and Arbitration

Nearly every agreement establishes procedures for handling employee complaints and disputes over the interpretation of contract terms. In most cases these procedures include arbitration of unresolved differences by an impartial third party. Grievance handling is a continuing process and represents the primary source of union-management contacts at times other than when negotiations are in progress. As such it may easily become embroiled in conflict. Efforts to minimize this eventuality will be considered in the section that follows.

Administering the Contract

The contract provides a backdrop and a guide for day-to-day relations between union and management. But it does not inevitably eliminate conflict in these relations or provide a blueprint for subsequent events in all cases. It is not at all uncommon for a company to give the union a great deal more than it is actually entitled to under the contract. This is an effort to minimize conflict and maintain friendly relations. Situations of this kind are most frequent when the union is new on the scene and the leaders militant. As the bargaining relationship matures, the trend is for management to reassert its rights under the contract and to insist on stricter enforcement (39).

In many plants there is considerable informal cooperation between local management and union representatives on a continuing basis. At times there are even private agreements to ignore major provisions of the contract in the interest of harmonious relations (10). Although practices of this kind are often helpful at the moment, the long-term result may well be continuing union pressure for informal concessions to the point where productivity goals are seriously imperiled. Thus, the advances in organizational maintenance are achieved at a heavy price. Eventually, as personnel changes occur, administration of the contract may verge on the chaotic.

Under a more formal approach, local plant managers are encouraged to notify top management of any contract provisions that are creating problems so that they may be modified through collective bargaining, rather than subverted on an informal basis. Another aspect of such an approach is for management to act on a unilateral basis, except as consultation with the union is specifically required in the contract. The union may then protest under the grievance process, if it desires. Thus, the grievance machinery, which was originally established to ensure equity in handling the complaints of individual employees and to provide a channel for upward communication, is used in addition as a method of interpreting the contract.

Grievance Procedures

The grievance process is set in motion by the employee, either alone or in conjunction with the steward, discussing a complaint with his immediate supervisor. From there the complaint is processed through successively higher levels of management and union officials to a point where an outside arbitrator may be called upon to resolve the issue. Settlement may of course occur at any point in this upward movement. The details of the procedure between the first and final steps vary from company to company. As indicated in Figures 19-3 and 19-4, the number of steps tends to be a function of company size.

Figure 19-3. Typical Grievance Procedure for Small Plants

Step number	Union Representative		Employer Representative
One	Union Steward or Committeeman or Employee or Both	Takes up grievance with	Representative of the employer (foreman)
Two	Union representative	Takes up grievance with	Owner or Manager
Three	Arbitration		

Source: A. L. Gitlow. *Labor and Industrial Society.* Revised Edition. Homewood, Illinois: Richard D. Irwin, Inc., 1963, p. 497.

Figure 19-4. Typical Grievance Procedure for Large Plants

Step number	Union Representative		Employer Representative
One	Steward and aggrieved employee or Steward alone or Aggrieved employee alone	to	Foreman
	(Additional appeals may be made by the steward to higher line supervision, or the foreman may consult his superiors before giving the steward his answer.)		
Two	Union business representative or Chief plant steward or Chairman grievance committee	to	Higher line supervision
Three	Plant grievance committee	to	Top local management or Industrial relations office
Four	International office of union (regional or district representative)	to	Company director of Industrial relations
Five	Arbitration		

Source: A. L. Gitlow. *Labor and Industrial Society*. Revised Edition. Homewood, Illinois: Richard D. Irwin, Inc., 1963, p. 498.

Besides the number of steps, other differences from company to company concern such matters as time limits at each level, requirements for presenting complaints in writing (usually this is first required at the second step), pay to union representatives for time spent in grievance handling, and personnel responsible for different phases of the total activity. Some procedures call for a joint labor-management grievance committee to meet on a regular weekly or monthly basis.

In nonunion facilities, or for groups of employees not represented by a union, some firms have established procedures that are in many ways comparable to union-negotiated grievance procedures. Some of these utilize higher-level line and staff executives (the latter primarily in the personnel area), some provide for a grievance committee elected by employees, and some specify a board of review consisting of company executives. Arbitration by an outsider is not normally included as a final step. These formalized grievance processes in nonunion situations are found primarily in large corporations. In addition, certain firms have informal appeal systems permitting some complaints to go beyond the immediate supervisor. Nevertheless the majority of nonunion companies do not make specific provision for the handling of employee complaints (32).

Arbitration

Nearly all union contracts specify that grievances that are not resolved by the parties themselves must be decided by arbitration—a quasi-judicial process that has both advantages and disadvantages from a management viewpoint. Although arbitration provides an orderly method of settling disputes and is ordinarily accompanied by a union no-strike pledge, which is unquestionably beneficial to management, the process may also serve to limit severely a company's freedom of action. For this reason a number of firms have insisted on contract provisions that clearly establish the scope of arbitration. These usually specify a limitation to matters involving the interpretation of the contract or exclude such concerns as general wage issues, production standards, and management rights.

In general the arbitrator is chosen on an *ad hoc* basis; that is, a different individual may be selected for each case. Some contracts call for an arbitration board, consisting of union and management representatives, with an impartial chairman. In some large companies or where an association-wide agreement exists, a permanent umpire or arbitration panel may be appointed to handle all disputes during the term of the contract. This has the advantage that the arbitrator can become familiar with contract provisions and problems and thus will not have to spend the same time acquiring background information that an *ad hoc* appointee would.

The arbitrator must be a mutual choice of both parties. Usually, if agreement on an individual cannot be achieved, the contract will require that the arbitrator be appointed by an impartial agency such as the Federal Mediation and Conciliation Service or the American Arbitration Association.

The expenses associated with arbitration can be considerable. Normally they are shared equally by union and company, although some contracts require the loser to assume the whole burden. The cost of arbitration, both in terms of fees charged and time lost from work, can be a decisive factor for a small company or a union with limited resources. Thus, a strong pressure for settlement at lower levels in the grievance process often exists.

The Effectiveness of Grievance Machinery

The grievance procedure is usually the most important aspect of labor relations insofar as conflict minimization is concerned. When the process operates fairly and efficiently, employees will have little need to resort to slowdowns, strikes, and similar disruptive actions to draw attention to their problems. The grievance machinery provides a readily available channel for upward communication.

By studying the use of the grievance procedure, a personnel manager can often become aware of potential focuses of conflict before they become disruptive. Any time there is a decided increase in grievance activity at a particular location or in an employee group, it can be assumed problems exist that may subsequently become critical. There may be an overeager union steward trying to make a name for himself through the expansion of minor incidents into full-scale grievances; there may be a concerted attempt to "get" an unpopular foreman; there may be considerable and widespread discontent over a change in production standards. In any event increased grievance activity is likely to portend trouble.

Yet a complete lack of grievances can also raise questions. There have been numerous instances in which foremen have permitted employees to violate the contract repeatedly to keep grievances down and avoid an image of dissension at higher levels. Thus, extremely low grievance rates may reflect supervisory overpermissiveness and may be obtained at considerable cost in other areas.

Because grievances almost invariably begin with a complaint to first-line supervision, and because the attitudes and behavior of supervisors have a direct relationship to the grievance rate (16), it is extremely important to keep the lower levels of management well informed in this area. This is particularly crucial in large organizations in which foremen often feel that they have little voice in contract negotiations. It is not "their" contract and they may tend to reject it, merely because they do not understand the reasons for certain provisions. Management development programs dealing with contract changes, grievance settlements, and arbitration awards are widely used to serve this need for continuing information.

In spite of these efforts there are many firms that are not able to make the grievance machinery operate effectively as a method of draining off anger and reducing controversy. Foremen often become disillusioned when their decisions are reversed at a later stage of the grievance process. The next time they may decide not to take disciplinary action, enforce production standards, or risk antagonizing their subordinates in some other way. The prospect of being reversed once again is more than they wish to face. Such difficulties can be overcome through effective communication among those responsible for management's answers at various steps in the grievance process. Unfortunately, however, this is not always achieved, and as a result the grievance machinery may serve to foster ineffective supervision much more than it serves to reduce conflict.

Another contributory factor in instances in which the grievance approach fails to achieve its full potential can be the nature of the relationship between union leaders and union members. A union steward or higher official may push an employee complaint to arbitration even though it is apparent to him that there is little likelihood of success. This is done to prove to the employee involved, and to others, that the leadership of the union does in fact have the interests of the membership in mind. Ironically, this sort of action tends to occur most frequently when union-management relations are tranquil, and the leadership may feel it is under some pressure to demonstrate a degree of militancy. Furthermore, there are times when it is difficult to convince an employee that his grievance has no merit. Under such circumstances it is often easier to let an arbitrator tell him than to withdraw the grievance against his opposition. A high proportion of grievances going to arbitration is often indicative of a leadership that feels powerless relative to the rank and file. This assumes, of course, that the union has a sizable treasury and can afford to use the arbitration process to placate the membership.

In recent years a number of different approaches have been developed to improve the effectiveness of the grievance machinery. Many of these involve some type of management development effort stressing aspects of the communications process. One company required the union to submit all grievances in writing and then made it mandatory for the foreman involved to consult with the personnel department before taking any action. In this way the company was able to assure that the foreman acted with full knowledge of relevant contract provisions and company policy (39). In another instance the approach was reversed. The formal writing of grievances was suspended; union and management representatives were encouraged to settle employee complaints orally and on the spot. The result was that the number of grievances submitted for arbitration was reduced substantially (28). Other companies have resorted to what amount to group therapy sessions in which supervisors discuss their grievance-handling methods and the reasons behind them. This approach has also been reported to be successful (36). Clearly, unique aspects of each situation contribute to the effectiveness of these approaches. What works to make the grievance process function more efficiently as a means to organizational maintenance in one firm may not achieve the same result in another.

Union-Management Conflict

Situations leading to major disputes between management and a union may result from an organizing drive, from an impasse during collective bargaining, from unresolved grievances, or from widespread employee dissatisfaction. When such disputes are not resolved to the satisfaction of the unionized employees, open conflict can result. The ultimate weapon available to the union at such times is a strike or some other type of work stoppage. A sizable breakdown of organizational maintenance can occur, and contributions to productivity goals are decreased or entirely eliminated.

During the 1930's the major factor in instances of open conflict was some kind of organizing effort. As indicated in Table 19-2, this situation has now changed. In recent years work stoppages have resulted primarily from disputes over general wage changes and other bargaining issues. This is true at least in part because most contracts include some type of no-strike pledge from the union. Because these pledges hold for the duration of a contract, it is only when an agreement has terminated, without a new one being signed, that the union can strike, unless it is willing to take the risk of being held liable for damages.

Table 19-2.   Major Issues in Work Stoppages Involving 1,000 Workers or More (1965)

Issue	*Stoppages, %*
General wage changes	40.7
Supplementary benefits; no general wage change	3.0
Wage adjustments	4.5
Hours of work	.4
Other contractual matters	3.0
Union organization and security	7.5
Job security	9.3
Plant administration	25.4
Other working conditions	2.2
Interunion or intraunion matters	4.1

Source: Bureau of Labor Statistics, United States Department of Labor, *Analysis of Work Stoppages 1965*, Bulletin No. 1525. Washington, D.C.: the Bureau, 1966, p. 4.

Union Tactics in Conflict

Strike actions may be categorized on a number of bases. The major consideration is the nature of the demand made on the company. An *economic strike* is one in which the demands relate to wages, fringe benefits, or some other factor having economic value. Usually it is an outgrowth of bargaining. An *unfair labor practices strike* represents a protest against an alleged illegal labor practice involving management, such as discrimination on the basis of union membership. *Jurisdictional strikes* may result when there is a dispute over representation—one of the unions involved uses this tactic to enforce a demand for recognition as the sole bargaining agent. *Sympathy strikes* occur when a union has no direct dispute with the company but merely wishes to register support for the demands of other strikers.

In any of these cases the strike may be *authorized,* in that it has been approved by a vote of the membership and by the national executive board, or *unauthorized,* in that such support has not been obtained. Unauthorized strikes are frequently referred to as *wildcat strikes.* Employees participating in them take considerable risk, because they may be disciplined by the union as well as the company (20).

The *slowdown* is another tactic that may be used by any group of employees, whether unionized or not, to indicate protest and to provide pressure in support of demands. Usually the employees stay on the job but slow production in various ways; sometimes they report sick in disproportionately large numbers. Approaches such as these are used during the term of a contract when a no-strike clause bars more direct action and when the situation does not appear to warrant the risks of a wildcat strike.

Unions may engage in *picketing* either in conjunction with a strike or separately. This tactic provides a means of informing outsiders regarding the nature of a labor-management dispute, with a view to discouraging buying, cutting off suppliers, or gaining the support of sympathy strikers. Picketing against a company with which the union has no dispute, merely to force the company not to handle products of another firm with which it does have a dispute, is considered a *secondary boycott,* and is illegal under Federal labor law.

As indicated earlier, the use of the various union tactics is hedged by a number of legal constraints. And there are certain things management may and may not do in retaliation. For instance, a company may institute a suit for damages against a union participating in a secondary boycott or an illegal strike. Economic strikers may be replaced, and thus lose their jobs permanently; unfair labor practice strikers retain their employee status. Any use of mass picketing to block access to a plant, or violence on the picket line, however, can result in loss of reinstatement rights. At certain times, such as the period just prior to contract termination, all strikes are illegal. Ordinarily a company that is struck can retaliate with a *lockout,* excluding all workers whether on strike or not. This is frequently done in association bargaining; the union will strike one plant or company, and the association responds with a lockout extending throughout its ranks. The union is thus faced with a considerably increased burden in terms of strike benefits.

The Decision for Conflict

Generally, management has a fairly good idea as to whether a union is in a position to strike in an effort to achieve its demands. Yet there are times when, even though the union clearly has the backing of its members and the resources to conduct a strike, the issues at stake are of such fundamental, long-term significance to the organization that there is, in fact, little choice. Management can lose more by giving in to a union than it could possibly lose by accepting a strike.

Both sides have much to consider before forcing such an open conflict. The union is much more likely to risk a strike in times of high employment and profits, when internal problems facing the leadership are minimal, when membership support for such action is strong, where the national union has given its approval and made strike funds available, and in an environment in which community and general public support can be anticipated. One of the most common and most serious miscalculations on the part of management relates to the support of the membership. In a number of cases in which there has appeared to be dissension within the union ranks, a firm stand by the company has served to polarize opinion and unite the membership against management. These and other considerations in the decision for or against open conflict are noted in Table 19-3.

In the early 1960's it appeared that there was a trend toward less strike activity on the part of the unions. Beginning in late 1964, however, this trend was reversed. Not only did the number of strikes increase, but they were of longer duration, presumably in part at least because of the availability of large strike funds accumulated over a period of time under long-term contracts (6).

Yet there is reason to believe that certain unions, at least, are finding strikes less attractive, especially in industries such as petroleum and the utilities, where operations are increasingly automated and production can continue at near normal levels despite a walkout (38). Furthermore, many current issues appear to be far too complex to be solved under the pressure of a strike. Accordingly, companies and unions in a number of industries have been experimenting with new approaches involving formal plans for cooperation, either written into the contract, or supplementing it, or in a few instances entirely outside it.

Table 19-3. Union and Company Alternatives in a Bargaining Situation and Related Consequences

Company	Union
Alternative 1: Giving in to union demands	Alternative 1: Accepting company counteroffer
Perceived *consequences:*	Perceived *consequences:*
1. Lessening of investor return	1. Loss of membership support
2. Loss of competitive standing	2. Loss of status within union movement
3. Setting bad precedent	3. Setting bad precedent
4. Avoiding costly strike	4. Avoiding costly strike
5. Avoiding government and public ill will	5. Avoiding government and public ill will
Alternative 2: Refusing to accede to union demands	Alternative 2: Sticking to original demands
Perceived *consequences:*	Perceived *consequences:*
1. Due to potential strike, loss of investor return	1. Prove strength and determination of union to members
2. Due to potential strike, loss of competitive standing	2. Due to potential strike, loss of member income
3. Loss of government and public good will	3. Due to potential strike, loss of member support
4. Maintenance of company prerogatives	4. Loss of government and public good will
5. Breaking union power	5. Teach company a "lesson"

Source: R. Stagner and H. Rosen, *Psychology of Union-Management Relations*, p. 103. Copyright 1965 by Wadsworth Publishing Company, Inc., Belmont, California. Used by permission.

Union-Management Cooperation

In recent years a number of particularly difficult situations have developed, not only in regard to bargaining, but also in day-to-day contract administration. In their efforts to remain competitive in a technological sense, certain firms have met considerable resistance. Archaic work rules and negotiated restrictions against such practices as contracting out maintenance and other work have been invoked repeatedly by unions (9). Nevertheless, automation has made headway, in some cases a great deal of headway. The number of production jobs is declining relative to the total labor force, and union strength has suffered accordingly.

Other sources of difficulties have been the trend toward larger bargaining units, encompassing entire multiplant corporations or even entire industries, and the resort to long-term contracts. When the issues build up over two or three years, it is often impossible to settle differences to the satisfaction of both parties in the two or three months normally allocated for negotiating a new contract.

As alternatives to open conflict in these situations, a number of plans calling for formal union-management cooperation on a continuing basis have been undertaken. Such plans are not entirely new, of course. Companies have utilized joint committees in areas such as accident prevention, suggestion systems, and job evaluation for some time. What is new is the assumption that a great many problems of a bargainable nature are too complex for hurried solution. Thus, there has been a tendency to study a much more varied set of issues jointly, often with the help of outside labor relations experts (21).

An example is provided by the Armour and Company negotiations. In 1959 the company closed down a number of plants, and as a result the union exerted considerable pressure for contract provisions protecting job security. Because of the many problems involved, there was not an adequate chance to reach an agreement during the 1959 bargaining. Accordingly the company proposed establishing an automation fund of $500,000 and a joint committee with an impartial chairman to study and report on ways to handle the job security issue. By the time of the 1961 negotiations, this committee had produced its report, and agreement was reached on various contract changes, providing for such things as transfer of seniority rights, payment of relocation costs, technological adjustment pay, improved severance allowances, and early retirement benefits. Also, the joint committee was continued. Although the attitudes of those involved changed very little, a much better understanding of mutual problems was achieved, with the result that open conflict was minimized (19).

The basic steel industry provides another example. Negotiations in 1959 produced a strike lasting more than 100 days, as well as considerable governmental pressure on both parties. The agreement that was finally attained in January 1960 included provisions for a Human Relations Research Committee to study and recommend solutions to various mutual problems. This committee developed suggestions on seniority and grievance procedures that were included in the 1962 contracts, and it has continued to conduct studies in other problem areas. Although this approach has eased some of the stress associated with bargaining, there is reason to believe that the union membership as a whole may have become disenchanted with the emphasis on human relations rather than dollars-and-cents benefits. The president of the Steelworkers Union, who was widely credited with having a major role in establishing the Human

Relations Research Committee, was not reelected to office in 1965, in part apparently because of dissatisfaction over such matters.

One of the most widely discussed agreements with regard to automation is the one covering longshoring operations on the West Coast. During the 1930's and 1940's open union-management conflict was frequent and intense. The union consistently opposed changes in work rules and the introduction of new methods. Concerned about the decline in work opportunity in the industry, the union leaders finally organized a special conference on the subject in 1957. The result was a proposal to cooperate with employers in developing a plan to modernize work methods without jeopardizing job security.

The resulting deliberations extended over three years. The 1960 negotiations produced an agreement permitting the employers to change work methods and introduce labor-saving devices on a large scale. In return the longshoremen were guaranteed pay for thirty-five hours a week whether they worked the full period or not. Also, there were various provisions for early retirement and lump-sum payments by the company at the time of retirement, disability, or death. Financing came from a trust fund to which the employers paid a total of $5 million each year for five and a half years. As it developed, even with the introduction of new methods, the thirty-five-hour work week was generally maintained. Consequently, at the end of 1966, $13 million from the fund was distributed to more than 10,000 union members. The pay guarantee was eliminated as unnecessary from the five-year contract signed in 1966, but the new agreement did provide for a special lump-sum bonus of $13,000 for any longshoreman who was willing to retire at age sixty-two to make way for more dock machines.

Another aspect of the longshoring and similar agreements is the emphasis on continuing day-to-day contact between the parties, aimed at solving problems before they become acute. Thus, local port arbitrators are charged with handling disputes on the docks. The result has not been a total elimination of controversy, but conflicts have diminished and actual work stoppages are now rare.

Whether the type of cooperation described provides a key to the labor relations of the future remains an open question. The great majority of these approaches have evolved from long-standing and mature bargaining relationships. The parties involved have been aware of a mutual need for new types of problem solving and for greater understanding.

References

1. Bakke, E. W., C. Kerr, and C. W. Anrod, *Unions, Management, and the Public.* New York: Harcourt, Brace, 1960.

2. Barkin, S., *The Decline of the Labor Movement*. Santa Barbara, Calif.: Center for the Study of Democratic Institutions, 1961.

3. Beal, E. F., *The Practice of Collective Bargaining*, 3rd ed. Homewood, Ill.: Irwin, 1967.

4. Blake, R. R., H. A. Shepard, and J. S. Mouton, *Managing Intergroup Conflict in Industry*. Houston, Texas: Gulf, 1964.

5. Blum, A. A., "The Prospects for Office Employee Unionism," in G. G. Somers (ed.), *Proceedings of the Sixteenth Annual Meeting*. Madison, Wisc.: Industrial Relations Research Association, 1964, pp. 182–193.

6. Bureau of Labor Statistics, United States Department of Labor, *Analysis of Work Stoppages 1965*, Bulletin No. 1525. Washington, D.C.: the Bureau, 1966.

7. Bureau of Labor Statistics, United States Department of Labor, *Directory of National and International Labor Unions in the United States, 1965*, Bulletin No. 1493. Washington, D.C.: the Bureau, 1966.

8. Bureau of National Affairs, Inc., *Basic Patterns in Union Contracts*, 6th ed. Washington, D.C.: BNA, Inc., 1966.

9. Chandler, M. K., *Management Rights and Union Interests*. New York: McGraw-Hill, 1964.

10. Dalton, M., "Some Pros and Cons of Union-Management Cooperation," *Personnel Administration*, Vol. 28, No. 6 (1965), 3–5, 38–43.

11. Derber, M., W. E. Chalmers, and R. Stagner, *The Local Union-Management Relationship*. Urbana, Ill.: Institute of Labor and Industrial Relations, Univ. of Illinois, 1960.

12. Dubin, R., "A Theory of Conflict and Power in Union-Management Relations," *Industrial and Labor Relations Review*, Vol. 13 (1960), 501–518.

13. Dubin, R., "Leadership in Union-Management Relations as an Intergroup System," in M. Sherif (ed.), *Intergroup Relations and Leadership*. New York: Wiley, 1962, pp. 70–91.

14. Dunnette, M. D., and W. K. Kirchner, *Psychology Applied to Industry*. New York: Appleton-Century-Crofts, 1965.

15. Estey, M., *The Unions—Structure, Development and Management*. New York: Harcourt, Brace and World, 1967.

16. Fleishman, E. A., and E. F. Harris, "Patterns of Leadership Behavior Related to Employee Grievances and Turnover," *Personnel Psychology*, Vol. 15 (1962), 43–56.

17. Ginzberg, E., and I. E. Berg, *Democratic Values and the Rights of Management*. New York: Columbia Univ. Press, 1963.

18. Gitlow, A. L., *Labor and Industrial Society*, rev. ed. Homewood, Ill.: Irwin, 1963.

19. Healy, J. J., *Creative Collective Bargaining*. Englewood Cliffs, N.J.: Prentice-Hall, 1965.

20. Heneman, H. G., and D. Yoder, *Labor Economics*, 2nd ed. Cincinnati: South-Western Publishing Company, 1965.

21. Hildebrand, G. H., "The Use of Tripartite Bodies to Supplement Collective Bargaining," *Labor Law Journal*, Vol. 12 (1961), 655–663.

22. Hilgert, R. L., "When an Office is Unionized—Its Meaning for Management Policy," *Personnel Administration*, Vol. 28, No. 2 (1965), 33–38.

23. Kassalow, E. M., "The United States," in A. Sturmthal (ed.), *White Collar Trade Unions.* Urbana, Ill.: Univ. of Illinois Press, 1966, pp. 305–364.
24. Kerr, C., "The Collective Bargaining Environment," in C. S. Golden and V. D. Parker (eds.), *Causes of Industrial Peace Under Collective Bargaining.* New York: Harper & Row, 1955, pp. 10–22.
25. Kerr, C., *Labor and Management in Industrial Society.* Garden City, N.Y.: Doubleday, 1964.
26. Kornhauser, A., R. Dubin, and A. M. Ross, *Industrial Conflict.* New York: McGraw-Hill, 1954.
27. Levine, S. B., and B. Karsh, "Industrial Relations in the Next Generation," *Quarterly Review of Economics and Business,* Vol. 1 (1961), 18–29.
28. McKersie, R. B., "Avoiding Written Grievances by Problem-Solving: An Outside View," *Personnel Psychology,* Vol. 17 (1964), 367–379.
29. Muench, G. A., "A Clinical Psychologist's Treatment of Labor-Management Conflicts," *Personnel Psychology,* Vol. 13 (1960), 165–172.
30. Northrup, H. R., and G. F. Bloom, *Government and Labor.* Homewood, Ill.: Irwin, 1963.
31. Purcell, T. V., *Blue Collar Man.* Cambridge, Mass.: Harvard Univ. Press, 1960.
32. Scott, W. G., *The Management of Conflict.* Homewood, Ill.: Irwin, 1965.
33. Shils, E. B., *Automation and Industrial Relations.* New York: Holt, Rinehart and Winston, 1963.
34. Slichter, S. H., J. J. Healy, and E. R. Livernash, *The Impact of Collective Bargaining on Management.* Washington, D.C.: The Brookings Institution, 1960.
35. Sloane, A. A., and L. B. Valant, "Changing Status of the Union Steward," *Personnel Journal,* Vol. 44 (1965), 295–300.
36. Speroff, B. J., "Group Psychology in Labor Relations," *Personnel Journal,* Vol. 39 (1960), 14–17.
37. Stagner, R., and H. Rosen, *Psychology of Union-Management Relations.* Belmont, Calif.: Wadsworth, 1965.
38. Stern, J. L., "Declining Utility of the Strike," *Industrial and Labor Relations Review,* Vol. 18 (1964), 60–72.
39. Strauss, G., "The Shifting Power Balance in the Plant," *Industrial Relations,* Vol. 1 (1962), 65–96.
40. Thompson, K. M., "Human Relations in Collective Bargaining," *Harvard Business Review,* Vol. 31, No. 2 (1953), 116–126.
41. Walton, R. E., and R. B. McKersie, *A Behavioral Theory of Labor Negotiations.* New York: McGraw-Hill, 1965.

Questions

1. Why does the mere presence of a union represent a threat to organizational maintenance? What factors associated with the union serve to determine the extent of this threat?
2. Why do workers join unions? What factors keep workers from joining

unions? Considering these two forces and the apparent future trends in labor force composition, what do you feel will be the pattern of union participation in years to come?

3. What are the pros and cons of free collective bargaining versus direct governmental intervention as approaches to industrial conflict?
4. Distinguish between the following:
   a. Union security and job security
   b. Closed shop and agency shop
   c. Craft unions and industrial unions
   d. Containment relationships and accommodation relationships
   e. Mediation and arbitration
   f. Jurisdictional strikes and sympathy strikes
   g. Organizational picketing and secondary boycotts
   h. Authorized strikes and wildcat strikes
   i. Union shop provisions and right-to-work laws
   j. Escalator clauses and checkoffs
5. Under what circumstances may the grievance process serve to
   a. Reduce the effectiveness of supervision
   b. Protect union leaders
   c. Interpret the contract
   d. Provide a means to conflict reduction
   e. Identify problem areas in the company
6. What are some of the newer approaches to grievance handling, collective bargaining, and union-management cooperation in general? Why does each of these approaches appear to have positive value as a means to organizational maintenance?

20

Employee Benefits
and Services

The number and variety of benefits and services provided by companies for their employees have grown rapidly in recent years to the point where items of this kind represent a major factor in total compensation. These so-called fringe benefits range from costly insurance and retirement programs to the use of company facilities in connection with the activities of various employee groups. They may be provided by the company on an entirely unilateral basis or they may emerge out of extended bargaining with a union. They may have as their immediate goal the improvement of working conditions (music in the plant), the provision of more leisure time (vacations and holidays), or the guaranteeing of security in times of personal adversity (group hospitalization insurance and supplemental unemployment pay).

Although part of the total compensation package, these items are not intended to encourage task motivation. Little effort has been made to use fringe benefits as inducements or rewards, with a view to maximizing the effectiveness of role behavior. Thus, differentials related to merit or productivity are not a characteristic aspect of their application. The ultimate goal of employee benefits and services is to further organizational maintenance by contributing to high morale, a sense of security, and the general job satisfaction of employees. In this way internal stress within the organization is minimized, but there is no reason to believe that productivity will necessarily be fostered as a result (2). In addition, benefits may be used as an inducement to continued organizational membership. A further objective, which is often noted, is that such benefits are a valuable asset in recruiting potentially effective employees.

The latter factor may not be as important as many have believed. Young people just entering the labor force, in particular, are unlikely to be influenced by liberal retirement provisions and life insurance plans. Even more mature job seekers are often not as concerned with such matters as with basic wage rates and advancement opportunities. Furthermore, those firms with the most liberal benefit plans also tend to be the ones with the highest wage scales and the most desirable working conditions (16). In other words, a good place to work is a good place to work, and employee benefits are unlikely to be the deciding factor when a man agrees to accept employment. On the other hand, a program in this area that is markedly deficient, relative to those of other companies, may make this a salient concern for a prospective employee and lead him to accept work elsewhere.

This same consideration—that benefit programs can hurt a company if they are below expectation levels but contribute very little to goal attainment in a positive sense if they are more liberal than expected— applies to existing employees as well. Yet some benefits clearly do contribute to a more stable work force. Thus, such things as the length of paid vacations and the amount of monthly retirement payments are normally dependent upon length of service and therefore do make a contribution to organizational stability.

Irrespective of the significance benefit programs may have for maintenance and recruiting, they nevertheless do represent a major aspect of the personnel function in most firms. Much time and effort is spent on surveys and studies of alternative benefit practices, in negotiating with unions on such matters, and in administering existing programs. Furthermore, a high percentage of all payroll costs are paid out in this form.

The Pattern of Growth

Various programs providing benefits and services to employees have been in existence since the beginnings of industrialization. Thus, it is not so much the existence of these practices that differentiates the present from the past as the frequency with which they are found and the costs involved.

Types of Benefits

The earliest employee benefits such as company housing and company stores were provided largely out of necessity where adequate facilities were not otherwise available to employees. By the first years of the present century there were occasional instances of companies giving paid vacations and holidays, and even retirement and insurance benefits. These spread still further during the 1920's with the advent of so-called paternalism. The benefits were usually granted unilaterally by the company, although it can be assumed that in some cases the primary intent was to prevent unionization. Actually, however, the most pronounced increase occurred among white-collar and salaried groups. In any event, many benefit plans inaugurated during the 1920's were short-lived. The depression produced major cutbacks in this area, so that by the mid-1930's few firms provided benefits of any real significance. For production workers they were almost nonexistent (18).

Yet at the present time practically all employees in the United States, at all levels, enjoy several paid holidays and a paid vacation each year, more than half are enrolled in some type of private pension plan, and about three-fourths are covered by a health and welfare program. This very marked change over the past thirty years can be attributed in large part to policies adopted by the Federal government and to the constraints on company personnel decisions that have resulted.

GOVERNMENTAL EFFECTS. As noted in Chapters 5 and 6, various laws of the new deal era had considerable impact. The Social Security Act influenced pension planning; the Wage-Hour law increased premium pay; the Wagner Act served to support unionization, and thus ultimately gave unions the strength to bargain for fringe benefits. During World War II, and again during the Korean War, the fiscal policies of the Federal government were important. Under the wage controls in effect at these times, companies were discouraged from raising wages, but they were often permitted to provide longer vacations, additional paid holidays, and other fringe items. Excess profit tax provisions served to encourage companies to set up retirement or health and welfare funds, because this could be done at very little immediate cost.

UNION EFFECTS. Although these governmental actions encouraged the growth of employee benefits, even to force them upon companies in some instances, the effects were often mediated by the unions. Until the end of World War II the major union emphasis was on raising wages; on benefits related to wages, hours, and work schedules, such as shift differentials, rest periods, and cleanup time; and on benefits requiring paid time away from work, such as holidays, vacations, and certain kinds of leaves. After the war, perhaps influenced by the number of plans established unilaterally by companies under the favorable wartime tax laws, the major unions began to demand bargaining with regard to retirement plans and health and welfare programs.

Initially there was considerable doubt as to whether these union demands were legally justified. However, in 1948 the National Labor Relations Board ruled in favor of the unions, indicating that companies must bargain on such matters.[1] Consequently the decade that followed produced a dramatic growth, both in the number of companies providing retirement and health benefits and in the level of the benefits themselves. The wage controls and tax provisions invoked during the Korean War of the early 1950's gave additional impetus to this upswing.

By the mid-1950's pension and welfare plans were well established throughout most of manufacturing. Union attention then shifted to methods of providing worker security against seasonal layoffs, as well as against technological displacement. In the automobile industry demands for a guaranteed annual wage produced extensive supplemental unemployment benefits at company expense. In other industries where automation threatened job security, union demands centered on benefits such as retraining allowances and severance pay, again with some success. However, the majority of these items are tailored to the specific problems of a particular industry. Thus, none has achieved widespread acceptance. In recent years the primary source of growth in the employee benefits area has been the increase in the level of existing provisions—longer vacations, additional insurance, higher retirement payments, and the like.

Costs of Benefits

One method of measuring growth in employee benefits is in terms of their cost to employers. Because of differences of opinion regarding the specific items to be included and varying methods of computing costs, it is often difficult to make meaningful benefit comparisons between companies. However, the Chamber of Commerce of the United States has conducted reasonably standardized surveys of fringe benefit costs every two years since 1947, and these findings are useful as a general indicator of trends over time.

The results of the 1965 survey indicated that payments for employee benefits and services ranged from 7 to over 70 per cent of payroll. The average for all companies included in the survey was 24.7 per cent of payroll (71.5 cents per payroll hour, or $1,502 per year per employee). By contrast the best available estimate of average benefit costs for the year 1929 is 3 per cent of payroll (6).

The figures in Table 20-1 are based on benefit costs reported by the eighty-four companies that have been included in all Chamber of Com-

---

[1] *Inland Steel Company v. NLRB,* NLRB77, 1(1948).

merce surveys since 1947. In absolute terms these results presumably are not typical for industry as a whole. The trend of the data does provide a good index of growth, however. Because of rapidly rising wages over the period, the increase as a per cent of payroll amounted to roughly 75 per cent; the actual increase in company costs, either in terms of cents per payroll hour or dollars per year per employee, exceeded 300 per cent. Most of the increase took the form of pension and welfare benefits and payments for time not worked, the two areas in which the unions have been most active.

Table 20-1. Comparison of 1947–1965 Fringe Payments for 84 Companies

Type of payment	1947	1955	1965
1. As per cent of total payroll	16.1	22.4	28.1
Legally required payments (employer's share only for Social Security, Unemployment Compensation, Workmen's Compensation, etc.)	2.6	2.9	4.2
Pension and other agreed-upon payments (employer's share only for pensions, insurance, health and welfare benefits, etc.)	5.0	7.5	9.9
Paid rest periods, lunch periods, etc.	1.6	2.4	2.4
Payments for time not worked (vacations, holidays, leaves, etc.)	5.6	7.7	9.6
Profit-sharing payments, bonuses, etc.	1.3	1.9	2.0
2. As cents per payroll hour	22.1	48.5	88.8
3. As dollars per year per employee	450	1,004	1,875

Source: Chamber of Commerce of the United States, *Fringe Benefits—1965*, Washington, D.C.: the Chamber, 1966, p. 27.

Legally Required Payments

Included in the Chamber of Commerce figures are payments required of employers by state or Federal law. Such payments serve to provide Social Security benefits at retirement, medical care for the elderly, compensation for injury on the job, and support for the unemployed. Because these subjects have been treated at length in connection with the discussion of legal constraints in Chapters 5 and 6, they will receive only limited attention here. Such legally required plans are of interest at this point primarily as they influence the specific private benefit programs developed by various companies.

Direct Monetary Benefits

A major category commonly included within the definition of employee benefits involves various direct payments to employees. These may occur (a) as part of regular earnings, (b) in lieu of regular earnings in cases associated with layoffs, and (c) in addition to regular earnings as with certain types of bonuses. In unionized situations such payments are a matter for negotiation and are specified in the contract. Generally nonunion firms attempt to maintain these direct monetary benefits at levels that are typical for the specific labor market and/or industry.

Payments Related to Time Worked

Almost all companies make some payments to their hourly workers that are in addition to the straight time rate for hours spent on the job. These payments are sometimes subsumed under wages and salaries for purposes of cost computation, but the more frequent practice appears to be to consider them as fringe benefits. Included are payments for daily or weekly overtime at rates above those for straight time; differentials for work on a second or third shift; premium pay for work on weekends, holidays, or under hazardous or undesirable conditions; call-in, reporting, and call-back pay; pay for wash-up or travel time; and paid coffee breaks, rest periods, or lunch hours.

Of course, some of these are required by law. Other payments related to time worked are specified in the union contract. Still others are provided by the company at its own discretion as a contribution to organizational maintenance. In large part the extent of such payments depends on the nature of the firm's operations. A manufacturing plant on a twenty-four-hour day and a seven-day week will have much higher costs in this area than a nonmanufacturing organization on a regular workweek.

Paid Time Off

Another group of benefits includes items designed to provide employees, whether hourly or salaried, a certain amount of time off without loss of pay. Holidays, vacations, and leaves are all of this kind.

HOLIDAYS. Nearly all firms give their employees at least six paid holidays; some give as many as nine or ten a year. Employees (other than managers and professionals) required to work on these days are normally compensated with an extra day's pay or more. Usually, eligibility for holiday pay is contingent on the employee working his regularly scheduled day before and after the holiday.

The most common holidays are Christmas, Thanksgiving, July Fourth, Labor Day, New Year's Day, and Memorial Day. Beyond these there is a great deal of diversity. Days off range from Election Day to various state holidays to the employee's birthday (4). There appears to be a trend recently to give more than one day off at Christmas or Thanksgiving, rather than to extend the number of isolated holidays. In any event it seems clear that the total paid time off for holidays is likely to continue its upward climb under the pressure of union demands.

VACATIONS. Provisions for paid vacations, varying in length from one to four weeks, are now a standard practice throughout industry. In nearly all cases the length of the vacation depends on the duration of employment with the company. For example, one week after one year of service, two weeks after three years, three weeks after ten years, and four weeks after twenty years. As with holidays, employees must usually meet certain work requirements to be eligible for a paid vacation. Some companies close down operations for vacation periods. Where this is not the practice, employees are likely to be given some choice in the scheduling process. First choice normally goes to those with the most seniority.

In industries characterized by casual employment, such as construction, employer associations or unions may establish a vacation fund from which workers receive benefits based on the number of hours worked during the year. In the business world generally it is not uncommon to make payments in lieu of a vacation, especially if an individual terminates employment prior to exhausting his allotted number of days. Thus, vacations are increasingly taking on the status of an earned right.

A new concept involving periodic extended vacations, or so-called sabbaticals, has been introduced in the steel and related industries in recent years. Aimed at providing more jobs for younger employees, cutting down on layoffs, and encouraging earlier retirements, the plan calls for ten weeks' vacation, in addition to the regular three or four weeks, once every five years. There is little indication that such plans are expanding to any marked degree beyond the confines of this one industry.

LEAVE. Unscheduled time off with pay, due to personal illness or to death or illness in the family, is provided by a number of companies. This type of benefit is most likely to apply to salaried employees, but many hourly production workers are now covered by insurance plans that accomplish much the same result. Time off to vote, required by law in a number of states, and time for jury duty are additional forms of paid leave often provided.

In addition there are a variety of unpaid leaves that, although they involve only negligible costs to the company, have important implications for job security. Thus, most firms permit employees to take unpaid leaves of absence for such reasons as maternity, military service, union business, civic duty, education, or merely "personal reasons" without any loss in seniority.

Payments in Lieu of Earnings

Several types of benefits are designed to maintain some income for employees during periods when work is not available. Some companies guarantee all regular employees a certain number of hours or a certain amount of pay per week. Or they guarantee so many weeks of work during the year. Provisions of this kind have been in existence for as long as thirty or forty years. More recently certain unions have negotiated plans calling for the payment of supplemental unemployment benefits. Generally these plans are financed by company contributions to a trust fund and, as the name implies, the benefits are paid as a supplement to state unemployment compensation. Thus, during the period of a layoff, such as the annual retooling period in the automobile industry, employees are able to maintain an income level close to their regular earnings.

Other benefits, such as severance or separation pay, retraining allowances, and technological adjustment pay, serve to maintain income to employees who are separated. The idea is to help them in the process of finding new employment, although some such payments extend well beyond the period normally required for this purpose. The minimum amount would appear to be about two weeks' pay; the maximum approximately a year's pay. Length of prior service is the determining factor in establishing the total payment.

Payments in Addition to Regular Earnings

Other types of cash payments, although not as widespread as those previously noted, are found in some companies. These usually take the form of a Christmas or year-end bonus. The amount of such a bonus may or may not be related to profits, but it is common practice to do so. Other factors that may influence the amount received are the total time worked during the year, length of service, and job level. A number of the profit-related plans introduced in recent years have carried a provision that all, or a large share, of the bonus go into a trust fund, so that actual payment does not occur until retirement or termination of employment. Thus, profit sharing becomes a means to enforced savings.

There are, in addition, a number of savings or *thrift plans* that do not necessarily have this enforced character. The usual practice under these plans is for the company to match a certain proportion of the employee's pay, which he chooses to contribute into the fund. Thus, an employee may put in perhaps 5 per cent of his earnings, and the company will contribute an equal amount. There is a set maximum that the employee can allocate for this purpose, and it is not uncommon to provide the company share in the form of stock, usually nonvoting. In most cases payment of the company contribution is contingent upon meeting some length of service requirement. Thus, this benefit is used to foster continued employment; organizational maintenance is directly involved.

Finally, mention should be made of various cash bonuses paid for long-term service to the company, for good attendance, as prizes for the winners of employee contests, and as awards under suggestion systems. In some cases such payments have an incentive quality that is closely tied to productivity. Many, however, represent an attempt to foster continued employment and employee satisfaction in a general sense. As such they contribute to the maintenance goal.

Group Insurance

The greatest activity over the past twenty years, insofar as employee benefits are concerned, has occurred in the areas of retirement planning and group insurance. In the latter instance the growth rate, whether computed in terms of the number of firms involved, the number of employees covered, the types of plans in force, or the amount of insurance provided, has been little short of phenomenal. Even when the company does not pay a share of the cost, group insurance of this kind represents a sizable benefit to the employee. He obtains the savings associated with group rates, and certain kinds of protection that are not practicable on an individual basis now become available to him.

Types of Group Insurance

Almost all the group insurance available today through company programs falls into three categories—life, sickness and accident, and medical.

LIFE INSURANCE. Life insurance policies provide either a lump-sum payment, or a guaranteed income, or some combination of the two to an employee's family in case of his death or, frequently, for dismemberment also. Special provisions may relate to accidental death, or separate insurance may be available for this purpose. In some instances there is an opportunity to insure the lives of other family members in addition to that of the employee.

SICKNESS AND ACCIDENT INSURANCE. Sickness and accident insurance policies pay weekly benefits to employees who are temporarily disabled by nonoccupational sickness or accident. Benefits of this type are required under the compulsory temporary disability benefit laws existing in the states of California, New Jersey, New York, and Rhode Island. There are, in addition, some income protection plans that guarantee a proportion of income against permanent disability.

MEDICAL INSURANCE. Medical insurance policies are extremely diverse. They cover costs associated with hospitalization, medical and surgical treatment, visits to a physician's office, and so on. Although many policies have relatively limited coverage in terms of costs, there are also *major medical* plans that provide protection against the costs associated with medical catastrophe and extended treatment. A typical plan might, for instance, pay 80 per cent of all costs not covered by other forms of medical insurance, up to a maximum of $10,000 a year. Recently a form of comprehensive medical insurance has been developed that combines basic protection and major medical in the same policy.

Financing Employee Insurance Benefits

The decision making associated with establishing and administering an employee insurance program can become an extremely complex process. There are hundreds of plans available through different private insurance companies in each of the three major categories, all with variable benefit amounts at variable costs (7). For this reason many companies, particularly smaller firms, provide insurance benefits through a trust fund established on an industry or area basis. These funds may be administered by representatives of the member companies, by a corporation or partnership made up of insurance specialists, or by a joint union-management committee—or, on occasion, they may be controlled by the union alone. The company pays into the fund on the basis of a cents-per-hour-worked formula, or as a percentage of total payroll. The trustees of the fund establish the types and levels of benefits to be paid within the limitations imposed by the union-management contract. Usually insurance is purchased commercially to guarantee these payments; sometimes the fund operates on a pay-as-you-go basis through what amounts to self-insurance.

In some areas and industries union-controlled funds have expanded to a point where they now cover all types of medical expenses including prescriptions, dental care, and psychiatric treatment. There are a number of union-operated clinics. Under such circumstances the company not only loses control insofar as specifying the benefits to be provided for its employees, but the union rather than the company tends to be credited with making the benefits possible. Furthermore, in most cases only employees represented by unions are eligible to receive benefits from the fund, with the result that nonunion employees including management must be covered in some other way. In instances of this kind certain immediate advantages in terms of ease of administration and greater predictability of benefit costs are achieved at considerable expense in other respects. A major opportunity to obtain a maximum return on investment, in terms of employee satisfaction and company loyalty, is lost.

EMPLOYEE CONTRIBUTIONS. Although there is a strong feeling that employees are more aware of benefits and more appreciative of them when they contribute part of the cost, there is a clear trend for companies to assume more and more of this burden, especially in unionized firms. One reason is that for group insurance plans to operate at any savings over individual plans, a certain percentage of the total employee group must be covered. In the case of life insurance, for example, if the employee group includes a large proportion of women without dependents, who would not choose to be covered if they had to pay part of the cost, the only way to obtain coverage for employees who desire it, at any saving, is for the company to pay the premium. One suggestion for alleviating this problem is for the company to pay the full cost of basic levels of insurance and then make certain additional benefits available on a contributory basis (19).

Dependent coverage is usually provided on such a contributory basis for most types of medical insurance, the company paying only the employee portion. Yet in some cases companies assume all premium costs for the individual and his family. Retired employees continue to be covered by company insurance programs in many cases, although usually life insurance benefit amounts are reduced. The matter of continuing to cover the retired for health benefits is of less concern now that Medicare has been established under Social Security.

Pensions and Retirement

Retirement plans, like group insurance, have experienced a sizable growth since the late 1940's when they became clearly established as a union bargaining goal. Even those company plans that existed prior to that time have undergone drastic changes as a result of recent developments.

Financing Retirement Plans

Most retirement plans that have been negotiated with a union are established so as to provide certain specified monthly benefits payable to the employee on retirement. The matter of how to guarantee these payments normally is left to the company. In the case of contributory plans, where the employee pays part of the cost, the contribution is a set amount or percentage of salary, and the company's share is the remaining amount necessary to provide the specified benefits. Such contributory plans are more commonly applied to nonunion, salaried workers and to management than to a unionized work force. If the pension is paid through a deferred profit-sharing arrangement, of the kind discussed previously under direct monetary payments, the monthly benefit payable at retirement depends on the equity built up over the years of employment by the individual employee.

Depending on such factors as the level of the benefits specified, the company financial position, the average age of the work force, and the proportion of females employed, pensions may be financed on a pay-as-you-go basis, by establishing a trust fund and/or through the purchase of annuities. The financial aspects of pension planning are complex and subject to many tax and other legal constraints. Thus, decisions in this area normally involve financial executives and/or consultants knowledgeable in areas other than personnel management (5). Of growing concern to financial specialists and economists are the huge reserves being accumulated in pension trust funds and their impact on the investment market. Union spokesmen have urged that these funds be used to finance low-cost housing or for other investments of social value (15). Although considerations of this kind do have implications for a company's retirement program, personnel managers in general have been much more concerned with the various ways in which retirement provisions may relate to internal stresses and organizational maintenance.

Normal Retirement

A common argument for retirement benefits, whether provided under the Federal Social Security program or by a private plan, is that the availability of such benefits will encourage older workers to leave the labor force, and thus make room for younger individuals, who are presumed to be more productive. Yet this assumption of an age-related productivity differential may or may not be grounded in fact, depending both on the individual and on the nature of his work. As indicated in Chapter 3, managerial performance may well improve in certain respects with age, whereas certain kinds of factory jobs are clearly adversely affected. The evidence suggests that in the white-collar area, generally, productivity does not increase (17).

The original Social Security legislation established age sixty-five as the earliest point at which monthly retirement benefits could be paid. This subsequently became the standard retirement age under most private plans. Some firms make retirement at sixty-five compulsory; others consider this as normal, but do not require retirement until age sixty-eight; still others attempt to maintain a flexible policy, with the compulsory provision invoked only when it is clearly required in a particular case.

Compulsory retirement at a fixed age, such as sixty-five, does have certain advantages in that all employees are treated alike and thus complaints of unfair treatment are kept to a minimum. From a social viewpoint it serves to increase turnover during periods of high unemployment and thus provides opportunities for younger workers with families to support. If new technology results in a reduced manpower need, the required attrition can be handled in many cases through normal retirement and less senior workers do not have to be released.

A flexible approach is much more difficult to administer, and it can become a source of dissension if certain employees feel that the policy as applied to them is unjust. Yet it does permit the retention of older individuals who remain effective. Senior employees need not be forced out, if they are clearly capable of making a contribution, and many, without doubt, are extremely capable. This is a particularly important consideration in times of labor shortage when older employees are likely to possess skills that are difficult to locate in the available labor market. Thus, it would seem that the flexible policy places greater emphasis on productivity considerations, whereas a fixed retirement age tends to foster organizational maintenance through a reduction in internal dissension.

As to the preferences of employees themselves, there is at least one major study indicating that a rather high proportion of workers would choose to retire at the normal age, even if in good health and capable of continued work, provided their retirement income was sufficient to live comfortably (9). Thus, the adequacy of pension payments may be the critical factor. Other studies demonstrate that those employees who are closest to retirement are the ones who favor it least, presumably because the prospect of a reduced income is more immediate for them (10).

There are various formulas for computing pension payments, most based on either a flat amount or a percentage of average annual earnings times years of service. In either case longer service with the company makes for a higher level of retirement pay. Yet even with relatively long service the normal pension amounts to only between one half and two thirds of previous earnings. It is little wonder that a sizable group of workers do not desire retirement under existing circumstances.

Another consideration is that most plans pay the same monthly benefits for the remainder of the individual's life, irrespective of changes in living costs. Some of the earliest plans negotiated with unions provided a flat monthly amount that included Social Security payments. Thus, even raises in the Federal benefits as a result of revisions in the law did not serve to increase the amount received. Most such instances have now been corrected, and certain changes have also been introduced in some cases to adjust for the rising cost of living. Yet it remains true, generally, that a man who retires at sixty-five and lives into his late seventies may see his pension shrink considerably in purchasing power over the intervening years.

Disability and Early Retirement

Another aspect of most retirement plans is a provision for payment of benefits before normal retirement age under certain circumstances. Most commonly there is some kind of protection against permanent and total disability. To be eligible for such a disability pension the employee must generally have a specified amount of service and have reached at least the age of fifty.

Early retirement for reasons other than disability is also permitted under some plans. This practice has become increasingly common in the past ten years. Employees with the required length of service are allowed to retire voluntarily at age sixty, or even fifty-five. Where the company has no great interest in encouraging these retirements, the monthly benefits tend to be lower than those provided with normal retirement. However, a number of companies have considered early retirement attractive as a method of reducing the work force, when technological changes produce decreased manpower requirements. It is minimally disruptive and creates few problems with the unions. Under such conditions companies have tended to escalate the rewards for accepting an early retirement. Thus, relatively high benefits may be paid, at least until the employee becomes eligible for Social Security.

Vesting Provisions

In recent years there has been considerable discussion regarding the effects of pension provisions on labor mobility. Partly out of economic considerations and partly out of a desire to foster a stable labor force, companies have tended to withhold the *vesting* of pension rights as long as possible. Thus, they have attempted to delay the point at which an employee attains a full right to the company's contribution to the retirement fund and therefore the time when he can be sure of achieving a full pension.

Union spokesmen and many economists have argued that workers are in fact loath to change employers when this means losing pension credits accumulated over the years (and of course company contributions as well). They have argued further that this represents an undesirable state of affairs, because job opportunities may be greater elsewhere. Although the question of the impact of pensions on the mobility of workers remains debatable, particularly in cases involving family relocation (14), there has been a definite trend recently toward vesting short of retirement. Under the pressure of union demands, this potential source of employee stability has been curtailed, so that it cannot make the same contribution to organizational maintenance now as in years past. Yet it is still true that the typical vesting provision, even now, requires ten or fifteen years service before an individual can retain the company contribution should he change jobs, and often he must be over age forty as well.

Much of this leverage toward employment stability is lost in the case of some of the multiemployer retirement plans that now exist, paralleling the health and welfare plans. In these cases each company contributes a set amount to ensure a given pension to its employees at retirement. Usually a single union represents the covered employees in all member companies. Under these circumstances an individual maintains his pension rights should he shift from one employer to another within the member group, and so there is no particular pressure to remain with a company. One of the earliest of these arrangements was established by the United Mine Workers in the coal industry. Under it, the various mine operators paid a flat royalty per ton of coal mined into the pension fund. On the other hand, maintenance considerations are relatively unimportant insofar as multiemployer plans in the construction industry are concerned. Here and in many similar situations employee mobility is an inevitable aspect of the work, and delayed vesting would have little significance in any event.

Employee Services

In contrast to direct monetary benefits, group insurance, and pensions, the various employee services are much more likely to be given at management's discretion, are not in any sense a reflection of public policy, are usually of limited concern to unions in collective bargaining, and are provided at relatively low cost to the company. A number of the services now available were initiated before the depression of the 1930's as part of the paternalistic emphasis that characterized that period. Recreation programs are typical. Some services are a function of plant location, i.e., transportation and eating facilities. Type of industry is clearly a factor in granting employee discounts on company products, because only consumer goods manufacturers have anything to offer in this regard. Certain services, such as free medical examinations, are closely related to other aspects of the personnel function. In some instances there is a good possibility that the company may benefit as much as the employee. This is particularly true of tuition refund programs and other types of educational sponsorship. It is probably impossible to mention all such employee services, but the following listing is reasonably comprehensive. Any one company, of course, will provide only a limited number of these:

1. *Services related to type of work performed,* including subsidies for the purchase and upkeep of work clothes and uniforms, as well as for various types of tools used in connection with the work.
2. *Eating facilities,* including company restaurants, cafeterias, lunch rooms, and vending machines. Under certain circumstances meals may be provided free of charge. More frequently the charge is at cost or somewhat below.
3. *Transportation facilities,* including parking lots, bus service, company cars, and assistance with arrangements for car pools.
4. *Housing services,* including company-owned or -constructed hous-

ing projects, rental lists, assistance with home financing, guarantees on the purchase of homes owned by employees transferred to new locations, and payment of moving expenses.

5. *Financial and legal services,* including sponsorship of credit unions, help in preparing income tax forms, and many types of legal assistance available through the company legal department. In addition, a number of companies operate loan services for employees, although these are usually restricted to hardship cases.

6. *Purchasing services,* including company-owned or -operated stores and discounts on company products and services.

7. *Recreational, social, and cultural programs,* including sponsorship of company athletic teams, social clubs, summer camps, country clubs, recreational areas, orchestras, and libraries.

8. *Medical and community services,* including plant infirmaries, clinics, and hospitals, with the more extensive facilities being found largely in isolated areas or foreign countries. In addition, companies provide physical examinations, visiting nurses, counseling services, and referrals to various community social service agencies.

9. *Educational services,* including sponsorship of off-hours courses, educational leaves, tuition refund plans, and scholarships or educational loans for employees and their children. Under certain conditions companies operate complete educational systems for the children of their employees.

Benefit Programs for Management

In the matter of employee benefits, as in many other aspects of the personnel function, special considerations and policies typically apply in the case of management, particularly at the higher levels. It is not at all uncommon for a firm to have an entirely different benefit structure for individuals in the ranks of management. This is due in part to the fact that many legal constraints, such as overtime payment requirements, do not operate at this level. In addition, collective bargaining agreements do not apply to management in most cases, although they may cover foremen in certain industries such as construction and printing. Finally, different traditions and requirements exist with regard to management employees; for example, holidays and paid vacations were well established for them long before they were applied to hourly workers. On the other hand, many of the services noted in the previous section have little meaning for managers.

Although there is considerable variability from one company to another, benefit levels tend to be somewhat higher for nonproduction and managerial employees; the differential, however, does not reach that in the salary area. In the matter of temporary disability, salaried employees are usually guaranteed paid sick leave under which the company continues their full salary for a specified period. Hourly workers are more likely to be covered by a sickness and accident insurance policy that pays benefits below the level of weekly wages.

On the other hand, salaried employees generally, and managers in particular, are more likely to contribute part of the cost of insurance and retirement benefits (3). Whether this will remain the case in the future is an open question. One argument in favor of noncontributory benefit plans is based on tax considerations. Employee contributions are part of taxable income for the individual, whereas company payments into pension and welfare funds are treated as an operating expense and thus are not subject to taxation, provided they meet certain Internal Revenue Service criteria.

Tax considerations become increasingly important generally as one moves up the management hierarchy. Thus, many complex executive benefits, like certain types of productivity-oriented compensation (see Chapter 16), have evolved as ways of deferring income and otherwise providing a tax shelter.

The Benefit Program as a Whole

Aside from the ever-increasing cost aspects of employee benefits and services, the major problem for personnel management in this area relates to matters of planning and control. Union pressures combined with a natural desire to maintain a competitive position vis-à-vis benefits offered by other firms have created a situation in some companies that borders on the chaotic. Pronounced imbalances exist between the various benefits, and the relationship of the total benefit package to organizational goal attainment is often unclear.

More than any other consideration in collective bargaining, fringe benefits have been used to achieve face-saving settlements by union and management alike. When demands for wage increases could not be justified, union leaders have often turned to employee benefits instead, even though the specific item had little appeal to the rank and file. Under such circumstances the leadership could at least point to some gain to compensate for an unchanging paycheck, although the gain might not actually be realized until after retirement.

On the other hand, a number of companies have succumbed to a "follow-the-leader" approach in bargaining on fringes. Rather than risk a strike, they have granted benefits negotiated elsewhere without concern for cost considerations that are unique to a particular situation. On occasion this approach has resulted in an agreement to provide benefits that make no sense at all when applied to a specific employee group. Or there may be a sizable overlap with programs already in effect.

The result of these processes has been that a number of firms have found themselves saddled with a hodgepodge of benefit programs, the costs of which are clearly unreasonable in relation to what is gained in employee satisfaction and organizational maintenance. There is little doubt that a more positive approach is needed. The cost of each fringe item should be determined, the objective in granting it to employees should be established, and a total package should be formed that is logically consistent and devoid of overlap and that provides the greatest return to the company in terms of its goals (8). In collective bargaining both union and management negotiators need to stop treating fringes as nonessential gifts and consider them, alternatively, as techniques for satisfying important employee motives (12).

Administration of the Benefit Program

The technicalities of most employee benefits and the amount of clerical work involved in their administration can present a sizable problem. For small employers the costs of administration can come to more than the amount paid for the benefits themselves. This is one reason why multiemployer arrangements that establish benefit funds are so attractive to smaller firms. The processing of forms and the handling of employee complaints regarding payments for all member firms are the responsibility of the fund's administrators. The economies of scale, insofar as administrative costs are concerned, are considerable.

Benefits specified in a union contract can represent a major source of grievance activity. Rights to vacation or holiday pay, for instance, may be questioned where the eligibility requirements as stated in the agreement are ambiguous and subject to multiple interpretations. Loose contract language can also result in overlapping benefits. A worker may be eligible to collect weekly benefits as paid sick leave and as workmen's compensation for the same period of time, unless the contract is very clear on this point. Thus, he could receive a higher income while absent than while present on the job, and the whole amount, ultimately, could be charged completely to the company. Such difficulties can be minimized with care in contract wording, particularly in dealing with eligibility requirements for various benefits (1).

In larger firms administrative difficulties are particularly frequent when benefit practices vary from plant to plant or department to department. This problem becomes especially acute when the firm has grown by acquisition and thus taken on a great diversity of benefit packages. Even where one policy is in effect, this policy may be interpreted differently at various company locations. On occasion several departments or divisions within the firm may be involved in administering benefit programs, with the result that conflicting statements are issued to employees. All this argues strongly for the centralization of responsibility for benefit planning and control in a single personnel executive, who can provide for effective policy communications that are neither ambiguous nor conflicting (11).

Employee Attitudes

Company benefit programs are often criticized for including items that fulfill no real employee need and that accomplish little in terms of goal attainment. A number of benefits that were initiated as legitimate motive satisfiers have now become standard in most firms. Against the background of current practice, it would appear that liberalizing them further has very little appeal for employees. After benefits reach a certain level, wage increases are preferred to more benefits (9). On occasion union leaders have had to sell the membership on the value of a particular fringe item, particularly where there is some feeling that a wage increase has been traded for a benefit that might well not be realized personally, as with higher retirement pay. Benefit plans that require employee contributions may, in fact, have a negative impact on employee attitudes. It is not particularly pleasant to find money deducted from one's paycheck for benefits that are not desired, even if, under a certain amount of social pressure, one has signed an authorization form.

Nevertheless, it can be assumed that many benefits are considered important by the majority of employees. This is illustrated in Table 20-2. In a few instances, such as major medical insurance, there is apparently a strong motive that is not being met on a widespread basis. On the other hand, group life insurance is ranked at the very bottom of the various insurance benefits even though 70 per cent of the firms provide it. From this and other studies it is apparent that the various types of medical insurance are of considerable importance to employees (13).

Among the noninsurance benefits there are some discrepancies also. One of the most notable is in the case of profit sharing, which is ranked fourth by the employees but is provided by only 15 per cent of the firms included in the study. There is some reason to believe that this may be an area of major concern to unions in the future. The United Auto Workers have indicated considerable interest in the idea of automatic wage supplements, to be granted whenever a company's profits rise above a specified level. In effect, this would suggest less emphasis on the usual fringe items in future bargaining, and more concern with ways of increasing basic compensation.

The significance of various work-force characteristics is stressed in another study (13), which dealt with the preferences of over 1,000 members of a union local (International Brotherhood of Electrical Workers). Overall, hospital insurance was most preferred of the six items considered. But, as Figure 20-1 indicates, there were sharp differences

Table 20-2.   Employee Preferences for Selected Employee Benefits

Benefits	Employee rank	Employees in 111 firms indicating that the benefit was of great importance, %	Total firms providing the benefit, %
Insurance benefits			
Hospitalization	1	79.6	93.2
Doctor bill	2	73.9	94.4
Major medical	3	64.8	45.7
Retirement plan (other than Social Security)	4	63.5	70.4
Disability income	5	61.3	53.7
Accidental death and dismemberment	6	58.8	53.1
Group life	7	55.9	70.4
Noninsurance benefits			
Paid vacation	1	87.0	81.5
Paid holidays	2	81.0	98.1
Paid sick leave	3	54.1	25.9
Profit-sharing plan	4	42.2	15.4
Credit unions	5	38.7	24.1
Paid rest periods, lunch	6	38.2	71.0
Other paid leaves	7	38.0	46.9
Free medical exams	8	31.0	30.2
Layoff allowances, SUB	9	28.0	11.1
Stock options	10	20.6	8.6
Merchandise discounts	11	18.0	55.6
Free or low-cost meals on premises	12	14.5	n.a.

Source: M. R. Greene, *The Role of Employee Benefit Structures in Manufacturing Industry.* Eugene, Oregon: School of Business Administration, Univ. of Oregon, 1964, pp. 24–25.

associated with age. Pension preference rose sharply and steadily in each older group from the thirties on, although pensions were not clearly favored over hospital insurance until the fifties. Sex differences could not be studied in this instance because only males were included. It can be presumed, however, that variations would emerge on this basis also. Thus, young, predominantly female office workers probably prefer more vacation benefits to most types of insurance.

✳ Irrespective of what benefits and services a firm provides, they can have little value as a means to encouraging pride in the organization, loyalty, and satisfaction unless employees know about and understand them. Many workers are entirely unaware that the company pays for

Figure 20-1. Benefit Preference by Age

Mean
preferance

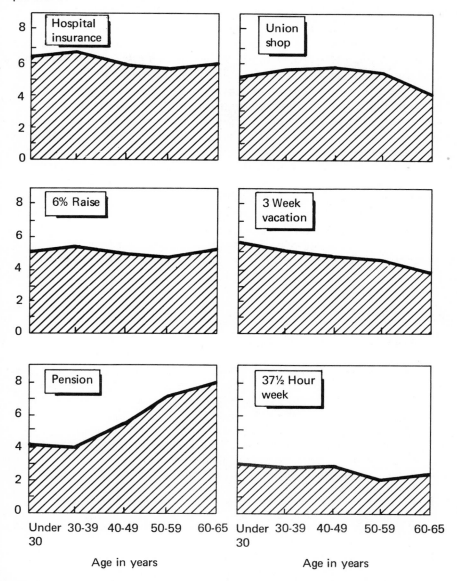

Age in years   Age in years

Source: Nealy, S. M., "Determining Worker Preferences Among Employee Benefit Programs," *Journal of Applied Psychology,* Vol. 48 (1964), p. 8.

unemployment compensation and contributes sizably to Social Security. A large number appear to have little knowledge of the private benefits available to them through the company (9). Frequently a union receives the credit for employee benefits and services, particularly those administered under union sponsorship, even though the funds derive entirely from company sources.

Thus, it becomes important to inform employees regarding the nature of the benefits provided and the company's role in their financing. This does not mean that a firm should claim full credit for benefits that are in fact provided at least in part as a result of legal constraints or union pressure, but it is desirable to make employees aware of what they are getting and of the costs incurred as a result of benefit payments. Where items are provided on a unilateral basis by the company, employees should know of this.

To get maximum return from an investment in fringe benefits, a company must have an effective communications program to inform employees regarding what is available, when they are eligible, and what procedures are involved in obtaining benefits. Managers, in particular, should be knowledgeable in this area, because employees normally turn to their immediate superior in search of benefit information. Various techniques and other aspects of internal communications are discussed in the next chapter.

References

1. Becker, C. A., "How to Forestall Benefit Giveaways," *Personnel,* Vol. 41, No. 2 (1964), 31–40.
2. Brayfield, A. H., and W. H. Crockett, "Employee Attitudes and Employee Performance," *Psychological Bulletin,* Vol. 52 (1955), 396–424.
3. Bureau of Labor Statistics, United States Department of Labor, *Health and Insurance Benefits and Pension Plans for Salaried Employees, Spring 1963,* Bulletin No. 1405. Washington, D.C.: the Bureau, 1964.
4. Bureau of National Affairs, Inc., *Basic Patterns in Union Contracts,* 6th ed. Washington, D.C.: BNA, Inc., 1966.
5. Bureau of National Affairs, Inc., *Pensions and Profit Sharing,* 3rd ed. Washington, D.C.: BNA, Inc., 1964.
6. Chamber of Commerce of the United States, *Fringe Benefits—1965.* Washington, D.C.: the Chamber, 1966.
7. Eilers, R. D., and R. M. Crowe, *Group Insurance Handbook.* Homewood, Ill.: Irwin, 1965.
8. Foegen, J. H., "Product Mix for Fringe Benefits," *Harvard Business Review,* Vol. 39, No. 4 (1961), 64–68.
9. Greene, M. R., *The Role of Employee Benefit Structures in Manufacturing Industry.* Eugene, Oregon: School of Business Administration, Univ. of Oregon, 1964.

10. Mathiasen, G., *Flexible Retirement*. New York: Putnam's, 1957.
11. McLaughlin, D. J., "Bring Order Out of Chaos in the Benefits Program," *Personnel*, Vol. 42, No. 1 (1965), 27–34.
12. Metzler, J., "Are Fringe Benefits an Answer?" *Personnel Administration*, Vol. 29, No. 4 (1966), 41–44.
13. Nealey, S. M., "Determining Worker Preferences Among Employee Benefit Programs," *Journal of Applied Psychology*, Vol. 48 (1964), 7–12.
14. Scanlan, B. K., "Effects of Pension Plans on Labor Mobility and Hiring Older Workers," *Personnel Journal*, Vol. 44, No. 1 (1965), 29–34.
15. Stein, E., "Union and Management Interests in the Investment of Pension Funds," in G. G. Somers (ed.), *Proceedings of the Eighteenth Annual Winter Meeting*. Madison, Wis.: Industrial Relations Research Association, 1966, pp. 297–321.
16. Tilove, R., "Pensions, Health, and Welfare Plans," in L. Ulman (ed.), *Challenges to Collective Bargaining*. Englewood Cliffs, N.J.: Prentice-Hall, 1967, pp. 37–64.
17. United States Department of Labor, *Comparative Job Performance by Age: Office Workers*. Washington, D.C.: Government Printing Office, 1960.
18. Wistert, F. M., *Fringe Benefits*. New York: Reinhold, 1959.
19. Zollitsch, H. G., "Fringes—Benefits or Burdens?" *Personnel*, Vol. 41, No. 4 (1964), 54–59.

Questions

1. What are the various types of direct monetary payments that are considered fringe benefits? How do the type and costs of such benefits vary with the nature of the business and the character of the work force?
2. What are the advantages and disadvantages of the various multiemployer fund arrangements for administering health and welfare and retirements plans?
3. What are the various arguments pro and con as regards having employees contribute their own money for the benefits they receive? What is the trend of the times insofar as contributory plans are concerned?
4. How should a company go about evaluating a given fringe benefit item before deciding to grant it to employees? What forces have operated to determine benefit choice in the absence of such realistic evaluations?
5. What types of employee benefits would appear to be particularly appropriate where the work force is constituted along each of the following lines:
   a. Primarily older, male production workers
   b. Primarily highly paid managerial and professional workers
   c. Primarily older married females whose husbands also work
   d. Primarily young, unmarried females

21

Internal Communications

This chapter will consider those communications procedures that personnel management can utilize directly to foster goal attainment—a limited perspective in comparison with a discussion of organizational communication processes as a whole. Yet, as indicated in the Preface, personnel management cannot be all things to all people. If it attempts to be so, it loses its identity as a separate profession and area of study. Just as with such topics as leadership, employee motivation, and work group dynamics, extended treatment of organizational communication generally seems more appropriately left to courses in principles of management and organizational behavior. The present focus, then, will be on those internal communications techniques that a personnel manager can bring directly to bear in utilizing a company's work force effectively. With only a few exceptions communications procedures of this kind have been directed toward the goal of organizational maintenance.

Although the present chapter will devote little space to the matter of superior-subordinate communications as they occur on a day-to-day basis in the workplace, it should not be assumed that interactions of this kind are totally unrelated to personnel management. As a part of the general management process they are of concern to managers in all aspects of the business, including managers in the personnel area. In addition, such topics as semantics in communications, communications skills, barriers to communications, and two-way communications are widely included in management development programs. It is thus indirectly, through management development, that personnel management achieves much of its impact on the primarily productivity-oriented superior-subordinate communications process.

Management development is not the only indirect approach that personnel managers can use to influence communications within the firm. Role prescriptions characteristically indicate rather specifically who is to communicate with whom and regarding what topics. Organization planning and job analysis both contribute to the establishment of formal communications channels by indicating expected reporting relationships; through such procedures the personnel function can influence organizational communications to a considerable degree. Yet there is no guarantee that communications will necessarily follow the patterns thus established in every respect. Role behavior may deviate from role prescriptions. A subordinate manager may "go over his superior's head" to discuss certain matters with a higher-level executive, even though such behavior is not generally condoned. Considerations of this kind involve personnel management because of their relationship to organization planning and management appraisal, but they can be directly influenced at a point in time only by the particular managers themselves. For this reason such malfunctioning of formal communications channels is probably best treated in discussions of the managerial process as a whole. Within personnel management superior-subordinate communications are in many ways more closely related to output considerations of the kind discussed in Part III than to the internal communications techniques covered in this chapter.

Rumor and the Grapevine

The rumor transmission process also fails to meet the specifications for extended treatment here. But in this case it is not the lack of *direct* control over the communication process that leads to the exclusion; rather it is the lack of any control at all. There is very little that a personnel manager, or any manager, can do to purposefully utilize the *grapevine* as a means to goal attainment.

As a result rumors probably do at least as much to subvert organizational goals as to foster them. They may well serve to stir up dissension. They are frequently contrary to fact. In one study carried out within six companies, sixteen of the thirty rumors checked were found to be false (13). Finally, rumors rarely reach everyone. Research has repeatedly indicated that the grapevine is spotty in its coverage and that a relatively large proportion of employees will not hear any given rumor (5,21).

Accordingly, it seems appropriate to conclude that the rumor transmission process is not only unusable as an internal communication technique, but that it is, in fact, so poor as an input-output mediator and often so harmful in its effects that every effort should be made to suppress it. A key to how this may be accomplished is the finding that rumors become most rampant in departments where the manager in charge deliberately withholds information as a means of exercising power and control (16). It would seem, then, that if employees are given maximal and valid information in areas of major interest to them, the grapevine will have little opportunity to thrive. In fact, under most circumstances the number of rumors circulating in a particular environment, and the rapidity with which they spread, provide a good index of the effectiveness of other communications procedures.

This view, that the grapevine is the antithesis of effective communications and that considerable effort should be devoted to minimizing its impact, is reflected in the *rumor clinic* concept. Clinics of this kind provide a specific locus where employees may go to obtain valid information with regard to rumors they have heard. No doubt, with ideal communications procedures in other respects, techniques of this kind would not be necessary. Yet it also seems apparent that the rumor process can rarely, if ever, be entirely eradicated.

Communications Downward

Various techniques are used to transmit information from the higher levels of an organization directly to individual members, with the objective of creating a sense of belonging. The overall cohesiveness of the company as a social unit is fostered and presumably employees will be more satisfied with their work situation. Downward communications should pull the entire organization together and unite it behind particular task objectives. Occasionally this may require a concerted effort to subvert the goals of a union, which does or is attempting to represent the company's employees, because unions can produce a major divisive force within the firm.

The media used by different companies to achieve these goals vary considerably. Among them are company magazines and newspapers; mass meetings, for all or groups of employees; employee letters, sent directly to the home or inserted in paychecks; information racks containing circulars and pamphlets; employee handbooks and manuals; bulletin boards and posters; bulletins and memoranda to management; and tours of company facilities. Annual reports, news items in the popular media, and even commercial advertising are used on occasion to communicate with employees. (In such cases external media are used for internal purposes.) Other downward communications techniques involve the use of speeches, telephone, teletype, films, public address systems, slides, radio, and television.

It is important that the internal communication system operate rapidly and with maximal validity. To the extent the system produces information that later proves to be incorrect, or lags and so yields its data subsequent to public or other media, it will be viewed as lacking in value by employees and will lose much of its audience. Without an audience it can have little impact as an input-output mediator.

The Selection of Media

Any medium of communication must meet certain requirements to be effective (22). It must reach all employees for whom it is intended. It must be official in the sense that the information is perceived as originating with individuals who are in a position to know. It must convey a certain type of information consistently, so that employees will look to this source when they desire to know about a particular matter.

Table 21-1. Mean Accuracy of Recall Scores for Information Transmitted Using Various Media

Method of presenting information	College student sample		Manufacturing employee sample		Retail store sample	
	Mean recall score	Number	Mean recall score	Number	Mean recall score	Number
Oral and written	6.54	281	7.30	30	7.70	102
Oral only	5.31	161	6.38	13	6.17	94
Written only	4.58	279	4.46	28	4.91	109
Bulletin board	3.52	152			3.72	115
Grapevine only	2.88	157	3.00	13	3.56	108

Source: T. L. Dahle, "An Objective and Comparative Study of Five Methods of Transmitting Information to Business and Industrial Employees," *Speech Monographs*, Vol. 21 (1954), pp. 24, 26, and 27.

Given these conditions, is there any evidence that some media are inherently more effective than others in getting information to employees? The data of Table 21-1 bear on this point. In this instance three separate studies were conducted—one with a large group of college students enrolled in a public speaking course at Purdue University; one with the production employees of a building materials manufacturing plant; and one with the employees at a single facility of Spiegel's, a mail order-chain store organization (4). The same information was transmitted in various ways, including oral presentations by professors or supervisors, written handouts or letters, and posting on a bulletin board. Information retention was measured with a ten-item questionnaire administered approximately two days after the original communication. In all cases a control group was included that could learn only through the grapevine. The bulletin board method was not used in the manufacturing plant.

The results are surprisingly consistent. A combination of written and oral media is clearly preferable. As between the two, however, oral presentations at a meeting are more effective. Posting an item on a bulletin board appears to accomplish relatively little, being indistinguishable from the grapevine, when standard tests of statistical significance are applied.

The superiority of oral face-to-face communication does not appear to be limited to information transmission. At least one large-scale investigation indicates that employees prefer it (20). In another instance certain comparisons were made between two almost identical plants, one of which relied upon regular monthly meetings conducted by foremen to transmit information, whereas the other did not. As might be expected, the employees in the plant with the meetings were much more likely to feel well informed, and they were also more likely to feel that they really belonged in the company (62 vs. 29 per cent) and to be highly satisfied with it as a place to work (45 vs. 20 per cent) (10). Thus, the meetings not only served to provide information; in doing so, they made a sizable contribution to organizational maintenance.

It should be emphasized that in this specific instance the meetings involved a two-way communications process. Employees were encouraged to ask questions, either with a view to clarifying points made by the foremen or for the purpose of eliciting new information. In general, such an approach seems to be highly advantageous in fostering employee satisfaction (1). A one-way system can create considerable frustration if the material is at all ambiguous or important aspects are omitted, whereas providing an opportunity for questioning can increase understanding markedly. But it can also produce a greater feeling of trust, openness, and belonging as regards the company. One major difficulty with written media is that it is very difficult to integrate them with communication upward in a meaningful way.

In using oral communications, with or without a two-way approach, a great many companies go to considerable trouble to stage and program their presentations. Materials are often prepared in advance and the manager who is to do the speaking may receive coaching from various training specialists. Presentations involving the company's financial position, in conjunction with the annual report, are particularly likely to involve considerable preparation. In other cases information may be transmitted to management via various memorandums or bulletins. The latter then serve as a basis for oral communications to appropriate employee groups. During union negotiations, a strike, or an organizing attempt, these management bulletins appear quite frequently.

It is important to recognize that the mere fact that employees have accumulated a large amount of information about their company provides no guarantee that organizational maintenance will be fostered. This is apparent from Table 21-2. In only one instance (firm D) is the correlation between information level and attitude level significant. The companies surveyed were a public utility, a trucking company, a wholesale distributing firm, a textile manufacturing firm, and an electrical equipment manufacturer (18).

Table 21-2. Correlations Between Information and Attitude Scores for Samples of Employees from Five Firms

Firm	Number of employees	Correlation
A	95	.06
B	59	.12
C	105	.12
D	90	.27
E	108	.12

Source: D. Perry and T. A. Mahoney, "In-plant Communications and Employee Morale," *Personnel Psychology*, Vol. 8 (1955), p. 342.

A firm that refuses to provide any information, or does so on a very minimal basis, will almost certainly suffer negative consequences. But given that communication is attempted at some meaningful level, the crucial considerations are how and what rather than how much. The advantages of a two-way approach have already been noted, and certainly the tone inherent in any communication can influence attitudes. But even more important is the content. Certain kinds of information may well make employees less satisfied, as, for instance, the knowledge that the firm has been put up for sale or merger. If no effort is made to utilize the communication system to convince employees that they are part of a worthwhile organization, then favorable attitudes are unlikely to result. Neutral communications may increase information tremendously but have little impact on how employees feel about the company.

Combining oral and written media to convey a piece of information with maximum effectiveness will contribute to goal achievement only if the information is of a kind that creates favorable attitudes. This is not to say that unpleasant information should be withheld or distorted. It is important that employees trust management and its information channels. A communication system that does not yield important information that is expected of it will soon lose its audience. But communication procedures can appropriately be used to encourage pride in the organization; to point up real advantages of employment, such as benefits and services; to state company, as opposed to union, viewpoints; and to demonstrate the advantages of the economic system that makes the company's existence possible.

With this orientation, a company should use those media that will convey maximal information and yield maximal recall. Without such a goal-related orientation there is a question whether the expense of a comprehensive internal communication system can be justified at all. Over the years a number of firms have failed, for various reasons, to use their publications and other media to encourage favorable employee attitudes. Presumably it is this fact that is reflected in the data of Table 21-2. The positive implications of the information transmitted, insofar as the company is concerned, apparently have not been emphasized in four of the five firms. Further evidence on this point will be presented in the next section.

Company Magazines and Newspapers

Almost all large corporations and a great many smaller ones publish a company magazine, usually on a monthly basis, that goes to all employees. Many firms have additional publications for separate departments, geographical regions, or plants. When these internal media are combined with those of an external nature directed to stockholders and the public, the total journalistic effort is very comprehensive indeed.

Yet for many years these publications said practically nothing about the company as an organization and did little to develop favorable employee attitudes. During and after World War II there was some shift away from chit-chat and personal news of individual employees but much still remained (6). Even when information about the company, including such matters as its economic position, organization, products, equipment, methods, benefits, and services was included, it was usually presented in an entirely factual manner. There was little attempt to provide employees with a company viewpoint and thus to encourage cohesiveness and loyalty. This remains largely true today.

Comparative studies of union and company publications have consistently pointed up the differential emphasis on economic matters, bargaining issues, and political action (7, 9). Company magazines practically never deal with these matters, whereas union publications invariably devote considerable space to them. Yet during a strike, companies are much more likely to move into the center of the communications arena. The company magazine may now take up the issues, letters are sent to employees at their homes, and the public media may be used to present the company viewpoint (8). Thus, the typical pattern is complete silence on labor relations matters prior to open conflict and then considerable utilization of company publications for persuasive purposes.

The reason often given for avoiding persuasive material, and even information regarding the company as an organization, is that too much stress on such matters will result in a loss of readership. Many company editors have maintained that if an employee does not find frequent mention of himself or people he knows in the pages of the magazine or newspaper he will cease to read it. In particular they have argued that "propaganda" should be avoided. The feeling has been that the audience must be held at all costs, and this cannot be done if one moves directly into the realm of organizational maintenance. This viewpoint involves certain quite testable assumptions about the nature of employee readership preferences and patterns. And, in fact, evidence does exist regarding reading differentials for material that is totally unrelated to company goals, company-oriented material, and material that is persuasive to a company viewpoint.

READERSHIP SURVEYS. One relevant study dealt with readership patterns among employees of The Atlantic Refining Company (17). Fifteen articles, which proved to be relatively evenly spaced along a scale of company orientation, were selected from various prior issues of *The Atlantic Magazine* and reprinted in a questionnaire. Scale position was determined by judges. None of the items dealt with economic, political, or union considerations, so that persuasion to a company viewpoint on such matters was not a factor in this particular study. Headlines for typical items judged to be highly company-oriented, in the middle range, and not company-oriented follow:

Company-oriented:
    Retirement System Ends 25th Year
    New-Products, Applications, Customers
    Questions and Answers on Company's Recent $55 Million Issue
       of Debentures!
Middle range:
    Safe Drivers Are Honored
    Atlantic Congratulates Its Faithful Employees Who Celebrate
      Service Anniversaries
Not company-oriented:
    Two at Pittsburgh Avid Stamp Collectors
    Egg Magic (four recipes)

In each instance the employee was asked to indicate whether he usually or only rarely read this particular type of item in the magazine. Questionnaires were sent to a representative sample of 600 employees; 251 were returned. Subsequent follow-up studies of the nonrespondents indicated that had all 600 employees returned questionnaires, the readership results obtained would not have differed from those derived with the 251.

The findings presented in Table 21-3 indicate that the employees not only did not object to company-oriented material, they actually preferred it. The major conclusion derived from the study was that the company magazine was viewed as the primary source of information regarding the firm's level of success. Thus, through such company-related material as appeared, employees could determine whether they were associated with an effective organization that could provide them with both security and opportunity. With the exception of the female employees, most of whom were young and would not stay long, there was a consistent tendency toward more widespread readership of the company-oriented articles. There was no evidence that chit-chat was necessary to maintain readership—quite the opposite. This conclusion has since been supported by other research (23).

Table 21-3.   Rank-Order Correlations Between Scale Values on Degree of Company Orientation for 15 Company Magazine Articles and Extent of Readership of the Articles

Group	N	Correlation
Total sample	251	.72
Sex		
Male	218	.70
Female	33	.40
Job level		
Supervisory	58	.72
Nonsupervisory	193	.74
Company service		
0–10 Years	92	.79
11–20	65	.68
21+ Years	94	.77
Education		
0–11 Years	67	.63
12 Years	79	.72
13+ Years	96	.79
Unknown	9	

Source: J. B. Miner and E. E. Heaton, "Company Orientation as a Factor in the Readership of Employee Publications," *Personnel Psychology*, Vol. 12 (1959), p. 615.

A second study goes beyond the matter of company orientation to the use of directly persuasive items (12). In this instance articles from past issues of the *Illuminator*, published by the Washington Water Power Company, were judged both as to their degree of company orientation and their degree of persuasiveness to a company view. The readership survey questionnaire contained twenty items: five each in the categories of high company orientation and high persuasiveness, high company orientation and low persuasiveness, low company orientation and high persuasiveness, and low company orientation and low persuasiveness. Examples of the four types of articles are as follows:

> High company orientation and high persuasiveness:
> Extras That Count—Liberal Sick Pay Program is Protection
> Vacation Time; Relax . . . With Pay
> You'll Want to Know These Pertinent Facts about Rate Proposal
> High company orientation and low persuasiveness:
> Branzell is Now President; Robinson Retains Key Role
> Canadian Line to Give WWP Third Gas Source
> Low company orientation and high persuasiveness:
> Union Magazine Looks at Power
> Ideals of Socialists Survive though Party Declines, Says Writer
> What is Profit? Recent Graduates Didn't Know Answer
> Low company orientation and low persuasiveness:
> Tight Races Feature all Bowling Leagues
> Bad Weather Brings These Driving Tips

In this instance the persuasive communications related to the company tended to stress what the company was doing in the area of employee benefits, and certain arguments bearing on governmental constraints applied to the utility industry. In addition, the magazine devoted space to matters concerning the economy generally and union activities. The persuasive material tended to be well written and relevant to company goal accomplishment.

Employees were asked to indicate whether they usually or rarely read items of the kind presented. A "usually" response was given a score of 3, a qualified response a 2, and a "rarely" response a 1. The mean scores for the 230 respondents in the four categories are presented in Table 21-4.

The data indicated clearly that, at least with the approach used in this company, persuasive material does not result in any loss of readership. In fact, it appears to be read with a frequency almost identical to the nonpersuasive material. Again, however, the conclusion must be qualified with reference to female employees. Their readership scores were consistently below those for the males, not only on the company-oriented items, but on the persuasive as well. Only in the chit-chat area (noncompany and nonpersuasive) did female readership equal that of the males.

It seems apparent that the widespread assumptions regarding loss of readership when company publications are oriented specifically to the goal of organizational maintenance do not meet the test of the research evidence. Articles of the kind described as company-oriented in *The Atlantic Magazine* and company-oriented and/or persuasive in the *Illuminator* can be used. In fact, this is what many employees appear to want from company publications.

Table 21-4. Mean Readership Scores for 20 Company Magazine Articles Varying in Persuasiveness and in Degree of Company Orientation

Persuasiveness	*Company orientation*		
	High (5 items)	Low (5 items)	Combined (10 items)
High (5 items)	2.67	2.36	2.51
Low (5 items)	2.79	2.22	2.51
Combined (10 items)	2.73	2.29	

Source: C. O. Henderson, *The Company Magazine as a Medium for Communicating Persuasive, Management Oriented Subject Matter*, DBA Thesis. Eugene, Oregon: Univ. of Oregon, 1964, p. 46.

Yet there is one important consideration if employee attitudes are to be influenced. The company magazine must not be viewed as an organ of extremism. It must be considered a trusted source of information; it must be accepted as a legitimate medium for transmitting the particular kind of material it contains; it must have a reputation for moderation (1). Given these conditions, there is every reason to believe that an appropriate selection of content along the lines suggested can make company publications a meaningful factor in organizational goal attainment.

The Problem of Readability

During the late 1940's and early 1950's there was a rather widespread concern in the business world regarding the reading level of material published for employees. A number of studies indicated that much of what was produced as part of the downward communication process was far above the comprehension level of the intended audience. Although the emphasis on this topic did yield considerable change in readability levels, the matter remains an important one. An employee who is continually exposed to material that he finds difficult or impossible to understand is unlikely to view the source of this material favorably. Such communication is most likely to yield feelings of inferiority and defensive criticism of the publication, perhaps also of the company as well.

An example of the problem is presented in Table 21-5. This particular study dealt with employee handbooks published by a number of major corporations. These handbooks covered such topics as attendance, safety, health, health insurance, promotion, recreational activities, formal training facilities, financial benefits, grievances, company history, employee services, vacations, holidays, pay, and working hours. Some dealt with other matters as well, such as permanence of employment, suggestion systems, and disciplinary rules (3). From the data presented it appears that seven of the eleven handbooks were written at a level above that of their intended readers; in some cases the discrepancy was sizable.

Table 21-5. A Comparison Between Flesch Reading Ease Score in Terms of Educational Level Required for Eleven Employee Handbooks and Median Educational Level of Unskilled Employees

Corporation	Educational level required by handbook	Educational level
1	Some high school	Fifth grade
2	Some high school	Eighth grade
3	High school or some college	One year of high school
4	Seventh or eighth grade	Seventh or eighth grade
5	High school or some college	Eighth grade
6	Some high school	Four years of high school
7	Seventh or eighth grade	Four years of high school
8	High school or some college	Eighth grade
9	Sixth grade	Sixth grade
10	Some high school	Eighth grade
11	College	Fourth grade

Source: C. Carlucci and W. J. E. Crissy, "How Readable are Employee Handbooks?" *Personnel Psychology*, Vol. 4 (1951), p. 385.

The readability problem appears to arise because employee publications are written by individuals with at least a college education, to be cleared by managers both within and outside the personnel area, who are equally well educated. Thus, handbooks, magazines, and practically anything else written for employees can easily represent difficult reading for those whose education is more limited. Fortunately, industrial editors have become increasingly conscious of this problem, and at the same time the educational level of the population has been rising. Thus, the gap is clearly narrowing. In all probability differentials of the kind found in corporation 11 of Table 21-5 are now to be found only in a few isolated instances.

Communications Upward

Communications from the bottom to the top of the organizational hierarchy are of significance for two reasons. First, it is primarily through some type of feedback process that management is able to obtain the information needed to evaluate and perhaps correct its downward communications. Feedback of this kind is needed to determine whether employees have received and understood the messages directed to them through the company media and supervisory channels. Second, without some mechanisms through which employees can ask questions, express dissatisfactions, register complaints, or make suggestions regarding company policies and procedures, management may remain completely unaware of major problem areas and threats to organizational maintenance for extended periods of time. The consequence can be a continual festering of problems until open conflict, mass resignations, or even disintegration of the organization occurs.

In contrast to downward communications, techniques of communicating upward are rather limited in number, and it is often difficult to control them, so as to keep the focus on goal-related information. As noted in the last section, the content of items initiated from the top can easily shift to areas, such as bowling leagues and cooking, that have little to do with company goals; this problem is accentuated many times when transmission is initiated at lower levels.

In part the difficulties of upward communication are inherent in the nature of business organizations, with their stress on hierarchy and their underlying premise that those at the upper levels should tell individuals below them what to do and how to do it, not the reverse (14). Furthermore, because a manager or supervisor has the power to control the work situation in many of its aspects, employees are not likely to communicate upward anything that might reflect negatively on them. Should an individual complain to his superior, or make a suggestion, he can have no feeling of certainty that the matter will go to higher levels. The supervisor may consider it unimportant or be too busy to take any action, or he may deliberately fail to report it to his superior because it implies that his own performance has been less than perfect. Even within the ranks of management, upward communications may be severely stifled or distorted, particularly where a subordinate has strong aspirations toward advancement in the organization (19).

Techniques in Upward Communication

From what has been said, it is apparent that the barriers and distortions that plague downward communications are magnified many times in the upward situation. Because of the uncertainties associated with the use of the superior-subordinate channel, various techniques have been devised that permit employees to bypass their immediate superiors in registering complaints or making suggestions. Other approaches, such as gripe boxes, permit employees to express dissatisfactions on an anonymous basis. Yet the existence of these techniques does not necessarily mean that employees will use them extensively.

Table 21-6 is based on a survey of personnel executives (2). It indicates quite clearly that in the opinion of these individuals the superior-subordinate channel remains the most effective, despite its inadequacies. First-line supervision is stressed in more companies than is any other technique, and this emphasis is particularly pronounced in the larger firms. Several of the other approaches to upward communication involve the superior-subordinate channel, also. This is true of both informal discussions and formal meetings, for instance, although both have downward, as well as upward, components in most cases.

Table 21-6. Most Effective Upward Communications Techniques in a Sample of 112 Companies

	All companies, %	Larger (over 1,000 employees), %	Smaller (1,000 employees or less), %
First-line supervisors	39	48	23
Informal inquiries or discussion	36	25	59
Formal attitude surveys	26	25	33
Formal meetings	23	24	20
Counseling or interviewing techniques	17	9	30
Gripe boxes	13	17	—
Union representatives	13	11	16
Formal grievance procedure	13	14	10
Question-and-answer column in plant newspaper	9	—	25
Grapevine	4	4	3

Source: Bureau of National Affairs, Inc., *Upward Communications*, Personnel Policies Forum Survey No. 76. Washington, D.C.: the Bureau, 1964, p. 4.

Although some companies do rely on union representatives for information, it is generally conceded that reports from this source need to be carefully evaluated. Often union leaders are more concerned with promulgating the union viewpoint than with providing an honest appraisal of a situation to the company. Other techniques, whose value has been questioned, include gripe boxes, which seem to have little appeal to the employees themselves, and question-and-answer columns in company publications. The latter normally involve considerable delay before answers are forthcoming. As a result they do not elicit widespread activity in most cases.

Some of the other techniques noted in Table 21-6 have already received considerable attention in other connections.

ATTITUDE SURVEYS, INTERVIEWING, AND COUNSELING. Employee attitude measurement, including the use of interviewing approaches, was discussed at length in Chapter 10 in connection with the treatment of performance evaluation. Yet this is, in some ways, as much an upward communications device as an evaluation procedure. The communications aspects become particularly evident when questions are included that seek to determine the extent of employee information on such matters as company policies and benefit programs.

Employee counseling was discussed in Chapter 18 as one of the corrective procedures used in connection with performance control. Although counselors will rarely transmit specific problems of specific employees to higher management, because in doing so they might create mistrust and thus prevent other employees from coming to them in the future, they may provide general impressions of employee attitudes. If a company does utilize counseling on a wide scale, this can be a valuable upward communications technique. Yet counseling is rarely, if ever, introduced for its upward communications value alone. The communications aspect tends to emerge subsequently, as a by-product.

GRIEVANCE AND COMPLAINT PROCEDURES. Grievance handling was considered at some length in Chapter 19 as an approach in labor relations. Procedures of this kind may also be viewed as devices to facilitate upward communications, even though when used with any frequency, they tend to reflect a breakdown or blockage within the superior-subordinate channel. The major difficulty from a communications viewpoint is that the grievance machinery may be used largely to further union goals. Thus, it may not provide valid information on real sources of employee dissatisfaction.

Suggestion Systems

A rather widely used technique for upward communications, which has not been considered previously in any other context, is the suggestion system. In many respects this approach is unique. It is not characteristically designed to provide feedback with regard to downward communications; those at lower levels must initiate largely in terms of their own ideas. It is not intended as a means to the expression of complaints so much as to permit employees to communicate upward in a positive and constructive fashion. The ideas communicated may relate to either productivity or maintenance goals; they may deal with more efficient production methods or with procedures for improving job satisfaction. Yet the existence of an effective suggestion system per se contributes primarily to organizational maintenance. The use of this technique can well yield a considerable feeling of involvement in the organization, a belief that one's contributions count and will be rewarded. Thus, loyalty, cohesiveness, and commitment are likely to be fostered. On the other hand, suggestion systems may also function to provide financial rewards for creative effort. Under these circumstances they are more than a technique of upward communication.

Suggestion systems may take a variety of forms. In some cases they are tied to specific objectives, as with work-simplification and cost-reduction programs, or they may be built into an incentive payment procedure. The system may be company-wide or it may apply only to a segment of the work force. Thus, some companies maintain entirely independent suggestion systems for production, office, and managerial employees. Usually, operation is continuous, but on occasion a definite time limit is established. In such cases the scope may also be restricted, to ideas related to safety, for instance.

OPERATING PROCEDURES. Suggestion systems need to be carefully administered, if they are to make a positive contribution to organizational maintenance. There is always a risk that feelings of inequity and injustice will be aroused, with the result that conflict may be the only observable consequence. For this reason most effective suggestion systems have standard forms for employees to use in submitting ideas. They set specific time limits for acknowledging the receipt of suggestions, investigation by the department concerned, and acceptance or rejection by the suggestion committee. They establish procedures to ensure the anonymity of those making suggestions during the review process. The suggestion committee itself is usually constituted primarily from among rank-and-file employees; often the only management representative is someone from the personnel department. However, to the extent top management can be involved, support for the suggestion system is likely to be increased. The union may well have formal representation, although this is by no means a universal practice.

Applicable rules and regulations normally attempt to ensure that the employee who first submits a suggestion receives credit for it and that suggestions are not rejected without a full explanation. The usual practice is to exclude ideas that fall within the normal scope of the individual's job. Thus, if the role requirements are such as to indicate that ideas of a certain kind *should* be produced by a particular individual, such ideas are ineligible for a suggestion award.

AWARDS. Probably the most difficult aspect of suggestion systems is determining the award for an acceptable suggestion. Most plans provide for awards in cash, although some firms award an equivalent amount in savings bonds or company stock certificates. There are also plans which make no formal provision for payment. The employee receives only a certificate of merit or a letter of commendation. But a copy of this goes in his personnel file. Thus, pay raises, promotions, and other personnel actions may well be influenced, even though direct payment is lacking.

Where cash awards are made, the minimum payment can vary from $15, or in some cases even less, to $25; the maximum can go as high as $10,000, or there may be no specified upper limit. Employees whose suggestions yield measurable savings to the company ordinarily receive an award amounting to a percentage, usually 10 or 20 per cent, of the anticipated savings during the year subsequent to adoption. Such awards may well run into thousands of dollars. Some companies conduct a special review at the end of this initial year to determine actual savings. Should these be greater than originally anticipated, a supplemental award is made; should they be less, the employee is permitted to keep all money paid on the estimate.

Determining awards for suggestions where the value cannot be stated in monetary terms, even though there is some definite intangible value to the firm, is more complex. Unfortunately, in many employment situations suggestions of this kind are much more frequent than those involving identifiable savings. The usual procedure is to award points to the suggestion in terms of the particular factors considered to be relevant. The approach has much in common with certain types of job evaluation. The points awarded on each of the factors are totaled, and this point score is then converted to a dollar amount using a standardized award scale. An example of a typical form used in evaluating intangible suggestions is provided in Figure 21-1.

FACTORS IN EFFECTIVENESS. It is widely recognized that, in spite of their tremendous potential contribution, many suggestion plans exist in a semi-dormant state. Few suggestions are submitted, and the contribution to goal attainment is probably not sufficient to justify the cost of maintaining the machinery. This is particularly likely to be the case where monetary awards are minimal or nonexistent, but it can occur under other circumstances as well.

The major factor in effectiveness appears to be the attitude of first-line supervision (11). Does the supervisor create the impression that good suggestions are desired and important? Or does his attitude imply that submitting suggestions is merely a troublesome method of attempting to curry favor? Even in departments where supervision actively promotes the suggestion system it may not operate very effectively. In a study of office workers in a large corporation, it was found that numerous suggestions were submitted by employees in a department with poor productivity, but the level of monetary awards was quite low. In another high-productivity department fewer suggestions were submitted, but awards averaged almost three times as high as in the department with low productivity (15). Apparently supervisors must transmit attitudes related to both quantity and quality for maximal results to be realized.

Figure 21-1. **Typical Form for Evaluating Suggestions with Intangible Value**

Suggestion No. _____

	Points
Nature of Benefit	
1. Has definite therapeutic value	16 to 20
2. Results in a definite improvement in safety	16 to 20
3. Produces a marked improvement in operations	16 to 20
4. Improves employee relations	6 to 15
5. Improves working conditions	6 to 15
6. Of only limited importance-minor improvement	1 to 5
Distribution of Value of Benefit	
1. Company-wide application	21 to 25
2. More than one department or installation	16 to 20
3. Single department or installation	6 to 15
4. Single operation or section	1 to 5
Ingenuity	
1. Very resourceful	11 to 25
2. Average	6 to 10
3. Uninventive	1 to 5
Cost of Adoption	
1. Less than $25	0
2. $25 to $100	−5
3. Over $100	−10
Effort Involved	
1. Considerable personal research	11 to 15
2. Average substantiation	1 to 10
3. No research at all	0
Completeness of Proposal	
1. Facts clearly presented, so that little further effort is required to put idea into effect	11 to 15
2. Basic facts are sound, but needs some refining to put into effect	6 to 10
3. Not completely or clearly presented, thus requiring considerable clarification	1 to 5

Total Points _____

Award Scale

Less than 25 points	$ 5	61 to 64 points	$ 55
25 to 28 points	$10	65 to 68 points	$ 60
29 to 32 points	$15	69 to 72 points	$ 65
33 to 36 points	$20	73 to 76 points	$ 70
37 to 40 points	$25	77 to 80 points	$ 75
41 to 44 points	$30	81 to 84 points	$ 80
45 to 48 points	$35	85 to 88 points	$ 85
49 to 52 points	$40	89 to 92 points	$ 90
53 to 56 points	$45	93 to 96 points	$ 95
57 to 60 points	$50	97 to 100 points	$100

Total $ _____

Aside from the attitudes of supervision, there are other factors associated with effectiveness. Most of these represent aspects of downward communication. The suggestion system should be actively promoted in the downward media. Information regarding awards should be publicized. Special attention should be given to particularly meritorious ideas. In this way high-quality participation can be stimulated. Also, management must take steps to ensure that employees feel entirely free to submit suggestions. An idea that would almost certainly leave a man without a job, or result in layoffs for others, or reduce incentive payments, is not likely to be submitted. There must be guarantees against negative consequences such as these.

Suggestion systems, like all the communications techniques mentioned in this chapter, do not operate in a vacuum. For internal communications devices of any kind to contribute maximally to goal attainment, there must be a constant downward-upward interaction. Initiation may come from any point in the system, toward the top or toward the bottom, but in any event there must be some feedback to the source. This is what is actually meant by two-way communication. It is an essential condition for continued organizational effectiveness, i.e., for integration of effort in pursuit of mutual goals.

References

1. Bass, B. M., *Organizational Psychology*. Boston: Allyn and Bacon, Inc., 1965.
2. Bureau of National Affairs, Inc., *Upward Communications*, Personnel Policies Forum Survey No. 76. Washington, D.C.: the Bureau, 1964.
3. Carlucci, C., and W. J. E. Crissy, "How Readable are Employee Handbooks?" *Personnel Psychology*, Vol. 4 (1951), 383–395.
4. Dahle, T. L., "An Objective and Comparative Study of Five Methods of Transmitting Information to Business and Industrial Employees," *Speech Monographs*, Vol. 21 (1954), 21–28.
5. Davis, K., "Management Communication and the Grapevine," *Harvard Business Review*, Vol. 31, No. 1 (1953), 43–49.
6. Dover, C. J., *Effective Communication in Company Publications*. Washington, D.C.: Bureau of National Affairs, Inc., 1959.
7. Foy, F. C., and R. Harper, "Round One: Union vs. Company Publications," *Harvard Business Review*, Vol. 33, No. 3 (1955), 59–67.
8. Haas, G., and H. Zagat, "Communicating on Labor Relations: A Survey of Company Practices," *Personnel*, Vol. 34, No. 1 (1957), 84–89.
9. Haas, G., and H. Zagat, "Trade Union Journal vs. Company Magazine," *Personnel*, Vol. 34, No. 6 (1958), 59–65.
10. Habbe, S., "Does Communication Make a Difference?" *Management Record*, Vol. 14 (1952), 414–416, 442–444.

11. Hardin, E., "Characteristics of Participants in an Employee Suggestion Plan," *Personnel Psychology,* Vol. 17 (1964), 289–303.

12. Henderson, C. O., *The Company Magazine as a Medium for Communicating Persuasive, Management Oriented Subject Matter.* DBA Thesis. Eugene, Ore.: Univ. of Oregon, 1964.

13. Hershey, R., "The Grapevine—Here to Stay But Not Beyond Control," *Personnel,* Vol. 43, No. 1 (1966), 62–66.

14. Katz, D., and R. L. Kahn, *The Social Psychology of Organizations.* New York: Wiley, 1966.

15. Katz, D., N. Maccoby, and N. C. Morse, *Productivity, Supervision, and Morale in an Office Situation.* Ann Arbor, Mich.: Institute for Social Research, Univ. of Michigan, 1950.

16. Martin, N. H., and J. H. Sims, "Thinking Ahead: Power Tactics," *Harvard Business Review,* Vol. 34, No. 6 (1956), 25.

17. Miner, J. B., and E. E. Heaton, "Company Orientation as a Factor in the Readership of Employee Publications," *Personnel Psychology,* Vol. 12 (1959), 607–618.

18. Perry, D., and T. A. Mahoney, "In-plant Communications and Employee Morale," *Personnel Psychology,* Vol. 8 (1955), 339–346.

19. Read, W. H., "Upward Communication in Industrial Hierarchies," *Human Relations,* Vol. 15 (1962), 3–15.

20. Redding, W. C., and G. A. Sanborn, *Business and Industrial Communication: A Source Book.* New York: Harper & Row, 1964.

21. Sutton, H., and L. W. Porter, "A Study of the Grapevine in a Governmental Organization," *Personnel Psychology,* Vol. 21 (1968), 223–230.

22. Walton, E., "Communicating Down the Line: How They Really Get the Word," *Personnel,* Vol. 36, No. 1 (1959), 78–82.

23. Walton, E., "Project Office Communications," *Administrative Management,* Vol. 23, No. 8 (1962), 22–24.

Questions

1. What types of communications media, utilized in what ways and under what circumstances, are most likely to prove effective as input-output mediators?

2. What is a readership survey and how is it conducted? Why is it important for a company to conduct readership surveys at periodic intervals?

3. What is the readability problem? Why does it occur and what are its consequences? What appears to be the future of the problem?

4. What are the upward communications techniques in widespread use? What special problems plague the use of upward communication channels? How successful are the various techniques in overcoming these difficulties?

VII

Theoretical Summary: Personnel Management in the Context of Organization Theory

22

The Model of the Personnel Management Function

In bits and pieces the preceding chapters present a rather comprehensive model of the personnel management function. This model follows the conceptual approach of the input-output system, an approach that appears to be winning considerable acceptance in organization theory generally (2,3,4,5,6).

Until now, however, the various elements of this conceptual framework for a company's utilization of human resources have not been brought together in a unified presentation. It seemed more appropriate to develop the various aspects of the theory as they were needed to explain specific features of personnel practice. At the same time the model served to specify those particular topics that should legitimately be included in a textbook on personnel management, as distinguished from a book dealing with administrative process, organizational behavior, management, or human relations.

It is now time to pull together the threads of theory running through the earlier chapters. What follows, then, represents an integration and recapitulation. Little new is added. Yet, when the various fragments are joined together into the whole, each may take on new meaning.

Goals and Constraints

The theory posits that organizations have certain goals that provide a degree of focus for their activities. These goals tend to be established not so much by the members of the organizations themselves, as by the next larger social unit, the society. In a sense the goals of a company are the role prescriptions established for organizations of this particular type within the framework of the total social structure. They provide a definition of what the organization is expected to contribute. Yet, while society tends to specify goals for its organizations, indicating how necessary functions are to be allocated among the various societal sectors, it also establishes restrictions on the means used to reach these objectives. Thus, society operates both to set the goals of business firms and to introduce constraints that limit the paths to goal attainment.

Company Goals

Business organizations, comprising the economic sector, operate with two primary types of goals under a capitalistic system. To the extent a firm is attaining both of these, it may be presumed to justify its creation and existence within society. These goals serve to guide all facets of organizational activity. As such, they are relevant for personnel management, just as they are for marketing, manufacturing, accounting, and other functions.

THE PRODUCTIVITY GOAL. All organizations have one or more task objectives. In the United States the economic sector of society is expected to operate in accordance with the capitalistic system. Thus, the task objective of business organizations is closely allied not only to the production of goods and services, but to the maximization of long-term net profit as well. Society expects business firms to produce as much as possible and make as much profit as possible within the limitations imposed by existing constraints and the organizational maintenance goal.

THE ORGANIZATIONAL MAINTENANCE GOAL. At the same time that companies are productive, they must also take steps to ensure survival on other grounds. The organization must be maintained as an ongoing social unit in the face of both internal and external pressures and stresses. Internal stress derives from intergroup conflict, low morale, and widespread dissatisfaction. It may under extreme circumstances result in a total disintegration of the organization, as members leave and subunits split off. Such matters have been the special concern of psychologists and sociologists. External stress, on the other hand, derives from the pressures imposed by governments, public opinion, and other economic organizations. Here economists and political scientists have been particularly concerned.

In a historical sense one of the major problems of the personnel management field, and one of the factors accounting for its occasional low status, has been that a large number of its representatives have chosen to emphasize the maintenance goal at a time when the great majority of managers were almost exclusively concerned with productivity and profit. As a consequence of the welfare tradition, transmitted into personnel management first through social work and later from certain segments of psychology, the field acquired a soft, almost weak, image. There was a time when many personnel managers seemed much more concerned with matters of employee happiness than with corporate profitability. At present the profession appears to have lined up more solidly behind *both* goals. As a result, its current detractors no longer appear to be emphasizing these goal considerations in their attacks (1).

Constraints on Personnel Decisions

Decisions made to implement the attainment of company goals are severely restricted by a whole host of constraints. There are a number of things that, at a given point in space and time, a personnel manager cannot do in carrying out his function. Either they are physically impossible or the consequences are such as to make them distinctly unattractive. These constraint systems, which impinge upon decision making in the personnel area, are of two kinds.

INTERNAL CONSTRAINTS. The major internal factors that serve to limit personnel decisions are the characteristics of the company's labor force, the existing structure of role prescriptions, and the union contract currently in effect. Individual differences, as they are reflected in a particular work force, in all probability have the most pronounced impact. At a particular point in time a company's employees are characterized by specific distributions of abilities and personalities. These distributions serve to limit personnel action, although, with time, the internal constraints thus imposed can be overcome through the hiring of new employees, training, and other procedures. Yet many companies have experienced serious difficulties because the constraints imposed by the nature of an existing work force have not been fully recognized. Accordingly they have committed themselves too rapidly to major product diversification, office and plant automation, or a strong research orientation. And consequently they have failed because current employees did not have the required capabilities and could not adapt to the new mold.

Restrictions are also imposed by the existing procedures for segmenting the total work effort, as a result of organization planning and job analysis. When a particular structure has been developed, with prescribed lines of authority, status, and communications, limitations are automatically imposed on personnel decisions. These limitations can be overcome through a restructuring of the organization or through job redesign, but at a point in time they represent a clear-cut constraint system. Similarly, the union contract specifies what can and cannot be done in certain areas, with regard to the utilization of human resources. It, too, can be changed, but rarely with ease, and then only when the next occasion for collective bargaining presents itself.

EXTERNAL CONSTRAINTS. Constraints imposed from outside the organization are even more resistant to change than those of an internal nature. This is particularly true of external constraints introduced by the culture. In Japan discharging a man for incompetence has long been considered reprehensible, and the particular equalitarian value system of the communist countries has served effectively to bar almost all psychological testing. Similarly, the high incidence of illiteracy in many under-developed countries tends to restrict company training efforts severely.

Within a country, geographical differences may also introduce significant constraints. Existing attitudes may place major barriers in the way of hiring particular groups of individuals for certain types of jobs. Differences in the educational, intellectual, and other characteristics of regional populations may force much more intensive recruiting efforts, expanded training, or even a curtailment of expansion plans.

Similar constraint systems may characterize entire industries. Differences in the propensity to strike impose limitations on the extent to which organizational maintenance considerations can be ignored. In years past, in industries such as mining and lumber, it was essential to devote considerable effort to such matters; in agriculture and the utilities, it was much less so. Again, in fields such as petroleum refining, where advancing technology has markedly reduced manpower needs, selection is not available in most cases as a means of upgrading a labor force; new refinery workers are only rarely hired. Industry constraints of much the same kind operate in other sectors of the economy.

Finally, there are the great variety of legal constraints that serve to restrict personnel actions. Perhaps most widely known are the Federal labor laws, the Wagner Act and the Taft-Hartley Act. But there are also numerous state laws in the labor relations area, as well as laws that limit employment decisions, at all levels of government. The Fair Labor Standards Act, fair employment practices legislation, the Social Security Act, Workmen's Compensation and so on, in addition to various court and commission rulings, can be cited as examples. These laws and rulings impose constraints on the payment of wages, working hours, selection procedures, separations, safety procedures, the utilization of older workers, and employment in a research capacity.

There is reason to believe that a major source of difficulty experienced by many personnel departments has been a tendency to become overconcerned with efforts to change a particular type of external constraint, often at the expense of other activities. Thus, certain companies have become so enmeshed in civil rights matters, on one side or the other of the issue, that other personnel functions have suffered. The tendency to devote very sizable resources to fighting certain specific legal constraints provides another example. Such an overcommitment in one area can contribute to major imbalances within the total personnel activity and consequently threaten organizational goal attainment.

Inputs and Outputs

Internal and external constraints operate on an organization, which may be most appropriately viewed as a behavioral system, performing in accordance with the input-output model. Insofar as the personnel function is concerned, the input side deals primarily with people, although for other purposes financial resources, materials, facilities, and technology may also be treated as inputs. People become available to the organization as a result of the employment process. They enter the firm with abilities, skills, personality characteristics, and cultural values that, as previously noted, operate to impose certain constraints on personnel decisions. But individual differences are also the raw materials, in a human resources sense, through which productivity and maintenance goals are achieved.

On the output side the major consideration insofar as personnel management is concerned is the behavior of employed individuals as organization members. The latter involves three aspects: (a) the things that people who work for the company say and do, (b) the things that people who work for the company are expected to say and do, and (c) the relationships between expectations and what members of the organization actually say and do.

Role Prescriptions

The things that people who work for a company are expected to do may be labeled as role prescriptions. These role prescriptions are developed to contribute most effectively to goal attainment. At least this is the intent. Unhappily, exact methods of determining whether a given structure of organizational roles is maximally supportive of productivity and maintenance goals are not generally available. Thus, there is usually considerable guesswork involved, even though experience can be a useful guide.

Nevertheless, after such role prescriptions are established, they become at a given point in space and time a set of internal constraints on related decisions. They impose limitations on personnel actions, just as individual differences do. At the managerial level a major contributor in introducing role expectations is the process of organization planning. At lower levels in the company some form of job analysis is used to perform this function, although on occasion aspects of a formal job analysis program are extended upward into the ranks of management.

At all levels it is important that the role prescriptions established be clear and that they be accepted within the organization as legitimate. In part this is necessary as a means to gaining the full advantages of division of labor in the pursuit of maximal productivity. But clear-cut jurisdictions, with little overlap and widespread acceptance, are also an important means to internal conflict reduction. Thus, the process of setting role prescriptions can make a sizable contribution to both major types of organizational goals.

Role Behavior

The things people are expected to do on the job are known as role prescriptions; the things they actually do are known as role behaviors. To the extent these role behaviors approximate a perfect match with the appropriate role prescriptions, an individual is said to be effective or successful. It is assumed that he is in fact contributing to company goal achievement.

Performance evaluation is essentially a matter of determining the degree of this matching. It is an attempt to take organizational goal attainment down to the level of the individual contribution. Or, put somewhat differently, it represents an evaluation of the behavioral output in terms of its contribution to the total firm. What is really important, insofar as an organization is concerned, is not how much an individual does, but how much of what he does is organizationally relevant as determined by his role.

As with the establishing of role expectations, the evaluation of role behaviors tends to be differentiated on a vertical scale. Management-appraisal techniques are utilized at the upper levels and employee evaluation at the submanagerial levels. In the former instance considerable emphasis is usually placed on the performance of the group managed as well as on the performance of the manager himself; below the ranks of management only the performance or role behavior of the individual himself is of concern.

The Input Side

In presenting this theoretical model the output side is discussed first because the selection of individual inputs must be carried out with a view to maximizing future role prescription–role behavior matching. An organization should pick those individuals for membership who subsequently will be most effective on the job. To fully understand personnel selection, then, one must be aware of what the concept of effective performance implies.

This means that studies should be conducted, using longitudinal and concurrent selection models as appropriate, to establish procedures that will in fact identify those individuals within an applicant group who are most likely to succeed. Unfortunately, some firms use a cumbersome and often very expensive selection apparatus that falls far short of accomplishing this objective. In such cases the selection process may contribute only very minimally to goal attainment. Certainly there is little point in extensive recruiting if a company does not select from among those recruited the specific individuals who will contribute most on an organizationally relevant basis.

This requirement that selection techniques be evaluated in terms of their contribution to the company holds for all approaches. Such techniques for the evaluation of individual inputs to an organization are of two types. First, there are those that utilize information on past behavior to predict future behavior. Among these are most selection interviews, application blanks, biographical inventories, reference checks, and the more comprehensive background investigations. Second, there are the techniques that utilize information on current behavior and functioning to predict future behavior. Among these are physical examinations, ability testing, personality testing, and skill or achievement testing.

The Input-Output Mediators

A final aspect of the model, perhaps the most important in that it covers more different types of personnel activities, is that of the input-output mediator. Such techniques are used to sustain or improve upon the original input so that the output is maximized. These mediators may be grouped in several ways.

Structural and Functional Mediators

One basis for grouping is in terms of structural and functional characteristics. The structural mediators are the techniques for establishing role requirements discussed previously. These techniques provide a basis for evaluating role behaviors, but only the role behaviors themselves represent actual organizational outputs. The structural mediators are procedures for grouping organizational tasks and establishing role requirements so as to channel the behaviors of organization members in the direction of goal attainment. This is accomplished through organization planning and job analysis. After these role prescriptions are set, they represent internal constraints.

The functional mediators influence organization members through procedures that impinge on the individual directly, rather than through role prescriptions. Included in this category are management development, training, wage and salary administration, safety management, counseling, discipline, medical treatment, labor relations activities, fringe benefits, and employee communications. All the techniques used to influence organizational input discussed in this book, with the exception of organization planning and job analysis, are functional in character. Yet the current listing is not meant to be definitive. Fifty years from now approaches that at present are not even under consideration may well have achieved widespread acceptance.

Productivity-Oriented and Maintenance-Oriented Mediators

As previously indicated the structural mediators normally serve both types of organization goals. They segment work, permitting specialization and thus more efficient productivity, while at the same time establishing jurisdictions that serve to limit internal conflict. Although in any given firm the major emphasis in developing role prescriptions may be on productivity or on maintenance considerations, both factors are likely to receive some recognition.

The functional mediators, on the other hand, appear to be much more susceptible to differentiation in terms of the type of organizational goal fostered. Yet even here there may be some overlap. Thus, although management development techniques generally appear to be strongly oriented toward productivity, certain human relations programs and sensitivity training are clearly directed toward organizational maintenance. This suggests that, at least potentially, many of the functional mediators could be focused on either type of goal or on both. In actual practice, however, there has been a tendency to use a particular type of mediator primarily for one purpose or the other.

Thus, management development, training, wage and salary administration, safety management, medical procedures, counseling, discipline, and the like tend to be applied most frequently toward the end of increasing productivity. The various approaches in the labor relations area, employee benefits and services, and communications procedures are characteristically maintenance-oriented.

Input Improving, Input Sustaining, and Control Mediators

In many of its applications the input-output model has included a feedback or control procedure. Thus, when the operation of part or all of the system drops below a certain level, or deviates too much from certain predetermined standards, corrective forces are activated in much the same way that a thermostat serves to activate a heating system when the temperature falls below a preset level.

Although this feedback or control concept is useful in understanding the functioning of some input-output mediators, it is not adequate to the task of explaining the whole gamut of techniques. At least two other types of mediators must be considered. These two categories, along with the control concept, provide a way of viewing mediators as they relate to the input side of the system.

One group of mediators is oriented toward the improvement of inputs so that role behavior eventually exceeds the level that could have been anticipated merely from a knowledge of the original input. Thus, the objective is to improve performance above and beyond what was manifest at the time of hiring. The structural mediators certainly contribute to this process, because in channeling effort and motivating individuals, they attempt to maximize output in the form of role behavior. The most obvious examples of input-improving mediators, however, are management development and training. Here an effort is made to change the individual in some way so that he now either is more capable of performing effectively or has a greater desire to do so. Various payment plans are also initiated with a view to mobilizing individual motivation behind organizational goal attainment. In all these instances the primary stress is not so much on correcting deviations from a preestablished standard, as on actually making the individual more effective than he was when he entered the organization.

Second, there are a group of mediators that serve primarily to sustain the behavior potential existing in the input. Such approaches are essentially preventive. They attempt to keep the situation from getting worse, rather than to make it much better. Most of what is done in the organizational maintenance area is basically of this kind. Approaches in labor relations, employee benefit programs, and communications efforts tend to focus on protecting the organization against stresses that might threaten its survival. Few firms are concerned with totally eradicating internal conflict or maximizing employee satisfaction. It is sufficient to establish conditions and utilize procedures that prevent such internal stresses from becoming disruptive and that keep people at least as satisfied as they were when they joined the company originally. Similarly, activities in the areas of safety management and preventive medicine are of an input-sustaining nature. The objective is to maintain the individual in the same state, insofar as his performance potential is concerned, that existed at the time of hiring.

Finally there are mediators that operate selectively to control negatively deviant cases. In these instances the feedback concept is adequate to explain what occurs. Individuals whose behavior departs from role requirements so markedly as to fall below a preestablished standard are identified, the sources of the failure are determined, and an appropriate corrective process is set in motion. Medical treatment, discipline, reassignment, and employee counseling operate in this manner. On occasion, mediators that are more commonly applied in an input-improving or input-sustaining context may also be utilized in a corrective sense and thus fulfill a control function. Thus, job redesign, training, payment procedures, and the like may be used at times for purposes of performance control.

The various elements of the total model are presented in Figure 22-1.

Figure 22-1.   The Model of the Personnel Management Function

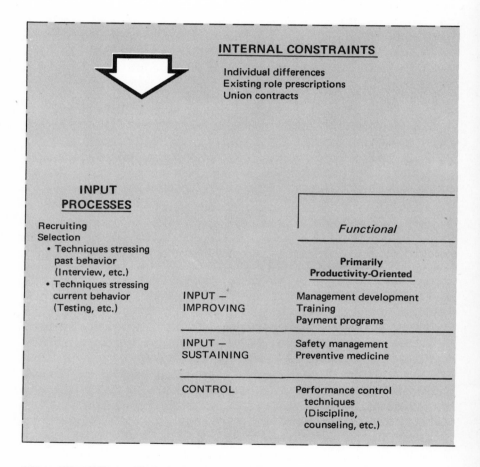

EXTERNAL CONSTRAINTS

Cultural, geographical,
   and industry characteristics
Labor relations laws
Employment laws

INTERNAL CONSTRAINTS

Individual differences
Existing role prescriptions
Union contracts

**INPUT
PROCESSES**

Recruiting
Selection
 • Techniques stressing
   past behavior
   (Interview, etc.)
 • Techniques stressing
   current behavior
   (Testing, etc.)

Functional

**Primarily
Productivity-Oriented**

INPUT —
IMPROVING

Management development
Training
Payment programs

INPUT —
SUSTAINING

Safety management
Preventive medicine

CONTROL

Performance control
   techniques
   (Discipline,
   counseling, etc.)

The Problem-Solving Approach
to Personnel Management

The model that has been developed implies a problem-solving approach to the personnel field. Specific strategies must be designed depending upon the particular task objectives and constraint structure of

GOALS

Productivity

Maintenance

- Against external stresses

Organizational
boundary

- Against internal stresses

MEDIATORS ———————————

Functional

Structural

**OUTPUT
PROCESSES**

Management appraisal
Employee evaluation
- Rating systems
- Attitude surveys

**Primarily
Maintenance-Oriented**

**Productivity- and
Maintenance-Oriented**

Organization planning
Job analysis

Approaches in labor relations
Employee benefits and services
Internal communications

a given organization. The input processes, mediators, and output processes that will maximize goal attainment in one situation are unlikely to do so in another. It is in the development and implementation of such overall strategies for corporate human resource utilization that the managerial approach to the personnel field achieves its fullest expression. Yet it is an unfortunate fact that personnel management has attracted a great many individuals who are strongly committed to certain specific techniques, rather than to broad managerial problem solving. The techniques vary, but the degree of commitment remains the same. Thus, there are psychological testing specialists, management development specialists, labor law specialists, compensation specialists, and many others. In each case the major concern has been with finding as many applications for a specific technique as possible. In many instances the individual may have very little knowledge of personnel management beyond the limits of his specialized skill.

This emphasis, where solutions are more important than problems, creates a situation in which techniques are often applied indiscriminately, with little attention to whether they are, in fact, appropriate to the need. In addition, particular approaches may be belabored long after they have outlived their usefulness. After a given technique has been introduced in a firm and has gained acceptance, there is little incentive to find new solutions in that particular problem area or to adopt other techniques. A problem-oriented approach, on the other hand, can provide protection against becoming technique-bound in this sense and thus can serve to foster creative thinking with regard to human resources utilization, as well as to promote the adoption of new and more appropriate techniques of personnel management.

References

1. Dunnette, M. D., and B. M. Bass, "Behavioral Scientists and Personnel Management," *Industrial Relations,* Vol. 2 (1963), 115–130.
2. Katz, D., and R. L. Kahn, *The Social Psychology of Organizations.* New York: Wiley, 1966.
3. Robin, D. P., "An Input-Output Model of Employee Behavior," *Academy of Management Journal,* Vol. 10 (1967), 257–268.
4. Stogdill, R. M., *Individual Behavior and Group Achievement.* New York: Oxford Univ. Press, 1959.
5. Stogdill, R. M., "Basic Concepts for a Theory of Organization," *Management Science,* Vol. 13 (1967), 666–676.
6. Thompson, J. D., *Approaches to Organizational Design.* Pittsburgh, Penn.: Univ. of Pittsburgh Press, 1966.

Index of Authors or Sources Cited

Subject Index

Randall Library – UNCW

HF5549 .M522   NXWW
Miner / Personnel and industrial relations; a mana

304900129233–